Engaging the Ottoman Empire

MATERIAL TEXTS

Engaging the
OTTOMAN EMPIRE

Vexed Mediations, 1690–1815

Daniel O'Quinn

PENN

University of Pennsylvania Press
Philadelphia

Published by
University of Pennsylvania Press
Philadelphia, Pennsylvania 19104-4112
www.upenn.edu/pennpress

Printed in the United States of America on acid-free paper
10 9 8 7 6 5 4 3 2 1

Library of Congress Cataloging-in-Publication Data
Names: O'Quinn, Daniel, 1962– author.
Title: Engaging the Ottoman empire : vexed mediations, 1690–1815 / Daniel O'Quinn.
Other titles: Material texts.
Description: 1st edition. | Philadelphia : University of Pennsylvania Press, [2019] |
    Series: Material texts | Includes bibliographical references and index.
Identifiers: LCCN 2018020835 | ISBN 9780812250602 (hardcopy : alk. paper)
Subjects: LCSH: Turkey—Foreign relations—Europe—History—18th century. | Europe—
    Foreign relations—Turkey—History—18th century. | Turkey—Relations—Europe—
    History—18th century. | Europe—Relations—Turkey—History—18th century. |
    Europe—Civilization—Turkish influences—History—18th century. | Diplomats—
    Turkey—History—18th century. | Intercultural communication—Political aspects—
    Turkey—History—18th century. | Intercultural communication—Political aspects—
    Europe—History—18th century.
Classification: LCC DR479.E85 O78 2019 | DDC 327.560409/033—dc23
LC record available at https://lccn.loc.gov/2018020835

For Eli

Contents

Introduction

Misunderstandings are the medium in which the
noncommunicable is communicated.

—*Theodor Adorno,* Prisms

It is the spring of 2013, the Rijksmuseum is still closed for renovation, but I am in Amsterdam to see a cache of paintings of Ottoman life by the French-Flemish artist Jean-Baptiste Vanmour. The curator in charge of the Calkoen collection has generously been standing by as I work painting by painting in the museum stores. On my final day she has kindly made an appointment for me to go to the office of the museum's director to see one final painting. To my surprise, he is there. He walks over and greets me warmly, and the three of us stand back to look at the enormous *View of Istanbul from the Dutch Embassy at Pera* (ca. 1720–37), which is bolted to the wall opposite his desk (Plate 1). It is a labored, confused painting. Time passes. In so many words, the director indicates that he will be happy not to look at this painting when he moves to his new office. Since I have occasioned reflection upon a daily irritant, I suddenly feel compelled to speak about this picture that I have only just seen, about why I am here.

By any standards, Vanmour's monumental landscape is a remarkably clumsy picture. Something about the task of representing Istanbul on this scale proved to be beyond his means.[1] The stone balcony in the foreground is perhaps the most discomfiting element of the painting: the tiles and stones defy any coherent sense of perspective and these spatial deformations are only exacerbated when we attempt to make sense of the roofs and houses beyond. Furthermore, the figures are not terribly well integrated. The central group of Europeans discoursing about what lies before them seems to come from an entirely different representational economy than the laborer on the left and the man with the horse on the right. These figures appear to be directly out of contemporary costume albums, and there is no apparent rationale for their presence here except as signs of exoticism. One could say something similar about the smoking figure seated on the balustrade—unlike the Europeans whose gestures connect them to the scene, he could be anywhere in the Ottoman dominions. But these disjunctions between the figures and their relative distance from one another are revealing because they demonstrate a failure to successfully devise a pictorial solution for intercultural relations. The very thing that unsettles this picture—its dubious command of the foreground elements—points to that which unsettles any European artist's practice in this space. How can the descriptive techniques of Dutch and French painting (Vanmour was trained in these traditions), and the sociability that they imply, be modified to adequately render the artist's and the viewer's situation.

I use the word "situation" advisedly because one of the thrilling things about this picture is the degree to which the image gains confidence the farther one moves into the landscape and away from the city. In other words, the evocative treatment of the mountains and the Bosphorus in the background highlights the aesthetic struggle to represent the urban world of Istanbul. That the primary elements that gave order to the Western aesthetic tradition—perspective and ocular description—are vexed by what would seem to be the simple task of rendering this balcony gives a very clear sense of the degree to which Vanmour and other cultural practitioners were forced to reimagine their practice. We could suggest that hybridizing the representational economies of landscape and the costume painting into the same picture has generated a spatial deformation, a kind of representational disturbance that actually captures the vexed relationship between European and Ottoman subjects in this represented space. Europeans and Ottomans had a great deal of mediated social intercourse in the capital, but devising a genre capable of capturing this extraordinary ordinariness called into question the way that social relations were represented. Time and again in this book we will encounter examples of this kind of representational discord. My objective is to track these disturbances as they surface in order reflect upon what they indicate about intercultural sociability and about mediation itself. My contention is that these representational disturbances, or vexed mediations, offer auspicious sites for considering social relations beyond fantasies of the selfsame: they are historical gifts for a time when the urgency of speaking, living, and being with others demands a fierce reckoning with Europe's own preconceptions of discursive legitimacy.

Such an exercise poses significant challenges for historical narration and conceptual organization. Rather than offering a grand narrative of European-Ottoman relations or a rigid conceptual framework to organize the archive, I have chosen to explore a series of intimate encounters, some of which have large geopolitical ramifications, using the tools of microhistory and cultural analysis. Thus, the overall effect is far more constellatory than cumulative. Every chapter of this book follows the fortunes of notable European—primarily British, Dutch, and French—diplomats to the Sublime Porte of the Ottoman Empire. These ambassadors were charged not only with representing their respective states at the Ottoman court, but also with maintaining vital trade relations in the Mediterranean. At times I look at their activities in great detail, because their complex mediatory role forces us to think carefully about intercultural communication itself, both in its intimate performance and in its geopolitical significance.[2] That said, every chapter of this book also attends to extremely important aesthetic representations of the Ottoman Empire produced by or under the aegis of these same diplomats. The European embassies in Pera were multifarious social spaces in which artists and writers engaged with the foreign world around them. Engagement in this sense has to do with how genres and forms of representation were deployed and modified to take stock of the spaces and subjects under Ottoman rule. As I work through a very mixed archive of drawings, maps, letters, dispatches, memoirs, travel narratives, engraved books, paintings, poems, and architecture, I argue that the repository of European representations of Ottoman culture constitutes a valuable resource not only for Ottoman cultural history but also for media archaeology in the eighteenth century. One of the primary theses of this book is that engagement and the later disengagement with the Ottoman world forced symptomatic alterations and deformations in European genres and media.[3] By closely analyzing these deformations and modifications it is possible to scale out to larger claims, first, about intercultural communication and sociability and, second, about recurrent patterns of national and imperial exchange. In its most provocative moments, this book argues that understanding European modernity requires an engagement with the Ottoman Empire.

These are large claims, especially since many of the materials I am analyzing here have either been marginalized in mainstream eighteenth-century studies, or they have only ever been handled in an illustrative fashion.[4] Some of the texts, paintings, and engravings that I deal with have appeared in essays and books as somewhat transparent representations of social practices—this is especially the case of the writings of Lady Mary Wortley Montagu and the paintings of Jean-Baptiste Vanmour. One of my primary objectives in this book is to radically complicate the relationship between these representations and that which they represent. There is a referential relationship between the images and texts I consider and the subjects they represent, but that relationship is tempered as much by European practices and expectations as it is by any challenges posed by the referent. Yet those challenges are manifest. Engaging the Ottoman world involves combined acts of translation, mediation, and invention such that these representations often draw attention to their own vexed status. And that vexation is only complicated further by the changing political desires vis-à-vis the Ottoman state.

The eight chapters that make up this book intermittently work very close to the evidence and draw back for the long view, a tactic employed by many of the representations I consider. What this means is that the book itself is faced with a challenging balancing act between historical narration and cultural analysis. It is my strong belief that achieving this balance is crucial for understanding the importance of the interface between European and Ottoman culture in this period for we will be encountering far more similarities than conventional wisdom and much scholarship has led us to believe. In the ensuing sections of this Introduction I sketch out three primary propositions that weave their way through all of the chapters: (1) careful attention to formal problematics and generic change allows us to discern important social and cultural tensions in this mediated archive; (2) scrutiny of spatial and temporal itineraries reveals a complex relation to Europe's past that haunts many of my primary observers' present experiences in Ottoman lands; and (3) matters of affect and power are crucial for understanding both formal deformation and historical consciousness in these works because they are so thoroughly entwined with wartime. Formal disturbances and collisions often point to competing temporal itineraries that ultimately leave an affective imprint of deep historical significance.

As these formal, historical, and affective concerns coalesce, I think we can discern crucial developments both in the formation of "Europe" as a concept and in the representation of the Ottoman Empire. In many ways, Europeans representing Ottoman culture and politics found themselves reexamining, or perhaps examining for the first time, the ways and means in which they represented themselves. In some cases, this self-scrutiny led to remarkable acts of cosmopolitan imagination; in others, challenges to the self opened onto either hyper-aesthetic acts of introversion or genocidal fantasies of domination and extirpation of the Ottoman Empire. Significantly these two poles of engagement correspond to separate eras of intercultural exchange, and thus this book is divided into two sections: the first covers the period from 1690 to 1734, and the second focuses on the period between 1763 and 1815.[5] But before laying out the book's structure and its overall narrative arc, I want to situate this book in relation to eighteenth-century studies and the scholarship on empire and globalization more generally. The following three sections of this Introduction elaborate on how form, historical itineraries, and emotion operate in this book.

"I Am Now Got into a New World": The Consolations of Form

For scholars of the eighteenth century, Lady Mary Wortley Montagu's *Turkish Embassy Letters* is the most widely acclaimed record of intercultural encounter with the Ottoman world.[6] One of the earliest letters addressed from Ottoman territory declares to an unknown addressee that "I am now got into a new world," and it is perhaps worth pausing over the modifiers that give the letter its aura of urgency and excitement.[7] The adverb "now" and the adjective "new" not only isolate her in an impossibly narrow present condition, but also disconnect the space she inhabits from its past, from its well-known history. Denys Van Renen argues that this clause "indicates that she is willing to let the setting dictate her outlook" and that "trying to make an impossible temporal category possible, Montagu employs her 'now' to create a perpetual present and to involve imaginatively the recipient in her experiences, eliding a past that interferes with 'their' total immersion in a new culture."[8] It is important to recognize just how artificial this gesture is. Both the "now" and the "new" are counterintuitive constructions. Writing can never capture the present; it is precisely the time that eludes inscription, and this ostensibly "new" world had been in place for centuries. The Ottoman Empire was founded under Osmân I in 1299 in northwestern Anatolia; but from Mehmed the Conquerer's conquest of Constantinople in 1453, the empire had exerted significant hold on the European imagination. As numerous scholars of early modern Europe have demonstrated, the "Turk" is almost coextensive with the imagination of Christendom itself. Significant recent arguments have shown that what we now identify as "news" came into full generic competence with the Battle of Lepanto. In the wake of that epochal event, the Ottomans became the preeminent example of a contemporary "empire" for the European imagination, only to be superseded by nascent imperial formations following the Seven Years' War.

This is an important and often forgotten point. Empire, from the sixteenth to the eighteenth century, was generally the subject of comparative analysis. And, crucially, not all of the empires being compared were European. Prior to the Treaty of Westphalia—which ended the Eighty Years' War between Spain and the Dutch Republic, established the precedent of peace treaties negotiated by diplomatic congresses, and ultimately instituted political order in Europe based on coexisting sovereign states—Europeans had direct political experience, affective involvement, and historical engagement with five very different imperial formations.[9] One, the Roman Empire, was inexorably a part of the past, but its cultural, legal, and social lineage remained imaginatively alive. Spain's vast overseas empire signaled the renewed viability in the present of economic and territorial control on a global scale; although with that possibility also came the specter of religious tyranny. This is not the place to survey the impact of the Spanish example on the political and social developments of every other region of what is now called Europe. At the risk of overstatement, no other imperial power had such wide-ranging effects on the domestic politics of regions outside its control, and this is why the Peace of Westphalia occupies such a constitutive place in the consideration of sovereignty, nationalism, and international law. The Dutch Republic's mercantile empire of the seventeenth century offered a rather different model, whose legacy is felt most forcefully in the English and French mercantile networks of the first half of the eighteenth century.

Two other empires—the Habsburg Empire and the Ottoman Empire—also engaged the European imagination during this period. Both predated and continued to operate outside the Westphalian system, and both laid claim to the frontiers between "Europe" and "Asia."[10] But they animated the European imagination in radically asymmetrical fashion. Because the Habsburg Empire drifted in and out of the Holy Roman Empire, and perhaps because the Habsburg Empire's statecraft did not cohere into an easily representable form until the late seventeenth century, it tended to disappear behind the alterity of its territorial rival. As numerous scholars have now demonstrated, the Ottoman Empire, by the time of the Battle of Lepanto, had very quickly acquired the status of Europe's defining other. With the Atlantic Ocean as that which brackets Europe's western expanse, then the geographical location of the Ottoman Empire allowed it to operate as the eastern bracket required for a wide range of polities to see themselves as somehow related. Looking at the vast archive of maps from the early modern period, Palmira Brummett argues conclusively that the combined force of location and religious difference allowed French, Dutch, Italian, English, and German observers of the Ottoman Empire to overcome the sectarian differences that otherwise made "Europe" other to itself.[11] In that regard, Islam worked as the absolute other that enabled "Christendom" to cohere as an ideology and as a political project. Despite remarkable levels of social exchange and a long history of porous borders in eastern Europe, Ottoman rule came to stand for this difference. It is important to recognize that this opposition was largely a discursive effect, activated to legitimate aggression or to constitute sameness; thus declarations of a "clash of civilizations" mistake an effect for cause. Even a cursory analysis of the Ottoman example demonstrates an extraordinary flow of foreign subjects into and through its territories and a remarkable toleration of difference among its subject populations.

This book shows that this specious activation of "Turkish" alterity also permeates the history of both print and performative media. My intention is to correct the relative lack of scholarly attention, especially among cultural critics, that has been paid to the abundance of informational literature and media about the Ottoman Empire that circulated in eighteenth-century Europe. Current secondary literature on "Turkish" topics in eighteenth-century studies tends to gravitate toward exoticism, the Oriental tale, and a generalized sense of the East as it registers in various fictional genres. Unlike scholarship on British India or on the circum-Atlantic, a large proportion of this work does not deal with the Ottoman Empire as a political and economic reality, in part because there is a mistaken assumption that readers did not know this world. Yet accounts of the Ottoman world pervade the print culture of many European locales. After all, the Ottoman state was the subject of extensive historical inquiry in Europe almost from its inception. It became a key comparator for Western theories of governance, and not only as the chief example of despotism. As numerous scholars have now shown, the highly organized Ottoman bureaucracy and its standing military were often as not seen as models of good governance.

To put this provocatively, the Ottoman Empire, before the advent of modernity, carried much of the heterocosmic import of that term. A functioning empire, in existence now, operating according to decidedly alternative social, legal, and religious structures would have looked remarkable to a merchant in London or Leiden as much as to a courtier in France or Sweden.[12] It should thus come as no surprise that the Ottoman world was represented in—and influenced the development of—a variety of European media. For example, Brummett has shown the constitutive place of the Ottoman Empire for the history of cartography in Italy, France, England, the Low Countries, and the Habsburg Empire. We can observe a similar phenomenon in other media. Andrew Pettegree has recently demonstrated not only how instrumental the reporting of the Battle of Lepanto was to the formal development of the news, but also how crucial the reporting on conflict with the Ottomans was to newsletters and newspapers in the seventeenth century.[13] Taking my cue from these recognitions, this book opens by looking closely at the mediation of the Treaty of Karlowitz in a wide range of printed matter in order to establish the everydayness of this information for readers in London and Paris.

By the time Lady Mary Wortley Montagu writes "I am now got into a new world," this new world was old news. In fact, that is what allows Montagu's text to stage its primary critique: she assumes that her readers have knowledge of the histories written by Richard Knolles and Paul Rycaut, of the journey writing of Jean de Thévenot, George Sandys, Ottaviano Bon, Aaron Hill, and others, of the maps coming out of Holland, of the plays and operas being acted in London and Paris, of the specific deployment of Ottoman examples in political treatises by John Locke, Thomas Hobbes, and others, and in the routine presence of Ottoman affairs in the daily press.[14] In fact, the assumed level of knowledge in Montagu's letters is no less a sign of epistolary intimacy than that rhetorically achieved by the temporal shifter "now" and the somewhat specious "new": they are part of the same effect of writing that is based on extensive acts of collective reading.[15]

Montagu's Letter-book is a useful heuristic here because the slow shift in how her text has been read tells us a great deal about eighteenth-century studies.[16] In the immediate wake of Edward Said's *Orientalism* and the postcolonial turn in cultural criticism, it makes sense that most essays and chapters on Montagu focused on specific scenes of exoticism, on acts of aestheticization, and on the deployment of the East as a utopic space. What is revealing is that the ensuing canonization of the *Turkish Embassy Letters* has been partial. Anthologies are content to give the hammam letter, the meeting with Fatima, perhaps the letter on the rights of Ottoman women in marriage. In short, attention to the book has been dominated by its most ideologically freighted space, the seraglio, and by its most fraught subjects, Ottoman women.[17] This disparity in the distribution of scholarly attention becomes all the more pronounced when we realize that more than half of the *Turkish Embassy Letters* focuses specifically on European spaces and social encounters.[18] When we grant the European sections of the *Turkish Embassy Letters* as much attention as scholars have paid to the Ottoman sections, we can see that Montagu soberly compares the Habsburg and Ottoman Empires in order to conduct a highly complex analysis of the ongoing war between the two powers that animated her husband's diplomacy.[19] Van Renen argues persuasively that to ignore the European sections of the *Letters* is to shred the text of much of its political argument, which he locates in Montagu's writings on fashion. In my fourth chapter, I will be pushing his argument much further by suggesting that Montagu addresses the issue of empire and war in the very historical discourses most conventionally utilized for these discussions—that is, epic poetry and classical history. I feel that this is necessary because Montagu's intervention has implications for the history of form, for aesthetics, and for the way that "European" discourses mediated their constitutive outsides.

Every page of this book, every argumentative thread, follows the information networks through which Europeans represented the Ottoman world and carefully tracks the search for formal and generic aptitude. Because so much of this book turns on pivotal moments when peace dissolves into war or when violence haunts attempts to represent the real, "crisis" is an important concept throughout. Following Lauren Berlant, I see "crisis" as "not exceptional to history or consciousness but a process embedded in the ordinary that unfolds in stories about navigating what's overwhelming."[20] That navigation involves a careful attention to form and genre for, as she states, "Affect's saturation of form can communicate the conditions under which a historical moment appears as a visceral moment, assessing the way a thing that is happening finds its genre."[21] The cultural products that make up the archive for this book share a common revisionary relation to genre and form. Europeans visiting or residing in the Ottoman Empire attempt to adapt or modify familiar forms to render distinctly unfamiliar experiences—in some cases they even learn from specifically Ottoman cultural practices. It is not an exaggeration to say that cultural difference was to some degree overwhelming for these observers, and we can trace the complex feelings instantiated by these encounters with social and historical alterity in the generic and formal innovations devised, on the spot as it were, to navigate this world.

Caroline Levine's capacious understanding of form proves to be useful in this context. For Levine, "'form' always indicates *an arrangement of elements—an ordering, patterning, or shaping. . . .* Form, for our purposes, will mean all shapes and configurations, all ordering principles, all patterns of repetition and difference." Like Jacques Rancière, she understands politics as a matter of imposing order on space and organizing time. In other words, "There is no politics without form."[22] This is a salient matter here because European representations of the Ottoman Empire involve colliding forms. European strategies of narration and description are used to render the forms of Ottoman sociability and statecraft with varying degrees of success. The formal structures of Ottoman state processions and celebrations will prove to be particularly important here because they constituted both a political and a formal challenge for European representation. Social performance is translated into a cultural artifact, and the formal translation will tell us a great deal about everyone involved.

For this reason I pay a great deal of attention to the specific forms and media used to communicate information about the Ottoman Empire. How did Europeans in London or Paris learn about this faraway place? Much of the scholarship on European knowledge of the East focuses on travel literature and Oriental tales. The former, for all its inaccuracies and inventions, is usually treated differently than the latter, which is rightly traced back to the extraordinary commercial success of Antoine Galland's *Les mille et une nuit* (1704–17), a proto-translation of the *Layla wa Layla*, which circulated in England as *Arabian Nights' Entertainments* (1706). Recent scholarship on Oriental tales has shown that they were an extremely elastic genre, often deployed for scrutinizing or critiquing European governmentality and society.[23] In a sense their generic flexibility and their explicit relation to fantasy and magic made them suitable for a wide range of historical and political applications. At the same time that these kinds of writings were permeating the print culture of eighteenth-century Europe, another kind of textual and visual engagement with the Ottoman world was suffusing the mediascape. There is a vast array of printed and visual materials purporting to offer more referential knowledge of the Ottoman Empire: travel narratives to be sure, but also engraved books, memoirs, scholarly disquisitions, histories, and new hybrid genres attempted to describe with increasing specificity a space and forms of sociability that most readers would never experience or see.

This book is very much about these latter materials, and the changing status of description is a crucial issue throughout. As Cynthia Wall has cogently argued in relation to the development of prose fiction in this period and Svetlana Alpers has vividly shown with regard to seventeenth-century Dutch painting, description has a complex discursive and political history.[24] Not only does description itself change over time, its function within prose narratives and within visual art alters significantly as the century progresses. Benjamin Schmidt has argued further that the efflorescence of "exotic geography" in the late seventeenth and early eighteenth centuries involved a rebalancing of narrative and description in favor of the latter that had a significant effect both on ethnography and geography itself.[25] We will be acutely aware of these epistemological and discursive changes across the century-long period of this book, but because my archive is both textual and visual (and sometimes a hybrid of the two) my consideration of description will be multivalent and often quite extensive. One of the things I want to argue here is that the frequent combination of textual and visual description in the archive I am considering opens onto metacritical reflections on the relationship between representation and referent. This reflection often takes the form of rather strange exculpations, because in many cases the authors and artists are describing events or people that they could not see. Because the referent—most famously Ottoman women—was inaccessible, description was either conducted at second hand or replaced by highly symptomatic forms of invention. The former implies that the empirical act of description was always already mediated; the latter calls into question the epistemological basis of description itself. One of the most important things that we will see throughout this book is that the writers and artists I deal with were not only aware of these problems in representation, but frequently made them the occasion for considering representation's volatile place in intercultural relations.

Even though the powers of western Europe—Britain, France, and the United Provinces—did not hold territorial possessions in or near Ottoman lands, the Ottoman Empire is a crucial site of imperial fantasy. This is in part because the Ottoman Empire functioned as a preeminent example of empire, as discussed above; and it is in part because it was a site of projection for European fantasies about another, historical, preeminent example of empire: Rome. Anyone who wants to understand British imperial desires during this period, and especially how these desires get routed through Roman fantasies and the classical past, needs to look carefully first at how Rome was deployed to understand the Ottoman Empire and then how Greece was imaginatively extricated from Ottoman control. In both cases, we get a new sense of the political function of classical material in eighteenth-century life. What I show in the last four chapters of this book is the degree to which that which is temporally distant comes to mediate that which is most difficult to reconcile in the present, namely, cultural difference itself. As we will see, allegory plays a vital role in this story and the complex temporal deferral at its heart is crucial to the historical melancholy that suffuses many of the texts I consider. It strikes me as somewhat counterintuitive that this study of intercultural exchange may help to reorient scholarship on philhellenism and the legacy of classical learning in the eighteenth century, but this is one of its inexorable conclusions.[26]

Spatial and Temporal Itineraries: Historical Involutes

Itineraries are as much about time as they are about space. As we move through space and time in this archive, we can trace changing relations not only to the object of knowledge, but also to the epistemological subject. One can discern a shifting field of desire vis-à-vis the Ottoman world that ultimately speaks just as clearly to emerging understandings of European identity.[27] If we look broadly across the archive of cultural materials purporting to represent the Ottoman Empire in the eighteenth century, we discover that substantial portions of these publications are devoted to representations of the Holy Lands, Greece, Egypt, and/or Syria. One would be hard pressed to determine whether the primary audience for these texts was drawn to the accounts of Constantinople and Ottoman manners and customs, or whether this material was a vestigial supplement to the antiquarian gaze.[28] Because these scenes of antiquarian interest were under Ottoman control, the vast majority of these texts brought multiple spatial and temporal genres into the same conceptual space, often with some significant discursive disjunctions. The complex relation between the "now" of Ottoman sociability and the "what has been" of antiquity is frequently marked in spatial terms.[29] The widely read histories of the Ottoman Empire, Richard Knolles's *The Generall Historie of the Turkes* (1603) and Paul Rycaut's *The Present State of the Ottoman Empire* (1665), and, in its own way, volume 7 of J. F. Bernard's *Cérémonies et coutumes religieuses de tous les peuples du monde* (*Ceremonies and Costumes*, 1737), with its extensive illustrations by Bernard Picart, use the device of episodic compilation to capture the successive iterations of political regimes and religious practice.[30] As Alain Grosrichard, Ros Ballaster, and others have demonstrated, these texts and the repetition of their primary episodes in political treatises and encyclopedic writing consolidated phantasms of the East. Spaces, dispositions, events become folded into a prevailing economy of despotism. The seraglio, the sultan's gaze and his handkerchief, the assassinations of the vizier coalesce into *doxa* long before Montesquieu would instrumentalize the tropes for a theory of governance.

But alongside of these accretions of cultural *doxa* one can also discern a responsiveness to historical change and lived social relations in prominent texts in this pre-disciplinary representation of the Ottoman Empire that is much more attentive to the disjunctive qualities of historical experience. Pre-disciplinarity is a valuable concept here because both "histories" and journey literature are often an extraordinary miscellany of knowledge practices. An example is helpful here. Cornelis de Bruijn's immensely influential *Reizen van Cornelis de Bruyn, door de vermaardste deelen van Klein Asia* (Delft, 1698) in many ways sets the terms for illustrated journey writing for the first fifty years of the eighteenth century. It was quickly translated and published throughout Europe. The English edition, *A Voyage to the Levant* (1702), like its Dutch and French predecessors, contains over two hundred copperplate engravings. These are roughly divided into four types of images: (1) maps and topographical views; (2) costume illustrations; (3) architectural drawings (exterior and interior); and (4) a small number of natural curiosities. These are matched by corresponding discursive types: (1) geographical descriptions that set the itinerary of both the journey and the book itself; (2) proto-ethnographic remarks on the manners and customs of the current residents of Constantinople, Cairo, and so on; (3) antiquarian discussions of ruins and buildings; and (4) fleeting remarks on natural history. The key recognition is that these images and discourses are not evenly developed, nor are they separate enterprises. This is most obvious when one attends to the relationship between built environments and architecture. In spite of the fact that half the book concerns Constantinople, De Bruijn's interest in Ottoman architecture is minimal. In part because the seraglio can only be observed from outside, the built environment of Constantinople is folded into topographical views, and the descriptions of prominent buildings are relegated to discussions of his itinerary. In the sections of the book devoted to Ephesus, Alexandria Troas, Rhodes, Jerusalem, Egypt, the visual interest in architecture intensifies and the built environment is the subject of numerous antiquarian illustrations. In fact, accounts of Ottoman manners and customs structurally separate the proto-geographical account of urban Constantinople and the antiquarianism that dominates the second half of the book.

We could argue that the journey to the "periphery" of the Ottoman Empire, that is, to Greece, Egypt, Aleppo, and Jerusalem, is no less concerned with social relations; it is just that they operate in a ghostly fashion. Only signaled in the text, the world of the Bible and of classical learning haunt the second half of *A Voyage to the Levant*; therefore we can recognize a crucial set of oppositions. First, De Bruijn's geographical itinerary always already invokes and gravitates toward the ancient world. Travel in the present carries with it an implied journey to past spaces: spaces that are known through biblical, Latin, and Greek texts and thus constitute pre-Ottoman historical formations. Second, De Bruijn's proto-ethnography of Ottoman society always already implies and consolidates a classical/biblical ethnographic fantasy. This is more than simply stating that De Bruijn's Orientalizing gaze is grounded in a prior Occidentalism. Rather, it is indicating that such as spatial separation involves a double temporal deformation. Unlike the allochronic aspects of ethnography discussed by Johannes Fabian, De Bruijn locates the ethnographic observation of Ottoman culture firmly in the "now" because he is going to find "Europe" in the "what-has-been" spaces of the Ottoman periphery.[31] This is why the links between preexisting biblical and classical learning and the antiquarianism of the text are not described: they are everywhere implied by the artifact, by the ruin, and are thus more phantasmatically potent as the silent *doxa* that counterbalances the loquacious accounts of Ottoman marriage and funeral practices, religious beliefs, and so on. What this means is that those aspects that immediately involve the narrating subject, his itinerary, his topographical observations, and his desire for a past effectively negate his own intercultural sociability (we get very little sense of interaction with his sources) and result in a hypostatization of Ottoman social practices as an object of proto-disciplinary knowledge. The key recognition here is that proto-ethnography and antiquarianism are two parts of the same narrative, discursive and subjective self-realizations.

In De Bruijn these discourses are basically in balance: he devotes roughly the same visual and textual attention to both. This is most obvious in the book's most spectacular engravings. There are two immense foldout views measuring more than two meters: the first is a topographical view of Constantinople (Figure 1); the second is a view of Jerusalem of similar scale and intent. In a sense, this makes his text the epitome of European engagement with the Ottoman Empire for the post-Karlowitz era. The epochal Treaty of Karlowitz of 1699 curtailed the westward expansion of the Ottoman Empire and, in many senses, set the terms for phantasmal oppositions between "Europe" and "the East." De Bruijn conducted his travels during the war between the Holy Roman Empire and the Ottoman Empire, but the engravings of the book were completed just after the Battle of Zenta. Thus his book and, perhaps more important, the translations circulated at a moment when, as the traveler Aaron Hill stated, the "Leviathan" was hooked.[32] In that regard, the text exhibits the anxieties that attend wartime and the hopes associated with peace. One way of reading the balance between proto-ethnography and antiquarianism is to suggest that the former has instrumental possibilities for European individuals and nations seeking to expand commercial engagement and the latter embodies enlightenment aspirations to historically contextualize the ancient texts that had until only recently grounded Western culture.

In many ways, De Bruijn's text is a consolidation of preexisting knowledge. But the massive expansion on those prior texts' illustrations and especially the rendering of Constantinople itself mark an important shift both in European representations and in Ottoman society. As Schmidt has argued, this shift toward visual representation is crucial to the emergence of "exotic geography" and the entire phantasmatic economy that relies on the exotic to consolidate notions of Europe.[33] Schmidt's argument focuses on Dutch publications from the period between 1660 and 1730, but their influence is wide and deep. Even as late as Charles Perry's

Figure 1. Cornelis de Bruijn, *Panoramic View of Constantinople*, engraving, in *Reizen van Cornelis de Bruyn, door de vermaardste deelen van Klein Asia* (Delft, 1698). Courtesy of the Getty Research Institute, Los Angeles.

A View of the Levant (1743), we can see the structural remains of these pre-disciplinary miscellanies. But at roughly this same time period we begin to see the emergence of discipline-specific publications. For example, the manners and customs chapters of De Bruijn morph into volume 7 of Bernard and Picart's *Ceremonies and Customs*. As important as Bernard and Picart's deployment of "Mahometism" in debates on Deism is, the disconnection of their treatise from a traveler's itinerary on the one hand and classical antiquarianism on the other is a significant development. Likewise, the intermittent description of geology and natural history that peppered De Bruijn's text become the subject of full-scale illustrated books like William Hamilton's *Campi Phlegraei* (1776). For our purposes, the most significant development is the separation of antiquarian discourse from representations of the Ottoman Empire. Those sections of *A Voyage to the Levant* dealing with ancient Greek, Roman, and Egyptian and Assyrian ruins become a separate genre unto themselves. Julien-David Le Roy's *Les ruines des plus beaux monuments de la Grèce* (1758), Robert Wood's *The Ruins of Palmyra* (1753) and *The Ruins of Balbec* (1757), and James Stuart and Nicholas Revett's *The Antiquities of Athens and Other Monuments of Greece* (1762), all notably devoted to specific elements of the cultural patrimony, tend to downplay the itinerary of the observing traveler. In all of these texts the presence of local society and regional governors associated with the Ottoman Empire poses both a narrative problem and an occasion for complex meditations on the relationship of past and present empires.

This uncertainty regarding ancient authority and modern sociability is perhaps nowhere more elegantly explored than in the work of James Stuart. Stuart's travels in the Peloponnese came during an extended period of peace in the Ottoman Empire. If we look at his preparatory illustrations for *The Antiquities of Athens*, we can see Stuart devising a pictorial method for capturing the collision of his-

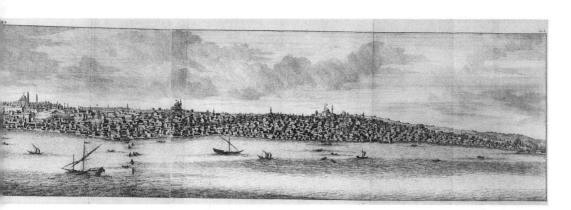

torically distinct cultural forms. The most interesting of these involve X-like compositions whereby one temporal regime crosses another. For example, in the 1755 watercolor studies for *Propylaea of the Hippodrome Seen from the Courtyard of a Private House, Salonica (Thessaloniki)* (Figure 2) and *View of the Temple of Augustus (Also Known as the Temple of Rome and Augusta), Pola (Pula), and Surrounding Buildings*, Stuart depicts two intersecting planes such that the classical ruin crosses the contemporary domestic space. Two temporal regimes intersect in this space, and the effect captures a historical disjunction. As these strategies make their way into *The Antiquities of Athens*, they begin to take on stadial significance: the contemporary Greek/Ottoman built environment interrupts an older more advanced cultural form. This would seem like a simple point, but other watercolors allow us to go further. James Stuart's *View of the Monument of Philopappos, Athens*, prepared during the same expedition, is typical of Stuart's innovative depiction of classical ruins in that it fully integrates figures, including the artist, into the scene (Plate 2). As stated in the catalog of the Royal Institute of British Architects, "the group of gentlemen on the left is Stuart, Nicholas Revett and James Dawkins."[34] Stuart and Revett adopted local dress at times to facilitate their travels, but choosing to portray themselves in this way poses a number of significant questions. We know from Stuart and Revett's placement of figures wearing robes and turbans in *The Antiquities of Athens* that these elements of costume are often deployed in a stadial argument about the degrees of civility of populations living in these spaces. As Jason Kelly has argued about Stuart's famous image of the acropolis that makes up the first engraving of *The Antiquities of Athens*, Turkish figures are incorporated to highlight not only the Ottoman subjugation of contemporary Greek communities but also their pillage of the patrimony of ancient Greece.[35] Stuart's images always tell a story of historical loss and displacement that sets the stage for an argument for the reconstitution of ancient liberty by enlightened European observers like himself.

Figure 2. James Stuart, *Propylaea of the Hippodrome Seen from the Courtyard of a Private House, Salonica (Thessaloniki)* (1755), gouache. Courtesy of the Royal Institute of British Architects.

In Stuart's drawing of the monument at Philopappos, Stuart and Revett mimic the "Turk," and they are in a sense negotiating with the conspicuously European figure. By taking the Turk's place, these artists have moved from a place in front of the picture plane (where the drawing is being produced) to a place within the historical exchange being represented. In this sense, the watercolor instantiates a desire to simply replace the Ottomans, to occupy Greece and appropriate its ancient ruins through a rhetorical sleight of hand that conveniently doesn't require the actual historical displacement of Ottoman governance, for that would require actual war. In this regard, the drawing enacts a desire to *own* this ruin in a fashion geopolitically similar to the Ottomans, but in a manner that is culturally more "informed." By integrating himself into the picture and by obscuring his role in the production of it, Stuart's desire is made manifest, and that is why I believe he appears to be looking outward at the viewer (or at himself). In a sense, this moment of recognition sums up the fantasy of appropriation at the heart of the kind philhellenism initiated by the Society of Dilettanti.[36]

But what are we to make of the other figure in the watercolor drawing? I'm hesitant to even call this a figure because it is not worked up in the same way as the others. Close inspection reveals the figure to the immediate left of the monument to be an underdrawing, likely in pencil or ink, perhaps a remnant of an earlier moment of composition. It is the ghostly quality of this figure that makes the overall

Figure 3. James Stuart, *View of the Monument of Philopappos,* engraving, in *The Antiquities of Athens* (1768). Courtesy of the Getty Research Institute, Los Angeles.

picture seem unfinished; but it is also the element that speaks most powerfully to the desiring relation already encoded into the trio of figures on the left. What kind of a figure is this ghost? He appears to be a Roman soldier lurking in this space, a reminder of a different moment when this space was under the control of a different empire altogether. If we are willing to accept the presence of this ghost, then the picture overlays three imperial regimes, all of whom controlled this geopolitical space, and postulates the emergence of a fourth. This fourth regime is, of course, Rome's uncomfortable avatar, Great Britain, and thus the picture's vestigial element (that which probably should have been erased) discloses the desiring relation that organizes the picture's historical engagement. I'm drawing attention to this errant moment in the watercolor and pursuing an advisedly errant reading of it because the execution of this drawing comes at the end of long period of peace in the Ottoman Empire and in many ways it captures the desires of Europeans looking at what they perceived to be a vulnerable political entity. This same drawing was later engraved for *The Antiquities of Athens* in the immediate wake of the disastrous war with the Russians that ended with the Treaty of Küçük Kaynarca (1774) (Figure 3). In its engraved form, the ghost of Rome has been transformed into a mere local subject, and there remains only one candidate for the future imperial domination of this space. In this regard we could argue that Stuart's images are as symptomatic of their moment as De Bruijn's were of his own and, more broadly, that the shift from pre-disciplinary representations of the Ottoman Empire to proto-disciplinary accounts of phenomena and objects in Ottoman territories marks a significant shift in Europe's political assessment of the Ottoman Empire's global significance. As we will see, this shift has important implications for both the diplomatic and aesthetic engagement with the Ottoman world.

That said, there is no hard and fast generic or medial shift; it is more a matter of one kind of knowledge practice slowly receding as another was emerging. Often we see a blend of epistemological positions and representational strategies. There is often an extraordinary divergence between the visual and textual economies of these texts wherein the visual description would seem manifestly at odds with its textual explication. Furthermore the rich array of printed materials pertaining to the Ottoman Empire is marked by the incessant repetition, citation, and appropriation of precursor texts that Said and others have famously identified as a hallmark of Orientalist representation. The sheer repetition of episodes from Knolles, Rycaut, de Thévenot, Jean Chardin, and Barthélemy D'Herbelot in later histories, travel narratives, treatises, and encyclopedic writings has a double effect on reading. On the one hand, repetition generates sedimented *doxa* that numbs analysis and critique; on the other hand, fleeting moments of variation or disjunction spring forth and shatter fantasies of received wisdom.

Even the most unsympathetic accounts of Ottoman history and society emerge from some level of intercultural exchange. Whether it is foregrounded or not, textual information about the Ottoman world implies a whole chain of mediating figures: dragomans, translators, guides, and assistants. And there is ample evidence of undisclosed reliance on Ottoman visual culture in the engraved books and paintings produced in the seventeenth and eighteenth centuries. Kishwar Rizvi argues that the engravings of sultans in Rycaut's *The Present State of the Ottoman Empire* were derived from Ottoman miniature painting.[37] Whether explicitly stated or implicitly evident, we see a willingness and a need for collaboration, adaptation, and exchange. But we also see resistance to this, a desire for the reassertion of representational boundaries and social efficacy. We could describe this as a tension between openness and closure, between interculturalism and the reinforcement of identity. The balance between these forces sometimes tilts more toward openness; sometimes closure to the demands of alterity comes all too quickly. My contention throughout this book is that learning to read this tension formally at the level of the text and images opens the way for more complex theories of social interaction. As we will see, the formal translation of this tension is intimately tied to historical and geopolitical forces. The pressure of war, the vicissitudes of peace, and the economic forces restructuring the interaction of European nations and Ottoman dominions in the Mediterranean and eastern Europe generate moments of openness and activate foreclosures of various kinds. What this means is that the formal resolution of these representational tensions are historical signs. They are instances where history, in all its affective power, finds its genre. Thus learning to read this push and pull makes us more sophisticated analysts not only of these representations of historical situations, but also of intercultural conflict and accommodation.

Subject to the Sultan: Feeling Power

When I initiated this project I simply wanted to look at the performance of intercultural sociability in the diplomatic and frontier spaces between Europe and the Ottoman world, especially in times of violent conflict. These moments of interaction were well represented in the archive and thus amenable to analysis. That now appears hopelessly naive, in part because I have had to break new ground by talking about sociability in a non-European context, and in part because I have had to come to terms with the cancellation of social relations that is inherent to wartime. Peace keeps slipping into war, and the affective cost of that slippage has been hard to measure. What has emerged is the recognition that intercultural sociability and violence exert pressure on representation itself and that similar problems and strategies emerge in a wide range of media to deal with representational disturbance. In part I think that this has become recognizable because the British, the French, and the Dutch were not directly involved in colonizing Ottoman space, however desperately they may have wanted to at certain points in the eighteenth century. My principle figures had the remarkable experience of living within Ottoman territory, technically under the auspices of the sultan, and that toleration of their foreign presence, for better or worse, allowed for ideational and representational acts to occur. Thus, without the impetus of colonization and not directly implicated in imperial warfare against the Ottoman Empire, the writers and artists I discuss in the ensuing chapters had the time and the space to imagine life after peace and beside war. In a curious way that capacity was a function of their reluctant subjection to sultan.

Compared to other diplomatic postings in Europe, legations to the Sublime Porte had a singular relation to foreign power. Since the mid-fifteenth century when the Ottomans first entered contractual agreements with their trading partners, the capitulations, or *ahdnames*, that regulated relations between the Ottoman Empire and its European trading partners lapsed with the death of the sultan.[38] With the advent of every new sultan or the appointment of a new ambassador, the capitulations had to be reconfirmed. Through a series of ritual performances ambassadors were forced to perform physically their subjection to the sultan's rule. Representations of these acts of subjection recur again and again in the archive of intercultural engagement, and, as I mentioned, it was these representations that first sparked my interest in this project. Like other forms of Ottoman state ritual, an ambassador's audience with the sultan or with the grand vizier followed strict protocols that remained unchanged for hundreds of years. In the mid-1760s Sir James Porter was complaining about the same acts of ritual humiliation as his predecessors in the late sixteenth century.[39] I want to take a moment to look at two such representations from the early eighteenth century because each in its different way not only demonstrates the degree to which the Ottoman state cast Europeans in a spectacle wherein their very presence instantiated the sultan's power over them, but also shows how Europeans resisted this kind of interpellation at the level of representation.

On 10 March 1701 Sir Robert Sutton had his public audience with Sultan Mustafa II in Adrianople.[40] Sutton's predecessor, Lord William Paget, had just successfully mediated the Treaty of Karlowitz. We will be discussing this treaty negotiation in detail in Chapter 1, but the important thing to recognize at this point is that Paget's skillful handling of the treaty negotiations allowed the Ottomans to save face after a series of catastrophic defeats to the Habsburg Empire; thus England was in favor at the Ottoman court. Sutton's eight-page relation of his audience constitutes one of his most extensive diplomatic dispatches and one of the most detailed accounts of this ritual that we have. Sutton recounts every aspect of the ceremony from the grand vizier's declaration that the grand signor has set a date for Sutton to be brought to him to the spectacular procession arranged for his transportation to the seraglio and his ensuing progress through the various courtyards to the divan itself. Perhaps the most salient aspect of the dispatch is the overwhelming sense of enforced passivity. Sutton's performance is scripted completely by Ottoman officials: his retinue, his time of departure, his route through the city, his horse and even its livery are either dictated or borrowed from his handlers. Significantly, his account breaks roughly in half. The first few pages focus entirely on his procession to the seraglio. The spectacle of the ambassador and his retinue accompanied by a vast array of janissaries is crucial to the event: the Ottoman state was essentially performing its control over the foreign legate for its own observing subjects. This explains the sheer excess of people and jewels on display. Michael Talbot cannily notes the polysemy of the procession: the English members of the procession could read the event as a sign of their importance at the same time that the residents lining the streets of Adrianople could read the event as a sign of the ambassador's obeisance to the sultan.

Once Sutton dismounts and passes through the gate of the seraglio on foot (none but the sultan was allowed to enter on his horse), the function of the spectacle is inverted:

The Chiaus Baski and Capigilarkihayasi (who performs the Office of Introductor of Ambassadors and came to the gate to receive his Excellency) walked before him, each of them having a silver staffe of Ceremony with which they beat the ground as they went. In passing the Court we saw on the right hand and bottom thereof about 3000 Janissaries ranged in Battalia, and keeping great order and silence, till upon a signal given they ran with all their force but with the same silence as before, to gather the rice soupe which was placed for them at certain distances in great dishes upon the grasse.[41]

This long-standing ritual of the symbolic payment of the janissary corps with rice was staged repeatedly for visiting ambassadors as a sign of strength and loyalty. What interests me about Sutton's account is his discursive insouciance at this display of force. With these three thousand martial bodies bearing down upon him in the closed space of the courtyard, the text merely states "The Ambassador being arrived near the Divan Hall, Signor Maurocordato . . . came to meet him, and receive him, and conducted him in the Hall, at the Entrance." The distancing effect of the passive voice rhetorically undermines the import of what amounts to a theater of martial dominion. Because this staging of the janissaries' loyalty to the sultan was so frequently rehearsed, and perhaps because the janissaries themselves were in such a weakened state at this point in the history of war between the Ottoman and Habsburg Empires, it has been diminished into a curiosity.

Like all ambassadors before and after him, Sutton was then greeted by the grand vizier and entertained with a sumptuous meal. Sutton's account spends a great deal of time emphasizing the grand vizier's knowledge of English affairs and concern for the health of William III. This scene of hospitality establishes a quasi-intimate relationship between Sutton and the grand vizier that discursively mitigates in advance his ritual humiliation. That moment comes during the final stage of his audience, when he is brought before Mustafa II (here referred to as the "grand signor"). After an elaborate ritual signaling the sultan's readiness to give the English ambassador audience, Sutton was

conducted . . . into the adjourning gallery, where his Excellency was vested with a Caftan, the two Signori Maurocordato's [sic], the Gentlemen that accompanied his Excellency, the Secretary of the Embassy, & the Officers & Pages to the number of 34 in all, during which the Vizir, the Caimacam Abdullah Pasha, & the Nissangi Pasha, as Vizirs of the Bench passed by along the gallery into the Gr. Signor's Audience Hall. At the same time the Presents (consisting of fine English cloth, satin, velvet, flowered stuffs & cloth of Gold) were exposed before the gate of the Gr. Signor's apartment held by several Officers appointed for that purpose. Soon after came two Capugi Bashis to take his Excellency and support him under the arms, after the Turkish civility & respect, conducting him with the 12 Gentlemen allowed to follow him into the gate & thro' two rows of White Eunuchs, who guard the room within, which leads to the Audience Hall where the Gr. Signor sate upon a Throne in the form of a Bed placed in a corner.

The moment at which Sutton is physically dragged before the sultan, when he is actually taken into custody, is an act of ritual subjugation. Sutton's attempt to discursively recharacterize this "support" as an expression of "Turkish civility & respect" can't fully dispel the performance of bodily capitulation. The text's very attempt to euphemistically reconfigure this performative assertion of power as a species of friendship or civility is perhaps the strongest sign that it was not experienced as in any way respectful. The entire ritual is aimed at making the ambassador feel in his body the lack of freedom before the sultan, and Sutton's text, with its recurrent emphases on the sultan's singular respect for the English, is working to dispel the lingering sense of subjection.

At one level Sutton's text describes the entire day of 10 March 1701 in remarkable detail, but one can detect disturbances in its representation of events that point to very specific experiences of intercultural discomfort. In the face of such enforced passivity it is as if Sutton is attempting to reconstitute his agency at the level of writing. It is not an exaggeration to suggest that refiguring the act of being physically taken into custody as the expression of civility or hospitality is necessary for Sutton to retain his veneer of diplomatic autonomy. We can detect a similar form of representational resistance in visual renderings of the same rituals. In his three paintings of the Dutch ambassador Cornelis Calkoen's audience with Sultan Ahmed III on 14 September 1727 in Constantinople, the expatriate artist Jean-Baptiste Vanmour focuses his attention on the events that happen in the seraglio and divides the event into the three separate spaces in which they occur.[42] This eliminates the ambassador's procession altogether—the place where the Ottoman state exhibited its dominance to the people—and thus significantly nullifies the sense of passivity that so strongly imbues the early stages of Sutton's account. This nullification is crucial because it allows Vanmour to reconstitute Calkoen's agency. How he does that is revealing.

Cornelis Calkoen on His Way to His Audience with Sultan Ahmed III shows the Dutch ambassador striding across the seraglio courtyard at precisely the moment that the janissaries descend upon the silver bowls of rice (Plate 3). Almost every detail in the painting matches Sutton's account of this event, but more intriguingly Vanmour replicates the discursive insouciance of Sutton's text by putting the gaze of the viewer and the ambassador at cross purposes. The viewer sees the janissaries surging toward the ambassador and toward the picture plane. The ambassador and his retinue take no notice of this display of active power, they simply stare ahead of them, out to the left. This has the effect of contrasting the ambassador's lack of interest in the janissaries with the viewer's excessive interest in the very theatricality of the scene. We could say simply that the ambassador's absorption makes the viewer aware of his or her overinvestment in the theatricality of the picture, his or her overinvestment in the spectacle of the sultan's power. This rhetorically diminishes the importance of the janissaries and quite literally foregrounds the importance of Calkoen. That importance is reinforced by the glowing red and gold of his brocade coat.

The pictorial rhetoric of *Cornelis Calkoen on His Way to His Audience with Sultan Ahmed III* is almost a perfect visual translation of Sutton's diminishment of the spectacle of the payment of the janissaries. We could even argue that the bifurcation between foreground and background in this painting replicates the sudden shift from the description of the three thousand janissaries silently running toward Sutton to the bare narration of his progress to the "Entrance of the Seraglio Hall." A similar level of correspondence can be seen in Vanmour's rendering of the grand vizier's entertainment of the ambassador: virtually every detail of Sutton's account of the grand vizier's hospitality is replicated in *The Meal in Honour of Ambassador Cornelis Calkoen* (Plate 4). When compared to the first painting, it is clear that the viewer's gaze is mapped onto that of the ambassador. If we think of the bifurcation between foreground and background in the first picture as an intercultural threshold, then that threshold has switched to the table and the viewer is placed eye to eye with the grand vizier Damad İbrahim Pasha. That mutual recognition both elevates the viewer and establishes a level of intimate connection with the grand vizier. As we will see, this important surrogative gesture sets the stage for the remarkable act of resistance encoded into the final painting in the series.

As in Sutton, it is the final stage of the audience that warrants our most serious attention and allows us to be more specific about the relationship between representational distortion, subjection, and the reassertion of agency. In the third picture, *Ambassador Cornelis Calkoen at His Audience with Sultan Ahmed III*, Vanmour uses composition and light to radically decenter the sultan (Plate 5). The representation of his throne matches Sutton's description perfectly, but here it is used like a kind of cell: pushed off to the left and looking out at the viewer, Ahmed III is isolated from all of the other figures in the painting. It is Calkoen with his glowing khalat (*khil'ah*) who is given pictorial centrality: he is not only located in the center and thus aligned with the light from the central window, but he is also engaged with the grand vizier on the far left. In other words, the absorptive alignment of Calkoen with the grand vizier in the second painting is redeployed here, but by turning their gaze ninety degrees, the entire picture highlights their colloquy and diminishes the exchange between the viewer and the sultan. As in the first painting, the painting's manipulation of viewpoint undermines the theatrical elevation of the sultan's power and forcefully establishes Calkoen's agency. With all of the viewer's attention converging on Calkoen, the most salient detail becomes visible. Unlike the other seven Europeans in the picture who are conspicuously being held by two flanking guards, Calkoen's hands and arms are free. He is not in physical custody. Vanmour not only negates the ritual sign of physical subjection to the sultan but also relegates Ahmed III to the background. If Sutton rhetorically attempted to recast subjection as hospitality, Vanmour goes one step further by asserting autonomy and perhaps even precedence.[43] Such a deviation from the audience protocols is a sign of precisely how uncomfortable Europeans were with this ritual: Vanmour would seem to be fully aware that his patron would prefer this version of the event and that the verisimilitude that de-fines his painting practice could itself obviate any lingering sense of humiliation. In short, it is Vanmour's pictorial rhetoric that allows Calkoen to retroactively reassert his subjective agency.

We will be seeing these diplomats and artists again, but I have presented these two examples in order to foreground key topoi and fundamental methodological concerns. In both Sutton's account and Vanmour's painting discomfort in the way that intercultural engagement is being framed by the Ottoman state generates productive distortions at the level of representation. Both the account and the paint-ing claim a certain level of descriptive verisimilitude, but close observation reveals subtle ruptures that allow for a retroactive reassertion of European autonomy— even when that autonomy is physically traduced by Ottoman state ritual. These ruptures often arise on discernable representational frontiers. In the Sutton text, the space where description meets narration allows for the careful reinscription of authority. The first and third Vanmour paintings establish thresholds of visual ex-change and use conflicting visual axes to diminish the theatricality of the sultan's power and elevate the absorptive subjectivity of the ambassador. Significantly, Van-mour's paintings effectively teach the viewer not to be drawn to that which is most pictorially spectacular and instead direct the viewer's attention to the small-est, yet most salient detail, namely Calkoen's free hands. In short, the historical/sociopolitical defensiveness of these textual and visual representations can be traced in the most local aesthetic and formal decisions, and thus they require a combina-tion of close analysis and deep historical contextualization.

After Peace and Beside War

This book is divided into two parts. The first, entitled "After Peace," focuses on the period from the late 1690s to the 1730s in the Ottoman Empire—from the epochal Treaty of Karlowitz in 1699 to the period just after the Patrona Halil rebellion. The first part of this period was marked by recurrent conflict with Habsburg Austria and its allies in the Holy Roman League dating back to the mid-seventeenth century. As recently as 1683 the Ottomans had been on the verge of conquering Vienna itself. Conflict between the Habsburgs and the Ottomans had been a fact of life for almost two hundred years—the first Ottoman siege of Vienna took place in 1529—but 1683 was a particularly perilous moment for the Habsburgs. Vienna was seriously weakened by the plague, and the Austrians were besieged by a large force of Ottoman janissaries, spahis (cavalry corps), and infantry. Strategic errors by the Ottoman commander, the grand vizier Kara Mustapha Pasha, allowed the Habsburg capital to be relieved by the Polish forces of Jan Sobieski. The alliance between the Holy Roman Empire and the Poles marked a turning point in the history of conflict between the Habsburg and Ottoman Empires. War continued for sixteen years after the Battle of Vienna and would flare up again in the second decade of the eighteenth century, but never again would Ottoman military forces progress this far westward.

The Treaty of Karlowitz (1699) and the Treaty of Passarowitz (1718) are crucial events for understanding the limitations on the westward expansion of the Ottoman Empire. These two moments of peace, arising from significant losses in the field, saw the Ottomans losing key territories and strategic positions in eastern Europe, while temporarily strengthening their grip on the Peloponnesian peninsula. The ensuing recalibration of Ottoman statecraft generated a period of great cultural efflorescence and a period of increasing social resentment between elite constituencies and more common people. As the Ottoman Empire turned its military attention to the dissolving Safavid Empire on its eastern borders in the 1720s, significant lines of fracture emerged in Ottoman society, and European observers found themselves witness to unparalleled modes of conspicuous consumption and social turmoil. Thus the narrative arc from the 1690s to the 1730s travels from constitutive scenes of war on the western borders of the empire to the most revolutionary scene of internal unrest in the history of the Ottoman capital.

The first chapter of the book serves as an introduction not only to the problem of intercultural sociability but also to the questions posed by peace. Chapter 1 examines the mediation of the Treaty of Karlowitz in two senses of that term. First, I offer an analysis of the mediation conducted by the British and Dutch ambassadors to the Ottoman Empire, Lord Paget and Jacobus Colyer. The chapter takes the reader from the horrific Battle of Zenta through the treaty conference to the celebrations that accompanied the ratification of the peace by attending to the mediation of these events in the scene of negotiation and in the capitals of Europe. Second, I analyze the mediation of the treaty negotiations in the European mediascape. This latter component involves readings of the newspapers, broadsides, engravings, and printed books that mediated these events for European audiences. Aside from establishing how information flows at this stage of engagement, I work this archive to show how mediation became a spectacle in itself. In doing so I introduce a number of shared strategies used by European and Ottoman states to make themselves visible both to each other and to their subjects. We will be looking at how processions, ritual gift exchange, and actual diplomatic performance were deployed and represented to figure forth the theater of peace.

My survey of the mediation of the Karlowitz negotiations demonstrates that the peace was achieved by establishing the social parameters whereby parties with different worldviews could communicate errantly to achieve incompatible goals. In fact, the differential qualities of translation allowed the Ottoman and Habsburg delegations to interpret the terms, derived from Roman law, in a fashion that maintained the integrity of both empires. Throughout my analysis it is evident that the very act of rendering what happened during the negotiations and what would happen in the post-treaty world was vexed. This sense of vexation will become a recurrent theme.

My second and third chapters focus explicitly on the crises in description that riddle the work of a longtime resident of Galata, the painter Jean-Baptiste Vanmour. Vanmour is, in my opinion, an extremely important figure not only because his work raises so many important issues for intercultural representation, but also because he lived in the Ottoman Empire for much of the thirty-seven-year period covered in the first section of this book. Because so little has been written on Vanmour, I undertake a full survey of the extant work produced during his career in the Ottoman capital. As I work through the widely circulated engravings of his costume images in Chapter 2 and his genre paintings in Chapter 3, I show that a sea change occurs in his work at roughly the time that he was commissioned to paint a portrait of Lady Mary Wortley Montagu. I will be discussing her *Embassy Letters* in depth in Chapter 4, but Montagu's text will prove to be useful in Chapter 2, in part because she is a likely source of information regarding the sequestered world of Ottoman women, and in part because her text engages with many of the descriptive problematics established by Vanmour in his costume engravings. Much of Chapter 2 builds on the discussion of processions in Chapter 1 to look not only at how Vanmour contains Ottoman state ritual but also at Montagu's subtle critique of these containment strategies. By comparing the work produced prior to and after Montagu's sitting for Vanmour, and by analyzing that portrait in some detail, I argue that we can discern significant disturbances in the descriptive aspect of Vanmour's art. His commitment to descriptive verisimilitude, inherited from the legacy of Dutch and French genre painting, is put into crisis by his desire to render that which he cannot see—specifically women and the revolutionary events of the Patrona Halil rebellion. Chapter 3 examines how he deals with this crisis in representation by pitting verisimilitude against itself and adopting a singular set of allegorical strategies to capture the social and historical transformations around him. If I am right about these strategies, then Vanmour's art offers a resonant archive not only for comprehending changes within the Ottoman culture he was observing but also for considering the political and historical import of description itself.

The fourth chapter extends this analysis of the politics of description by showing how the dynamics of translation, allusion, and allegory allow for even more complex representational interventions. I zero in on the volatile period immediately prior to and immediately following the Treaty of Passarowitz by closely engaging with Lady Mary Wortley Montagu's *Embassy Letters*. Montagu's Letter-book is arguably the most canonical source in this study and has certainly been the object of the most sustained critical scrutiny. One of the great virtues of Montagu's Letter-book is its self-conscious understanding of the problems posed by description and translation in an intercultural context. Her thoughts on translation are themselves revealing, and I deal with them at the outset of the fourth chapter in order to link back to similar problems that arose during Lord Paget's mediation of the Treaty of Karlowitz. But I have consciously placed this chapter after my consideration of Vanmour because I want the reader to have a full sense of Ottoman sociability in this period, before turning to Montagu's harrowing account of its desecration.

She famously offers some of the most compelling textual representations of intercultural sociability, but it is my contention that these moments are haunted by heretofore unrecognized formal and rhetorical qualifications—qualifications that seriously impinge on eighteenth-century European understandings of empire. By focusing on her complex analysis of war and peace in the region, I significantly shift the frame of analysis from prior studies of her text. I argue that to understand the full affective importance of her text and its remarkable generic innovations we need to follow closely the mediating function of classical literature and actual artifacts of ancient Greece in her text. Repeatedly Montagu uses scenes from Virgil and Homer to figure the ongoing conflict between the Ottoman and Habsburg Empires. In this regard, her text has much more to do with her husband's ambassadorial mission than we tend to acknowledge, and it has a great deal to say about the place of translation, mediation, and representation in a world at war. Dealing with this aspect of her Letter-book will necessarily open onto intense affective problematics, and I will argue that the Letter-book constitutes one of the most profound attempts to register, however indirectly, the visceral sense of historical crisis. Understanding this will require us to attend to the issue of hospitality, something that Montagu herself continually returns to as she brushes up against the tangible effects of war. To modify a phrase from Lauren Berlant, I argue that the Letter-book aesthetically mediates affective responses to exemplify a shared historical sense, but it does so in a way that questions the very notion of a "shared" history in a divided world.[44]

If we return momentarily to Vanmour's *View of Istanbul from the Dutch Embassy at Pera* (ca. 1720–37), we can postulate a comfort in distance and a disease with proximity. The closer one gets to intercultural exchange, the more one can discern the struggle to represent, describe, and narrate. At the risk of being reductive, the Vanmour picture can stand heuristically for this combination of representational equanimity and distortion. The archives from which the four chapters of "After Peace" derive exhibit many of these same problems, but in one remarkable way they move in an entirely different direction. As we will see, in contrast to Vanmour's outward-looking view of Constantinople, the accounts of the Treaty of Karlowitz, Vanmour's costume and genre paintings, and Lady Mary Wortley Montagu's Letter-book all exhibit a drive to get indoors. That is where the people are and that is where sociability, hospitality, negotiation, and exchange take place. These are the zones where representation is most vulnerable and precarious because there are either no common linguistic or social norms for interaction or too many. Crossing the threshold into these interior spaces, with the concomitant implication of gaining some sense of the interiority of Ottoman subjects, is no small task. I use the term "task" advisedly, because, as Walter Benjamin used the term in "The Task of the Translator," it emphasizes the ongoing errant process of exchange over any kind of transparent, closed meaning.[45] Benjamin's thoughts on translation are helpful because the desired sociability implied by the drive to "get indoors," if you will, always already involves the revelations and frustrations of translation. Translation is endemic to the preferred methodological terms of this book—sociability and mediation—and, as the epigraph from Adorno indicates, the strange combination of successful and failed communication is our topic.

"After Peace" excavates fundamental questions about war, peace, and sociability from instances in which representation is tangibly deformed or distorted by the challenges posed by intercultural exchange. By showing how eras of supposed "peace" are repeatedly punctured by complexly imagined fantasies of violence that draw their affective pull from wartimes of the deeply distant yet seemingly always present classical past, "After Peace" asks if there is *ever* any alternative to "wartime" affect.[46] Peace, as it is encountered here, seems to happen nowhere and in no time, which is not to say that it doesn't happen. As we will see, spatial voids and temporal lacunae are imagined, constituted, and maintained for peace to occur. But these respective acts of imagination, constitution, and maintenance do not operate outside war's jurisdiction: they happen within wartime, and that is why peace can never be separated from war. Even when hostilities and violence are not actively traducing the body, they inhabit memory as that which pertains to the past but that happens now. This is a strange statement because life requires that we recurrently forget this: that we imagine discrete moments of conflict that open onto death and moments of phantasmatic calm wherein we, as subjects, thrive. In its most provocative formulation, wartime is time itself and peace is what happens in its interruption—an interruption that is as much aesthetic as temporal.

Hospitality and intimacy seem to be what comes to stand in place of the "void" of peace in this book. Paget and Colyer choreograph the negotiations at Karlowitz such that representatives from the warring parties can cross a threshold and perform a historically vital experiment in intercultural sociability. Vanmour's descriptive art progresses when he devises a way of deploying the picture plane as an intercultural threshold: we will see what it means to be kept outside and what it means to enter the world he describes. And Lady Mary Wortley Montagu brings both the necessity and the violence of hospitality into the open in her Letter-book. For her unwavering act of witnessing the conditions of possibility for hospitality, intimacy, and sociability, I hope the reader will be grateful. It is chiefly in my reading of her Letter-book, and by extension its deployment of the *Aeneid*, that I have come to appreciate the precarious value of these terms.

As the preceding paragraph suggests, all four chapters of Part I demonstrate that the local pressures of intercultural communication and sociability and the global pressures of war converge in the materials I am discussing, thus my analysis has implications beyond the specific social and cultural milieu at hand. That said, one of the peculiar aspects of this archive is that all of the major figures I discuss knew one another: Paget was Lady Mary's relative; Lady Mary sat for Vanmour and may have been an important informant for his studio practice. What this means is that the large geopolitical narrative that holds these four chapters together is shadowed by an intimate network of social exchange. Paget, Colyer, Montagu, her husband and her various Ottoman acquaintances, Vanmour and his patrons Charles de Ferriol and Calkoen all lived in the same neighborhood, and although not necessarily directly acquainted with one another they would have relied on many of the same individuals to mediate their everyday relations with both the Ottoman state and the commercial world around them. If anything this is more intensely the case in the second part of this book. With the exception of Lord Byron, the primary figures I discuss all knew one another as friends, associates, enemies, rivals, or competitors in the cultural marketplace. And thus I pursue two levels of narrative engagement: one suited to capturing the large-scale conflicts between the Ottoman Empire and Russia in the late eighteenth century and one suited to rendering the interpersonal relationships between the classically inclined artists and diplomats stationed in Galata. As we will see, my readings of their cultural productions and their political acts serve to link these micrological and macrological concerns in a fashion that argues for the necessity of keeping both levels of analysis in play.

Part II of the book is entitled "Beside War," and it too follows upon another world historical peace, but this time a peace in which the Ottomans played no part. The Treaty of Paris of 1763 that concluded the Seven Years' War quite literally altered the shape and flows of global power, but the Ottoman Empire avoided what was otherwise a global conflict. The long peace from 1740 to 1764 was an era of prosperity for the Ottoman Empire, but it may have done more damage to the empire's future than any of its past military reverses.[47] During the Seven Years' War, most of the surrounding powers, specifically Austria and Russia, radically modernized their logistical and military capabilities. With the onset of war with Russia in 1764, the Ottomans found themselves technologically and strategically out of step with political entities threatening the northern and western borders of the empire.[48] The second half of the book looks at this period when Russia decisively defeated the Ottomans in two successive wars, thus precipitating an important era of governmental and military reform. It is during this period that Europeans start actively imagining a post-Ottoman world, and I carefully look at these genocidal imperatives and the complex acts of aesthetic resistance staged by some Europeans with long histories of living in Ottoman territory. In this period, Europeans keep looking toward Asia Minor—maybe even looking more than they did before in terms of the upswing of archaeological interest—but they stop *seeing* Ottomans. The second half of the book comes "after peace" in more than one sense: first, it takes place during the renewal of hostilities between the Ottomans and various other powers, and, second, it witnesses (at least in the archives I've assembled here) the cessation of a certain kind of sociable hospitality that animates Part I.

Crucial to Part II is the reconstitution of fantasies of ancient Greece from the rubble on the ground of Asia Minor. At one level, the first three chapters in this part offer a history of philhellenism as practiced and fostered by the diplomats stationed in Galata, but significantly there is an underappreciated connection to Lady Mary Wortley Montagu's writings. Chapter 5 focuses on the Ionian expedition sponsored by the Society of Dilettanti and the mediation of their findings in London. Montagu's *Letters of the Right Honourable Lady M——y W——y M——e: Written during her travels in Europe, Asia and Africa, to persons of distinction, men of letters, &c. in different parts of Europe; Which contain, among other curious relations, accounts of the policy and manners of the Turks* was published in 1763 and avidly read by the members of the expedition. In fact, their first act was to explicitly rehearse her exploration of Alexandria Troas, which I discuss at length in Chapter 5; thus one can argue that the expedition was continuing work first initiated by Montagu. The three primary figures in the expedition, William Pars, Nicholas Revett, and

Richard Chandler, not only collaborated on extremely influential publications of the Society of Dilettanti but also chose to exhibit, design, and write supplemental materials that significantly complicate the mission's empirical objectives. As we will see, the recent history of the Seven Years' War prior to the expedition and the outbreak of war between the Ottoman Empire and Russia shortly after the trio's return significantly inflected their accounts of what they observed. By bringing the trio's enlightenment project into close contact with their complex engagement with war, I argue that all three members of the Ionian expedition develop distinctly counter-enlightenment fantasies that ultimately postulate a nostalgic escape from the violent history that was reshaping the world around them.

If Chapter 5 is about art's auratic power to instantiate a retreat from history and violence, then Chapter 6 is about the incitement of violence in the name of art and culture. This chapter focuses on the activities of the Comte de Choiseul-Gouffier both prior to and after his appointment as the French ambassador to the Ottoman Empire in 1784. The first half of the chapter offers a detailed analysis of the genocidal imperative encoded into both the text and the engravings of his deeply influential *Voyage pittoresque de la Grèce* (1782). Choiseul-Gouffier's project was based explicitly on the example of the Society of Dilettanti publications, but he developed a number of key narrative strategies that significantly tilted his project away from ostensible empirical observation toward a highly ideological appropriation of Greek culture for the French Enlightenment. This appropriation came not only with a symptomatic derogation of Ottoman society and culture, but also with direct calls for the extirpation of Ottoman rule. The linked deployment of reproductive sexuality as a sign for the potential to reinvigorate Greece and of the sodomitical Turk as a sign of the barrenness of Ottoman culture is crucial to the Choiseul-Gouffier's rhetorical strategy in the *Voyage pittoresque*, and it remained a crucial issue for both his followers and those who chose to resist his example.

Once he became ambassador, his interventions were the focus of much concern, especially for Great Britain, because he felt that his political and aesthetic desires could be fulfilled by abetting Russian aggression in the region. The second half of Chapter 6 looks at Lady Elizabeth Craven's *A Journey Through the Crimea to Constantinople*. Craven was an interesting figure in her own right, and her fascination with the classical world drew her to the company of Choiseul-Gouffier once she arrived in Constantinople. Her travel memoir can be read as a sophisticated meditation on the function of ancient art and as a deeply disturbing rewriting of Montagu's *Embassy Letters*. What I show here is that her collaboration with Choiseul-Gouffier, her fetishization of ancient Greek art, and her anti-Ottoman resistance to Montagu's observations constitute a significant reworking not only of Choiseul-Gouffier's incitements to war but also of Montagu's melancholic contemplation of cosmopolitan peace. Craven translated Choiseul-Gouffier's opposition between reproduction and sodomy into an economy of female beauty with desirable Greek women at one extreme and repulsive Turkish women at the other.[49] Thus the deployment of sexuality in the *Voyage pittoresque* was differentially written onto the bodies of women under Ottoman rule, "Greek" and "Turkish" alike.

Chapter 7 examines the political and aesthetic resistance to Choiseul-Gouffier's attempt to turn his fantasy of liberating Greece into policy. Britain's ambassador Sir Robert Ainslie was Choiseul-Gouffier's chief diplomatic rival at the Sublime Porte and a notable classicist in his own right. Under his aegis, the artist Luigi Mayer produced a series of extraordinary watercolors that engage not only with the history of the Russo-Turkish wars but also with Choiseul-Gouffier's representation of Greek subjugation. In his dispatches and in the paintings he commissioned, Ainslie actively countered Choiseul-Gouffier's political and aesthetic designs and presented a remarkable view of collaboration between European and Ottoman subjects. After introducing the question of collaboration and remediation via a brief consideration of Ignatius Mouradgea d'Ohsson's *Tableau général de l'Empire othoman* (1787–1820), another cultural artifact that uses Choiseul-Gouffier's formal innovations to repudiate the political argument of the *Voyage pittoresque*, I demonstrate how Ainslie and Mayer's interest in cultural collaboration opens onto a very different understanding of the relationship between ancient and modern history. My argument here delves into one watercolor that not only counters Choiseul-Gouffier's genocidal imperatives but also activates the very homoerotic desires he so insistently abjures. Because Mayer's drawing of the Achilles sarcophagus at Ephesus is itself a remediation of two crucial engravings from *Voyage pittoresque de la Grèce*, it is as much an engagement with ancient Greek sexuality as it is with Choiseul-Gouffier's occlusion of it. With great subtlety and seriousness I believe that Ainslie and Mayer disclose their own intimacy as a bulwark against a world at war.

Chapter 8 builds on this reading of Mayer's meditation on the relationship of war, love, and empire to look at two masterworks of French and British Romanticism—Antoine-Ignace Melling's *Voyage pittoresque de Constantinople et des rives du Bosphore* (1807–24) and Lord Byron's *The Giaour* (1813). Both Melling and Byron pose significant questions regarding the relationship between emerging notions of normative sexuality and racial identity on the one hand and the practice of empire on the other. Melling's elephant folio and Byron's fractured poem both bear the imprint of Napoleon's military incursion into the Levant, and both use formal disjunction to engage with imperial nostalgia. Working in Constantinople first for the French and then for other embassies, Melling was commissioned by Sultan Selim III to execute a number of architectural projects for the sultan and for his sister Hatice Sultan. These projects were incorporated into one of the most important European renderings of the Ottoman capital, Melling's magisterial *Voyage pittoresque de Constantinople*. Like Vanmour's work in the 1720s and 1730s, Melling's work in the first decade of the nineteenth century offers a view of the Ottoman Empire in a state of internal transition. Again, close analysis of his drawings and engravings and their divergence from the accompanying texts written by his editor Jean-Charles-Dominique de Lacretelle opens onto a more extensive discussion of European-Ottoman relations during a period of wide-ranging governmental and military reform in the Ottoman Empire known as *Nizâm-i Cedid*. Because these reforms were initiated in the wake of humiliating losses to the Russians in the late eighteenth century and explicitly set about to modernize the Ottoman state on European principles, this material allows us to conclude our discussion of visual representations of the Ottoman Empire with a sustained meditation on a series of problematics that run through the entire book—the relationship between war and cultural change, the function of art in fantasies of intercultural détente and/or cultural supremacy, the status of modernity as experienced in this zone of varying rates of modernization, and the very problem posed by observation, representation, and desire between cultures.

Desire will prove to be a crucial bridge to my concluding analysis of the intersection of form, affect, and history in *The Giaour*. There is a palpable disjunction between the deployment of gender and sexuality in Lacretelle's Orientalist explications of Melling's engravings and the sociability implied by the images themselves. I argue that the tension between Lacretelle's ascription of desire and Melling's interest in intimate exchange with his patrons opens a gap in the text that allows us to crystallize a particular moment of imperial nostalgia. In *The Giaour* there is a similar tension between the notes and the poem, and between various fragments of the verse proper, and my objective is to show how Byron mobilizes these formal disjunctions in a critique of emerging British imperial policy in the nineteenth century and its reliance on heteronormative tropes and narratives to derogate both nonreproductive sexualities and the kind of intercultural exchange so vividly presented in the letters arising from his tour of the Levant in 1809 and 1810. As is well known, Byron's letters register his impatience with antiquarianism, his fascination with the people he meets in the Morea and in Constantinople, and his pursuit of queer desire in a space of relative sexual freedom. By attending to these three topoi, the full implications of my reading of the function of gendered figures in Choiseul-Gouffier and Craven's texts and Mayer's resistant homophilia fully unfold because Byron insistently destabilizes the sexualized norms that were so crucial to Britain's fantasy of a civilizing mission. Marilyn Butler's famous reading of *The Giaour* recognized Byron's critique many years ago, but I expand the purview of her analysis in a manner that draws up all of the chapters in "Beside War."[50] I contend that *The Giaour* returns to the moment of American decolonization to think through the local and global implications of imperial history—both British and Ottoman—in the wake of the Seven Years' War, and thus Byron's remarkable poem can be read in dialogue with Pars's anxious sense of entropy, Choiseul-Gouffier's will to power, and Ainslie and Mayer's attempt to think about other forms of desire and history. Thus my concluding remarks on *The Giaour* emphasize both the intimate and extimate negotiations with a new world order.

It is my hope that the struggle to give form to these desires—some of which are deeply disturbing and some of which seem to point to the possibility of liberation—that characterizes the chapters that make up "Beside War" will keep the reader in a continual state of uneasiness. Many of the same topoi explored in the opening four chapters recur—the fleeting condition of peace, the strange volatility of hospitality, the importance of intimacy and sexuality to this archive—but in this later historical moment everything seems to gravitate toward the selfsame. With the exception of the resistant strategies of collaboration discussed in Chapters 7 and 8, the phantasmatic subsumption of Greece in the imaginary of western Europe was facilitated by the Russian domination of the Ottomans in the final thirty years of eighteenth century. For British and French observers of this process, and of the weakened condition of the Ottoman Empire, this seemed to open a door for imaginatively acquiring the Ottomans' prize possessions.

Significantly this appropriation of the patrimony of ancient Greece did not happen through territorial acquisition. By operating "beside" war, the French and the British connoisseurs and antiquarians were able to obviate intercultural sociability altogether and thus substantively avoid many of the affective risks so dramatically on display in the chapters that make up "After Peace." "Beside" has the connotation both of adjacency and removal, proximity and distance. It is my sense that this spatial obfuscation in which violence is heralded and ignored is crucial to late eighteenth-century philhellenism and its corollary anti-Ottoman proclivities. Thus one could propose that the temporal loophole that made peace and intercultural sociability imaginable in the first part of this book has been transformed into a spatial loophole—a space adjacent to but affectively disconnected from the space of war. In the former case, the temporal loophole, because it became coextensive with time itself, allowed for an assessment of life. In the latter case, the spatial loophole becomes privative in order to allow for appropriation: relations among people become relations between people and things. In the most disturbing versions of this latter substitution, time itself collapses and, as we will see in the work of Choiseul-Gouffier, genocidal fantasies driven by the auratic power of art billow forth. And yet, it is the very force of these phantasmatic investments that generates the divergent acts of aesthetic resistance mobilized by Ainslie, Mayer, Melling, and Byron. Intercultural sociability reemerges as a crucial element of their resistant practices and artifacts.[51]

All this is to say that this study's consideration of the European engagement with the Ottoman world finds that the pressure of finding forms for intercultural sociability generates complex meditations on the nature of representation and history. In this regard, I hope that the book provides a useful counterpart to the current turn within Ottoman studies toward cultural history. In a sense this book may well operate like a photographic negative of the scholarship on Ottoman social, political, and cultural history by figures like Rifa'at Ali Abou-El-Haj, Halil Inalcik, Mehmet Sinan Birdal, Suraiya Faroqhi, Palmira Brummett, John-Paul Ghobrial, Virginia Aksan, Michael Talbot, and others that will surface throughout the ensuing chapters. I have neither the expertise nor the linguistic skills to engage with Ottoman materials directly, thus I find myself in a position not unlike many of the figures I discuss in this book. Thus translation, mediation, and, at times, speculation are vital methodological tools for engaging with this archive. In a very real sense, I am arguing that this quite literally comes with the territory and that, like the cultural practitioners I discuss, my own awareness of the complexity of intercultural exchange can be productive above and beyond any notion of transparent comprehension. It is my hope that I can translate the palpable weakness of my engagement into a strength—something that I think is exemplified by moments in Paget and Colyer's mediation, Vanmour's vexed descriptions, Montagu's errant translations and her vulnerable allegories, William Pars's entropic designs, Ainslie and Mayer's affective refigurations, Melling's hybrid inventions, and Byron's formal interventions.

PART I

After Peace

CHAPTER 1

Theatrum Pacis

Mediating the Treaty of Karlowitz

When and where does one find peace? Peace, if it is ever established, has a fleeting existence, and thus writing its history invariably becomes a historiography of conflict and war. In spite of the challenges posed by representing peace, it plays a vital role in this book's consideration of European descriptions of the Ottoman world in the eighteenth century. As we will see, the intermittent cessation of hostilities between the Ottoman Empire and its neighbors throughout the century had a deep impact on what I am going to loosely call an art of engagement. *Engagement* is a valuable word here because it has both geopolitical and aesthetic connotations, and this book will repeatedly make the transit from one to the other of these meanings. This chapter is about the mediation of the single most important interaction between Europe and the Ottoman Empire in the history of both domains. The Treaty of Karlowitz of 26 January 1699 fundamentally altered the rules of engagement for diplomatic relations between the Ottoman Empire and its European neighbors. In the words of Mehmet Sinan Birdal, "the signing of a peace treaty with a Christian state and the adoption of an international rule represented a radical break with imperial unilateralism. The ensuing treaties, which were negotiated for the first time by Ottoman diplomats of scribal rather than military origin, set clearly demarcated political boundaries and imposed respect for territorial integrity."[1] As this chapter unfolds we will be attending to the role played by Lord William Paget, the English ambassador to the Ottoman Empire, and Jacobus Colyer, his Dutch counterpart, in mediating this epochal agreement between the Holy Roman League and the Ottoman sultan. But my analysis of their actions cannot be separated from how the treaty negotiations were mediated for European audiences. Thus I will be considering "mediation" in two senses of the word. In order to comprehend diplomatic mediation we will be looking at its representation in scribal networks, official and unofficial correspondence, newspapers, pamphlets, maps, engravings, and illustrated books. My primary objective is to use this informational archive, especially the interaction of text and image, to understand a repertoire of particularly auspicious intercultural performances—performances that quite literally changed the world.

The year 1699 is frequently invoked as the beginning of the decline of the Ottoman Empire in that the treaty marked the end of its westward expansion. The fact of the matter is that the borderlands in eastern Europe remained very much in contention for the first half of the eighteenth century, and the Ottoman Empire itself remained a significant territorial power for a further two hundred years.[2] But 1699 marked a moment of transition, both historical and representational, in relations between the Ottoman world and Europe.[3] The Treaty of Karlowitz was the first diplomatic engagement in which the Ottomans were not negotiating from a position of strength. In prior treaty negotiations, the Ottomans were victorious in the field and merely sent representatives from the military to dictate terms.[4] This peace was also the first negotiated by civil servants: the Ottoman delegation was composed of the *reis efendi*, referred to in European publications as the secretary of state, and the chief dragoman, or interpreter, to the grand vizier.[5] The activities of these two men inaugurated a new era in Ottoman diplomacy and governance in which the Ottomans seemingly accepted the basic structural principles of international law promulgated in the post-Westphalian era.[6]

This was a conflict and a negotiation between empires with radically different legal histories and styles of legitimation that were slowly transforming into absolutist states.[7] Birdal emphasizes that the Habsburg and the Ottoman Empires transformed from self-declared global imperial powers to absolutist states according to very different chronologies.[8] At the time of the Treaty of Karlowitz, the Habsburgs were effectively an absolutist monarchy with residual links to the other states in the Holy Roman League. The Ottomans retained the posture of universal empire throughout the eighteenth century and only began the full transformation to an absolutist state form in the nineteenth century.[9] This makes the legal procedures adopted during the Treaty of Karlowitz quite complex. The Ottomans came to the table accepting the principle of *uti possidetis*—that is, that the various parties to the treaty would retain territories captured during the war—but the very notion, derived from Roman law, was translated to suit an Ottoman view of world affairs. Provisional acceptance of this principle did not imply that the Ottomans thought they were negotiating with equally sovereign powers—there was no recognition of foreign sovereignty. And it is clear from Abou-El-Haj's analysis of Rami Mehmed Efendi's "relation" of the negotiations that the Ottoman negotiator was working from a fundamentally different understanding of the preliminary agreements: one that understood the agreed-to procedures, principles, and evacuation clauses in ways that were in keeping with past modes of Ottoman negotiation and state legitimation.[10] What we have then is an act of political and legal mistranslation that enabled the Ottomans to retain their own self-image in a seemingly post-Westphalian situation. One could argue that the entire negotiation operated much like a Lyotardian "differend," where mutually exclusive phrase regimes were brought together in a way that enabled a kind of improvisatory interface between these state forms.[11]

The protracted war with the Holy Roman League that included Austria, Poland, Venice, and Russia dated back to the final months of 1682 and was, on the whole, a period of substantial loss for the Ottomans. The war started with the failed siege of Vienna in 1683, and its end was precipitated by the catastrophic Battle of Zenta in 1697. On 27 September 1697 readers of the newspapers in London would have encountered the following supplement dated Vienna, 14 September:

The Emperor has received advice by several Expresses of a signal Victory obtained by his Army over the *Turks*, on the 11th instant, near *Zentha*, with the following particulars: Prince *Eugene* of *Savoy* being reinforced with 7000 men from *Transylvania*, under the command of General *Rabutin*, resolved to fight the *Ottomans*; and accordingly marched the 9th instant with the Cavalry 18 hours together: the 10th he lay within 2 *German* leagues of the *Turks*, and the Foot came up. The 11th day early in the morning he advanced with Prince *Vaudemont* to view the disposition of the Enemy, and found 24000 Janizaries and 6000 Horse encamped on a very advantageous Post, for the security of which they had cast up three Intrenchments; the main body of their Army being encamped on the other side of the River *Theysse*; whereupon a Council of War was held, wherein it was resolved to attack the Enemy while they were divided, and immediately the Artillery was posted on a rising ground, with orders to fire upon the Bridge of the *Turks*, and hinder their passage; and the whole Imperial Army attack'd them with so much vigour, that tho the Intrenchments were defended with 72 pieces of Cannon, they took the first in an hour, and the others [sic] two in 3 hours more. The Slaughter was so great, that 10000 *Turks* were killed on the spot, with the Grand Visier and the Aga of the *Janissaries*. The rest endeavoured to get over the *Theysse*, but they were in such a confusion, that the greatest part were drowned. They left all their Cannon, Baggage and Ammunition. We had about 1000 men killed and wounded. Expresses have been dispatched to the King of *England*, the States, and the Elector of *Bavaria*, to acquaint them with this welcom News.[12]

Figure 4. Jan van Huchtenburg, *Vue et representation de la bataille de Zenta . . . 11 Septembre 1697*, etching, 1725. Trustees of the British Museum.

Prince Eugene of Savoy essentially destroyed the sultan's infantry: between 25,000 and 30,000 Ottoman soldiers, including most of the officer class, lost their lives in a single day of action. Of these dead, up to 20,000 drowned trying to flee across the river Tisa in present day Serbia.[13] With the river fully clogged with rotting corpses, the Austrians were forced to relocate their camps to avoid the stench.[14] As one might expect, engravings celebrating the near-total victory were immediately put into print that emphasize the sheer number of Ottoman soldiers and cavalry killed by the forces of the heroic prince on horseback. Versions of these images were still being produced in the 1720s (Figure 4).

The Battle of Zenta prompted "an extraordinary procession" in Vienna and something close to panic in Constantinople: according to letters from Vienna published in the London press, the grand signor "is inconsolable for his defeat which he frequently bewailes with Tears in his Eyes, and 'tis confirmed, that of all his Infantry only 2500 escaped."[15] A subsequent issue of the same paper describes elaborate scenes of self-castigation initiated by the Ottoman sultan, the extremity of which likely points to their fictionality. Declaring that the sultan attributed the loss of 30,000 men to a failure "to attone the anger of God, and appease his great Prophet," the paper reports that an edict had been issued demanding a multiday fast and specifying that the "*Mufty* and his Domesticks shall . . . appear first in the open Streets, and afterwards in the Churches in Sackcloth, girt about their Wastes with Ropes, and shall with mournful Countenances, Gestures and lamentable Outcries repeat *JA AAGIB JA ALLAH ALLAH* (O Wonderful God! O God.)"[16] This is merely the prelude to the following directions for a procession—ostensibly from the sultan—that confirms preexisting European views of Ottoman fanaticism and ferocity, this time turned inward:

> A great Chest full of dead Bones, broken Sabres and Muskets shall be carried, by 6000 Persons in Sackcloath, barefooted, without Turbants, and girt about their waste with ropes.
>
> 3000 *Mussulmen* shall sprinkle Blood and Ashes upon the Ground, Crying, Howling, Shreiking, and renting their Garments.
>
> 6000 Persons half naked shall scourge their Breasts and Shoulders with Thorns, till their Blood stream out upon the Ground, and it shall not be dried up.
>
> 3000 *Spahys* [spahis] without Turbants shall carry the Chest of the Prophet in the middle of this procession, and 300 Bassa's [pashas] with naked Sabres, shall go up and down, and if any man presume to stare upon the said Chest, he shall be immediately cut in pieces, and his Body thrown to the Dogs.
>
> At every Miles end a Christian Slave and a Jew shall be cut in pieces, and left to dye wallowing in their Blood.[17]

The spectacle of humiliation and staged exculpation fills multiple columns in the paper, and, in spite of the fact that processions were part of the Ottoman political repertoire, it is hard not to read texts like this as a form of wishful thinking on the part of Europeans used to fearing Ottoman aggression in eastern Europe and the Mediterranean. Broadsides featuring Ottoman religious officials tearing their beards out in consternation crystallized this scene of abjection (Figure 5).

But this gloating over Ottoman suffering is quickly replaced by reports on the progress of peace:

> Vienna, Aug. 23. We hear that the Principal points of the Peace with the Turks viz. That the Principality of Transylvania, and all other Conquests made during this War, shall remain in the Emperors Full Possession, and the *Turks* keeping of *Belgrade,* are adjusted by the English Ambassador, the Lord Paget; we will also try to divert the Turks from pretending the demolition of *Peterwaradin*; but the question is, whether they'll agree to the dismantling of *Temiswar,* which the Emperor insists upon; yet it seems that this Peace is look'd on by both parties as good as Concluded.[18]

Figure 5. Anon., *Abbildung der Türckischen Muffty, Welche Wegend es grossen Verlust ihrer Armee*, engraving, 1697. Trustees of the British Museum.

The principle of *uti possidetis*, *alahaleh* in Ottoman usage, had been proposed on numerous occasions by Paget but was only accepted by the Ottomans in an imperial rescript of July 1697.[19] For the Ottomans this would mean giving up Transylvania and other parts of Hungary—vast losses that could only be mitigated by retaining the Banat of Temeswar and certain strategic sites on the newly established territorial limits.[20] Working out these limits in a way that saved face for the sultan was the primary task of the Ottoman negotiators.

Coverage of the treaty negotiations in the London press worked by printing letters sent from more proximate sites to the news. In this case, initial reports from Vienna gave way to reports from Belgrade and finally readers in November and

December of 1698 started reading accounts marked and dated from Karlowitz.[21] These reports are remarkably detailed. For example, the press was especially attentive to the wretched weather. Reporting on the first day of negotiation, the *Post Boy* for 1–3 December states: "Both Parties have sent away most part of their Guards, retaining only as many as are actually necessary, by reason of the excessive Cold, which occasion'd divers of the Turks to desert, and an *Arabian* belonging to the Lord *Paget* died with Cold." This report ties in with others about Paget's ill health, but it either arises from a correspondent in the encampment or is meant to give that impression. As the same report indicates, "the Tents were surrounded with a Guard of Imperialists and Turks, with divers Officers of both Nations, who see all, tho' not hear it." More substantive remarks pertaining to the actual negotiation itself would seem to arise from the gossip collected by those adjacent to, but not immediately part of, the talks. And some of these remarks are more specific than any of the post-treaty publications: "the chief Debates are about settling the Limits, on which the Turkish Ambassadors desired, That since the Sultan, their Master, renounc'd his Right to a whole Kingdom, and so many Provinces, some insignificant things might be granted them in the Limiting of Frontiers."[22] This is not represented speech, but this summary's mimicking of the *reis efendi*'s idiom almost operates as free indirect discourse and thereby feigns a kind of immediacy. Staging moments of immediate witnessing was as much a part of the representational economy of the "news" as it is today. None of the retrospective accounts published after the ratification of the treaty offer this kind of detail about specific points of discussion even though there is evidence that these texts utilized the newspapers as source material. As we will see later in this chapter, these later compiled texts actively withheld the scene of speech from the reader.

As this brief sample of the reports on the Battle of Zenta and on the treaty preparations indicates, the news networks linking the European powers with the Ottoman world were remarkably rich. Even at this early date, printed intelligence operated to keep observers at great distances aware of developments in the war. The emergence of the newspaper as an informational genre builds on the already complex network of oral and handwritten communication that John-Paul Ghobrial argues tied together the Ottoman Empire and the European world.[23] But the press also generates a demand for information that activates other forms of mediation. By the end of this chapter I hope that this accelerating desire for information flow will be more palpable. I believe that this increased demand for information is not merely a function of print.[24] Rather, I want to suggest that there is something inherent to the treaty itself that warrants particular interest because the negotiations that ended this war, perhaps more than any previous diplomatic interaction with the Ottoman Empire, were about the very problem of intercultural communication. The chief mediators, Paget and Colyer, developed specific communication protocols to enable negotiation; and the primary mediations invented representational strategies suitable for capturing the performance of peace.

But rather than focusing on the mediators, I start by looking at one of the most puzzling aspects of the visual mediation of the treaty. This will draw our attention to the ludic space of negotiation itself, to its theater, if you will, and will prepare us for a consideration of the remarkable tableaux and processions staged by the various powers. Paget and Colyer attempted to contain these ritual ceremonies, and we will need to think about how one "sees" the state once its primary mode of visual exemplification is put in temporary abeyance. I say "temporary" because in ratifying the peace both the Habsburgs and the Ottomans quickly reasserted visual and material protocols for their recognition in the post-treaty world.

Describing the Void

There are moments when the archive itself points the way to what is salient. The vast array of documents surrounding the Treaty of Karlowitz is staggering. The texts temporally closest to the events are manuscript sources, but these are quickly supplemented by various genres of printed matter. Official diplomatic dispatches from all of the players are now held in national collections. These are unevenly distributed and preserved. Because of the long-standing tradition of Venetian diplomatic *relazioni*, there is an extensive narrative account of the negotiations and a 650-page bound volume of supporting documents in the collections of the Biblioteca Nazionale Marciano in Venice.[25] This impulse to retain every scrap of paper was partly business as usual in the Serene Republic, but there was also a clear sense that the Treaty of Karlowitz was a world historical event. Among Venetians it was seen as a high point in seventeenth-century Venetian diplomacy. At the core of this volume, interspersed with a remarkably complete record of official documents and key correspondence between Carlo Ruzzini, the chief Venetian emissary, and Paget, is a day-by-day diary of negotiation, most likely recorded by Ruzzini's secretary.[26] It would appear that the 650-page volume provided Ruzzini with the primary documents for the composition of a separate narrative entitled *Relatione del Congresso di Carloviz e dell'ambasciata di Vienna di Carlo Ruzini Cavalier*. In addition to summarizing the peace negotiations, this latter text provides "a detailed map in color put at the end of the volume, locating Karlowitz, Petrowardein, and other important places as well as the quarters occupied by the Turks, the imperialists, the English and Dutch mediators at Karlowitz, together with the *domus conferentiarium* and the seating of the conferees."[27]

We will be returning to this supplemental image in a moment, but it is useful to compare the Venetian to the English archive. In the eyes of many participants,

Venice was more of an irritant than anything else. The Venetian ambassador was both indecisive and constantly obliged to consult the council at Venice, thus his reluctance to act rendered him a minor player in the negotiations. Lord Paget, the chief mediator and driving force in the negotiations, was a crucial figure, yet the official record of his activities is far more scant. Paget had been in Constantinople since 1693 and had been pressing for peace since his arrival. Despite extensive discussion of his proposals for peace throughout the 1690s, his own dispatches are silent about the negotiations themselves. There are plenty of letters up to 9 May 1698 regarding the slow agreement of all the powers to accept the basic precept of *uti possidetis*, but official correspondence breaks off until 16/26 January 1699, when Paget writes to Whitehall to declare the conclusion of the treaty.[28] In other words, there is a gap precisely during the period in which Paget and the Dutch mediator Colyer progressed to Belgrade and convened the conference. The fractious negotiation over the actual site for the conference, the regulations pertaining to processions and ceremonies, the actual negotiations and ratification of the treaty are not part of the official English record.

This does not necessarily mean that Paget wasn't sending reports home to Whitehall. As Ghobrial states with regard to the embassy of Sir William Trumbull, English ambassador at Constantinople ten years earlier, England had not yet adopted a central record office for the secretary of state for the southern region: "the absence of any formal process for the deposit, storage, and consultation of ambassadorial dispatches along the lines of the *relazioni* meant that a good deal of this activity depended on the initiative and direction of individuals."[29] With no systematic compilation of information, Paget's dispatches may have been lost. Or the lack of records may be a function of his sensitive role in the negotiations. As mediator, his primary communicative function would have been between the active parties and not with the Crown. This is why the bulk of Paget's written record of the Karlowitz proceedings is held in his private papers and correspondence. The Paget Papers run to nineteen boxes of manuscripts in the School of Oriental and African Studies special collections at the University of London. These "private" records include large quantities of official documents. For example, all of Paget's specific instructions from William III and the declarations giving Paget the power to mediate are in this collection. Likewise copies of many of the drafted articles of peace and the counterproposals from Austria, Venice, Poland, Russia, and the grand vizier that were circulated prior to the agreement to negotiate were kept by Paget in his private papers. But interspersed with these governmental documents, Paget's papers also include private correspondence and a remarkable diary that allow us to reconstruct some of the complex interchanges that brought the peace to fruition. We will be returning to some of these personal materials later in this chapter.

The gap in the Foreign Office records is interesting because it is in stark contrast not only to other manuscript archives but also to the remarkably detailed accounts of the negotiations in the newspapers of major European capitals. There is a startlingly efficient network of scriptorial informants able to keep the newspapers well apprised of developments. The delay in news coming via Vienna was sometimes as little as four weeks. Readers in London were remarkably well informed about the mediation of their ambassador Lord Paget. As soon as the articles of peace were ratified, they were translated and sent all over Europe and of course to the sultan. The articles were then almost immediately circulated in print via newspapers and broadsides.

Soon to follow were printed narrative accounts of the proceedings that utilized previously circulated manuscript, print, and oral information. As early as 1700, the events were quickly incorporated into a new text by Paul Rycaut entitled *The History of the Turks: Beginning with the Year 1679; Being a full Relation of the Last Troubles in Hungary, with the Sieges of Vienna, and Buda, and all the several Battles both by Sea and Land, between the Christians, and the Turks, until the End of the Year 1698, and 1699; In which the Peace between the Turks, and the Confederate Christian Princes and States, was happily Concluded at Carlowitz in Hungary, by the mediation of His Majesty of Great Britain, and the States General of the United Provinces.*[30] A sequel of sorts to Rycaut's hugely influential *Present State of the Ottoman Empire* (1665), this volume was then added to all subsequent editions.[31] Similarly quick aggregations of information were printed in Austria, France, and the Netherlands. In Vienna a heavily illustrated book devoted entirely to the proceeding was published in 1702. The text, entitled *Gründ- und Umständlicher Bericht Von Denen Römisch-Kayserlichen Wie auch Ottomannischen Gross-Bothschafften, Wodurch Der Friede oder Stillstand Zwischen Dem Roemischen Kayser Leopoldo Primo und Dem Sultan Mustafahan III Den 26. Januarii, 1699; Zu Carlowiz in Sirmien auf 25. Jahr geschlossen Und darauff auch an denen respectivè Höffen Zu Wienn und Constantinopel bestaetiget worden,* not only gives an account of the peace but devotes considerable attention to the visits paid by the Viennese ambassador to Constantinople and by the Ottoman ambassador to Vienna immediately after the treaty.[32] A remarkable broadside engraving entitled *Theatre de la paix entre les Chrestiens et les Turcs* was published at roughly the same time at the Hague.[33]

By the time these illustrated accounts of the treaty negotiations were published something strange begins to occur. As information about this world historical event begins to cohere, there suddenly emerges what would seem to be excessive interest in the small building constructed to house the negotiations. As noted earlier, Ruzzini's *Relatione* concludes with a colored map that carefully delineates the *domus conferentiarum*. After portraits of King Leopold I and Sultan Mustafa II, the Viennese *Bericht* combines a bird's-eye view of the encampment at Karlowitz with diagrams of the conference building. Likewise, the elaborate Dutch engraving of the event, *Theatre de la paix entre les Chrestiens et les Turcs*, provides not only diagrams of the building but also images of key players in each of the rooms. Furthermore the entire composition of the Dutch map is attuned to the building itself. In all of these accounts of the treaty negotiations, detailed front views and annotated floor plans dominate the visual representations of the events. But their sheer simplicity seems to defy analysis. This simple four-room building is accorded more representational importance than the myriad processions that inaugurated the talks and the subsequent presentation of gifts after the treaty was ratified. Because of their ritual importance, these processions are attended to in the narrative accounts, and there is a careful tallying of presents, but we are being asked to look closely at the most mundane aspect of the event. There is also little interest in representing the plenipotentiaries and mediators: the stage is accorded far more attention than the actors. There are no explicit portraits of Paget or Colyer or of the chief negotiators for the Holy Roman League or the Ottoman sultan.[34] What about these simple wooden walls bears consideration?

The Italian manuscript and the Viennese and Dutch publications imply a desire to see where the negotiations happened. This is because the conference took place in the middle of nowhere. Much to the surprise and annoyance of Paget and the Austrians, the Ottoman plenipotentiaries refused the Austrian invitation to meet at Vienna. The two Ottoman negotiators, the *reisülküttab* Rami Mehmed Efendi and the chief dragoman Alexander Mavrocordato, insisted that the parties meet at "an appropriate place" on the frontier. Paget's letter to the imperial plenipoteniaries in Vienna gives a clear sense of his reservations:

> Sirs,
> We have now arrived near Crushendal [Krušedol], where it took Us quite a lot of time to inform Your Excellencies that the place is very inconvenient for a congress, because there is no water, nor any of the things necessary for Our Camp, which is why We have been thinking that we really need to move to another place, and go camp in the Carlowitz plain, where we can get plenty of what We are missing here, and where at the same time we will have the honour of being close to Your Excellencies.[35]

Paget's ill health made protracted talks outdoors in the winter unappealing. The Ottomans responded to his objections by guaranteeing tents and by allowing the Viennese to construct a building for the proceedings: "We were surprised to hear the day before that Your Excellencies appointed a wooden House for Us, although as we did not know it beforehand, We were unable to inform you, that We have been accommodated (some time ago) in an Imperial tent. We do not refuse to build a wooden house, provided that we pay for it, and we cannot give up this intention."[36] After much negotiation, Karlowitz, a small town on the Danube, was chosen because it had sufficient harbor facilities.[37] As Abou-El-Haj states, meeting in this space required a decree from the sultan and the Austrian kaiser to establish a neutral zone: "Hostilities were forbidden on the waters of the Danube and Sava Rivers. A truce was declared in the territory between these two rivers from Zemlin up to Ilcek and from Belgrade to the confluence of the Bosut River with the Sava—an area of about seventy-eight miles in length in the eastern parts of Slavonia."[38] With this neutral zone in place the various delegations camped at a short distance from the site of the conference house.

Perhaps the best sense of the degree to which the conference took place in an interstitial, marginal space can be gleaned from Rycaut's account of the proceedings: "On the 20th/30th [October] the Plenipotentiaries were showed to each other; and shortly after the Conferences began; but first the Preparations were making for building the House for Conferences: But in the mean time to supply that Convenience, a great Tent was rais'd in the midst of that void place which was between the Tents of the Mediators; where it was farther ordered, That instead of Chambers for the several Parties, there should be Tents pitched on both sides."[39] This "void place" is, of course, a fiction, but it is a necessary abstraction of neutrality. The importance of this indeterminate zone can be gleaned from Rycaut's own repetition: "On the 3/13 of November, the Ambassador from the Emperor, appeared in the Camp of *Carlovitz*; as also did those from the Sultan, who placed themselves on both sides, not far from the House appointed for the Conferences to be held, and not far from the Places where the Mediators had their Lodgings, in which void Places several Magnificent and Stately Tents were erected."[40]

Just as the very notion of mediation implies a forgetting of the interest of the mediators—it would be naive to think that the English and the Dutch were wholly disinterested; they wanted to end this war so that the Habsburgs could turn their attention to France in the War of Spanish Succession—so too does peace require a temporary suspension of convention and order. The very notion of "mediation" requires not only the postulation of an abstract space somehow adjacent to the immediate field of representation and action, but the articulation of a performance space wherein a new sociopolitical paradigm can emerge and eventually feed back into the surrounding politico-legal domains that temporally and spatially surround the negotiation. In other words, the "void place" is remarkably similar to the kind of ludic time space of liminality explored by Victor Turner and other anthropological theorists of ritual and play.[41] Here the void is established by the mediators, but it relies on the mutual decree of temporary neutrality by the sultan and the kaiser.[42] In other words, the void is surrounded by a carefully delineated military cushion whose importance will become obvious when we consider the visual materials associated with the treaty.[43]

The various accounts and illustrations of the Treaty of Karlowitz seek to "describe" this "void place" in three ways. If we look at the visual archive first, each of the illustrations locates the negotiations in geographical space—they locate the meeting on a particular site on the bank of the Danube. With these basic topographical coordinates in place the illustrations then situate the mediators and plenipotentiaries in the conference house. This is done with varying degrees of specificity: all three images provide a floor plan; the Dutch and the Italians provide a seating plan; but significantly only the Dutch map provides supplemental illustrations of the various named ambassadors in their respective rooms. What we can see from these simple distinctions is that each of the illustrations handles pictorial space in slightly different ways. By looking more carefully at these pictorial matters, we can begin to discern some crucial political distinctions.

The Italian map can be distinguished from the others because it is a singular entity (Plate 6). Hand drawn in ink and watercolor, it may have been prepared by Ruzzini himself. A similarly evocative town plan of Belgrade, dated 1699, appears to be drawn by the same hand (Figure 6). Both maps are aerial topographical maps curiously oriented such that North is at the bottom. The large-scale map has an inset Latin scroll whose text commemorates the peace:

> Theatrum Pacis.
> Quod inter
> Serenissimos et Potentissimos IMPERATOREM
> Romanerum Regem et Republicam Polonarium
> Rempublicam Venetam, Czar Muscovia' et Sereni
> ssimum, et Potentissimum Imperatorem Turcarum
> Iuxia
> Oras Danuby, et Eucrsi dim Oppidi
> Carlovitz
> 26 Mensis Octobris 1698
> apperiri Coeptem est.

What does it mean to call this the theater of peace? Is this an ironic play on *Theatrum Belli*, or "Theater of War": the title of numerous maps in the era? Despite its title, the map's top three-quarters bears all the traces of a military document. Each of the towns surrounding Karlowitz, marked by red churches, is located in relation to detailed renderings of fortifications. In this regard, the more detailed map of Belgrade is a helpful heuristic because we can see that both maps' precise

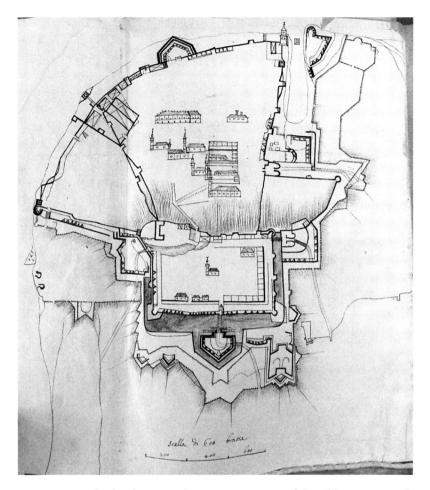

Figure 6. Map of Belgrade, 1699, ink on paper. Courtesy of the Biblioteca Nazionale Marciana, Venice.

rendering of the interaction between topography and fortification is strategic. The mapmaker uses green to denote the river and floodplain/marshland; hills and cliffs are rendered by close hatching. The orientation of each fortress is carefully documented. So the map is curiously double: it celebrates peace and records how best to proceed on this frontier should the peace dissolve.

That said, the large map also marks the location of the encampments of all the plenipotentiaries and the mediators and of the "Domus Conferentiarum." These ordinal marks are then presented in more detail across the bottom of the map. To the left, we have the orientation of the mediator's camps in relation to the conference house. To the right, we are presented with the rectangular arrangement of the plenipotentiaries' camps. In the center monument we have a floor plan of the building entitled "Ichnographia Conferentiarum" (Figure 7). The inverted T-shaped structure shows how each of the negotiating parties could retreat from the central

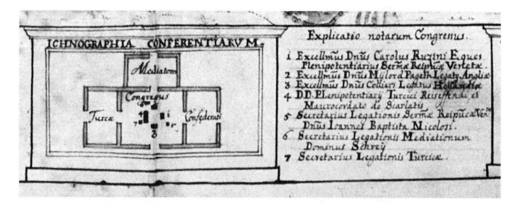

Figure 7. Detail, Carlo Ruzzini, *Theatrum Pacis*, ink and watercolor map. Courtesy of the Biblioteca Nazionale Marciana, Venice.

conference room in opposite directions. In the central room, the map records in detail the position of the mediators, the Ottoman delegation, and, because this is a Venetian document, the location of Ruzzini and Nicolosi his secretary. Although it does not give a scenographic rendering of these talks, for some reason the map makes its viewer aware of the position of the players in relation to the set. In spite of its ordinal explication, the descriptive impulse inherent to this rendering of the "Domus Conferentiarum" feels interrupted and stands in lieu of narrative. In this regard, the map could simply be seen as a descriptive supplement to Ruzzini's narration of events in the *Relatione*. But in comparison to the clearly strategic information presented in the upper three-fourths of the map, the bottom fourth provides information of dubious utility. Is the arrangement of tables in a room supposed to fulfill a commemorative function? Is it supposed to allow the viewer to imagine more vividly the dramatic events that took place in this theater? If so, then why are the actors withheld from view and why is the section of the map devoted to representing people subordinated to the rather decorative patterning used to denote marsh and hills? Is mapmaking so wholly subservient to military usage that devising a map for peace is riven by discontinuous signs? Strangely enough, I think we can get some purchase on what is going on here by looking at a far less detailed visualization of this event.

By the standards of late seventeenth-century engraving, the Viennese diagram from the *Bericht* is not terribly refined, but that is itself important (Figure 8). It is neither a map nor a narrative composition, but a combination of both visual modes. The engraving is divided in half across its length. The bottom half of the image provides a floor plan and a frontal view of the building in what appears to be the same scale; and these views are separated by a lettered key that identifies components of both sections of the engraving. The top half of the image uses a bird's-eye view to situate the building in the space of the encampment. Comparison with

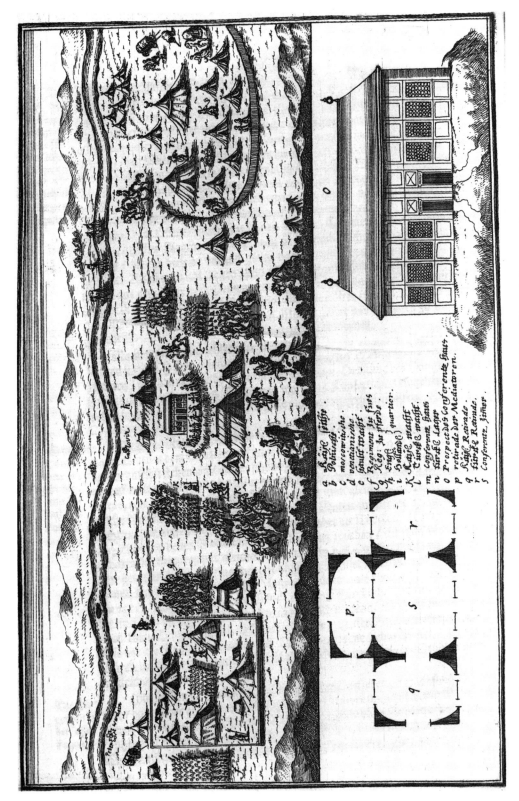

Figure 8. Map of camp, in *Gründ- und Umständlicher Bericht Von Denen Römisch-Kayserlichen Wie auch Ottomannischen Gross-Botbschafften*, engraving, 1702. Courtesy of the Getty Research Institute, Los Angeles.

the Italian map shows that this diagram is not terribly interested in the coordinates of the encampments: at the very least there is discrepancy about where the river should go. What was crucial to the Venetian map—strategic location—is of no concern here; rather the mountains and the river are compositional devices. Carefully situated between the mountains in the foreground and the river and mountains in the background, the building's centrality to this part of the engraving is emphasized first by the careful array of cavalry and infantry on each side and then by the visual renderings of the rectangular European encampment on the left and the circular Ottoman encampment on the right. The building is further framed in the top half of the engraving by the English mediator's tent on the top and the Dutch mediator's tent on the bottom. It is significant that these tents are both identical to each other and different from the tents of the other powers. However crudely, the engraving emphasizes not only the distinction of the mediators from the negotiating plenipotentiaries, but also the distinction between the Holy Roman League and the Ottoman Empire.

But there are a number of subtle gestures here as well. The rendering of the camp of the Holy League (the alliance of Austria, Poland, Venice, and Russia) is based in fact—apparently the only way that the mediators could mitigate the problem of precedence among the powers was to settle on a rectangular deployment of tents[44]—but close perusal reveals that the left side of the engraving is far more militarized than the right. The Holy League encampment is filled and flanked by troops, and there are four prominently represented sentries. The Ottoman encampment is less organized and is filled with figures conspicuously smoking. The smoking Turk, like the crescent-topped tent poles presented here, is, of course, a stereotypical visual sign, but the paucity of janissaries in the camp—as opposed to the ceremonial figures immediately adjacent to the conference building—is a subtle sign of the depleted Ottoman military. The emptiness of the Ottoman camp underlines the merely ceremonial exhibition of strength just to the right of the building. When we recognize that the Venetian map didn't even bother to render the Ottoman encampment, it becomes evident that this contrast is a vital concern for the Austrian document.

All of the textual accounts of the negotiations emphasize the splendor and sheer size of the Ottoman delegation—Abou-El-Haj reports that Ottoman accounts talk of an escort in excess of twelve hundred officers and troops: "Each [Ottoman delegate] had more than three hundred *curbacilar* (officers of the corps of the janissaries), dressed in their red flowing robes, trousers, plumed headgear and yellow light boots. Several hundred cavalry, infantry officers and troops from various divisions of the Ottoman armed forces, with scores of musketeers carrying their silver embossed muskets, marched in front of the Ottoman delegation."[45] But in the Viennese engraving that magnificence is recontextualized as a face-saving gesture, as a performance that ultimately testifies to weakness. At one level, this is hardly surprising; after all, this a Viennese publication and the Austrians had essentially routed the Ottomans and forced the ulema and the sultan to enter into a peace process that they had publicly rejected until the very last moment.[46]

But it is the crescent-shaped group of figures immediately below the conference house that warrants our most serious attention. At the center of the crescent, just below the doors to the house, two figures shake hands. Presumably the chief Austrian negotiator, Count Ottingen, and Rami Mehmed Efendi are performing an act of good will immediately prior to entering into negotiations.[47] The number of attendants and the mediators is roughly correct, so we would seem to be on the verge of the negotiation itself: this is the last moment that both parties are visible before getting down to business. In this regard, the building becomes a bit of a black box: the walls impede visual observation and that necessitates the floor plan below. But when we turn to the floor plan, what we get are four carefully arranged "voids." The diagram locates the spaces apportioned to the Habsburgs and their alliance, the Ottomans, and to the mediators, and shows how the building's design does not accord precedence to any of the negotiating parties. Significantly, the mediators are located on a different axis than the Holy League and the Ottomans, thus replicating the overall spatial organization of the upper half of the engraving. The pictorial organization of the upper half of the engraving— that is, of the encampment—is modeled on the architectural organization of the building, and this correspondence is meant to exemplify the conditions of negotiation.

But the more one looks at this crucial symbolic floor plan, the more that the central room becomes an ovoid cipher. At a certain point intercultural communication had to occur in this space, the performance of negotiation had to unfold. But it is precisely this social interaction that eludes this image. This is odd because the text shows no such reticence:

> In accordance with this plan the Imperial and Turkish legates had a number of beautiful tents pitched on either side of the conference house early in the morning of November 13th, towards the site where the mediators had been standing earlier. The Imperials drove thereafter to the first congress around nine o'clock, in four carriages with six horses and a large entourage. Around the same time the Turkish legate appeared in said place with much splendour and many people on horseback. After the mediators welcomed each party, first the Imperials and then the Turks in their tent, they walked together into the conference house in equal steps on either side of the mediators. They very courteously greeted one another there, in which the mediators and Imperials as well as Mauro Cordato, being a Chris-

tian, uncovered their heads. The Reis Efendi, however, bowed in Turkish manner with his right hand pressed on his left breast. They sat down on some chairs which were positioned quite near each other on a rug; the Imperials' chairs were cloth-draped fauteuils, and the Turks had gold- and silver-leaf covered Vesper chairs, not unlike footstools.[48]

The disjunction between image and text is deeply significant because the crucial early negotiations between the Austrians and the Ottomans did not happen in this room. Because the building was not yet complete, the first phase of the negotiations between the Austrian delegation and the two Ottoman negotiators took place in a special tent provided by the sultan. This is revealed in a slippage in Rycaut's account:

> about Nine in the Morning, the Emperor's Ambassador arrived, being attended with Four Coaches of State and a Numerous Retinue.
>
> And in the first place they went to the Tents of the Mediators, where at the same time appeared the *Turkish* Ambassador, attended with a very stately Retinue . . . Where after the Salutations, and Complements on both sides, sufficiently Courteous and Obliging, they took their Seats in the middle of the *Tent*, purposely set, and laid for them, one directly against the other, in such a Manner, that no Person could take Exception against his Place, or Seat appointed for him.
>
> This being agreed and settled, the first Conference began, which was to determine this Great and Solemn Peace, which was the first of this kind, that ever passed between the *Christians* and the *Turks*.[49]

That the negotiations started in this tent is important for various reasons. First of all, the first three or four days of negotiation established the pattern and precedents through which negotiation would take place. The Austrians came to the treaty talks in an obvious position of strength. They had decisively vanquished the sultan's forces on the battlefield and stood to gain vast amounts of territory in Hungary and Transylvania that had long been under Ottoman control. But the Austrians were also pressed to end hostilities in the East so that they could focus more military attention on the French threat to western Europe, especially in the Low Countries. As Jeremy Black demonstrates, this had a significant impact on Austria's ambitions during the treaty. In contrast, the Ottomans came to the talks severely weakened and stood to lose a large amount of territory.[50] In the face of these setbacks, "an Imperial rescript, dated July 22, 1698 . . . named the Grand Vezir, his deputy (*vekil*) in the settlement of peace, with delegated authority to appoint an Ottoman peace mission fully accredited and empowered to treat, negotiate and sign the peace. However, it was stipulated that in their conduct of the negotiations both the Grand Vezir and the Ottoman plenipotentiaries were not to act, under any circumstances, contrary to the honour (*irz*) and the dignity (*namus*) of the Sultan."[51] "Given the sultan's 'ideological role' as the ruler who constantly expanded the borders of the Islamic world by victorious campaigns," the Ottoman delegation not only had the task of minimizing territorial losses, but also had to avoid a humiliating peace.[52]

Rami Mehmed Efendi and Alexander Mavrocordato responded to this difficult task by adopting a startling strategy. By obstinately laying claim to Transylvania—a territory they had already lost and had agreed to give up by acceding to the precept of *uti possidetis*—the Ottomans initiated a crisis. With the Austrians threatening to leave, the Ottomans essentially gave up what they had no claim to in exchange for something contested: the Banat of Temeswar. The Austrians controlled much of this territory, but the Ottomans argued that because they still held the capital and because they had "given" up Transylvania already in negotiation, then they should regain control of Temeswar. The tactic worked and set up the pattern for the next contentious problem: establishing the border. In much the same fashion as the Transylvania/Temeswar "trade," the Ottoman negotiators succeeded in forcing the Austrians to negotiate the evacuation of forts and towns in succession all the way along the military frontier. This was a radical divergence from the preferred Austrian solution to this problem. As Paget stated in a letter prior to the congress: "The Imperialists propositions are large and full of words, and so mathematically disposed by notions of [drawing crossed out] imaginary lines to be drawn for distinction of frontiers, that I fear the Turks will never digest them, and I dare affirme they will not pass, except they be very much altered."[53] Paget implicitly understood that the visual paradigms used to understand space were culturally specific—that is, that any kind of geometric rendering of space typical of seventeenth-century European maps would alienate the Ottoman delegation.[54]

As Suraiya Faroqhi states with regard to the Ottoman tendency to disregard officially drawn "line borders," "When truces were negotiated, which according to the stipulations of Islamic religious law had to be strictly temporary, it was usually the possession of individual fortresses that was considered crucial rather than the course of a line on the map."[55] So rather than assenting to global abstract solutions proposed in writing by the Austrians, the Ottomans succeeded beyond Paget's predictions to shift the terms of negotiation. It appears that the negotiation proceeded by avoiding such visual representations of territorial limits and opted instead for textual descriptions and narrative accounts of territorial space.[56] Mehmed Reis Efendi would continually horse-trade strategic position for strategic position all along the frontier. As Abou-El-Haj argues, these tactical gains at the negotiating table were remarkable, considering the weakness of the Ottoman position, and they allowed the Ottomans to foreground the retention of Temeswar as a "victory" in spite of the fact that they permanently lost vast tracts of land in Hungary and Transylvania.[57]

This strong performance by the Ottoman plenipotentiaries occurred while the negotiations were held in the tent provided by the sultan. That tent was specially designed with four separate entrances to obviate problems of precedence, but its erasure from the Viennese illustration suggests that the Austrians were discomfited by the fact of the early negotiations taking place in an environment both materially and visually aligned with the sultan. To put this Ottoman tent at the middle of the engraving would be to radically reorient the conflict and the treaty itself because it would suggest that the Ottomans' good showing in the negotiation was in some sense a function of the fact that it took place on "their ground." In short, the tent in which the negotiations between Austria and the Ottoman officials took place had to be erased not only to consolidate the fantasy of neutrality but also to reassert Austrian domination of the proceedings. The important thing about the conference house then is that it is so palpably not a tent; that empty central room is a historical screen designed to obfuscate rather than clarify what happened in these negotiations. I would contend that the centrality of this building in all of the visual representations of the treaty in European sources serves to formally displace the Ottomans both from pictorial space and from historical time. It is a supplemental gesture aimed at asserting Habsburg domination both during the negotiations and after the peace.

The conference house was completed at roughly the same time that the key aspects of the deal between the Habsburgs and the Ottoman sultan were in place, and upon its completion the negotiations followed the earlier pattern of negotiation, only now the Ottomans met with each of the other powers in turn. We can get some sense of the disruptive qualities of the negotiation tent by turning to the elaborate Dutch engraving *Theatre de la paix entre les Chrestiens et les Turcs* (Plate 7/ Figure 9). Despite the obvious increase in refinement and detail, this document also uses the building as a compositional device.[58] The central axis provides the topographical location of the house in the central upper view and a combination of frontal view and floor plan in the lower central rectangle. The floor plan itself, set into a bit of sculptural ornament, is similar to the Venetian map in that it provides the arrangement of chairs and tables. But basically these two central sections aggregate and arrange the spatial information in much the same way as the Viennese engraving. Both focus attention on topography, on the ceremonial display of arms, and both use the house to organize visual and political space. This is perhaps most forcefully seen both in the way that the escorting troops are deployed to draw the

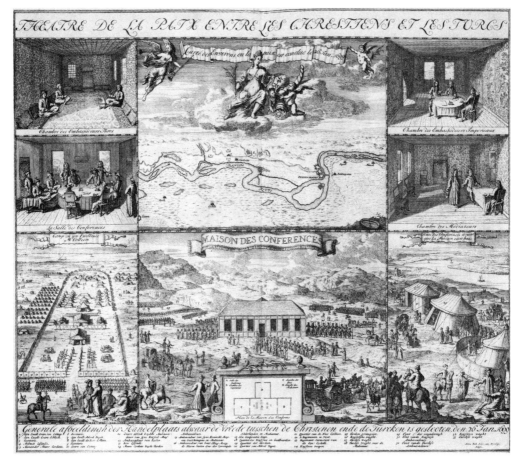

Figure 9. Anon., *Theatre de la paix entre les Chrestiens et les Turcs*, engraving, ca. 1704. Courtesy of the Albertina Museum.

eye to the house itself and in the pairing of the ornamental figure for peace on the top of the image with the ornamental sculpture that carries the floor plan. Both ornaments are adorned with lilies to signify peace and prosperity.

However, unlike the Viennese engraving, this document tells the story of the Dutch mediator, and thus it contains three things ignored in the Austrian text. On the bottom right there is a detailed representation of the negotiations, entitled "Tente des Conference avant que la Maison estoit batie." The title is a misnomer because the engraving shows three separate and very different tents. As Rycaut states, "not far from the Places where the Mediators had their Lodgings, in which void Places several Magnificent and Stately Tents were erected." The conference tent is in the middle, and it is flanked by two different styles of tents: to the left is a rectangular structure with semicircular end walls and bearing the Habsburg arms on its roof and to the right is a large circular tent surrounded by a second exterior wall and surmounted by an Ottoman crescent. Intriguingly the central tent appears to be an architectural hybrid of the Austrian and Ottoman tents: it has the basic footprint of the Austrian tent, but its walls flare outward like the Ottoman structure. All insignia have been removed, and only the tent poles are adorned by neutral blossom-like finials.[59] Whether this was the case is aside from the point: the engraver has decided to construct a blended structure for these unprecedented negotiations. This is also reflected in the unusual doorways. As many reports indicated, the central negotiation tent had four evenly spaced doors in order to obviate matters of precedence upon entry and exit to the zone of negotiation. Each of these subtle details is part of a larger argument about extra-sovereign exceptionalism: this is the impossible place of peace where the cultural, political, and social determinants that are inscribed into space itself merge.

If one looks closely at this inset image the negotiations are ongoing—one can just make out the backs of the negotiators in the two visible doors. Because the tents are set in a line and access from tent to tent is restricted by conduit like ranks of soldiers and janissaries, we see into the end of the tent from the Ottoman side. The midway door is that of the mediator, most likely Colyer, because the entire engraving tracks his activities but never quite gives us his presence.[60] In a sense, what the organization does is show how Colyer, or Paget, for that matter, can be traced by following how space is arranged to accommodate their mediate position. In the bottom right insert we have two carefully articulated axes set at right angles. There is the axis linking the negotiating powers that passes through all three tents and incorporates the ancient ruined fortress at Karlowitz. This linear conjunction is not incidental because, of course, the fortress and the field tents are scenographically vital to the theater of war. At right angles to that axis of conflict, there is the axis of mediation that runs through the two coaches and right through the middle door of the conference tent. These coaches are intriguing because they exist in stark contrast to the ranks of infantry and cavalry deployed elsewhere in the engraving. They seem to carry a demilitarized signification and promise the possibility of civil society arising from this unlikely frontier encounter. We know from accounts that the Austrian envoy Ottingen also arrived in a coach, and it is represented at the far end of the Austrian tent, but for that reason it is folded into the axis of antagonism that diagonally bisects this inset image.

These minor compositional details become increasingly significant when we cross the engraving and compare them to the pictorial rendering of the "Camp du son Excellence Mr. Colliers." This bird's-eye view of Colyer's encampment depicts a specific moment—the arrival of the mediator before his vast retinue. We know from Rycaut that the mediators were escorted from Adrianople by a vast procession of janissaries and that their passage over the Sava River was marked by cannon salutes. They preceded the other plenipotentiaries to the general environs of Karlowitz, but their eventual presentation at the conference site was the occasion of a joint reception: "Upon the Arrival of the Mediators at *Carlowitz*, they were received by the *German* Horse and Foot, and a Captain-Lieutenant and a Standard, with 50 Horse, and an Ensign, with 70 Foot, which were appointed to each Ambassador for the Mediators Guards. The *Turkish* Soldiers were at the Right of the *English* Ambassador and at the Left of the *Dutch*."[61] The image of Colyer's encampment does not necessarily depict this moment, but it does mark a moment of formal reception with Austrian and Ottoman guards carefully arranged to the left and right of the arriving carriage of the mediator. Everything about this part of the engraving is about order, number, and magnitude. If one looks closely, one can establish the number of horses, carriages, and tents in part because they are laid out with almost mathematical precision. In contrast to the dynamic diagonal bisection of the inset image on the bottom right, this view is rigorously perspectival and balanced on a vertical axis. This contrast is not incidental, because the camp of the mediator is meant to figure a world in orderly balance, the world to come from the negotiations depicted on the bottom right.

In a sense, this pictorial contrast allegorizes mediation itself, and this is borne out by the figures in the foreground of each inset image. From their costume the figures in the right foreground are of various nationalities, but the crucial detail is their disparate placement. No one occupies or speaks on the same level. By contrast the prominent pair of figures in the foreground of the bottom left inset stand on the same ground and converse directly eye to eye. They are flanked by three other seated figures, more Turkish looking, again in direct conversation. It is no accident that the mediator's carriage emerges from behind this rendering of equal colloquy. Nor is it surprising that horses of different scale traverse the pictorial space of the bottom right image—they have the compositional task of figuring forth disequilibrium.

With some sense of the allegorical importance of the relationship between bodies and spaces in this engraving, it behooves us to consider its most remarkable feature. Unlike the Venetian or the Viennese documents, the *Theatre de la paix* provides the viewer with detailed representations of each room of the convention house and with labeled portraits of each of the primary players in situ. These portraits are obviously not likenesses, but they stress the social interaction of specific bodies in specific spaces in much the same way that contemporary engravings and drawings of set designs capture moments of dramatic incident.[62] In the "Chambre des Mediateurs," "Syn Excell Milord Paget" and "Syn Excell de Heer Colliers" are seated at the table conversing with an unnamed "Secretaris." The "Chambre des Embassadeurs Imperieaux" and "Chambre des Embassadeurs Turcs" provide labeled figures of each of the plenipotentiaries along with unnamed secretaries in their respective rooms in the conference house. All of the figures are then brought together as a group negotiating in the "Salle des Conferences" (Figure 10). This is

Figure 10. Detail, "La Salle des Conferences," *Theatre de la paix entre les Chrestiens et les Turcs*, engraving, ca. 1704. Courtesy of the Albertina Museum.

precisely what was absent in the other images, and it is interesting to consider how the Dutch illustrator fills the void. If one looks carefully at each of the rooms, one notes that they are decorated in distinctly different styles. With the exception of the "Salle des Conferences," attention has been paid to wallpaper and furniture. The space surrounding Rami Mehmed Efendi and Alexander Mavrocordato is obviously the most distinctive—the carpet, the divan, and typically floral wall coverings all mark the space as Ottoman. But no less attention has been paid to the distinction between the Austrian rooms and the mediator's room on the right; decorative style is being carefully deployed to register cultural and national difference. At one level this is little more than an extrapolation from the period's tendency to use costume to make national and racial distinctions. And this of course extends to the image of negotiation itself, where each party is identified and differentiated by clothing, posture, and chair.

But this specification takes on a different significance when we look more closely at the "Salle des Conferences." Whatever distinction we can find around this table is a function of the body of the plenipotentiary. We know that after the second day of negotiation a divan of sorts was installed to accommodate the Ottoman delegation unaccustomed to sitting in chairs, and it is fitting that the only distinction in furniture in this image reflects a widely reported bodily need. But rather than making this alteration the occasion for further specification, the surrounding space of negotiation is devoid of ornament. The walls are bare, and even the carpet on which the *reis efendi* and Mavrocordato sit, unlike that of the "Chambre des Embassadeurs Turcs," is free of pattern and texture. This is how *Theatre de la paix* renders the "void" of neutrality. As with a theatrical production that strips the stage bare, this scenographic gesture focuses attention on communication it-self, on gesture, on represented speech, and on the only props available—namely, the implements of writing. Notably no one around this table is writing: the pens and papers are there for future use. But there is a great deal of gestural commu-nication signifying colloquy. What is so remarkable about this image is how the bareness of the space heightens the sense of intimacy required to fill the void.

We can now see that the Dutch engraving is carefully designed to instantiate the desire for intimate communication. The central house and the floor plan in the center of the picture operate as moments of blockage—the entire composition directs us to them but they are like ciphers. Likewise the complex bottom insets operate dialectically to give a sense of the push and pull of negotiation. Both bird's-eye views show the need for and the promise of peace by contrasting pictorial discord on the right with order and balance on the left. That neither image brings us into the space of negotiation, but each merely signals its ongoing presence, is crucial because this generates a need for further elucidation that is achieved by the detailed views of the rooms in the top of the picture. In a sense, these rooms constitute the elusive dialectical resolution to the historical conflict presented in the bottom of the engraving. *Theatre de la paix* demands that the viewer con-ceptually place these rooms in the plan and that firmly locates the rooms of the plenipotentiaries and the mediators on the periphery of the central "Salle des Conferences." What this means is that one has to actively place this image from the left of the engraving into a central conceptual zone. Further, it is clear from the vertical arrangement of spaces that the centrality of this space of intimate colloquy is appended to or made possible by the "Chambre des Mediateurs." The viewer is called upon to bring the negotiation into the center, as it were, to carry out a conceptual act that mimics the act of negotiation itself in that one has to give up firm spatial demarcation, break the rules of normal pictorial organization, and adopt new rules established by the image of the "Salle des Conferences" itself.

The circular arrangement of figures around the table and the complex play of glances and gestures operates very differently than the play of vertical and hori-zontal lines that organize the overall pictorial space of the map. Just as the diago-nal axis in the bottom right image constituted a remnant or reminder of war's disturbance of the *Theatre de la paix*, so too does the circular composition of the "Salle des Conferences" show us not only how conflict will be terminated but also how one must read the engraving's representation of that termination. Just as the plenipotentiaries look back and forth around this table, the viewer of the *Theatre de la paix* needs to take in its various components, overcome its conventional rec-tilinear arrangement, process all its different views, and finally recognize the world-historical importance of that which is conventionally displaced—intimate exchange and colloquy. The engraving's complex displacement of the "Salle des Conferences" and its replacement by the centrally located frontal view of the house speaks volumes about how the mediation of peace requires the suspension of conventional historiographical form, forms that invariably give us limited views of events and persons. What I would suggest is that like the mediators themselves, the *Theatre de la paix*'s mediation of the negotiations brings us into a rarely adopted representational loophole where the small gestures and words only discernible through intimate contact emerge as the most salient matters at hand. As these displaced experiences migrate to the conceptual center of this "theater," it becomes clear why the writing implements on the table are untouched. It is not simply that we are witnessing a moment prior to the treaty's formal composition and ratification. We are being asked to consider and actively create, by reorganizing the image, the conditions of possibility for peace. And this involves imagining a cosmopolitan world where two Ottomans, an Englishman and a Dutchman, and two Austrians and their multilingual secretaries communicate orally at table.

The Spectacle of Mediation

Significantly, the challenges of imagining that performance were anticipated by the mediators themselves when they established the rules of negotiation. As Rycaut reports, on 6 November 1698 the mediators pressed all the parties to agree to six "Articles for Facilitating the Negotiation." The first was the most brief and the most important: "To take away Notifications, and Visits of Ceremony and Precedence." Paget and Colyer were extraordinarily cognizant of the problems posed by state ceremony and protocol. The entire congress was almost scuttled by the Russians who, through poor planning, arrived at Karlowitz at the same time as the Venetian delegation, thus precipitating a crisis of precedence. Working out who would alight onto the shores of the Danube first was a delicate matter.[63] Navigating these matters of protocol took skill and knowledge. Perhaps the most revealing example of the perils of failed ceremony came shortly after the treaty was ratified. In two rather bemused letters, Paget writes about the humiliation of the new French ambassador Comte de Ferriol. Ferriol insisted on wearing his sword to his first audience with the sultan and was rather brusquely shown the door, followed by his presents.[64] Shortly after this diplomatic faux pas he made the error of setting out in a roofed galley that surpassed the sultan's in opulence. He was thrown in jail for eight days and the *bostanci*, or palace guards, demanded that the offending vessel be destroyed.[65] He would remain out of favor for four years. What would seem to be petty matters were actually of great consequence because for all of the parties the rituals of state ceremony and public procession were crucial to the visualization of state power.

This was famously the case for the Ottomans who, Birdal argues, were in a constant struggle to assert the legitimacy of the state.[66] We know from Ottoman miniature painting and from the remarkable Ralamb paintings arising from the Swedish delegation to Constantinople in 1657–58 that processions were crucial to the state form in the seventeenth and eighteenth centuries.[67] Elaborate systems of protocol governed their performance; as Nurhan Atasoy states,

> the rules of protocol were observed in every area of court and state rela-tions. These rules preserved a sensitive balance based on the rank, author-ity and responsibilities of every official. Meticulous importance was attached to them, and any adjustments and changes made to these rules were recorded in the protocol registers. These registers even include detailed descriptions of how each person should dress.
>
> Processions marking various events were not only watched by citizens, but by foreigners visiting or living in the country, and so were an interna-tional mirror reflecting the image of the Ottoman world.[68]

The guild processions or the sultan's procession to his military encampment would span an entire day and involve thousands of participants. These processions were both spectacular manifestations of Ottoman power and ritual performances of continuity and tradition.

The most widely read English language accounts of the Ottoman world—Knolles's *Generall Historie* and Rycaut's *Present State of the Ottoman Empire*—had little to say about these processions. This lacuna suggests a certain anxiety, an un-willingness to give these performances of Ottoman state power their due. To get some sense of their singular importance one need only consult Antoine Galland's *Voyage à Constantinople (1672–1673)*. Galland's entry for "Samedy" [sic], 7 May 1672, is by far the most lengthy in his journal because he attempts to record in detail all the elements of the sultan's ceremonial procession to Adrianople to engage in the summer campaign against the Poles:

> I had never seen anything resembling the beauty of the radiance and the surprising appearance of the exit that His Highness made outside Andri-anople today to launch his campaign. All the depictions of entrances, tri-umphs, tournaments, carousels, masquerades and games made for pleasure, that I can remember reading in novels, cannot in any way be compared with the prestige that I could actually witness with all the other Christian strang-ers who were there, and who could all, and this would be in complete disinterest and without any concern, testify to this truth.[69]

From this opening gambit Galland argues that the procession exceeds the expectations of romance, that an accurate description of it would fit seamlessly into one of the lengthy Oriental novels of Madeleine de Scudéry and that it is almost impossible to remember what passes before one's eyes. This latter point is particularly important because it is clear from Ottoman protocol registers and from Galland's own catalog-like description that these processions demanded a very intense and highly ordered mode of viewing. To make sense of the procession's spatialization of power relations one would need to attend to the passage of each passing component through time. Because viewers remained largely static—usually viewing the procession from buildings lining the streets—the procession became like a moving list whose structure was discernible from shifts in costume and "furniture." But the procession's internal hierarchies only made sense in relation to its totality; therefore it always already made a performative contract with its viewers and participants that brought them from beginning to end. This occupation of time and memory was as important as the occupation of the streets of Constantinople itself.

Galland's description explicitly indicates that he has witnessed many things like this before. His list of "all the depictions of entrances, triumphs, tournaments, carousels, masquerades and games made for pleasure, that I can remember reading in novels" points to the ubiquitous nature of these ritual performances. Every European monarch had recourse to a similar repertoire of state processions to mark significant dates in the calendar. Even the news could generate this kind of performance: "Vienna, September 25. On Sunday last the Emperor and the whole Court assisted at an extraordinary procession, upon the account of the late Victory [at the Battle of Zenta], which is the greatest that ever has been obtained over the Turks during this present War."[70] But Galland's list is revealing because there is no distinction between descriptions of triumphal processions such as this Viennese celebration of Eugene of Savoy's rout of the Ottomans at Zenta and "games made for pleasure": they are all seen as performative fictions or symbolic rituals of social affiliation in which a part stands for the whole. In the case of the sultan processing to his martial encampment, the six sections of janissaries and the complex subcategories of the guilds described by Galland emblematize the structural coherence of the Ottoman military. In the case of the less strongly scripted Viennese procession to celebrate victory at Zenta, the court itself operates as a synecdoche for the rather abstract totality of the Holy Roman Empire. As exercises in figuration, processions not only assumed that they would be interpreted but also presupposed that successful interpretation arose from the internalization of previous performances.

The sheer conventionality of state procession meant that viewers gained a certain facility with the genre, and thus these events had the potential not only to exemplify control and power but also to testify to moments of desperate overcompensation. As we have already seen from our reading of *Theatre de la paix*, emphasis on Ottoman pomp and magnificence could easily operate as a symptom of their weakness in the field. But it is clear from Paget's papers and from the printed accounts of the negotiations that procession was a vital component of the conference at Karlowitz. A great deal of planning went into the formation and scheduling not only for the procession of each power but also for that of the mediators themselves.[71] In fact, the various delegations all set up staging grounds at a distance from Karlowitz and then proceeded according to a particular calendar.

The procession of the mediators took precedence above all others. Here is how the London press recorded the event in a report from Belgrade dated 20 August:

> The Lord *Paget*, Ambassador from the King of *Great Brittain* to the Port, has made his publick Entry into the Camp before this City, with as great splendor and magnificence as the Heer *Colliers*, Ambassador from the States General of the United Provinces lately did. The *Turks* are in great hopes that by their Mediation they shall have an end put to the War very speedily, and their inclination thereto is so great, that 'tis said the *Prime Visier* will undertake nothing with his Army this Campaign, for fear of procrastinating the Peace. Their Excellencies are caressed where ever they go, and are more honoured and respected by the *Turks* than ever any Ministers was before 'em. They have sent notice to the Imperial Court of their Arrival here, so that we hope suddenly to hear of the Christian Plenipotentiaries being come to *Selankement*. In the mean time the *Turkish* Plenipotentiaries are ready to set out, but will stay at *Hysassick* about 5 miles from this City, till they hear of the arrival of the Christians at the place of Treaty.[72]

Paget and Colyer's companies had been moving from Adrianople from the late summer until this point, but it was not until 19 October that they left Belgrade, crossed the river Save and approached Karlowitz. Rycaut devotes considerable space to describing this procession:

> In passing this River this Order was observed.
> First went an Allai-Bey, or the Marshal of the Show, with about 50 Horse.
> Then 60 Chiauses on Horseback.
> A Guard of Janisaries, being about 330 Men, all on Foot.
> An Aga belonging to the Ambassadors, with his own Servants, and six Domestick Janisaries.
> After which followed two Flags; one with the *English* Coat of Arms, and the other was a large Red Cross in a White Field.

Then followed the *English* Ambassador's 6 led Horses covered with very rich Furniture, followed by the Gentleman of the Horse to my Lord Ambassador, attended by a *Giovane di Lingua*, or a young Druggerman, or Interpreter.

Then came up the two Interpreters attending His Excellency the Lord Ambassador, on each side of his Horse, and they attended with two *Hey-dukes* [*hajduks,* or Hungarian mercenaries] in their own Country Habit; and on both sides 10 *Chiabadars* [çuhadâr], or Servants, who carry the Cloaks, or Vests of Great Men, in White Vests, with their Carbines on their Shoulders.

The Brother to the Lord Ambassador road afterwards with six *Chio-badars*.

Then followed the Secretary, and Doctor, with two *English* Gentlemen; one from *Aleppo*, and the other from *Tripoli*.

Also six Pages with the Lord Ambassador's Coach, with a Turkish one, which went before the Common Servants, who marched all on Horseback, two and two.

At their Passage over the Bridge of the *Save*, which was lined with Janisaries, three Guns were fired from the Castle; and the Gallies, Saicks, and the Frigats as they passed fired each a Gun.

About half the way to *Semblin*, the Chiaus [attendants], and others, whom the Vizier had sent along with them, made a Halt, and having wished a good Journey to those whom they conducted, returned back.

About an Hour after these Matters had passed, the *Dutch* Ambassador followed, and was used with the same Civility as those preceding.[73]

I've presented this tedious catalog for two reasons. First, it asks us to consider why Rycaut would consider this worthy of so much attention. At one level, it attests to the importance of Paget and Colyer's mission, but I think there is more at stake in the details. Careful attention—the kind of attention regularly demanded by processions—reveals that this is a celebration of communication. Rather than cavalry and sword bearers—the appropriate props of the sultan—we have the dragomans, secretaries, and *giovane di lingua* (interpreters) employed by the British embassy—the very embodiments of mediation in both senses of the word.[74]

This procession, perhaps more than any other element of the peace negotiations, testifies to the complex and profound role played by translation, interpretation, and the circulation of documents to the prosecution of peace. The flurry of documents set into motion by Paget and Colyer from late 1697, when it became clear that the Ottomans would accept Paget's long-standing suggestion of a peace based on *uti possidetis*, encompassed texts in Latin, Italian, French, Ottoman, English, and to a lesser extent Polish, German, and Russian.[75] Paget's communication with Austria, Poland, and Russia was primarily conducted in French and Latin. His communications with the Ottomans took place in Latin and Italian. There is an extensive body of correspondence between Paget and Alexander Mavrocordato—the second Ottoman delegate—in Italian. Letters from the *reis efendi* or the grand vizier are typically translated into Latin. French and Italian appear to be the working languages for negotiation itself, although much would have traveled through translators. Needless to say, each set of plenipotentiaries had to overcome these same communicative challenges, but here the mediators are using the art of procession to assert a kind of communicative prowess that exceeds the pretensions to military supremacy that so often defined procession in times of war.

Second, and perhaps more important, this procession is not a visualization of sovereignty. With its borrowed janissaries and its singular aggregation of English national props and servants, this is an ad hoc incarnation not of the state but rather of an interstitial delegation that will bring discrete states together. In other words, working in a necessarily improvisational mode, the mediators are using the genre of processional performance to confer status on a group beyond or above that of the state form. When we realize that the typical Ottoman procession is the embodiment of the self-styled Supreme Celestial Power on Earth, it is hard not to regard this procession as a parodic sublation not only of the negotiating powers but also of their conventional modes of performative realization. From this recognition, it is not difficult to see that the mediators' procession into the neutral zone is but a precursor to the dissolution of state-specific ceremony and ritual during the negotiations themselves.

This is borne out by Rycaut's narrative, because the arrival of the Austrian and Ottoman delegations are handled as almost cursory events—in spite of the fact that we know from other sources that all of the plenipotentiaries arrived with much pomp and circumstance.[76] In Rycaut the various powers only come into representation when they are adjacent to the mediators:

> Upon the Arrival of the Mediators at *Carlowitz*, they were received by the *German* Horse and Foot, and a Captain-Lieutenant and a Standard, with 50 Horse, and also with another Captain-Lieutenant, and an Ensign, with 70 Foot, which were appointed to each Ambassador for the Mediators Guards. The *Turkish* Soldiers were at the Right of the *English* Ambassador, and at the Left of the *Dutch.*
>
> On the 20/30th the Plenipotentiaries were showed to each other; and shortly after the Conferences began.[77]

As Rycaut's narrative approaches the scene of negotiation, state spectacle, in the form of grand procession, dissolves and we are drawn to the table in "the midst of that void place." This compression of narrative duration effectively deprives the negotiating powers of their most dynamic spectacle, and attention is focused on a scene of speech that is consistently withheld.

The representation of the first day of negotiation is effectively the last time we "see" the negotiating states as spectacular entities until the treaty's ratification. Within the logic implied by the procession of the mediators this makes sense; spectacles put on for and by competing states will be temporarily suspended so that the states' representatives can talk. So Rycaut presents one last scene of pageantry before introducing the characters and describing their placement at the negotiating table:

> On the 3/13 of *November*, the Ambassador from the Emperor, appeared in the Camp of *Carlovitz*; as also did those from the Sultan, who placed themselves on both sides . . . at which, about nine of the Clock in the Morning, the Emperor's Ambassador arrived, being attended with four Coaches of State, and a Numerous Retinue.
>
> And in the first place they went to the Tents of the Mediators, where at the same time appeared the *Turkish* Ambassador, attended with a very stately Retinue of Cavaliers, well mounted on Horses of the finest Shapes that could be found in all Quarters of the *Eastern* World, and besides their Cloathing which was very rich, they made as beautiful an Appearance as the *Germans* had done before them.[78]

There are subtle rhetorical moves here. The relative lack of detail about the Austrian contingent somehow makes the opulence of the Turks seem desperate. But the most salient issue here is that these ceremonial acts are staged to be rhetorically eliminated. Rycaut turns away from the fine horses and costumes to describe in detail the tent and the dramatis personae of a drama that, as we will see, he will not represent:

> The Tent appointed for this Congress had four Doors, which fronted each other, at one of which entered the Imperial Ambassador, and the opposite thereunto entered the *Turkish*; and at the two others, which were likewise opposite, entered the Mediators.
>
> The Imperial Ambassador, was Named the Most Excellent Lord the Count of *Ottingen*: And on the *Turkish* side was the *Reis Effendi*, which I take to be the principal Secretary of State with us.

Behind the Emperor's Ambassador the Secretary of the Embassy was placed; as also at a small Table behind the *English* Mediator, was placed the *English* Secretary: and behind the *Ottoman* Ambassador the *Turkish* Secretary, called *Mauro Cordato*.[79]

It is remarkable that he has withheld the identity of major players to this point, but I think that this has a crucial rhetorical effect. Suddenly we are dealing with named figures, and with the introduction of names comes attention to their dispositions. Much is made of the seating posture of the *reis efendi* and of Mavrocordato—the latter starts out standing, but "afterwards was ordered to sit on the Ground after the Turkish Fashion."[80] Where cultural difference had only a few paragraphs earlier been registered by row upon row of horse and foot, we are now attending to individual bodily comportment and gesture.

At this point one would think the representation of speech would become crucial to the text, except this is precisely what Rycaut doesn't provide. Having established zones of narrative intimacy he backs away and simply reports on the length of negotiation. This is surprising because some of the newspaper material that he incorporates into his text exhibits no such reticence: as noted earlier, the papers pushed on the very limits of discursive summary to give the texture of the Ottoman delegates' demands.[81] What happens at that table is the discursive enigma that drives Rycaut's narrative and, in a sense, our own desire to comprehend what happened in this void place.[82] Summary allows the text to jump over the scene of intercultural exchange and thus keep this central enigma intact. Once the treaty is ratified a number of retroactive gestures will be employed to replace the process with the product: Rycaut's text, like all other accounts, records the final treaty articles, and in a way they seem that much more valuable because of his reticence regarding the performance of negotiation itself. One of the upshots of this is that the printing of the treaty inaugurates a whole new set of processions and celebrations. With the process over, the suspension of the state form's performance of excess is itself suspended. But before we look at this return to business as usual, I want to take some time to look more directly at that which Rycaut, for whatever reason, refused to narrate.

At Table

In the previous section I implied that Rycaut's text uses the desire to reconstruct what happened in these negotiations as a kind of narrative enigma—as that which Roland Barthes has argued inculcates desire in the reader. Rycaut pulls you to the table and then catapults you past the negotiation into the post-treaty world. Perhaps it is too uncomfortable to stay too long, even in narrative, in a space beyond the reach of any one state form. But for someone sifting through this archive of material, Rycaut's text and the other printed documents instantiate a desire for the script beyond the usual historiographic yearning for the kernel of truth at the heart of an event. Because Rycaut's text and the *Bericht* pay so much attention to performance and spectacle and because the visual record is so obsessed with scenographic matters, it becomes difficult not to begin to represent the event as theater. Rycaut, I would argue, gestures to this possibility when he gives us the dramatis personae just before negotiations begin. Likewise, the *Post Boy* instantiates a scene of theatrical reception when it speaks of "divers Officers of both Nations, who see all, tho' not hear it."[83] The *Bericht* uses a similar trope: "Several officers stood in both the Imperial and Turkish doors and were able to see everything, but hear nothing."[84] But as noted in the previous sections, both the textual accounts and the visual representations bring us to the playhouse, and some documents like the *Post Boy* and the *Theatre de la paix* pretend to show us communication with the sound turned off, as it were, in a sort of described video for the early era of print culture.

Such a refusal to record the negotiations was not an option for the mediators or the plenipotentiaries. They had to keep track of what transpired, but this kind of transcription would be necessarily ephemeral—proscribed from circulation by the very rules of negotiation but nonetheless necessary for the nightly preparation for the next day's talks. We are extraordinarily fortunate that fragments of these ephemeral scripts still exist. Both Paget's and Ruzzini's secretaries took careful notes of the negotiation, but I am more interested in the script of mediation.

Buried deep in Paget's correspondence is a fascicle tied together with delicate thread. On its pages are recorded the conversations at the negotiating table. Peter Cernovodeanu has published an accurate transcription of this document, but as he states it is incomplete.[85] It is composed of forty-four pages, but it is clear that the outermost pages of the fascicle are missing. This means that the reader enters the negotiation in medias res, as it were, on Friday, 11/21 November 1698, and follows the negotiations to Monday, 16/26 January 1699.[86] According to Rycaut the peace talks commenced on 3/13 November when the Austrian and Ottoman delegations first sat down in the tent with the mediators, so most of the crucial debates over Transylvania, Temeswar, and the territorial limits took place during the period prior to those in the extant pages of the diary. In keeping with the order of negotiation, the first pages of the extant diary cover discussions with the Polish and Muscovite delegations; near the end the diarist records the meetings in which the Austrian and Ottoman delegations reiterate the final articles and finalize the specific wording of the treaty.

While working through the Paget Papers at SOAS, I found one of the missing outer sheets, and, as one might expect, it refers to a meeting held earlier in the conference on 6/16 November, the day after Emperor Leopold's birthday. Mavro-cordato and Count Schlick, the secondary plenipotentiaries for the Ottomans and Austrians respectively, are trying to hammer out the territorial limits of Temeswar and come up with some kind of agreement on access and use of the rivers that make up the new border. This was arguably the most complex article of the treaty, and some sense of the stakes can be gleaned from the diary.[87] Because this missing outer sheet is such a singular document I am going to present a full translation and then discuss its particulars.

Solis 6 Nov[em]bris [Sunday, November 6[th]]

Mauroc[ordato] goes to the Reis Effendi with this proposition. They come together, and after some talking they decide to dictate the article 2d.

C. Schlick proposes, since we are doing so fine, and are on a roll, that we should go on.

Mauroc[ordato] is happy, and that we are talking about the land, which is located between the Tibisque[88] and the Danube.

C. Schlick. It is unnecessary to discuss the fact that all this land is in the hands, and possessed by, the Emperor.

Mauroc[ordato] that this land is deserted if we also want it to remain within the State where it is located, let's not build any further fortifications.

C. Schlick says since we have not accepted their proposition on the Marosh [the river Mureș], therefore etc.

Mauroc[ordato]. whatever they say, this land must remain as it is. and Tithil[89] must not be fortified any futher.

C. Schlick does not believe, that this will happen, because the place is inconvenient, but that they do not want to commit themselves.

Since the place is not that important, they move on and cross the Danube.

C. Schlick enters in Esclavonie.[90] Since it is controlled by the Capital Cities of Essek[91] and Peterwaradin,[92] it belongs to the Emperor from the Drave[93]—and along the Danube—to the Save.[94]

Mauroc[ordato] Will do all that is humanly possible. They cannot refuse the offer he is going to make. As the demolition of Petrovaradin will be very costly for the Emperor. offers to define a line from the Tysa estuary, to the Bossut[95] estuary. Finally that one does whatever they want with Peterwaradin.

Solis 6 Nov[em]bris (Sunday, November 6[th]) [continued]

Mauroc[ordato] The argument of the desert is flawed, as it is against religion, which suffers from depopulation.

C. Schlick concedes the dwelling of the land located an hour away from the bank, but the rivers must be theirs.

Mauroc[ordato] insists on the use of rivers; begs that it should not be refused to them.

C. Schlick we must leave these two rivers to them, as we leave the Themes[96] and Beg[97] to the Turks.

Mauroc[ordato] Pray the Mediators to accommodate this difference.

My Lord says, when they themselves talk with the other Plenipotentiaries, they cannot do a proper mediation

Mauroc[ordato] says that they are going to leave and they stand up.

Messrs the Mediators confer with the Imperial Ambassadors. It was decided to grant them the use of the water, to fish, and for other necessary needs, but not for sailing, and with these words the Mediators go see the Turks. They come back, and say, that they only wish to build a couple of watermills, without disturbing their sailing, or their watermills. They once again go see the Turks, to tell them, that later on, when they need a watermill, they could use the Germans', as friends.

Messrs the Imperial Ambassadors stand up with firmness, to not grant the watermills.

Maroc[ordato] comes and the Imperial Ambassadors.

Maroc[ordato] says that we should not discuss the ownership of the rivers, that we could put off this difficulty until after the peace is concluded, and they will content themselves with what they will be granted.

C. Schlick that it is not in their power to do it.

My lord proposes, that the rivers are part of the peace terms, but that the use and the way of inhabiting must be determined after the Peace treaty.[98]

The text is clearly the work of one of Paget's secretaries—most likely George Schreyer—because Paget's interventions are referred to as coming from "Milord" or "my lord."[99] What is so striking here is the way that the conventions used for mediating theatrical performance are redeployed to represent the negotiations. Mavrocordato and Schlick's remarks are rendered as dialogue. Significantly, Paget's statements are not presented as direct speech; less attention is paid to his specific words. In part this is because the secretary is most concerned with recording the mediator's actions. When the discussion of the use of rivers seems to be at an impasse, the secretary seamlessly shifts from summary of Paget's remarks to narrate the movement of Paget and Colyer first to a private meeting with the imperial delegation and then to a similarly separate meeting with the *reis efendi* and Mavrocordato. With an interim solution in hand the secretary returns to recording the statements of Mavrocordato and Schlick.

This script-like diary uses two discursive modes to distinguish between two types of participants at the negotiations. On the one hand, dialogue is accorded to the plenipotentiaries; on the other hand, Paget's role as mediator is represented primarily through narrative and at times through summarized speech. This has the effect not only of equalizing the parties to the negotiations but also of elevating the mediators into a position of narrative agency. Put bluntly, the various delegates make proposals and counterproposals, but Lord Paget makes things happen; Mavrocordato and Schlick are characters, but Lord Paget has the agency of a focalizer capable of taming irreducible differences into a narrative totality. Significantly, we see how this distinction is maintained by Paget himself in one of the recorded interventions above. In response to Count Schlick's intransigence about the usage of rivers on the border, Mavrocordato projects his desired position onto that of the mediators: "Pray the Mediators to accommodate this difference." Lord Paget responds with "when they themselves talk with the other Plenipotentiaries, they cannot do a proper mediation." Aside from maintaining a certain level of neutrality, Paget is deploying the yet-to-be-held discussions with the Venetians and the Poles as a check not only on attempts to draw the mediators to one side or the other, but also on intransigence. What Mavrocordato and Schlick do here, he is implying, has an impact on his efficacy as a mediator later on and thus on his capacity to resolve more crucial issues elsewhere in the negotiation. In a sense, what Paget is doing is foregrounding the narrative agency of the mediator—he must be able to tell the story and situate the dialogue in a manner that will drive the talks toward a successful resolution. And to do this it is crucial that he be able to ensure narrative continuity and continuance.[100]

If we look at the rest of the diary, Paget's strategy of pushing off currently irresolvable issues to a later date proved to be essential. In the final days of negotiation it became clear that many of Venice's concerns could not be met because Ruzzini had not been given sufficient power by the doge to sign the articles. In the end many issues including specific resolutions to border disputes and the Venetian ratification would be delayed until after the conference.[101] However, at the level of representation something quite startling happens at the end of the diary. As the treaty comes to fruition, the plenipotentiaries no longer appear as characters in a play; rather they emerge as narrative agents operating on a similar discursive level as the mediator:

Solis 15 January 1699 (Sunday, 15 January 1699)

The discrepancies—found in the Preface and Epilogue of the Instrument—in some words of the Ambassador of Venice were discussed and adjusted.

Lunae 16/26 January 1699 (Monday, 16/26 January 1699)

Messrs the Ambassadors of Germany and Pologne came, and at the same time the Turkish Ambassadors, and after verifying the instruments, the Peace was signed and the Instruments were given to the Parties by Messrs the Mediators.[102]

The subtle shift from names such as "Mauro C." and "Schlick" to the general noun "ambassadors" signals the slow reemergence of the state. With the theater of negotiation at an end focus now shifts to the circulation of signed documents, to the movement of texts. At this point the diary ends because the fictional theater of negotiation has dissolved.

The shift from one representational economy to another is immediately apparent when we consult Paget's correspondence immediately following the peace. On 16/26 January 1699 Paget sends a dispatch to London declaring "the conclusion of the treatys of Peace which have ben debated here above 3 months, with danger of breaking off severall times."[103] In the same letter, he also indicates that his primary correspondent during the negotiations has been Sir Robert Sutton, the British envoy at Vienna, and it is with a letter to Sutton dated 21/31 January 1699 that I wish to conclude this section. Of all the letters extant from the conference, this text is invaluable not only because it gives us a sense of Paget's personality, but also because it draws attention to a different kind of table. Rycaut and others report upon the social activities of the delegations, but Paget's letter gives us an intimate description of the celebrations that concluded the peace:

since the Business is over we have passd the time as jovially as we could, in entertainments [ ] &c The day the Peace was signed (Monday 26th in . . .) OS all the Ambrs, Turks as well as Ch[ristia]n and all their attendants and all the Country I think (for we had about 4, or 5,000 people) did me the favour to dine with me [and were merry]; the Emperor [&], the King our Masters the good and lasting continuance of the concluded peace were warmly drunk, and all the solemnities the place could afford, and we were heartily merry.[104]

This remarkable scene of concord, hosted by Paget, is a prominent feature of Rycaut's account as well:

Monday the 16/26th of *January*, was the Solemn Day of Signature, the which having been passed in the Morning, all the Ambassadors, *Turks* as well as *Christians*, with all their Attendants, Guards, &c. with many Persons of Quality out of the Country, making about 5000 Persons, Dined at my

Lord *Paget*'s Quarters, at whose Table, the King of *England*'s Health was the first that was drank, then the Emperor's, and the lasting Continuance of the Peace, which was Signed that very Day: And then we may believe, and fancie, that most People there present were all heartily Merry, with as much Solemnity as that Place could afford: And amongst other things of Mirth it was observed, That my Lord *Paget* had an Oxe Roasted whole for the Soldiers, a thing never known before in those Parts.[105]

The repetition of phrases from Paget's letter in Rycaut's text tells us something about the discourse networks at play here—citation and repetition are crucial mechanisms. But, more important, it is clear that this rather unusual celebration—recognized as a heretofore unheard of event—paradoxically marks the return to prior norms of sociability and sovereignty.

As Paget's letter continues, it becomes clear that this first celebration was but the precursor to increasingly more elaborate entertainments that would seem more typical of the embassy circuit in Galata than the harsh frontier:

Tuesday? We dined with the Imperial Ambrs where were like [thanks]givings (fire works, fountains of wine, discharge of great and small guns &c) Wednesday pas'd in visits so did Thursday. Friday were [ ], today by Imperial Ambrs return the compliments, tomorrow the Turks visit. Then Monday the Turks take their leave because the Tuesday the Imper return the visit, and wensday or at farthest Thursday morning. Then we shall God willing, begin our voyage toward Belgrade, parting all of us well contented with what has been done.[106]

As this letter unfolds we witness the reinstitution of matters of precedence and obligation—visits to the Austrian plenipotentiaries instantiate reciprocal visits, and then a similar set of visits are enacted with the Ottoman delegation. Likewise, the penchant for spectacle, now in the name of peace, is reengaged, but significantly what Paget records is not procession, but rather far less hierarchical displays. For a brief period improvisatory celebration trumped state and—as the remarks on wine indicate—religious protocol.

As these ceremonies proceed, the delegations slowly begin to depart the zone of neutrality. Considering the snows and the weather, it is not surprising that Paget's letter exhibits impatience for his voyage to Belgrade. But as the letter concludes, we see in miniature much of what is to come:

The Polish abmr left us the 26th at Night, and at parting made me (amongst many other) a particular great compliment; he told me he would make haste home to his wife (for it seems he has lately Married a young pretty lady) think upon me, and get a sense who have my name, for memory of the fortunate agreement I had given to the successful conclusion of these intricate negotiations which had been agitated in this place. The Moscovite Ambr. Presented me 20 pair of sable skins with great compliments this Day, so the middle of the next week will be the congress houses is bestowed by Ct. Offing on the Franciscan fryers who, for the memory of what has passd here intend to make a church of it, etc.[107]

The amusing remarks about the Polish ambassador's ardor—perhaps the most intimate statement about any of the participants in the archive—modulates into Paget's account of gift exchange and then of the transformation of the conference building into a memorial to peace.[108] In a sense, this latter issue is the beginning of the fetishization of the conference house. Ottingen's bestowal of the house on the Franciscans renders it holy and thus makes it the most important symbol of peace.[109] Out of the void comes a monumental icon that will be represented in text and image repeatedly in the ensuing years. Interestingly, no reference is made to the fact that in doing this Ottingen makes it a site of Christian control and reverence. But, as we have seen, this is implicit in the visual renderings of this building across Europe. Paget's lack of commentary on the politics of Ottingen's gesture is entirely in keeping with the building's stark iconicity. But it is important that we not let this building occlude the other little things referred to here.

Peaceable Things

If the representation of the conference house at the end of Paget's letter presages the auratic power of its bare exterior walls in later representations, his remark on the opulence of the Muscovite ambassador's gift of twenty pairs of sable skins is the first indication of the importance of gift exchange in the subsequent months. Gift exchange was a vital component of diplomatic relations with the Ottoman Empire, and the arrival of new diplomats at the Sublime Porte, like the processions that enacted the sovereign power of the sultan, was subject to long-standing rules of protocol. The exchange of presents was crucial not only to these rituals but also to the everyday practice of business between European and Ottoman officials.

But the exchange of diplomats and presents after the Treaty of Karlowitz was distinct from these oft-repeated ceremonies. This is most evident from the extraordinary attention to their particulars in the print sources. As recorded in both Rycaut's text and the *Bericht*, the Treaty of Karlowitz instantiated the exchange of ambassadors between the Habsburg and Ottoman Empires. On orders from Emperor Leopold, Ottingen, Schlick, and their retinue proceeded to Constantinople. Shortly thereafter Rami Mehmed Efendi attended the Habsburg court in Vienna. The *Bericht* spends more time discussing these visits than on the treaty negotiations, and, in a gesture that confirms my argument about the reinstitution of state spectacle above, presents elaborate engravings of the ambassadors' processions to each capital (Figures 11 and 12). There are no corresponding images for the period leading up to or during the treaty negotiations. Only after considerable study can one differentiate between the two diplomatic delegations in these post-treaty processions; both entourages are presented according to the same economy of excess. The visual enjambment required to fit the procession to the page indicates the superfluity seemingly required to declare legitimacy and sovereignty. Paget did everything in his power to prevent an Ottoman ambassador from being dispatched to England because he was intensely aware of the expenses that would accrue to the Crown. Ottoman diplomacy, like all aspects of Ottoman statecraft, turned on the exchange of exceedingly expensive presents. As Michael Talbot and others have noted, this present exchange was not simply a form of bribery.[110] It had far more symbolic significance than mere corruption. In fact, present exchange was crucial to how the Ottoman sultan exerted his power over visiting diplomats. To understand this we need to look at the kind of exchange that typically took place when a new ambassador was appointed to the Ottoman Porte.

Looking at accounts of ambassadorial audiences at the Ottoman court, one is immediately struck by the continuity of these practices. Foreign ambassadors would be entertained on two separate occasions. In the first audience, the ambassador would cross the Golden Horn from Galata by boat and then progress to Topkapi with an appointed escort. Upon reaching the palace, he would then enter the outer courtyard and move inward until finally meeting with the grand vizier. Presents would be exchanged, most often in the form of multiple ceremonial garments, or khalats, and the audience would conclude with a display of Ottoman hospitality usually in the form of a feast. This event introduced the ambassador to the protocols that would govern his audience with the sultan. In this second audience, the same preliminary progression took place, but the feasting inside the palace came before the ambassador was brought into the sultan's presence. The final meeting was structured such that the ambassador quite literally performed his subjection or capitulation to the sultan's rule. In both cases, the ambassador's movements and actions as well as his gifts were folded into a preexisting ritual whose primary function was to assert the supremacy of the Ottoman state. The key issue here, as with the performance of processions discussed earlier, is that a continuous history of gift-exchange protocol was enacted to essentially write the representative of a

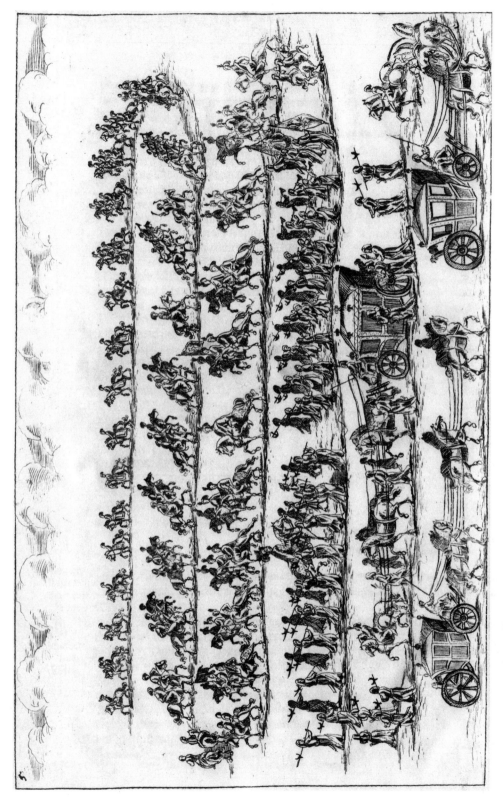

Figure 11. Procession (engraving), in *Gründ- und Umständlicher Bericht Von Denen Römisch-Kayserlichen Wie auch Ottomannischen Gross-Botbschafften* (1702). Courtesy of the Getty Research Institute, Los Angeles.

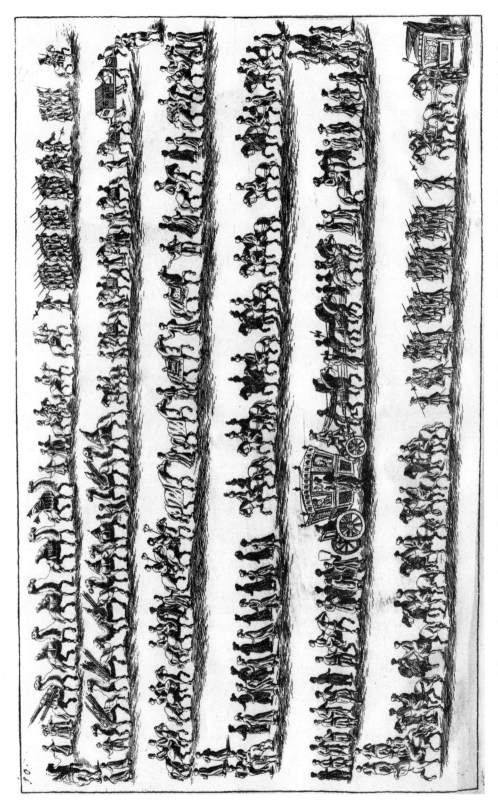

Figure 12. Ottoman delegation (engraving), in *Gründ- und Umständlicher Bericht Von Denen Römisch-Kayserlichen Wie auch Ottomannischen Gross-Bothschafften* (1702). Courtesy of the Getty Research Institute, Los Angeles.

foreign power into a narrative that was controlled by the Ottomans. Many later ambassadors brayed at this, but for the most part the diplomatic corps was well aware that these performances could not be separated from the capitulations or from the everyday business in the court.

If we look at the retrospective accounts of the Treaty of Karlowitz, we find that there is extraordinary interest not only in the processional theater of diplomacy but also in the specific gifts offered by the sultan and the emperor. Rycaut's description of Ottingen's arrival in the Ottoman capital is exceedingly interesting on this point because he so clearly subordinates the spectacle of Ottoman protocol to that of the visiting delegation:

> On the 29th of *January*, O.S. Count *Otting*, the Emperor's Amassador, made his publick Entry here: First, marched the Basha of *Nicopolis*, with his Retinue, who conducted the Ambassador from *Rutsick* hither; after him an Oda of Janisaries, with their Aga and Officers; then came the *Dutch* Ambassadors Gentlemen of the Horse, his led Horses, my Lord *Pagett's* Secretary, with three Gentlemen, and 12 Men in Liveries, all the English Nation; and then followed the Chiousses, Visier Agas, the *German* Ambassadors Officers, five Led horses, the Gentlemen Hautboys, Trumpeters, Noblemen, and he himself on Horseback, having 20 Trabants on both sides, his Drugoman, and the rest of his Retinue: He came in by *Adrianople* Gate, through part of the City, and out again by *Fenar*-Gate on the Water-side, so to *Ujup*, *Kehathana*, and finally to *Pera*, where he is lodged in *Hattum Hussein* Aga's House, not far from my Lord *Pagett's*.
>
> The 3/13th Instant he had his Audience of the Vizier, where he was Clothed with a Sable Vest, and his Gentlemen to the number of 100 with Caftans.
>
> The 6/16th his Excellency went in Pomp to the Sultan.[111]

In all of these events, Ottingen's actions are scripted by his Ottoman hosts, but Rycaut's text shifts the emphasis to suggest that the Austrians are processing in triumph. But that sense can only be maintained by first obfuscating the ambassador's relation to the janissary escort and then literally eliding any account of his audience with the sultan. In the final phase of that audience, Ottingen, like all other foreign diplomats, would have been physically restrained by *kapĭcĭs*, the palace gatekeepers, and then forced to bow low before the sultan. As Talbot has argued, this ritual of deference was always on the verge of becoming a scene of humiliation, but this was kept at bay by a discourse of security.[112] Here it is simply erased altogether in favor of a far more detailed account of Ottingen's visits with other European ambassadors. These later scenes of diplomatic hospitality among the Europeans are given far more emphasis than Ottingen's audience with the sultan. In other words, Rycaut's text does everything in its power not only to subordinate the sultan and the Ottoman state but also to elevate European embassies. One could say that Ottingen's embassy is portrayed more like an occupation.

Similar gestures can be found in the *Bericht*. As in Rycaut, Ottingen's entry into the city is given great prominence and his subordination to the sultan is barely touched upon. In a singular moment of appropriation, the *Bericht* provides a map of Ottingen's audience with the sultan and in so doing penetrates the seraglio in a fashion that visually lays claim to the space (Figure 13). The careful delineation of the seraglio and the confident fixing of the representatives of Ottoman power in place break with all previous forms of visualization in the *Bericht*. This map subjects the sublime power of the sultan to quantifiable measurement. He is a mere point, identified by a letter, roughly 250 meters from the outer door, and thus he is subtly transformed into an ornamental object within a human structure. Furthermore, the representational flattening implied by this image is felt throughout the accounts of the post-treaty world because actions and negotiations find themselves subordinated to catalogs of objects.

Rycaut demonstrates the close relationship between subordination and a very specific deployment of things when he handles the Ottoman delegation's visit to the Austrian court. The very acts that one normally finds in accounts of European audiences with the sultan are subtly enacted in the emperor's palace:

> On the 16th of February, N.S. the Turkish Ambassador had Audience of the Emperor, and was conducted to the Palace. The Emperor received him in the Council-Chamber, seated on his Throne under a rich Canopy, and attended by his Principal Ministers of State. . . . The Ambassador when he entred the Room, made a low Reverence, another in the middle of the Chamber, and the third near the Throne. He went up the Steps of the Throne, presented his Credentials, and laid them on the Table that was before the Emperor, and then returned to the Place where he made his Speech in his own Language, containing an Assurance of the Sultan his Master's Friendship, and sincere intentions, strictly to observe the Treaty between the two Empires lately concluded. . . . Then the Ambassador ordered his Steward to bring in the Grand Signor's Presents; a List of which he laid upon the Table, with a Letter from the Grand Vizier, and going once more up the Steps to the Throne, kissed the Border of the Emperor's Robe, his Attendants at the same time making a very low Reverence. After which the Ambassador withdrew, walking backwards while he was in the Emperor's Presence, and making three Reverences in like manner as when

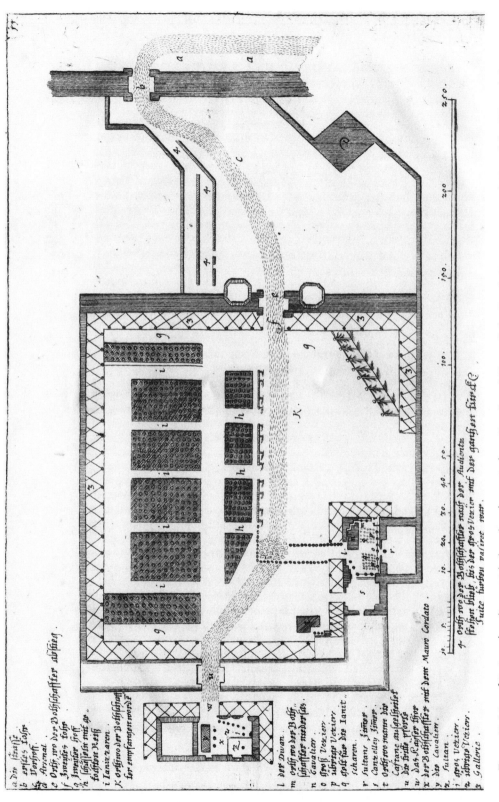

Figure 13. Map of Ottingen's audience with the sultan (engraving), in *Gründ- und Umständlicher Bericht Von Denen Römisch-Kayserlichen Wie auch Ottomanischen Gross-Bothschafften* (1702). Courtesy of the Getty Research Institute, Los Angeles.

he came into the Room, and was reconducted to his House, and nobly entertained.[113]

If one compares this passage to Robert Sutton's extremely detailed account of his audience with the grand signor of 10 March 1711, one discovers that every component of Rycaut's representation of the Turkish ambassador's audience above rehearses the ritual performance of the European ambassador before the sultan.[114] The description of the "throne," the attendants, the number of reverences, and the display of presents is virtually identical. One could argue that the Ottoman delegation is merely performing in a way that makes sense to their own comprehension of diplomatic protocol, but this would be contrary to the Ottoman state self-conception and performance. Rather, I think Rycaut's gesture here is entirely his own and may well be based on his own experience of these performances. He is forcing the Ottoman delegation to perform reverence in precisely the fashion that European delegations are forced to capitulate before the sultan. When one takes into account that the physical act of deference is not narrated in the account of Count Ottingen's embassy, it is clear that Rycaut's text is using the very protocols of the Ottoman state to enact its subordination to the emergent powers in Europe. In short, Rycaut's account of the Treaty of Karlowitz does not end with the representation of a kind of détente but with a highly charged assertion of European domination. Whatever neutrality was momentarily engaged during the negotiations themselves is superseded by a forceful appropriation of Ottoman ritual.

This is not to say that these kinds of performance were not also a part of European court theater. What interests me here is, first, the specificity of Rycaut's substitution and, second, his relentless cataloging of presents in the ensuing pages. Rycaut's account of the diplomatic audiences in both capitals is almost eclipsed by a detailed list of presents; he would seem to provide the very text that each ambassador ostensibly gave to the sovereign.[115] He starts with "A List of the Presents presented to the Emperor by the Turkish Ambassador" and then provides "Particulars of the Presents which the Emperor by his Ambassador gave to the Grand Seignior." The order is significant because the first list is almost an anatomy of Ottoman excess. Luxury items are listed complete with the precise number of jewels: "A Plume of Red and White Feathers, set with 52 Diamonds great and small. A Bridle covered with Gold, and enamelled with Red and White, set with 531 Diamonds, and 338 Rubies."[116] As the list unfolds the reader's attention is drawn from ornamental tack (saddles, bridles, and so on—the accoutrements of the sultan's own processional theater) to jewels to silk, brocade, and other cloth, only to end with valuable live animals, Arabian horses and tamed leopards. In a sense these presents would seem to represent both the political and the mercantile signs of the Ottoman Empire. Significantly, there is no mention of the traditional forms of diplomatic presents—khalats and the like. Rather, these presents step beyond prior ritual to envisage a different world and a different historical situation. What is so disturbing here is that it is difficult to see Rycaut's list as anything other than wishful thinking because it is as though the ambassador lays the signs of the sultan's power and the empire's chief luxury commodities before the emperor's feet. In the context of the post-treaty world Rycaut's list is suspiciously close to a symbolic pillage.

This sense of symbolically acquiring the Ottoman Empire is reinforced when Rycaut lists the "particulars" of the emperor's presents to the sultan. Again it is a list of luxury items, but the traditional garments (khalats and so on) are nowhere mentioned. According to Rycaut, the Austrian ambassador has arrived with altogether different kinds of presents. There are no jewels, but rather an array of technological manufactures: "Ten hanging Clocks, in Silver emboss'd Frames. Eight great Clocks, in form, like the Pedestal of a Pillar, and the Clock-work in the middle"; "A pair of Tongs, Fire-Shovel and Proger of polished Steel, with Silver Heads. Twenty-four Silver Sconces, with Looking-Glasses in the middles of them"; and various examples of European silverware and cabinetry.[117] The list of Ottoman presents to the emperor amounts to a list of luxury resources to be extracted from the empire: jewels, fabrics, horses. The list of Austrian presents to the sultan constitutes a catalog of luxury manufactures for Ottoman consumption. What I would suggest is that the presents, as represented by Rycaut, establish a nexus of trade. In this symbolic exchange luxury resources come out of the Ottoman Empire and are laid before the feet of the Austrians; the Austrians for their part are displaying the attractions of technological modernity, the clocks and the metalware that they would so heavily promote in future trade relations with the Ottomans. As Michael Talbot has argued, the manufacture of clocks and watches for the Ottoman present economy was part of a concerted effort to open up the Ottoman Empire as a market for European luxury goods.[118]

Thus the "things" of peace carry a multivalent meaning here. Rycaut's text subtly suggests that the presents have an intrinsically different meaning for each party. The Ottoman luxuries seem mired in an earlier economy of excess: their value lies in their ornamentality. The Austrian luxuries seem to signify an emergent manufacturing economy: their value lies in their use value, especially, as Michael Talbot has suggested, since timekeeping was so important to religious practice in Ottoman lands.[119] In other words, these lists capture two different moments in the early accumulation of capital. The accounts of the visits of each ambassador clearly indicate that Rycaut sees Europe in the ascendance, and thus the Austrian presents would seem to be developing a market for new commodities. As we will see, these present catalogs essentially establish future patterns for luxury consumption both within the Ottoman Empire and within Europe that will heavily influence representations of the Ottoman Empire in the 1720s. But it is important for us to recognize the way that these things, and the symbolic imbalance between ancient luxury and modern technology inscribed into their exchange, presage the unraveling of the accord achieved at Karlowitz. Paget's mediation momentarily ceased hostilities and established borders, but Rycaut's mediation, in a different sense, reinscribed conflict in the scene of diplomatic exchange in a way that explicitly activated the struggle for economic, political, and, ultimately, territorial precedence. The only place of rest was an imaginary house conjured out of nowhere and now irrevocably in the past. Peace does not abide.

CHAPTER 2

A Costume Empire

Describing the Social Matrix

At the end of his chapter on the Ottoman military, the English traveler Aaron Hill offers a condensed metaphor for the state of the Ottoman Empire in the post-Karlowitz era: "When a Man who seriously reflects on what he sees, becomes a Witness of the numberless Attendants, Trains, and Carriages of the Turkish Armies, he cannot but with Wonder bless that God, who curbs in Mercy the Ambitious Arms of this prodigious Government, and has kindly plac'd a powerful Hook in the presumptuous Nostrils of their Great Leviathan."[1] Hill is far from a reliable source, but his combined assertions of inestimable strength and constitutive decay are symptomatic of European theories of Ottoman decline. Anxiety over the power of the Turks is activated in order for it to be suspended. The decline thesis has been widely discredited as little more than wishful thinking on the part of European observers, but Hill seems invested in a fantasy of absolute stasis, of an empire interrupted by Providence.[2] This is perhaps most evident in the way that everything in his text converges on the explication of his "map" of the seraglio. Located in the center of his text and prominently referred to in the "Advertisement," Hill's rendering of the seraglio is above all a container, a prison of pleasure, that as much as any external restraint constrains the Ottoman Empire from within. Alain Grosrichard's *The Sultan's Court* thoroughly anatomizes this political fantasy and demonstrates how, like a particularly hardy weed, it propagates through eighteenth-century political thought.[3]

Despite the suffusion of this fantasy through a host of European discourses, it was evident that the Ottoman Empire was anything but static in the early years of the eighteenth century. As Virginia Aksan emphasizes, the preface to the Ottoman Turkish version of the Treaty of Karlowitz justifies the peace as only a temporary stopping point in a longer journey:

> The Austrians, Poles, Russians . . . and Venetians had so strongly united to-
> gether and attacked Muslim frontiers from all sides, from land and sea,
> that it was impossible to divide and conquer them. Suspending hostilities
> and seeking peace was to be interpreted as the equivalent of *jihad*, and there-
> fore good for the supreme state. . . . Jurists were reinterpreting the con-
> cept of holy war to permit a legal state of peace, basing it on the rationale
> of the good of the Muslim community—*malasha*—a term evoked by later
> treaties. In other words, peace was another way to continue war.[4]

This rationalization would become less tenable later in the century when significant losses to the Russians would make the need for military and governmental reform all too evident, but by 1709 peace had reverted to war and the Great Leviathan had clearly thrown its hook. The grand vizier Baltaci Mehmed Pasha gained substantial victories against the Russians at the Battle of the Pruth River, and his successor, Silâhdar Damad Ali Pasha, took the Peloponnesian peninsula from the Venetians in 1715. But shortly afterward the Ottomans were routed again by Eugene of Savoy at the Battle of Petrovaradin in the summer of 1716. Silâhdar Damad Ali and over 30,000 troops lost their lives in that battle, and the Ottomans were further deci-mated at the siege of Belgrade in 1717. After substantial losses, the Ottomans once again found themselves negotiating for peace. Like the Treaty of Karlowitz, the Treaty of Passarowitz of 1718 allowed the Ottomans to convert substantial losses into palpable gains, for the loss of Belgrade and strategic sites in eastern Europe was offset by the reacquisition of the Peloponnesian peninsula. The Treaties of Karlow-itz and Passarowitz set the Danube as a practical western border on the empire, but they also signaled the permanent dissolution of Venice as a military threat. Fur-thermore, the dissolution of the Safavid Empire on the eastern borders reoriented Ottoman policy. The new grand vizier Damad İbrahim Pasha's extraordinary suc-cesses would be determined in the eastern, rather than the western, theater.

As we will see, the backlash against Damad İbrahim Pasha's eastern policies and the very way he conducted his grand vizierate would rock the streets of Con-stantinople, but prior to the Patrona Halil rebellion of 1730 one can discern a clear period of consolidation in the Ottoman Empire. Both major treaties with Austria and Venice had a positive effect on trade in the region. After Karlowitz and the loss of much of Hungary, the court returned to Constantinople from Adrianople and, as Shirine Hamadeh argues, consolidated its presence in the Ottoman capital.[5] As readers across Europe contented themselves with the usual itinerary of sights—Topkapi, the Hippodrome, the Hagia Sophia, the Great Pillar—Sultan Ahmed III, who acceded to the sultanate in 1703, undertook ambitious restoration and rebuild-ing plans. The ritual performances that attended Ottoman statecraft—processions demonstrating guild loyalty, celebrating the circumcision of the sultan's sons, and those conspicuously displaying the sultan himself—were once again part of daily life. In one sense, this reconsolidation can be seen as a response to the humiliation of Zenta and Karlowitz, but in many ways the empire was resurgent during this period. As Ariel Salzmann states, "At the crossroads of the early consumer revolution, Ottoman townsmen and women were pivotal actors in global trade. Given state policies that encouraged the circulation of luxuries and commercial manufactures to its growing cities, Ottoman townspeople and merchants mediated the flow of manufactures and design between west Asia, Africa, and Europe. They affected the monetary and importation policies of Mediterranean merchants and states."[6] Consumption, particularly of cultural objects, was significant in its own right and as a sign of the state's vibrancy; thus it is a vital lens for understanding not only the stability or instability of Ottoman society in this period of turbulent internal change but also the capacity or incapacity of European observers to assess the shifting world around them.

This chapter and the next look at the descriptive strategies of two European observers—Jean-Baptiste Vanmour and Lady Mary Wortley Montagu—who attempted to catalog this matrix of state power and economic transaction. Montagu is the more famous of the two, and her Letter-book, conventionally referred to as *The Turkish Embassy Letters,* has now achieved canonical status in eighteenth-century studies.[7] The Letter-book was composed during and after her time in Constantinople where she accompanied her husband on his embassy to the Sublime Porte. One of my primary contentions regarding Montagu's text is that there is complex interweaving of a discourse that aspires to verisimilitude and of an allegorical mode that pushes beyond description to engage with her literary forebears. My in-depth engagement with Montagu in Chapter 4 concerns this under-discussed allegorical dimension of the Letter-book and will argue that Montagu's writings can be profitably engaged as a complex meditation not only on how cultural dislocation opens a space for the subject to become other to itself, but also on the aestheticization of imperial history in Virgil and Homer. But in the current chapter I look closely at the scope and texture of descriptive discourse in Montagu's Letter-book in order to open up an avenue for discussing the descriptive strategies of the artist Jean-Baptiste Vanmour who resided in Pera from shortly after the Treaty of Karlowitz to well into the 1730s. If Montagu is steeped in the classics, Vanmour's art is deeply embedded in Dutch and French genre painting, another tradition where the relationship between descriptive verisimilitude and allegory is always at stake.[8] As we will see, the relationship between description and allegory in Vanmour also provides a model for thinking about these two interlocking modes in Montagu's writing.

Vanmour's costume paintings, the engravings derived from them, and his related paintings of Ottoman state theater were extraordinarily influential, but their restrictive visual economies allow us to see something about how forms collide in this liminal intercultural space. The subtle analysis of social and political crisis that we find in Vanmour's work emerges from and relies upon bending the northern European pictorial tradition to fit the exigencies of the Ottoman world. Vanmour was cognizant of the tradition of costume engraving, and as Alexander Bevilacqua and Helen Pfeifer argue, his costume images were in dialogue with Ottoman costume images,[9] but he was also witness to the highly choreographed performance of processions in Constantinople and his relation to these performances is intriguing. At one level, they were occasions for precise observation of the vast array of people that he would codify in the costume album that made him famous across Europe. But I would also suggest that processions generated significant levels of discomfort, both political and representational. As events designed to declare the supreme power of the Ottoman state, they undermined the efficacy of European observers. And their performative totality in space and time exceeded conventional European forms of visual narrative and description. We can perceive this discomfort in Vanmour's procession paintings. In the first two sections that follow in this chapter I will suggest that Vanmour's costume images attempt to supplant and thus contain the threat posed by the narrative structure of Ottoman processional theater. The third section of the chapter turns to Montagu's Letter-book for a critique of the visual stasis that characterizes costume images. As we will see, her critique is applicable to both Vanmour's rendering of the state officials he could see and the various sequestered figures that he had no access to. Montagu's rehearsal of Vanmour's descriptive strategies will push beyond static forms toward scenes of intercultural transaction, often economic, but also erotic and intimate. The final section brings these two remarkable figures together for an analysis of Vanmour's 1717 portrait of Lady Mary.

Empire as Album

France's ambassador to the Ottoman Empire, Marquis Charles de Ferriol, took up his post in Constantinople in 1699 and immediately found himself out of favor with the Ottoman court. As discussed briefly in Chapter 1, successive failures to observe the rules of state protocol rendered his embassy highly ineffectual in its early years, but he eventually turned his career around and served in the post until 1711. When he was appointed, Ferriol invited the French-Flemish painter Jean-Baptiste Vanmour to join him on his journey to Constantinople. Vanmour was born in 1671 in Valenciennes, a town that shifted from Spanish to French rule in 1678. His father was a master cabinetmaker, and he was apprenticed to the painter's guild.[10] It is likely that Ferriol selected Vanmour to work on behalf of the embassy because of his skill in portraiture and in minor decorative painting. But Vanmour is an exception to most ambassadorial painters because his sojourn in Constantinople was not defined by his French patron. Vanmour established a studio in Pera and worked in the Ottoman capital until his death in 1737, producing work for a wide range of Frankish patrons.[11] As Eveline Sint Nicolaas states, the length and social rank of his client list was a significant factor in the dissemination of his work.[12] His most important patron was the Dutch ambassador Cornelis Calkoen who also had a conspicuously long career in Ottoman territory. We have already discussed some of the ambassadorial portraits that Vanmour produced for Calkoen, and we will return to his work in oils shortly, but first I want to look at the influential work produced in the first decade of his residency in Pera for Ferriol.

Almost immediately upon arrival, Vanmour was commissioned to produce one hundred paintings of various notable types of people exercising or living under Ottoman rule. The resulting paintings, produced in 1707 and 1708, had a dual life. In the first instance they were transformed into engravings and published in 1714 under the title *Recueil de cent estampes représentant différentes nations du Levant* (commonly referred to in short as the *Recueil Ferriol*) immediately after Ferriol's return to Paris. The engravings were executed in 1712 and 1713 by a team of engravers that included Gérard Jean-Baptiste Scotin, Philippe Simonneau fils, and Jean-Baptiste Haussard.[13] Explanatory notes for each plate were provided by Ferriol and the book's publisher Jacques Le Hay. The book was pirated almost immediately, and the original publishers reprinted the book on numerous occasions. Because it was translated into multiple languages and so widely circulated, it defined the visual ethnography of the Ottoman domains for much the eighteenth century. Vanmour's costume images were also the basis for a host of highly influential later images. Bernard and Picart's famous account of Islam in volume 7 of *Cérémonies et coutumes religieuses de tous les peuples du monde* (1737) prominently copies twenty-six engravings from the *Recueil Ferriol*, including his stunning view of the dervish ceremony.[14] As Palmira Brummett notes, versions of his engravings were incorporated into Henri Chatelain's *Atlas historique, ou Nouvelle introduction a l'histoire* (1739), John Hamilton Moore's *A New and Complete Collection of Voyages and Travels* (1785), and a host of other geographical and historical publications.[15] The same images were also the source for a remarkable compendium of Eastern types specifically for masquerading.[16] There is little doubt that his representations were replicated for the theater and thus were dynamically altered and supplemented as the century unfolded. Vanmour's visualization of Ottoman life dominated the mediascape of early eighteenth-century Europe.[17]

In addition, these same small paintings were also copied in oil and sold both within the local market in Constantinople and within a larger circuit of exchange. As Sint Nicolaas summarizes, "Calkoen bought a series of thirty-two costume paintings. He gave these to his employers, the Directorate of Levant Trade to decorate their office in Amsterdam's town hall. . . . Calkoen's costume paintings served a practical purpose: they enabled merchants who visited the office to familiarize themselves with the empire's inhabitants. The paintings were numbered and a framed legend provided an explanation."[18] These paintings were not executed by Vanmour, but rather by employees of his studio working from his designs. These divergent modes of dissemination—one along political channels and one through the networks of commerce—capture quite eloquently the double modes of European engagement with the Ottoman Empire. Just as the diplomats who employed Vanmour found themselves constantly balancing and blurring commercial and political interest, so too did the artist find himself producing and collecting images to suit the commission. The Calkoen costume paintings are a case in point because they constitute only a third of the images produced in this manner. The selection is telling: it is largely a mix of Ottoman officials and the merchant middlemen of the Aegean. The extensive array of religious and military figures and the heavily eroticized women that are so important to the structural and textual apparatus of the more complete *Recueil Ferriol* are notably absent because they aren't part of the immediate pedagogical objective of the Amsterdam town hall exhibition.

I have been careful not to refer to these images as portraits because they derive from the long tradition of costume albums that extends back to the earliest published images of encounter with the Ottoman Empire.[19] Formats and organization vary, but every generation seemed to have its own market demand for these albums.[20] As early as 1568, Nicolas de Nicolay, in *Les quatre premiers livres des navigations et peregrinations orientales*, established the single-page format adopted by Vanmour, but the close links between costume and geography can be seen in the way that they are intertwined in de Bruijn's highly influential *A Voyage to the Levant*.[21] If one flips through de Bruijn's text topographical views of Constantinople give way to engravings of architecture and finally the reader comes upon costume images of the people that inhabit these spaces.[22] But the images of people seem to emerge from a very different pictorial tradition than the empirical observation of spaces, and it is worth considering the kind of epistemological work they performed. As Bronwen Wilson argues, costume albums present the viewer with types of people rather than specific likenesses and thus are akin to other modes of visual classification.[23] In all but a few cases, the subjects are identifiable not by their countenance but by their dress. The exception, of course, are those "types" whose very singularity means that they must refer to a specific person; for example, engravings of the sultan or of the *kislar aga* (chief eunuch) approach the condition of portraiture, but no claim is made to likeness. Eschewing likeness, costume albums implicitly map a perceptual and conceptual field.[24] If we take the *Recueil Ferriol* as our primary example, it is clear that the sum of the one hundred engravings is far greater than the visual impact of each plate, because as a group they provide a de facto map not only of the Ottoman state but also of Ottoman commercial society. This mapping function implies a need in the viewer/reader that clearly reflects the practical realities of the post-Karlowitz world, a need to know where power lies.[25]

This is everywhere visible in the organization of the *Recueil Ferriol*. The first forty engravings present the officials and functionaries of the Ottoman state. The book opens with two complementary images of the sultan, referred to as the "grand seigneur"—one in his ceremonial religious costume and one showing his "private" dress, complete with obligatory handkerchief—that establish divergent but overlapping visual intineraries through the book. The virtuoso first engraving shows the sultan in ceremonial habit worn for his procession during the festival of Bayram (Figure 14). This was one of the most significant public processions in the Ottoman calendar, and it was an occasion where the sultan's status as supreme political and religious leader was made manifest in the streets of the Ottoman capital. Vanmour would have been able to carefully observe his costume and the elaborate equipage of his horse and retinue. Unlike earlier costume albums, the *Recueil Ferriol* uses the very signs deployed by the Ottoman master of ceremonies to organize its composition. On the streets, the grand signor's status would be marked by his differential relation to an ongoing series of passing men and horses: it is a linear articulation of power. In the hand-colored engravings, the same figures, the janissaries and the caparisoned horse, frame the yellow central figure in brackets of red. The horse and sword operate as fairly straightforward signs of military efficacy. Nothing in the background detracts from this full-frontal exhibition of confident rule.

Following the political/religious thread initiated by this first engraving, engravings 4 to 27 take us through the ranks of the sultan's household. Quite early on the reader becomes aware of Ferriol's mediating presence. For example, the accompanying text for engraving 14 gives a long exculpatory account of the dispute—now fourteen years in the past—over Ferriol's disastrous insistence on wearing his sword during his audience with the sultan in 1699. The text cites precedence for wearing the sword and fulminates over the pettiness of Ottoman officials. This multipage account brings the illustrated characters into the narrative and thus enhances the images' claims to veracity and contemporaneity; in a

Figure 14. P. Simonneau, engraving after Jean-Baptiste Vanmour, *Le Grand Seigneur en habit de Ceremonie le jour du Beiram* (1714), plate 1 in *Recueil Ferriol*. Courtesy of the UCLA Library Special Collections, Charles E. Young Research Library, UCLA.

sense, Ferriol and Le Hay's supplemental commentary ties the costume album to scenes of official witnessing. The length of this text is somewhat anomalous; for the most part we are introduced to the religious and legal officials of the state with little discussion, until we come upon the grand vizier. The somewhat sober image of this powerful figure is radically recontextualized by Ferriol and Le Hay's explication:

> The Grand Vizier is the Lieutenant General of the Empire, a Commander
> in Chief of the Armies, Superintendent of Finance, without giving an ac-
> count, distributing dignities and graces, and having all authority in his
> hands; but subject to great reverses. There have been twenty since the
> year 1690, two of which were killed in Hungary, Cupruly at the battle of
> Salenkemen (he was the brother of the man who took Candia), and
> Mehmet Dalmas Pasha at Sentha. The others were strangled, or died in
> their beds; there are still two or three living, who are governors of the
> provinces.[26]

This blunt account of the precariousness of the grand vizier's life emphasizes the
danger posed not only by the enemy but also by the very forces he commands. The
unnamed assassins of the final sentence come from the ranks of the ensuing
thirteen engravings, because they lay out the structure of the Ottoman military.
These images of the military, epitomized by the *Le Jannissaire-Aga ou Commandant des Jannissaires* in engraving 29 are among the most sumptuous in the book
and consistently place these figures in an exterior ground where troops are always already prepared for war (Figure 15). In short, an entire argument about
Ottoman despotism and militarism is encoded into the first forty engravings of
the *Recueil Ferriol*.

Ferriol and Le Hay's commentary allows us to see the importance of stasis to
Vanmour's project. As Wilson states with regard to earlier albums, "The repeated
use of frames . . . call attention to the category of identity designated by the costume. In contrast to the body as the means to convey moral values . . . here the
figures are cut from any narrative context in which their actions or movements
could be interpreted. The use of frames emphasizes the isolation of the figures
and focuses the viewer on the vestments."[27] Without the commentary, the book
effectively isolates and atomizes a highly integrated and organized set of political
and social relations. In contrast to the repeated performance of affiliation and
power in Ottoman state theater, the *Recueil Ferriol* is a surrogate for the people
and practices from which it is derived. Control over the "procession" of figures is
now in the hands of the printer and the reader, and thus each of these figures
"performs" for the observer. This effectively puts the long tradition of Ottoman
processional practices in abeyance and supplants it with the browsing prerogative
of the *Recueil Ferriol*'s consumer. Le Hay's commentary adds a further level of
narrativization that incessantly pulls Vanmour's descriptions toward preexisting
doxa regarding Ottoman society and culture. Increasing layers of visual and textual mediation push the performative repertoire on the streets of Constantinople
further and further away from the scene of reading, and with that distantiation

Figure 15. G. Scotin, engraving after Jean-Baptiste Vanmour, *Le Janissaire-Aga ou Commandant des Janissaires* (1714), plate 29 in *Recueil Ferriol*. Courtesy of the UCLA Library Special Collections, Charles E. Young Research Library, UCLA.

each individual image becomes increasingly detachable from the fabric of Ottoman life. It is not hard to see how specific images could then reemerge in other texts or be translated into theatrical and masquerade costume as more or less portable objects. However, this combination of static containment and distantiation was less available to Europeans in Constantinople itself where processional theater and everyday life were ongoing. One could say that the pressure of contemporaneity demands that Lady Mary Wortley Montagu and Vanmour address the problem of the gaze and the difficulty of bringing description and narrative together. This address, whether explicit or implicit, ultimately brings the act of observation back to the self and to the very problem of representation.

Processing

If we look closely at Montagu's Letter-book we can discern a careful engagement with the politics of looking and with the problem of giving form to Ottoman social performances. This is most obviously the case with regard to Ottoman processions and related forms of state theater. When Montagu and the French ambassadress witness Sultan Ahmed III's procession to the mosque in letter 29, her text would appear to operate much like Vanmour's representation of the sultan in engraving 1.[28] The signs of election coded into the processional narrative are condensed into the sultan's clothing and deportment, and the linear hierarchy of the procession itself is reconfigured into a concentric set of bracketing tropes. The centrality of the grand signor is almost typographically identifiable by the ascription of a numerical value to his clothes:

> I went yesterday along with the French Ambassadress[29] to see the Grand Signor in his passage to the mosque. He was preceded by a numerous guard of janissaries with vast white feathers on their heads, *Spahis* and *Bostangees*, these are foot and horse guard, and the royal gardeners, which are a very considerable body of men, dressed in different habits of fine lively colours, so that at a distance they appeared like a parterre of tulips. After them the Aga of the janissaries in a robe of purple velvet, lined with silver tissue, his horse led by two slaves richly dressed. Next him the *Kuzlir Aga* (Your Ladyship knows this is the chief guardian of the Seraglio ladies) in a deep yellow cloth (which suited very well to his black face) lined with sables, and last his Sublimity himself in green lined with the fur of a black Muscovite fox, which is supposed worth £1000 sterling, mounted on a fine horse with furniture richly embroidered with jewels. Six more horses richly furnished were led after him, and two of his principal courtiers bore, one his gold, and the other his silver coffee pot, on a staff. Another carried a silver stool on his head for him to sit on. It would be too tedious to tell your Ladyship the various dresses and turbans (by which their rank is distinguished) but they were all extreme rich and gay, to the number of some thousands, that perhaps there cannot be seen a more beautiful procession. (29.110–11; H 1:323)

We have already discussed how the theatricality of Ottoman statecraft enacted in the streets of Constantinople was translated into the pictorial economy of the

Recueil Ferriol—the arrangement of images in descending order of status en-hances the visual singularity of the sultan in the opening plates. Here it is being reconfigured to suit the descriptive textual economy of Montagu's letters. Because the text unfolds in linear time, Montagu can replicate the order of procession, but her close attention to how color acts as a metaphorical framing device is indebted both to Vanmour and to the Ottoman state itself. Her metaphorical comparison between the procession and the parterre of tulips partakes of the very tropes used by the Ottoman state to figure the beauty and stability of the empire.

But in the process of relaying the ideological significance of Ottoman pro-cessional performance for her European readers, something crucial happens. The intimate relationship implied by the direct visual address between Vanmour's sul-tan and the consumer of the *Recueil Ferriol* is transferred to the grand signor and Montagu's narrative persona: "The Sultan appeared to us a handsome man of about forty, with a very graceful air, but something severe in his countenance, his eyes very full and black. He happened to stop under the window where we stood, and (I suppose being told who we were) looked upon us very attentively, that we had full leisure to consider him, and the French Ambassadress agreed with me as to his good mien" (29.111; H 1:323–24). We are suddenly watching this exchange be-tween Montagu and the sultan both within the narrative and at the level of repre-sentation. The reader is put in a position of watching the scene of description and its composition. The reader, unlike the viewer of the *Recueil Ferriol*, operates some-where adjacent to the axis of observation, and this means that we are necessarily considering the relationship, both representational and social, between the ambassadresses and the grand signor.

This effectively replicates the external representational protocols of state pro-cession and state performance. As Atasoy argues, processions need to be consid-ered as events that delineate the sinews of power.[30] They do so not only by rigorously articulating internal hierarchies but also by scripting the social location of exter-nal observation. In the case of the sultan's procession to the mosque, the reader of Montagu's Letter-book is asked to look at the scene of viewing first from the ambassadress's perspective and then from the perspective of someone in the street or in an adjacent house—we watch the visual exchange between these specific women and the sultan.[31] When the text subtly shifts perspective the reader is forced to recognize that both women are subordinate to the gaze of his "Sublim-ity" in spite of the fact that one of them has ostensible control over the text in our hands. Note how it is only when the sultan looks at her that Montagu is at leisure to consider him, and only after he passes that the two women return to an evaluation of his "mien."

This is in marked contrast to Vanmour's painting of a similar procession en-titled *The Grand Vizier Crossing the Atmeydani* (Figure 16). Unlike the visual economy

Figure 16. Jean-Baptiste Vanmour, *The Grand Vizier Crossing the Atmeydani* (ca. 1720–37), oil on canvas. Courtesy of the Rijksmuseum, Amsterdam.

of the *Recueil Ferriol*, this later painting (composed sometime between 1720 and 1737 for the Dutch ambassador Cornelis Calkoen) eschews the metaphorical centrality of its key figure. One has to look hard to find the grand vizier, in part because the painter seems distracted by the representation of architecture and in part because the viewer is distanced from the scene. Condensing three of the most frequently described sights in the Ottoman capital into one image, the accurate portrayal of famous buildings and landscape interrupts the meta-geography of power encoded into the event. In this regard it operates much like a picture postcard, a souvenir of a place rather than an event, and in so doing refuses to accept the theatrical economy of state procession. This is why the painting largely elides observers; their presence would alter the status of the grand vizier and usurp power from the artist himself.

The same evacuation of the observing population informs Vanmour's more typical procession paintings. Olga Nefedova records at least five such depictions of processional theater by Vanmour, led variously by the grand vizier or the sultan.[32] In *The Procession of Sultan Ahmed III*, the procession winds around the picture plane like a snake and is thus recursively flattened (Plate 8). As in the engravings of processions in the *Bericht* discussed in Chapter 1, the very act of framing is an exercise in control and pictorial containment (see Figure 12). But the most startling thing about these pictures is that the relative subordination of the onlookers—both in social standing and number—suggests not only that the procession is a form of representational overkill, but also that it is being enacted for two viewers: the artist and a peasant in the foreground. This effectively makes the observer the occasion for this pomp and circumstance, and thus the grand vizier or the sultan quite literally performs, excessively, for the viewer. That this excess signifies little is amplified by the diminished rank of the peasant observer and by the fact that the other foreground figures quite literally ignore the procession. I think we can get some sense of Vanmour's diminishment of the sultan in this painting by comparing it to a similar picture, *The Ambassadorial Procession of the Venetian Bailo Francesco Gritti* (ca. 1725) (Plate 9). In this painting the richly caparisoned diplomatic legation is observed by a conspicuous group of observers in the middle ground, and Vanmour has been careful to render the observers' clothing in equally rich colors to signify their rank. Furthermore, it is clear that as we move into the picture that the entire city of Constantinople lies in wait to see the Venetian ambassador process. Subtle details also signify here: the ambassador's rearing horse aligns him with martial portraiture, thus firmly separating him from his janissary guard, in spite of the fact that his role in this performance was strictly dictated by Ottoman protocol. If *The Procession of Sultan Ahmed III* diminishes the claims of the sultan, then *The Ambassadorial Procession of the Venetian Bailo Francesco Gritti* enhances the status of the ambassador; but crucially both pictures achieve their divergent strategies of diminishment and enhancement by consolidating the power of the viewer/artist in front of the picture plane.

It is this latter point that separates Montagu's representation from Vanmour's visual practice: she discloses something about the marginality—and hence the vulnerability—of her position in this foreign place, whereas he defensively forecloses on such a recognition by asserting the power of his gaze to fix the grand vizier or the sultan in his view. And this effectively subordinates the particular official in question. In the case of *The Procession of Sultan Ahmed III*, the act of subordination is coterminous with Vanmour's elevation of the viewer's position. In the case of *The Grand Vizier Crossing the Atmeydani*, this strategy is even more pronounced by heightening that elevation and deepening the pictorial space. Damad İbrahim Pasha is rendered minuscule by the long history registered in the careful rendering of the Hagia Sophia, the remains of the Byzantine hippodrome, and the remnants of the Egyptian obelisks.[33] In other words, the well-worn itinerary of famous sights from the journey literature drowns out the present. Thus Vanmour meets the procession's claim to preeminence with a historical argument about the inability of any one person or culture to remain dominant in the *longue durée*.

In contrast, Montagu's treatment of processions understands that the performance is making phantasmatic claims to the endurance of power. As Zeynep Yelçe summarizes, these were occasions not only for the sultan to demonstrate his care for his subjects and his respect for religious leaders, thus reassuring his subjects of his power, but also to impress foreign dignitaries.[34] Montagu's understanding of the politics of state theatricality is no doubt indebted to her own experience of overdetermined court performances in London and Vienna. Court masque, although not strictly processional, makes similar metaphorical claims to inalienable timeless power even at moments of great monarchical insecurity.[35] This is perhaps why she is such a cogent reader of pageantry, for it is remarkable how attentive she is to the significant allegorical details. She would not have been able to decode the allegories without interpretive help, but her experience with court performance meant not only that she recognized that these were multivalent signs, but also that she knew to ask about their multiple signification.

One of the most remarkable aspects of Ottoman state theater is that while it was always "about" the sultan, he was often its primary audience: thus watching the sultan watching added another performative element of his validation.[36] Montagu's extensive description of the guild procession in letter 35 draws the reader's attention to how specific signs are mobilized by each profession to visually express its allegiance to the sultan as he prepares for war. Again, this was a highly scripted and conventional practice, and Montagu narrates its unfolding meaning from a very specific vantage point. In fact, the entire description is framed by two reciprocal acts of viewing: "The Grand Signor was at the Seraglio window to see the procession, which passed through all the principal streets. . . . The whole show lasted near eight hours, to my great sorrow, who was heartily tired, though I was in the house of the widow of the Captain Bassa (Admiral), who refreshed me with coffee, sweetmeats, sherbet, etc., with all possible civility" (35.137–39; H 1:356–57). As in her earlier procession description, Montagu is careful to lay out the spectatorial dynamics that condition its performance. This event is different from the earlier one because now the guild members process before the sultan and other notable observers such as the widow of the *kapudan-i deryâ* (grand admiral of the Ottoman fleet) and Montagu herself. Montagu's position, like that of her host, is clearly subordinate to the sultan, but it is superior to those expressing their allegiance in the streets. Through the rhetoric of hospitality, Montagu almost seamlessly integrates herself into the social matrix instantiated by the guild procession. She is now aligned with a prominent Ottoman official and thus partakes of some of the processing individuals' tribute. Significantly, the passage subtly moves us from a position where we are watching the sultan's act of observation to a position that may be physically distant from this initial point of view, but that is in many ways rhetorically more proximate to his power. This rhetorical sleight of hand is made possible by the fact that Montagu only discloses her position at the end of the description; the reader is forced to retroactively elevate her from the street, as it were, and recognize that her position is a sign of her acceptance into the realm of those who serve the Ottoman state.

The detailed description framed by these two acts of observation is broken into two sections. The first describes the careful deployment of people and objects, and the second turns its attention to less scripted acts of allegiance:

> The rear was closed by the volunteers, who came to beg the honour of dying in his service. This part of the show seemed to me so barbarous I removed from the window upon the first appearance of it. They were all naked to the middle, their arms pierced through with arrows left sticking in them, others had them sticking in their heads, the blood trickling down their faces, and some slashed their arms with sharp knives, making the blood spout out upon those that stood near, and this is looked upon as an expression of their zeal for glory. I am told that some make use of it to advance their love, and when they are near the window where their mistress stands (all the women in town being veiled to see this spectacle) they stick another arrow for her sake, who gives some sign of approbation and encouragement to this gallantry. (35.138–39; H 1:357)

This is a revealing passage because it so easily overcomes the charge of barbarism—there is barely a pause between the representational impasse registered in the second sentence to the prolixity of the third. She continues to look—avidly—because this practice was widely described and prominently rendered in many venues, including the *Recueil Ferriol*.[37] In Vanmour's image, this act of self-mutilation, entitled *Amant Turc qui se perce le bras devant sa Maitresse pour preuve de son amour*, is contained within the scene of erotic desire—it is rendered as an act of the extremity of passion not as an expression of political affiliation (Figure 17). Montagu fundamentally alters our understanding of the practice by placing it within the context of a prior, more political act of viewing. Montagu insinuates that the act of self-mutilation is a sign of erotic constancy because it is a repetition of an act of loyalty to the sultan that was witnessed by "all the women in the town being veiled to see this spectacle." This allegorical link between political allegiance and erotic constancy not only makes the erotics of the processional economy explicit but also suggests that Montagu sees Ottoman society as a coherent performative totality. Thus "reading" the scene of viewing is as important as describing what is seen.

Figure 17. G. Scotin, engraving after Jean-Baptiste Vanmour, *Amant Turc qui se perce le bras devant sa Maitresse pour preuve de son amour* (1714), plate 43 in *Recueil Ferriol*. Courtesy of the UCLA Library Special Collections, Charles E. Young Research Library, UCLA.

Describing Description

This relationship between the erotic and the political is important to the *Recueil Ferriol* in a different way. If the movement from engravings 1 to 40 can be understood as an atomized presentation of the Ottoman state and the military, then there is a cognate argument initiated in engravings 2 and 3, but not brought into full prominence until the middle section of the book. Engravings 41 to 60 focus

Figure 18. P. Simonneau, engraving after Jean-Baptiste Vanmour, *Le Grand Seigneur dans le Serrail, avec le Kislar Agassi* (1714), plate 2 in *Recueil Ferriol*. Courtesy of the UCLA Library Special Collections, Charles E. Young Research Library, UCLA.

primarily on the everyday life of women and servants. This group of people represents those under the immediate control of the sultan's household and thus directly harks back to the image of *Le Grand Seigneur dans le Serrail, avec le Kislar Agassi* in engraving 2 (Figure 18) and that of *La Sultane Asseki, ou Sultane Reine* in engraving 3 (Figure 19). If the text on the strangling of the grand vizier reiterates one of the chief tropes for Ottoman despotism circulated from at least the time of Knolles's *Generall Historie of the Turkes* (1603), then these two images reengage the

B.   *La Sultane Asseki, ou Sultane Reine.*   3.

Figure 19. G. Scotin, engraving after Jean-Baptiste Vanmour, *La Sultane Asseki, ou Sultane Reine* (1714), engraving, plate 3 in *Recueil Ferriol*. Courtesy of the UCLA Library Special Collections, Charles E. Young Research Library, UCLA.

primary erotic fantasies associated with the seraglio. If anything they anatomize the two primary directions of these fantasies. *Le Grand Seigneur dans le Serrail* quite powerfully conjoins the fantasy of unlimited sexual consumption associated with both the sultan and the *kislar aga*, and subtly insinuates that excess leads to lassitude and impotence. *La Sultane Asseki* simultaneously activates the specter of petticoat government that was by this time associated with European representations of the harem, and the primary homophobic trope through which it was demonized. The intimate glances between the *kislar aga* and the grand signor and between the sultana and her female servant signal a whole economy of perverse

Figure 20. G. Scotin, engraving after Jean-Baptiste Vanmour, *Femme Turque qui repose sur le Sopha sortant du bain* (1714), plate 46 in *Recueil Ferriol*. Courtesy of the UCLA Library Special Collections, Charles E. Young Research Library, UCLA.

desire. If the former culminates in the violent homosocial world of the grand vizier, where every official ultimately finds himself alone in the gaze of the sultan—this is why the album so relentlessly shows these officials in solitary poses—then the latter reaches its destination in the array of eroticized female figures that populate the center of *Recueil Ferriol*.[38]

This fits the conventional sense of Ottoman society as represented by Rycaut, Hill, and other travelers. And certainly images such as engraving 46, *Femme Turque qui repose sur le Sopha sortant du bain* (Figure 20), or engraving 54,

Figure 21. G. Scotin, engraving after Jean-Baptiste Vanmour, *Tchinguis, ou Danseuse Turque* (1714), plate 54 in *Recueil Ferriol*. Courtesy of the UCLA Library Special Collections, Charles E. Young Research Library, UCLA.

Tchinguis, ou Danseuse Turque (Figure 21), could well operate as illustrations to writings by Aaron Hill or other similarly leering travelers. But the *Recueil Ferriol* is more than a reiteration of preexisting fantasies of despotism and Eastern sexuality because it breaks its own fascination with the seraglio to depict an entirely different level of control. Engravings 66 to 99 provide the reader/viewer with images of the various ethnic populations under Ottoman rule.[39] Within this grouping there is a finely calibrated presentation of ethnic difference among the residents of the Greek islands and then a sequential rendering of Wallachians,

Hungarians, Bulgarians, Armenians, and finally more far-flung figures who have felt the tentacles of Ottoman influence: Tartars, Persians, Arabs, Indians, Africans, and Moors. In this regard, the *Recueil Ferriol* offers a human census of Ottoman territorial governance that implicitly speaks to the Ottoman tolerance of religious, social, and cultural difference within its imperial borders.

Significantly, the catalog of people under the internal and external control of the sultan is interrupted by a very different group of figures. Engravings 61 to 65 show the commercial middlemen of the empire—starting with a Frankish merchant, the *Recueil Ferriol* moves on to images of a Jew and a Jewish woman, only to conclude with the remarkable image *Femme Juive, courtier qui porte ses Marchandises aux Jeunes Dames Turques qui ne peuvent sortir* (Figure 22). The image of the female Jewish intermediary occurs in other sources, and aside from the opening engraving and the double portrait of the sultan and the *kislar aga* in engraving 2, this may be the most significant image in the collection because it refers so explicitly to the commercial connections that enable everyday economic and social exchange. This image of commercial agency signals a whole set of social concerns that were vital not only to Vanmour's local diplomatic patrons, all of whom were charged with facilitating trade in Ottoman domains, but also to the potential consumers of this rather elaborate and expensive book. Engravings 61 to 65 operate as the connective tissue that links all of the groups of people presented in the album into a dynamic economic organism. Put succinctly, this image speaks directly to the expanding market in female luxury goods that was so crucial to the efflorescence of the economy and culture during Ahmed III's reign. Speaking in strictly historical terms, this rather innocuous illustration may be the very epitome of socioeconomic relations in the period.[40]

Further, this image of the Jewish woman bringing goods to the women of the seraglio explicitly resonates with engraving 62, *Femme d'un Franc allant au Bain* (Figure 23). Again we have women aligned either directly or indirectly with the merchant class entering the spaces where Ottoman women socialize with one another. This is important because, as Montagu states, Ottoman women devoted themselves to "visiting, bathing, or the agreeable amusement of spending money and inventing new fashions" (43.172; H 1:406). Montagu is sensitive to the economic dimensions of sociability because they are so much a part of her experience of rank both prior to and during her journey.[41] But I have drawn attention to the images of the Jewish woman and the Frankish woman going to the bath, and to Montagu's words because these very characters figure so prominently in the Letter-book. In letter 30, Montagu's famous remarks on the "liberty" instantiated by the *ferigée*, or veil, are explicitly linked to the social and economic importance of Jewish mediation between Ottoman women and those with whom it is ostensibly difficult for them fraternize:

Femme Juive
Courtiere qui porte ses Marchandises
aux Jeunes Dames Turques qui ne peuvent sortir.

Figure 22. P. Simonneau, engraving after Jean-Baptiste Vanmour, *Femme Juive, court-ier qui porte ses Marchandises aux Jeunes Dames Turques qui ne peuvent sortir* (1714), plate 65 in *Recueil Ferriol*. Courtesy of the UCLA Library Special Collections, Charles E. Young Research Library, UCLA.

'Tis very easy to see, they have more liberty than we have, no woman of what rank soever being permitted to go in the streets without two mus-lins, one that covers her face all but her eyes, and another that hides the whole dress of her head, and hangs half way down her back; and their shapes are also wholly concealed by a thing they call a *ferigée*, which no woman of any sort appears without. . . . You may guess how effectually this disguises them, that there is no distinguishing the great lady from her

Femme d'un Franc
allant au Bain

Figure 23. P. Simonneau, engraving after Jean-Baptiste Vanmour, *Femme d'un Franc allant au Bain* (1714), plate 62 in *Recueil Ferriol*. Courtesy of the UCLA Library Special Collections, Charles E. Young Research Library, UCLA.

slave, and 'tis impossible for the most jealous husband to know his wife when he meets her, and no man dare either touch or follow a woman in the street.

This perpetual masquerade gives them entire liberty of following their inclinations without danger of discovery. The most usual method of intrigue is to send an appointment to the lover to meet the lady at a Jew's shop, which are as notoriously convenient as our Indian houses, and yet even those that don't make that use of them do not scruple to go to buy pennorths and tumble over rich goods, which are chiefly to be found amongst that sort of people. (30.114–15; H 1:328)

This passage has been the focus of an extraordinary amount of commentary, but I want to draw attention to how Montagu links liberty and commerce here. Note how in this passage the boundary between erotic and commercial exchange becomes blurred, how pleasure and consumption become mutually constitutive components of sociability within the Ottoman capital.[42] Furthermore, the social analysis is clinched by a comparison to social practices in London: the invocation of "Indian houses" as sites of social, sexual, and commercial exchange folds her observations into familiar metropolitan experiences.

Montagu's observation comes from a place that is neither inside nor outside any one woman's specific purview: it rhetorically includes any veiled figure moving through these spaces including Montagu herself.[43] Montagu's understanding of this complex and foreign mode of sociability is conditioned by or operates much like the costume album itself. She literalizes the interchangeability of character and clothing that lies at the heart of the costume album's proto-ethnography. This is particularly acute when she describes her "Turkish dress" item by item, and layer by layer to her sister Lady Mar earlier in letter 30. The link to visual description is explicit when she introduces the topic: "I will try to awaken your gratitude by giving you a full and true relation of the novelties of this place, none of which would surprise you more than a sight of my person as I am now in my Turkish habit, though I believe you would be of my opinion that 'tis admirably becoming. I intend to send you my picture; in the mean time accept of it here" (30.113; H 1:326). During her stay, Montagu had her portrait painted twice by Jean-Baptiste Vanmour, thus she was well aware of his practice.[44] We will be considering one of these portraits shortly, but for the moment it is worth considering what Montagu means when she insinuates that the following passage is a "picture" akin to the ones executed by Vanmour:

The first piece of my dress is a pair of drawers, very full, that reach to my shoes, and conceal the legs more modestly than your petticoats. They are of a thin rose coloured damask, brocaded with silver flowers. My shoes are of white kid leather, embroidered with gold. Over this hangs my smock of a fine white silk gauze, edged with embroidery. This smock has wide sleeves hanging half-way down my arm and is closed at the neck with a diamond button, but the shape and colour of the bosom very well to be distinguished through it.—The *antery* is a waistcoat made close to the shape, of white and gold damask, with very long sleeves falling back and fringed with deep gold fringe, and should have diamond or pearl buttons. My *caftan*, of the same stuff with my drawers, is a robe exactly fitted to my shape and reaching to my feet, with very long strait falling sleeves. Over this is the girdle, of about four fingers broad, which all that can afford have entirely of diamonds or other precious stones. Those that will not be at that expense, have it of exquisite embroidery on satin, but it must be fastened before with a clasp of diamonds. The *curdée* is a loose robe they throw off or put on according to the weather, being of a rich brocade (mine is green and gold) either lined with ermine or sables; the sleeves reach very little below the shoulders. The headdress is composed of a cap, called *talpock*, which is in winter of fine velvet embroidered with pearls or diamonds, and in summer of a light shining silver stuff. This is fixed on one side of the head, hanging a little way down with a gold tassel, and bound on either with a circle of diamonds (as I have seen several) or a rich embroidered handkerchief. On the other side of the head, the hair is laid flat, and here the ladies are at liberty to show their fancies, some putting flowers, others a plume of heron's feathers, and, in short, what they please; but the most general fashion is, a large bouquet of jewels, made like natural flowers, that is, the buds of pearls, the roses of different coloured rubies, the jessamines of diamonds, the jonquils of topazes, etc. so well set and enamelled, 'tis hard to imagine anything of that kind so beautiful. The hair hangs at its full length behind, divided into tresses braided with pearl or ribbon, which is always in great quantity. (30.113–14; H 1:326–27)

I've presented this passage at length because it is only when one considers the incremental attention to detail and the organization of the entire passage that one is able to fully understand its status as an innovative act of picturing. If we merely summarized or quoted excerpts of the passage, we could mistake her description for one of Vanmour's descriptive strategies in the *Recueil Ferriol*. She supplements the painter's practice by rendering costume from the inside out, and thus her description condenses multiple images in Vanmour's series. She is inside these images and thus can offer an account of precisely what was withheld from readers/viewers of the *Recueil Ferriol*—intimate contact not only with the body but also with Ottoman material culture and the social forces that impinge upon it.[45] By augmenting Vanmour's necessarily external scopophilic catalog, Montagu effectively argues that costume albums offer ethnography without people because they are fundamentally disconnected from the experience of wearing these items. The very act of pictorial observation enforces a distance between observer and observed.[46] This is why she so systematically places each element of her dress in a matrix of commercial and social value. Each successive remark on the value of this or that jewel, or the inability to afford such and such a clasp radically supplements the representational economy of Vanmour's work with implicit accounts of lived social relations.[47]

Readers of Montagu's Letter-book have long been aware of the importance of spectatorial matters to her text.[48] The prominence of her remarks on Guido, Titian, and Charles Jervas in letter 27—the famous hammam letter—is only the most obvious case in point (27.100–3; H 1:312–15). In every encounter with Ottoman women she carefully sets the scene by providing detailed descriptions of the interior spaces of women's private quarters before describing the person she is meeting. In other words, these letters are constructed according to strict protocols of figure and ground. This dynamic is most forcefully at play in those parts of Montagu's text that resonate most directly with the *Recueil Ferriol*. As noted above, when we look at engraving 62, *Femme d'un Franc allant au Bain*, it is hard not to recognize that Montagu was textualizing and, most important, contesting a pre-existing visual economy. Montagu's description of herself in Turkish costume both tallies with engraving 62 and exceeds its truth claims by describing not only her experience *in* these clothes, but also her interactions with women whose bodily comportment was defined by an intimate history of dressing and undressing. Thus her description of the hammam—as one might expect—has no counterpart in Vanmour's series. His *Femme Turque qui repose sur le Sopha sortant du bain* is a conventional odalisque whose very isolation renders her an object of the gaze rather than a subject of sociability (see Figure 20).

Before looking at how Montagu supplements this kind of image it is important to register how the pillow in the right of the figure seems just as desirable as, if not more than, the woman. I believe this has something to do with the manner of execution: the precisely rendered pillow, likely from Vanmour's studio, is drawn from scrupulous observation whereas the clumsily drawn woman stands in for what the artist cannot see. Thus her conventionality, drawn from nude goddesses and odalisques that hark back to Titian, makes her an empty sign. In this engraving, the object at hand is paradoxically more engaging than the object of desire because the former is available for consumption. When Vanmour offers a scene of the bath in engraving 49, *Fille Turque a qui l'on tresse les cheveux au bain*, we find ourselves in a representational impasse—the dynamism that characterizes the other plates is gone in part because the figures are so poorly observed and in part because there are no supplemental objects for visual and material consumption (Figure 24). This image from the very center of the *Recueil Ferriol* almost seems to stand outside it. Montagu was well aware of this problematic, and it should come as no surprise that her revisionary account of the hammam lies at the very center of the Letter-book.

Montagu's careful descriptions of her interactions with Ottoman women mark out important areas of divergence from Vanmour's highly influential album. Put simply and somewhat metaphorically, Montagu's letters repeatedly take us from

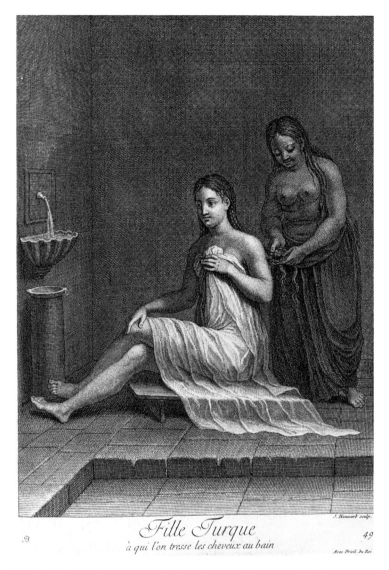

Figure 24. J. Haussard, engraving after Jean-Baptiste Vanmour, *Fille Turque a qui l'on tresse les cheveux au bain* (1714), plate 49 in *Recueil Ferriol*. Courtesy of the UCLA Library Special Collections, Charles E. Young Research Library, UCLA.

the representational paradigm defined by Vanmour—she describes the ground and then places the figure within it—and then undoes its restrictions by drawing the reader into the representational field to watch her looking at and finally interacting with the women who inhabit these spaces. In doing so she invariably demands that her reader move beyond the act of aestheticization implicit to her proto-ethnographic gaze by narrating acts of intercultural exchange that involve multiple figures. Rarely is an Ottoman woman encountered in a one-on-one exchange as in Vanmour's engravings. This is most famously the case in letter 27. As Elizabeth A.

Bohls has argued, the hammam letter explicitly aestheticizes the women in the bath in order to counter prevailing masculininst modes of viewing.[49] The way Montagu stages this counter-aestheticization is important; first Montagu renders the women much as Vanmour does in the *Recueil Ferriol*, and then she draws attention to her act of erotic idealization: "They walked, and moved with the same majestic grace which Milton describes of our General Mother. There were many amongst them as exactly proportioned as ever any goddess was drawn by the pencil of Guido or Titian, and most of their skins shiningly white, only adorned by their beautiful hair divided into many tresses hanging on their shoulders, braided either with pearl or ribbon, perfectly representing the figures of the Graces" (27.101–2; H 1:313–14). The choice of comparisons is not incidental: Montagu is evoking Milton at his most erotic, and her references to Guido and Titian are meant to invoke the apogee of feminine desirability.[50] But this is a setup for the remarkable repudiation of painting in an ensuing sentence:

> To tell you the truth, I had wickedness enough to wish secretly that Mr. Gervase could have been there invisible. I fancy it would have very much improved his art to see so many fine women naked, in different postures, some in conversation, some working, others drinking coffee or sherbet, and many negligently lying on their cushions, while their slaves (generally pretty girls of seventeen or eighteen) were employed in braiding their hair in several pretty manners. In short, 'tis the woman's coffee-house, where all the news of the Town is told, scandal invented, etc. (27.102; H 1:314)

Titian and Guido were up to the task here because they carefully observed the female form; Jervas, she implies, hasn't been looking closely enough. In terms of the argument I have been developing here, we could easily substitute Vanmour for Jervas. But this is only an incidental joke in the overall trajectory of the sentence because all this talk of visual verisimilitude is literally overwhelmed by the sociability of women.

As this sentence unfolds the visual becomes subordinated to conversation, to intimate acts of friendship and colloquy, some of it benign, some of it scandalous. In short, Montagu's letter moves ineluctably into the realm of social exchange. It is telling that she does not compare the hammam to a drawing room or a salon. By invoking the coffeehouse she is explicitly linking this social world to the extramural world of exchange: the comparison of this space to the London coffeehouse implies that these women are as much a part of the commercial world as their male London counterparts. In this context, it makes sense that the letter ends with the foremost women of the hammam attempting to draw Montagu into this scene of social and commercial exchange—this is what this social network was designed to do—and thus her resistance at this point in the text is also due to a

lingering sense of her rank. When Montagu insinuates that her husband's desire
to see the stones of Justinian's church is not only woefully disconnected from any
engagement with the present state of Ottoman society but also embarrassingly
blind to the power of women in this world, she succinctly critiques the very acts
of distancing that have distorted views of Ottoman life.

Montagu's indirect critique of her husband in letter 27 aligns well with her
engagement with Vanmour: both men fail to fully comprehend that women's sociability permeates their world, and thus they find themselves unable to fully account for women's agency. Because they have no access to the world Montagu
represents here these men resort to strategies of avoidance or obfuscation. Montagu's satirical remarks on her husband's burning desire to look at a heap of stones
constitute a singular instance of avoiding the other through an act of antiquarian
tourism.[51] Vanmour's representations of Ottoman women in the early part of his
career tend toward the condition of obfuscation. At best, the *Recueil Ferriol* can
only piece together fragments of cloth; it cannot represent the act of wearing clothing: only the latter carries the vestige of life. This radically separates Vanmour's
images of Ottoman women from those of the men and women (Greek, Armenian,
Jewish) that he was able to observe. It is for this reason that engravings 40 to 60
seem unable to live up to the phantasmatic weight placed on them in the *Recueil
Ferriol*—they are less visually satisfying than, say, the plates of the grand signor
or the janissary aga. That said, I would suggest that the paradoxes that destabilize
Vanmour's practice are perhaps most fruitfully engaged by considering his paintings of Lady Mary herself, because it is here that we see his struggle to balance
the generic demands of costume painting and portraiture. What I want to suggest
is that Vanmour is struggling to find a genre that suits the historical condition of
his practice. The commission for Ferriol is mired in an obsolete genre, although
I will be arguing in the next chapter that in the late pages of the *Recueil Ferriol*
we can also discern the kernel of a new direction in his work. His portrait of Lady
Mary is another barometer of change.

Inside Out/Outside In

Vanmour's portrait of Lady Mary Wortley Montagu and her son held in the National Portrait Gallery in London comes from a transitional period in his career
(Plate 10). It must have been painted during her residence in Pera, so it postdates
the publication of the *Recueil Ferriol* in 1714 and predates her departure in 1718.[52]
It is a curious picture both within Vanmour's oeuvre and within the broader context of early eighteenth-century portraiture. Vanmour produced other paintings
of identifiable figures, most notably his series of paintings depicting Cornelis

Fille Turque,
jouant du Tehegour.

B   *51.*

G. Scotin maj. sculp.

Avec Privil. du Roi.

Figure 25. G. Scotin, engraving after Jean-Baptiste Vanmour, *Fille Turque, jouant du Tehegour* (1714), plate 51 in *Recueil Ferriol.* Courtesy of the UCLA Library Special Collections, Charles E. Young Research Library, UCLA.

Calkoen's audience with the grand vizier.[53] Smaller in scale than these later paintings and compositionally less complex, this portrait of Montagu nevertheless places her within a social environment. But unlike the audience paintings, it is difficult to say where this is or even what kind of occasion it is intended to depict. The carpet, the divan, and the background image of Constantinople seem almost generic. This is exacerbated by the other figures in the picture. The woman on the left was clearly modeled on one of the paintings for the *Recueil Ferriol*—engraving 51, *Fille Turque jouant du Tehegour* (Figure 25)—and the man on the right is a blend of various figures from early in the album. The painting is an uneasy blend of costume album and portraiture: uneasy because the former practice focuses on types—it drains its subject of specificity—whereas the latter attempts to provide a specific likeness to render a singular subject. The problem here is that the sequential composition and the uniform scale of the figures makes them uncomfortably alike—the costume figures seem to aspire to specific subjectivity and the central portrait seems to partake of the reproducibility that defines the costume engraving.

This uneasy blending of genres is perhaps most forcefully felt in the rather noncommittal transitional spaces between each figure. These spaces seem necessary to separate Montagu from the other figures, but the strong horizontal line that links the base of the divan to the edge of the platform ineluctably ties her to those around her. We could simply argue that Vanmour's work on the costume album has made him a less than successful portraitist, but I want to argue forcefully in the other direction. Unlike other painters who rendered Montagu à la Turque, Vanmour is subtly embedding her within a chain of social relations. The messenger on the right delivers a letter—the very sign of communication and the emblem of what she would become: one of the masters of epistolary discourse. Whether he was instructed to include this detail, or he invented it himself, Vanmour signals the network of exchange that defines Montagu's engagement with the Ottoman world.

The relationship to the female musician on the left is no less resonant, for it links her to the pleasures and to the homosociality that she was at pains to record in the Letter-book. From this perspective, it becomes clear that Vanmour is presenting Montagu as a hybrid figure. The left part of the picture embeds her in the private spaces occupied by Ottoman women. The relationship between her and the servant is akin to that of an elite Ottoman woman and her slave. The right part of the picture marks her difference from this subject position by placing her in direct communicative contact with a male functionary and thus the public world of the embassy. This private/public division is coded into the background: the painting invents a kind of dark internal space on the left to separate her relationship with her female slave from the external reach of her interaction with the male servant. The strange, almost impossible lighting necessitated by this division of the pictorial space is an eloquent sign of Montagu's mediate position. Privacy seems to inhere in the midst of landscape.

Significantly, this bifurcation in the background is not balanced, the dark drapery extends past the midpoint of the painting to suggest that Montagu's subjectivity, like the overall deportment of her figure, tends toward the social world sketched for us in the left of the frame. This is also why her son is placed between her and the female slave. Throughout her text she emphasizes that Ottoman women see themselves first and foremost as mothers.[54] By deploying her son in this way, Vanmour aligns her far more forcefully with Ottoman femininity than Jonathan Richardson's deployment of a slave boy in his 1725 portrait of Lady Mary (Plate 11). Richardson's painting is a more conventional portrait—nothing pulls our eye from the sitter. The slave boy, like the turban on her head, operates as a blank sign of the "East," but this reduces Montagu's interaction with the Ottoman world into a preexisting fantasy of Eastern slavery—in an odd way it is a portrait that finally operates like a costume picture.

In order to capture Montagu's engagement, Vanmour has had to produce a far less satisfying image, it is less coherent, less sumptuous and eroticized than Richardson's picture, because it is attempting to find a genre somewhere beyond portraiture that can adequately characterize Montagu's historical and social situation. Vanmour used the devices of costume painting to produce a painting of Montagu's personality and thus shifted the objective of portraiture from physical likeness to conceptual verisimilitude. Both pictures depict Montagu with slaves, but Vanmour's hybrid image implies that she conducts herself according to the practices learned from Ottoman women of her own rank while maintaining vital ties with European world. Although not explicitly addressed in the picture, the fact that Montagu had her son inoculated for smallpox at roughly the time this painting was composed speaks to the example she represents.[55] Willing to integrate her child into these specifically Ottoman practices, she essentially describes herself traveling in the very direction depicted by Vanmour in this painting. That she was so forcefully condemned for this action upon her return to England is in many ways the clearest sign of its cultural and social importance and of the significance of Vanmour's decisions here.[56]

CHAPTER 3

At the Limits of Verisimilitude

Vanmour's Allegories of Social Cohesion

Readers of eighteenth-century accounts of Constantinople would expect to find descriptions of the same sights—the Hagia Sophia, the Hippodrome, the Great Pillar, the Seven Towers, and the Serpent Pillar—so any variation in itinerary is of palpable importance. In 1743 readers in London were introduced to two new sights in Charles Perry's *A View of the Levant*. Perry was in the Ottoman capital in 1741 at the beginning of a prosperous period of peace and tranquillity in the Ottoman Empire. As we will see in Chapter 5, this peace came at great cost, but elements of Perry's text can serve as a useful introduction to Vanmour's genre paintings of the 1720s. After conceding that it is impossible to describe the Grand Seraglio because access is barred, Perry declares that "we got Entrance (by virtue of that powerful Mediator and Intercessor, Gold) into some of the Royal Seraglios without the City, of which there are several, both on the *European* and *Asiatic* Shores; but what appeared to us the most elegant and curious . . . are *Besheictash* [Beshiâtash] and *Sadabat*, which are situate upon the *European* Shore, near the Entrance into the Canal of the *Black* Sea."[1]

Commissioned by the grand vizier Damad İbrahim Pasha and constructed in 1722, Sa'dabad was an extensive garden palace on the Kagithane River. Perry's description of the site is remarkable both for its precision and for its attempt to accurately identify what type of structure it is:

> That Pleasure-house, called *Sadabat*, is sometimes styled a *Kiosk*, and some-times a *Seraglio*; others again call it The *Kiosk* and Seraglio of *Sadabat*. This Kiosk is embellished in a very splendid and elegant manner; its Roof is covered all over with Lead, resting upon little Arches, which are sustained by 30 small Pillars: The Intercolumniations are filled with Sheets of green Canvas, which, when stretched out, may serve as Umbrellas. The Entrance

is through a Pair of Brass Folding-doors, which are fixed in a Case of white Marble; between the Pillars in each Space rises a Balustrade about Two Feet from the Ground, upon which was a Sofa of very rich Brocade; in the Middle is a lovely Fountain, which plays its Water through a Cluster of little gilded Pipes, starting out of a Marble Cistern, against a large gilt Wall hung with Tassels: From thence the Water is reflected upon a noble Tivan, or Ceiling, of gilded Fret-work, which beats it down again in little sprinkling Showers. Immediately before the Kiosk lies a spacious Meadow, where the Courtiers exercise themselves in Throwing the Girst.[2]

Perry's description warrants our sustained attention for two reasons. First, as the description unfolds, it becomes apparent that Perry is most impressed by what is most ephemeral about the building. He is less interested in hard structure than in the use of fabric design elements and the extraordinary manipulation of water around the site. Perry aligns the transient water effects of reflection and showers with the sociability of the "courtiers" in the final sentence. The leisure of these courtiers shares a certain lightness with the building itself that Perry quickly aligns with the pastoral.

But he doesn't know what to call this place. He vacillates between terms, and that uncertainty is instructive because it encapsulates something crucial about Sa'dabad's historical significance. From its very commission Sa'dabad's status as a sign has been contested and debated.[3] Rarely has such a temporary structure been forced to bear the historical weight placed upon it. During Damad İbrahim Pasha's grand vizierate it functioned as sign of elite privilege and of conspicuous consumption. In spite of the reverses that precipitated the 1718 Treaty of Passarowitz, Ahmed III was able to legitimate his rule by downplaying the loss of the key strategic city of Belgrade by playing up the reconquest of the Peloponnesian peninsula. In the period between the signing of the treaty and the construction of Sa'dabad, Ahmed III and Damad İbrahim Pasha significantly reorganized the border defenses on the new western margins of the empire.[4] But the majority of the state's attention after the construction of the pleasure garden was directed to the east. The collapse of the Safavid Empire afforded opportunities and presented complex challenges for governance.

Between 1723 and 1730, when the Ottoman capital was rocked by the Patrona Halil rebellion—an uprising that cost Damad İbrahim Pasha his life—the social structure of the empire went through a crucial bifurcation. Elite constituencies associated with the grand vizier consolidated their social, economic, and political power, and in the process fostered a cultural efflorescence. But the conspicuous consumption that characterized their sociability contrasted sharply with the economic hardship inflicted on the *esnaf* (artisans) and the military by the heavy taxation needed to sustain military operations against Persia. To these increasingly impoverished constituencies, Saʻdabad and the other pleasure palaces along the Golden Horn were signs of corruption, licentiousness, and dissipation. The imputation that libertine practices flourished within the precincts of Saʻdabad made it a particularly easy target for conservative members of the ulema.[5] When Patrona Halil was encouraged by dissident kâdîs to lead fractious members of the *esnaf* and disaffected members of the janissary corps against the sultan in the fall of 1730, the rebels almost simultaneously demanded the execution of Damad İbrahim Pasha and destroyed the pleasure garden so frequently associated with his dissipation. In having the grand vizier killed and partially destroying Saʻdabad, the rebels were committing convergent acts of real and symbolic violence.[6] Two loci of bodily pleasure were canceled and the new political dispensation attempted to harness a different set of signs for its legitimation. Put crudely, the valorization of worldly pleasure as a sign of wealth and power was superseded by investments in spiritual signs of election. The new sultanate of Mahmûd I would style itself according to traditional tropes of Sunni rule, and religion would come to play an increasingly important hegemonic role in Ottoman governance.

Damad İbrahim Pasha's grand vizierate was one of opulence and luxury, but as Ariel Salzmann has argued, similar patterns of consumption can be charted among European and Ottoman elites in this time period.[7] In fact, one could argue that the followers of Patrona Halil shared much in common with critics of the licentiousness and profligacy of the European aristocracy. Scholars of early eighteenth-century European society and culture are accustomed to observing the coexistence of the preexisting valorization of luxury, wealth, and libertinism as signs of aristocratic and monarchical power with the emergent value structures endemic to commodity culture. What is crucial for us to recognize is that this period was marked by parallel developments in Ottoman consumer society as well.[8] The production and circulation of luxury goods accelerated during this period largely to meet the demands of elite women clientele.[9] Ottomans and Europeans alike were struggling to make sense of a world where commercial capital was changing the social and cultural significance of consumption itself.

For contemporary observers, Saʻdabad and all the practices that ostensibly took place within its precincts were turned into symptoms of social cohesion and wealth on the one hand, and of social dissipation and corruption on the other.[10] Perry's treatment of the site is revealing because he incorporated an extensive narrative account of the Patrona Halil rebellion as a major selling point for his text.[11] His account, like others circulating in Europe and Constantinople, unequivocally characterizes the rebels as threats to established order and reinforces notions of elite rule. Even if he can't quite place the structure within an architectural repertoire, Saʻdabad fulfills his expectations for elite consumption. His even longer description of Beşiktaş catalogs the splendor and he concludes: "This Seraglio was built by Mehmed IV and has swallowed up such an immense Treasure, as none but so powerful and proud a Monarch was capable of expending on a House, merely for his Pleasure and Recreation."[12] For Perry, the building signifies power and wealth. His description of the workmanship of the building and the various pleasures devised for its female inhabitants figures forth social and political stability. Perry, even with the benefit of hindsight, reads these spaces as indicators of rank, status, and power, not as signs of excessive expenditure or profligacy.[13]

Jean-Baptiste Vanmour was present in Constantinople for the entirety of Damad İbrahim Pasha's grand vizierate, and, as one might imagine, the very question of the Ottoman Empire's stability and resilience animated Vanmour's practice in this period. In this chapter I consider Vanmour's genre paintings from the post-Passarowitz era as engagements with imperial continuity and radical historical change. Vanmour's work in this manner relied on informants, and although it cannot be proven, it is hard not to speculate that he gained valuable information about the sociability of Ottoman women from Lady Mary and other Frankish women who circulated in Ottoman female society.[14] Vanmour's portrait of Lady Mary, for all of its uneasiness, can be seen as a transitional work in his oeuvre. It clearly shows how he repurposed his costume paintings for more ambitious commissions, and it begins to give some sense of the complex signification of internal and external space that would characterize his work in the 1720s and 1730s. The paradox that runs through Vanmour's studio practice—the fact that he often could not see that which he so carefully described—constitutes a cultural phenomenon perhaps more valuable than any particular image he produced during his long career in Pera. The itinerary of Vanmour's work from the earliest phases of his employment at the French embassy through to his work as an independent master craftsman in the 1720s allows us to track crucial developments in Ottoman society during the first thirty years of the eighteenth century. By looking closely at his studio practice, we will be able to discern an important anatomy of consumption, strong visual arguments for social cohesion, intimations of social corruption, and, ultimately, attempts to capture and make sense of insurrection. Looked at as a whole, his work shows the tight causal links between these four topoi and thus operates as a revealing cultural diagnostic. But recognizing that diagnostic imperative requires that we attend to the allegorical dimensions of his later work.

In the first two sections of the chapter I consider the preponderance of marriage pictures as a group in order to give a sense of the palpable transformations in his art in the 1720s. While maintaining a commitment to visual description, his forms afford allegorical potential. As we will see, the depiction of marriage processions and attention to movement in general not only contrast with his static practice in the *Recueil Ferriol*, but also offer an implicit commentary on pictorial allegory's capacity to move conceptually from the referent to world historical narratives of imperial continuity and stability. The third section of the chapter shows how the depiction of pleasure uses kinesthetic uncertainty to allegorize the potential for even the most stable social forms and governmental regimes to unravel. The final section engages with that unraveling by comparing Vanmour's struggle to represent the Patronal Halil rebellion to similar representational impasses in the writings of European diplomats trying to assess the state of affairs as events unfolded in the capital. Vanmour returns to his earlier descriptive strategies but in new ways. In one case he sets descriptive and narrative modes at odds with one another to capture the affective charge of political uncertainty; in another, he redeploys the static potential of costume description to figure forth the reassertion of order in the Ottoman capital. In these visual and textual struggles we can see the degree to which radical historical ruptures impinge on description and force us to consider the undescribable.

An Arborial Emblem

Many of the finest paintings in Vanmour's post-Passarowitz oeuvre depict scenes of marriage and lying-in, and they all hark back to the most complex engraving in the *Recueil Ferriol*. The *Recueil Ferriol* concludes with three engravings that substantially deviate from the costume album format of the first ninety-nine engravings. They are double-sized foldout engravings showing a Turkish marriage, a Turkish funeral, and the dervishes in their temple at Pera. Engraving 100, simply captioned *Mariage Turc* (Figure 26), comes first and establishes a new compositional norm: all three engravings depict large groups of figures moving horizontally through a landscape (although the dervish picture is enclosed within a building, it maintains this pictorial arrangement). The extraordinary attention to deep space feels like a release from the flatness of the costume engravings, and with that expansion comes an opportunity for narrative. However, that expansion is downplayed in the explication of the plate because its primary objective is to identify the various participants: "The Bride is sitting on a horse, under a canopy held by four men: the Bride's parents are preceding the canopy, the father, uncle and parents are following it. The Janissaries, wearing their mitres, are heading the procession: some kind of Pyramid is carried among them, and sometimes, several [pyramids] adorned with streamers, golden sequins and jewelry: the Music is following the Janissaries" (21). Both the picture and the explication describe the practice of fetching the bride, or the *gelin alma*, a ceremony in which the bride is led from her home to that of the groom. Roughly equidistant from the left and right margins of the engraving we have the mounted bride under her pavilion and the

Figure 26. J. B. Scotin, engraving after Jean-Baptiste Vanmour, *Mariage Turc* (1714), plate 100 in *Recueil Ferriol*. Courtesy of the UCLA Library Special Collections, Charles E. Young Research Library, UCLA.

symbolic *nahil* being carried by the janissaries. The *nahil* was a phallic surrogate crucial to both bridal and circumcision procession and it symbolizes the potency of the groom (or in the case of the circumcision ceremony, the sultanate)—this is why the *nahil* points to the groom's house.[15]

However, the way in which Vanmour integrates these figures and props into the landscape is deeply significant. The central group of trees plays a key role in the composition of the engraving. At one level, the trees separate the musicians and the janissaries carrying the *nahil* on the right from the bride and her relations on the left. Her immediate male relatives are partially obscured by these rather intrusive trees, but we can clearly make her out from under the portable canopy. When we factor in the dark triangular foreground on which they are perched, these trees act as a fulcrum for the overall composition. There are actually three trunks: a dead trunk on the left, a vibrantly burgeoning tree on the right flank, and a central trunk whose leaves are turning. Reading left to right the trees become increasingly younger, more alive, and more fecund; thus, they allegorize the progression from barrenness to fecundity in a manner that resonates with the overall progression of the marriage party toward the groom's residence. The trees divide the engraving in two, and they provide a structuring principle of disjunction—the very principle of allegory itself.[16] The movement from ruination to birth, from past to present, is firmly coded into the picture's architectural elements. The antique ruin on the left mimics the immediately adjacent blasted trunk; the rightmost tree's full foliage intimates the future condition of the husband's house on the right. The fading tree stands in for the wife's parents, and thus attests to their own mortality. This characterizes marriage as mode of filial continuation that guarantees the survival of a culture and a society in spite of the death of its individual members and generations. That the ruins are conspicuously classical and the house is in the Ottoman style implies that the passage from generation to generation is a force more intransigent than the historical supersession of empires.

Looked at in this way, the engraving suggests that marriage's function is inextricably tied to matters of reproduction. But as the explication continues it becomes far more concerned with questions of exchange: "This is how the Bride is taken to her Husband's house. He may be happy if she happens to be pretty and of good character; because he has never seen her. When the dowry is comprised of gemstones, money or herds, the father sends her on Camels the day before, or on the day of the wedding; or he has her carried by Slaves" (21). The strangeness of Ottoman marriage practice, argues Ferriol, lies in the husband's passivity in the marriage market. He has not seen his future wife, he has no sense of her character, thus his satisfaction is far from guaranteed. This sudden characterization of the husband as a less-than-informed consumer is part of an overall tendency in the passage to think of marriage as commodity exchange. The final sentence details how the groom's father moves the goods that will accompany the wife to her future husband's household, and the earlier remarks explaining the pyramid carried by the janissaries focus the reader's attention on these items. What interests me is how widely these remarks on the traffic in women diverge from Vanmour's image. There is little emphasis on these signs of exchange; they are overshadowed by the demonstrable allegorical work on the passage of time, regeneration, and continuity. In this light, the explication seems intent on redirecting the image toward European understandings of marriage.

This is important because, as Montagu and many previous travelers emphasized, Ottoman marriage law diverged radically from European practices around questions of female property and divorce. As Montagu states in letter 30, an

Ottoman woman comes into marriage with a certain amount of property, and it is not subject to her husband's control (30.115; H 1:329). Should the couple divorce—and divorce was possible—women retained their property. It is this set of conventions that ultimately undergirds Montagu's sense that Ottoman women had more liberty than European wives. Elsewhere in her writings, Montagu explored how coverture made marriage into a dangerous prison for European women, but in the Letter-book she is also careful to describe an alternative system of value. If women in European marriages of alliance were valuable for the property they brought into the marriage state, Lady Mary contended that Ottoman wives' value lay in their reproductive capacity. Of course Ottoman women brought prestige and property into marriage, but Montagu's extensive consideration of reproduction in letters 36 and 40 is part of a larger systemic analysis of Ottoman sexuality. She argues that this deployment of reproductive sexuality—and its internalization as a marker of ultimate social value—is inextricably tied to the independence of women's property under Ottoman law. To her eyes, this is the most fundamental distinction between Ottoman and European society.[17] One way of thinking about Montagu's interaction with Ottoman women is to suggest that she saw the future of social relations and recognized that reproduction, no less than property, would render women subject not only to their husbands but also to their own understanding of bodily value.

Vanmour did not share Montagu's experiences, nor was it likely that his analysis of the sexual economy of either European or Ottoman society was as sophisticated. At this stage he likely had little understanding of these issues. But *Mariage Turc* is significant because it so forcefully subordinates the issues of exchange brought forward in the explication to matters of reproduction. And it does so by utilizing the opportunities afforded by the expansion of pictorial space to build allegory into the image. The expansion of the compositional tools at hand allows Vanmour to develop proto-ethnographic narratives, rather than merely present ethnographic types. The procession itself captures the movement of figures through time and space and thus fulfills a narrative function. But the cluster of trees and the adjoining buildings capture temporal flow in a different, more complex fashion. The synchronic movement of the figures is interrupted and linked to a diachronic sense of intergenerational history by the triadic group of tree trunks. And the architectural elements frame the entire image in a historical narrative of imperial succession. This deeper temporal engagement turns on allegory.

The argument so carefully built into the composition of *Mariage Turc* is further reinforced by the succeeding engraving. *Enterrement Turc* shows a funeral procession and can be seen as part of a long-standing fascination with Muslim burial practices (Figure 27). Almost every travel narrative to the Ottoman Empire describes graveyards and funeral rituals.[18] The explication for plate 101 in *Recueil*

Figure 27. G. Scotin, engraving after Jean-Baptiste Vanmour, *Enterrement Turc* (1714), plate 101 in *Recueil Ferriol*. Courtesy of the UCLA Library Special Collections, Charles E. Young Research Library, UCLA.

Ferriol repeats much of this *doxa*, but what immediately strikes the viewer here is the resituation of the cluster of trees from the previous engraving. This is clearly a different space than that of *Mariage Turc*, but the allegorical triad of blasted, waning, and thriving trees has migrated from image to image. Now situated on the left, the trees are laid over the cemetery. With the trees no longer in the center of the composition, the dead body essentially divides the image in half. To the left, we have death, despondency, and grief, here figured by the lone contemplative figure at the base of the trees in the foreground. Colored versions of the engraving drive home this left/right separation by contrasting the vibrant costumes of processional figures with the restrained palette used to render the graveyard. However, as soon as one recognizes the left/right distinction it becomes clear that the sequencing of the trees repeats the direction of the funeral procession from a condition of living to one of death. This repeated alignment not only shows us how this image's compositional balance essentially argues for the inevitability of death, but also how the previous engraving emphasized how reproduction operates against this flow. If we return to *Mariage Turc* after looking at *Enterrement Turc*, it becomes clear that the marriage procession runs counter to the direction of the tree's inscription of the stages of life. The bride quite literally moves from the realm of death, figured by the ruins and the blasted trunk that frame her, to a condition of futurity and birth, figured by the thriving tree and the groom's home that frame the musicians. As a pair, these two engravings use the allegorical cluster of trees and basic compositional devices pertaining to visual direction to constitute an argument about how social norms and practices inhere in spite of the passing of its individual members.

The Marriage State

Vanmour's interest in the relationship between marriage, reproduction and the renovation of the social is even more apparent in his later pictures on this theme. His *Wedding Procession on the Bosphorus* (Plate 12) offers an obvious point of comparison to *Mariage Turc*. Superficially this painting (ca. 1720–37) would appear to replicate the earlier image from the other side as it were. Rather than progressing from left to right, the marriage procession moves from right to left. All of the key groupings are re-presented, but the *nahil* is now on the left and the bride on the right. The *nahil* itself has changed shape and as we will see that is deeply significant. The janissaries carrying the *nahil* are followed by the musicians, who are followed by the male members of the bride's family; next comes the bride herself concealed beneath a pavilion and then a host of veiled women, presumably family members, relations and friends. As in the *Mariage Turc* engraving, the male family members occupy the center of picture, only here they are not obscured by the trunks of allegorical trees. In this picture, the male relations stand out in part because of the way Vanmour handles color and light, and in part because the central foreground figures point in their direction.

The elimination of the central allegorical device does not mean that Vanmour has abandoned his interest in the reproduction of the social, rather allegory now permeates the entire picture. If we look closely at the procession we see that the topic of reproduction has been moved from this central motif to the outer edges of the painting. Children now lead the procession outward toward the left side of the picture; and nestled below the crowd of women on the right is a little boy watching his mother breast-feeding her infant. These two groups of figures frame the world of men and subtly mirror each other: Vanmour uses the white head-dresses and similar shades of dress to link mothers on the right to the children on the left. These descriptive strategies are enhanced by the verisimilitude of the landscape behind the procession. Set on the banks of Bosphorus, this painting handles landscape much differently than the earlier engraving in that it takes place in a recognizable topographical space. The painting shows the Rumelihisari on the west side of the Bosphorous—a structure ineluctably tied to Sultan Mehmed II's conquest of Constantinople and thus to foundational events in the history of the Ottoman Empire. The structure of the walls and the towers of the fortress are carefully rendered, and the adjoining neighborhood is presented in detail. This is a significant departure from the deployment of the ruin and the house in the engraving *Mariage Turc*, because this painting is clearly committed to a present view. It is not making a historical argument about the relationship between the present Ottoman dispensation and the ruined legacy of ancient Greece or Rome; rather Vanmour is proposing that his viewer consider this world on its own terms and in relation to its own history. Verisimilitude carries its own ideological message here.

I think this is also why the painting's handling of space is so flat. Rather than a deep space of diagonals receding away from the viewer, Vanmour presents four horizontal bands: the marriage procession, the Bosphorus, the inhabited embankment, and the sky. This breaks the side-to-side viewing pattern so crucial to the engraving's allegorical gestures and replaces it with an up-down comparison between social practice in the foreground and built environment across the water. Vanmour is bluntly stating that it is the cohesiveness of familial and social relations—here exemplified by marriage and childbirth, and augmented by discrete signs of religious observance such as the Koran in the boy's hands—that makes the fortress and the city across the water such a stable and prosperous entity. This connection between near and far, between micrological social norms and macrological governmental control, is quite forcefully drawn by the *nahil* in the janissary's hands. This fine thread of paint links the procession to the tower on the far shore. This is an extraordinary move on Vanmour's part because he is supplementing the extant symbolic function of the *nahil* in the marriage procession with the very meaning that it comes to hold in the circumcision ceremonies that were so important to state theater at this moment. As Babak Rahimi argues, the *nahil* uses the tropes of phallic potency and reproductive force to signify the power and endurance of the sultan's line.[19] Without presenting the circumcision ritual, Vanmour nevertheless makes the same connection by linking the reproductive tropes of the wedding procession with key images of the military and governmental history of the Ottoman Empire.

The elongation and placement of the *nahil* is a subtle visual gesture, but it unlocks a series of parallel constructions. The procession itself, like the arrangement of towers on the far shore, is shaped like a wedge—higher on the right and diminishing toward the left. With the pyramid tying the front of the procession to the leftmost tower, the bride's pavilion pairs quite nicely with the central tower on the shoreline immediately opposite: its flags mimic the barely visible minarets in the distance. And finally, the group of women in the right foreground maps onto the array of houses between the two minarets that mark out a neighborhood to the right of the fortified towers and walls. If the engraving of *Mariage Turc* used flow and counterflow to make an allegorical argument about social continuity, this painting is using repeated visual arrays in each of its compositional bands to argue for the sedimentation of social custom. In each horizontal band, the viewer's gaze is encouraged to move from right to left such that the marriage party, the Bosphorus, the city, and even the sky all move in the same direction. It is hard to imagine a more forceful statement of the embeddedness of a culture in a time and place.

But it is worth asking why Vanmour chooses not to represent the circumcision rituals or other forms of state theater that so clearly informs this later work? I have already argued that Vanmour's paintings of state procession refuse to accept the spectatorial economy scripted by the Ottoman state.[20] *The Grand Vizier Crossing the Atmeydani* (see Figure 16) subordinates the enactment of ritual power to static architectural observation and thus deprives the state of its claim to vitality. This claim to life, fecundity, and potency was crucial to Ottoman state theater, and we can see in retrospect that the *Recueil Ferriol* was also committed to breaking up the flow of processional theater—many or most of the Ottoman officials depicted in the engravings were most likely observed in these processions, and it is their performative relationship to each other and to the guild associations that carried the most political meaning. Only vestiges of the performance of state cohesion and power are retained in the sequence of the *Recueil Ferriol*; for all intents and purposes the costume album bleeds the liveness out of state theater. In that regard, *Wedding Procession on the Bosphorus* subtly reactivates some of the performative objectives of Ottoman state theatre by indirectly calling up some of its most vital signs. The indirection—i.e. the refusal to paint state procession per se—is a continuing sign of Vanmour's resistance to professions of Ottoman supremacy; but the multivalence of the *nahil* in this picture shows that Vanmour wants to represent how and why this society thrives both at the level of the family and at the level of politics.

Wedding Procession on the Bosphorus is clearly a revision of the earlier *Mariage Turc* that replaces culturally nonspecific arguments about the transience of life with a very particular argument about the resilience of Ottoman society. Nonspecific signs of antiquity, death, and fecundity are replaced by visual descriptions of a specific place and time, of a specific historical formation. The importance of this pairing of social actants and observed landscape becomes evident when we compare *Wedding Procession on the Bosphorus* to another wedding painting that seems almost to replicate many of its visual devices. *Armenian Wedding* is from the same period, and again we have a procession moving from right to left with what appears to be the Bosphorus in the middle ground (Plate 13). Armenian wedding practices were the locus of intense fascination and descriptions; they figure prominently in travel narratives. Montagu's account is instructive:

> What is most extraordinary in their customs is their matrimony, a ceremony I believe unparalleled all over the world. They are always promised very young, but the espoused never see one another till three days after their marriage. The bride is carried to church with a cap on her head in the fashion of a large trencher, and over it a red silken veil which covers her all over to her feet. The priest asks the bridegroom whether he is contented to marry that woman, be she deaf, be she blind? These are the literal words, to which having answered yes, she is led home to his house accompanied with all the friends and relations on both sides, singing and dancing, and is placed on a cushion in the corner of the sofa, but her veil never lifted up, not even by her husband, till she has been three days married. There is something so odd and monstrous in these ways that I could not believe them till I had enquired of several Armenians myself, who all assured me of the truth of them, particularly one young fellow who wept when he spoke of it, being promised by his mother to a girl that he must marry in this manner, though he protested to me he had rather die than submit to this slavery, having already figured his bride to himself with all the deformities in nature. (43.176; 1:411–12)

I have presented this passage at length because Montagu's charge of monstrosity is directed at those whom she calls "the devoutest Christians in the world" (43.176; H 1:410). Her account of "Turkish" marriage ceremony, by contrast, is an occasion for her to argue that "the Turkish ladies have at least as much wit and civility, nay liberty, as ladies among us" (43.173; H 1:407). Montagu's horror has to do with an understanding of marriage that assumes the agency of the both the bride and the groom. This is the only occasion in the Letter-book where she recoils at the practice of veiling, and it is because she understands it as privative and, most important, as the opposite of Ottoman veiling practices. In contrast to Ottoman "liberty," Montagu sees Armenian veiling is part of an economy of slavery.[21] This somewhat counterintuitive distinction—both societies have prearranged marriages, and both Ottoman and Armenian men have restricted access to their future brides—lies not in the veil itself but rather in the distinction between Ottoman and Armenian relations to extramarital sex and divorce. The discussion with the

Figure 28. J. Haussard, engraving after Jean-Baptiste Vanmour, *Fille Armenienne, que l'on conduit à l'Eglise pour la marier* (1714), plate 87 in *Recueil Ferriol*. Courtesy of the UCLA Library Special Collections, Charles E. Young Research Library, UCLA.

young Armenian man that concludes this passage works from the assumption that Christian marriage is irrevocable.

Like *Wedding Procession on the Bosphorus*, Vanmour's *Armenian Wedding* is a revision of an earlier image, engraving 87 in the *Recueil Ferriol*. I think some of what disturbed Montagu comes through in the earlier engraving, *Fille Armenienne, que l'on conduit à l'Eglise pour la marier* (Figure 28). The bride in this image is the only fully veiled figure in the book. Unlike all the other women, and men for that matter, she is being held by other figures. Whether that grasp is coercive is unclear precisely because we cannot observe the bride's face. A question is raised that we cannot answer. This gains added weight when we remember that Vanmour regularly shows us the faces of Ottoman women: he shows them at leisure, caring for one another, engaged in private activities that he had no access to. Like so many "observers" before and after him, Vanmour is willing to compensate for this epistemological void in a manner that not only repeats prior conventions, but itself relies on repetition to build a fantasy of accessibility. But the Armenian bride is being handled differently than other women in the book—she both stands for and is embedded in a narrative enigma. That is not to say that she isn't also the locus of erotic fantasy—the way that Vanmour renders her breasts through the semitransparent veil is a sure sign of fascination—but the occlusion of her eyes acts as the very sign of disfigurement referred to in Montagu's rendering of the groom's vow. This conspicuously Christian bride operates as a double sign of attraction and repulsion. Could we not argue that this is the most direct, because indirect, rendering of Vanmour's relation to the women of the harem?

I pose the question in this way because Vanmour uses the technique of semitransparency so hauntingly worked out here to render the bride's pavilion in *Mariage Turc*. In other words, there is a commutability already nascent in the *Recueil Ferriol* that is altered in quite significant ways in the later paintings. If we return to *Wedding Procession on the Bosphorus*, we see that Vanmour has carefully registered the texture of the bride's processional pavilion, but the viewer cannot make out her shape. The female figures around her horse can act as visual substitutes, but the bride is withheld from view. I would suggest that this is crucial to the overall de-eroticization of the image: the bride is de-eroticized in order to more solemnly invest in her reproductive sexuality. This subtle play between eroticism and sexuality is crucial to Vanmour's marriage pictures. In *Armenian Wedding*, the simple act of shifting the viewer's perspective from a full frontal view of the bride to this side view cancels the shadowy eyes that so conspicuously disfigured the earlier engraving. This considerably changes the erotic economy of the image: note how the later painting draws even more attention to her form by echoing the shape of the bride's breasts in each of the women around her. Again comparison to the engraving is helpful: the bride's attendants in the earlier image are desexualized, and this goes some way to rendering plate 87 in the *Recueil Ferriol* a scene of coercion. In contrast, the vibrant palette of *Armenian Wedding*, its deployment of female forms, and, above all, its subtle but powerful shift in the rendering of the bride herself make this an image of social pleasure.

Unshackled from the burden of rendering social stability and political continuity that we saw in *Wedding Procession on the Bosphorus*, this picture very quickly adapts the signs of pastoral to its primary ends. The dancers and muscians, the bucolic landscape, and its de-specified spatial coordinates point to erotic pleasure, not reproductive capacity and filial continuity. In this picture, the party seems categorically distant from the obscure buildings on the far shore: they are part of but not inherently connected to that sign of Ottoman settlement. And that I think is the key point. The Armenians are a subject population, but Vanmour is showing the viewer that under Ottoman governance they retain cultural and social autonomy. The fear and fascination of the earlier engraving has been superseded by a larger political allegory about hegemonic imperial relations with minority populations. This helps to explain why the outward signs of coercion—the attendants' hold on the bride's arms—are only minimally shown here. Within the descriptive economy of this painting this aspect of the ceremony has been subordinated to myriad signs of erotic desire and festive sociability. In short, Vanmour is showing us something that he did not understand earlier in his career; namely, that Ottoman political domination is made possible by according social and cultural freedoms within the realms it controls: pleasure can be part of a larger strategy of rule. It is telling that no one in the wedding party responds to the inquiries of the seated man in the foreground. Unlike the similar figure in *Wedding Procession on the Bosphorus*, whose outstretched arm was used to visually link the groom's family to the built environment on the far shore, he is simply ignored. And that refusal to engage with his gaze amounts to a repudiation of Vanmour's earlier engraving, for this is precisely the spectatorial and epistemological stance—the very viewing position—articulated by the *Recueil Ferriol*'s treatment of this social practice.

We have now looked at four weddings and a funeral, and in the process have argued for a substantial shift not only in Vanmour's visual practice whereby his interest in verisimilitude becomes entwined with specifically allegorical objectives, but also in his understanding of the Ottoman world. By the time of the composition of this later group of paintings, Vanmour had resided in Istanbul for at least twenty years, maybe as much as thirty-five (depending on how we date the paintings). We have postulated that increasing contact with informants, and, frankly, more visual observation, changed his style and his objectives as an artist. This is perhaps nowhere more evident than in an additional marriage painting, entitled *Greek Wedding* (Plate 14). Unlike the other wedding images this is not a ritual procession, although some figures process across the picture plane; it does not correspond to an event that he could have witnessed in the exterior world. This is especially remarkable in that of all the populations he could have observed, the Greek residents of the capital would have been the most readily accessible. Greek weddings were the subject of frequent representation in traveler's texts, and Vanmour himself has a quite striking painting of Greek men and women dancing the *khorra*—an activity described in detail in Montagu.[22]

Unlike Vanmour's paintings of wedding processions, *Greek Wedding* engages with the private world of women's sociability: he depicts the centrally seated Greek bride receiving visitors and gifts prior to her wedding. Presented with almost mathematical precision, the relatively shallow space is rigorously divided and subdivided by the decorative elements of the room. The pattern in the foreground carpet clearly marks out converging lines of perspective. Framed between flanking draperies and walls, the three windows organize the divan into three equal sections and also locate the room in relation to an external pastoral world. The careful placement of figures, windows, and wall decorations makes the middle ground of the image absolutely stable, almost static. The stillness of this central element allows the social activity in the foreground to become that much more pronounced: visitors press in from the left; women converse freely on the right. But the most striking thing about this picture is its focus on commodities. Every figure is an occasion for the painting of brocade and embroidery. The attention to the texture, sheen, and variety of textiles is remarkable; it goes far beyond any of the pictures seen thus far, including those from the *Recueil Ferriol* that were ostensibly focused on costume. Each jewel is carefully picked out by the painter's brush. Not only are consumer goods carefully and realistically portrayed, the entire painting is about the circulation of goods from the visitors to the future bride. The visitors carry presents, the bride inspects a gift, the basket before her contains more things: Vanmour's painting is about the gift economy of marriage. The painting's composition does everything possible to maximize the display of commodities—it is organized like a shop or a catalog.

We have already seen Vanmour's interest in the reproductive dynamics of marriage to figure larger notions of social and political continuity. This image supplements this earlier concern by showing that women's consumption of goods—both through ritual and through everyday sociability—drives production and thus the economic vitality of the empire. The three scarves hanging on the wall are commodities pure and simple, and the viewer is asked to link them to the immediately adjacent world visible through the windows. What happens in here, Vanmour suggests, cannot be separated from what happens beyond these walls and the lines of connection are sexual, social, and economic. The traffic in women and the traffic in luxury goods are so fully intertwined in this picture as to be indistinguishable. This is a significant elaboration on or supplementation of the arguments regarding social stability in the earlier marriage paintings. The social force of marriage and reproduction are now being connected to the economic force of women's consumption of commodities with ritual gift giving as the prime example of expenditure. That this is a Greek wedding is, I think, significant because Vanmour is emphasizing the importance of Greek intermediaries to the commercial cohesion of the Ottoman capital. As we will see, his treatment of the interior world of

Ottoman women also emphasizes their relation to the world of consumer goods, but he subordinates their pleasure in consumption to their reproductive capacity.

Greek Wedding rather bluntly presents us with the bride as consumer; in the related painting *Lying-in Room of a Distinguished Turkish Woman*, we can see Vanmour's most complex engagement with marriage, reproduction, and commodification, but this time he is explicitly dealing with Ottoman women (Plate 15). At first glance the painting's composition seems almost identical to the *Greek Wedding* painting, but slight variations carry great significance here. We still have a shallow interior space: there is carpeted foreground, a kind of dais in the middle ground, and a vestibule akin to that of the *Greek Wedding* painting, only here there are no windows opening onto the deep pastoral space of the verdant external world. The almost mathematical segmentation of the *Greek Wedding* picture and its emphasis on receding lines of perspective are mitigated here by repeated circular motifs. The contrast between the foreground carpets in each picture is only the most obvious assertion of circular compositional tools, but circles abound: the table, the brazier, and the cradle break up the foreground. The two groups of women on the right and the left are arranged in absorptive ellipses: they look either at each other or at their work—none of them look at the reclining mother or her child, although everyone is contributing to her sense of well-being. The servants on the right are preparing the child's cradle. The other four servants on the carpet are preparing coffee, sherbet, and rosewater for the entertainment of both the mother and the group of women on the left. In contrast to the *Greek Wedding* picture, this painting demands that the viewer interpolate the relationship between the women rather than simply catalog the commodities in the room. This is not to say that the image is any less sumptuous or unconcerned with women's consumption: there is a similar attention to textiles and goods as evidenced by the repeated motif of the hanging scarves. Only here the viewer considers the commodities in the picture not solely as objects of exchange but also as material items with specific use values. For that reason we get little visual lessons in the preparation of sherbet and coffee, in the arrangement of the bassinet.

Continued viewing of the picture slowly reveals that it is primarily a picture about labor and class stratification. All of the women in the foreground are involved in specific tasks. It is as though the carpet and the adjoining area on the right are the province of the harem's slaves. They are separated spatially from the group of elite women on the left and from the mother herself by a simple but telling elevation. But significantly the picture both marks this separation and continually contravenes it. All of the slave women's bodies are spread over the ostensible horizontal line separating them from the elite women in the middle ground.[23] There is also remarkably little distinction made at the level of dress (the seated ladies have more brocade and jewels, but it requires sustained observation to make this recognition) or at the level of detail in which the figures are represented. If anything the slaves are the primary locus of observation, in part because they are most actively moving through pictorial space.[24]

That said, the most forceful gesture in *Lying-in Room of a Distinguished Turkish Woman* is Vanmour's rendering of the bed in the middle ground. This deep red rectangle is the hub around which all of the social and domestic labor revolves. And it clearly marks the mother and child as the occasion for all of this interaction. The mother and child pair is the hinge that links the labor in the foreground to the conspicuous consumption that is registered in the costume of the other women in the middle ground and in those scarves on the wall. Looked at in this way, the Ottoman household becomes a dynamic nexus where reproduction, sociability, and consumption are deeply interfused. This is why the picture uses so many devices to link what would otherwise be distinct images of social, reproductive, and domestic labor. The very shallowness of the space, and its resistance to the spatial segmentation of *Greek Wedding,* affords Vanmour the opportunity to present an image of a vibrant social, familial, and commercial network. The fact that this tightly composed knot of figures and actions revolves around the red maternal bed and is effectively surrounded by the green draped walls should not elude our notice. These related visual devices indicate that this realm is a self-sustaining social mechanism, a zone that both produces and reproduces the Ottoman world. The world of women is not simply a market or a zone of phantasmatic investment but constitutes a formidable productive force.

Vanmour did not see this space. He likely used information gleaned from Frankish women in Istanbul, but it would be a mistake to see this as a realistic painting. It uses the tools of pictorial verisimilitude to make an argument about its subject, an argument in striking contrast to most European representations of the harem prior to and after this period. It even stands distinct from Montagu's generally celebratory rhetoric in its resistance both to classicizing gestures and to explicit eroticization. A brief glance at her representation of an Ottoman bride's prenuptial ceremony is instructive:

I was three days ago at one of the finest in the town and had the opportunity of seeing a Turkish bride received there and all the ceremonies used on that occasion, which made me recollect the epithalamium of Helen by Theocritus, and it seems to me that the same customs have continued ever since. All the she-friends, relations and acquaintance of the two families newly allied meet at the bagnio; several others go out of curiosity, and I believe there was that day at least two hundred women. Those that were or had been married placed themselves round the rooms on the marble sofas, but the virgins very hastily threw off their clothes, and appeared without other ornament or covering than their own long hair braided with pearl or ribbon. Two of them met the bride at the door, conducted by her mother and another grave relation. She was a beautiful maid of about seventeen, very richly dressed and shining with jewels, but was presently reduced by them to the state of nature. Two others filled silver gilt pots with perfume and began the procession, the rest following in pairs, to the number of thirty. The leaders sung an epithalamium, answered by the others in chorus, and the two last led the fair bride, her eyes fixed on the ground with a charming affectation of modesty. In this order they marched round the three large rooms of the bagnio. 'Tis not easy to represent to you the beauty of this sight, most of them being well proportioned and white skinned, all of them perfectly smooth and polished by the frequent use of bathing. After having made their tour, the bride was again led to every matron round the rooms, who saluted her with a compliment and a present, some of jewels, others pieces of stuff, handkerchiefs, or little gallantries of that nature, which she thanked them for by kissing their hands. (43.172; H 1:406–7)

Montagu's allusion to Theocritus and her description of women in a state of nature rehearses memorable moves from letter 27, but here there is an equal interest in the ritual exchange of gifts and presents. If Montagu's initially excessive aestheticization of Ottoman women in the hammam letter was corrected by supplementary accounts of women's sociability, here Montagu leaves the transformation of the bride into an aesthetic object intact and in a sense augments it by attending to her ritual ornamentation.[25] The interest in "jewels, other pieces of stuff, handkerchiefs, or little gallantries of that nature" is similar to that of Vanmour, but she seems to imply a commutability between polished bride and polished stone. That commutability would seem to arise from her status as a bride—as the object of exchange. When Montagu considers married women or widows much of this aestheticization dissolves, and she too focuses her attention on the relationship among women of all ranks. In other words, Vanmour's erotic restraint in these later paintings has more in common with Montagu's description of Fatima, the *kethüdâ*'s lady, than with either his earlier practice in the *Recueil Ferriol* or Montagu's initial accounts of Ottoman female beauty. As Vanmour's work progresses, the women in his wedding/lying-in paintings become less objects of exchange than agents of social interaction and commerce. They are the hub that organizes a whole host of social vectors. Their placement in such a network goes some way toward separating them from a preexisting European fascination with the harem and the hammam as sites of erotic engagement. To put this in somewhat more provocative terms, these images make the middle plates of the *Recueil Ferriol* obsolete.

At the same time that we can read *Lying-in Room of a Distinguished Turkish Woman* as a complex meditation on the cohesion of economic production and re-production in the Ottoman Empire, we must also understand it as one of Van-mour's most explicit representations of conspicuous consumption. As a descriptive painting, it presents its viewer with a whole world of goods for their consideration. In a sense, the picture wraps fecundity, plenitude, and social pleasure into a sin-gular image of contentment. It is no accident that the baby's bassinet is arguably the most ornamental object in the room: by simply describing the object in this way Vanmour aligns child and commodity in a mutually constitutive figure of cultural value.

It is intriguing that this fusion of maternal and commercial pleasure is ren-dered through the descriptive techniques most commonly associated with Flem-ish and Dutch genre painting. This may reflect the taste of Vanmour's primary patron after 1720, the Dutch ambassador Cornelis Calkoen. The argument I have been building about the transition in Vanmour's work suggests a developmental model but it is clear that his studio was still churning out costume paintings well after the departure of Ferriol. Furthermore there are two other bodies of work in the Calkoen collection that seem to coexist with these modes that seriously com-plicate our image of Vanmour's practice. The first grouping pertains to the ques-tion of pleasure itself—paintings of women that clearly operate contrary to the moralizing arguments of the genre paintings discussed in the previous section; paintings that seem to fit more comfortably into the tradition of rococo French painting. And there is a second, even more unusual set of paintings of the Patrona Halil rebellion that break with Vanmour's Dutch and French models in order to deal with a historical crisis. I will deal with these latter paintings in the final sec-tion of this chapter, but first I want to consider the painting of pleasure because I think it is inextricably tied to the Patrona Halil pictures. In order to understand this somewhat counterintuitive statement we will need to look carefully at how the rebellion was represented in other media. For the moment, however, we need to address the function of pleasure as an allegorical counterweight to the wedding pictures.

Consumed by Pleasure

Despite the importance of *Lying-in Room of a Distinguished Turkish Woman*, it would be a mistake to see it as the culmination of Vanmour's engagement with women's sociability without also considering what I believe is Vanmour's finest achievement: *Ladies' Outing at Hünkâr Iskelesi Along the Bosporus* (Plate 16). To my mind these two paintings operate like the two sides of Vanmour's portrait of Lady Mary Wortley

Montagu. *Lying-in Room* uses the compositional constrictions of interior space to capture the tight weave of maternality and women's sociability; *Ladies' Outing* uses the opportunities afforded by the deep space of the external world to explore further the importance of pleasure to his understanding of Ottoman society. Just as the full complexity of Lady Mary's situation could only be captured by artificially linking interior and exterior worlds, so too must we read these two paintings as part of a dialectical whole.

More than any other painting in Vanmour's oeuvre, *Ladies' Outing* resembles a *fête galante*, particularly Antoine Watteau's paintings of 1716 and 1717. The treatment of landscape, the very subject of a party of pleasure and the ambiguous movement of the figures, would seem to recall paintings like *L'Embarquement pour Cythere* of 1717. But we have to be cautious about reading the painting through this lens. Vanmour would not have seen any of Watteau's work in this manner, except perhaps through engravings.[26] Watteau's work was reproduced, but whether these engravings would have been available to Vanmour is unlikely. This is important because the term *fête galante* was invented by the French Royal Academy of Painting and Sculpture to describe Watteau's innovative rendering of pleasure and courtly dissipation. His paintings combine theatrical figures from the Parisian fairs with aristocratic figures to represent a mode of performative pleasure distinct from the courtly world of Louis XIV. This is not the place to explore the performative politics of his paintings, but the comparison helps us to comprehend what is *not* happening in Vanmour's picture. The picture does not portray the progress of love or desire as in Watteau: there simply are no male lovers here. The *kislar aga*—forcefully presented at the center of the painting—signals that men are excluded from this space at the Sultan's Pier. In that regard, the picture brings Ottoman women out of the harem but maintains a pretense of enclosure so that they can be observed. Significantly, the picture locates this party in a specific place; much like *Wedding Procession on the Bosphorus*, the simple act of location allows Vanmour's gestures toward verisimilitude to take on a larger significance.

The painting is nothing if not well observed. All of the groups of women are handled in great detail, and the viewer is able to make very subtle social distinctions. The liberal use of deep red and blue pigments and the wonderful use of white highlights clearly mark the central group in the foreground as superior to all of the other figures. They are attended on the left and right by slaves and immediately associated with the luxurious commodities of sweetmeats, rosewater, and coffee. Immediately above this group we have a second group of women, sumptuously dressed but in paler colors and unattended. Within this group, the unveiled foursome on the right appear to greet or bid farewell to the more covered four women on the left. Behind this central group of eight figures Vanmour presents a third group of veiled women either embarking or disembarking from the galleys in the deep middle ground. I am being intentionally vague about the direction of movement because I think this ambiguity—are women arriving or leaving?—is important to establishing the preeminence of the central woman in the foreground group. Everyone else is in motion and thus peripheral; she is calmly reposed and thus the locus of most prestige. Only the *kislar aga* exhibits a similar static power, and this affiliation further establishes her status. For that is what this picture is about. Each element of the painting shows different elements of social pleasure, but that pleasure is clearly anchored by the rank of the foremost lady. Significantly, Vanmour utilizes light itself, rather than mere compositional location to show this. Despite the fact that the central group of eight figures is bathed in light pouring through the opening in the forest, and thus immediately catch the eye, the woman with the white headdress in the foreground group seems to radiate light from within. She actually seems to illuminate those around her. Rank produces light. In a sense, Vanmour has replicated the stability of the internal world of the harem in the central foreground of the picture: like the *Lying-in* painting, the bottom third of the painting figures this woman's household as a centripetal locus of power nominally presided over by the *kislar aga* from without—note his abnormally long shadow—but actually maintained by the luminescent elite woman at its core.

This is important because her status is upheld not only from within but also by the arrangement of the allegorical objects around her. Each of the attending groups of slaves presides over circular objects—a bowl and baskets on the left and coffee brazier on the right. As in the *Lying-in* painting, these objects are signs both of domestic use value and of conspicuous consumption, but they resonate both with the circular group of women in the center foreground and the large carved melon in the foremost woman's lap. This prominent symbol of fertility and the circular framing gestures replicate the key ideological strategies of the *Lying-in* painting. Consumption, fertility, and rank are coterminous. But this picture does something else as well. The carefully arranged parties of women in the center of the painting define linked modes of sociability and privacy. Through the simple play of light—whether it comes from within the most prominent woman or is cast on the elite women who move either toward or away from her presence—Vanmour charts the topography of social influence according to rank. Light here emanates from or picks out valorized modes of sociability, consumption, and production. But these areas of luminescence are surrounded by far more ambiguous areas of darkness. What precisely is happening in the area behind the structure on the right? There are rather obscure tents in the forest that suggest different kinds of interiors than we have seen thus far. What are the women doing in the shadow of the trees in the left foreground? They appear to be dancing, and they seem fully disconnected from the central groups of women.

Figure 29. Jean-Baptiste Vanmour, *Turkish Women in the Countryside near Istanbul* (ca. 1720–37), oil on canvas. Courtesy of the Rijksmuseum, Amsterdam.

I think we can postulate different zones of pleasure in these dark parts of the painting akin to those referred to by Montagu when she suggests that the very Ottoman social customs that afford women liberty "give them so many opportunities of gratifying their evil inclinations (if they have any) [and] also puts it very fully in the power of their husbands to revenge them if they are discovered" (43.173; H 1:407). Vanmour's contrast between clear observation in the center of the painting and obscurity on its margins gets at a sort of shadow economy separate from the appropriate modes of production and consumption figured by the melon and the richness of the elite women's clothes. In the shadows we have pleasure disconnected from reproduction, and it is exceedingly difficult to perceive the conspicuous consumption that co-legitimated women's sociability in the rest of the painting. Again the *kislar aga* plays a crucial role in the painting's argument, for he does not see what is happening in the dark but simply symbolizes the legitimacy of what is enclosed in the light.

Vanmour's treatment of the dark zones of this painting gains some depth when we consider what would appear to be anomalies in his practice: *Fête Champêtre with Turkish Courtiers Under a Tent* (Plate 17) and *Turkish Women in the Countryside near Istanbul* (Figure 29). Both paintings were painted for Calkoen, but they seem to militate against the strictly descriptive paradigm of the paintings considered thus far. The *Fête Champêtre* is an explicitly erotic picture: not only does it render women in states of undress and sexual congress, but the array of items in front of and handled by the woman in yellow emblematically refer to licentiousness and corruption.[27] She is pouring wine and the phallic vessel itself clearly casts her as equivalent to the waiting cup. The message is redoubled by the *semits* and the grapes that flank her. But most conspicuous here is the broken melon. That hanging rind, when compared to the fecund melon of *Ladies' Outing at Hünkâr Iskelesi*, is a sign of corruption and dissipation, of pleasure disconnected from reproduction. The darkness of the surrounding tent seems consonant with the dark zones of *Ladies' Outing at Hünkâr Iskelesi*—there are similar shaped tents in the forest on the right. But in that painting the modes of legitimate sociability and consumption are protected by a kind of prophylactic penumbra of light. Significantly, the *Fête Champêtre* painting not only makes no space for legitimacy, it also ruptures any sense of cohesive women's sociability: men interrupt the scene, the figures are jumbled, sensuality has imbued the composition with chaos. Could this be what lies in the darkness of *Ladies' Outing at Hünkâr Iskelesi*? If so, is Vanmour saying something about hedonism and the erosion of social cohesion. It would seem at the very least that the model of consumption presented in *Fête Champêtre* is different: women have been moved out of the categories of producers and consumers and now figure for that which is consumed. The women in this picture bear none of the signs of elite rank that we have seen in other paintings, and I would suggest that the picture exhibits a certain fascination with and anxiety regarding the middle ranks of society—an anxiety that owes as much to Vanmour's experience of shifts in European society as it does to transitions visible in the Ottoman capital.

The other "dark" painting from this period is no less of a sign of social and cultural disintegration. If the *Fête Champêtre* partakes of a rather formulaic fantasy of the sexual availability of Eastern women, the rather mysterious *Turkish Women in the Countryside near Istanbul* (Figure 29) seems to come straight out of Galland's *Les mille et une nuit*. The genie-like figure dancing in the sky seems so at variance not only with the verisimilitude of the rest of the painting, but also with the descriptive impulses that govern Vanmour's practice that it is tempting to see this picture solely as an anomalous experiment or as the request of a patron. But we could also see it as testing the market for pleasure. Could Vanmour develop a market for explicitly fantastic images or for images that reconstructed the Muslim world as a world of superstition? If we recall the deployment of light and dark in *Ladies' Outing at Hünkâr Iskelesi* it is not hard to make an argument for the alignment between darkness and superstition that would fit into emergent narratives of enlightenment. This would suggest that Vanmour's rendering of Ottoman women's sociability, much like that of Montagu, uses the tropes of enlightenment to valorize Ottoman marriage and reproduction, without losing sight of the dark side, here figured by sensuality, fantasy, and superstition. Vanmour's compositional tools render literal this dialectic of enlightenment: lurking on the edge of his celebrations of the order of elite society lays the threat of chaos.[28] Significantly, these two paintings indulge in the conventional tropes regarding Muslim women and religion, thus Vanmour may well be suggesting that European fantasies of Ottoman culture constitute its dissolution. In other words, if there is a cultural decline implied here, Vanmour seems to be suggesting that the Ottomans risk becoming what Europeans think they are. And here I believe we see the harsh edge of Vanmour's verisimilitude. That which is visually reliable in Vanmour—that is, that which eschews fantasy and symbolic overdetermination—is aligned with Ottoman social cohesion and resilience. The *Fête Champêtre*'s lack of conviction and the excessiveness of *Turkish Women in the Countryside near Istanbul* operate as a critique of the market for pleasure that they may have been executed for.

As we have seen, Montagu also engages in a subtle form of the dialectic of enlightenment, only she addresses reason's dark side by bluntly reporting on the fact of domestic violence—the body of the bleeding bride from letter 43 is Montagu's sobering reminder of injustice. But Montagu's interest in violence, both domestic and political, is a helpful heuristic for understanding a key aspect of Vanmour's later work. I have been attempting to show how Vanmour's work in the Calkoen collection renders the solidity, the power, and the resilience of the Ottoman state through his representation of seemingly quotidian matters. Rather than rendering state theater—the Ottomans' own preferred mode of asserting the power of the sultan—Vanmour's attention is on the domestic economy in all senses of that phrase: marriage, reproduction, and consumption become plangent signs of a dynamic, thriving empire. And these signs of social, political, and economic vitality are insistently aligned with the households of elite women. Rank, above all, is the bedrock of this society, and this helps to explain why the seemingly anomalous images of sensuality and superstition in *Fête Champêtre* and *Turkish Women in the Countryside near Istanbul* eschew the signs of wealth and power. These fantasias come from outside the ruling class, maybe from outside the Ottomans' own self-image (if we see them as critiques of their client's desires).[29] What I would suggest is that Vanmour and his patrons, no less than the ruling orders of Ottoman society, were anxious about the shifting demographics of economic power. Mercantile capital's unsettling of traditional vectors of power and control was as much a factor in the rearrangement of the social structures of Europe as it was of the Ottoman Empire. Vanmour's strict demarcation of cultural and social legitimacy is crucial for understanding the most unusual paintings in his oeuvre: his paintings of the Patrona Halil rebellion.

Insurgency's Demands

On the morning of 28 September 1730 a small group of men entered the covered bazaar of Istanbul and started what has been referred to as the most significant uprising in eighteenth-century Ottoman history.[30] As numerous commentators have noted, rebellions were not uncommon in the Ottoman Empire, especially in the peripheries, but as Robert Olson states, "it was not until 1730 that certain ulema, a former bastion of the sultan's power base, collaborated with dissident *esnaf* [artisans or skilled craftsmen] and unemployed migrants to perpetrate the first large-scale social, religious and political revolution in the Ottoman Empire."[31] The causes for the rebellion were manifold. The period following the Treaty of Passarowitz saw a large migration of agrarian workers to the Ottoman capital from both the west and the east; in addition to the movements of refugees from the Caucasus, the onset of war with Persia in 1723 saw a similar flow of refugees from eastern Anatolia. As Constantinople's population swelled, so too did social unrest. Arson became the preferred mode of protesting the luxury and dissipation of the Ottoman court.

But more than anything else the high cost of waging war led to the institution of multiple taxation regimes and limitations on military pay that alienated both the *esnaf* and the janissaries. As the military's wages declined or went further in arrears, they started moving in on the *esnaf*'s business. This unsustainable situation came to a head when Nadir Shah (the future shah of Persia) invaded Azerbaijan in 1730 because Damad İbrahim Pasha was compelled to raise taxes for the impending war. The grand vizier and Sultan Ahmed III went to Üsküdar, the Asian side of Istanbul, to mobilize for an eastern campaign, but the preparations went on for months. As Olson states, "the *esnaf* who had paid their campaign taxes felt that they had been deceived and that the government was spending their tax money for something other than the war against Persia."[32] This inherent suspicion about the government's profligacy was only one of a number of factors undermining support for Damad İbrahim Pasha in the ulema. A faction of influential kâdîs fomented rebellion in part because they objected to government corruption, in part because they felt that İbrahim Pasha's treaty with the Russians in 1724 was contrary to Islamic law, in part because they personally objected to Damad İbrahim Pasha's licentiousness,[33] and in part because they themselves had much to gain from the grand vizier's demise. Many of these men had been the grand vizier's disciples, but the actual uprising was led by Patrona Halil and Deli Ibrahim, men of decidedly lower rank.

Once under way the rebellion was rapid and effective. On 28 September, a holiday, most state officials were not in the capital, and therefore communication was vague and the response was slow. Because the uprising was not shut down quickly, the insurgents were quickly joined by disgruntled janissaries in the capital. Within two days it became clear that Patrona Halil had direct connections with the dissident members of the ulema. On 30 September, Ahmed III was forced to sacrifice Damad İbrahim Pasha and his two nephews to the rebels. An extraordinary amount of gold and jewels were recovered from their treasuries, thus confirming many of the suspicions regarding corruption. On 2 October, Ahmed III was deposed and his nephew Mahmûd I was proclaimed sultan. In five days the foremost officials of the empire were eliminated, and over the next two months Patrona Halil's supporters and the dissident members of the ulema radically transformed the direction of Ottoman governance and destroyed many of the symbols of Damad İbrahim Pasha's and Ahmed III's power. Most significant among this symbolic violence was the destruction of the pleasure palaces and kiosks on the Golden Horn. Sa'dabad was partially razed, and a new, more sober, ostensibly more observant, social order was set in place. However, by the end of November, Mahmûd I was in a position to consolidate his power and set about eliminating the forces of rebellion. Patrona Halil and other key leaders of the uprising that deposed Ahmed III were executed in the seraglio on 24 November 1730. In the days following, Patrona Halil's supporters were hunted down, tied into sacks, and drowned in the Bosphorus.[34]

Vanmour's two pictures of Patrona Halil in the Calkoen collection bookend the rebellion of 1730 and would appear to mark an entirely different mode of painting from that encountered thus far.[35] One is a portrait—although it is certainly not drawn from life—whose scale and composition are unlike any of Vanmour's paintings of individuals. It is roughly three times the size of portraits of Ahmed III and Damad İbrahim Pasha from a similar time period. The other is a painting whose primary objectives are narrative—albeit its narrative strategies will force us to ask some important questions about Vanmour's relation to Ottoman visual culture. Aside from breaking new ground in terms of genre, they also seem to mark a new relation to the world around him—a more embedded sense of urgency seems to emanate from these pictures. When compared to the *Recueil Ferriol* or to the marriage paintings, these images convey a sense of historical crisis by presenting a twofold argument about the relationship between private virtue and the state. And yet they share one fundamental thing with his paintings of the everyday life of women in the Ottoman Empire: they are representations of events and people that he had no access to. They render information secondhand, and I think it is useful to think about the pictures first in terms of mediation, because the rebellion they represent generated a remarkable demand for information.

John-Paul Ghobrial's extraordinary account of the flow of information regarding the rebellion that deposed Sultan Mehmed IV in November 1687 provides a useful template for considering the mediation of the Patrona Halil rebellion.[36] Ghobrial demonstrates that in the case of the earlier rebellion, the English ambassador William Trumbull gathered information about events from mediating informants and consolidated information by comparing narratives with other European diplomats and merchants in Pera. The internal circulation of oral and written reports in Constantinople was matched by a corresponding circulation of scribal material in London as Trumbull sent his dispatches to Whitehall. Fragments of these letters found their way into the daily press and received wider circulation. In a final stage of mediation, authors with immediate contacts within the Levant Company, most notably Paul Rycaut, gained access to these governmental documents and compiled all of the information into prose accounts of the sultan's deposition. The relevant passages in Rycaut's 1700 *History of the Turks, Beginning the Year 1679* are a collation of all of these prior discourse networks.[37] We can chart a similar flow of information in the case of the Patrona Halil rebellion. Oral testimony from a wide array of sources—some close to the events, some merely interpreting the gossip—found its way into diplomatic dispatches, and these eventually began to circulate in print in London, Paris, and Amsterdam. In this case the final product is the *Particular Account of the Two Rebellions* (1737)—a translation of a French text that also appeared in the Netherlands.

If we look at the correspondence of two of the most informed European observers of the Patrona Halil rebellion we are able to discern key patterns of information dissemination that ultimately lead to a very specific interpretation of the uprising and its meaning. Like many other European and Ottoman officials, the recently appointed English ambassador George Hay, 8th Earl of Kinnoull, was not in Constantinople when the uprising commenced:

> I was in the Country at Belgrade Village about 14 Miles from Pera on Thursday where I first received an account of the Rebellion. I came to Town on Fryday with all our Merchants who retire there in the time of the Plague; and found our part of the Town as quiet as if nothing had happen'd, only the shops were shut and few people in the streets: My Gate being shut for the Plague I kept it so and have had no sort of disturbance from the Rebels and after Sunday that the new G. Signor was proclaimed the Frank Ministers have visited one another as usual, and our Merchants walk the streets with great safety.[38]

This account of Kinnoull's movements comes quite late in a long dispatch to the Duke of Newcastle after a series of paragraphs that narrate the sequence of events leading to the execution of the grand vizier and the deposition of Sultan Ahmed III. This narration includes moments of summarized speech, and it is clear from phrases such as "it is said that" that Kinnoull's narrative of the rebellion is constructed from oral and perhaps written communication gathered from both Ottoman informants and other European residents in Pera and Galata. His dispatch clearly indicates that the Frank ministers were able to communicate freely during the unrest. In fact, this very document was sent to Newcastle via French diplomatic channels because Kinnoull feared that overland correspondence to Vienna would be too slow.

If we look at the correspondence of Cornelis Calkoen, Vanmour's patron and one of the longest serving diplomats in the Ottoman capital, it is possible to discern shared narratives of the events. For example, Calkoen's account of the transition of power from Sultan Ahmed III to Mahmûd I focuses on the specific statements of the deposed sultan that clearly resonate with passages in Kinnoull's dispatch. After the execution of the grand vizier, the rebels moved to depose the sultan. According to Calkoen:

> The Sultan, hearing the news, rose in amazement, saying that he referred his case to the justice of God to decide whether he had deserved such a fate, and asking for the reasons; afterwards he showed a great indignation and affliction, saying that he had been deceived all the time. . . . After which Pasmaci-zade and the Kislar agasi went to the harem to invite Sultan Mahmud to leave his rooms. Upon seeing him, Sultan Ahmed went out to meet him and kissed him on the head. . . . Subsequently, he ordered the Mufti to draw up a legal document stating that he, of his own free will, ceded the Throne to Sultan Mahmud, furthermore recommending his children and himself to the new sovereign . . . and advising him to benefit by the example of the late Sultan Mustafa and himself, never to put too much affection and trust in his Grand Viziers . . . this being a source of all disasters . . . but to govern according to his own enlightened ideas, asking for counsel, but never completely relying upon anyone.[39]

Kinnoull's version of these events is not a word for word transcription, but virtually every detail is replicated:

> This naturally pleased the Mob, and he was conducted with great acclamations of Joy to his predecessors throne in the Seraglio and the late sultan Ahmed was carried to Sultan Mahmuds Prison, where he had lived shut up these 27 Years.

It is said, that the old Sultan made the new one a very handsome Speech and told him, That he had the good fortune to govern the Ottoman Empire for 27 Years. That now the Janissarys were weary of his Government and would not have him for their Emperor any longer. Therefore he very willingly resign'd the Government to his Nephew, whom they had chosen, and that he had three Requests to make to him,

    1. That he would preserve his Life

    2. That he would protect his Children and

    3. That he would never give himself up to be blindly govern'd by his G. Vezir, but would change his G. Vezirs every two years.

That he would use no other Arguments to prove this to be a wholesome Advice but the Examples that he had before him of his Fathers Fate and his Uncles present fate, which were both occasion'd by their being blindly govern'd by their G. Vezirs, and by continuing them too long in power; and that he wish'd him a prosperous and happy reign.

It is said that the new Sultan was affected with this discourse and that they both show'd a good deal of concern at parting. He told him that since the Janissarys had chosen him for their Emperor he would do every thing in his power for the good of his Subjects. As for himself that he should always have a great Regard for his Person and his family.[40]

Unlike Calkoen, Kinnoull almost obsessively marks the recited events as hearsay—"it is said" is repeated throughout—and this may say something about Kinnoull's relative distance from his sources of information. We know that Calkoen had unusually high access to insider reports; Kinnoull's information may well have come via the Dutch ambassador or from other better informed Europeans. But what interests me here and the reason why I have quoted these two passages in full is that both diplomats felt the need to provide a dramatic scene of succession for their readers in Amsterdam and London. It is clear from the rest of their dispatches that Sultan Ahmed III's fate was not sealed by his decision to abdicate the throne; rather, he was presented with no other option by the forces in the street and the ulema. He was fighting for his life. But within the representational economy of these dispatches, the deposed sultan is almost a tragic figure—a victim of his unreliable grand vizier. This means that the dispatches have already built an interpretation of the rebellion that coincides with the deposed sultan's exculpation. The shaming of the grand vizier is already under way, and importantly the agency of the "street" is radically diminished.

This is significant because both Calkoen and Kinnoull are deeply uncomfortable with the fact that this is a popular uprising. In a letter to the States-General, the States of Holland, and the Amsterdam Burgomasters of 13 November 1730,

Calkoen states that on the morning of 28 September "a small group consisting of a 'miserable Albanian called Patrona Halil, because he had served as a sailor on the Patrona (admiral's) galley; of a certain coffee-shop owner called Muzlu,' and of another fifteen or twenty 'miserable, mostly indigent people' created havoc in the Covered Bazaar and ordered shopkeepers to close."[41] At no point does Kinnoull identify the chief rebels—they don't seem to warrant a name—but he too emphasizes their low rank for a rather different purpose:

> During this whole affair the Rebels (who are common Janissarys and the lowest of the Trades People, and whose new Aga or Gent. is but a mean man, and all their new Officers chosen out amongst themselves) have acted as if they had been statesmen all their lives, and have conducted this affair in all circumstances with the greatest Skill; on the other side the Courtiers and Statesmen who have govern'd this Empire for 13 Years with great Art and good fortune, In this affair have behaved themselves like fools and Cowards, were struck at once with a panick sat still and waited for their doom.[42]

Kinnoull expresses something implicit in Calkoen's remarks; namely, that in this event there has been a complete overturning of ranks: men ostensibly unfit to govern due to their low station show far more skill than those born to rule the empire. As he goes on to argue, "if one Man of Courage had sally'd out of the Seraglio with 1000 Men on Thursday night or fryday morning against the Rebels, they had put an end to the Rebellion at once."[43] In other words, for Kinnoull the success of the rebellion had less to do with the legitimacy of rebels' cause or their strategic acumen, but rather with the court's utter failure to live up to its governmental responsibility. But there is also a begrudging recognition that these low figures have skill.

To Kinnoull, the speed with which the grand vizier was executed and the sultan deposed was the most telling symptom of governmental ineptitude, and this prompts rather ironic reflections on English governmental practices:

> Upon the whole this great Event has been conducted with so much good Sense, and carried on with so much prudence and order; and every thing has pass'd so quietly, that it appears to me at this hour like a dream and I can scar[c]e yet perswade my self that it is possible.
>
> There is more bustle and disturbance at the Election of a Mayor of a Town in England, than has been in this great City to overthrow the Government of this great Empire and to change their Governors from the G. Signor down to the lowest officers about the Court, and all this begun

and finished in four days. [W]hat more Changes may happen God only knows: but certainly their fever is not over, and for some time we must expect a great many Irregularitys in their proceedings.

I don't doubt but your Grace will be astonish'd at this sudden change. It is something very surprising to those that live under a regular Government. Happy are Englishmen who are govern'd by a good King and wholesome Laws! The more we see of the Effects of the Constitution of other Governments, the more we have reason to thank God for our own happy constitution and Government.[44]

Kinnoull's expressions of patriotic loyalty are intriguing here because he was a long-standing Jacobite and hence always under suspicion—in fact, his appointment was contested and he was recalled because of excessively close ties with the French. Is Kinnoull defensively distancing himself from the revolutionary energy he has just described because it looks a bit too much like his politics? Or do these remarks point to a certain level of frustration? He must have seen these events as discouraging in more ways than one. In the wake of the failure of the 1715 Jacobite uprising, a rebellion made up of a similar mixed constituency of tradesmen, indigents, and disaffected members of the court with aims to reassert an ostensibly lapsed religious order and put the son of an earlier ruler on the throne would seem rather familiar. But the sheer speed of the Patrona Halil rebellion, its effectiveness, and the "skill" of its perpetrators would seem to speak not only to the ineptitude of his political allies, but also to the resilience and fortitude of the Protestant English monarchy.

Whichever way we read Kinnoull's sudden act of comparative politics, it is a useful starting point for considering Vanmour's unusual painting of Patrona Halil standing victorious within the precincts of Topkapi on what would seem to be the fourth day of the rebellion (Plate 18). We can be specific about the date because, although Vanmour has inscribed the stone on the left "Kalil Patronia / chef / de la Revolte / arrivee / a Constantinople / le 28 de 7bre / de l'annee 1730 /de Vanmour / pinxit," the activity in the courtyard clearly shows three dead bodies being removed from the precincts of the palace's outermost courtyard. The grand vizier and his nephews were delivered to the rebels on 30 September, and the rebels (now fully reinforced by the janissaries and other military personnel and goaded on by the ulema) entered the seraglio on 1 October. So in the area behind the foreground figures, Vanmour's painting collapses events from 30 September and 1 October into the same image. When this background is appended to the foreground figures and the inscription, the painting compresses the narrative time of the rebellion even further than the reports he was most likely to be working from. The picture presents a four-day period in one simultaneous image, but in so doing refuses to represent the fifth day of the rebellion. The events of 2 October—the dramatic scene of Sultan Ahmed III's deposition and the transferal of power to Mahmûd I—are held in abeyance, implied but not brought into representation.

This also alters the story of Damad İbrahim Pasha's demise. The removal of carefully shrouded bodies depicted right behind Patrona Halil stands in marked contrast to Kinnoull's aide's summary of events:

> on Saturday the Rebels demanded of the G. Signor the persons of the G. Vezir, the Vezir Chehaia, and the Captain Pasha accordingly the G. Signor had them all three strangled in the Seraglio, and sent them out on Sunday morning in a Cart drawn by Buffalos, to be delivered to the Rebels, who mangled the Bodys of the Vezir and his Chehaia in a most miserable manner and afterwards threw them to the Dogs to devour them. But they suffered the Captain Pasha's Body to be buried.
>
> It is said when the Vezir heard that the G. Signor had taken the resolution to deliver him up, that he poyson'd himself, and that the Officers who were sent to strangle him, found him already dead in his room. They say to confirm this, that four of the Dogs that eat [sic] of his Body were poysoned and dy'd.[45]

Kinnoull's repetitions and his corroborations—that is, the story must be true because the dogs died—emphasize the degree to which information of these events among Europeans was highly imperfect. But Vanmour's moves here don't seem to reflect a lack of knowledge—they are too symptomatic for that. The bodies of the dead are prepared for burial, and he has taken great pains to show that they are cared for by the surrounding male and female figures. He is reinventing the circumstances of Damad İbrahim Pasha's execution. In other words, in a painting that otherwise collapses the temporal span of the rebellion into an instant, he nevertheless avoids the desecration of the body of the grand vizier and the humiliation of Sultan Ahmed III. In light of both Calkoen and Kinnoull's dramatization of precisely these events how are we to interpret this restraint?

We know from both Vanmour's audience paintings and from portraits in the Calkoen collection that the artist had produced images not only of Damad İbrahim Pasha but also of both Ahmed III and Mahmûd I. The portraits of Damad İbrahim Pasha and of Ahmed III show none of the generic qualities of the engravings of the grand vizier and the sultan in the *Recueil Ferriol* because Vanmour saw these figures on numerous occasions as part of his embassy duties (Figures 30 and 31).[46] Vanmour's strengths as a descriptive painter are on display here. In contrast, his painting of Mahmûd I is much less assured (Figure 32). It is in many ways a simple duplication of his painting of Ahmed III: the costume and pose are

Figure 30. Jean-Baptiste Vanmour, *Grand Vizier Nevşehirli Damat Pasha* (ca. 1727–30), oil on canvas. Courtesy of the Rijksmuseum, Amsterdam.

precisely the same, and the background figures are repeated with less attention to detail. But there is a crucial distinction: Mahmûd I appears stranded between interior and exterior spaces whereas Ahmed III is perfectly enclosed in the natural world around him.[47] What I would like to suggest is Vanmour's portrait of Mahmûd I appears to be a return to many of the representational strategies of the *Recueil Ferriol*—strategies that I would argue have their basis in visual and epistemological uncertainty.

I believe a similar uncertainty permeates Vanmour's portrait of Patrona Halil. Vanmour clearly knows how to represent Damad İbrahim Pasha and Ahmed III as vibrant rulers, but the narrative of the rebellion itself has canceled that assur-

Figure 31. Jean-Baptiste Vanmour, *Sultan Ahmed III* (ca. 1727–30), oil on canvas. Courtesy of the Rijksmuseum, Amsterdam.

ance. Rather than confront the task of representing the dead grand vizier or the humiliation of the sultan, Vanmour has chosen instead to invest in the body of Patrona Halil himself as a subject of heroic narrative. But the very act of rendering Patrona Halil in this way and at this scale (none of Vanmour's other figurative works approach this size) not only suppresses the narrative of the passing of the old regime but also poses two questions about the subject. First and most obvious, does this man warrant this kind of attention? The sumptuous treatment of his robes, his pose, and his direct address to the viewer all seem to emulate the norms of heroic portraiture. But there is also something unreadable about him as well. What are we to make of his companions' gaze? Two of the figures on the

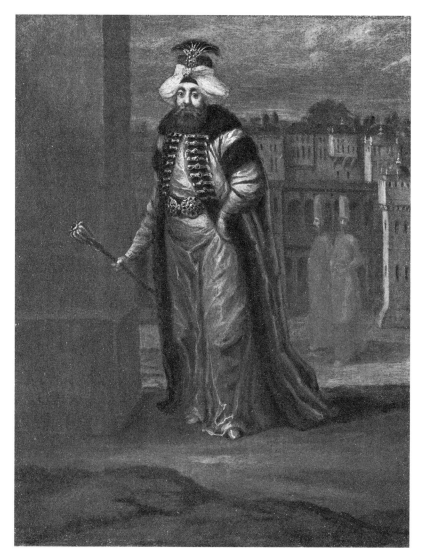

Figure 32. Jean-Baptiste Vanmour, *Sultan Mahmud I* (ca. 1730–37), oil on canvas. Courtesy of the Rijksmuseum, Amsterdam.

right ignore him. The other doesn't look at Patrona Halil in admiration, but rather looks at us as if asking for our approbation or judgment. Sustained observation shows that Patrona Halil is remarkably isolated in the image. The stone and the figures in the foreground bracket him, but they seem to testify to his presence rather than offer any clues as to the value of his actions. And where exactly is this parapet where the artist's inscription so radically contravenes the fiction of verisimilitude?

These equivocations lead us to the second question, and this one has more to do with the handling of pictorial space that we have already seen to be so crucial to Vanmour's practice. This painting superimposes the two different phases of Vanmour's career. The foreground is very similar to the pictorial strategies of the *Recueil Ferriol*: the primary figure dominates the picture plane in a central composition and it has a caption. Like the portrait of the sultan from the *Recueil Ferriol*, ancillary figures are used to frame the primary figure, and thus we can in some ways see this as an apt substitution. Patrona Halil rests in the foreground like the sultan he helped to depose in the earlier engravings. But the background is highly reminiscent of Vanmour's more complex paintings of Ottoman sociability executed in the 1720s: paintings that focused on processions and other symbolic performances of social and cultural cohesion. In fact, one could argue that Patrona Halil's figure interrupts what is essentially a makeshift burial procession. In this regard the painting overlays two representational modes that in Vanmour's practice have tended to work at variance to one another. The question posed by this painting thus becomes "Does the scalar expansion of the foreground figure so dominate the picture plane that it eclipses the careful social observations that it interrupts?" If the intention was to celebrate Patrona Halil as a kind of working-class or bourgeois hero, then why represent the countervailing images of loss in the background?

The painting's collapse of narrative time, its isolation of Patrona Halil, its lingering attention to loss, and its almost respectful treatment of the old regime create an unsettling image of cultural and social rupture. This rupture is coded not only into the tension between foreground and background, but also within the figure of Patrona Halil himself. Vanmour almost certainly had no occasion to see Patrona Halil, but I think we can see where he found the materials to portray him. Patrona Halil was an Albanian sailor, and Vanmour has fused elements of his costume portraits of *Leventi, ou Soldat de Marine* and *Dgi-Guerdgi Albanois qui porte au Bezestein des Foyes de Mouton pour nourrir les Chats* (Figures 33 and 34). From the former he has derived Patrona Halil's headdress, his belt, and his dagger; from the latter he has derived his countenance and his pose. But the most prominent element of the "portrait" is Patrona Halil's fur-lined robe—a sign of rank—and it closely resembles that used for his engraving of *Bey, Capitaine de Galere* in the *Recueil Ferriol* (Figure 35). In other words, Patrona Halil is a composite figure whose adoption of the bey's robe literalizes his insubordination. Vanmour is hybridizing both his pictorial strategies and his representation of the central figure, and the key question is can this hold together? Thus the internal contradictions of the painting itself—the tension between front and back and the hybridization of costume—are being mobilized to ask whether this is a viable historical development, can this rebellion generate the kind of social cohesion and resilience so thoroughly portrayed in the rest of Vanmour's work from the 1720s and 1730s? Everything about this painting is asking precisely the question implicit

Leventi
ou Soldat de Marine.

Figure 33. C. N. Cochin, engraving after Jean-Baptiste Vanmour, *Leventi, ou Soldat de Marins* (1714), plate 38 in *Recueil Ferriol*. Courtesy of the UCLA Library Special Collections, Charles E. Young Research Library, UCLA.

in Calkoen's description of the rebels and made explicit by Kinnoull's remarks on the "uncertainty" generated by this rapid shift in power.

That question is answered with extraordinary weight and gravitas by Vanmour's second Patrona Halil painting (Plate 19). If *Patrona Halil* was deceptively simple, *The Murder of Patrona Halil and His Fellow Rebels* is easily the most complex painting produced by Vanmour while in Pera. It depicts the moment on 25 November when Patrona Halil and his lieutenant Manay Muslu were killed in the inner courtyard of the seraglio. As the dissident members of the ulema consolidated their

Figure 34. G. Scotin, engraving after Jean-Baptiste Vanmour, *Dgi-Guerdgi Albanois qui porte au Bezestein des Foyes de Mouton pour nourrir les Chats* (1714), plate 60 in *Recueil Ferriol*. Courtesy of the UCLA Library Special Collections, Charles E. Young Research Library, UCLA.

position, they began to take steps to isolate and ultimately remove the popular elements of the uprising. Under the pretense of appointing the rebel leaders to key military posts on the Persian frontier, Mahmûd I had the men executed in turn. Kinnoull's account gives a clear sense of the violence:

> The Grand Signor having got Patrona Khalil, the Janissary Aga, and Musolo who had lately been made Koul Kyassi and the greatest Part of the

Figure 35. G. Scotin, engraving after Jean-Baptiste Vanmour, *Bey, Capitaine de Galere* (1714), plate 37 in *Recueil Ferriol*. Courtesy of the UCLA Library Special Collections, Charles E. Young Research Library, UCLA.

Chiefs of the Rebells within the Seraglio, order'd that Gates to be shut, and had them all cut in Pieces together with their Attendants. Their Bodies were exposed at the Gate of the Seraglio for several hours to the People, and afterwards thrown into the Sea.

So soon as this News was known in the City the Remains of the Rebels (who had escaped this sudden blow) dispersed and hid themselves, but in a few Days most of them were found and put to Death.[48]

Vanmour's painting shows this scene of execution. Different clusters of figures en-acting different moments of murder are dispersed across the picture plane. Read-ing from right to left, we see that the arches frame the primary insurgents. On the right, Patrona Halil, wielding a pistol, is attacked by three sword-wielding fig-ures. That he is carrying a firearm marks him as separate from this world—a kind of modern man perhaps. Two very similar looking figures—one of them ostensi-bly Muslu—are cut down in two connected scenes in the center of the painting. And the background left captures the subsequent roundup of the remaining rebels.

But the repetition of violent acts in the picture is no less important than the careful deployment of identifiable figures of state power to reassert visually the dominance of the Ottoman regime. The "Grand Vizier" is given great visual prom-inence in the central arch. The "Tchorbadgi, Captain of the Janissaries," with his vast plumed headdress, asserts his authority over the entire left side of the image. And the right arch is dominated by the "Kadi Askeri," or chief military judge, who, through a simple manipulation of scale, towers over the scene of execution. I've identified all of these figures in quotation marks because they are clearly inlaid from patterns developed for the *Recueil Ferriol*. But unlike the unsettling hybrid-ization of costume figures to form the central figure of *Patrona Halil*, each of these figures is rendered in a highly conventional fashion—Vanmour replicates these earlier well-circulated images to reassert their continuity with the past. They look on, unmoved, as the rebels are cut to pieces, placidly overseeing business as usual. Each of them is integrated into the picture in a fashion that stabilizes their role in an otherwise chaotic scene. Thus the entire picture works to cancel not only the threat posed by the rebels but also the demands placed on representation by insur-rection. Thus repetition both of violent acts and of past figures of stability becomes Vanmour's key narrative device.

By placing repeated multiple acts of murder in the same image, Vanmour once again collapses time but in doing so he emphasizes the ejection of the rebels from the larger narrative of Ottoman state continuity, here figured by the redeployment of costume figures. In this regard, this painting works in exactly the opposite way as *Patrona Halil*: the strategies employed in the *Recueil Ferriol* are not set in ten-sion to his more mature representation of groups in landscape, but rather are used to enhance the feeling of closure in each of the narrative cells of the painting. Each official presides over a different scene of death and thus assists in the elimination of rebellion. And each of these scenes is forcefully contained in architectural frames that signify both historical continuity and governmental stability. This is, I be-lieve, why Vanmour strays from the historical narrative slightly, because the exe-cutions took place in the innermost regions of the seraglio. The picture is set in an outer courtyard so that Vanmour can show the full restoration of state power in all areas. The two primary arches show the settling of the interior world of the seraglio by the sultan's chief minions; and the deep space on the left side of the picture shows that the sultan has full control of the external world through force of arms.

In both paintings we see Vanmour pushing on the very limits of his practice, indeed turning different aspects of his work on itself, in order to deal with the uncertainty generated by historical crisis. It seems fitting that the *Murder* painting dovetails so forcefully with the European powers' desire for stability in this time frame. For both the Dutch and the English, stability was synonymous with maintaining the free flow of commodities, and both Calkoen and Kinnoull happily report the violent return to business as usual. That Vanmour should be willing to explore the anxiety of these events is, I think, remarkable and instructive because it shows how larger anxieties about broad economic and political shifts in the period infused description itself. Vanmour's verisimilitude has this unsettling quality because it allows us to see both what he saw and what he could not see. That he engaged the "unseen" world with the tools of description led to crises in pictorial legitimacy that he cannily harnessed when questions of political legitimacy emerged so forcefully in the Ottoman world. It is here that his reticence regarding the death of Damad İbrahim Pasha and the deposition of Ahmed III is so resonant, because he chose not to represent that which he had clearly seen, in favor of rendering that which he had only secondhand access to. Aside from preserving the dead and deposed from further scrutiny, the very fact of not being beholden to sight enabled Vanmour to explore the ideological questions posed by the Patrona Halil rebellion at the level of composition. That he ultimately answered these questions in a fashion in line with his patron's—and his—interest should not blind us to the fact that he posed them at all.

The representational space between *Patrona Halil* and *The Murder of Patrona Halil and His Fellow Rebels* seems to beg the question of what one does in the face of an unknown or unknowable future. Vanmour, like the Ottoman state itself, chose to replace the unknown with the familiar, to eject the shock of the new. From this recognition I think it is possible see the modernity of *Patrona Halil*. The sheer challenge it poses both to description and narrative alike is akin to that of imagining the post-Ottoman world, or, perhaps more generally, a post-absolutist polity. The harsh rejoinder of *The Murder of Patrona Halil and His Fellow Rebels* shows that Vanmour could not imagine or chose not to envisage such a possibility. As we will see in Chapters 5 and 6 some of his notable successors were all too willing to imagine and visualize such a future.

CHAPTER 4

Critical Alignments

Lady Mary Wortley Montagu's Classical Counter-Memory

Jean-Baptiste Vanmour's paintings of the Patrona Halil rebellion exhibit an aesthetic at the very limits of its capacity. This chapter will be looking at a similar dynamic, one in which violence and historical crisis exert intense pressure on representation. Chapters 2 and 3 showed not only how description's referential effects can make worlds, but also how these same referential effects can become the ground for allegories of social stability and/or crisis. This complex interplay of verisimilitude and allegory also animates Montagu's writing, and we will see a remarkably similar layering of historical moments but this time in the act of translation and the practice of allusion. Translation, allusion, and allegory are all bridging activities and as such they are apt models for Lady Mary Wortley Montagu's self-imposed task in her Letter-book.

Translation takes one from one linguistic environment to another; allusion specifically joins textual domains; and allegory systematically aligns multiple layers of signification. But what Hanneke Grootenboer says of allegory is true for all three processes: "allegory's structural principle is disjunction, since the allegorical sign never contains its own meaning, but refers to other signs in a discontinuous temporal relation."[1] All three processes generate polysemy: their differential qualities open up communicative loops in a manner that always exceeds any singular application. Translation makes one aware of errancy and miscommunication; allusion heightens one's sense of proliferating intertextuality; and even in its most controlled Scholastic practice, allegory's palimpsestic gestures consign the reader to a complex multiplicity of meaning. As Grootenboer summarizes, "The term 'allegory' is a contraction of *allos,* which means 'other,' and *agoria,* 'to speak.' The allegorical sign stands at a distance from its meaning, which is marked by a constant deferral. This deferral is not a progressive but a regressive process: the allegorical sign refers to another sign that precedes it, but with which it will never be able to coincide."[2] This constitutive temporal deferral means that allegory has an important relation to history and to the perception of alterity. The primary contention of this chapter is that these three processes have been underappreciated in criticism of Montagu's writing and that a clear reckoning of the rhetorical potential they offer is crucial for understanding both the complexity of her Letter-book and her achievement as a theorist of empire and intercultural relations. As we move from Montagu's own theorization of translation to her complex recusative acts of allusion and finally to her Virgilian allegories, we can track two coextensive performances. The first pertains to her specific understanding of authorship and the second involves a stunning recognition of how authority, complicity, and allegory come together in her understanding of history.

Unlike the previous chapter, which followed the arc of one artist's practice over a thirty-year period, this chapter focuses quite insistently on the crucial two-year period from 1716 to 1718 that concluded with the Treaty of Passarowitz and on a single cultural product: Lady Mary Wortley Montagu's Letter-book, now commonly referred to as *The Turkish Embassy Letters*. It has taken on that name because it was composed during and after her journey through Europe to Constantinople in the company of her husband, the newly minted British ambassador to the Sublime Porte of the Ottoman Empire. Edward Wortley Montagu was charged with the daunting task of negotiating an end to the Austro-Turkish war that had broken out in 1716. In many respects his mission was a failure; he was recalled to London early in 1718 and played little role in the mediation of the peace between the Ottomans and Habsburgs largely because Austrian military success in the field made his contributions vestigial. The talks were overseen by Jacobus Colyer, the ambassador who played such a vital role in getting the principle of *uti possidetis* accepted at the Karlowitz negotiations, thus bringing the Ottomans into the orbit of European diplomatic affairs.[3]

The ineffectual British ambassador and his highly educated wife returned to England in the fall of 1718. Lady Mary Wortley Montagu's surviving Letter-book, which records these travels, is among the greatest achievements of eighteenth-century literature, yet, in comparison to the work of her peers, the text has received decidedly less commentary than it deserves. No doubt part of this neglect can be traced back to the scorn directed at her by Alexander Pope and Horace Walpole.[4] Intelligent and witty, like many women who rebelled against gender conventions, she was the target of vicious attacks. The combination of a damaged reputation and, more generally, the historical neglect of women writers means that her writing has only recently regained its canonical status. But character assassination and systemic neglect are only part of the issue. The Letter-book itself poses many critical challenges that ultimately raise questions about the very practice of reading, writing, and interpretation in a global framework.

As soon as one starts reading this work, a number of issues relating to its production, circulation, and reception immediately arise. Like any eighteenth-century woman of her rank and education, Montagu carried on an extensive correspondence with other aristocratic women in England and with a number of prominent literary men. However, very few of the letters actually sent from the stopping points on her journey to Constantinople and back again survive, and it is not safe to assume that the missives that make up the her Letter-book are transcriptions of actual correspondence. The text—variously known as *The Turkish Embassy Letters*; *Embassy to Constantinople: The Travels of Lady Mary Montague*; *Letters from the Levant During the Embassy to Constantinople, 1716–18*; and *Letters of Lady Mary Wortley Montague: Written During Her Travels in Europe, Asia, and Africa*—is derived from two leather-bound volumes of continuous fair-copy text carefully written out by Montagu and an unknown copyist. The text likely was composed sometime between her return from Constantinople in 1718 and 1724. We can establish this time frame because Montagu loaned the Letter-book to the feminist writer Mary Astell in 1724, and Astell inscribed a note "To the Reader" and a brief poem about the text in the blank pages at the back of the second volume. This was how the Letter-book circulated for roughly the first forty years of its existence.

Literary historians tend to think of the eighteenth century as the era in which the print public sphere inexorably dominated the field of literary production. But the old model of scribal coteries exchanging handwritten manuscripts did not immediately die out with the emergence of periodicals such as *The Spectator* and the rise of the novel. Alongside the commercial world of print, one can discern literary subcultures or coteries where the circulation of manuscripts was an end in itself. As Margaret Ezell and others have argued, "rather than being a nostalgic clinging to an outdated technology representing a fading aristocratic possession of the world of letters, the older practice of circulating scribal texts was instead a choice."[5] Authors such as Pope, who are conventionally associated with the emergence of commercial print culture, also partook in scribal production: important works including Pope's *Pastorals* and his poem "Windsor Forest" circulated as fair-copy manuscripts well before they were printed.[6] Like Pope, Montagu addressed both public and private audiences via print and scribal production: she prepared some texts, such as her essay on smallpox inoculation and her magazine *The Nonsense of Common-Sense*, for print publication, but wanted her identity kept secret; and she circulated other works, such as the Letter-book, to friends and acquaintances.[7]

Because publicity itself was deemed inimical to a sound reputation, women's relation to print was always more complex than that of their male contemporaries, and Montagu was certainly not alone in using pseudonyms or anonymous publications to avoid public censure in the world of print. Like many women writers, she attempted to control when, where, and how her works were printed, but at times her works were pirated from manuscript copy and put into circulation, often at significant personal cost. When Edmund Curl published some of her "Town Eclogues" in 1716 (under the title of "Court Poems") without her consent, she found herself misread and suddenly out of favor at court.

Based on the practices of other scribal coteries it is reasonable to assume that the loan to Astell was not a singular event. The Letter-book would have been shared with friends and like-minded acquaintances in the period between its composition and Montagu's death. Letter 31 has all the hallmarks of scribal exchange: both commentary on the flow of texts between Lady Mary and her addressee and the transcription of poems both received and original are typical of the scribal miscellanies of the late seventeenth and early eighteenth century.[8] The notion of what Ezell refers to as "social authorship" has important ramifications for the form of the Letter-book because Montagu chose to present the text as a series of letters to friends and acquaintances. Even without identifying the addressees of the letters, epistolary discourse establishes a relation of intimacy between the writing subject and the letter's ostensible recipient.[9] Elsewhere in Montagu's manuscripts there is a key to the addressees of the letters, but a number of the recipients remain unknown and are perhaps fictional. However, for readers of the Letter-book, part of the interpretive process involves characterizing the addressees: for some readers in Lady Mary's immediate circle, the addressees would have been not only identifiable but actual acquaintances, relatives, friends, or enemies. Needless to say, the intimacy that conditions both the circulation of the Letter-book and its formal strategies plays a crucial part in its interpretation.[10]

Montagu's letters to her husband during her stay in Constantinople are more obviously "private," detailing both practical and intimate concerns, but eighteenth-century epistolary discourse was also a public medium. Letters, like other texts, were often read aloud. All through the late seventeenth and early eighteenth centuries, manuals were published to help mostly aristocratic men and women exhibit an air of sophistication and civility. Letters were also not an uncommon medium for published disquisitions on philosophy, science, religion, history, and politics. And of course the emergence of the novel is inextricably tied to epistolary fictions. Thus when Montagu veers into these areas of enlightened inquiry, she is not deviating from generic expectations, but rather merely shifting discourses within an already hybrid and elastic form.

Near the end of her life, Montagu returned to London from a period of voluntary exile in Italy. The immediate reason for her return to London in 1761 had to do with legal matters relating to her estranged husband's estate, but on her journey she gave the Letter-book, which she carried with her for most of her life, to

Benjamin Sowden, a British clergyman in Rotterdam. It is generally assumed that she intended Sowden to shepherd the Letter-book into print, but in return for two hundred pounds he handed it over to Lord Bute, the husband of Lady Mary's daughter and at that time the First Lord of the Treasury. However, Sowden did lend out the Letter-book to two English travelers for a night; it was hastily transcribed and published after Montagu's death in 1762. One of the copyists was related to the bookseller Thomas Becket, and an error-laden version of the Letter-book was published in three volumes as *Letters of the Right Honourable Lady M——y W——y M——e: Written, during her Travels in Europe, Asia and Africa, to Persons of Distinction, Men of Letters, &c. in different Parts of Europe; Which contain, Among other curious Relations, Accounts of the Policy and Manners of the Turks* by Becket and De Hondt in London in 1763. In 1767 another edition from the same bookseller added five spurious letters.[11]

Walpole affirmed that it was Montagu's deathbed wish that these letters be published, and it seems she wrote them with publication in mind. Highly crafted and aesthetically coherent, the Letter-book frequently engages with the conventions of travel narratives that had preceded hers, and the sequential breakdown that she offers, which is rarely ever discussed,[12] organizes the text not by addressee, but by place and topic, as was typical of the genre. Montagu herself further signals the connection to journey writing by explicitly engaging with prior travelers' texts. Her objections to Aaron Hill and others are both explicitly presented and valuable indexes of where and how her writing diverges from the legacy of travel narratives pertaining to the Levant and the eastern Mediterranean. As Srinivas Aravamudan argues, her refutation of prior travelers' representations of Ottoman women and of domestic affairs foregrounds not only the gendered nature of knowledge acquisition, but also her privileged access to the private domains that preoccupied European fantasies of the East.[13] Significantly, Montagu invokes journey writing as a way of bolstering her claims to empirical truth.

The book's printed title and preface, derived from Astell's commentary, suggest that while Montagu had "condemned it to obscurity during her life," her Letter-book was also written as a direct challenge to male travel narratives so "that the world should see, to how much better purpose the Ladies travel than their Lords."[14] As soon as the book appeared in print, it was glowingly reviewed, gained immediate notoriety, and twenty-three editions were published between 1763 and 1800. At the head of each entry in the Letter-book Montagu provides a date and place of ostensible composition. For readers first encountering the book in its printed form, all of the narrated events would have taken place roughly fifty years in the past; and the geopolitical coordinates referred to would have accrued new significance in the interim. Furthermore, some aspects not only of Anglo-Austro-Ottoman relations, but also of British social history would have receded into historical oblivion.

Thus Montagu's print readers would now be recovering a past moment, and the significance of many of her critiques and observations would be measured in ways very different from those who read the Letter-book prior to its publication.

This complex history of production, circulation, and reception means that care must be taken not to mistake the letters for actual letters, and the performance of writing needs to be constantly at the fore of the contemporary reader's mind. Furthermore, attention needs to be paid to Montagu's complex engagement with earlier travel narratives, histories, and literature about the Ottoman Empire, with classical literature, and to the Letter-book as a stylistic whole. Conditioned by, but also significantly critical of, the emerging Orientalist discourse of the eighteenth century, the intercultural challenges posed by the text are fascinating. It is important to recognize that Orientalism itself has a complex history that impinges directly on the reception of this text during the period of its manuscript circulation, following its initial publication, and for that matter, at the moment of its present reading in the twenty-first century. My primary objective here is to show how Montagu develops implicit theories of errant translation and allusion in order to fully register the complexity of social and cultural dislocation. As we will see, the pressure of intercultural sociability leads to remarkable acts of historical layering. Significantly, her thoughts on translation and her idiosyncratic use of allusion quite radically misremember classical texts for present purposes and thus open a space for the subject to become other to itself. The frontier between literal meaning and allegorical design is a crucial issue in the Letter-book, and, as we shall see, it is through allegory that she makes her most radical historical interventions. In my reading below, I argue that these strategies are a fundamental part of Montagu's reckoning with war and empire and that she pushes them to a point where her own complicity becomes shockingly visible.

Intimate Translations

The importance of journey writing and epistolary practice to how the Letter-book is to be read is incontestable: we have already seen the way in which her descriptions engage with and intervene in the preexisting archive of travel writing and costume albums. But Montagu also provides key examples of intercultural reading practice within specific letters that I believe offer supplemental accounts of reading that significantly expand her rhetorical objectives. To my eye, these internal heuristics have not been sufficiently attended to, and they both pertain to questions of translation.[15] Translation is key to intercultural exchange, and Montagu is careful to indicate both its necessity and its limitations. Significantly, Montagu's account of intercultural relations with Ottoman subjects demonstrates not only her increasing fluency in Ottoman Turkish, but also her heightened awareness of the complexity of translation itself. And this does not simply apply to her sojourn in the Ottoman Empire—her lack of German means that social relations in the Viennese court, for instance, are mediated in French or through the assistance of a translator. The problematic is introduced in letter 8 in which she relates her reliance on a female translator to help her comprehend the performance of a comedy based on the Amphitryon story staged in the Viennese court. But the importance of the issue is magnified when she crosses the frontier of the Ottoman Empire. In letter 25's representation of her encounter with Achmet Beg in the contested border city of Belgrade, she states that she is likely to learn Arabic, that her host mistakenly believes that she understands Persian, and she concludes the letter by saying that Achmet Beg "has had the curiosity to make one of our servants set him an alphabet of our letters, and can already write a good Roman hand" (25.98; H 1:308). In letter 27, her visit to the hammam concludes with a famous misunderstanding regarding the purpose of her stays that allows Montagu to speak truth to power in an altogether different sphere. I will be discussing these letters in detail later in this chapter, but for the moment it is enough to recognize that Montagu carefully inscribes the desire for intercultural communication among all parties. Unlike some travelers who stressed the unwillingness of Ottomans to socialize, Montagu immediately establishes a mutual desire to communicate in any way possible: through a transposition to shared languages, through the acquisition of language, through gesture and performance. And, I would argue, the continual reinscription of this desire is constitutive: it defines both Montagu's text and her view of sociability.

But her explicit reflection on translation is only retroactively engaged. After her initial encounters in letters 25 and 26 and important descriptions of Ottoman society in letters 27 through 30, she presents a key letter whose topic is translation itself. Letter 31 is addressed to Alexander Pope, and it opens quite conspicuously with an untranslated Latin quotation from Virgil's *Georgics* and a long paragraph in which Montagu declares that those elements in Homer or Theocritus that she once saw as exotic or "romantic" (31.118; H 1:332) are simply descriptive: the people of the present country being simulacra of the Greek peasants of pastoral antiquity. This sets the stage for her commentary on Pope's translation of the *Iliad*:

> I read over your Homer here with an infinite pleasure and find several little passages explained that I did not before entirely comprehend the beauty of, many of the customs and much of the dress then in fashion being yet retained, and I don't wonder to find more remains here of an age so distant than is to be found in any other country, the Turks not taking

the pains to introduce their own manners as has been generally practiced by other nations that imagine themselves more polite. It would be too tedious to you to point out all the passages that relate to present customs, but I can assure you that the princesses and great ladies pass their time at their looms, embroidering veils and robes, surrounded by their maids, which are always very numerous, in the same manner as we find Andromache and Helen described. The description of the belt of Menelaus exactly resembles those that are now worn by the great men, fastened before with broad golden clasps and embroidered round with rich work. (31.119–20; H 1:332–33)

The first two volumes of Pope's translation of Homer were published before Montagu's departure from England, and in a letter of June 1717 Pope indicates that he has sent her the third volume.[16] Her remarks here are complex because she does not have Greek, and thus prior to her time in the Ottoman Empire she relies on translation for her access to Greek antiquity and to the acknowledged urtext of Western civilization. By informing Pope that things have not changed and that the society Homer represents is alive and well before her eyes because the Ottomans have not made it their practice to extirpate conquered cultures, Montagu not only marks out a distinguishing factor in Ottoman imperial practice, but also suggests that her present social experience acts as a supplement to Pope's translation. It is not a flat out refutation of the importance of Pope's text, but it does suggest that reading his Homer is now only a precursor to a richer level of intercultural and textual engagement. It is tempting to read this as precisely the kind of allochronic gesture described so powerfully in Johannes Fabian's critique of ethnography's temporal dislocations: these people before me are not of this time but conform to my preexisting sense of culture derived from ancient texts.[17] But at another level, Montagu's declaration is radically of the present: she informs Pope that his translation is confirmed by present empirical observation. Significantly, he has no awareness of this; Montagu subtly indicates that she is better placed, in spite of her linguistic limitations, to render this pastoral world.[18]

This presentist critique is borne out immediately when she shifts from Pope's translation of Greek to the challenges posed by translating Ottoman Turkish:

I should have told you in the first place that the eastern manners give a great light into many scripture passages that appear odd to us, their phrases being commonly what we should call scripture language. The vulgar Turk is very different from what is spoke at Court or amongst the people of figure, who always mix so much Arabic and Persian in their discourse that it may very well be called another language; and 'tis as ridiculous to make use of the

expressions commonly used in speaking to a great man or a lady as it would
be to talk broad Yorkshire or Somersetshire in the drawing room. Besides
this distinction, they have what they call the sublime, that is, a style proper
for poetry, and which is the exact scripture style. (31.120; H 1:333)

In a remarkable gesture of exemplification, she goes specifically to a contemporary
literary production by none other than the future grand vizier Damad İbrahim
Pasha that suggests far more intimate connection to the Ottoman court than she
could reasonably claim:

> I believe you would be pleased to see a genuine example of this, and I am
> very glad I have it in my power to satisfy your curiosity by sending you a
> faithful copy of the verses that Ibrahim Bassa, the reigning favourite, has
> made for the young Princess, his contracted wife, whom he is not yet per-
> mitted to visit without witnesses, though she is gone home to his house.
> He is a man of wit and learning, and whether or no he is capable of writing
> good verse himself, you may be sure that on such an occasion he would not
> want the assistance of the best poets in the Empire. Thus the verses may be
> looked upon as a sample of their finest poetry, and I don't doubt you'll be of
> my mind that it is most wonderfully resembling the Song of Solomon,
> which also was addressed to a royal bride. (31.120–21; H 1:333–34)

This passage opens with three sentences on Ottoman usage that imply a level of
expertise beyond that of her male addressee. She then follows with the stated
example for Pope's edification. And then she presents Damad İbrahim Pasha's
poem twice. In the first instance she presents a version mediated by unknown
translators and indicates that she has "taken abundance of pain to get these verses
in a literal translation, and if you were acquainted with my interpreters, I might
spare myself the trouble of assuring you that they have received no poetical
touches from their hands" (31.122; H 1:335). In the second instance she recasts
the poem "into the style of English poetry" (31.123; H 1:336) and concludes the
letter with further commentary on her translation. If we look at the overall arc of
the letter, then what we have is a decisive, if politely rendered, claim to authority
that can be summarized as follows: thanks for your translation of Homer; I can
confirm that aspects of your translation are accurate; I enclose my translation of a
typical Ottoman poem in the sublime style; you are in no position to question its
merits as a translation.

What interests me about this move on Montagu's part is the degree to which
she locates the success of a translation in terms of intercultural sociability. In both
versions of the poem, her claims for its merit both as a poem and as a translation

turn on her knowledge of the social condition of its production and reception. In her prelude to the first version of the poem, she carefully provides the backstory that provides the rationale for Damad İbrahim Pasha's passionate performance. After she cites the poem, her commentary folds in Pope's experience as a translator to verify her own judgments:

> In my opinion (allowing for the inevitable faults of a prose translation into a language so very different) there is a good deal of beauty in them. The epithet of stag-eyed (though the sound is not very agreeable in English) pleases me extremely, and is I think, a very lively image of the fire and indifference in his mistress' eyes. Monsieur Boileau has very justly observed, we are never to judge of the elevation of an expression in an ancient author by the sound it carries with us, which may be extremely fine with them at the same time it looks low or uncouth to us. You are so well acquainted with Homer, you cannot but have observed the same thing, and you must have the same indulgence for all oriental poetry. The repetitions at the end of the two first stanzas are meant for a sort of chorus and agreeable to the ancient manner of writing. The music of the verses apparently changes in the third stanza, where the burden is altered, and I think he very artfully seems more passionate at the conclusion as 'tis natural for people to warm themselves by their own discourse, especially on a subject where the heart is concerned, and is far more touching than our modern custom of concluding a song of passion with a turn which is inconsistent with it. (31.122; H 1:335–36)

Montagu's representation of the task of the translator explicitly calls for a recognition of, or in her words an "indulgence" for, not only the fact of linguistic difference, but also of the value of difference itself. In her view, the language of the poem arises from the culture and thus has a constitutive relation to its source. In a remarkable act of ventriloquism, she attributes the same view to French poet and literary critic Nicolas Boileau and to Pope.

And this of course is not a frivolous concern. It is difficult to overstate the importance of classical translation for Augustan literary practice. Dryden's rendering of Virgil and Juvenal, and Pope's experiments with Homer and Horace, and Swift's even more eccentric practice quite literally set the parameters for poetic discourse. In all three cases, there is a famous willingness to deviate quite forcefully from the original. This is especially the case when the translator is rendering the Latin or Greek with an eye to contemporary politics. As we will see, both Dryden and Pope freely added material to the *Aeneid* and the *Iliad* in order to address factional concerns in England. When we recognize that Montagu's journey and her experiment with authorship are permeated by the far-reaching politics of empire and the intimate politics of the British sex/gender system, then it should come as no surprise that we see her reconceptualizing the task of the translator to meet her immediate needs. As Helen Deutsch states, "long before her travels through space, the young Lady Mary—who taught herself Latin, translated Epictetus in prose, and imitated Ovid, Catullus, Horace, Virgil, and Sappho in verse—travelled through time in her father's library. Her long sojourns in ancient Greece and Rome immersed in a pastoral landscape that framed her perception of her travels abroad."[19] In my readings of Montagu's remarks on translation and on her idiosyncratic allusions to the *Aeneid*, in this section and the next, I argue that Montagu develops an understanding of the function of classical texts that diverges from her Augustan colleagues in order to speak to her status as a woman writer and, in the case of the Letter-book, as a foreign observer.

When Montagu offers her rendition of Damad İbrahim Pasha's poem in English, she, like Pope, moves toward recognizable English metrics and the rhyming couplet. And she takes the original poem's invocation of the nightingale to invoke the familiar myth of Philomel, but she retains certain rhetorical features of the original in order to emphasize the poem's filiation to her fantasy of Ottoman or Oriental society: "I could not forbear retaining the comparison of her eyes to those of a stag, though perhaps the novelty of it may give it a burlesque sound in our language. I cannot determine upon the whole how well I have succeeded in the translation. Neither do I think our English proper to express such violence of passion, which is very seldom felt amongst us, and we want those compound words which are very frequent and strong in the Turkish language" (31.124; H 1:337). The objective of the translation is to capture the "violence of passion" that ostensibly characterizes the future grand vizier and by extension his culture. As the letter closes she returns again to the translator's medium to indicate the limits she is up against. She not only says that this level of emotional intensity is alien to the English, but indicates that the proof can be gleaned from our language's lack of compound expressions. There is an isomorphic parallel between the relative lack of compound structures and the equanimity of Englishness.

I am spending some time on this not to emphasize Montagu's ethnocentrism, but rather to draw attention to her attempts to move beyond these limitations. For Montagu, Pope's Homer is valuable because it enables the reader to get beyond the self.[20] In her representation of her pastoral experiences and in her presentation of Damad İbrahim Pasha's poem there is an implicit investment in the value of moving beyond historical and geographical barriers to exchange. But translation does not dissolve difference; rather it repeatedly presents itself as that failed communicative act that makes difference truly discernable. It may seem paradoxical, but failure here is folded into a fantasy of increasing cosmopolitan expansion. It is for this reason that I have shifted into the language of acquisition and exchange. Montagu's version of enlightenment implicitly assumes that knowledge will be acquired from outside in order to transform the self.

This is nowhere more powerfully presented than in her other account of translation in the Letter-book. Because letter 31 is addressed to Pope, its register is in some senses directed at the republic of letters: the Virgilian tags, the discussion of Homer, the analysis of Damad İbrahim Pasha's poem, her invocation of Boileau, and the overall tone of intellectual exchange mimic the tone and the content of periodical criticism. We are not that far from Mr. Spectator here. That Pope is the addressee is apt because he lies at the very frontier of this public world for Montagu. But letter 31 is supplemented by a much more radical meditation on translation, this time addressed to an unknown woman. The difference in the gender of the addressee is important because the translated document comes from the sequestered world of women's private correspondence. Like letter 31, letter 41 provides a full citation of an Ottoman textual artifact, but the artifact itself magnifies the complex interweaving of translation, cultural difference, and desire. With this letter, Montagu is credited with introducing the *sélam* into Europe. Jean Dumont and other travelers describe similar letters composed of objects rather than words: "But wou'd you not be surpriz'd, instead of a *Billet-doux*, to find nothing but bits of *Charcoal, Scarlet Cloth, Saffron, Ashes,* and such like Trash, wrapt in a Piece of Paper. 'Tis true, these are as significant as the most passionate Words; but 'tis a Mystical Language that cannot be understood without a *Turkish* Interpreter."[21] The *sélam* was supposedly a game played by women in the harem, where a message composed of flowers and other objects was sent to a lover and was in turn decoded based on a word that rhymed with the object.

This is one of the only letters in the Letter-book that focuses on a specifically Ottoman aesthetic practice. She refers to the box of objects as a verse and provides an object-by-object translation:

> I have got for you, as you desire, a Turkish love-letter, which I have put in a little box and ordered the captain of the *Smyrnoite* to deliver it to you with this letter. The translation of it is literally as follows. The first piece you should pull out of the purse is a little pearl, which is in Turkish called *ingi*, and should be understood in this manner:

Pearl	Sensin Uzellerin gingi
Ingi	Fairest of the young.
Caremsil	Caremfilsen cararen Yok

A clove	Conge gulsun timarin yok
	Benseny chok tan severim
	Senin benden haberin Yok
	You are as slender as this clove;
	You are an unblown Rose;
	I have long loved you, and you have not known it.
Pul	derdime derman bul
a Jonquil	Have pity on my passion.
Kihat	Biîlerum sahat sahat
paper	I faint every hour.
ermut	ver bize bir umut
pear	Give me some hope.
sabun	Derdinden oldum Zabun
Soap	I am sick with Love.
chemur	Ben oliyim size umur
coal	May I die, and all my years be yours!
Gul,	ben aglarum sen gul
A Rose	May you be pleased, and all your sorrows mine!
hazir	Oliîm sana Yazir
a straw	Suffer me to be your slave.
Jo ha	ustune bulunmaz Paha
cloth	Your price is not to be found.
tartsin	sen ghel ben chekeim senin hargin
cinnamon	But my fortune is yours.
Gira	Esking-ilen oldum Ghira
a match	I burn, I burn, my flame consumes me.
Sirma	uzunu benden ayirma
Goldthread	Don't turn away your face.
Satch	Bazmazun tatch
Hair	Crown of my head.
Uzum	Benim iki Guzum
Grape	My eyes.

tel   uluyorum tez ghel
Gold Wire   I die—come quickly.

And by way of postscript:

biber   Bize bir dogru haber
pepper,   Send me an Answer.

You see this letter is all in verses, and I can assure you there is as much fancy shown in the choice of them as in the most studied expressions of our letters, there being (I believe) a million of verse designed for this use. There is no colour, no flower, no weed, no fruit, herb, pebble, or feather, that has not a verse belonging to it; and you may quarrel, reproach, or send letters of passion, friendship, or civility, or even of news, without ever inking your fingers. (41.160–62; H 1:388–89)

I have presented the *sélam* in full in order to stress the certainty in Montagu's translation: there is no equivocation, no vagueness, no sense of idiomatic struggle, only assumed knowledge. As Robert Halsband notes, there is a literal translation of these verses in Montagu's commonplace book at the Fisher Library, University of Sydney, and it appears that the verse was first rendered in Latin script from the Ottoman, but this is all carefully suppressed.[22] This is because the important issue here has little to do with linguistic facility and everything to do with declaring intimacy. Montagu handles this aesthetic object for which there is no European counterpart as a species of allegory: the literal object activates a higher level of meaning. But she is careful to point out that the allegorical translation relies on the implicit construction of intimate communication among women. In other words, the preexisting sociability of the communicants allows for a prior agreement on the signification of each object. In the specific case at hand, one must move past the aesthetic appreciation of the pearl to comprehend its affective significance. The radical upshot here is that true intercultural translation requires intimacy. This lesson, I believe, lies at the core of Montagu's practice in the Letter-book.

If we return to Montagu's remarks on Pope's *Iliad* we see a similar sequencing: she opens with an aesthetic appreciation of Pope's text and then supplements his translation with her own intimate experience with those present men and women who correspond to Homer's characters. Throughout the Letter-book, cultural alterity is understood through acts of aestheticization; as often as not classical examples and narratives are mobilized to comprehend and valorize Ottoman culture. Mary Jo Kietzman's discussion of this dynamic in the famous hammam letter (letter 27) is apposite here.[23] After much attention to the space of the bath, her first encounter with the women in the bath involves an act of linguistic translation: "I believe in the whole there were 200 women, and yet none of those disdainful smiles, or satiric whispers that never fail in our assemblies, when any body appears that is not dressed exactly in the fashion. They repeated over and over to me, *Uzelle, pek uzelle*, which is nothing but *Charming, very charming*" (27.101; H 1:313). There are very few moments of direct translation like this in the Letter-book, but this one establishes intimacy and elicits an immediate aestheticization:

> The first sofas were covered with cushions and rich carpets, on which sat the ladies, and on the second their slaves behind 'em, but without any distinction of rank by their dress, all being in the state of nature, that is, in plain English, stark naked, without any beauty or defect concealed, yet there was not the least wanton smile or immodest gesture amongst them. They walked, and moved with the same majestic grace which Milton describes of our General Mother. There were many amongst them as exactly proportioned as ever any goddess was drawn by the pencil of Guido or Titian, and most of their skins shiningly white, only adorned by their beautiful hair divided into many tresses hanging on their shoulders, braided either with pearl or ribbon, perfectly representing the figures of the Graces. (27.101–2; H 1:313–14)

Much has been said about this transformation of the women of the hammam into aesthetic objects, but less has been said about how Montagu immediately undoes this aestheticization in the following two paragraphs. She imagines the presence of the painter Charles Jervas only to argue that the potential for empirical observation would improve his art. This disparaging account of art's capacity to operate autonomously without sufficient attention to the world opens the way, first, for her assertion that "'tis the woman's coffee-house" and, second, for the intimate communication regarding her stays (27.102–3; H 1:314–15). In other words the aestheticization marked by the invocation of Milton, Guido, and Titian is supplemented and displaced by affective exchange. For Montagu this staging of affect is crucial for satisfying acts of translation and intercultural exchange because it occasions new forms of (feminist) aesthetic intervention that are exemplified by the Letter-book itself.[24]

   That this is all keyed to the expression of love and desire should not go unnoticed. The hammam letter is suffused by a desire for further intimacy among women that is interrupted by her husband's desire to contemplate "the ruins of Justinian's church, which did not afford me so agreeable a prospect as I had left, being little more than a heap of stones" (27.103; H 1:314). Having overcome her own act of aestheticization two paragraphs earlier, she finds the ruins of antiquity boring. This is intriguing because one could argue that she is saying something similar about Pope's *Iliad*: in this place, among these people, I am less interested in your rendering of Homer than in the passion of İbrahim Pasha and my own attempt to comprehend his desire for the sultana. In that case, she is still struggling to find an idiom suitable to mediate these ostensibly alien passions; but by the time she discusses the *sélam*, it goes without saying that she has achieved a sufficient level of intimacy with the women of the harem (and sufficient linguistic competence) to offer a definitive interpretation of the objects that has no recourse to identifiable European aesthetic precursors.

What is remarkable about the Letter-book is that she takes the example of "reading" the *sélam* and applies it to far more familiar "texts" that are by their very nature "alien"—texts whose strangeness lies in their historical rather than their geographical dislocation. I am referring, of course, to how she handles the panoply of classical texts that she deploys to comprehend or mediate cultural difference. As Palmira Brummett argues, classical learning has been deployed in European representations of the Ottoman Empire since its emergence, but Montagu handles this classical heritage in a singular way.[25] For Montagu, fragments of classical culture operate much like the objects in the *sélam*: their literal signification instantiates allegorical relations. I will eventually be arguing that the way classical references are handled in her texts is similar to the *sélam*, and thus we can isolate a certain appropriation and modification of Ottoman culture at the formal level of the Letter-book. Like Pope, who explicitly recognized Homer's alterity in the preface to his translation of the *Iliad*, Montagu's practice makes the classical tradition, which is supposed to be incorporated into fantasies of European hegemony, foreign again. As we will see, this almost Kristevan inversion of the foreign is of great strategic importance for Montagu not only for her attempts to think through the problem of cosmopolitanism but also to think through war's potential to radically cancel any possibility for intercultural practice.[26] The following section develops these issues by exploring a rather unlikely example of how Montagu uses classical material differently than important precursors like Pope and Dryden. As with the hammam letter it will require us to pay close attention not only to the social interactions between women but also to her subtle assertion of textual authority.

Veiled Allusions

Because so much of the scholarship on Montagu has focused on her representation of Ottoman culture, very little has been said either about her stay in Austria—in spite of the fact that the "European" portion of the Letter-book takes up half of the text—or about the way that geopolitical conflict permeates the letters. This section attempts to correct these critical lapses by attending to Montagu's representation of a women's shooting match in Vienna. It is one of the earliest accounts of a sporting event written by a woman, and I believe it reveals a great deal about Montagu's rhetorical strategies in the letters, as well as the complex ways in which bodily acts are mediated in her text. The actions of these gun-wielding women are afforded far more cultural significance than they would seem to warrant, and they point to very subtle historical arguments about war and empire. These historical arguments rely on a retroactive allusion to one of the most famous representations of sport in all of literature: the archery contest held in honor of Anchises in book 5 of the *Aeneid*. Both Virgil's archery contest and Montagu's allusion to it are temporally complex because they impinge on the present action of the narrative and yet refer to events well in the future. My intention is to demonstrate how these temporal folds allow Montagu to engage critically with the very imperial conflict that was the focus of her husband's failed mediation.

The relative lack of commentary on the Viennese letters is due to inattention to the formal design of the two-volume Letter-book. Most editions of the text follow Halsband's *Complete Letters* and break the order of the Letter-book by integrating pieces of actual correspondence. If one attends solely to the fair-copy Letter-book that was circulated among her coterie and from which the first 1763 edition was pirated, one discovers not only that the text has a carefully constructed internal structure, but also that many of its formal gestures are explicitly and implicitly in dialogue with important textual precursors. There is an obvious engagement with travel writing, but there is a less frequently discussed negotiation with the *Aeneid* and the *Iliad*. Montagu's interest in these texts is hardly surprising: Pope's translation of Homer was in her luggage, and she was traveling through the very spaces represented in these epic texts. But more important, Virgil and Homer provide important models for thinking about and writing about war.

This was a period of constantly changing borders, of conquests and reconquests, and of shifting allegiances. The Ottoman and Habsburg Empires had been at war all through the late seventeenth and early eighteenth centuries. Although we can now, in retrospect, view the 1699 Treaty of Karlowitz as a decisive step in the contraction of the Ottoman Empire, the period immediately preceding Edward Wortley Montagu's term as ambassador was one of Ottoman resurgence. Having successfully defeated the Russians at Pruth River in the Russo-Turkish War (1710–11), and having reconquered the Morea from the Venetians in 1715, the Ottomans, spurred on by pro-war factions, set out to regain Hungary. Leaving some troops at home to guard against a possible attack by the Russians and sending others to Albania to guard Corfu, the grand vizier and sultan's son-in-law, Silâhdar Damad Ali Pasha, was perhaps overly confident as he marched north. Eugene of Savoy, the talented Austrian Habsburg military leader, who had fought at the Battle of Vienna and had defeated the Ottomans at the Battle of Zenta in 1697, was once again victorious at Petrovaradin on 5 August 1716, and the grand vizier died from his battle wounds. Within a year and a half the Austrians would take Belgrade and force the Ottomans to submit to the Treaty of Passarowitz.

Lady Mary Wortley Montagu's acute sensitivity to the fact of war in the region is registered both locally in highly allusive scenes of conflict and more generally at the level of textual structure. We will be discussing her representation of the Battle at Petrovaradin and her unsettling account of Belgrade in the next section of this chapter, but before crossing the frontier it is important to consider her whimsical presentation of how war permeates Viennese culture and society. Roughly one month after Prince Eugene's victory at Petrovaradin and only a couple of months prior to her perilous encounter in Belgrade, Montagu sends the following account of a "diversion" in the court at Vienna to her sister Lady Mar:

> The next day I was to wait on the Empress Amalia, who is now at her palace of retirement half a mile from the town. I had there the pleasure of seeing a diversion wholly new to me, but which is the common amusement of this court. The Empress herself was seated on a little throne at the end of the fine alley in the garden, and on each side of her ranged two parties of her ladies of honour with other young ladies of quality, headed by the two young arch-duchesses, all dressed in their hair, full of jewels, with fine light guns in their hands, and at proper distances were placed three oval pictures, which were the marks to be shot at. (9.63; H 1:268)

This account, like so many representations of elite leisure, operates on a number of levels. Because it is marked as a "common amusement of this court" it becomes emblematic of Austrian character. We are treated to the spectacle of aristocratic women exhibiting their marksmanship, and as Montagu emphasizes later, watching women handle guns is the "favourite pleasure of the emperor, and there is rarely a week without some feast of this kind, which makes the young ladies skillful enough to defend a fort" (9.63; H 1:268–69). So we are placed somewhere just adjacent to the male viewers of this scene. This is a subtle move on Montagu's part, quite typical of the Letter-book as a whole, in that she separates her femininity from that of the women she is observing and also implies that the male courtiers are positioned much like her. As we will see, this ascription of femininity is crucial to Montagu's designs.

At one level Montagu is suggesting that such an amusement is entirely fitting for such a heavily militarized society. And yet the gender inversion turns the entire scene into an emblem of the perversion of social relations and thus a sign of social corruption that attends continual war. As we will see, Montagu also points to a certain level of gender insubordination when she encounters Prince Eugene of Savoy. While on leave from the theater of war, Eugene is explicitly feminized in the text; and here women are masculinized in telling ways. Montagu is intrigued by their erotic agency: in this scene they are quite literally valued by the observing men for their martial qualities.[27]

Drawing out Montagu's ascription of nonnormativity to the scene tallies well with the subversive components of the game itself. If we look closely at the targets, we find that all of them portray the usurpation of phallic agency: "The first was that of a Cupid, filling a bumper of Burgundy, and the motto, '*Tis easy to be valiant here.* The second a Fortune holding a garland in her hand, the motto, *For her whom Fortune favours.* The third was a Sword with a laurel wreath on the point, the motto, *Here is no shame to the vanquished*" (9.63; H 1:268). In the first instance, the shooter shoots the shooter to preserve her erotic autonomy. In the second case, the shooter quite literally pierces the "lucky lady" of Fortune. In the final target, the bullet destroys the sword with the laurel wrapped around its tip. All of the mottoes are playful and draw attention to the allegorical potential of female marksmanship. But what is so interesting is the way that these allegories get layered. At the lowest level of signification, the bravery that comes with drinking, the favoritism that comes with luck and the lack of shame that comes with vanquishing phallicism all allegorize female erotic agency and autonomy.

But erotic allegory takes on a more political overtone when the empress allocates the prizes:

> Near the Empress was a gilded trophy wreathed with flowers, and made of little crooks, on which were hung rich Turkish handkerchiefs, tippets, ribands, laces, etc. for the small prizes. The Empress gave the first with her own hand, which was a fine ruby ring set round with diamonds in a gold snuff-box. There was for the second a little cupid set with brilliants, and besides these a set of fine china for a tea table, enchased in gold, Japan trunks, fans, and many gallantries of the same nature. All the men of quality at Vienna were spectators, but only the ladies had permission to shoot, and the Arch-Duchess Amalia carried off the first prize. (9.63; H 1:268)

Montagu's specificity here is significant. All of the prizes have distinctly Eastern connotations, and the text moves from explicit reference to Turkish goods to other commodities that would have come by way of Ottoman lands. The specific prizes would seem to signify little more than luxury except that this scene of mock battle is embedded in an actual theater of war between Austria and the Ottoman Empire. What is confusing is that the political allegory is disconnected from enemy combatants—the scene seems far more concerned with lines of amity than with lines of enmity.

But in a gesture typical for the Letter-book, Montagu provides the allegorical key in a seemingly offhand remark whose retroactive application allows us to comprehend the rhetorical function and historical import of this diversion: "I was very well pleased with having seen this entertainment, and I do not know but it might make as good a figure as the prize shooting in the Aeneid, if I could write as well as Virgil" (9.63; H 1:268). Montagu's *recusatio*, her refusal to adopt the strategies of epic even in this brief interlude, feigns modesty in order to question the genre itself. By invoking Virgil at this point, Montagu would seem to be skirting on the domain of mock-epic. As with the card game in *The Rape of the Lock*, attention to detail unlocks another level of meaning. The funeral games held in honor of Anchises in book 5 of the *Aeneid* is one of the strangest parts of the poem;[28] that Montagu is reading the shooting match through this lens is indicative of her neoclassical pretensions, but it is also a sign of her sly politicization of seemingly trivial encounters. For Aeneas and his soldiers the funeral games are a respite from the violence of the Trojan War and a diversion from the deeply unsettling encounter with Dido. They are also a transitional point in the text. Prior to the hiatus of the games, Aeneas and his followers are essentially refugees beholden to the hospitality, first, of Dido and, second, of Acestes. After the games and the burning of Aeneas's ships, those who follow Aeneas are firmly embarked on the conquest of Latium and the prosecution of war foretold by Anchises's prophecy. Because Acestes is strongly associated with Troy in the poem, book 5 marks the end of the retroactive view of the Trojan War and anticipates the series of narrative events that culminate in the formation of the Roman Empire.

But what are we to make of Montagu's comparison between the shooting match in the Viennese court and the archery match from the funeral games for Anchises? She doesn't explicitly play out the terms of the comparison, but rather marks the nascent potential in an act of writing that could unfold if she had epic pretensions. It is a lacuna that calls on the reader to finish her thought. If we back out from the scene, at least one of the implications is clear: this is a transitional moment in the text. At this point, Montagu, like the Austrians, is approaching the frontier on the eve of Prince Eugene's assault on Petrovaradin. After they cross the frontier, she and her husband are in Constantinople when the Austrian forces raze Belgrade to the ground and thus force the Ottomans into accepting the Peace of Passarowitz in 1718. This action effectively ended Edward Wortley Montagu's diplomatic mission and forced an early return to England. Since the Letter-book is composed after the establishment of this chronology of Austrian ascendancy, the shooting match

Plate 1. Jean-Baptiste Vanmour, *View of Istanbul from the Dutch Embassy at Pera* (ca. 1720–37), oil on canvas. Courtesy of the Rijksmuseum, Amsterdam.

Plate 2. James Stuart, *View of the Monument of Philopappos*, Athens (1755), gouache on paper. Courtesy of the British Architectural Library, Royal Institute of British Architects, London.

Plate 3. Jean-Baptiste Vanmour, *Cornelis Calkoen on His Way to His Audience with Sultan Ahmed III* (1727–30), oil on canvas. Courtesy of the Rijksmuseum, Amsterdam.

Plate 4. Jean-Baptiste Vanmour, *The Meal in Honour of Ambassador Cornelis Calkoen* (1727–30), oil on canvas. Courtesy of the Rijksmuseum, Amsterdam.

Plate 5. Jean-Baptiste Vanmour, *Ambassador Cornelis Calkoen at His Audience with Sultan Ahmed III* (1727–30), oil on canvas. Courtesy of the Rijksmuseum, Amsterdam.

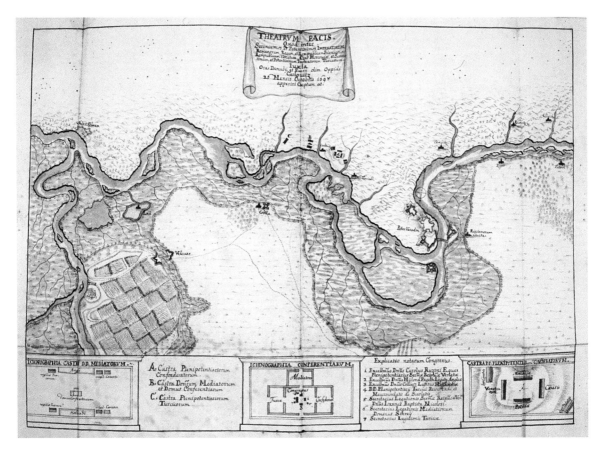

Plate 6. Carlo Ruzzini, *Theatrum Pacis*, ink and watercolor map. Courtesy of the Biblioteca Nazionale Marciana, Venice.

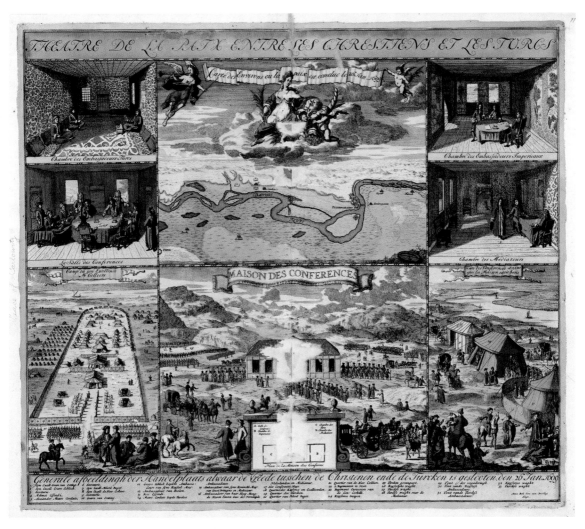

Plate 7. Anon., *Theatre de la paix entre les Chrestiens et les Turcs*, hand-colored engraved map, from Anna Beeck and Gaspar De Baillieu, *A Collection of Plans of Fortifications and Battles, 1684–1709: Europe* (S.l.: s.n., 1709). Courtesy of the Library of Congress.

Plate 8. Jean-Baptiste Vanmour, *Procession of Sultan Ahmed III*, oil painting. Private collection. Photograph courtesy of Sotheby's.

Plate 9. Jean-Baptiste Vanmour, *The Ambassadorial Procession of the Venetian Bailo Francesco Gritti* (ca. 1725), oil on canvas. Courtesy of the Orientalist Paintings Collection, Pera Müzesi, Istanbul.

Plate 10. Jean-Baptiste Vanmour, *Lady Mary Wortley Montagu and Her Son* (ca. 1717), oil on canvas. Courtesy of the National Portrait Gallery, London.

Plate 11. Jonathan Richardson (attrib.), *Lady Mary Wortley Montagu in Turkish Dress with Page* (ca. 1725), oil on canvas. Private collection. Reproduced by permission of the private collection/Bridgeman Art Library.

Plate 12. Jean-Baptist Vanmour, *Wedding Procession on the Bosphorus* (ca. 1720–37), oil on canvas. Courtesy of the Rijksmuseum, Amsterdam.

Plate 13. Jean-Baptiste Vanmour, *Armenian Wedding* (ca. 1720–37), oil on canvas. Courtesy of the Rijksmuseum, Amsterdam.

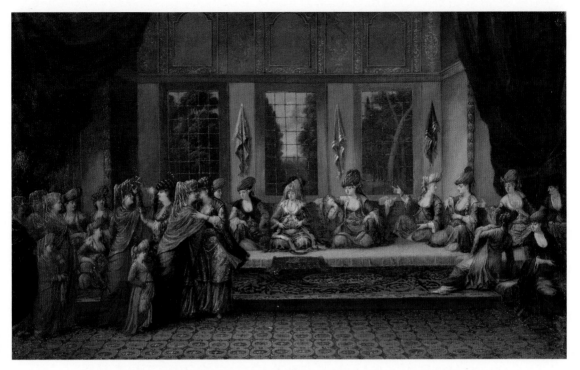

Plate 14. Jean-Baptiste Vanmour, *Greek Wedding* (ca. 1720–37), oil on canvas. Courtesy of the Rijksmuseum, Amsterdam.

Plate 15. Jean-Baptiste Vanmour, *Lying-in Room of a Distinguished Turkish Woman* (ca. 1720–37), oil on canvas. Courtesy of the Rijksmuseum, Amsterdam.

Plate 16. Jean-Baptiste Vanmour, *Ladies' Outing at Hünkâr Iskelesi Along the Bosporus*
(ca. 1720–37), oil on canvas. Courtesy of the Rijksmuseum, Amsterdam.

Plate 17. Jean-Baptiste Vanmour. *Fête Champêtre with Turkish Courtiers Under a Tent*
(ca. 1720–37), oil on canvas. Courtesy of the Rijksmuseum, Amsterdam.

Plate 18. Jean-Baptiste Vanmour, *Patrona Halil* (ca. 1730–37), oil on canvas. Courtesy of the Rijksmuseum, Amsterdam.

Plate 19. Jean-Baptiste Vanmour, *The Murder of Halil Patrona and His Fellow Rebels* (ca. 1730–37), oil on canvas. Courtesy of the Rijksmuseum, Amsterdam.

Plate 20. William Pars, *The Stadium at Laodicea* (1765), drawing, pen and ink and watercolor. Trustees of the British Museum.

Plate 21. William Pars, *The Theatre at Miletus with Party Crossing in a Ferry* (1764), watercolor drawing. Trustees of the British Museum.

Plate 22. *Ruin near the Port of Aegina—the Temple of Apollo on the Island of Aegina* (1764–65), watercolor drawing. Trustees of the British Museum.

Plate 23. Luigi Mayer, *Veduta esteriore dei padiglioni del gran-visir nel Campo di Daud Pasha vicino di Constantinopli* (1788), watercolor. Trustees of the British Museum.

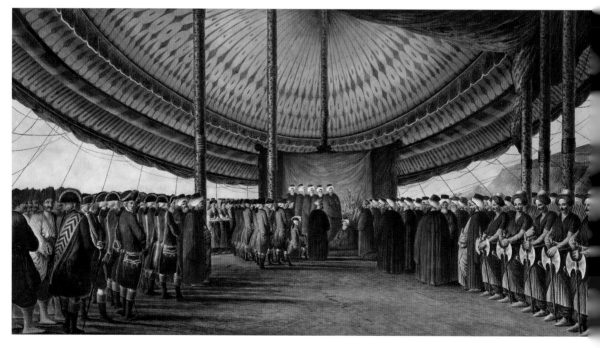

Plate 24. Luigi Mayer, *Veduta interna del padiglione del gran-visir ove riceve li ministri Europei* (1788), watercolor. Trustees of the British Museum.

Plate 25. Luigi Mayer, *Veduta della gran tribuna del Tempio di Diana d'Efeso* (1788), watercolor. Trustees of the British Museum.

Plate 26. Luigi Mayer, *Veduta di frammenti di scultura ed architettura; che si osservano nell'antica città di Efeso* (1788), watercolor. Trustees of the British Museum.

Plate 27. Antoine-Ignace Melling, *Vue de la pointe du Sérail et l'entrevue du général Sébastiani avec le Grand-Seigneur le 2 mars 1807* (1808–12), oil on canvas. Courtesy of the Napoleon Museum Thurgau, Arenenberg Palace, Salsenstein, Switzerland.

bears more than fleeting comparison to the archery match in book 5 of the *Aeneid*, for it too has a complex relation to prophecy and narrative composition.

Virgil's archery contest is a very strange event. Aeneas orders a dove to be tied to the mast of a ship and four archers take part. The first arrow, from Hippocoon, strikes the mast. The second, fired by Mnesthes, cuts the cord that fixes the dove. As the dove flies away, the third archer, Eurytion, aims and kills the bird as it tries to escape. The fourth archer, Aeneas's host Acestes, will not be outdone:

> Acestes, grudging at his lot, remains,
> Without a prize to gratify his pains.
> Yet, shooting upward, sends his shaft, to show
> An archer's art, and boast his twanging bow.
> The feather'd arrow gave a dire portent,
> And latter augurs judge from this event.
> Chaf'd by the speed, it fir'd; and, as it flew,
> A trail of following flames ascending drew:
> Kindling they mount, and mark the shiny way;
> Across the skies as falling meteors play,
> And vanish into wind, or in a blaze decay.[29]

In the Latin text, the flaming arrow is compared to a shooting star, and here in Dryden's translation the reader is presented with a flaming meteor. Dryden's translation skews the meaning by figuring this as "a dire portent." The negative connotation is not present in the Latin because it resonates with another shooting star in book 2 that portends the future glory of Julius Caesar. As numerous commentators have argued, these shooting stars have conventionally been read as precursors or "allusions to the famous comet of 44 B.C. that was considered a sign of the apotheosis of Julius Caesar. . . . The comet appeared at a time of incredible tension between Marc Antony and Octavian, just after Caesar's assassination, when it was very unclear whether or not civil war would erupt at once between the two rivals."[30] This comet coincided with another celebratory sporting event. Caesar had established games in honor of his divine progenitor Venus, and they were eventually moved to July, his own birth month, by Octavian in 44 B.C., the first summer after Caesar's death. The comet was read not only as Caesar's apotheosis, but also as a sign of the piety of Caesar's adopted son Octavian. In other words, the comet prefigures Octavian's rise to power. When we remember that Octavian and Antony would eventually split the empire into West and East, and that Octavian ultimately would send his general Agrippa to vanquish the Easternized Antony, whose claim to true "Roman-ness" was undermined by his relation to Cleopatra, then the significance of the omen both in Virgil and Lady Mary becomes more clear.

In Virgil, Acestes's arrow foreshadows the ascendance of Virgil's patron Octavian and the reunification of the Roman Empire into a vast amalgam of Europe and Asia. Of course, the link between comet and burning arrow, between the present world of the *Aeneid*'s composition and this narrative moment in book 5, relies on the retroactive anticipation that characterizes Anchises's prophecy and the poem itself. As David Ross states, "The Trojan past, having reached a finality through the unreality of Virgilian inversion, has suddenly, with this dread omen, become the Roman future."[31] Montagu's gesture here is more playful, but no less complex. Composing the Letter-book after the Treaty of Passarowitz, she can jokingly suggest that the shooting match has certain prophetic qualities: the Austrians will vanquish the Ottomans in the future. The grave Charles VI of Austria finds himself aligned with the pious Octavian; Eugene of Savoy gets to be the Agrippa in this story, and this diversion portends the eventual expansion of Austrian imperial control eastward. This helps to explain why Montagu keeps both herself and these historical figures at an observational remove from the contest: like Octavian, the emperor "reads" the scene played out before him from a distance, and thus it is Empress Amalia, like Aeneas, who convenes the games and distributes the prizes. And Montagu, like Virgil, takes on the task of prophetic representation. Montagu doesn't play out the allegory in detail, not least of all because there is no astronomical event, no exhibition of filial piety, and the conflict is less of a civil war than a clash of empires, but also, as is typical of *recusatio*, because she has other objectives.

Most notably, she recognizes that the shooting match, like the games sponsored by Octavian, honor Caesar's progenitor Venus. As John T. Ramsey argues, the games combined *ludi Veneris Genetricis* and *ludi funebres* in a fashion that laid the foundation for the imperial *ludi Victoriae Caesaris* that were such a prominent feature of Octavian's rule after he took the name Augustus.[32] In the Viennese contest, the language of love and language of empire are thoroughly entwined, thus the event rehearses the Roman games alluded to by Virgil. Montagu's attention to the games as erotic spectacle not only reinforces the allegorical connection to Caesar's funeral games even when the comet fails to appear, but also suggests that the interpenetration of love and war exhibited in the shooting match is itself a symptom of corruption comparable to the excesses of later Roman *ludi*.

But Montagu's most interesting rhetorical move has to do with fear. In the *Aeneid*, the burning arrow is immediately understood as an omen. Because its significance can be perceived only by the reader, the immediate witnesses to this supernatural event are bewildered. But their wonder quickly gives way to terror when the women in Aeneas's party, under the influence of Iris, set fire to the Trojan ships. Sent by Juno to foil Aeneas's destiny, Iris persuades the Trojan women to fire the ships by instigating gossip about endless war and maternal sacrifice. In other words, Iris plays on the women's desire for security, an implicit recognition of "their fear of a continuing, omen fraught voyage."[33] Virgil is remarkably restrained in his representation of the Trojan women. The blame for the destruction of Aeneas's fleet is placed squarely at Juno's feet in part because the Trojans who choose to stay in Sicily with Acestes go on to found the city of Segesta, a key Roman ally in the First Punic War.

There is no explicit omen in Montagu's rendering of the shooting match, but as soon as she invokes Virgil there is an explicit articulation of fear: "This is a favourite pleasure of the Emperor, and there is rarely a week without some feast of this kind, which makes the young ladies skillful enough to defend a fort, and they laughed very much to see me afraid to handle a gun" (9.63; H 1:268–69). Montagu emphasizes her own fear and the fear of those who do not handle weapons. The significance of this move becomes apparent when we compare her gesture to the most famous English translation of the *Aeneid*. Dryden referred to his act of translation as "Bringing Virgil over into Britain," and he consistently makes the thematics of exile, revolution, invasion, and usurpation consonant with recent British political life. As Richard Morton argues, Dryden's translation of the archery contest highlights the fear of the Trojans upon witnessing the flaming arrow:

> The Trojans and Sicilians wildly stare,
> And, trembling, turn their wonder into pray'r.
> The Dardan prince put on a smiling face,
> And strain'd Acestes with a close embrace;
> Then, hon'ring him with gifts above the rest,
> Turn'd the bad omen, nor his fears confess'd.
> "The gods," said he, "this miracle have wrought,
> And order'd you the prize without the lot.
> Accept this goblet, rough with figur'd gold,
> Which Thracian Cisseus gave my sire of old:
> This pledge of ancient amity receive,
> Which to my second sire I justly give."[34]

This image of the trembling Trojans and of Aeneas putting on a brave face is largely Dryden's construction. He manipulates most of adjectives to emphasize the timidity of the Trojans who choose to stay in Sicily, and he has the spirit of Anchises add this advice to the original: "The wholsome counsel of your friend receive; / And here the coward train and women leave."[35] In Dryden, the heroism of Aeneas and those who choose to go to war relies on the shaming of women and effeminate men—that is, on a consolidation of martial masculinity.

Recent readings of Dryden's *Aeneid* have emphasized the links between Aeneas and William III, and I don't think it is difficult to see how Dryden's attempts to find favor with the new regime are served by these highly gendered interpolations.[36] But Dryden's alterations of Virgil help us to see what Montagu is not doing. By owning her fear, she firmly aligns herself with the Trojan women who value security over wars of conquest. In doing so Montagu implicitly accepts the full ramifications of Juno's willingness to unleash civil war and of book 12's unrestrained violence. As W. R. Johnson argues, a full reckoning with these aspects of the poem opens onto a very different vision of epic than that established by Homer.[37] In contrast to Dryden's slavish consolidation of heroism and his avoidance of historical and moral vulnerability, Montagu opens herself to the full horror of Juno's intervention and thus her Virgil is one attentive to Dido's claim and the cost of heroism itself to Aeneas's character.[38] As the Letter-book unfolds it becomes clear that she not only abhors war itself but also comes to favor the Ottoman side of the conflict. She states this explicitly in letter 25 and in letter 33, where she refers to the fall of Belgrade as a "loss" (33.127; H 1:340), but it is perhaps most profoundly articulated in the way that she deploys sexuality. As we have seen, the Viennese women's facility with guns is a figure for their sexual agency—they are the dominant figures in heterosexual relations. The letter immediately following the description of the shooting contest is about the Viennese women's practice of publicly maintaining lovers with the assistance of their husbands. But for all her amusement, Montagu resists these kinds of practices: she will not take a Viennese lover, even when one is offered, and she will not pick up a gun, even if only for sport.

When she crosses the dangerous frontier into Ottoman territory, she puts fear behind her while at the same time emphasizing her gender normativity. In a sense, she posits a different kind of femininity than that deployed by Dryden. This feminine figure is not a scapegoat or a rhetorical trope, but rather is a narrator, or to put it more forcefully, an author "Bringing Virgil *with* her into the Ottoman world." Her subtle play—and I think that is the best way to describe her practice here—with the funeral games of both Anchises and Caesar is only the first of numerous textual interactions with the *Aeneid*. And I would argue that it is the maintenance of her gender and class normativity that leads Montagu to represent the Ottoman women she encounters as more appropriately "European" than the women she meets in Austria. Unlike even the Empress Amalia, whom she admires, she recognizes and celebrates the freedom and the agency of Ottoman women at the same time that she physically separates them from the culture of war. Indeed once the text fully enters Ottoman space, the events of the Austro-Turkish war are not remarked upon, but the presence of war is felt in frequent allusions to the anguish of the Trojan women.

Thus the shooting contest allows Montagu to do two things simultaneously. By deploying the funeral games themselves in a way almost as mysterious as the ominous flaming arrow, she plays out the historical ascendance of the Habsburg Empire by invoking and reenacting Virgil's allegorical celebration of Octavian and Julius Caesar. Her *recusatio* is a subtle way of testifying to the slaughter that would ensue. Her reticence here is itself a compelling rehearsal of Virgil's own open-ended figure. But this is a reenactment with a difference because it foretells Habsburg victory without celebrating Austria.[39] Unlike Dryden's rendering of Virgil, whose treatment of Aeneas's conquest of Latium is thoroughly, and at times tortuously, intertwined with Roman self-validation and hence the celebration of empire, Montagu is in a position adjacent to these historical narratives and thus can take up a position of critique. Montagu's Virgil is arguably more true to what makes the *Aeneid* such a significant recasting of the *Iliad*: namely, its open-ended comprehension that war heralds "the disintegration of justice and truth."[40] W. R. Johnson's assessment of Virgil's achievement in the *Aeneid* aligns well with Montagu's objectives: "no poet, not Homer himself, has shown how precious and how fragile are the formation and equilibrium of man's integrity of spirit. The multiple allegories of Vergil reveal in their shifting configurations the reality of goodness and the unspeakable nonbeing of evil. . . . Or, to put it another way, Vergil's poetry can let us ponder for ourselves what society, justice, and being mean because it has closed with and faced what their absence is and means."[41] It is for this reason that Montagu's most famous letters celebrate hospitality not war: the sanctuary afforded by Achmet Beg in war-torn Belgrade, her stopover in the hammam at Sophia, and her visits to the harem of Fatima, the *kethüdâ*'s lady. After her withering remarks on Austrian sociability, these are all posited as constitutive spaces of a different kind of empire, one based on peaceful cosmopolitan intercultural exchange, not territorial acquisition and the enforcement of conformity to the norms of the conqueror.

With the invocation of exchange here, I think we can elucidate one last element of Montagu's account of the shooting match. As noted above, Aeneas quells the anxiety activated by the flaming arrow by giving Acestes a conspicuously Trojan gift—a Thracian cup owned by Anchises. The reward is an affirmation of identity and cultural continuity. But in the Austrian shooting match, the Empress Amalia's prizes are all conspicuous commodities from the Levant trade—they are valuable for their exotic luxury. Thus the reward here is an appropriation of difference that ultimately emphasizes the hollowness of Habsburg imperial designs. These games do not commemorate the glory of one's forebears, but rather indulge in acquisition pure and simple. Montagu's subtle gesture toward mock-epic is critical not only of the validation of the selfsame as it appears both in the shooting match and in Dryden's translation of its allegorical precursor, but also of Austria's bellicose pretensions to "vanquish" alterity (whether that is understood in geopolitical or gendered terms). What emerges from Montagu's allusion to the funeral games is a political, social, and authorial position distinct from these two violent fantasies of empire in which Montagu becomes other than herself. But the full extant to which that is the case can only be appreciated by turning more directly to the question of war's human cost, to the very issues that concerned Virgil in the treatment of Dido and in the horrifying narrative arc of book 12.

Brutal Allegories

The following extract is from a letter sent by Edward Wortley Montagu from Pera in his capacity as British ambassador to the Ottoman Porte on 2 August 1717 to Secretary of State Joseph Addison regarding the progress of the Austro-Turkish war: "When I writ my letter of the 18 of the last month neither the French Ambassador nor the Dutch nor my self had any certain advice of what passed at the Camp, or Belgrade. All letters between the Court and this place were stop'd for a time, and it has been for some days believed by almost every body even the Officers of the Camacham that Belgrade was taken after a siege of a month. The people were extremely uneasy. But within two or three days many have been put in prison for having spread that news which 'tis now said is false and that Belgrade has only been blocked up."[42] Because he is at a distance from the action Wortley's letter is mired in uncertainty, but there is something peculiar about the way that the letter discloses and suppresses the information it carries. Even after it is confirmed that Prince Eugene of Savoy has razed the city to the ground and that over 20,000 Ottoman troops have been killed, Wortley is reticent: he simply states that "the Turks were intirely routed."[43]

Wortley's remarks are terse, but they are considerably more loquacious than those of his more famous wife. The regular pattern of correspondence in Lady Mary Wortley Montagu's Letter-book is disrupted for precisely the period when the siege and fall of Belgrade took place. The six-month gap between letter 38 and letter 39 consigns the destruction of Belgrade to textual oblivion. This in spite of the fact that Prince Eugene's victory spelled the end of her husband's diplomatic attempts to resolve the conflict and likely marked the violent end of one of her most valued friendships. Nor is there any mention of the fact that Montagu and her husband were only recently residents of Belgrade. There is only silence. This section of the chapter is about the affective weight of this silence and about how the information suppressed by the gap in the letter book re-emerges in a sustained meditation on the relationship between war, hospitality, and the epic tradition.

Wortley's reticence and Montagu's silence stand in marked contrast to their dispatches from Belgrade only six months earlier. In March and early April, both were witness to the tangible effects of warfare not only on the flesh but also on what we would conventionally call sovereignty. In a letter addressed to Alexander Pope from Belgrade, Lady Mary reports: "we pass'd over the fields of Carlowitz, where the last great victory was obtained by Prince Eugene over the Turks. The marks of that glorious bloody day are yet recent, the field being strewed with the skulls and carcasses of unburied men, horses and camels. I could not look without horror on such numbers of mangled human bodies, and reflect on the injustice of war, that makes murder not only necessary but meritorious" (25.95; H 1:305). For some time I was unaware of the strangeness of this passage. The Austrians had defeated the Ottomans at Petrovaradin on 5 August 1716, so it is important to remember that during this phase of her journey Lady Mary is effectively passing through what was six months earlier a war zone. But by referring to the fields of Karlowitz, Montagu's observations become curiously doubled. The name of Karlowitz carries with it ties to the notorious Battle of Zenta (1697), where Prince Eugene of Saxony defeated the grand vizier, killed over 30,000 Turkish troops, and secured the Peace of Karlowitz in 1699. The action at Petrovaradin in 1716 was not a massacre, so in the phrase "that glorious bloody day" Montagu conflates the two events in a manner that gives the impression that the physical bodies of the dead from the epochal earlier battle are still present as a sign of history.

The flesh of the unburied men elicits both horror and an ethical argument.[44] War here commits violence against the idea of justice itself. This recognition opens onto an explicitly theoretical consideration that disconnects human nature from rationality:

> Nothing seems to me plainer proof of the irrationality of mankind (whatever fine claims we pretend to reason) than the rage with which they contest for a small spot of ground, when such vast parts of fruitful earth lie quite uninhabited. 'Tis true, custom has now made it unavoidable, but can there be a greater demonstration of want of reason than a custom being firmly established so plainly contrary to the interest of man in general? I am a good deal inclined to believe Mr. Hobbs, that the state of nature is a state of war, but thence I conclude human nature not rational, if the word reason means common sense, as I suppose it does. (25.95; H 1:305)

Significantly, Montagu does not go on, as Hobbes does, to suggest that in the face of such irrationality it is necessary to seek protection under a sovereign power. Instead, she gives a detailed account of the political situation in Belgrade, where she and her husband were detained before entering the Ottoman Empire. Her account of the situation in Belgrade is harrowing, and I believe instructive, because it demonstrates how little control the sovereign has over the military.

While in Petrovaradin she and her husband were informed that the people of Belgrade were weary of the war and had killed their pasha in a mutiny because he had taken bribes to allow the Tartars to ravage the German frontiers. As she states, "We were very well pleas'd to hear of such favourable dispositions in the people," but when they arrived in the garrison they found an altogether different situation:

> The late Bassa fell under the displeasure of his soldiers, for no other reason, but restraining their incursions on the Germans. They took it into their heads from that mildness, he was of intelligence with the enemy, and sent such information to the Grand Signior at Adrianople. But redress not coming quick enough from thence, they assembled themselves in a tumultuous manner, and by force dragged their Bassa before the *Cadi* and *Mufti*, and there demanded justice in a mutinous way; one crying out, why he protected the Infidels? Another, why he squeezed them of their money? that easily guessing their purpose, he calmly replied to them that they asked him too many questions, he had but one life, which must answer for all. They immediately fell upon him with their scimitars (without waiting the sentence of their heads of the law) and in a few moments cut him in pieces. The present Bassa has not dared to punish the murder. . . . You may imagine, I cannot be very easy in a town which is really under the government of an insolent Soldiery. (25.96–97; H 1:306–7)

Montagu's narrative resonates with much of the Tory writing in England against the notion of a standing army, but the story is important because it so carefully represents the frontier as zone of violence, corruption, and fear.[45] The janissaries, in sidestepping the kâdî, who administers both Islamic and Ottoman law, are explicitly operating against the very state form that they ostensibly serve. Montagu is bluntly showing us something about Hobbes's protection racket that goes unsaid when she first invokes the notion of war as the state of nature: namely, that the state's monopoly on violence—even in a state taken to be the very essence of absolutism—far from protecting the people, actually perpetuates a cascade of violence precisely because the military acts according to its insatiable desires. And the violence flows in all directions, thus instituting a condition of "uneasiness," to borrow a euphemism employed by both Montagu and her husband.[46]

If we understand Montagu's representation of the dead at Petrovaradin and of the crisis in Belgrade as a critique of Hobbes's argument for sovereign power, then the rest of her letter from Belgrade offers an important counterexample. Trapped in Belgrade under the military rule of the corrupt pasha for roughly a month, Montagu suddenly recounts a remarkable scene of hospitality:

> In the mean time we are lodged in one of the best houses, belonging to a very considerable man amongst them, and have a whole chamber of janissaries to guard us. My only diversion is the conversation of our host, Achmet-Beg, a title something like that of count in Germany. His father was a great Bassa and he has been educated in the most polite Eastern learning, being perfectly skill'd in the Arabic and Persian Languages, and is an extraordinary scribe, which they call *Effendi*. This accomplishment makes way to the greatest preferments, but he has had the good sense to prefer an easy, quiet, secure life, to all the dangerous honours of the Porte. He sups with us every night, and drinks wine very freely. You cannot imagine how much he is delighted with the liberty of conversing with me. He has explained to me many pieces of Arabian poetry, which, I observed are in numbers not unlike ours, generally alternate verse, and of a very musical sound. Their expressions of love are very passionate and lively. I am so much pleased with them, I really believe I should learn to read Arabic if I was to stay here a few months. He has a very good library of their books of all kinds and, as he tells me, spends the greatest part of his life there. I pass for a great scholar with him by relating to him some of the Persian tales, which I find are genuine. At first he believ'd I understood Persian. I have frequent disputes with him concerning the difference of our customs, particularly the confinements of Women. He assures me there is nothing at all in it, only says he, we have the advantage that when our wives cheat us, no body knows it. He has wit and is more polite than many Christian men of Quality. I am very much entertained with him. (25.97–98; H 1:307–8)

United by their rank and education, Montagu and Achmet Beg pass their time in conversation and conviviality.[47] But everything about this scene of cosmopolitan hospitality is shadowed by violence and ethnic partition. Because the scene of hospitality itself is surrounded by the janissaries, they are part and parcel of its constitution. Achmet Beg's house acts as a kind of sanctuary from this historical zone of violence, irrationality, and death, but we also need to recognize that Achmet Beg is himself in a form of internal exile: he has avoided the preferments of the Porte because such an accession to a position of power is inherently dangerous in an absolutist state. In short, nonparticipation in the political world of the Porte is a precondition of the ideal converse presented here. Perhaps this is why no mention is made of Wortley in this passage. Because he is a minion of the state, he quite literally cannot come into the same discursive space as Montagu and Achmet Beg, in spite of the fact that he clearly shared the same house. In this context, the sanctuary afforded in Achmet Beg's house and his library is both extra-political and gendered. The discursive exclusion of Montagu's husband is not incidental. It is part of a larger pattern of reserving domestic sites of intercultural exchange for women that is most famously registered in letter 27's representation of the hammam and in the account of the *kethüdâ*'s harem in letter 34.

I have spent some time with letter 25 not only because it establishes the importance of hospitality to Montagu's notion of cosmopolitan interculturalism, but also because the sanctuary afforded by Achmet Beg is so radically traversed both in the text and in the history of the Austro-Turkish war. When Belgrade is captured and burned by Prince Eugene in the summer of 1717 what happens to Achmet Beg? As Isobel Grundy notes, the fate of Montagu's friend Achmet Beg is unknown.[48] In this context, the gap between letters 38 and 39 consigns his life and probable death to obscure silence.

When one recognizes that the gap in the letters erases personal loss and failed diplomacy, then one can discern that it marks a crucial structural bridge in a larger argument about war, hospitality, and empire in the text. The gap lies between Montagu's explicit attack on the war in letter 25, where her horrified observations of the dead bodies from the carnage inflicted by Prince Eugene at Karlowitz and Petrovaradin escalate into a full-fledged declaration of man's irrationality, and her allegorical attack on the glorification of war in letter 45, in which she recounts her journey from Constantinople to Tunis. In that latter letter to the Abbé Conti, she parodies a section of George Sandys's *Travels* by reorienting his allusions to the *Iliad* with subtle references to the horrors suffered by the Trojan women after the fall of Troy.[49]

Bracketed between these two meditations on war, the silence regarding the subversion of Wortley's diplomacy and the death of her closest Ottoman interlocutor, Achmet Beg, becomes the traumatic core of the Letter-book. Silence substitutes not only for the death of intimate enlightened conversation, but also for the collapse of diplomatic and cultural exchange that had defined British relations—not just Montagu's—with the Ottomans under the capitulations granted with the formation of the Levant Company. In short, that silence marks a crucial melancholy turn in Montagu's personal history of cosmopolitan enlightenment. "Cosmopolitanism" is a term so imbued with hope that we need to ask what it means for it to be inextricably tied to mutilation, loss, and the tangible relics of slaughter. As we will see, it is precisely this melancholy link that makes her text so formally and ethically complex.

My emphasis here is in part formal because Montagu prepares the reader for this complex historical and personal rupture in a fashion that is reminiscent of the classical texts that she was avidly reading during this period. As already noted with regard to letter 31, Montagu explicitly brings together her proto-ethnographic observations with her reading of the second volume of Pope's translation of the *Iliad* and argues that there is historical continuity between Homer's description of the social world of Troy and the present environs of Adrianople:

> I can assure you that the princesses and great ladies pass their time at their looms, embroidering veils and robes, surrounded by their maids, which are always very numerous, in the same manner as we find Andromache and Helen described. The description of the belt of Menelaus exactly resembles those that are now worn by great men, fastened before with broad golden clasps and embroidered round with rich work. The snowy veil that Helen throws over her face is still fashionable; and I never see (as I do very often) half a dozen old Bashaws with their reverend beards, siting basking in the sun, but I recollect good King Priam and his counselors. (31:119–20; H 1:332–33)

This gesture is different from the allochronic tendencies that Johannes Fabian identifies in much European ethnography. Montagu does not erase everyday Ottoman life in favor of a fantasy of ancient culture. Rather, she suggests that practices reported in the ancients are still vibrant in the present moment.[50] These historical and rhetorical links between the Trojans and the Ottomans—and especially between the women of Troy (Helen here is in the complex role of captive) and Ottoman women—play an important role in the text on the eve of the Ottoman defeat at Belgrade.

But the full import of Montagu's linkage between the Ottoman people around her and the Trojans specifically represented in Pope's translation lies in an acceptance of an important divergence from Homer. As Aaron Santesso has recently argued, Pope's translation deploys pastoral discourse to highlight the cruelty and violence of the Greek heroes. Santesso demonstrates how Pope recasts or invents encounters between proto-Virgilian "swains" and the martial Greeks in order to critique Greek militarism. Pope's reservations about the Greeks were famously articulated in his preface: "Who can be so prejudiced in their Favour as to magnify the Felicity of those Ages, when a Spirit of Revenge and Cruelty, join'd with the practice of Rapine and Robbery, reign'd thro' the World, when no Mercy was shown but for the sake of Lucre, when the Greatest Princes, were put to the Sword, and their Wives and Daughters made Slaves and Concubines?"[51] Santesso's crucial observation is that in the translation of the *Iliad*, as in "Windsor Forest," Pope consistently deploys Virgilian pastoral discourse to figure forth a fantasy of Tory landed rule that, of course, was being made politically obsolete by the ascendance of the

Hanoverian line. In this representational economy, Greek cruelty is aligned with Whig bellicosity and expansionism; the people of Troy become "conscious swains" who either experience or observe the horrors of unnecessary aggression. As Santesso states, "The Arcadian setting of Pope's epic is meant for a peaceful pastoral shepherd; the warriors who have occupied it exhibit an utterly opposite demeanor, and the shepherd-witness notes the disparity."[52]

It is not difficult to see why this political allegory would appeal to Montagu. Her family and her circle of friends were attempting, with varying degrees of success, to adapt to this new Whig world.[53] Montagu and her husband were courting favor with the new dispensation, but her primary interlocutors in the Letter-book, Pope and Lady Mar, were notoriously associated with anti-Whig factions.[54] Furthermore, her husband's mission was to negotiate peace, and she consistently critiques the bellicosity of the Austrians. But significantly, Wortley is also working for the staunch Whig Joseph Addison, so there are key moments when he is excluded from the text.[55] As we will see, Montagu adopts Pope's pastoral rhetoric to represent the Ottomans as witnesses to war, but not without some crucial interventions of her own.

The first of these interventions is subtle but nevertheless significant. Pope's attack on the "barbarity" of epic heroism is especially pronounced in the representation of Achilles in the late books of the *Iliad*. As Santesso argues, Pope consistently translates Achilles's resolution and determination as a species of "manic, almost psychotic rage."[56] Montagu has her own "great man" to deal with and her portrait of Prince Eugene of Savoy opts for a different mode of attack. She meets him immediately after he repulsed the Turkish attempt to recapture the fortified town of Petrovaradin in 1716. Like Pope she recognizes greatness in the warrior hero, but offers a curious equivocation: "Now I have named that great man, I am sure you expect I should say something particular of him, having the advantage of seeing him very often, but I am as unwilling to speak of him at Vienna, as I should be to talk of Hercules in the court of Omphale if I had seen him there. I don't know what comfort other people find in considering the weaknesses of great men because it brings them nearer to their own level, but 'tis always a mortification to me to observe that there is no perfection in humanity" (21.85–86; H 1:295–97). According to legend the Lydian queen Omphale dressed Hercules in women's clothing and forced him to perform feminine tasks. Halsband suggests that Lady Mary was playing on his reputation as a Mars without a Venus. However, I read the passage differently. Montagu refuses to provide a portrait of Eugene in a domestic setting because he has a specific function in the text. He embodies a form of bellicose masculinity that reveals itself to be perverse when taken out of the theater of war. Using the spectacle of Hercules in women's clothing to figure for the oxymoronic conjunction of the martial hero and domesticity,

Montagu is doing more than "exposing the weakness of a great man." She is rigorously separating the theater of war from the intimate space of hospitality.

In contrast to Pope's "conscious swains," Montagu's witnesses come from the intimate space of hospitality to speak in a ghostly fashion about the prosecution of war. I have chosen my words carefully here because the gap in the text quite literally ghosts Achmet Beg: he exists in a liminal state, but his unresolved condition haunts the text even before he disappears. And this is signaled in a remarkable rehearsal of one the most famous ghost stories of all; one in which hospitality, love, and empire are tightly entwined. In her first letter from Belgrade-Village,[57] dated 17 June 1717, Lady Mary describes her sojourn as a liminal state between life and death: "I hope before this time, you have receiv'd 2 or 3 of my letters. I had Yours but yesterday, thô dated the 3rd of Feb., in which You Suppose me to be dead and bury'd. I have already let you know that I am Still alive, but to say Truth I look upon my present Circumstances to be exactly the Same with those of departed Spirits" (37.146; H 1:365). The letter starts out as a jest on reports that she has died, but she imagines herself in the Elysian fields:

> The heats of Constantinople have driven me to this place, which perfectly answers the description of the Elysian fields. I am in the middle of a wood consisting chiefly of fruit trees, watered by a vast number of fountains, famous for the excellency of their water, and divided into many shady walks upon short grass, that seems to me artificial, but I am assured is the pure work of nature, within view of the Black-Sea. . . . The village is wholly inhabited by the richest amongst the Christians, who meet every night at a fountain forty paces from my house to sing and dance, the beauty and dress of the women exactly resembling the ideas of the ancient nymphs as they are given us by the representations of the poets and painters. (37.146; H 1:365–66)

As in Pope's translation of the *Iliad*, the pastoral description is less Homeric than Virgilian, and as the passage unfolds Montagu eventually discloses her allusion to the *Aeneid*. The passage's overall tone resonates with Aeneas's entry into Elysium, and in many ways the description of her own desire to speak with those from whom she is separated parallels Anchises's desire to speak with his son:

> But what persuades me more fully of my decease is the situation of my own mind, the profound ignorance I am in of what passes amongst the living, which only comes to me by chance, and the great calmness with which I receive it. Yet I have still a hankering after my friends and acquaintance left in the world, according to the authority of that admirable author,

> That spirits departed are wondrous kind
> To friends and relations left behind,
> Which no body can deny,
> Of which solemn truth I am a dead Instance. (37.146–47; H 1:366)

Here her sequestration in Belgrade-Village is metaphorically aligned with a death of sorts whereby she is stranded from her friends in London and to a lesser extent Adrianople. What interests me is the careful account of her emotional state, because like Anchises she exhibits a kind of hospitality to Pope's correspondence. In this figural assemblage, letters pass from the land of the living to the land of the dead and are received with kindness and gratitude.

But this rhetorical gesture takes on another level of complexity when she goes to specific lines in the *Aeneid*:

> I think Virgil is of the same opinion, that in human souls there will still be some remains of human passions:
> —*Curae non ipsâ in Morte relinquunt*[58]
> and 'tis very necessary to make a perfect Elysium that there should be a river Lethe, which I am not so happy to find. (37.147; H 1:366)

The citation from the *Aeneid* is both apposite and surprising, for it is imbued with intense emotion but linked to an altogether different scene in book 6 than that which takes place in Elysium. The citation comes at the beginning of the passage in which Aeneas and the Cumaean sibyl come upon the dead who remain consumed by desire for their lovers. Halsband translates the line as "Not even in death do the sorrows [of love] leave them," but a roughly contemporary prose translation gives perhaps a more accurate view of the passage: "Not far from hence, extended on every side, are shewn the Fields of Mourning: For so they call those Fields by Name. Here By-paths remote conceal, and Myrtle Groves cover those around, whom unrelenting Love, with his cruel envenomed Darts, consumed away. Their Cares leave them not in Death itself."[59] Virgil's representation of this region of the underworld where Cupid's victims pine away is one of the most affecting moments in the text because it prefaces the confrontation between Dido and Aeneas in which the Carthaginian queen calls Aeneas to account for deserting her. Dido's palpable anguish quickly transforms into anger and detestation, and she leaves Aeneas to contemplate his guilt. Crucially, this is achieved by turning away silently and refusing to engage with him. Montagu's silence repeats this gesture.

By invoking this moment in the *Aeneid*, Montagu achieves a number of objectives simultaneously. First, she emphasizes the centrality of Aeneas's betrayal of Dido to her consideration of her epic forebears. After all, Aeneas's betrayal is as much a betrayal of Dido's hospitality as it is of her love. Second, she displaces the expected encounter in Elysium with this scene of anguish and mourning. This is crucial because Virgil's account of Aeneas's conversation with his father in Elysium opens onto a prophetic catalog that shows how Aeneas's actions in Latium are connected to the Roman Empire of Virgil's time. In the passage, Anchises explains how the heroes of Elysium cross Lethe, forget their former selves, and return to the world of the living to play a new role in history. This remarkable deployment of forgetting and reincarnation allows Virgil to literally link the Trojan heroes with their Roman offspring. The effect is an extraordinary consolidation of national and imperial fantasy with the process of forgetting. And yet this very recognition of the place of forgetting in imperial fantasy is itself an act of remembering: Virgil's epic reveals the constitutive place of the betrayal of hospitality in the history of Rome. What I would like to suggest is that Montagu takes up Virgil's task with an arguably more rigorous set of rhetorical imperatives. Like the *Aeneid*, her text will remember even as it forgets the cost of war.

In the gap between letters 38 and 39, Lady Mary "forgets" to narrate what happens in Belgrade. By displacing this material and linking the river Lethe with Dido's—and her own—predicament, Montagu reimagines the prophecies disclosed in the underworld. At a minimum these two rhetorical strategies interrupt the fantasy of imperial consolidation and reorient the scene such that it is about disappropriation, violence, and loss, rather than conquest and acquisition. Like Dido, Montagu cannot find the river Lethe, she cannot forget. But what are we to make of Montagu's metaphorical death before death and of her desire for forgetting? She gives no indication of what needs to be forgotten, but her citation of the *Aeneid* brings the reader right to the fundamental conflict between the claims of Dido's love and hospitality and Aeneas's bellicose imperial destiny. In other words, letter 37 quite literally travels between the poles of intimate sanctuary and imperial conquest. Does the phantasmatic scene allow a space for Montagu to explore the emotions that attend the death or displacement of her host before these events occur? It is important to recognize that this entire letter is directly linked to conflicted scenes of prophecy, for it is in book 6 that we discover not only that Aeneas and his men will be victorious in Latium but also that the betrayal of Dido will haunt his descendants in scenes of future carnage.

At least part of this prophetic capacity is a function of the scene of writing. Composing the Letter-book after the fact, Montagu has the ability to register grief before Achmet Beg's death. And she has the capacity to yearn for forgetting before the catastrophe. In short, it is her situation as writer and historian that puts her in a situation akin to that of Aeneas and the Cumaean sibyl—and for that matter Virgil. It is significant that she expresses the unfulfilled desire to forget prior to the enactment of that forgetting in the gap between letters 38 and 39. As we will see, the forgetting of the emotional bonds of friendship that is both yearned for and putatively satisfied in this section of the text is not without its repercussions. Montagu's engagement with the Trojan War is far from over because she has significant reservations about Pope's critique of Greek "barbarity." Furthermore, she reenacts Aeneas's betrayal in Carthage with remarkable specificity. As in Virgil, what she does after leaving the ruins of Troy has historical implications far beyond what appear to be merely private exchanges in foreign lands. This chapter will conclude by looking at these complex historical critiques in turn.

After six months of silence, Montagu's remaining letters are addressed either from Constantinople or from various ports and stopping points on her return journey. The description of various sights continues much as before, but her accounts of Ottoman hospitality exhibit a melancholic tendency. When she narrates her visit to Hafise Kadinefendi, one of four *kadĭns*, or formally recognized concubines, of Mustafa II, Montagu dramatizes the "agonies of sorrow" that attended her transfer from the sultan to the secretary of state Ebubekir Efendi (40.154; 1:381) after the sultan's death.[60] Her portrait of the grieving yet respected *kadĭn* is notable because Mustafa II assumed the sultanate in 1695 and was deposed in 1703 as mentally incompetent. He died at Topkapi Palace four months later. Under his reign the empire lost Hungary by the Treaty of Karlowitz in 1699. Thus this encounter with Sultana Hafise brings us back to the aftermath of the Battle of Zenta, to the period of political and social turmoil following Prince Eugene's epochal victory over the Ottomans. Montagu's narration of the sultana's transferral to Ebubekir Efendi focuses on the political implications of the fall of Mustafa II, but the full weight of the sultana's personal affliction is reserved for a later paragraph:

> She never mention'd the Sultan without tears in her Eyes, yet she seemed very fond of the discourse. My past happiness (said she) appears a dream to me, yet I cannot forget that I was beloved by the greatest and most lovely of mankind. I was chose from all the rest to make all his campaigns with him. I would not survive him if I was not passionately fond of the Princess, my daughter, yet all my tenderness for her was hardly enough to make me preserve my life when I lost him. I passed a whole twelvemonth without seeing the light. Time has softened my despair, yet I now pass some days every week in tears devoted to the memory of my Sultan.—There was no affectation in these words. It was easy to see she was in a deep melancholy, though her good humour made her willing to divert me. (40.157; H 1:384)

What this passage and others in the letters dated after Prince Eugene's capture of Belgrade in the summer of 1717 demonstrate is an overall sense of the emotional and physical cost of political conflict. And this is registered through a series of

scenes where women lose their husbands and lovers, lose their lives, or find themselves disposed of in ways that are reminiscent of the fate of the Trojan women
following the fall of Troy.

If this seems like an interpretive leap, think about how similar Sultana Hafise's
predicament is to that of Andromache mourning for Hector. Like Andromache,
her husband dies and his male children do not survive, and she is forced to
become a concubine to her husband's successor. In the same letter, the beautiful
kethüdâ's lady Fatima reveals herself to be of Polish descent, her mother having
been abducted during the siege of Kamieniec Podolski in 1672. With this information, it is possible read Fatima as the type of Helen: her beauty is overwhelming, but she hails from the parts of central Europe that had defeated the Ottomans
first at Zenta and then again at Petrovaradin. In fact, types of Helen proliferate in
this section of the letters because the tale of the abduction of a Spanish maiden by
an Ottoman admiral in letter 43 exhibits many of the equivocations of the classical sources regarding Helen's status in Troy. In this later letter, Montagu's raptur-
ous account of the Turkish wedding explicitly compares the bride to Helen as
represented by Theocritus (43:406). Is it then any surprise that the letter suddenly
turns to offer an account of "the bleeding body of a young woman, naked, only
wrapped in a coarse sheet, with two wounds with a knife, one in her side and another in her breast" (43.173; H 1:407) and a blunt indication that adultery begets
murder and revenge?

Epic Refugees

These are admittedly subtle alignments, and the text often does not draw explicit
references to the obvious classical texts. But I would contend that the changing
representation of the Ottoman women is part of a larger melancholy pattern in
the text that can only be retroactively constructed after the all-important letter
45. With the disappearance of Achmet Beg from the text and Montagu's unwilling departure from Ottoman lands, the *Embassy Letters* draw all of these anxious
threads together into a larger allegorical gambit that explicitly aligns her travels
with those of Aeneas after the fall of Troy. Addressed to the Abbé Conti from
Tunis on 31 July 1718, letter 45 fills the void between letters 38 and 39; it is here
that Montagu retroactively speaks to historical trauma. Its almost constant invocation of precursor texts and narratives forces the reader to confront key patterns
in world history and to carefully bring together the patterns of reference already
put into play.

This intertextuality is important because Montagu has three key texts in hand
when drafting this letter, and they are invoked on three different levels. The first

is Pope's translation of the *Iliad*, and it is literally at Montagu's side as she travels through the islands of Greece. In his letter to Montagu dated June 1717, Alexander Pope indicates that he sent her a copy of the recently published third volume of his translation of the *Iliad*. In light of our previous discussion of her reading of the second volume, it is worth imagining this book traveling by post across the Mediterranean, arriving at the embassy in Constantinople, and then resting in Montagu's hands in the state room of her berth on the *Preston* en route to Tunis. She does not refer to Pope's book in this letter, but the reader is well aware of her reading the translation. This is important because it raises again Pope's relation to Homer's epic and the celebration of martial culture. As Grundy and others have noted, Montagu's letters exhibit a certain resistance to Pope's thinly veiled erotic advances, but I want to suggest that she is countering Pope on an altogether different level.

Pope's letters to Montagu during the embassy continually return to questions of acquisition, first of a Circassian slave and later of Montagu herself. Montagu parries these letters by either disabusing Pope of his fantasies or by critiquing the commodification of women implied in his leering jests. This would seem to have little to do with Homer and Pope's translation, but it is important to remember what happens to the Trojan women after the fall of Troy. In book 24 of the *Iliad*, Homer—and Pope after him—registers the lamentations of Andromache, Hecuba, and Helen,[61] but the poem ends before the sack of Troy and thus before the dispersion of the Trojan women to their horrible fates as slaves of their Greek conquerors. Despite Pope's attempt to dissociate himself from Greek cruelty, he is not attentive to the ways in which sexual violence looms large in the overall story of the destruction of Troy. Furthermore, Pope's representation of the Trojan women earlier in the text is troubling. As Carolyn D. Williams has demonstrated, his representation of the rape of Helen, for example, is cynical, and he undermines Andromache by emphasizing her feminine weakness.[62] We could argue that his highly politicized deployment of pastoral swains to witness the horrors of war, while consistent with a coded Tory critique of Whig economic and imperial policy, exists separate from his representation of the most famous witnesses of all. In fact, space is crucial here. It is significant that Pope's translation inserts these swain-observers where there are none in Homer to highlight the gory reality of war in the field, yet consistently underplays a different, far more affective form of witnessing within the walls of Troy itself, because it dissociates politics from the domestic sphere and from women.[63] If, as Santesso argues, Pope aligns himself with these swain-observers, then the external scenes of carnage and the external political world thoroughly infuse one another. In aligning himself with the victims of "barbarity," Pope nevertheless reserves a rhetorical position to attack his Whig adversaries.[64] As we will see, Montagu tracks violence from the external world to the interior spaces of hospitality and, in a remarkable act of counter-memory, will not accede to a feigned position of vulnerability. Instead, she will explore the aftermath of the Trojan War in a manner that attacks both Pope's blindness to gendered violence and her own rhetorical aggression.

Montagu supplies the supplemental material required to fully understand the tragedy of the fall of Troy in her account of the voyage from Constantinople to Tunis. Letter 45 follows closely in reverse George Sandys's progress through the Hellespont and the Aegean in his *Travels* (1615). As his biographer indicates, "Sandys was an observant, inquisitive traveller and his description of the foreign cultures he encountered is remarkable for moderation and tolerance."[65] As an important translator of the *Aeneid* and the *Metamorphoses*, his touchstones are Virgil, Ovid, and the Roman historians; thus the destruction of Troy is always understood as a precursor to the foundation of Rome. Approaching Troy, Sandys invokes Ovid:

> Who hath not heard of this glorious City, the former taking, the ten years war, and latter final subversion? which befell according to *Eusebius*, in the year of the world 2784 . . .
>> *So rich, so powerful, that so proudly stood,*
>> *That could for ten years space spend so much blood:*
>> *Now prostrate, only her old ruins shows,*
>> *And Tombs that famous Ancestors inclose.*[66]

This powerful statement of the bloodshed of the Trojan War is immediately followed by an argument for Virgil's rendering of the sack of Troy that refutes the imputation that Aeneas never left Troy. As Sandys progresses farther eastward, he recapitulates the long narrative of the Trojan War and its aftermath:

> Two not far disjoyning vallies there are that stretch to each other, and joyn in an ample plain (the theatre of those so renowned bickerments) where stood the antient *Ilium*, if not fortunate, not inglorious, nor un-revenged.
>> *Old Troy by Greeks twice sackt: twice new Greece rued*
>> *Her conquering Ancestors. First when subdued*
>> *By Rome's bold* Trojan *progeny; and now*
>> *When forc'd through* Turkish *insolence to bow.*[67]

By including the Byzantine and the Turkish conquests of Greece in this narrative, Sandys recasts the historical succession of empires as an extended revenge narrative arising from the cruelties inflicted on the once glorious city.

Montagu replicates Sandys's regular allusions to classical verse but with an important shift in emphasis and order. Like Sandys's, her allusions to Ovid, Virgil, and other texts focus on the tragic aftermath of the Trojan War across a broad historical span. Women play a prominent role in these allusions and in the related nods to Greek mythology and Byzantine history. Letter 45 could be considered a complex parody of Sandys's masculinist classicism, and it works by merely reversing the order of narrative disclosure. As the *Preston* makes its way through the Hellespont toward the ruins of Troy, Montagu explores first the tale of Hero and Leander—at the very minimum, a tale of the death of a male lover that precipitates the grief-stricken suicide of the priestess Hero (45.181; H 1:416). At the level of tone and theme, the tale continues the series of stories of dead lovers and grieving women from the preceding six letters.

In my discussion of these earlier letters, I suggested that the various Ottoman women are allegorical types of the Trojan women. It should come as no surprise that Montagu then turns specifically to the horrors faced by Hecuba: "Not many leagues sail from hence, I saw the point of land where poor old Hecuba was buried, and about a league from that place is Cape Janizary, the famous promontory of Sigæum, where we anchor'd" (45.182; H 1:417). Sandys is more specific about Hecuba's fate. Upon entering the Hellespont, Sandys states, "Bounded on the left hand with the *Thracian Chersonesus* (vulgarly called *St. George*'s arm) a *peninsula* pointed to the South-west: whereon stood the Sepulcher of *Hecuba*, called *Cynossema*, which signifieth Dog: fained to have metamorphosed into one, in regard of her impatiency. She in the division of the *Trojan* Captives, contemned, derided, and avoided of all, fell to the hated share of *Ulysses*: when to free her self from shame and captivity, she leapt into the *Hellespont*."[68] But Montagu's elaboration on coming to the site of Hecuba's grave moves in a different direction: "my curiosity supplied me with strength to climb to the top of it to see the place where Achilles was buried and where Alexander ran naked round his tomb in his honour, which, no doubt, was a great comfort to his ghost" (45.182; H 1:417). For readers acquainted with the classical texts, this invocation of Achilles's tomb carries with it a harsh reproof. In Euripides's *Hecuba*, the ghost of Achilles becalms the Greek ships on their return from Troy and demands the sacrifice of Hecuba's daughter Polyxena. Polyxena is horrifically sacrificed, and news comes that Polymestor has murdered Hecuba's son. The play's representation of the doubly grieving mother is unrelenting, and in spite of Hecuba's revenge on Polymestor, the audience is left with an overwhelming sense of desolation and anguish.

As we have already seen, from letter 39 forward Montagu's representations of women have repeatedly gravitated toward scenes of loss and grief. But this invocation of Hecuba captures the horror of war in quite specific ways. Her text suddenly turns to what appears to be a simple description of the ruins of Sigeum (or Sigeion), but her description of a marble monument on or near the Temple of Minerva brings the scene of dead children and grieving mothers into harsh relief:

Figure 36. Sigeion *trapeza* [funerary monument], marble (ca. 350 B.C.). Trustees of the British Museum.

On each side the door of this little church lies a large stone, about ten foot long each, fuve in breadth, and three in thickness. That on the right is very fine white marble, the side of it beautifully carved in bas relief. It represents a woman who seems to be designed for some deity sitting on a chair with a footstool, and before her another woman weeping and presenting to her a young child that she has in her arms, followed by a procession of women with children in the same manner. This is certainly part of a very ancient tomb, but I dare not pretend to give the true explanation of it. (45.183; H 1:418)[69]

This marble bas-relief, now in the collection of the British Museum, becomes a kind of counter monument to the tomb of Achilles venerated by Alexander (Figures 36 and 37). If the latter scene, derived again from Sandys, celebrates martial prowess by linking mythic and historical conquerors, then Montagu's encounter with the monument to grieving mothers effectively figures forth the cost of war. In this regard, Montagu's subtle engagement with the fate of the Trojan women in previous letters reaches its destination, because it is here that she is commemorating the loss not simply of Hecuba, Andromache, and their children, but more subtly the loss of life that attended the horrific slaughter at Zenta in 1697 and at Belgrade in 1717.[70] Through this figural connection, established in the earlier letters, she has extended Sandys's account of imperial war to the present, only now it is the Ottomans who find themselves figurally aligned with the defeated Trojans.

This brings us to the third text that I would argue animates letter 45. Because the letter is addressed from Tunis, we need to think carefully about the letter's relation to the *Aeneid*. As the *Preston* approaches Malta, Montagu's text's intense

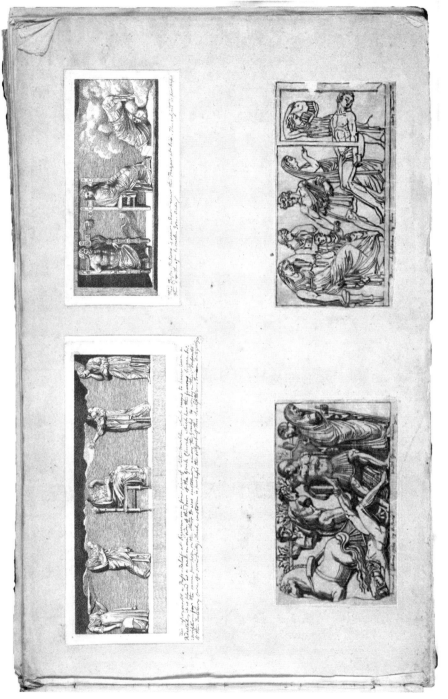

Figure 37. Page from an album of prints and drawings compiled by William Young Ottley c. 1791. In the top left corner is pasted the headpiece to preface, "To the Reader," *Ionian Antiquities* (1769), engraving after William Pars's drawings of the Segeion base at Alexandria Troas (see Figure 52). Trustees of the British Museum.

engagement with Sandys's *Travels* dissolves. It is quite literally blown away by a highly significant storm: "Off of this Island we were toss'd by a severe storm, and very glad, after 8 days, to be able to put into Porta Farine on the Africk shore, where our Ship now rides" (45.190; H 1:424). This storm is remarkably similar to the storm thrown up by Juno in the opening section of book 1 of the *Aeneid*, and Montagu, like Aeneas, finds herself seeking sanctuary in the vicinity of Carthage. When we recognize that the scene of narration of the letter itself is akin to the scene of Aeneas's retroactive account of the sack of Troy while enjoying the hospitality of Dido, a whole series of rhetorical gestures become more salient. Like Aeneas, Montagu has been narrating the horrible aftermath of the Trojan War, but unlike Aeneas she reorients the story to focus on the suffering of the Trojan women. This narrative alignment between Aeneas and speaker in the letter has a significant impact on the overall meaning of letter 45, because I believe that Montagu has Virgil's larger epic argument in mind. The *Aeneid*'s martial narrative fulfills the demands of the genre, but the complex betrayal of Dido, the prophetic invocation of the brutal Roman conquest of Carthage, and the demonstrable darkness of the poem's final eruption of unmitigated slaughter underscores the violence that subtends the triumph of empire.

That Montagu stages this letter in Tunis is important, because like the *Aeneid*, her critique of empire is brought home by her changing representation of hospitality. After the storm, she states that "We were met here by the English consul who resides at Tunis. I readily accepted of the offer of his house there for some days, being very curious to see this part of the world, and particularly the ruins of Carthage. I set out in his chaise at nine at night; the moon being at full, I saw the prospect of the country almost as well as I could have done by day light, and the heat of the sun is now so intolerable, 'tis impossible to travel at any other time" (45.191; H 1:424–25). As is well known, the retrospective narration of the fall of Troy in the first five books of the *Aeneid* is framed by a narrative of Dido's noble hospitality. It is the security offered to the refugee Trojans that in some senses enables both the narration of their past and the progession to their future in Latium. Aeneas has to break the bonds of love and scorn Dido's hospitality in order to fulfill his imperial and epic destiny. Thus hospitality and empire find themselves radically at odds in Virgil's text in much the same way that these two imperatives work at cross-purposes throughout Montagu's letters.

But the clearest indication that Montagu understands this predicament comes when she dramatizes her own betrayal of cosmopolitan hospitality at the close of the same letter. Here, near the site of Carthage, Montagu suddenly loses the capacity for affective or intellectual exchange with the peoples of this land. The first indication that something is awry comes in a passage that literally replays her earlier account of country people dancing and singing at Belgrade-Village in letter 37 but rather than adopting the pastoral discourse of the earlier letter, she veers toward repulsion:

> We saw under the trees in many places companies of the country people, eating, singing, and dancing to their wild music. They are not quite black, but all mulattos, and the most frightful creatures that can appear in a human figure. They are almost naked, only wearing a piece of coarse serge wrapped about them, but the women have their arms to their very shoulders and their necks and faces adorned with flowers, stars, and various sorts of figures impressed by gun-powder; a considerable addition to their natural deformity, which is, however, esteemed very ornamental amongst them, and I believe they suffer a good deal of pain by it. (45.191; H 1:425)

Many critics have been shocked by the sudden ethnocentric turn in Montagu's letter, but I believe it cannot be dissociated from the overall critique mounted in the text.[71] This becomes clear when Montagu comes to Carthage itself, and the text adopts an explicitly racist and xenophobic stance:

> I went very early yesterday morning (after one night's repose) to see the ruins of Carthage. I was, however, half broil in the sun, and overjoyed to be led into one of the subterranean apartments. . . . I found in many of them broken pieces of columns of fine marble and some of porphyry. . . . They are now used as granaries by the country people. While I sat here, from the town of tents not far off, many of the women flocked in to see me, and we were equally entertained with viewing one another. Their posture in sitting, the colour of their skin, their lank black hair falling on each side their faces, their features and the shape of their limbs, differ so little from their own country people, the baboons, 'tis hard to fancy them a distinct race, and I could not help thinking there had been some ancient alliances between them. (45.193; H 1:426–27)

Just as Aeneas's betrayal of Dido begets a history of enmity that results in brutal conquest and enslavement, so Montagu rehearses the imperial narrative that underpins her own culture. Unlike previous scenes of intercultural exchange, Montagu registers alienation from the conspicuously racialized women in what should be yet another space of hospitality. In a moment of intense alienation, guest and host change places, and the betrayal of hospitality happens so quickly that it barely even registers as a possibility. Racial hatred is made manifest in precisely

the place where Romans had before destroyed and enslaved their erstwhile enemies, and thus Montagu makes herself both the prophet and the embodiment of
imperial guilt and sadness. At this point my argument reaches its breaking point for
it is difficult to do more than speculate about intention here; perhaps it is best to see
this section of the text and my own desire to comprehend it within a narrative of
self-critique as symptoms whose larger ramifications need to be recognized.

As part of an imperial society that has also brutally enslaved African peoples,
Montagu shares more than a cultural inheritance with Virgil. Both Virgil and
Montagu are complicit beneficiaries of the very violence they critique in their work.
This retroactive enactment of complicity, both in the *Aeneid* and the Letter-book,
is inextricably tied to the melancholy loss of cosmopolitan exchange—whether it
be in the siege of Belgrade or on the plains outside ancient Carthage. And we
should be struck by the historical layering, by the play of allegory, how the fall of
Troy gets repeated again and again in the narrative, as a precursor to imperial ascendance and imperial decline. Thus as Montagu progresses on to continental
Europe and England, the text brings us closer and closer to the present situation
of global empires. Crucial to this layering effect is the suggestion that the most
recent fall—the defeat of the Ottomans at Belgrade—first elided in Montagu's text,
will be retroactively narrated as part of a prophetic narrative of counterinsurgency.
The currently ascendant imperial powers of Austria will find themselves brought
to account for their bellicosity. This carries with it the implication that the Ottomans will rise again against the powers of Europe after the Treaty of Passarowitz.[72]

But what is so remarkable is that Montagu's text effectively brings itself to account by enacting its own melancholy betrayal of its enlightenment principles of
hospitality and cosmopolitan exchange. What could be more painful than the recognition that one is historically excluded from the principles that made the possibility of peace and love seem suddenly within one's grasp? But it would be granting
Montagu a great deal of self-reflection to suggest that she was fully cognizant of
the problematic inscribed in the Letter-book. It is perhaps more appropriate to
conclude that the letters are displaced from themselves. Let us call them "refugee
letters," caught in a horrible melancholic state where grief and loss return again
and again to show just how precious are the moments of frontier hospitality narrated in letters 25 and 27. It is this ineffable sadness that makes these letters such
an important rejoinder to the martial predilection of the epic genre, especially as
it is rendered in Dryden's and Pope's translations.

The letters constitute a counter-epic that quite literally turns the tradition on
itself to reveal what it cannot adequately represent: the recurrent trauma of war.
As such they are a brilliant reading of the *Aeneid*, for they seem to prefigure that
sense of dread and darkness that Johnson so persuasively tracks through Virgil's

epic. For Johnson, the *Aeneid*, unlike the *Iliad*'s dialectical exploration of the heroism of Hector and Achilles,

> forces us to contemplate not so much man's dignity and courage as his vulnerability and . . . the mysterious forces that cause him to jeopardize his dignity and waste his courage. . . . Vergil found himself more and more constrained to imagine a world in which the prevalence of anger and unreason and sheer ignorance is so great that the human spirit is seen to be awesomely vulnerable and human effort is seen to be matched against dark forces that are as insuperable as they are mysterious. In such a world as this it is not impossible to talk of man's greatness of spirit, but it is more to the point to suggest that merely to be decent or adequate in such a world is hard enough.[73]

As the primary character in her own narrative, Montagu turns on herself, rendering herself like Aeneas, in her final malevolence, as the negation of her former manifestation of dignity and courage. It is in this negation that the historical forces of empire are brutally disclosed.

That Montagu's counter-epic, her recusal, is explicitly aligned with a proto-feminist critique of national and imperial culture should not go unnoticed. By comparison with Pope's factionalized pastoral critique of epic ambition in his translation of the *Iliad*, and his political deployment of pastoral discourse to subtly attack Whig models of empire in "Windsor Forest," the *Embassy Letters* offers a much less nostalgic and ultimately more troubling critique of national and imperial culture. By isolating the defensive quality of nostalgia in Pope's pastoral discourse and by ruthlessly anatomizing her own complicity in Britain's imperial culture, the text demonstrates the necessity of repeatedly reengaging with the recurrence of aggression in the present, even when it is enacted by oneself.[74] In this regard, the *Embassy Letters* raises the possibility of an act of overcoming, but nevertheless exhibits the very limits that constrain enlightenment as an attempt to live otherwise. Could we argue that the racist interlude in Tunis bears witness to the way that war eats away at cosmopolitan hope and thus needs to be presented, enacted, and scrutinized as a symptom beyond any simple moral calculation? Would such a process shift the ground from melancholia to mourning and thus to some sort of resolution of war's affective impact? Montagu's Letter-book, like the *Aeneid,* recognizes the historical and aesthetic necessity of such a task.

PART II

Beside War

CHAPTER 5

"As Are Yet to Be Seen"

The Dilettanti's Re-enchantment of the Ionian World

> Finding our guide ignorant and at a loss which way to
> go, we adopted the surer direction of antient history.
> —*Richard Chandler,* Travels in Asia Minor

Like the Treaty of Karlowitz, the 1763 Treaty of Paris fundamentally transformed global affairs. As the conclusion of the first truly global war, its impact on participants and non-participants alike was profound. The Ottoman Empire stayed out of the conflict, while Russia, its chief territorial rival, absorbed new technological and logistical advances developed during this war. Ottoman peace left it out of step with its enemies, and it would pay dearly at the hands of the Russians later in the century.[1] After early reverses in the Seven Years' War, Britain emerged as a truly global power. As Troy Bickham states, "The series of victories against France and its allies in Africa, the Americas, Asia and Europe drastically altered the British Empire not only demographically—the majority of people living under its control were no longer of European descent, but Asians in Bengal—but also in ways that transformed British culture at home into one that imagined the empire as intrinsic to the nation's economic prosperity and security."[2] Building on John Brewer's detailed analysis of the emergence of the military as the largest borrower, spender, and employer in the eighteenth century, Douglas Fordham has persuasively demonstrated that the Seven Years' War was a "pivotal moment" in the emergence of British art as an autonomous cultural entity.[3] The close links between imperial politics and artistic practice led to the founding of the Royal Academy by George III in December of 1768, and its role in mediating the vicissitudes of empire are well documented. In fact, Britain's new imperium was permeating everyday life like never before: disarticulating the local from the global was increasingly difficult. Fordham's detailed analysis of the convergence of art and arms at this historical moment demonstrates not only that "British art was forged in the crucible of war," but also that it was subsumed by uncertainty and contingency after peace.[4]

Just as there was an unforeseen cost to midcentury Ottoman peace, British victory in the Seven Years' War came at a steep price. In the immediate aftermath of the war this price tag was quite literally felt: the unprecedented debt generated by the war threatened to sink the economy. Furthermore, this newfound dominance outside of Europe almost immediately generated problems for imperial governance. The economies of its Atlantic empire and its new holdings in India operated on different principles, and early observers like Edmund Burke saw that Britain's rapid rise might be followed by a rapid decline. That decline was almost immediate, as the American crisis gained traction in the late 1760s and 1770s. In a series of ill-advised policies to offset the huge debt incurred by the Seven Years' War, successive governments in Westminster attempted to extract revenue from the American colonies, prompting a rebellion that sharply divided the nation and eventually shattered British imperial confidence. By the late 1770s it was apparent that Britain would lose much of its Atlantic empire, and by the next Treaty of Paris in 1783, American decolonization had rocked Britain's sense of imperial efficacy and prompted questions about the integrity of its national culture. These questions proliferated throughout the 1780s and were both reactivated and subsumed by the Revolutionary Wars with France in the 1790s.[5]

The vast majority of scholarship on the cultural impact of the Seven Years' War focuses either on the Atlantic world or on the Asian subcontinent. This is the first in a series of chapters that explore the interplay of imperial aspirations and uncertainties in the wake of this epochal declaration of peace, but they do so by integrating the representation of war in Ottoman dominions into this new world of global contingencies. That exploration starts with a literal act of exploration whose mediation reveals the tensions underlying both Britain's newfound imperial identity and its attendant cultural institutions and practices. If "the victories of the Seven Years' War resounded in English hearts for decades to come as a nearly mythic period of national unity and communal triumph," then this chapter recovers some of the hesitant articulations of how imperial triumph dissolves and disintegrates.[6] And it also takes stock of the aesthetic and political fantasies that emerged to put this sense of historical contingency in abeyance. As we will see, the radical spatial expansion of Britain's global empire meant that its culture was now being assessed and produced in relation to a vastly enlarged historical continuum.[7]

Early in 1764, the Society of Dilettanti, unlike many British institutions in the period following the Seven Years' War, discovered that it possessed a financial surplus. As reported in *Ionian Antiquities* (1769), "Various schemes were proposed for applying part of this Money to some Purpose which might promote Taste, and do Honour to the Society; and after some consideration it was resolved, 'That a Person or Persons properly qualified should be sent, with sufficient appointments, to certain Parts of the East, to collect Information relative to the former State of those Countries, and particularly to procure exact Descriptions of the Ruins of such Monuments of Antiquity as are yet to be seen in those Parts.'"[8] The resulting Ionian mission was the first archaeological expedition to Asia Minor to be sponsored and funded by a British institution. The administrators of the expedition chose two experts and a relative newcomer to carry out the task. Richard Chandler, a renowned expert in inscriptions, and Nicholas Revett, the architect now famous for his contributions to *The Antiquities of Athens* (1762), were joined by the twenty-two-year-old William Pars, a portrait painter who was enlisted to take views and render the various sculptures encountered on the journey. This chapter is about the activities of these three men during the collection and the complex mediation of information regarding the Ottoman-controlled regions visited on the journey. What I hope to demonstrate is how Ionia came to operate as a zone of phantasmatic compensation for the corrosive effects of early capitalist modernity because aesthetically engaging with its ruins demanded thorough scrutiny of the relationship between culture and violence—both in the present and the past. And I will be arguing that the complex representational strategies developed by these artists went far beyond laying the groundwork for much British and European philhellenism. As we will see, their work was significantly influenced by the aftermath of one imperial war and the onset of another: peace for these men was fleeting indeed.

On 9 June 1764, Chandler, Revett, and Pars embarked on the *Anglicana* bound for Constantinople and were put on shore at the Dardenelles on 25 August. The trio was in Ottoman territory for two years, and their itinerary is quickly summarized in the preface to *Ionian Antiquities*:

> Having visited the Sigéan Promontory, the Ruins of Troas, with the Islands of Tenedos and Scio, they arrived at Smyrna on the eleventh of September. From that City, as their Head-Quarters, they made several Excursions. On the twentieth of August, 1765, they sailed from Smyrna, and arrived at Athens on the thirty first of the same Month, touching at Sunium and Aegina in their way. They staid at Athens till the eleventh of June, 1766, visiting Marathon, Eleusis, Salamis, Megara, and other Places in the Neighbourhood. Leaving Athens, they proceeded, by the little Island of Calauria, to the Trœzene, Epidaurus, Argos, and Corinth. From this they visited Delphi, Patræ, Elis, and Zante, whence they sailed, on the thirty first of August, in the *Diligence* Brig, Captain LONG, bound for Bristol, and arrived in England the second of November following. (ii–iii)

This seemingly mundane itinerary should give us pause. It is the only account of the journey published until Chandler's *Travels in Asia Minor* appears in 1775. The book in which this itinerary appears is concerned with four sites in the immediate vicinity of Smyrna: precisely that part of the expedition almost dismissed in the telegraphic second sentence of the passage above. This stands in contrast to the careful listing of stopping points on the journey to and from Athens in 1765. Important views and drawings were collected on this latter leg of the journey, but they are disseminated at a later date in the second volume of *The Antiquities of Athens*.[9] In other words, this already minimal account of the expedition is a remarkably obscure preface to the *Ionian Antiquities* and to the Ionian expedition as a whole.

This would seem to be a minor point, but scholarship on the Ionian expedition tends to circumvent this information vacuum by reading *Ionian Antiquities* with Chandler's narrative of the expedition in hand. Jason Kelly, for instance, handles the range of publications as the "Ionian corpus."[10] At one level, this is an entirely understandable move. Both texts were sponsored and published under the aegis of the Society of Dilettanti. There are frequent references in Chandler's 1775 narrative to the 1769 *Ionian Antiquities*. In other words, Chandler's travel narrative retroactively provides the information needed to contextualize the documentation of the four primary sites. Without Chandler's text one has very little sense of the expedition's interaction with Ottoman subjects, with the fact that it took place in a "now" of intercultural sociability. My contention here is that the history of the dissemination of the information collected on the expedition—that is, the order in which the images and texts reached the public—is itself of historical and political significance. And it is important to consider each mode of dissemination in relation to its generic specificity. As Bruce Redford argues, "During the central two decades of the eighteenth century, the Dilettanti . . . sponsored expeditions and expedited publications that created a new genre, the proto-archaeological folio. This new kind of folio reaches back to seventeenth-century models and casts forward to the establishment of archaeology as rigorous scholarly discipline. It appears and thrives between 1753 and 1769, only to be overshadowed by imaginative interpretations of antiquity in the style of Piranesi and Adam, and by illustrated *voyages pittoresques*."[11] As we will see, this expedition and its representation are inextricably tied to events that both inaugurated new aesthetic and political formations and foreclosed certain futures for the past. As that sentence and the title of this chapter imply, the expedition's relationship to past, present, and future turned out to be extraordinarily complex, and I believe that temporality became one of the key thematic problems for Pars, Revett, and Chandler. In order to see this we need to disentangle the practices of these three men and pay close attention to how the order of disclosure affects our understanding of their work. Chronologies will be important here, but before submitting to the regimen of the calendar, I want to look closely at a cultural artifact that seems to stand outside of time but that captures many of the problematics to be explored in this chapter.

Timeless Peace

Perhaps the most curious thing about the entire Ionian expedition is that the single most compelling image collected during the journey languished in obscurity while far more prosaic images were immediately exhibited or engraved for circulation. After returning to London, Pars, Revett, and Chandler collaborated on the publication of the first volume of *Ionian Antiquities*.[12] For Chandler this meant drafting the texts to accompany the numerous plates in the book. The majority of the plates were the province of Revett—the elevations of the Temple of Bacchus at Teos, the Temple of Minerva Polias at Priene, the Temple of Apollo Didymaeus near Miletus, and the Heraeum at Samos, along with the drawings of the decorative elements of the pediments and such were chiefly his responsibility. But each of the four sites was introduced with a view engraved from Pars's topographical watercolors, and each section had head- and endpieces engraved from Pars's rendering of broken pediments and bas-reliefs taken in situ.[13] Significantly, some of Pars's most accomplished watercolors were passed over for the book project, but he chose to work up seven of these drawings for the inaugural exhibition of the Royal Academy of Arts in the spring of 1769. The drawings in the exhibition and those engraved for *Ionian Antiquities* entered the public at roughly the same time, but, as we will see, they have a supplemental relation to one another, and like all supplements, they recursively rebound on one another in a fashion that undermines their most sacrosanct assumptions and highlights their most tenuous rhetorical gestures.

But Pars's evocative *The Stadium at Laodicea* (Plate 20) was not exhibited in 1769 or in 1770 when Pars showed some of his paintings of the Parthenon. It is an image firmly located in the chronology of the expedition—its rendering of the caravan even represents travel within the frame—but for a significant period it was dislocated from the chronology of information dissemination. It was eventually engraved for the second volume of the *Antiquities of Ionia*, but that volume was not published until 1797.[14] The publication of this second volume was overseen by Sir Robert Ainslie after the death of Pars, and as we will see in Chapter 7, that in itself is an important issue, for the subject matter and the execution of this image operate differently than many of the images immediately circulated in 1769.

Most likely worked up from a brown-wash drawing executed on-site in the summer of 1765, Pars's picture meets one of the key objectives of eighteenth-century archaeological topography: it provides a precise visual description of the ruin.[15]

Laodicea became a notable city during the reign of Caesar Augustus, but after the disintegration of the Roman Empire the city was progressively abandoned. The site of numerous wars, Laodicea nevertheless featured the remains of two theaters, a stadium, and a number of large structures, including what the expedition assumed were a gymnasium and an odeon. Pars's picture records the existence of these structures on the left-hand ridge, but it is the stadium that organizes the overall composition. With the foreground dominated by the cluster of figures perched on the central lip of the stadium, the flanks of the stadium form two strong diagonals connecting the bottom corners of the painting to the horizon line of the landscape. This generates a strong central axis that gives the drawing extraordinary depth. The rippling effect generated by the rows makes it seem as though the landscape is almost biblically parted.[16] The viewer is forcefully incorporated along this central axis, and even though we are firmly located on ground level the view seems elevated because the stadium drops away out of view almost immediately. The visual effect is enhanced by a series of interior frames where the seats of the stadium—the ostensible subject of the view—provide a concentric device that brings the eye back to the quintet just below the center of the picture plane. Or is it the reverse? Does the central quintet provide the necessary focal point to organize the jumbled ruins in the middle ground?[17] There is a symbiosis here that becomes even more intriguing when we look at these central figures.

Five non-Europeans rest on the rim of the stadium, but they are subtly broken into two groups. The three unarmed men on the left—likely translators or intermediaries—wear turbans and are picked out by the rays of the sun. The same light casts the pair of armed figures on the right in relative shadow. Their headdress marks them either as janissaries or as armed mercenaries hired to protect the expedition, thus there is a social and ethnic distinction as well. This distinction between light and dark, unarmed and armed, divides the drawing and heralds a more subtle alignment. The three men on the left are in close visual proximity to the more well-preserved seats on the left diagonal. The armed figures are bracketed by the vestiges of destruction on the right. This contrast is further enhanced by the fact that three left-hand figures are deployed along the left diagonal of the stadium and city; the armed figures are arranged against the flow of the right-hand diagonal, and their rifles are the most conspicuous visual interruptions in the overall flow of the composition. Nestled in the center of this picture is a little essay on war, peace, and the effects of time. The central group stands for the combination of armed aggression and benign neglect that has rendered this remarkable ruin a metaphor for imperial destruction. Significantly, the space was one of Roman gladiatorial combat, so there are at least two crumbling empires and two regimes of violence superimposed in this picture. Looking down on the Roman ruins, the more recent empire, less accomplished, perhaps, than the old, presides over and organizes the space where the old empire came to be enter-tained by staged ludic violence.[18] As a pictorial metaphor for governance it is both authoritative and open to internal dissolution because the central group is itself divided. Like many European representations of Ottoman rule in the eigh-teenth century, the empire, as represented by this collection of multiethnic fig-ures, is divided against itself. But my sense is that this derives from the expedition's specific experience of regional ağas' resisting central rule and of growing unrest in the janissary corps. As we will, this sense of the Ottoman periphery unraveling is a crucial element of Chandler's *Travels in Asia Minor*.

It is important to remember that *The Stadium at Laodicea* is explicitly in dia-logue with the long tradition of such views and with the more recent example of James Stuart's topographical drawings taken during Stuart and Revett's 1750 expe-dition to Athens and published in *The Antiquities of Athens* in 1762. As Frank Salmon argues, "the key point of difference [between Stuart and Revett's practice and much prior representation of architecture] lay in their use of actual state topographical views, to provide 'authority, for our measures' and 'reasons' for every element of their restoration."[19] Andrew Wilton argues that Stuart's influence on Pars was sig-nificant and that Pars may well have seen Stuart's vibrant gouache paintings of Athens before his departure for Ionia.[20] Like Wilton, I also believe that Pars en-gages with Stuart's legacy in a manner that ultimately upends many of the assump-tions of the earlier artist's views, but it is helpful to consider first the ways in which Pars adopts Stuart's relation to the object of representation.[21] As Jason Kelly has recently argued, "Stuart's readers found that his topographies were landscapes of people as well as monuments." In a virtuoso reading of the first plate in *The Antiqui-ties of Athens*, Kelly demonstrates how Stuart deploys Ottoman figures to build a larger stadial argument about the progress and dissolution of civilizations that reso-nates with Johann Joachim Winckelmann's recently published and highly influen-tial thesis about Greek art and architecture. In his reading of the plate entitled *View of Athens* (Figure 38) and the explanatory note, Kelly underscores the dynamic ten-sion between the representation of antiquity and of the ethnographic subjects:

> Framing "Hasan Agà, the *Vaiwode* [local ruler] of Athens" within the Ionic entryway to the Reservoir of Hadrian, Stuart juxtaposed the ancient and the modern, the occident and the orient. . . . In his text, which supple-mented the view, Stuart spent as much space describing the characters as the monuments in his image. He told his readers that the Vaivode "de-lighted in Archery, and desired to be thus represented in this View; his greatest random shot was 1753 English feet." This seemingly offhand de-tail served as a device to refer readers back to his claim of objective and accurate observation. . . . The comment about the Vaivode served as a spur

for Stuart to discuss the "manners," the social structure, and the politics of modern Athens, however briefly. The Vaivode was "avaricious" and "cruel," while the modern Athenians had "more vivacity, more genius and a politer address than any other people in the Turkish Dominions."[22]

The broad contours of the stadial argument are nascent in the distinction drawn between the Ottomans and the Athenians. For Stuart, Revett, and other members of the Society of Dilettanti, the cyclical quality of history was supplemented by a hierarchy of civilizations based on their "spirit." In this historical fantasy, the Ottoman "spirit" exhibited neither genius nor aesthetic sensibility, and the contemporary Athenians, although retaining some elements of their ancient forebears, were a subject people and thus lacking the freedom to attain their full artistic and cultural potential.

The question of liberty proves to be crucial because the Dilettanti writings repeatedly align modern Britons with ancient Athenians: "Like the modern Britons, [the ancient Athenians] were a 'free, an affectionate, and a happy people,' 'blessed with the Arts of Elegance and those of Empire equally flourishing.' Unfortunately, the peak of their empire was followed by the loss of their freedom, thus depriving the Greeks of that essential element to the flourishing of the arts."[23] Kelly goes on to show how the framing devices of Ionic columns in the *View of Athens* carefully construct the succession of Athenian subjugation—"first under Minos, then under Rome, and finally under the Ottoman Empire."[24] This was almost the perfect inverse of David Hume's account of the progress of Liberty in *The History of England* (1754–61). This crucial first image in *The Antiquities of Athens* rhetorically situates the Ottoman Empire as the most recent, and most egregious, impediment to the progress of taste, elegance, and their lifeblood—Liberty. This rhetorical deployment of the Ottomans becomes a standard trope in the Dilettanti corpus. There are no shortage of scenes of Ottoman degradation in Chandler's *Travels in Asia Minor*, and Revett explicitly states that Ottoman destruction of classical remains was done "indiscriminately and without regret."[25]

But the alignment of modern Britain and ancient Athens, for all its self-congratulatory declaration of Britain's status as an erstwhile great civilization, comes with some significant risks.[26] Stuart's *View of Athens* was composed in 1750, but much to the dismay of many classical scholars including Winckelmann, the preparation of the text was a slow process, and *The Antiquities of Athens* was not published until 1762. As the images were engraved, Britain was in the throes of the Seven Years' War—a global conflict that would change utterly Britons' understanding of empire. After repeated losses in the early stages of the war, Britons faced the real possibility of imperial disintegration. That possibility was squelched by the annus mirabilis of 1759 in which Britain was victorious at Quebec and at

Figure 38. James Stuart, *View of Athens*, engraving, plate 1 from James Stuart and Nicholas Revett, *The Antiquities of Athens* (1769). Courtesy of the Getty Research Institute, Los Angeles.

Quiberon Bay, but Britons remained cognizant of the tenuousness of imperial domination right through the Peace of Paris in 1763 and beyond.[27] Even during the triumphal period immediately after the war, many Britons were deeply concerned about their capacity to maintain their imperial holdings. These concerns proved to be well founded, as the American colonists almost immediately began to agitate against incursions on their liberty. "Liberty"—the term that was so crucial to the Dilettanti's fantasy of Britain's link to ancient Athens—proved to be a deeply troubling matter because their own subjects were challenging the fantasy of civilized empire from within. How would one characterize the "spirit" of the Americans? This will become a key issue in subsequent chapters, where the complex problem of how to comprehend and move beyond American decolonization will be felt in seemingly disconnected zones of inquiry. But for the moment Liberty's volatility was an immediate problem within the metropole itself.

The internal crisis provoked by John Wilkes—a member of the Society of Dilettanti—revolved around the rhetorical and practical deployment of political liberty. David Solkin and Douglas Fordham have demonstrated that the debate around Wilkes and liberty had significant implications for artistic practice in the early stages of the Royal Academy of Arts.[28] But before turning to these issues, we need to think about *The Antiquities of Athens* and the Ionian expedition in relation to the uneasy topic of peace. I say "uneasy" because the patriotic discourses of wartime, however attenuated, tend to stabilize national fantasy. Peace is always on the verge of transmuting into war, and in a century of almost perpetual war it was far less the norm than conflict. However, the period between 1747 and 1768 was longest stretch of peace between the Ottoman Empire and Europe in its history. In a very real way, it was the fact of peace that allowed the firman—an edict from Sultan Mustafa III—to be granted to the members of the Society of Dilettanti that gave them access to Athens and to Ionia in the first place. It is also important to recognize that Stuart and Revett's travels were conducted during a period of peace prior to the Seven Years' War and that the Ionian expedition was conceived and conducted in the immediate aftermath of the Peace of Paris.

That said, the time of Stuart and Revett's trip and that of Chandler, Revett, and Pars would have felt very different on the ground. Because Stuart is imaging and imagining Athens, the rhetorical stakes are high, and thus the distinction between Ottomans and Greeks is starkly drawn. Faced with recording a less exalted site—Ionia was considered to be a culture progressing toward perfection, but clearly not on a level with Athens—Pars pursues a different historical fantasy and a different set of artistic protocols. This is registered in those areas of artistic practice where Pars diverges most forcefully from Stuart. Pars's subdued palette, his interest in fragmentary confusion, and his more subtle rendering of human subjects separate him from Stuart and can be linked to important historical transitions in the region.

As the peace of 1747–68 progressed, the Ottoman Empire became increasingly divided, rebellions emerged, and corruption became more and more acute. The janissary corps was undergoing internal transitions that would become a significant problem when that peace ended in 1768.[29] Further, the modular system of control in the Ottoman state meant that regional ağas could generate significant levels of resistance in times of diminished central control. As we have seen, Stuart is far from complementary about the vaivode of Athens, but his derogation of the ağa has none of the portentousness of Chandler's account of various forms of resistance and outright disrespect to the sultan's firman in *Travels in Asia Minor.*

Significantly, Chandler's discussion of the exploration of Laodicea and the ensuing attempt to survey Hierapolis is framed by harrowing accounts of regional ağas asserting their independence from the sultan.[30] Just prior to arriving in Laodicea, the janissary who was charged with protecting the expedition was arrested by the ağa:

> Mustapha, pleading our Fihrman and remonstrating, was seized, disarmed, and thrown into prison. In the mean time we were very uneasy at the tent, presaging no good from his long stay. After some hours, we saw him coming without his gun, pistol, or sabre; terrified and dejected. He exclaimed, we were among rebels and robbers; that the roads were beset to prevent our escape, and the Aga, if we hesitated to comply with his demand [for money], was determined to cut us to pieces, and take possession of our baggage.
>
> The Janizary described the Aga as uncommonly fierce and haughty, and bade us apprehend the very worst consequences from his intemperance and savage disposition. (223)

Faced with this situation, Chandler paid off the ağa, and the expedition turned to the site of Laodicea in earnest. But what I find striking here is that the strict separation of Europeans from Ottomans dissolves in the face of rebellion. For the first time in the text the janissary has a name. Chandler registers his emotions. And follows his advice. In other words, the threat of violence generates intercultural intimacy and momentary trust. Instability has fleetingly interrupted the rhetorical distinctions so crucial for Stuart's derogation of Turkish rule in spite of the fact that Chandler's narrative is nonetheless recording an instance of Ottoman ferocity. A similar thing happens at Hierapolis, where the company escapes an even more dangerous ağa.[31]

Suddenly Pars's drawing of the stadium reads differently. The central figures still operate as a metaphor for a society increasingly divided against itself and thus for the deteriorating condition of the peace (Figure 39). But they also accede to

Figure 39. Detail, William Pars, *The Stadium at Laodicea* (1765), watercolor drawing. Trustees of the British Museum.

the condition of portraits. Is this Mustapha glancing out at us, however obscurely? The very question challenges the generic expectations of the picture. The topographical view is supposed to depersonalize the ethnographic subject. It is not supposed to convey events. It is not supposed to lend itself to historical narrative.[32] By capturing the stillness of this moment, Pars has put history and life at stake. In the context of Chandler's narration of social insecurity those stakes are even more heightened because *Travels in Asia Minor* was published in 1775, immediately after the conclusion of the Russo-Ottoman War of 1768–74. The instability described by Chandler rendered the Ottomans susceptible to Catherine the Great's bellicose intentions. The war was disastrous for the Ottomans. In 1770 the Ottoman fleet was wiped out by the Russians near the Bay of Çeşme, roughly 150 kilometers west of Laodicea. Chandler invokes that defeat in his narrative (94), and it is apparent that it presages further Russian aggression in the region. We will have more to say later in this chapter about the historicity of Chandler's text, poised as it is at the end of one war and the beginning of another, but first I want to return to the 1760s, to Pars and the problem of peace.

Here in *The Stadium at Laodicea*, which predates the war, stillness reigns yet. A few short paces away from the viewer sit five men whose lives will be permanently altered by the Russian invasion and by the Ottoman defeat at Çeşme. The pictorial illusion of proximity between the viewer and these Turks—itself an effect of the drawing's great depth—is the cognate gesture to Chandler's subtle intimations of alliance with and concern for Mustapha. There is instability at the core of the picture, but the resulting anxiety, the anticipation of conflict, is part of the experience of peacetime. One could well ask in what time does peace occur if not in this fantasy of a timeless threshold between the present and past. Wartime seems to vacillate between nostalgia for prewar conditions and desire for conflict to end. Desire for the cessation of hostilities incorporates a specific form of historical consciousness.[33] Peacetime is marked by a desire for its continuance in the face of memories of carnage, thus the future of peace is committed to the cancellation of death. Pars's drawing gives us just that: an image of recurrent violent ruin out there below us, just past the threshold of conversation on the rim of this theater. In a strange way, these five men seem to hang on the edge of what is certain to happen yet again. Already coming apart at the seams, Ottoman peace was becoming dangerous; British peace, only just beginning, was starting to spawn images, narratives, and discourses of its dissolution. Almost simultaneously in the streets of London and Boston, a new future for liberty was altering the balance between the imperial state and its fantasy of civility and virtue.

Imperial Fantasy at the Royal Academy, 1769

David Solkin's groundbreaking analysis of the inaugural exhibition of the Royal Academy in *Painting for Money* opens with a lengthy citation from *Lloyd's Evening Post, and British Chronicle* that establishes a fundamental distinction between the kind of paintings on display in Pall Mall and those at the rival Society of Artists exhibition at Spring Gardens. As Solkin states, "The most striking feature of the Academy exhibits is the preponderance of classical titles, for both histories and portraits . . . such works were pointedly absent from the Spring Gardens show. . . . At the Society viewers seem to have taken especial pleasure in fairly small scale, highly particularized renderings of modern subjects, most them genre scenes or conversations, and in a surprisingly high number of pictures which featured the sort of dramatic illumination commonly associated with the seventeenth-century Dutch tradition."[34] Solkin's reading of the politics of that distinction is a classic of British art history, and I will be engaging with some of his theses shortly, but I think it is important to return to *Lloyd's Evening Post*'s list of notable paintings in the Royal Academy exhibition in order to think about Pars's contributions to the show:

> The Pictures that have this season chiefly attracted the attention of the Connoisseurs at the Royal Academy in Pall-Mall, are three by Sir Joshua Reynolds, viz. Diana disarming Cupid, Juno receiving the Cestus from Venus,

and Hope nursing Love; The Departure of Regulus from Rome, containing a great number of figures which are admirably characterized, and Venus lamenting the Death of Adonis, by Mr. West; Hector and Andromache, Venus directing Aeneas and Achates, by Mrs. Angelica, an Italian young Lady of uncommon genius and merit; The King and Queen at full length, by Mr. Dance; Lady Molyneux, by Mr. Gainsborough.[35]

Not surprisingly, Pars's drawings do not make the list. His seven watercolors were minor works: small in scale at roughly twelve by twenty-four inches, they were also classed as drawings; hardly the large-scale works in oil that caught the eye of the press.[36] Neither history paintings per se, nor portraits of the fashionable and political elite, Pars's pictures have much more in common with the genre paintings on display at the Society of Artists, but here they are in the same exhibition as these paintings by Benjamin West, Joshua Reynolds, Angelica Kauffman, Nathaniel Dance, and Thomas Gainsborough.

Take for example Pars's drawings of the *Cave of Archidamus* (Figures 40 and 41). The brown-wash study establishes the basic forms and the overall composition, but the more finished drawing carefully records the inscriptions in this cave and thus fulfills its documentary objectives. That said, its fascination with lighting effects makes it quite comparable to the candle-light paintings most famously associated with Joseph Wright of Derby and with the 1769 Society of Artists exhibition. Pars's painting makes an interesting comparison to Wright's *Three Persons Viewing the Gladiator by Candlelight* of 1765 that depicts three connoisseurs viewing a model of the *Borghese Gladiator* (Figure 42). Viewing antiquities by candlelight was a regular practice, therefore one could argue that Wright and Pars are recording the conditions of viewing. And yet the subject matter of Pars's watercolors, the ruins of antiquity, has a complex relationship to the idealized rendering of classical scenes and figures in the history paintings and grand manner portraits that dominated the Royal Academy exhibition and its mediation in the press.

What does it mean to consider the inaugural Royal Academy show from well below the line as it were, from a minoritized or marginal position? According to Greg Smith, in the Royal Academy's first home in Pall Mall "oil paintings, miniatures, watercolours and sculpture had been mixed in the same room" and "though there is no visual or textual evidence to suggest how drawing fared . . . , the absence of specific complaints about their placement suggests a rough and ready equality."[37] We can't offer a precise reconstruction of the hang, but Pars's drawings read quite strangely in this august company. On its own, Pars's diminutive *The Theatre at Miletus with Party Crossing in a Ferry* (Plate 21) is perhaps most legible in relation to Stuart's archaeological topographies.[38] This picture is arguably

Figure 40. William Pars, *Sacred Cave of Archidamus* (1765?), watercolor with pen and black and gray ink over graphite. Courtesy of the Yale Center for British Art, Paul Mellon Collection.

Figure 41. William Pars, *The Cave of Archidamus* (1765?), watercolor drawing. Trustees of the British Museum.

Figure 42. William Pether, after Joseph Wright of Derby, *Three Persons Viewing the Gladiator by Candlelight* (1769), mezzotint. Trustees of the British Museum.

the closest Pars came to mimicking Stuart's deployment of ethnographic figures and architectural observation in one image. For viewers familiar with *The Antiquities of Athens*, the composition of the picture would have been reminiscent of Stuart's *View of Athens* (see Figure 38). Rather than the Acropolis off in the distance at the top right of the picture, Pars has placed the Theater of Miletus in the center background. In the foreground left, we have a cluster of Ottoman and Armenian men attempting to help Revett and Pars board the ferry so that they can examine the theater more closely. Like the rendering of the vaivode in Stuart's picture, the handling of these figures emphasizes motion, but there is an important comic register. The drawing handles the problem of capturing a sudden event in much the way that British viewers would associate with Hogarth, and this I believe is intentional. If one looks closely at the two European figures alone it becomes apparent that they are out of proportion both with one another and with the surrounding Ottomans—the central figure, presumably Pars, and his horse are too small. There is also something puzzling about the presence of all three English travelers in the picture. Who is taking this view? Does uncertain handling of the figures betray the artifice of the allochronic distinction between ethnographic subject and the ostensibly empirical observer? The scale of the figures is disjunctive, the layering of the figures is hard to read, and the combined effect is to make the embarkation that much more comic.

This sense of pictorial unrest is enhanced both by the stillness of the ruin in the background and by the fact that the third European, presumably Chandler, is already on board calmly awaiting the embarkation of his colleagues. The subtle link drawn between the standing figure on the right and the ruin of the theater reveals a dyadic structure that resonates with the *View of Athens*. In its most crude reading, the comic, almost chaotic, strategies that dominate the left of the painting operate in stark contrast to the calm, carefully delineated representation of both the theater and Chandler on the right. As in Stuart, this lends itself to a derogation of the present Ottoman dispensation and an idealization of both the cultures of antiquity and the expedition's attempt to empirically describe the remnants of ancient Greek and Roman culture.

But the image also offers more subtle avenues for interpretation. The theater itself complicates the left/right, modern Ottoman/ancient Greece dyad, because although it dates back to the fourth century B.C. and to important schools of Greek philosophy and science, the ruin as presented is a vastly expanded structure built by the Romans. Reported to seat 15,000 spectators, the Roman iteration of the building was the scene of gladiatorial combat. As in Stuart's *View of Athens*, this vestige or overlay of a later imperial history allows for a stadial argument to unfold. In this picture, the representatives of historically less developed civilizations enable the ostensibly more advanced British observers to explore the remains of two noble yet different cultural predecessors. But this also raises a vexing problem. Because the picture so forcefully aligns the English figure on the right with the ruin of the theater we must eventually ask where his affiliations lie. Is there an identification with the ancient Greek theater (now incorporated into the Roman ruin) and thus to the democratic polis, or is the relationship more comfortably drawn between the English observer and the Roman stadium and thus to the altogether different connotations of empire and violence? The ghost of Rome in this picture subtly injects a subtext of violent unrest in the ostensibly still portion of the composition.[39]

This seemingly subtle point begins to loom large when we think about the image in the context of the rest of the exhibition. By far the most important work in the show, Benjamin West's *Departure of Regulus from Rome* is explicitly drawn from the history of the First Punic War (Figure 43). When George III commissioned the painting, he brought West to the relevant passage in Livy.[40] Solkin is no doubt correct in his assessment of the picture's political import:

> [West] had decided to make his mark with a large canvas in the uncompromisingly elevated manner of Nicholas Poussin; but more to the point,

Figure 43. Benjamin West, *The Departure of Regulus from Rome* (1769), oil on canvas. Courtesy of the Royal Collection/Bridgeman Art.

perhaps, West had also chosen a theme that celebrated the stoic fortitude of an exemplary civic protagonist. Regulus, after deciding on death for himself rather than dishonor for Rome, is shown literally turning his back on family and friends, sacrificing both his self-interest and all emotional attachments in favour of the greater good of the republic. . . . Regulus stands above the realm of sociality, and beyond the private viewer's capacity for emulation. Such a figure may command the respect of ordinary citizens, but he instantiates the virtues of a superior class of men.[41]

Regulus's disinterested nobility is pitched in contrast to the Wilkite notions of an expanded polity—here figured by the mob on the left side of the painting—and thus the picture folds into a rearguard action to shore up the political power of the Crown and affiliated elites.[42]

West's *Regulus* exemplified the Royal Academy's aspirations for history painting, and the painting, like its central protagonist, was meant to exemplify the disinterested public character of the institution. But the very claim to disinterestedness meant that the painting and Sir Joshua Reynolds's cognate theory of history painting were inherently politicized.[43] As Solkin argues,

To promote an agenda for grand-style historical art involved calling for the fusion of an elevated style with themes of ostensibly timeless significance. If this combination conferred nobility on the painter, it was also meant to define his chosen viewers as individuals who were morally, socially, and intellectually superior to that part of mankind attached to more vulgar, material concerns. As James T. Bolton has observed, this was precisely the strategy employed by the leading spokesmen for the government cause in the press and pamphlet war during the climactic period of the Wilkes affair.[44]

The way this is handled in the painting is intriguing because Regulus is literally surrounded by the very multitude he is resisting in his return to Carthage. West represents two types of people who are unable to see what is best for Rome. There is the vast majority, the friends and family who gaze at Regulus—at the man not the state's representative—and there is the small cluster of figures on the right of the canvas who don't notice Regulus at all. This conspicuously affluent pair—their attendant slave is a sign of wealth and decadence—stand for those whose obsession with material concerns blinds them to what is best for the nation. In the context of Wilkite London, this is an attack on "The People" and on "The Ton."

But there is a further political overtone here as well. Regulus's stoicism is part of the history of imperial war. West's painting instantiates a series of class problematics that attended the Wilkes affair, but George III's commission of the painting can't easily be separated from its martial narrative. The Regulus story seems to point back to the period prior to the annus mirabilis of the Seven Years' War when the question of an unfavorable peace was rejected in favor of further prosecution of the war. In 1768, George III could look back on that decision as an example of the very nobility he needed to activate yet again to deal with the impending crisis in the American colonies. The resistance to the Stamp Act and the Townshend Revenue Acts is the immediate backdrop not only for the king's desire for patriotic history painting, but also for much of Wilkes's agitation. In other words, the example of Regulus's stoicism in the First Punic War amounts to a powerful fantasy of sacrifice for imperial conquest. Choosing to think about this aspect of Roman history is part of an early investment in the subjection and, if necessary, the reconquest of the American colonies.

If we step away from the monumentality of West's painting and look at the rest of the show, it is hard not to notice a recurring interest in classical models of war and empire. The other painting marked out for singular praise in *Lloyd's Evening Post* is Angelica Kauffmann's *Venus Directing Aeneas and Achates to Carthage*. The significance of the image would not have been lost on the viewers already dealing

Figure 44. William Pars, *Arch at Mylasa* (1764), watercolor drawing. Trustees of the British Museum.

with West's rendering of the First Punic War because Aeneas's entry into Carthage not only enables the diasporic Trojans' eventual conquest of Latium and the foundation of Rome, but also the instantiation of Dido's curse that underlies all subsequent accounts of the enmity between Rome and Carthage especially during the Punic Wars. In a strange way, Kauffmann's painting is a prequel of sorts to West's *Regulus* that takes us from the foundation of conflict between Rome and Carthage articulated in the *Aeneid* to the exemplification of Roman imperial power. If we wanted to pursue this further we could also make links to Kauffmann's *Hector and Andromache* and to Reynolds's portrait of Lady Blake as *Juno Receiving the Cestus of Venus*. Such a move would trace the success of Rome over Carthage all the way back to the tragic destruction of Troy by the Achaeans. If we build this set of connections, then this grouping of paintings tropologically testifies to the cyclical nature of imperial war.[45]

We would seem to be a long way from Ionia, but Pars's little watercolors, by virtue of their empiricism, keep on drawing the viewer to a different view of Roman history.[46] If *The Theatre at Miletus with Party Crossing in a Ferry* subtly, or perhaps inadvertently, reminds the viewer that to align oneself with Rome is also to align oneself with its gladiatorial past, then a more accomplished picture such as *Arch at Mylasa* reminds the viewer that great empires quite literally disintegrate (Figure 44). Carefully observed, Pars's rendering of this second-century Roman archway quite obviously captures the passing of the Roman Empire, but it should also remind us of West's palpable antiquarian interests.[47] The architectural details of West's *Regulus* are not incidental framing devices; they are a manifestation of the stability and strength of the Roman republic. What is so startling is that West's grand picture replicates the composition of Pars's drawing. Both pictures feature enclosed spaces with an outlet to the right of the pictorial plane. Placed side by side one can't help but feel the absence of not only the hero but also the multitude that animates the interior space of *Regulus*. The mound of rubble to the left—both in size and shape—strangely seems to substitute for the mob in West. The figures in Pars, such as they are, draw the eye out of the ruin and subtly help to squelch any possibility for drama within the architectural space. In place of actants and drama, Pars gives us rubble that is rendered that much more stark by the extraordinarily flat lighting. If *Regulus* operates as a fantasy of elite class consolidation and unrestrained desire for imperial control, the *Arch at Mylasa* seems to capture disintegration and entropy in all their fearsomeness.[48]

Desolation becomes one of Pars's great rhetorical devices. We saw it at play in the *Stadium at Laodicea*, and it is perhaps most starkly exemplified by *Ruin near the Port of Aegina—the Temple of Apollo on the Island of Aegina* (Plate 22). We might ask what about this watercolor warrants viewing? When placed next to Stuart's vibrant gouaches—arguably the most important precursor images in this style—Pars's muted palette tends toward inconsequentiality. The painting is almost a canceled sign, and in its very negation of interest it gains its eloquence. My sense is that alone it is of little import, but in the context of the Royal Academy show it operates a bit like the child struck by the nakedness of King Midas. In the face of West's bluster and Reynolds's hyperbolic claims for history painting, this small-scale work of minimal visual intensity punctures the twofold fantasy of imperial desire and class ascendancy with startling matter-of-factness. In fact it is scale and even medium itself that signify here, for the very minority of the drawing—its inconsequentiality—enacts the entropy of the subject matter.

The reclining Ottomans in the center of the watercolor only serve to redouble the sense that all that remains is desolation. Of course, to say this, one has to place these same Ottomans in a category of noninterest. One could argue that this is a form of ethnocentrism far more powerful than Stuart's example, for Pars here renders the Ottomans as ghostly apparitions, alive but as inconsequential as the fragments they recline upon. But I don't think the overall import is that of a Lockean vacuum awaiting conquest and appropriation, nor is it simply a matter of Montesquieu's despotic lassitude washing through the center of the picture, although both fantasies of empire are signaled. My sense is that Pars's images are directly confronting the problem of imperial decay with pictorial strategies far more modern and potentially more disturbing than the highly theatrical deployment of antiquity in West or Kauffmann. If anything, the presence of these figures indicates that they too will disappear, and thus they are central to Pars's entropic argument. By incorporating the viewer into the scene of historical witnessing, Pars brings the viewer face-to-face with the erosion of civilization and with death itself.

Entropic Designs

This same sense of entropy and disintegration can't help but figure into the Society of Dilettanti's first publication from the expedition. Like Pars's Royal Academy submissions, *Ionian Antiquities* reached the public in 1769, and it attempted to provide "exact Descriptions of the Ruins of such Monuments of Antiquity as are yet to be seen in those Parts."[49] The temporal complexity of that verb construction— "as are yet to be seen"—signals an attempt to contain the sense of entropy, which, if left to do its historical work, can unhinge the kind of grand narratives mobilized to legitimize the Society of Dilettanti's commitment to classical art. The vestiges of Ionian culture that were the subject of Chandler, Revett, and Pars's corporate enterprise were, like the figures on the rim of the Stadium of Laodicea, on the very threshold of oblivion. The explicit objective of *Ionian Antiquities* was to capture the traces of four important ruins before they permanently pass away. This objective is easily stated but involves a complex representational sleight of hand that necessarily requires the very different contributions of all three members of the expedition. Pars's uncanny ability to capture entropy forms one half of a dialectical operation that is balanced by Revett's intense commitment to restore order from the rubble around him. This dialectical tension between Pars's views and Revett's elevations and schematic drawings enacts the very tension inscribed in that troubling expression used to describe the expedition's objective.[50] As a grammatical construction, "as are yet to be seen" combines a sense of the fleeting present with a sense of ongoing futurity to counteract the entropic force of history. Likewise, Revett's elevations and schematics have a strange relation to the future. As we will see, Chandler's text tends to mediate between the two diverging tendencies of Pars's and Revett's illustrations. When all three components are working properly, *Ionian Antiquities* is able to mobilize the sense of desolation already encountered in Pars's pictures in a broader project to bring order to a rapidly changing world.[51] In that sense, the book, like the Royal Academy exhibition of 1769, is symptomatic of an attempt to put disorder—both social and political—in abeyance. As we will see, this involves a complex deployment of Ottoman figures.

As I have already mentioned, *Ionian Antiquities* focuses on four archaeological sites: the Temple of Bacchus at Teos, the Temple of Minerva Polias at Priene, the Temple of Apollo Didymaeus near Miletus, and a temple at Iackly, near Mylasa.

Figure 45. Headpiece to chapter 1 of *Ionian Antiquities* (1769), engraving after a watercolor by William Pars. Courtesy of the Getty Research Institute, Los Angeles.

As Redford summarizes, "The folio associated with the Dilettanti is characterized by three discourses: a quasi-scientific discourse that stresses empirical exactitude; a nationalistic discourse that contrasts British gentlemen with the client of the French state; and an anti-picturesque discourse that deprecates theatrical exaggeration, both visual and verbal, in favor of clarity and precision."[52] As one might expect from a publication whose very generic cohesion turns on clarity, the organization of the book appears straightforward. The sites are handled in four separate chapters. Each chapter opens with a headpiece illustration by Pars, which is immediately followed by a general discussion of the site and by a series of commentaries on the ensuing plates. The textual commentaries are separated from the plates by a decorative illustration derived from Pars's watercolors. Revett's elevations and schematic drawings of architectural elements outnumber Pars's contributions by a ratio of roughly five to one. But the visual effect is far more balanced. Partly because of their placement and partly because of their composition and depth, Pars's views and his drawings of fragments give a strong sense of the disorder encountered by the expedition.[53]

This is perhaps nowhere more forcefully articulated than in the first headpiece: Pars's rendering of the mound of stones that was once the Temple of Bacchus at Teos (Figure 45). Compared to many of Pars's images this one is remarkably flat: the viewer is confronted with a horizontal array of fractured marble in the middle ground. It is difficult to pick out any organization to the fragments. But there are crucial details that in many ways make this the baseline image from which the entire text operates. The vegetation is very carefully observed, and it stands for nature's unending encroachment on the site. The other key detail is political. On the right side of the image are two Ottoman grave markers that have been fashioned out of fragments from the temple. They are both memento mori and explicit evidence of Ottoman depradations on the site. The figure in the bottom right is an Ottoman stonecutter fashioning gravestones from the remains of the temple.[54] All three members of the expedition were scandalized by the contemporary use of marble from the ancient buildings.[55] Local populations routinely used sarcophagi and other objects for water receptacles. But the issue of gravestones is particularly significant because it directly marks the Ottoman occupation of Teos and because the new artifact is repurposed to suit Islamic cultural practices. Thus imperial and natural succession are simultaneously invoked.[56] This image firmly locates the encounter in a chronological moment and raises the issue of that moment's passing.

But after this header image the expedition itself is virtually erased from the text. There is little or no sense of how the observers got from site to site. Unlike the 1821 reprint of the text, there isn't even a map to situate the ruins. The effect is disorienting because one is forced to consider each site in isolation. This essentially transforms the site into an artifact closed off from the world around it. The only narrativity associated with each site is to be derived from the ancient sources so copiously referenced in Chandler's commentary, thus the contemporary experience of encountering the sites is strictly relegated to the landscapes, which are rigorously tied to empirical observation of what lies on the ground. The plate commentaries and the architectural plates seem to eschew the present either because they refer to ancient discussions of the sites or because they restore the ruins to their imagined, undamaged state. Both processes involve a species of nostalgia, but the latter act of restoration is more complex than it first appears.

The temporal disjunction is evident when we turn to Revett's first plate in the volume (Figure 46). The commitment to order in his reconstruction of the Temple of Bacchus is as intense as Pars's visualization of entropy. As Redford states, Revett "took pains to insure that his onsite drawings were translated into the most informative plates possible."[57] But how does one get from the rubble of the archaeological site to this ideal frontal elevation? Chandler's commentary on Revett's plate explicitly raises the problem:

> As a description of the parts of any building, unaccompanied with a display of their Effect when united, conveys only imperfect Ideas of its beauty; the curious Reader will, it is hoped, derive pleasure and satisfaction from seeing this Temple restored. The liberties necessarily taken for this purpose, with the authorities on which they are founded, shall be laid before him, that neither the fidelity of the Author may be suspected, nor his judgement implicitly relied on.
>
> The disorder, in which this ruin lies, is so great, that no fragment of a Column, or portion of the Cell, is found unmoved from its original place.

Figure 46. Elevation of the Temple of Bacchus, *Ionian Antiquities* (1769), engraving after drawing by Nicholas Revett. Courtesy of the Getty Research Institute, Los Angeles.

No vestige of the Plan could be discovered, much less could the Aspect or Species of the Temple be determined, from its present state. But these two articles are supplied from Vitruvius, who, in describing the Eustylos, gives this Temple as an example, calling it Octastylos, by which he means Dipteros, specified from the number of columns in the Front. (6)

From the number of columns, Chandler and Revett work inductively to construct the image in the plate. Their arguments are supported by detailed footnotes to classical texts and by their own measurements, but ultimately the attempt to reconstitute the building from its present state relies on stylistic comparison to the Parthenon, a building both historically and stylistically distinct from this temple (7–8). The link between the geographically distant buildings is forged via the invocation of rules of proportion exemplified by another structure. My point here is not to contest the argument, but rather to demonstrate its conjectural quality.[58]

This is important because for all the talk of measurement in Chandler's commentary and Revett's drawings, there is also a commitment to what Chandler describes as a "liberty" to ensure that the reader "derives pleasure and satisfaction from seeing the Temple restored" (6).[59] When taken in sequence, Pars's image invokes a certain pathos or pain at irrecoverable loss, and Revett's elevation alleviates that pain through an act of aesthetic imagination.[60] This pattern is played out again and again throughout the book, both in the interplay between Pars's views and Revett's architectural drawings and within the sequence of Revett's plates.

Figure 47 (including facing page). Revett's illustrations for the ornamental cornices and columns for the Temple of Bacchus, *Ionian Antiquities* (1769). Courtesy of the Getty Research Institute, Los Angeles.

It may seem like a subtle point, but the act of giving the reader a plate of diagrams of ornamental cornices and pediments and then supplementing it with a shaded image is to bring these elements closer and closer to three-dimensional autonomy (Figure 47). It is as though one moves from plan to object, and in this context the addition of a verifiable light source gestures toward a reconstitution not simply of the temple but of the world around it.[61] In short, Revett's plates go well beyond restoring order to a disordered site; they drive toward a resistance to entropy itself.

And that drive cannot be separated from the two forces of entropy so eloquently coded into Pars's first view of the Temple of Bacchus at Teos. If his resistance to nature's encroachments on the temple's legacy seems merely fanciful, then his resistance to the Ottoman recycling of the materials confirms the stadial logic of much of the Society of Dilettanti's work.

What we need to recognize is that the rhetorical force of the reconstitution of the temple in Revett's drawings relies on the repeated destruction so vividly captured in Pars's views. Their dialectical relationship keeps reactivating pain and

Figure 48. Headpiece to chapter 2 of *Ionian Antiquities* (1769), engraving after a water-color by William Pars. Courtesy of the Getty Research Institute, Los Angeles.

pleasure, entropy and ideal order, and Chandler's commentary simply emphasizes that the reader's desire for Beauty is genealogically tied to the fact of its loss. Significantly the subsequent chapters do not present reconstructions of the other three temples. The Temple of Bacchus at Teos becomes an imagined—or, more accurately, an imaginary—touchstone as the book—like the marbles turned to gravestones—turns more doggedly to bits and pieces. This is signaled by the headpiece image to the second chapter, a beautiful rendering of a pair of capitals emerging from the ground (Figure 48). Half-buried, half-revealed, these marbles have a forlorn quality that is no less powerful than the subsequent view of the dilapidated site of the Temple of Minerva at Priene (Figure 49). If the latter image reactivates the sense of entropy temporarily put on hold by Revett's elevations and drawings, then the former does something subtly different. There are no figures here and no obvious signs of death as in the headpiece to chapter 1 (see Figure 44), but the perfectly matching swirls of the fragments instill a compositional balance that mimics the kind of order that characterizes the temple's architecture. In other words, the precarious inductive argument regarding the reconstruction of the Temple of Bacchus is replaced here by a deductive explication quite literally grounded in these capitals. It is no surprise therefore that Revett's reconstitution shifts from the building to these elements strewn about the site. I would argue that this goes one step further to fetishize that which remains both for its connection to the past structure and for its capacity to ground ideals whose realizations can only lie in the future. In other words, the same dialectic articulated in

Figure 49. *The Temple of Minerva at Priene*, chapter 2, plate 1, in *Ionian Antiquities* (1769), engraving after watercolor by William Pars. Courtesy of the Getty Research Institute, Los Angeles.

the first chapter between site and "building" is being compressed into one's relation to each individual fragment.

This points toward a progressively auratic relation to the fragments that actually runs counter to the ostensible empiricism of *Ionian Antiquities*. This is borne out in the headpiece image to chapter 3, which suddenly zeroes in on one of the carved images in a frieze at the Temple of Apollo Didymaeus near Miletus (Figure 50). With the knowledge that the ancients worshipped temple images, the presentation of this image brings us closer and closer to pagan religious practice, only now the cultic relation to the object is being absorbed into the aesthetic relation itself. Significantly, Pars's primary view of the temple represents a different religious practice (Figure 51). The Ottoman man heeding the call to prayer is involved in an act that separates him not only from the ruin in the background but also from the secular gaze of the observer in front of the image. But this is more than a derogation of Muslim superstition or fanaticism. The overall project of *Ionian Antiquities* seems to drive through empirical observation toward a fetishization of the bits and pieces of antiquity strewn about these sites. The resulting aestheticization of the past acts as a bulwark against the increasing secularization of eighteenth-century life. If we follow Weber and describe modernity as "the disenchantment of the world," then the dialectical process that I have been charting in the *Ionian Antiquities* amounts to a process of re-enchantment, an attempt to cling to the last vestiges of belief in the face of entropic death. As the viewer looks past the praying Ottoman to the ruins of

Figure 50. Headpiece to chapter 3 of *Ionian Antiquities*, engraving after a watercolor by William Pars. Courtesy of the Getty Research Institute, Los Angeles.

Figure 51. *View of the End of the Ruin of the Temple*, chapter 3, plate 2, in *Ionian Antiquities* (1769), engraving after watercolor by William Pars. Courtesy of the Getty Research Institute, Los Angeles.

the temple and feels the desire to reconstitute the ideal of Greek culture, he or she is always already involved in the central dilemma of modern art.

In part because of its subject matter and in part because if its historical situation, *Ionian Antiquities* offers a surprising glimpse of the stakes that attended the emergence of modernity not only in Europe but in the Ottoman Empire as well.[62] I don't think it is difficult to see the desire for auratic art at play in *Ionian Antiquities*. In fact, the flow from chapter to chapter not only pushes toward an increasingly autonomous art object but also moves toward an idealization of the viewing subject that will be realized in a fantasy of pure artistic spirit. The theorization of this in terms of Liberty's historical realization is in line with Douglas Fordham's argument regarding the links between artistic autonomy and British imperial politics in the wake of the Seven Years' War. But the Ionian corpus also signals the fragility of this aesthetic and political fantasy. Chandler's explicit statement that the liberty of imagination is necessary in the face of desolation is a remarkably prescient observation because within a few years the confidence that characterized British imperial policy and its aesthetic program at the Royal Academy would be interrupted by the forceful deployment of Liberty in the cause of American decolonization. As we will see in the ensuing chapters, the necessary realignment of the cultural patrimony in the wake of the American war would have an extraordinary impact not only on the imagination of the "East," but also on the deployment of antiquity.[63] For the moment, it is enough to recognize that Pars's ruthless act of witnessing—for that is what it is—elicits a departure from the present that paradoxically amounts to a future directed nostalgia. At a great distance from London, the epicenter of a dominant imperial power on the brink of capitalist modernity, Pars, Revett, and Chandler were faced with the prospect of permanent disconnection from the past. *Ionian Antiquities* is symptomatic of how that fearsome prospect could generate a leap forward whose legacy remains ambiguous because incomplete. One thread of this will lead not only to the actual architectural and artistic commissions in Great Britain and Europe that Jason Kelly tracks in his study, but also to a series of French interventions that will come to haunt British philhellenic and Orientalist fantasy. But another thread leads to somewhere far more dangerous and strange: to war in the region and to Chandler's 1775 account of the expedition in *Travels to Asia Minor*. This latter thread demands that we pay closer attention to the Ottoman Empire's complex struggle with modernization.

War Without End

By the time Pars's pictures were shown at the Royal Academy and *Ionian Antiquities* was in circulation, Britons would have been well aware that the region explored by the Ionian expedition was now a war zone. If anything, the ruins were in a more precarious situation. The Russian invasion in 1768 was well reported in all of the daily papers, but some Britons would have had a much more immediate sense of what was happening in western regions of the Ottoman Empire because prominent British veterans of the Seven Years' War were enlisted in the Russian cause.[64] At the same time that Pars's paintings were hanging in the Royal Academy exhibition, John Elphinston accepted a commission as a rear admiral in the Russian navy. Elphinston was an officer of exceptional merit who was raised in a naval family. During the Seven Years' War he advanced rapidly. He served under Lord Howe at St. Malo, Cherbourg, and St. Cas. He was taken captive at St. Cas, but returned to service after a prisoner exchange in time to play a prominent role in the capture of Quebec in 1760. His greatest successes came in the Caribbean campaign the following spring. His survey of the Old Bahama Passage allowed the British fleet to surprise the Spanish, and he then assisted Admiral Pocock in the successful siege of Havana.

Unlike the Society of Dilettanti, the Royal Navy came out of the Seven Years' War in a state of debt. The financial strains caused by the war would put extraordinary pressure on the ministry and would eventually precipitate the American crisis. As it had for many other veterans, the Peace of Paris led to a serious setback in Elphinston's career. Without the proper connections, even an officer of his distinction was quickly moved to half pay. When the Russians came calling in 1769, Elphinston and a number of other officers and seamen in the Royal Navy returned to active service under a different flag. It might be hyperbolic to say that the infusion of British expertise was a decisive factor in the Russo-Turkish War of 1768–74, but there is no doubt that Elphinstone and other British naval officers and seamen brought modern tactical thinking to the moribund Russian navy. As we will see, an account of one of his officers of the obliteration of the Ottoman fleet at the Battle of Çeşme is severely critical of the Russian fleet and its command, and in many ways it is centrally concerned with showing how British influence accelerated Russia's development into a modern naval power. *An Authentic Narrative of the Russian Expedition Against the Turks by Sea and Land* was published in London in 1772, and its narrative strategies bear comparison to accounts of the Society of Dilettanti's far less bellicose expedition to the same regions of the Ionian coast. As opposed to the Society of Dilettanti publications' subtle engagement with modernity, the question of modernization factors into the *Authentic Narrative* quite directly, and I believe it establishes an important vantage point for understanding Chandler's treatment of war, art, and antiquity in his *Travels in Asia Minor*.

The unnamed British naval officer's narrative opens with an account of the outbreak of war between Russia and the Ottoman Empire, and as one might expect from a mercenary working for Russians, its praise of Catherine the Great's objectives are unbounded. The war broke out in Poland, but Catherine decided to open a second front in the war by sending the Baltic fleet under the joint command of Vice Admiral Grigory Spiridov and Rear Admiral Elphinston to the Mediterranean where, under the command of Count Aleksey Orlov, a further campaign was to be conducted on sea and land in the islands and coastal regions of the Ionian coast. Significantly, the *Authentic Narrative* introduces the campaign in terms that resonate with British imperial discourse:

> Whilst her Majesty thus succoured her friends the Poles, and carried the terror of arms farther into the heart of the Turkish dominions by land, than any of her predecessors; she formed the design of sending her fleets from Petersburgh, on the north-east extremity of the Baltic Sea, into the Mediterranean, and up the Levant.
>
> The design was great, and worthy of her.
>
> All Europe was surprized and alarmed at seeing, for the first time the Russian flag flying among the islands of the Archipelago, chacing the Turkish marine, and inviting their miserable tributaries the Greeks, to arms and liberty.[65]

This restylization of territorial aggression as war to liberate Greece from Ottoman oppression is a persistent theme. But the British officer's self-serving representation of British subjects joining Catherine in the propagation of liberty dissolves quite quickly in favor of a different self-justification. *The Authentic Narrative* gives a detailed account of how the Russians destroyed the Turkish fleet in the Bay of Çeşme in spite of the outdated ships and the obsolete tactics of his Russian colleagues. Their success, according to the *Narrative*'s author, only came after Spiridov and Orlov adopted Elphinston's tactical innovations, and it was the various British officers and seamen employed in the firing of the ships who ensured the Russian victory.

The accuracy of this account has been contested, especially by Russian historians.[66] But I am much more interested in the way that the author builds his story, because he does so in a fashion that subtly links contemporary Britons—including himself—with the ancient Greeks. In the process, he not only separates himself from both Russians and Ottomans, but he also aestheticizes the entire theater of war. On the way from the Baltic to Portsmouth, where Elphinston has some of his ships repaired, the narrator indicates that Elphinston had concerns that the Russians under his command may be more committed to pleasure than war. By the time the fleet reaches the Aegean, it is clear that the relationship between Elphinston and Spiridov has devolved into a dysfunctional rivalry and that

Spiridov does everything in his power to undermine Elphiston's orders. But when the Russian fleet reaches Paros, the author of the *Narrative* mobilizes a powerful metaphor for the entire operation:

> The town of Paros is seated on the western coast of the island. . . . It was anciently famous for the uncommon fineness of its marble, and received additional lustre from the labours of two of its natives, Phidias and Prax-itelles, who were the most celebrated statuaries in the world.
>
> The town retains nothing of its former grandeur, and yet, like beauty in distress, it excites our particular regard: we cannot see without regret the many noble pieces of sculpture, consisting of basso-relievos, altars, &c. disgraced by serving as common fences to their fields, or to patch up their poor inconvenient habitations. (47–48)

This sudden invocation of classical antiquity and the suggestion that he is now protecting "a beauty in distress" instantiates a gendered discourse of honor and duty to preserve the remains of antiquity from the disgraceful neglect of the subjected contemporary Greek population. But it is striking that his final sentence could almost come verbatim from Revett or Chandler.

This would amount to little more than another derogation of Ottoman rule and Greek subjection except that this account of subsequent actions emphasizes that the Russians under Elphinston's command are little different from the Ottomans. This is in some degrees surprising because the Battle of Çeşme is figured as a repetition of the Holy League's epochal naval victory over the Ottomans at Lepanto two hundred years earlier. As the author states at the climax of his narrative of the battle, "The moment was now arrived when the Russian cross was finally to triumph over the Turkish crescent!" (76). Rendering the conflict as a clash of civilizations and, more important, as a religious confrontation is both typical of accounts of Lepanto and strangely out of step with the events. In this case the Russians were the aggressors and the Ottomans were trying check their advances through the Mediterranean. But I believe Lepanto figures here because the narrative subtly implies that the combat follows historically obsolete patterns and protocols. In other words, narrating this battle requires that one step back in time to a period when shipboard hand-to-hand combat was a prominent strategic concern in naval warfare. This retroactive gesture effectively portrays two naval forces and two imperial cultures mired in obsolescence. In this context, the Russians and the Ottomans are distinguished by their access to the modernizing influence of Elphinston, Samuel Greig, and other British sailors, whose "innovations," primarily the use of fire ships, are themselves based on strategic developments perfected in the seventeenth century. Significantly, this doesn't involve an argument for Russian technological superiority. Rather everything turns on the decisions and conduct of the veterans of the Royal Navy.[67]

The author of *An Authentic Narrative* breaks his account of the Battle of Çeşme into two radically different episodes. The first focuses on the Russian attack on the Turkish fleet on 7 July 1770 as it "lay at anchor in a line of battle, a little above the north entrance of Schisma bay, which is opposite to, and about four leagues from Scio[68] town" (53). After indicating that Ottomans had neglected to raise batteries on shore and thus gave up their immediate advantage, the author reports that Elphinston went to Orlov with detailed plans of attack that would minimize the potential for reverses against the Russian fleet. Orlov and Spiridov rejected Elphinston's tactical suggestions in favor of a plan that would bring both fleets into close proximity. The ensuing narrative is a horrifying account of the results of that decision. Within a paragraph, Spiridov and the kapudan pasha or grand admiral's ships are fully disabled, but cabled together:

> Grappled they fought hand to hand, for fifteen minutes; when a column of flame and smoak burst from the Turkish admiral's starboard-quarter-gallery; in a moment what dreadful confusion? the stoutest hearts among them now trembled. The fire increased every moment on board the Bashaw's ship, and with irresistible fury fired the rigging, mast, &c. of admiral Spiritdoff's ship.
>
> The crews of both, equally exposed to the same calamity, forgot their animosities, suspended firing on each other, and were only intent on how to escape those dreadful elements fire and water. (62–63)

This narrative is notable above all for its extended account of how panic accelerates through the scene, instantiating indiscriminate destruction and barbarity on all sides. A company of cuirassiers aboard Spiridov's ship is "cut to pieces by the Turks," and this prompts the Russians to kill Turks in the water fleeing the burning ships (66–67).

Perhaps the most remarkable thing about this account is the fact that the narrator devotes a scant paragraph to the ill-conduct of the Ottomans—it is perhaps merely expected—as opposed to five full pages on the barbarism of the Russian survivors killing the noble captain of the kapudan pasha's ship. In the text's most sentimental moment, the narrator underlines the emotional exchange of respectful glances between himself and the captain, first, as he attempts to save the man from the water and, second, as the man is shot against Elphinston's orders. As the narrator states, "All my soul was shocked at this more than savage insensibility. I was greatly distressed lest he should think I had betrayed him; but my anxiety was soon removed—I saw him again, and kept my eyes fixed upon him—he kissed his hand once more, and gave me every other proof in his power . . . that he was sensible how desirious I was of saving him" (71). This narrative of Russian savagery is deployed for very specific reasons. The tactical errors of Orlov and Spiridov had led to chaos, and chaos instantiated a devolution in character, a stripping away of humanity and honor. In this regard, military strategy becomes intimately tied to the capacity for humanity, and in this narrative that capacity is what separates the British narrator from both the Russians and the Ottomans.[69]

This complex representation of chaotic strategic failure and the barbarism of combat sets the stage for the second episode in the Battle of Çeşme. Both episodes are horrifying, but the terror conveyed serves different ideological purposes. This is altogether more visible because the chief source of terror—fire—is represented in such radically different ways. After the first encounter at the mouth of the Bay of Çeşme, the Ottomans retreated into the bay, and their entire fleet was closely contained. Elphinston and Samuel Greig advocated the use of fire ships to destroy the fleet, and the Russians allowed them to take the lead. The result was a universal destruction of the entire fleet and the death of between 9,000 and 11,000 Ottoman sailors and soldiers. As opposed to the chaos of the far less consequential first encounter, the second is susceptible to a very particular aestheticization:

> A fleet consisting of two hundred sail, almost in one general blaze, presented a picture of distress and horror, dreadfully sublime!
>
> This description will convey but a faint idea of the catastrophe of the Turkish fleet. While the flames with utmost rapidity were spreading destruction on all sides, and ship blowing up after ship, with every soul on board that feared to trust the waves to swim for shore, the Russians kept pouring upon them such showers of cannon balls, shells, and small-shot, that not one of the many thousands of their weeping friends on land, who saw their distress, dared venture to their relief!
>
> Nothing now remained but united shrieks and unavailing cries, which, joined to the martial music, and the loud triumphant shouts of the victors, served to swell alternately the various notes of joy and sorrow, that composed the solemn dirge of their departing glory. (78–79)

The distinction I have been sketching between the blend of chaos and sentimental attachment of the first encounter and the detached invocation of the sublime to render the conflagration of the Ottoman fleet as a kind of death fugue has two primary consequences. First, the narrative distinction between the two episodes allows the author to make the Battle of Çeşme a victory for modernity itself, not because of any particular technological advantage, but because it was an act of calculated reason. Second, this claim is bolstered by the aestheticization because this sublime fugue takes the horror of the first episode and meticulously reorganizes it such that enough purchase is granted to recognize the world-historical import of the victory. From this sublime distance, the particular strains of sound, horrific in their singularity, are rhetorically woven, but not seamlessly blended, into a complex harmonic entity. As an aesthetic figure for incipient modernity, the fugue both tames chaos and unleashes its full emotional power to resignify mass death as "departing glory." And it is important to recognize that that which is departing is no longer a group of people. It is now an era, and thus worthy of commemoration.

However, this assertion of modernity's ascendance is immediately undercut. As soon as the battle is concluded, Elphinston recommends that the Russians proceed immediately to the Dardanelles and assault Constantinople. Strategically he wants to capitalize on the panic generated by the defeat in order to complete Catherine's "liberal" plan. But his suggestions are dashed on religious grounds. The Greek Orthodox clergy who come out to celebrate the victory convince Orlov that "this day must be kept as a thanksgiving, and that the following must also be celebrated as a high festival" (87). Superstition rears up and momentarily stops the progress of enlightenment warfare. Although the author goes on to argue that the Russians ultimately chose to only blockade the Dardanelles, there is something about his presentation of the Russian hesitancy that suggests that they have not fully entered the secular world of total war. The remainder of the narrative painfully recounts how the Russians repeatedly fail to take the initiative and how the war fizzles out. In general, the author treats this hesitancy with scorn, but at times he also elegizes a passing world of honor and nobility.

This is a curious way of handling what was to be a resounding territorial and diplomatic victory over the Ottomans, and it is intriguing to look at how the author becomes fixated on scenes of martial obsolescence. It is as though blocked from pursuing the cause of liberty and capitalist modernity to the fullest, the *Narrative*'s author has room to register the passing of forms of honorable conduct that would find themselves replaced by the technocratic calculation of firepower and logistics. The first accords nobility to an Ottoman spahi, or cavalry officer, but firmly demonstrates how his nobility is aside from the point:

> We perceived an officer very richly dressed and finely mounted, endeavouring to rally them, and make them stand their ground: and notwithstanding the briskness of our fire, he continued galloping from one end of their front line to the other with great spirit. I wished him in a less dangerous situation. We loaded one of our bow-chaces with round ball and langrege shot, and looking on this gallant officer as the life of their whole force, the fatal minute being come, we fired, and the thundering messenger executed

the commission; for as soon as the smoke cleared up, I saw with that concern and pity, inseparable from humanity, his horse lying dead, and about twenty of his men carrying him off dangerously wounded. (104–5)

In the process of elegizing the Ottoman spahi, the narrator turns the entire killing into an occasion for the assertion of his own humanity. The quick and effortless passage from the rational calculation of the Ottoman's death and the declaration of pity is chilling.

A similar ascription of humanity is accorded to Count Orlov, only this time it folds into an Orientalist fantasy of protection. In response to their horrible defeat at sea, the Ottomans, according to the author, go on a killing spree in Smyrna. The fear of reprisals becomes a significant obstacle to Russian attempts to foment rebellion among the Greeks. In a gesture that resonates with the previously stated desire to preserve the beauty of Paros, Orlov saves a beautiful female captive and returns her to the Ottomans "to convince the Turks, that by such actions he wished to inspire them with the like sentiments of honour and humanity, and convince them that the true hero is greater, when treating the vanquished with generous pity, than in dealing destruction to his enemies in the field. Such was Scipio of Rome, who first convinced the proud Carthaginians, that they were not invincible" (112). In light of the manifest inhumanity of the Russians elsewhere in the narrative, the narrator's move here is concerned primarily with recuperating the Russian action for a view of modern Europe. But the recourse to classical examples is significant. Lines of affiliation are being drawn first between Scipio, Orlov, and Elphinston but secondarily between Catherine, her British allies, and the Roman republic. But more important, it is Scipio's amalgam of strategic acumen and philhellenic qualities that signifies here. What Elphinston, Orlov, and Catherine ostensibly share is a type of republican virtue exemplified by clemency and a commitment to British liberty. It is precisely the fantasy of virtue that J. G. A. Pocock has carefully tracked through eighteenth-century British political discourse and that would come under such intense pressure during the American crisis.[70]

In that regard, the rhetorical strain that comes from reconfiguring the Russian victory at Çeşme as a sign of a British veteran's capacity to see the broad historical ties between the ancient Greek polity and the ascendance of British political enlightenment in a new global empire is manifest. Ultimately, the struggle of the author of *An Authentic Narrative* to maintain the majority of Russian combatants and the entire Ottoman Empire as premodern—even barbarian—reads more like an anxious attempt to shore up the crumbling notion of honor that heretofore had structured elite British political and military life. In this light, the very real chaos unleashed in the combat scenes is immediately tied to the increasing deployment of incendiary weapons—weapons designed to instill fear and panic in the enemy.

What is so important here is that the same weapons of technological modernity activate a more subtle and less immediate fear, a fear that enlightenment war constitutes a decisive break from the social codes that were so crucial to maintaining the fabric of past and present empires. This, of course, includes the Ottoman Empire and that is why the scene of the murdered spahi is so important, because it marks a moment of irrevocable change, or more specifically, a sign of the future. In the case of the Ottomans, the necessity of reorganizing the military and the state would not be fully realized until the 1820s. For the British, the American crisis and the French Revolutionary Wars would permanently alter the military-state complex. For the Russians, the Battle of Çeşme and the ensuing military victories in the Balkans and the Crimea would consolidate the forces propelling it into modern statehood.[71]

Modernity's Scourge

The defeat of the Ottoman navy at Çeşme was followed by serious reverses for the Ottoman army at the Battle of Larga and the Battle of Kartal. After 1770 the Ottoman military was well on the defensive. To make matters worse, the Porte was dealing with rebellions in Egypt and Syria and territorial threats from Persia. Facing this panoply of disadvantages, the Ottomans signed the Treaty of Küçük Kaynarca on 21 July 1774 and under the terms of the treaty lost control of the Crimean Khanate and of the ports of Azov and Kilburun in the Black Sea.[72] The treaty provisions provided numerous opportunities for the Russians to resume hostilities against the Ottomans, and thus it is, perhaps, more accurate to see this as an intentionally temporary peace designed to give the Russians every advantage for a continued policy of conquest. We will be following that policy forward in time in the next two chapters, but I want to conclude this chapter in the period immediately following the end of the Russo-Turkish War and immediately prior to the onset of war between Britain and the American colonies.

Chandler's *Travels in Asia Minor* was published in 1775, shortly after the end of the Russo-Turkish War and just prior to the American crisis. The former fact is registered explicitly in Chandler's text and, I believe, has a significant impact on how we comprehend the legacy of the Ionian expedition: "We had been told that at Chismé, a town since noted for the destruction of the Turkish navy by the Russians, and distant about five hours from Erythrae, were spatious and handsome baths erected by the Genoese. We had intended seeing them, but were now informed that the place was almost abandoned, the plague having been carried thither from Scio" (94). Chandler's cursory remark is the only indication that the regions explored by the expedition have since been embroiled in a major war, and it is worth asking why this issue emerges at all. After all, the narrative focuses on events prior to the war's onset, and it is most concerned with the remnants of the distant past. But I would argue that this affectless historical note provides the key to comprehending a series of narrative obsessions in Chandler's text. On the one hand, Chandler's travel narrative allows us to situate the activities of Pars, Revett, and Chandler as it moves around coastal Anatolia; but on the other hand, Chandler's narrative does not so much contextualize their activities as reimagine the significance of archaeological observation for a postwar era.

The world Chandler is addressing is caught between one theater of war and another, and as we will see, that has a significant effect on the rhetorical structure of *Travels in Asia Minor*. But the text's relation to the question of modernity is perhaps most nakedly presented in its discomfort with the present. That is manifest in the distancing techniques used to contain most representations of intercultural exchange in the narrative. But there are moments when Chandler is remarkably direct in his derogation of commercial progress. As he states early in the narrative with regard to the impact of Ottoman imperial society, "Prosperity is less friendly to antiquity than desertion and depopulation" (53). This is less of an expression of desire for a depopulation of the region—although that would be one genocidal extrapolation of the text's derogation of Ottoman culture—than it is a recognition that prosperity, however inadvertently, destroys those elements of the past on the horizon of the Dilettanti's interest. Modernity is itself an agent of entropy, and whether one is considering the Ottoman's difficult transition to a modern empire or the model of enlightenment expressed in the Dilettanti publications, modernity can't be fully separated from the damage it incurs. Significantly, Chandler is cognizant that this process is taking place in both worlds as it were: in the world of the British observers and in the society of the Ottomans they encounter along the way.

Ostensibly designed to take the reader from archaeological site to archaeological site according to the itinerary of the voyage, *Travels in Asia Minor* is closely pegged to specific dates and precise locations on the map helpfully provided as a frontispiece to the text. But Chandler's text overflows this strict narrative itinerary and his ethnographic and historical effusions operate as a counter-discourse that ultimately undermines the ostensible empirical purpose of the text. What this means is that Chandler's narrative intensifies the precarious sense of entropy that permeates Pars's views and that Revett's drawings had aspired to contain in *Ionian Antiquities*. If anything, the historical problems posed by modernity that we have been charting both in the Society of Dilettanti publications and in *An Authentic Narrative* become even more vexed in *Travels in Asia Minor*, and we begin to see counter-enlightenment investigations of pagan worship, magic, and enchantment. What I wish to suggest in the final section of the chapter is that Chandler's narrative undoes the temporary equipoise achieved in *Ionian Antiquities* and projects his readers into a historical condition whose only consolations lie, on the one hand, in the realm of aesthetic contemplation and appropriation, and, on the other, in a very different set of ethnographic fantasies than those encountered thus far. Significantly, this is achieved primarily in places not publicly represented by Pars and Revett in 1769.

However, before turning to these regions and experiences, this section considers how Chandler supplements the information already in circulation. Chandler's treatment of the four sites discussed in *Ionian Antiquities* is both perfunctory and revealing: "The temple of Bacchus at Teos was one of the most celebrated structures in Ionia. The remains of it have been engraved at the expense of the society of Dilettanti, and published, with its history, in the *Ionian Antiquities*; and a beautiful Portico has since been erected at the seat of the Right Hon. Lord Le Despenser, near High-Wykeham, under the inspection of Mr. Revett, in which the exact proportions of the order are observed" (98). The shifting verb tenses of these three sentences very clearly manifest the objectives of the Ionian expedition: there was something important on this site, its remains have been salvaged, and it has since been reconstituted here in England. But significantly, that which has been salvaged and reconstituted is not material, but rather ideational. If we recall Chandler's remark in *Ionian Antiquities* that the design of the temple could only be presented as a provisional and tendentious work of the imagination, then it becomes apparent that the significance of the site was established from classical literature well before the expedition departed, the fantasy of the building was articulated after the expedition returned in the engraving of Revett's supposed elevation, and the new building near High-Wykeham (High Wycombe) will have clinched the entire phantasmatic revivification by the time Chandler writes his narrative.

This process is accompanied by a descriptive passage that acts as a contrast to the productivity of the previous paragraph: "The town has long been deserted. It has no ruins of churches, to prove it existed under the Greek emperors; nor of mosques or baths, to show it was frequented by the Turks. In the time of Anacreon, the Teians migrated from a love of liberty to Thrace, but some afterwards came back, and the city re-flourished. They are now utterly gone, and it is likely never to return. The site is a wilderness; and the low grounds, which are wet, produce the iris or flag, blue and white" (98). In many ways, this is the textual cognate to Pars's representation of historical dissolution and desolation. Even the more recent presence of Byzantine and Ottoman populations has been erased by the inexorable flow of time. But significantly, this sense of natural succession is supplemented, much like Pars's headpiece image of the temple ruin, by a resonant figure for Ottoman neglect: "The master of a Venetian scow, in the harbour at Segigeck, furnished us with a small quantity of wine, but of a poor quality; otherwise we should have drank only water on a spot once sacred to Bacchus, and able to supply a Roman fleet. The grave Turk, its present owner, predestines the clusters of the few vines it now bears, for his food, when ripened; or to be dried in the sun, as raisins, for sale" (99). Limited agricultural productivity is seen as a poor contrast to the remarkable achievement of Revett's portico at High-Wykeham. The satirical knife is turned one step further by the implicit suggestion that this amounts to a failure of the imagination on the Ottoman's part: because he does not know or care that these grapes were sacred to Bacchus and supplied a Roman fleet, he gets to trade in raisins—their withered counterparts—rather than exult in the culture of the Dionysiasts documented in the ensuing pages of Chandler's text or rule over the Mediterranean like the Romans. When we remember that Chandler has just informed the reader of the Ottoman loss at the Battle of Çeşme, this latter point is aimed explicitly at marking the waning influence of the Ottomans in the region.

Rhetorically, Chandler's brief account of the Temple of Bacchus at Teos replicates both the dialectical structure of Pars's and Revett's visualization of the site and the ethnocentric deployment of Ottoman figures in *Ionian Antiquities*. Likewise, his brief remarks on the Temple of Apollo Didymaeus pursues a similar aestheticization of the actual fragments on the ground as that discussed above in the third section of this chapter, but here something goes awry:

> The memory of the pleasure, which this spot afforded me, will not be soon or easily erased. The columns yet entire are so exquisitely fine, the marble mass so vast and noble, that it is impossible perhaps to conceive great beauty and majesty of ruin. At evening a large flock of goats, returning to the fold, their bells tinkling, spread over the heap, climbing to browse on the shrubs and trees growing between the huge stones. The whole mass was illuminated by the declining sun with a variety of rich tints, and cast a very strong shade. The sea, at a distance, was smooth and shining, bordered by a mountainous coast, with rocky islands. The picture was as delicious as striking. A view of part of the heap, with plates of the architecture of this glorious edifice, has been engraved and published at the expense of the society of Dilettanti. (151–52)

What is so striking here is that Chandler's "picture," for all of its invocation of the pastoral and the picturesque, is precisely what is not presented in *Ionian Antiquities*. In the 1769 publication we get extremely close-up renderings of specific ornaments; the only thing transferred over from Pars's images in the earlier publication to *Travels in Asia Minor*—aside from a lone pasturing animal—is the strong sense of dramatic lighting.[73]

But that lighting has significance in itself because the descending darkness is matched by an explicit invocation of death—first of a civilization, but then more troublingly of some unnamed person. "We found among the ruins, which are extensive, a plain stone cistern; many marble sarcophagi, some unopened, and one in which was a thigh bone, sunk deep in earth; with five statues, near each other, in a row, almost buried" (152). This scene operates like an emblem for the book as a whole, because nestled within the remains of ancient civilization one finds indexical signs of life. Just as Revett imaginatively reconstitutes the Temple of Bacchus from its scattered remains, Chandler restores flesh, and then spirit, to this wayward bone, but the way that he does this is remarkable for its incorporation of the ethnographic subjects so contemptuously handled elsewhere in the narrative.

It turns out that the goats browsing through the temple ruins are—as Pars's picture might lead us to believe—crucial, because they are an extension of the goat-herds who repeatedly offer hospitality to the expedition party. After surveying the Temple of Apollo Didymaeus, Chandler's narrative focuses on the journey to Priene, where the expedition will eventually explore the Temple of Minerva. But because the text is recording multiple excursions from Smyrna and because it gets quite digressive, the transit between these two sites is quite confusing. That confusion is matched by an account of getting lost on the way: "We were benighted, and perplexed, the track not being distinguishable, though the moon began to shine" (156). Thirsty and exhausted and scared by barking dogs, the party is rescued:

> Deceived by the light of the moon, we now fancied we could see a village, and were much mortified to find only a station of poor goat-herds, without even a shed, and nothing for our horses to eat. They were lying, wrapped in their thick capots or loose coats, by some glimmering embers among the bushes in a dale, under a spreading tree by the fold. They received us hospitably, heaping on fresh fewel, and producing Caimac or sour curds, and coarse bread, which they toasted for us on the coals. We made a scanty meal sitting on the ground, lighted by the fire and the moon; after which sleep suddenly overpowered me. (157)

This is one of many scenes of hospitality in the *Travels*, but any sense that this is a pastoral scene is immediately curtailed:

> On waking I found my two companions by my side, sharing in the comfortable cover of the janizary's cloke, which he had carefully spread over us. I was now much struck by the wild appearance of the spot. The tree was hung with rustic utensils; the she-goats in a pen sneezed, and bleated,

and rustled to and fro; the shrubs, by which our horses stood, were leaf-
less, and the earth bare; a black caldron with milk was simmering over the
fire; and a figure more ghaunt or savage, close by us, struggling on the
ground with a kid, whose ears he had slit and was endeavouring to cauter-
ize with a piece of red hot iron. (157)

This encounter is richly presented. The janissary's intimate care for the Europeans is signaled. The generosity of the goatherds, especially in light of their manifest poverty, is specifically recorded. The scene of care—for that is what it is—is
made even more powerful by the sense of desolation and the barrenness of the
landscape. But how are we to interpret the "savage" figure at the conclusion of
the passage? At one level, he is a representative of a primitive society, but at another level his concerns are with animal life, with survival in this harsh world.

That figure turns out to be a harbinger of sorts because the rest of the narrative
returns again and again to the problem of survival, to the project of living in this
world, and the perplexing issue of death. I use the word "perplexing" here advisedly, because death's finality keeps reasserting itself in the face of the Dilettanti's
desire for revivification. Significantly, this reassertion comes not from the ruins or
from the bones of the long dead, but from those recently deceased or on the verge
of passing from this life. The last eight chapters of the text are literally overwhelmed by the threat of the plague, and the narrative is caught in a state of in-
ertia. But prior to this, as the expedition moves farther away from the coast,
security becomes of paramount concern. I have already detailed the arrest and the
terror of the party's janissary Mustapha. His humiliation by the ağa is a precursor to
the far more dangerous conflict with a different ağa near Pammukale whose threats
curtail the expedition's exploration of Hierapolis. The ağa's disrespect for the firman that accords the expedition protection on its travels is an act of open rebellion that not only forces the party to retreat to the plague-ridden vicinity of
Smyrna, but also demonstrates that the sultan's control of the region is precarious. It is precisely this fracturing of the Ottoman polity that the Russians hoped
to exploit in their Mediterranean mission five years later. Even though the mass
death of Ottoman sailors at Çeşme happens after the time of the story, its prolep-
tic insertion at a midpoint in the narrative casts a salient shadow on the entire
text, but especially on its later events. The narrative brings the Ottoman dead
from the future and makes their presence felt in an earlier historical moment,
thereby giving the sense that events in 1764–65 are leading inexorably to the catastrophe of 1770. Thus the narration of the waning of the janissary's influence is
emblematic of a vulnerability overlooked by many prior to the success of the Russians in the early 1770s. At one level this resonates with much of the narrative's
investment in Ottoman decline, but there is a further overtone that implicitly

speaks to the condition of a British writer contemplating the cyclical quality of empires in 1775.

The Enchantment of the World

This strangely prophetic turn in the narrative takes various forms, but it unfolds with most intensity in relation to sites and encounters not represented in *Ionian Antiquities* or in the paintings exhibited at the Royal Academy in 1769. Pars took views of these sites, but they remained in obscurity until the 1797 publication of the second volume of the *Antiquities of Ionia*.[74] I want to look at three scenes where the present and the ancient past are brought immediately and uncomfortably adjacent to one another. As Joan Coutu has argued with regard to antiquarian collecting more generally, "the desire and attempt to juxtapose the classical and the modern or to invest the modern with the classical is entirely consistent with the mid-century generation's acknowledgment of the temporal distancing of the classical past while at the same time, paradoxically, eliding that temporality."[75] This temporal paradox is evident in Chandler, but the scenes where the distant past collapses into the present moment are suffused with affect and thus far more concerned with questions of subjectivity and sociability than the more documentary elements of the text. In these scenes of intercultural exchange, Chandler is confronted with intense expressions of emotion that elicit symptomatic strategies of displacement in the narrative.

If we return to the itinerary of the expedition published in the preface of *Ionian Antiquities*, we discover that the first encounter with the ruins of antiquity would have been extremely familiar. In early September of 1764, before meeting the British consul at Smyrna and receiving the sultan's firman, Chandler, Pars, and Revett explored the Sigeion Promontory and the ruins at Alexandria Troas. One of Pars's earliest drawings on the Ionian expedition was a careful rendering of the very metope that played such a key role in Lady Mary Wortley Montagu's melancholic account of the effects of war. This drawing became the first engraving that the reader encountered in *Ionian Antiquities* (Figure 52).[76] This is significant because her account of these sites was published less than a year before the expedition's departure and Pars, in a way, starts where she left off. It is not a huge step from Montagu's haunting evocation of this sculpture and Pars's entropic tendencies. Likewise, Chandler indicates that he has read her text and consulted the inscription that Edward Wortley Montagu took from Alexandria Troas and donated to Trinity College, Cambridge. As a student of inscriptions, Chandler would have been intimately familiar with the latter artifact. In other words, the expedition immediately retraces the steps of their famous British forebears. However,

Figure 52. Headpiece to preface, "To the Reader," *Ionian Antiquities* (1769), engraving after William Pars's drawings of metope at Alexandria Troas. Courtesy of the Getty Research Institute, Los Angeles.

Chandler is doing more than commemorating this earlier visit. Like Pars, he both amplifies the sense of overall destruction—"Confusion cannot easily be described" (27)—and condenses the dynamic relation between past and present already articulated in Lady Mary's letters.

As with Montagu's account of her sojourn with Achmet Beg discussed in Chapter 4, Chandler's description of the scene of hospitality outside Sigeum or Sigeion acts as a narrative threshold that first and foremost indicts Ottoman oppression:

> We left Enekioi, and landed again about midday on the beach without the Hellespont, not far from the Sigean promontory, and ascended by a steep track to Giaurkioi a Greek village, once Sigeum, high above the sea, and now resembling Enekioi in wretchedness as well as in situation. We were here accommodated with a small apartment in one of the cottages, but it required caution to avoid falling through the floor. The family to which it belonged was as poor as oppressed. The thin-voiced women scolding and howling in the court, we enquired the reason, and were told, they had paid a piaster for the privilege of keeping a hog; that the Turk, who collected this money for the Aga, demanded ten Peraus as his fee, that they were unable or unwilling to gratify him, and he was carrying the son to prison. (36)

The scene has none of the opulence and sophistication of Achmet Beg's hospitality, but in many ways the generosity of the hosts is magnified here by their manifest poverty. That poverty is clearly linked to the corruption of Turkish officials, something Montagu also carefully recorded in her account of crossing the frontiers of the Ottoman Empire.

Chandler appears to drop the Greek women's intense expressions of emotion for the incarcerated child—I think we are meant to equate incarceration with execution—but the next paragraph replays the relationship between mothers and children by deploying the same metope that also fascinated Lady Mary fifty years earlier:

> The city Sigéum stood antiently on a slope opposite to the part where we ascended. . . . A mean church . . . occupies the site of the Atheneum or temple of Minerva; of which the scattered marbles by it are remains. The famous Sigean inscription lies on the right hand, as you enter it; and on the left is part of a pedestal, of fine white marble, with sculpture in basso-relievo; of which the subject is the presentation of young children, with the accustomed offerings, to Minerva. Within the same building was found a marble, once reposited in the precincts of the temple, and now preserved in the library of Trinity college in Cambridge. (36–37)

Chandler goes on to interpret the inscription and to describe how Edward Wortley Montagu relocated the marble. At one level, this is a simple charting of provenance, but it can't help but raise the issue of Lady Mary's interpretation of the sculpture, then well in circulation. As we saw in Chapter 4, she explicitly reads the depicted scene of mothers and children in terms of mourning. By a subtle displacement, the concern for the wailing women that was discursively suppressed at the end of the previous paragraph reemerges in this intertextual relationship with Montagu's text.

Chandler is diverting some of the emotional intensity of that latter scene to face the problem of what to do about the fragments of the past in front of him. Unable to rescue the boy from the ağa's minions, Chandler calls instead for a different kind of rescue operation. After a brief excursus on the Sigean inscription, Chandler calls for the custodial care not of the boy but of the artifacts: "We copied these inscriptions very carefully, and not without deep regret, that a stone so singularly curious, which has preserved to us a specimen of writing antiquated above two thousand years ago, should be suffered to lie neglected and exposed. Above half a century has elapsed, since it was first discovered, and it still remains in the open air, a seat for the Greeks, destitute of a patron to rescue it from barbarism, and obtain its removal into the safer custody of some private museum; or, which is rather to be desired, some public repository" (39). A note in which Chandler sketches a plan for the removal of the marbles immediately follows. The language used to describe the kind of care envisaged here is striking. "Patron," "rescue," and "custody" all carry connotations of familial care. If the expedition members are powerless to resist Ottoman corruption and its palpable incursions on the lives of their Greek hosts, then the narrative argues that it may be within the power of the Society of Dilettanti, or some other such body, with the assistance of the

Levant Company, to resist the "barbarism" that threatens these orphan sculptures and inscriptions.[77] This kind of alibi for naked appropriation blandly substitutes things for humans and cynically instrumentalizes filial affect. And it is important to register how distinct this is from Lady Mary's engagement with the same issue. Having witnessed and lived through far more harrowing states of social insecurity, Lady Mary's appropriation of the classical artifacts, and the classical world in general, is limited to allegory. Allegorical substitution is a far more restrained procedure than the kind of substitution—both psychic and material—rhetorically enacted here.

That said, Chandler is not averse to narrating the actions of the expedition as rehearsals of classical narratives, or in some way connected to the observations and travels of the ancients. For example, shortly after his description of Sigeum, he venerates the ostensible barrow of Achilles and Patroclus (42). The janissary who accompanies them once the firman has been conferred is described in terms reminiscent of the *Iliad*: "our janizary was provided with a cloke of a dark colour, shaggy, and very thick, made without a seam, with a cape or rather a cowl for his head. Wrapped in this he lay down like Diomed in his bull-skin, in the open air, with his pistol and sabre by him, and his gun in his hand" (92). That this invocation of Diomedes comes immediately prior to Chandler's invocation of the Battle of Çeşme is not incidental, but it also has interesting ramifications. Aligning the janissary with the Achaean hero both ennobles him and links the Ottomans with the Achaeans. This may seem counterintuitive at first, but it is important to remember that for much of the eighteenth-century, and certainly for Pope, the Achaeans were disturbingly barbaric. If linking the janissary with Diomedes would seem to cast the Ottomans as the Achaeans and the Russians as the Trojans, this would imply that the Russian victory at Çeşme was akin to the Trojan advances on the Achaean ships. If we play this out to the end, Troy will fall—thus allegorically limiting Russian aspirations—but its heroes will be transmuted into the model of eighteenth-century imperial rule, Rome in all her glory. In addition to containing immediate Russian successes in a broader narrative of another empire's ascent, this has the salutary effect of allegorizing the Russo-Ottoman War in terms that can be subsumed into fantasies of British imperial power.

If we look at the broader context in which his remarks are embedded, then it becomes clear that Chandler's allegorical gestures are extremely unstable if not counterintuitive. This rhetorical instability precipitates a different kind of resolution, but to see this we need to look at moments where Chandler's ethnographic concerns open onto far more speculative historical displacements. As Chandler tries to imagine heathen subjectivity, it becomes evident that he longs for a re-enchantment of the world that lies broken before him. Almost immediately after the encounter with the goatherds, near the ruins at Priene, in a Greek village named Giaur-Kelibesh, Chandler's ethnographic observations reach a crescendo of sorts. Across five paragraphs we can see all the hallmarks of Chandler's ethnographic discourse, but I also think we can see something far more revealing about the ethnographer himself. After situating the reader, the text gives a typical account of the customs and manners "of the vagrant people, called Atzíncari or Zíngari, the Gypsies of the East," by describing a performance of trained apes (159). The link between animals and humans is symptomatic of a discourse of primitivism, and as the chapter unfolds each successive paragraph explores different instances of premodern superstition. The first, associated with Greek Orthodox religion, is anatomized in a fashion that highlights emotional excess and childlike cultural production. But again it is the occasion of mourning that activates Chandler's containment strategies:

> One evening, coming from the ruins, we found an old woman sitting by the church on the grave of her daughter, who had been buried about two years. She wore a black veil, and pulling the ends alternately bowed her head down to her bosom; and at the same time lamented aloud, singing in an uniform dismal cadence, with very few pauses. She continued thus above an hour, when it grew dark, fulfilling a measure of tributary sorrow, which the Greeks superstitiously believe to be acceptable and beneficial to the souls of the deceased. The next morning a man was interred, the wife following the body, tearing her long disheveled tresses in agony, calling him her life, her love, demanding the reason of his leaving her; and expostulating with him on his dying, in terms the most expressive of conjugal endearments and affection. (159–60)

This is unreason at its most naked and its most human. Chandler attempts to control the palpable emotion of the passage by casting it as superstition, but the final sentence almost grudgingly recognizes the power of love.

That power is transferred to a celebration of the resurrection in the ensuing paragraph, and it is significant that Chandler focuses the reader's attention on the intercultural exchange that occurs in this tiny village: "The Greeks now celebrated Easter. A small bier, prettily decked with orange and citron-buds, jasmine, flowers, and boughs, was placed in the church, with a Christ crucified rudely painted on board, for the body. We saw it in the evening; and before day-break were suddenly awakened by the blaze and crackling of a large bonfire, with singing and shouting in honour of the Resurrection. They made us presents of coloured eggs, and cakes of Easter-bread" (160). Chandler and the rest of the cohort are both socially and culturally separated from those around them, and this is marked by the "rudeness" of the Christ painted on the board. But the fact that they are folded into the ritual celebration of the resurrection not only implies a shared sociability but also speaks directly to the problem of the grieving woman in the previous paragraph. The resurrection offers a way of thinking through the desolation of death, and it is shared, to unequal degrees, by both communities. But significantly, the Greeks' superstition, which should make them more amenable to the consolations of religion, fails to satisfy the needs of mourning in the first instance. Chandler's enlightened Protestant position distances him from the affective investment in religious ritual, but he seems able to imagine a different form of consolation in the realm of art itself. Put bluntly, the acquisition and material transfer of antiquities will become, for Chandler and so many others, a secular but no less ritual act whose doctrine will be preservation.

But it is not the crude image of the crucifixion on the board that works on Chandler but rather a remarkable aestheticization of the natural world that is contingent upon a fantasy of being able to live in the world not as a superstitious Orthodox woman, but rather as a pagan subject:

> The weather had been unsettled. The sky was blue, but a wet, wintry north-wind swept the clouds along the top of the range of Mycale. We were sitting on the floor early one morning at breakfast, with the door, which was toward the mountain, open; when we discover a small rainbow just above the brow. The sun was then peeping only over the opposite mountain, and, as it got higher, the arc widened and descended toward us; the cattle, feeding on the slope, being seen through it, tinged with its various colours as it passed down, and seeming in the bow. This phænomenon is probably not uncommon in the mountainous regions of Ionia and Greece. (160)

This description of the rising sun operates both as a meteorological observation and as a figuration of the resurrection from the previous paragraph. This transit from tenor to vehicle moves along a well-worn metaphorical track, but Chandler displaces the Christian connotations of the sunrise with a remarkable attempt to imagine how the same phenomenon would operate in a different and far more ancient figural economy: "Let us suppose a devout heathen one of our company, when this happened. On perceiving the bow descend, he would have fancied Iris was coming with a message to Earth from Jupiter Pluvius; and, if he had beheld the bow ascend in like manner, which at some seasons and in certain situations he might do, he would have confidently pronounced, that the goddess had performed her errand, and was going back to heaven" (160). If the world of Greek Orthodox superstition appears alien to him, he seems far more comfortable with the metaphorical leaps of Iris descending from and ascending to the heavens. And well he might be, because the earlier scene of mourning and ritual is connected to immediate expression of affect and the fact of intercultural sociability in the present. Chandler's speculative investment in heathen subjectivity forecloses on the emotions and the sociability of the ethnographic subjects around him, and thus maintains the distance required for the consolidation of his own subjectivity in a temporal zone adjacent to but not part of the contemporary social world of Giaur-Kelibesh. That foreclosure not only ensures that his own ostensible modernity is not troubled by passion and superstition, but also attempts to subsume a patently pagan interpretation of this same world into his present. In other words, Chandler's text attempts to simultaneously embrace the disenchantment of the world that characterizes his European modernity and yet retain access to ideologically useful instances of re-enchantment. Seen in this light, Chandler's deployment of the Iris story amounts to a supplemental gesture that fills the gap left by reason's foundational critique of religion in the modern world.

This is even more explicitly demonstrated in the most extensive account of ruination in the narrative. The expedition's exploration of the ruins at Ephesus is both the most closely documented and historically rich portion of the text. Chandler's discussion of Ephesus takes up close to thirty-five pages, and it features what are by now familiar topoi. The wretchedness of contemporary Ephesus is bemoaned at some length, and the text takes full advantage of the elegiac mode (130–31). However, to make this lament for Ephesus really work Chandler presents the reader with an extensive account of the history of the city. That history is one of repeated conquest and almost endless war. He marshals all of the ancient and modern historical sources to show how the city was subsumed and ultimately destroyed by each successive empire. At this basic level, the discussion of Ephesus is replete with a sense of violent loss.

That is nowhere more intensely rendered than in the treatment of Ephesus's most famous monument. In ancient times, Ephesus was the site of a magnificent Temple of Diana—one of the wonders of the classical world. The building, which is described and referred to repeatedly in classical texts, is utterly gone. Unlike the other ruins in *Travels in Asia Minor*, the most important architectural achievement has left behind no tangible indexical sign: no stone walls, no marble fragments, not even a clear sense of the space it could be found in. The entropy that permeates Pars's views of other sites here reaches its fearsome, because totalizing, conclusion. But even without the traces of the building, Chandler counters this entropic tendency by suggesting that the legacy of the Temple of Diana inheres in the Marian cults of the Greek Orthodox residents of the region:

A people convinced that the self-manifestations of the deity before mentioned were real, could not easily be turned to a religion, which did not pretend to a similar or equal intercourse with its divinity. And this perhaps is the true reason, why, in the early ages of Christianity, besides the miraculous agency of the spirit in prophetic fits of extasy, a belief of supernatural interposition by the Panagia or Virgin Mary, and by saints appearing in daily or nightly visions, was encouraged and inculcated. It helped by its currency to procure and confirm the credulous votary, to prevent or refute the cavil of the heathen, to exalt the new religion, and to deprive the established of its ideal superiority. The superstitions derived on the Greek church from this source, in a remote period, and still continuing to flourish in it, would principally impede the progress of any, who should endeavour to convert its members to the nakedness of reformed Christianity. *Great is the Panagia* would be the general cry; and her self-manifestations, like those of Diana antiently, would even now be attested by many a reputable witness. By what arguments shall a people, filled with affectionate regard for her, and feeling complacency from their conviction of her attention to them and of her power, be prevailed on to accept our rational Protestantism in exchange for their fancied but satisfactory revelations? (136)

This would seem to imply that deep within the core of Orthodox religious superstition lie the vestiges of pagan practices now long gone, and thus the potential for a revivification or connection with the spirit of the ancient Greeks. But that potential spiritual reconnection requires intercultural exchange, and, as the passage above indicates, the terms of that exchange are predetermined in such a way that precludes access to the affective core of cultic or ritual practices. Since this avenue of historical contact and consciousness is already foreclosed by Chandler's commitment to rational modernity, everything falls to a kind of aesthetic contemplation that retains the power of ritual without any of the social risk.

The only problem is that this auratic displacement requires an aesthetic object. There is no object to venerate here, and thus the aesthetic subject is thrown into a state of panic:

The destruction of so illustrious an edifice deserved to have been carefully recorded by contemporary historians. We may conjecture it followed the triumph of Christianity. The Ephesian reformers, when authorized by the imperial edicts, rejoiced in the opportunity of insulting Diana; and deemed it piety to demolish the very ruin of her habitation. Hence, perhaps, while the columns of the Corinthian temple have owed their preservation to their bulk, those of this fabric, with the vast architraves and all the massive materials, have perished and are consumed. Though its stones were far more ponderous, and the heap larger beyond comparison, the whole is vanished we know not how or whither. An antient author has described it as standing at the head of the port, and shining as a meteor. We may add, that as such too it has since disappeared. (140)

As with so many other instances where "antient history" fails to provide an adequate guide, Chandler turns to a sublime figure from the phenomenal world, a figure for transience and catastrophe. But this meteor is immediately supplemented and thus undone by the postulation of a "writer" who could resolve the problem of temporal loss and thus of modernity's inexorable relation to entropy and death:

A writer, who lived toward the end of the second century, has cited a Sibyl as foretelling, that, the earth opening and quaking, the temple of Diana would be swallowed, like a ship in a storm, into the abyss; and Ephesus lamenting and weeping by the river-banks, would enquire for it, then inhabited no more. If the authenticity of the oracle were undisputed, and the Sibyl acknowledged a genuine prophetess, we might infer from the visible condition of the place, the full accomplishment of the whole prediction. We now seek in vain for the temple; the city is prostrate; and the goddess gone. (141)

The way in which the conditional tenses and sentences dissolve in this passage is perhaps the most eloquent demonstration of Chandler's vexed relation to both the present and the past. "If the authenticity of the oracle were undisputed," then we could make sense of time's entropic force. Chandler seems to say that in the face of all this destruction and catastrophe, all one can do is project oneself into the place of this oracle, tendentiously predicting and anticipating the loss, which is all too apparent on the ground, but which we don't want to see. And that applies as much to the emblematic yet vulnerable buildings of Ephesus as it does to the exemplary observers of all this ruination.

From this perspective I think it is possible to look back at the stark palette of Pars's watercolors with more clarity. Like Chandler he devised a method for conveying the panic instilled by a rupture in the temporal continuum. That method required a flattening out of both palette and composition that points toward the pictorial experiments of Turner at his most modern. Likewise, Revett's architectural idealizations are more clearly comprehensible as projections aimed at keeping loss in abeyance. They don't attempt to come up with a new pictorial language for modernity as much as ameliorate its immediate effects for those who could pay for a new portico at High-Wykeham. As we will see, the problems encountered by

Pars, Revett, and Chandler are not easily resolved. In Chapter 7, we will return quite specifically to Ephesus with Sir Robert Ainslie and Luigi Mayer, only this time the aesthetic object will be as unavoidable as the war once again raging in the region. The reading of specific objects in Chapter 7 will force us to reconsider the links between war and art in an even more pointed fashion. But before returning to Ephesus, we need to expand our engagement with the geopolitics of Russia's aggression and contemplate the artful obsessions of a different set of Europeans in Constantinople.

CHAPTER 6

Exoriare Aliquis

Choiseul-Gouffier's Needs and Lady Craven's Desires

But whoever shall appear with arms in their hands will
be welcome; and when that day arrives, heaven have
mercy on the Ottomans, they cannot expect it from the
Giaours.

—*Byron, notes to* Childe Harold's Pilgrimage

In Chapter 5 we looked at how the aleatory movements of three antiquarians in
Asia Minor coalesced into a complex dialectical engagement with the very foun-
dations of modernity. And we also demonstrated how that dialectic folded itself
into entropic representations of violence, both historical and contemporary, that
resonated with ongoing conflict in Ottoman territory. By bringing the activities
of Pars, Revett, and Chandler into contact with *An Authentic Narrative of the Russian Expedition Against the Turks by Sea and Land*'s account of the horrific conflagration in the Bay of Çeşme, I have endeavored not to separate the temporality of
war from the temporality of aesthetic contemplation. What I hope is evident from
the readings presented in Chapter 5 is that for those European subjects traversing
these contested spaces such a separation was not only impossible but also undesir-
able because so much of their investment both in their own narratives of discovery and in the narratives of that which they were ostensibly revivifying turned on
the consideration of historical violence. The key distinction between the author of
Authentic Narrative and the members of the Ionian expedition is that he was working for the Russians; he was an active agent of war. But we have also noted the
degree to which Pars, Revett, and Chandler participated in the derogation of Ottoman rule and specifically the Ottoman territorial occupation of Greece. Their

lament over ruination, as much as their subtle quest for "a re-enchantment of the world," implies a displacement of the Ottomans altogether.

In some sense, the primary agents in Chapter 5 necessarily play at a certain detachment or distance from the scenes of violence before them. Pars and Revett come upon ruin belatedly, and it is that temporal distance that instantiates the complex desire to eliminate it. Chandler writes about Çeşme after the fact and thus is able to contain some of its implications. The unnamed officer's *Authoritative Narrative,* although not afforded the luxury of temporal or spatial distance from the conflagration in the harbor, nonetheless deploys a sublime rhetoric in order to comprehend both the specific horror of death and the more nebulous emotion associated with world-historical change. All of these figures develop formal and rhetorical strategies to mediate their complex affective responses to these events, some of which unfold over centuries and some of which take less than a nighttime.

If Pars, Revett, Chandler, Elphinston and the author or *An Authoritative Narrative* found themselves looking for loopholes in modernity, ways out of the experience of contemporaneity, then the subjects of this chapter exhibited rather different dreams and aspirations.[1] This chapter examines two very distinctive journeys to Constantinople, both of which end up in the Palais de France in Pera. The first follows the Comte de Choiseul-Gouffier from his groundbreaking exploration of the Cyclades and Asia Minor in 1776–77, through the landmark preparation and publication of his *Voyage pittoresque de la Grèce,* to his appointment as French ambassador to the Sublime Porte in 1784. The second follows Lady Elizabeth Craven on her scandalous tour of the courts of France, Italy, and Russia en route to Constantinople. The former took considerably longer than the latter—one could say that a certain recursivity meant that it took thousands of years for Choiseul-Gouffier to reach his objective; but Craven's journey is of no less import for untangling the knot that ties together geopolitics, aesthetics, and ethnocentric fantasies of Ottoman domination into a particularly dangerous cultural formation. These are remarkable texts not only because they were written by aristocratic observers committed to a certain fantasy of Enlightenment, but also because both journeys were undertaken to be written about and thus were highly conscious of their immediate generic forebears. Choiseul-Gouffier's text is in explicit dialogue with a whole library of ancient and modern texts; Lady Craven's *Journey Through the Crimea to Constantinople* (1789) is most thoroughly engaged with Lady Mary Wortley Montagu's *Letters* but she too is well aware of Choiseul-Gouffier's important intervention. Both writers were obsessed with ancient Greece, held the three-hundred-year tenure of Ottoman rule in contempt, and had a conspicuous interest in the much more recent activities of the Russians. How these interests come together is my primary concern because it permeates every element of their texts and will come to play a significant part in the actual prosecution of war.

Comte de Choiseul-Gouffier's Grecian Fantasies

"All Hastened to Serve Me, to Anticipate My Needs"

On 4 April 1776 the French frigate *L'Atalante* set sail from Toulon under the command of Joseph-Bernard, marquis de Chabert de Cogolin, for the eastern Mediterranean. He made his name in the French Ministère de la Marine in 1740s and early 1750s for his hydrographic observations of the coast of Cape Breton, Nova Scotia, and Newfoundland. His *Voyage fait par ordre du roi en 1750 et 1751, dans L'Amerique septentrionale* (1753) was the most accurate hydrographic survey of the east coast of New France, and the maps from that survey were absolutely vital to French success in the early parts of the Seven Years' War. Although he did not see naval action in that war, his maps and his innovations in the science of cartography were part of the increasingly scientific basis of war at sea. In recognition of his achievement, Chabert was elected a member of the French Académie des Sciences for his contributions to the sciences of navigation and cartography. After rising steadily through the officer ranks, he was promoted to brigadier of naval forces in 1776. When France joined the American cause in 1778, he obtained command of the *Vaillant* in Vice Admiral Jean-Baptiste-Charles d'Estaing's West India squadron (1778–79), and he later served under Rear Admiral François-Joseph-Paul de Grasse (1781–82). On 5 September 1781 he was seriously wounded while engaging five ships of the line in Thomas Graves's fleet.[2]

But in the two years prior to fighting against the British in the West Indies, Chabert was embarked on a cartographic mission to the eastern Mediterranean and the Aegean Sea. His work was aimed at providing French ships with reliable maps so that they could more easily avoid piracy in the region. The mission was also part of Chabert's lifelong project of conducting a full hydrographic survey of the Mediterranean: he had done work in the Mediterranean early in his life, and this new voyage aboard *L'Atalante* was aimed at correcting earlier observations and taking new measurements. The results of his work were of obvious strategic interest to the Ministry of Marine and to the overall desire to promote trade in the Levant.

However, Chabert also had orders from Versailles to make room on board for a young aristocrat named Marie-Gabriel-Florent-Auguste, comte de Choiseul-Gouffier, and his party.[3] Both Chabert and Choiseul-Gouffier came from deeply entrenched families of the ancien régime, both had extensive military backgrounds, but they were also men of immense learning. Chabert had already distinguished himself as a mathematician and geographer; Choiseul-Gouffier, although considerably younger than Chabert, had very quickly established his credentials as an antiquarian and as a natural philosopher. Like many of the philosophes that he counted as his friends, Choiseul-Gouffier pursued an encyclopedic knowledge of the world both ancient and modern, which meant that he was as familiar with the French naturalist Buffon as he was with minor Greek poets and philosophers.[4] As his biographer Frédéric Barbier indicates, his family connections and his talent secured access not only to the enlightened salons of Paris but also to Chabert's expedition. While Chabert was conducting his hydrographic survey, Choiseul-Gouffier planned to conduct an archaeological expedition explicitly modeled on that of the Society of Dilettanti's earlier exploration of Ionia. Significantly, Choiseul-Gouffier himself understood Chabert's contemporary interest in the hydrographic survey and his own interest in the ruined landscapes of antiquity as divergent inquiries that were linked by a subtle militarism: "One could only expect from Mr de Chabert the maneuvers necessary for the seafarers, those which determine the directions and the anchorages. A true sailor, he had not allowed himself any incursion on land, and he did not even worry much about the exact configuration of the coastline, even less about Xerxes's itinerary or the Athenian flotilla's."[5] If Chabert's observations were ostensibly scientific, they also had military applications; likewise, as the remark above suggests, Choiseul-Gouffier's enlightened observations are rarely distant from narratives of military conquest and imperial conflict. For Choiseul-Gouffier the expedition became about much more than ruined architecture, and, significantly, his highly militarized maps would come to have a prominent place in his account of the region. By the time that Choiseul-Gouffier returned to Paris at the beginning of 1777, the idea for a new kind of antiquarian travel narrative began to coalesce. Choiseul-Gouffier's project would attempt to play water and land, ancient and modern off one another in quite politicized ways.

Choiseul-Gouffier's expedition was explicitly undertaken as a book project, and that project came to fruition under the title *Voyage pittoresque de la Grèce.* (1782). With the aim of preparing an illustrated travel narrative, Choiseul-Gouffier employed a *dessinateur* named Jean-Baptiste Hilaire to take views of the ancient sites and an architect named Jacques Foucherot, whose primary job was to take elevations and prepare architectural drawings of the ruins.[6] Choiseul-Gouffier also had considerable artistic talent, so the trio brought formidable visual skill to their task and that is everywhere evident in the product of the journey. As Barbier argues, the book is as much a product of Enlightenment science as it is of late eighteenth-century bibliophilia. One of the most expensively and elaborately illustrated books of its kind, the project was funded by subscription and executed in twelve separate *livraisons.*[7] As each *livraison* was published, notice was taken across the learned journals of Europe, and by the time the entire project was completed the *Voyage pittoresque's* importance was already assured. Perhaps the best sense of the book's reception is provided by one of its earliest notices in the *Bibliothèque des sciences et des beaux-arts*:

> If the Society of *Dilettanti* was so much praised and well deserved public attention by sending Messrs. *Chandler*, *Revett* and *Pars* to Asia Minor and to Greece in order to examine the ancient monuments that still remain there, how could we not applaud the noble ardor of a French lord, who has himself undertaken the journey to Greece with a couple of artists he has hired to follow him. . . . All these discoveries, all the observations of this interesting voyage, the drawings he made himself or which were made before his eyes, will be communicated to the public in a series of books that will make up two folio volumes. The book that we are hereby presenting comprises ten plates exceptionally engraved by Mr. Choffard . . . , a very beautiful small illustration [and] a tailpiece. [The] text matches the beauty of the figures, its style is elegant and pure, the narrations are interesting, the reflections are often clever and always judicious.[8]

The high quality of the engravings, Choiseul-Gouffier's elegant style, his narrative skill, and his philosophical meditations are all signaled here, and it is precisely these qualities that made the book exceedingly influential. It would secure its author a place in the Acadèmie Française and played no small role in his appointment as French ambassador to the Sublime Porte of the Ottoman Empire in 1784.

It is notable that this review also sees Choiseul-Gouffier's work as a continuation of the project of the Society of Dilettanti. At one level, this is almost certainly the case; but on another level Choiseul-Gouffier's book goes far beyond its immediate predecessors. The Dilettanti publications were exceedingly influential, and the *Voyage pittoresque* synthesizes modes of representation developed separately in *The Antiquities of Athens*, *Ionian Antiquities*, and *Travels in Asia Minor*. There is ample evidence throughout the text that Choiseul-Gouffier and his primary illustrator Jean-Baptiste Hilaire had fully absorbed Stuart's translation of stadial theory into an efficient visual rhetoric of Ottoman dissipation and of Grecian cultural decay. And I would argue that Hilaire was also familiar with the power of Pars's rendering of entropy. Both artists took views of the Roman gate at Mylasa, but Hilaire's 's view takes Pars's fascination with entropy and applies it to Pars's own image (Figure 53; see also Figure 44). Pars's detailed rendering of how the gate was integrated into the walls of later structures has been fractured to leave only the gate itself; the more contemporary buildings have

Figure 53. *Vue d'une porte de Mylasa*, and *Élévation de la même porte*, plates 90 (*top*) and 91 (*bottom*) in Choiseul-Gouffier, *Voyage pittoresque de la Grèce* (1782), engravings. Courtesy of the Getty Research Institute, Los Angeles.

evaporated. The forlorn gate is now contrasted with the members of the caravan in a gesture reminiscent of Stuart's visual practice, but the entire engraving is immediately paired with Foucherot's Revett-like engraving of what can only be described as the restored architecture. Choiseul-Gouffier uses these half-page pairings quite frequently in the text, and they are points of particular argumentative density. This single page in *Voyage pittoresque* takes the complex dialectic between entropy and reconstitution articulated in *Ionian Antiquities* and makes it

Figure 54. *Ruines du Temple de Mars*, plate 99 in Choiseul-Gouffier, *Voyage pittoresque de la Grèce* (1782), engraving. Courtesy of the Getty Research Institute, Los Angeles.

that much more palpable because one has to deal with both images in a single act of comparative viewing. Indeed this intensification of the visual rhetoric of the Dilettanti texts is consistent throughout, but the objective is not simply a matter of one-upmanship.

Voyage pittoresque's plate 99, *Ruins of the Temple of Mars*, demonstrates how the two pictorial strategies of Stuart and Pars are dynamically fused in Choiseul-Gouffier's book (Figure 54). The contrast between the ruin and the reclining Turks is very reminiscent of Stuart's views: it operates by simple visual contrast. The careful presentation of plants growing through the pediments is similar to Pars's interest in the historical depredations of the natural world. But Hilaire brings something new to the table. The temple appears to be crumbling before our eyes because the smoke from the campfire shades into the tumbling column. The "motion" of that smoke allegorizes a geopolitical argument. The temple has been eroded by the inexorable forces of nature, but the smoke suggests that the succession of empires and, in particular, the current state of Ottoman rule have accelerated the destruction of the cultural artifacts of antiquity. That fire has been set by the Turks, and, as we will see, smoke is hardly a neutral sign in this text. Again this engraving is supplemented by a set of "détails de ce monument" designed by Foucherot that restores geometrical order and solidity to the building (Figure 55). As I argued with regard to *Ionian Antiquities*, this supplemental relation between entropic views and idealizing elevations activates anxiety in order to contain it with

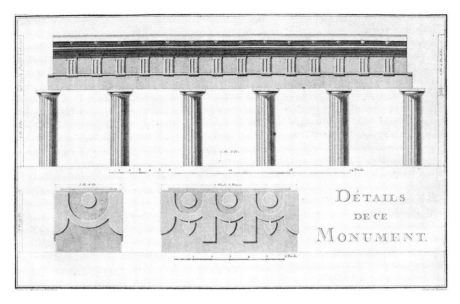

Figure 55. *Détails de cette monument*, plate 100 in Choiseul-Gouffier, *Voyage pittoresque de la Grèce* (1782), engraving.

a fantasy of mimetic truth that can exist only in the present of the volume itself. The rhetorical sleight of hand is literally one of smoke and mirrors.

This intensification of the pictorial strategies exhibited in *The Antiquities of Athens* and *Ionian Antiquities* is matched by a further innovation. Unlike *Ionian Antiquities*, which provided almost no narrative or cartographic information about the expedition, *Voyage pittoresque* is first and foremost a travel narrative. The author emerges as a character in the *Voyage*, and we are constantly brought back to the notion of an enlightened subject observing this distant world.[9] Copious and highly detailed maps constantly serve to orient the reader in space. By layering ancient and modern place-names and details, the maps also remind the reader of the chronology of historical events in the region.[10] It is as though Choiseul-Gouffier integrated Chandler's *Travels in Asia Minor* with *Ionian Antiquities* to generate a single organic whole. This innovation is signaled in the title itself for *pittoresque* is not being used here in the sense of the "picturesque," as it is commonly used in English, but rather in the sense of a voyage to be painted or worthy of visualization.[11] Like other Enlightenment travel narratives, *Voyage pittoresque* exhibits a broad range of interests. Its fascination with geological formations, best exemplified by the extensive discussion and illustration of a descent into the Grotto of Antiparos in plates 36, 37, and 38, is reminiscent of the geological passages in Goethe's *Italian Journey*. There are illustrations and discussions of volcanic formations no doubt inspired by Sir William Hamilton's *Observations on Mount Vesuvius, Mount Etna, and Other Volcanos* (1772) and *Campi Phlegraei* (1776).

As Frédéric Barbier has argued, Choiseul-Gouffier explicitly set out to produce a text whose readerly pleasures would suit men and women of taste. This means that the scholarly apparatus is subordinated to elegance of expression and narrative interest. Because there is far less activity in scholarly notes, the itinerary or plot of the expedition becomes increasingly important. And this foregrounding of the itinerary can be traced in both the prose commentary and in the sequence of illustrations; in fact it has structural implications.[12] The integration of the itinerary is deeply significant because Choiseul-Gouffier explores two different kinds of spaces on his journey, and the book is fundamentally divided by this spatial bifurcation.[13] The first six *livraisons* and plates 1 to 63 (precisely half the illustrations) are devoted to observations made in the "Grecian" islands of the Cyclades and the Dodecanese as Choiseul-Gouffier progresses from Koroni on the Peloponnesian peninsula through the Cyclades to Rhodes. *Livraisons* 7 to 12 and plates 64 to 126 are based on observations made on the mainland of Asia Minor. In other words, the first half of the text is devoted to maritime travel and tracks the relatively secure voyage of the *L'Atalante* and the second half of the text concerns a far more dangerous overland journey. The question of security is not incidental because it directly impinges on the kind of stadial arguments activated in each section of the text.

During the first half of the text, there are relatively few architectural elevations or studies of ornament. But there is a preponderance of stadial landscapes and a remarkable series of large figure ethnographic portraits. A set of paired engravings should give a sense of the pictorial strategies in this section of the *Voyage pittoresque*. After a series of ethnographic portraits and views of various ports and caves along the journey, the text presents two contrasting plates on the same page (Figure 56). The top engraving, *Vestiges d'un temple de Cybele vulgairement appellé l'ecole d'Homere*, is based on a drawing by Choiseul-Gouffier himself and epitomizes the argument of the entire text. There are only traces of the Temple of Cybele, but the reason for its disappearance is encoded directly into the composition. The mosque that dominates the left side of the picture is the sign of Ottoman occupation. The figures in the foreground all have their back to the staircase and the missing space where the temple should be. At best it is an image of ignorance and neglect—a resonance picked up by the title's use of the word *vulgairement*—at worst it is a sign of irrecoverable loss. The invocation of Homer is crucial because it allows Choiseul-Gouffier to both declare what is missing and correct a misconception. The author/illustrator marks an epistemic difference between himself and the figures in the image.[14]

This is only further emphasized by the juxtaposition of this engraving with the one below it made after a drawing by Hilaire, *Femmes de l'Ile de Scio*. *Voyage Pittoresque* is replete with these kind of ethnographic portraits. This one operates

VESTIGES D'UN TEMPLE DE CYBELE
vulgairement appellé l'ecole d'HOMERE.
A.P.D.R.

FEMMES DE L'ILE DE SCIO.
A.P.D.R.

Figure 56. *Vestiges d'un temple de Cybele* and *Femmes de l'Ile de Scio*, plates 47 (*top*) and 48 (*bottom*) in Choiseul-Gouffier, *Voyage pittoresque de la Grèce* (1782), engravings. Courtesy of the Getty Research Institute, Los Angeles.

on two registers. First the genre image of peasant life activates a whole cascade of associations regarding oppressive Ottoman rule. We are presented here with the poor Greek subjects of Ottoman imperial domination. That relationship is established again in the composition only this time the mosque occupies the right side of the picture plane. The outstretched hand of the central figure draws an explicit link between the condition of the peasant women and the most explicit visual sign of Islamic governance. If we look now at the entire page—that is, if we take both plates together—we have a kind of Z-shaped visual itinerary. In the top left and the bottom right, the artists give a straightforward representation of Ottoman rule—the minarets and domes carefully mirroring one another. In the top right and the bottom left we have the historical casualties, the desecrated and missing vestiges of ancient Greece in the top right and the impoverished peasant women, here a synecdoche for Greek subjugation, in the bottom center to the left of the mosque.

These female casualties are of singular importance because there are eleven full-length costume portraits of Greek women in the first half of *Voyage pittoresque*.[15] There is only one similar image of Ottoman subjects in the second half of the text, but it operates quite differently. We will have a great deal to say about that image shortly, but it is important to recognize at this stage how the proliferation of female ethnographic portraits feminizes the Grecian islands. It is not that there aren't ethnographic images of men throughout the text, but in general they are minor visual details: in the first half of the text, groups of Greek fishermen or shepherds are interspersed in the various topographical views and in the second half reclining Turkish smokers are ubiquitous. But the eleven female portraits in the first half of *Voyage pittoresque* constitute a significant deployment of sexuality. Usually grouped in intergenerational pairs or groups of three in the middle ground with the accoutrements of domestic life around them, these women are the object of both sociological and erotic engagement. The high degree of visual interest in their dress is supplemented by frequent remarks about their desirability in the prose commentary. In most cases, Choiseul-Gouffier complains about the inconveniences of the women's clothing, but in his commentary to plate 12, *Femmes de l'Ile de Nio*, he has the following to say:

> The way of dressing of the Women of Nio[16] is rather pleasant. A plain camisole marks their waistline, but does not constrict it; and their very short skirts, instead of alarming decency, only foreshadow the purity of their mores. They may seem too lightly dressed, but one will never find that they are immodestly dressed.
>
> The safely preserved customs of the inhabitants of this island, the way they live together, their consideration toward foreigners, everything evokes

the simplicity of the first ages. I enjoyed all its pleasantness: Masters, Women, Children, all hastened to serve me, to anticipate my needs. (20–21)

The accompanying engraving dutifully provides a view of the well-shaped calves of two young women, thus drawing attention to the shortness of the skirts at the same time that he argues that there was nothing immodest about their dress (Figure 57). Conjoining the revealing clothing with the assertion that the inhabitants of Nio are preternaturally inclined to respond to his needs and desires not only eroticizes the scene but also links it to a fantasy of the "premiers âges" of unrestrained desire and hospitality.[17]

It is also important to note that this is a portrait of a mother and her two teenage daughters because the portraits repeatedly attest to the fecundity of Greek women. Image after image shows women caring for young girls. If the *Voyage pittoresque* is any indication, these islands in the Aegean Sea are replete with mothers, infants, and mothers-to-be. Unlike similar gestures with regard to the South Pacific, this emphasis on reproduction extends beyond mere eroticization; the issue here, I would contend, has to do with literal potential and figural receptivity. Choiseul-Gouffier is committed to representing Greece as a region ready and willing to serve a new, more enlightened master, one committed to restoring the vibrancy of culture itself. As he states, "all hastened to serve me, to anticipate my needs," and thus it is important to recognize that this desire also declares a need. In the immediate context of hospitality, he imagines that these women will provide for his quotidian wants, but there is a further implication that these representatives of the "premiers âges" have the capacity to fill a cultural lack instituted by modernity itself.[18]

This is nowhere more evident than in the illustration used for the title page of the volume (Figure 58). This allegorical portrait of Greece features a chained woman reclining among the tombs of ancient Greeks known for their writings on liberty. As David Roessel has argued, this image of Greece as a female slave awaiting liberation conditioned much of the representation of Greece from its first publication right through the Greek revolution in the early nineteenth century.[19] The pose of the central figure is multivalent: it invokes a kind of classical repose and at the same time it signifies a kind of erotic receptivity that resonates with the deployment of sexuality in the ethnographic portraits (Figure 59). Significantly, the allegorical Greece is not represented like a piece of ancient sculpture: she is idealized, but she is also clothed in a sort of amalgamation of classical drapery and contemporary Grecian costume. It is crucial that she not be confused with the sculptural fragments around her or with the ruined temples in the background because these are signs of mortality. Because she is a figure, she is still alive and thus constitutes a potential bridge—albeit phantasmatic—with the glories of antiquity.

VUE DE LA VILLE DE NIO.

A.P.D.R.

FEMMES DE L'ILE DE NIO.

A.P.D.R.

Figure 57. *Femmes de l'Ile de Nio*, plate 12 in Choiseul-Gouffier, *Voyage pittoresque de la Grèce* (1782), engraving. Courtesy of the Getty Research Institute, Los Angeles.

Dessiné par J.B.Hilair.   FEMMES DE L'ISLE DE SIPHANTO.   *Gravé par A.J.Duclos.*

A.P.D.R.

Dessiné par le Comte De Choiseul-Gouffier.   VUE DE L'ISLE DE SIKINO.   *Gravé par Daniel Maceker.*

A.P.D.R.

Figure 58. Title page, Choiseul-Gouffier, *Voyage pittoresque de la Grèce* (1782), engraving. Courtesy of the Getty Research Institute, Los Angeles.

Figure 59. Detail from title
page, Choiseul-Gouffier,
Voyage pittoresque de la Grèce
(1782), engraving. Courtesy of
the Getty Research Institute,
Los Angeles.

Choiseul-Gouffier's "Explication du frontispice" on the ensuing page elucidates
the importance of the textual material inscribed on the monuments and rocks
around the central figure as follows:

> Greece, represented by a woman laden with irons, is surrounded by funer-
> ary monuments, raised in honor of the great Men of Greece who sacrificed
> themselves for its freedom; such as Lycurgus, Miltiades, Themistocles,
> Aristides, Epaminondas, Pelopidas, Timoleon, Demosthenes, Phocion,
> Philopoemen. She is leaning on Leonidas's tombstone, and behind her is
> the cippus on which is engraved the inscription Simonides made for the
> three hundred Spartans who died fighting in the Thermopylae.
>
> *Passerby, go tell Lacedaemon that we died here to obey his laws.*
>
> Greece seems to be bringing out the souls of those great Men, and on the
> next rock the words *Exoriare aliquis . . .* are written.[20]

The jumble of names in this passage mirrors the rubble around the allegorical figure and thus offers a textual equivalent to the entropic ruination of antiquity. But Choiseul-Gouffier's invocation of the Battle of Thermopylae moves away from parataxis in order to foreground a specific historical affiliation. Arguably the most famous battle of antiquity, Leonidas's last stand at Thermopylae against the far larger Persian army is conventionally understood not only as the epitome of patriotic valor but also as a sign of the superiority of Greek democracy over Persian despotism. In spite of their loss at Thermopylae and subsequent territorial losses to the Persians, the Greeks would eventually repel Persian conquest. For contemporary conservative ideologues such as Victor Davis Hanson, "contemporary Greeks saw Thermopylae as a critical moral and cultural lesson. In universal terms, a small, free people had willingly outfought huge numbers of imperial subjects who advanced under the lash. More specifically, the Western idea that soldiers themselves decide where, how, and against whom they will fight was contrasted against the Eastern notion of despotism and monarchy—freedom proving the stronger idea as the more courageous fighting of the Greeks at Thermopylae, and their later victories at Salamis and Plataea attested."[21] This is a reductive but oft repeated assertion that nonetheless resonates with Choiseul-Gouffier's deployment of famous elegiac couplet of Simonides:

Ὦ ξεῖν', ἀγγέλλειν Λακεδαιμονίοις ὅτι τῇδε
κείμεθα, τοῖς κείνων ῥήμασι πειθόμενοι.

Choiseul-Gouffier's translation, "Passant, va dire à Lacédémone que nous sommes morts ici pour obéir à ses loix," makes good use of the Greek epitaphic convention of addressing passing strangers to address the reader of *Voyage pittoresque*, but he gives the epitaph a specifically political inflection. Translations of Simonides move in one of two directions: one school emphasizes that the three hundred Spartans under Leonidas's command died following their orders, but the other declares that they died in fulfillment of the laws of Sparta.[22] Choiseul-Gouffier's translation is of the latter tendency, and this subtle distinction necessarily shifts the praise slightly from that of military discipline to superior governmentality.

Choiseul-Gouffier's invocation of the sine qua non of the clash of civilizations is not surprising, but the fact that the allegorical figure of Greece lies on the tomb of Leonidas has significant implications for understanding the role of embodied allegory in *Voyage pittoresque*. According to Herodotus, after the defeat of Leonidas at Thermopylae, the Persian leader Xerxes divagated from the Persian custom of venerating fallen heroes and ordered that Leonidas be decapitated and crucified. Forty years later, when the bones of Leonidas were returned to Sparta, he was buried with full honors, and funeral games were held annually to commemorate his heroism. The desecration of Leonidas's body became a sign of Eastern ferocity, and thus the relationship between the allegorical figure of Greece and Leonidas's remains depicted in the frontispiece is one of both explicit succor and implicit xenophobia. The recovery of the body of Leonidas forcefully asserts that despite the desecration inflicted on the heroic past by "Eastern" foes it can nonetheless be retrieved. Choiseul-Gouffier is suggesting that a similar liberation can be effected in the present moment.

The deployment of corporeal tropes is not confined to martial fantasies; it is also supplemented by a less straightforward erotic economy. The final sentence of Choiseul-Gouffier's "Explication du frontispice" brings the reader back to an important compositional detail on the title page. The entire composition is bracketed by two groups of cypress trees that draw attention to the inflammatory words carved into the rocks over her head. All the other text in this image is Greek, so the Latin "EXORIARE ALIQUIS" jumps out from the background with resounding effect. That effect is reinforced by the "Explication."[23] The famous phrase is from Dido's curse on Aeneas in book 4 of the *Aeneid* in which she calls for one of her kin to avenge Aeneas's betrayal: "Exoriare aliquis nostris ex ossibus ultor" (May you arise from my bones, you unknown stranger). Choiseul-Gouffier is picking up on the fact that Virgil uses the second-person subjunctive to address her avenger in person at some moment in the future. The unknown stranger implied here is the reader of *Voyage pittoresque*. The gesture is blunt but suggestive. Greece has been betrayed like Dido and thus her words apply. Someone must come forward who will avenge her subjugation and rise up against imperial occupation; the figural link between Carthage and Greece is important because of the politics of empire. These future Hannibals will aim their vengeance at the Ottoman not the Roman Empire. The crucial implication here is that those who would take up Hannibal's task and Choiseul-Gouffier's Dido-like injunction are defending their heritage and thus are laying claim to the cultural patrimony of ancient Greece. But the Latin inscription is also an important supplement to the inscriptions pertaining to the Battle of Thermopylae, because Dido's claim on Aeneas is erotic and thus his betrayal is a betrayal of both her capacity for love and her hospitality to strangers: precisely the combination of qualities attributed to the "Femmes de l'Ile de Nio." That these qualities ostensibly live on beyond allegory in the reproductive potential of the women of Greece is a deeply political sign and thus the ethnographic portraits and descriptions are tightly wound into a fantasy of a future cultural and social efflorescence that the text equates with vitality itself. As we will see, this deployment of reproductive sexuality is further activated by a crucial deployment of nonproductive homosexuality during Choiseul-Gouffier's travels on the mainland of Asia Minor.

When we turn to the second half of the text, the question of life becomes decisive because the mainland of Ionia is quite literally the space of death. The first

VUE DE LA MONTAGNE DES TOMBEAUX PRES DE TELMISSUS.

Figure 60. *Vue de la montagne des tombeaux près de Telmissus*, plate 67 in Choiseul-Gouffier, *Voyage pittoresque de la Grèce* (1782), engraving. Courtesy of the Getty Research Institute, Los Angeles.

five engravings pertaining to Choiseul-Gouffier's journey on the mainland of Asia Minor, plates 64–69, depict tombs and sarcophagi. It is the most insistent thematic unit in the entire text; no other artifact or issue is handled as insistently over a group of repeated images. If we remember that each *livraison* was published separately, then the publication of these tomb images with the seventh *livraison* would have announced a rupture in the thematics of the overall text (Figure 60). Choiseul-Gouffier's wide-ranging commentary on ancient monuments compares these tombs at Telmissus, "carved from living rock," to the similar veneration of the dead in Egypt and Persia and speculates that the consistency of the need to memorialize indicates that "the ancient peoples have communicated to each other" (121). In light of the celebration of Simonides's epitaph in the frontispiece, these remarks on monumental history become that much more significant. In the frontispiece, the tombs of Leonidas and others both support and are cared for by the allegorical figure of Greece. In the two views from this *livraison*, there are only Turks and their camels presiding over these invaluable links to the past. What this means is that the care of these ancient monuments—and hence the spirit of Greece—falls to Choiseul-Gouffier, his companions, and his readers. And the author's status as custodian is enacted by the diagrams presented in plates 65, 66, 68, and 69. In a sense, the demonstrable care that went into the creation of plate 68 (Figure 61), for instance, is a claim to a sort of larger cultural appropriation. After these six inaugural plates there are no longer comforting images of women, fecundity, and domestic calm; these tropes are replaced by images of physical desolation

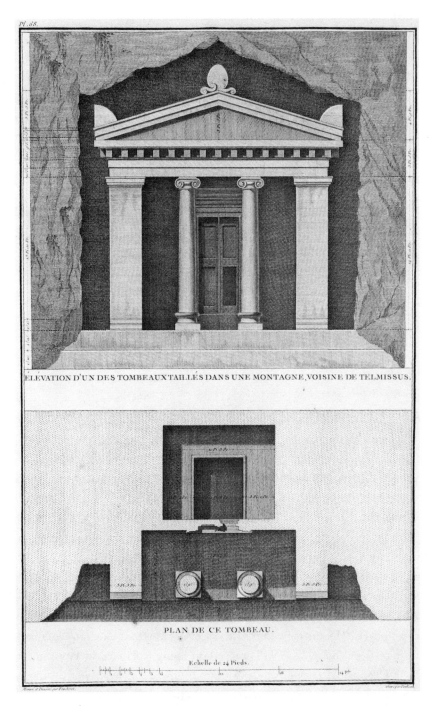

Pl. 68.

ÉLÉVATION D'UN DES TOMBEAUX TAILLÉS DANS UNE MONTAGNE, VOISINE DE TELMISSUS.

PLAN DE CE TOMBEAU.

Echelle de 24 Pieds.

Figure 61. *Élévation d'un des tombeaux taillés dans une montagne voisine de Telmissus*, plate 68 in Choiseul-Gouffier, *Voyage pittoresque de la Grèce* (1782), engraving. Courtesy of the Getty Research Institute, Los Angeles.

HALTE DES VOYAGEURS PRÈS DE DOURLACH, DANS LA CARIE.

A. P.D.R.

Figure 62. *Halte des voyageurs près de Dourlach, dans la Carie*, plate 74 in Choiseul-Gouffier, *Voyage pittoresque de la Grèce* (1782), engraving. Courtesy of the Getty Research Institute, Los Angeles.

and increasingly threatening scenes of male homosocial encounter between Choiseul-Gouffier's party and Ottoman peoples. In a sense, the presence of the frigate *L'Atalante* always provided the maritime part of the journey with a level of security that could not be sustained once Choiseul-Gouffier, Hilaire, and Foucherot started moving overland in the company of Ottoman guides and interpreters.

The transition from relative security to an economy of fear is registered first by the haunting tombs of plates 64 to 69 and then by the frequent representation of weaponry in views of the party's progress. Perhaps the most important of these latter engravings is plate 74, *Halte des Voyageurs près de Dourlach, dans la Carie* (Figure 62). Unlike the Dilettanti publications, this engraving does not pertain to the ruins of antiquity but rather to the exigencies of travel and intercultural encounter. Hilaire's image is dominated by a tree that provides shade for Choiseul-Gouffier, his companions, and his guides. This central grouping is flanked by two important signs of Ottoman alterity in the background: on the left we have the obligatory caravan and to the right two mosques. But it is the subtle distinctions between the European travelers and the Ottoman guides that are most resonant here. As Barbier suggests, the seated artist on the left is most likely Hilaire whose name is appended to the engraving; he is being directed by the standing figure of Choiseul-Gouffier. A third European—Barbier suggests that it is Chartier, Choiseul-Gouffier's valet de chambre—prepares a wild fowl for roasting on the fire in the background center. The seven Ottoman figures are marked by their supine lassitude. The contrasting poses mark a firm distinction between Occidental agency and Oriental passivity. In a sense, the active gestures of each European figure operate as signs of their cultural superiority. This is especially the case with regard to Choiseul-Gouffier's pointing finger: in a sense, the gesture is a condensed sign of authorship itself, especially since he is directing the attention of his *dessinateur*. This authority is amplified by the fact that he is standing, armed with a scimitar.

The arming of Choiseul-Gouffier needs to be read in relation to the pile of weapons in the foreground. Those weapons belong to the reclining Turks, and they signify both the danger of the overland journey—that is, the party needs an armed guard—and a crucial lack of confidence in the security provided by the Ottoman figures. If this party of reclining figures was to be attacked, they would not only be unprepared, their weapons would be at a distance. Choiseul-Gouffier is the only figure ready for action, and it is significant that he has appropriated a distinctively Ottoman weapon. This subtle gesture simultaneously attests to the dangerous volatility of the region and suggests that the inept Ottomans would easily succumb to the more vigorous leadership of a European like Choiseul-Gouffier. As we will see, this revelation of Ottoman vulnerability is not an incidental element of this engraving. Choiseul-Gouffier demonstrates throughout the text that the strength of the Ottoman Empire, based on the superior number of their forces and on their ostensible ferocity, is no longer a historical fact. The comparison to the ancient Persians is palpable. However, before turning to an explication of how this aspect of the text's politics inflects the first half of the text, it is important to look more closely at how fear is mobilized in the second half of the text.

Our discussion of the first section of *Voyage pittoresque* started from an analysis of a pair of half-page engravings based on observations on the Isle of Scio. If we look at a similar pair of images to those of plates 47 and 48 from the second half of the text, we can see how this economy of fear is folded into a very specific argument about the present moment.[24] In plates 112 and 113 we find stadial theory in its most stark manifestation (Figure 63). The landscape on the top of the page presents a view of the region near Latmos, showing animals, tents, a caravan, a ruined hovel; amid all the visual clutter one can just make out the remains of the Fountain of Byblis. There is no title to identify the fountain, only a passage from Ovid.[25] Here the supplemental text tells us what is missing from the view. In this passage from the *Metamorphoses*, Ovid relates the transformation of Byblis by Apollo. With little or no vestige of the ancient Temple of Apollo Didymaeus on the ground as it were, it has to be excavated from Ovid's text. The bottom image is an architectural elevation of the Temple of Apollo Didymaeus executed with an extraordinary mathematical precision. I don't think it is difficult to comprehend the political argument here. The top image locates the present state of degradation.

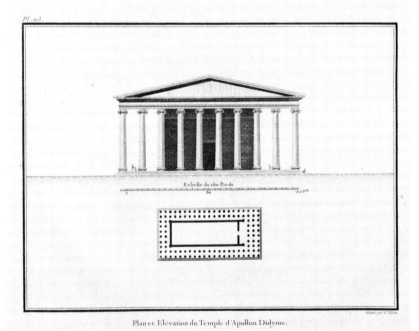

Figure 63. Two differing renderings of the Temple of Apollo Didymaeus, plates 112 (*top*) and 113 (*bottom*) in Choiseul-Gouffier, *Voyage pittoresque de la Grèce* (1782), engravings. Courtesy of the Getty Research Institute, Los Angeles.

What is less obvious is that the bottom image is also a rendering of the present, for it declares that the author and illustrator are the rightful heirs of the cultural heritage of Greece. It is an assertion of historical continuity that steps past the regressive image on the top of the page. Although it refers to that which is inexorably past, it enacts its reconstitution in the present. On this page there are two presents, but one is marked as historically obsolete and thus expendable. But the adjacency of these two claims on the present captures an important fear and a political paradox. The fear is that under Ottoman rule all that remains of Greek antiquity will rapidly disappear—that is, things will go the way of the top engraving. The political paradox is that preservation and imaginary reconstitution require the ongoing complicity and hospitality of the Ottoman Empire. Despite his contempt for contemporary populations and rulers, Choiseul-Gouffier, like Lord Elgin some years later, would eventually secure a *firman* from the Ottoman Porte that enabled him to remove valuable antiquities from the Parthenon and Attica, which would eventually make their way to the Louvre. In other words, Choiseul-Gouffier's philhellenism relies on the very Ottoman control of the region that he critiques.

This paradoxical relation to his Ottoman hosts is enacted in the most complex cultural encounter in the text. On the route toward Moglad, Choiseul-Gouffier's company was traveling in a region controlled by a relatively independent ağa named "Hassan Tchaousch Oglou."[26] Staged initially as an act of combined curiosity and politeness—that is, as an expression of his own persona's enlightened qualities—it becomes apparent that Choiseul-Gouffier needs the ağa's permission and protection to explore the region (136). Choiseul-Gouffier narrates his audience with the ağa twice in the commentary to plates 75 and 77. Both narratives serve to derogate the ağa, but they employ different strategies to attack Ottoman rule. Although the rhetorical strategies employed in the commentary to plate 75 are less extreme than those activated for plate 77, plate 75 itself presents an interesting conundrum (Figure 64). The engraving was executed by the notable academy artist Jean-Michel Moreau le Jeune from a sketch by the author. However, the author himself is the subject of the image, thus we are quite far away from the ostensible empirical illustrations elsewhere in the text. Executed in Paris well after the voyage this engraving is stylistically distinct from the rest of *Voyage pittoresque* in that it incorporates visual signs of "Turkish" otherness from precursor Orientalist painting and engraving. Nowhere else in *Voyage pittoresque* is there such multifarious attention to the clothing and facial expressions of Ottoman figures, and this is the only representation of this specific kind of interior space. And this is the only image where Ottoman figures are handled in a scale similar to that accorded to the Grecian women earlier in the text. At one level this is because the relationship of engraving to text is illustrative. Whereas the majority of the commentary in

RÉCEPTION DE L'AUTEUR CHEZ HASSAN TCHAOUSCH-OGLOU.

A.P.D.R.

Figure 64. *Réception de l'auteur chez Hassan Tchaousch-Oglou*, plate 75 in Choiseul-Gouffier, *Voyage pittoresque de la Grèce* (1782), engraving. Courtesy of the Getty Research Institute, Los Angeles.

the text operates as an explication of the associated plates, it is clear that Moreau is rendering the audience so that it fits the details of Choiseul-Gouffier's account. The text pays a great deal of attention to the formality of the divan and to the intense interest of the ağa's court in the French visitors (131). Everything about Moreau's composition works to amplify these two issues. In his rendering of the central grouping, Moreau uses the doctor/interpreter as a balancing device between the aged ağa and his young son on the left and Choiseul-Gouffier and his companion on the right. The mutual gaze of these four figures is replicated throughout the room all the way to both edges of the picture plane. The pose of every figure is carefully deployed to focus all attention on the intercultural encounter in the deep space of the image. The two vertical pillars further highlight this transaction.

However Moreau's deviation from Choiseul-Gouffier is telling. Because the ağa and his son are the smallest and most distant figures, they are handled with the least detail. Compared to the expressive rendering of the two turbaned figures in the right foreground they are of limited interest. In a sense Moreau's composition draws all internal attention to the ağa only to fall back on stock images of Eastern alterity in the foreground. This is contrary to Choiseul-Gouffier's highly detailed assessment of the ağa's character. When we look closely at the textual version of the audience, what we find is a thinly veiled essay on despotism. Choiseul-Gouffier starts out by emphasizing that the ağa is an unusually independent figure, but as his narration of the meeting unfolds he signals all the crucial signs from Montesquieu's *Spirit of the Laws*: luxury, corruption, pride, and violence are invoked in turn. The reader is presented with obligatory eunuchs, Arabian horses, and the sumptuous goods of Orientalist discourse. But these signs are only the backdrop for a political intervention. The ağa's repeated assertion of his independence from the sultan and his careful education and protection of his son slowly disclose the anxiety nascent in a volatile despotic state. As the ağa states, "I have never harmed the Sultan who does not know me, and in the name of whom they would have beheaded me, if I had not taken the precaution to expel from my land the Emissaries in charge of the commission. I only want my sons to be like me; to be able to defend themselves after I die, and to pass on their authority onto this child I cherish" (132). Choiseul-Gouffier makes everything transparent when he suggests that the ağa's situation is comparable to that of the conspirator Acomat in Racine's *Bajazet*: "I was listening to him, struck by his answers, and by some features of his which reminded me of the Vizier Acomat—whom Racine painted—when I saw his face brightening up, and, all of a sudden, after I looked at what he seemed to be staring at, I saw a remarkable face which contorted in a thousand ways, and spoke with great volubility" (132). The nod to Racine plays out the critique of despotism through literary allusion: the readers of *Voyage pittoresque* would have been familiar with the claustrophobic fear inculcated by Racine's tragedy.

Following Montesquieu, Choiseul-Gouffier suggests that fear of conspiracy and summary violence characteristic of despotic states ultimately undermines good governance. But the sudden turn to the ağa's fool is much more revealing. Choiseul-Gouffier is told that the fool amuses the ağa with his antics, and he is asked through the interpreter whether or not "Princes of my country had fools in their palaces" (133). He responds that this is now an obsolete practice and concludes with a pointed political comment: "If the Sultan had done the same, the efforts of his arms were better directed, then he would not have failed recently in front of a small number of Russians" (133). Suddenly the entire anecdote serves not only to separate modern European monarchies from their own dissipated past, but also to demonstrate that the sultan is too distracted by questionable pleasures to effectively lead his state in a time of war. The suggestion is that the Russians were successful in the recent Russo-Turkish War of 1768–74 because despotic governance is prone to such dissipation.

When we turn to the commentary to plate 77 (Figure 65, bottom), the xenophobia of Choiseul-Gouffier is no longer checked by a veneer of politeness: "After working all day on the measurements of the ruins—which I will talk about in the next articles—I went to see the Aga, Hassan Tchaousch Oglou's grandson. He was a young man, extremely ugly and absolutely stupid, and who will, in all likelihood, get strangled shortly after his grandfather's death; he first welcomed me with great

Palais de l'Aga d'Eski-Hissar.

Fête turque.

Figure 65. *Palais de l'Aga d'Eski-Hissar* and *Fête turque*, plates 76 (*top*) and 77 (*bottom*) in Choiseul-Gouffier, *Voyage pittoresque de la Grèce* (1782), engravings. Courtesy of the Getty Research Institute, Los Angeles.

arrogance" (136). The audience with the ağa is quickly related and supplemented with an account of a festivity whose implications for Choiseul-Gouffier's overall rhetorical objectives can't be overstated. The deployment of sodomy in the following passage is the rhetorical counterweight to the deployment of reproductive heteronormativity in the first half of the text:

> Shortly after I placed myself next to the Aga, we saw entering a Turk dressed in fine attire, his head covered with a hat loaded with pearls; after a few gambols and a lot of grimaces, he crouched down in the middle of the place, and with an almost crazed look, started singing a long succession of verses: he accompanied himself with some kind of guitar which made a loud and repeated noise, and which he did not stop hitting with his fingers all held together. He first celebrated the fearlessness and the victories of the brave Hassan,[27] like in Homer['s *Odyssey*], when Telemachus hears his father's praises being sung at Menelaus's table. Those war songs were soon followed by songs more alike the show that was being prepared: he celebrated the subject of his love, painted all their charm; but too faithful to the Ancients' examples, he only demonstrated the corruption of this region, and recalled Anacreon's amorality [les égarements d'Anacréon]. Then, four young persons came in dancing, and, next, played some kind of farce, whose obscenity was too revolting to even be possibly mentioned. The Aga's enthusiasm, the clapping and the ambient inebriation of the people, showed me to what excess the Turks push their depravity, which seems to be hereditary among the inhabitants of this region. (136–37)

There are two *égarements*, or aberrations in this passage. The first is the perversion of martial panegyric itself. To compare the discordant and frenetic song of praise to the ağa to the celebration of Odysseus's heroism is to emphasize the aberration of the former from the timeless example of the latter. However, this ironic gesture partakes less of the explicit language of perversion than Choiseul-Gouffier's treatment of the celebration of the ağa's sodomitical desires in song and in the ensuing dance. At first declared revolting, these "égarements d'Anacréon" are immediately associated with the climate—another debt to Montesquieu—but this raises a significant problem. In this analysis, ancient Greek culture would be no less aberrant and this is indicated by the fact that Anacreon's name substitutes for sodomy.

As soon as this problem surfaces, the text shifts gears and opts instead for obfuscation: any further description of the dance is too obscene to relate. And that representational erasure proves to be highly useful. At one level, this reticence is staged out of ostensible politeness, but at another level, representational lack here is about maintaining the sexual economy of the *Voyage pittoresque* by according visibility to Greek women and relegating Ottoman sexuality to a shadowy realm of perverse phantasm. As we have already seen, the entire first section of the text aligns Greece, both ancient and modern, with reproductive heteronormative desire. From the frontispiece to the ethnographic portraits of Greek women, maternal care operates as a sign of the potential to revivify Greek liberty. That rhetoric relies on a counterintuitive suppression of the widely known pederastic elements of ancient Greek culture and society. By accentuating the ağa's sodomitical character and by forcing his readers to imagine precisely what these young dancers are doing that is so revolting, he is effectively attempting to firmly align Ottoman rule with aberrant, nonproductive sexuality. That nonproductivity resonates with the repeated images of fear, death, and desolation in the latter seven *livraisons*. This issue will return with some urgency in Chapter 7 because Choiseul-Gouffier's chief diplomatic rival in Pera, Sir Robert Ainslie, will turn Choiseul-Gouffier's deployment of sexuality inside out to generate an extraordinary discourse of peace that turns on Anglo-Ottoman collaboration and the recognition of the heroic legitimacy of same-sex desire. And as we will see in the final chapter of the book, this intervention is not isolated: Byron will engage with the deployment of normative sexuality in his critique of imperial/antiquarian desire in *The Giaour*.

Collaboration with local powers and peoples is fundamentally inimical to Choiseul-Gouffier's project. Because the very same climatological argument that underwrites this territorialization of normative and aberrant desires applies to ancient and contemporary Greek culture, Choiseul-Gouffier ultimately delegitimates all the local populations in the region and chooses to deal with allegorical dreams of Greek receptivity and nightmares Turkish perversion. With the sexual and governmental arguments now fully explicated, it is clear that *Voyage pittoresque*'s primary objective has been to clear the ground for the appropriation of ancient culture by the European enlightenment here handily embodied by Choiseul-Gouffier himself and by extension his readers. This is hardly surprising, but what separates *Voyage pittoresque* from its predecessors is its explicit interest in the prosecution of war. In his encounters with the ağa, Choiseul-Gouffier begrudgingly admits that he relies on Ottoman hospitality for access to Greek antiquity.[28] Because this situation is presented as both morally intolerable and ultimately unsafe, the only solution is regime change.

Smoke and Mirrors

As noted earlier, Choiseul-Gouffier was himself a military man, and his expedition was appended to the cartographic mission of the Marquis de Chabert, captain of the frigate *L'Atalante*. He had orders to take hydrographic readings of the Ionian and Aegean Seas for strategic reasons. This helps to explain the preponderance of maps in the volume and the careful presentation of depth measurements throughout. The *Plan du Port de Naussa* (Figure 66) gives precise locations for the artillery batteries that protect the harbor and depth measurements for planning a successful assault. In case the military connotations would go unnoticed, the inset lozenge identifying the map is a compendium of naval cannon and ammunition that connotes the recent Russian naval victories over the Turkish fleet. In doing so, Choiseul-Gouffier's text goes further than incorporating the strategic observations of his colleague. *Voyage pittoresque* is explicitly interested in the recent war between Russia and the Ottoman Empire because Russia's victory demonstrates the vulnerability of the Ottoman military and the ineptitude of the Ottoman state.

This has already been noted in Choiseul-Gouffier's remarks on the fool in the ağa's court, but key events from that conflict have structural prominence in the first half of the volume. If one were to enter the shop of a Paris bookseller and open the compiled volume, the first illustration one would see after the "Discours préliminaire" and the maps of ancient and modern Greece is the headpiece to the first chapter (Figure 67). A complex and busy engraving, its import is perhaps most clearly realized in relation to the frontispiece discussed above. Again we have an allegorical figure flanked by two trees, but rather than a supine figure of feminized Greece reclining on the tomb of the fallen hero Leonidas, this engraving features an active warrior goddess straddling a compendium of maps, cannon, and other weapons. She leads a European army across the picture plane from right to left and pushes a group of chained and starving figures toward the dead tree on the left margin of the engraving. On the end of her lance is the turban-like helmet of the enemy, and the lance itself firmly divides the composition into two contrasting halves. To the right of the lance we have glorious victory (figured by the warrior herself), order (conspicuously rendered in the legion of troops), and vibrant life (here associated with the palm tree and the foreground vegetation). To the left of the lance we have subjugation (figured by the fleeing chained figures), destruction (the town burning in the background), and death (here figured by the hollow and blasted tree). The map, the minarets in the burning town, and the uniforms of the marching soldiers specify the war in question: this is an explicit celebration of Russian victory over the Ottoman Empire in the recent war. In a sense, the transition from the frontispiece to the headpiece of chapter 1 enacts the bellicose injunction encoded in the inscription on the rock above the allegorical figure of Greece. It is as though the Russian troops have arisen from Leonidas's bones, reclining Greece has transformed into a warrior goddess, and vengeance on behalf of "Liberty"—directed at a conspicuously Ottoman target—is under way.

But the most salient sign in the headpiece to the first chapter is the smoke that enshrouds the burning Turkish town and from which the chained figures emerge.

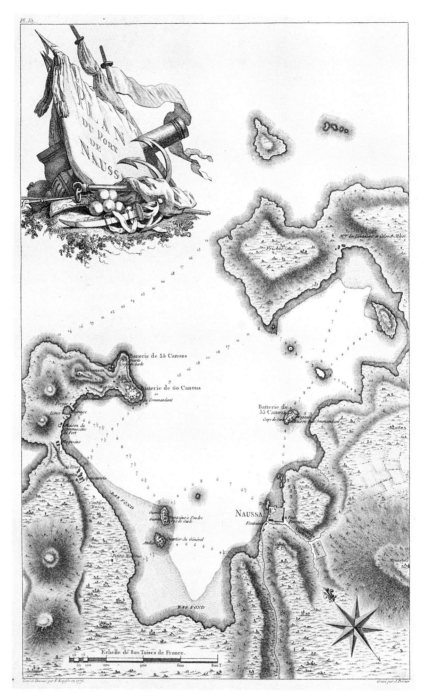

Figure 66. *Plan du Port de Naussa*, plate 35 in *Voyage pittoresque de la Grèce* (1782), engraving. Courtesy of the Getty Research Institute, Los Angeles.

Figure 67. Headpiece to chapter 1 in Choiseul-Gouffier, *Voyage pittoresque de la Grèce* (1782), engraving. Courtesy of the Getty Research Institute.

Throughout *Voyage pittoresque* smoke is used to figure violent change. In many of the topographical views from the second half of the text, fire and smoke are deployed as visual signs of danger and cultural dislocation. I have already noted this in regard to plate 99 where the smoke from the Turkish campfire is folded into a stadial argument about the ongoing Ottoman threat to the preservation of Greek antiquity (see Figure 53). One could also argue that the raging fire at the center of plate 74 (see Figure 61) is a further sign of the instability of the overland part of Choiseul-Gouffier's journey. But in the first half of the text engraved smoke has an altogether different connotation that mitigates these later threats because it is used to great effect in Hilaire's renderings of recent Russian victories over the Ottoman military. In fact the first full-sized plate in the volume emphasizes that Choiseul-Gouffier and his companions are exploring what was recently a war zone (Figure 68). In Hilaire's *Vue de la ville et du chateau de Coron, assiégé par le Rûsses en 1770* smoke is coming from the castle, and thus the Russian siege is ongoing. It is important to think about the aggressivity of this gesture because this engraving cannot be called a topographical view in the strict sense. The events depicted happened six years prior to the *L'Atalante*'s arrival at Koroni at the southern extremity of the Peloponnesian peninsula, thus this engraving hybridizes landscape observation and history painting. The Russian men-of-war in the foreground right and middle ground and the two Russian galleys have been integrated into a historically more recent view of the harbor. But I would venture that it is smoke that temporalizes the image; smoke visually ties the ships to the fortress in a fantasy of ongoing crisis, and it links this engraving back to the allegorical headpiece to chapter 1.

This sense of ongoing conflict is important because, as Choiseul-Gouffier recounts at length in the commentary to this image, this is not a representation of

VUE DE LA VILLE ET DU CHATEAU DE CORON,

dessiné par les Russes en 1770.

A. P. D. R.

Figure 68. *Vue de la ville et du château de Coron*, plate 1 in Choiseul-Gouffier, *Voyage pittoresque de la Grèce* (1782), engraving. Courtesy of the Getty Research Institute, Los Angeles.

Figure 69. *Soldats Albanois*, plate 2 in Choiseul-Gouffier, *Voyage pittoresque de la Grèce* (1782), engraving. Courtesy of the Getty Research Institute, Los Angeles.

Ottoman defeat. War between the Russians and Ottoman Porte had been ongoing since 1768. But in 1770 Greeks in the Peloponnesian peninsula, with the assistance of Grigory, Aleksey, and Fyodor Orlov, rose up against Ottoman rule. Ottoman administration of the region had become increasingly corrupt and ineffective to the point where Greek towns were regularly raided and ravaged by Albanian and other criminal forces. The significance of these armed Albanians is indicated by the fact that the second plate in *Voyage pittoresque* is devoted to an ethnographic portrait of their threatening presence (Figure 69). Taking advantage of the general state of insecurity, the Russians promised to support an emergent Greek revolution, but when they arrived in February 1770 with a small squadron of ships, the Greek insurgents lost faith in their ostensible allies. Despite initial victory over the Ottomans at Kalamata, the lack of cooperation between the insurgents and the Russians ultimately undid the revolution. The most significant sign of this failure came at Koroni, where the Ottomans withstood the Russian siege but then burned the town. Hilaire's image depicts this moment:

> The Count of Orlow [Orlov] finally decided to lift the siege of Coron on 26 April 1770. The Turkish garrison left the Castle as soon as they saw the Squadron casting off, and entirely destroyed the Greek city. The Traders' Shops—all French—were pillaged and burned. As soon as the siege had started, these unlucky people had decided to board a Trading vessel, which

got there by chance, and as it had been keeping perfectly neutral, had waited under the protection of both the Russians and the Turks, and thus their fate was sealed: they lost in one day the fruits of their labor. (4–5)

By suddenly turning to the impact of the failed revolution on French trade, Choiseul-Gouffier reminds his readers of their interest in the depicted moment and emphasizes that none of the combatants can adequately defend that which is valuable. With varying degrees of emphasis, Ottoman cruelty, Russian ineptitude, Albanian greed, and Greek immaturity are all signaled in Choiseul-Gouffier's multiparagraph discussion of this missed opportunity on the Greek mainland.[29] This subtly raises the question of who will take on the role of protector; again the phrase *exoriare aliquis* resonates with Choiseul-Gouffier's overall rhetorical objectives. But it is the willingness of the Ottomans to retaliate by burning the Greek village that Hilaire captures in plate 1, and it is this action—seemingly ongoing—that Choiseul-Gouffier chooses to open his travel narrative.

By opening with this retroactive view, Choiseul-Gouffier is not only establishing an ongoing sense of anxiety but also anticipating an extraordinary scene of violence already well known to his readers. Only two and a half months after the lifting of the siege at Koroni, Count Orlov, with the assistance of the British admiral Elphinston, would completely destroy the Ottoman fleet in the Bay of Çeşme. The burning of the Ottoman fleet at Çeşme is an epochal event in *Voyage pittoresque*. It is proof beyond all other that the Ottoman Empire can be defeated in spite of its superior numbers and for this reason the battle is given a prominent place in the first half of the volume. Choiseul-Gouffier's explication of the battle moves in two directions. His first rhetorical move is to emphasize that the Ottomans were defeated because the Russians had the benefit of English strategic innovations. The battle is first presented in the form of a map drawn and dated by Choiseul-Gouffier that tracks the movements of the Russian and English ships as they corralled the Ottoman galleys into the harbor (Figure 70). The map's title, *Plan du Port de Tchesmé et des manoeuvres de l'Escadre Russe le 5 et le 7 Juillet 1770* (Map of the Port of Çeşme and the Maneuvers of the Russian Squadron, the 5th and the 7th of July 1700), indicates that this is a two-dimensional rendering of a series of events that unfolded over three days. It may seem like a minor point but this visualization effectively compresses sequential time into a single observable arrangement of signs. Furthermore, the map's hydrographic measurements, its mathematical precision, and above all its veneer of scientific objectivity transform the horrific conflagration of the Ottoman fleet into a detached image of reasonable observation. In this crucial assertion of the power of scientific modernity, the very same skills that go into making this map are the ones that enabled the Russians and the British to outmaneuver and destroy the Ottomans. The link between mapmaking, ordnance

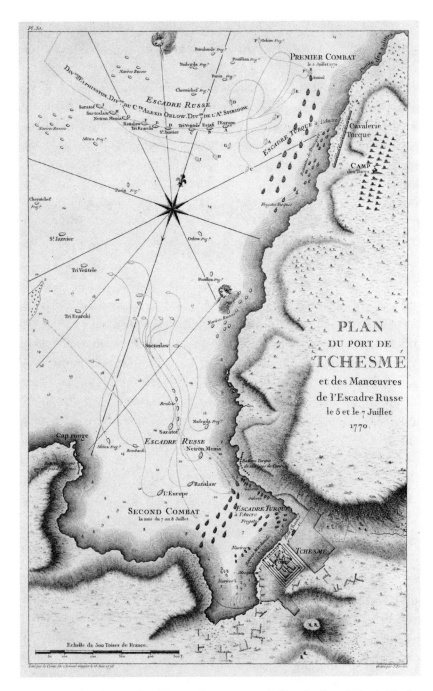

Figure 70. *Plan du Port de Tchesmé et des manœuvres de l'Escadre Russe le 5 et le 7 Juillet 1770*, plate 50 in Choiseul-Gouffier, *Voyage pittoresque de la Grèce* (1782), engraving. Courtesy of the Getty Research Institute, Los Angeles.

survey, navigation, strategic prowess, and authority is a powerful nexus because it fully aligns the reader with the map's maker and with the officers who enacted these maneuvers.[30]

When we recall the British officer's account of the battle (see Chapter 5), we can discern two different modes of distantion from the horror of war. In our discussion of the officer's *Authentic Narrative*, we demonstrated how he used the rhetoric of the sublime to apprehend the incomprehensible. This involved a temporal rupture and a figural compensation: metaphor was used to effect a representational transit past the witnessing of mass death. Choiseul-Gouffier's map and his ensuing narration of events have none of the affective force of the British officer's testimony:

> At midnight on the seventh, five Russian vessels crossed in front of the port, and started a dreadful cannonade supported by the perpetual firing of a bomb galliot; but they soon resorted to more dreadful means, which were of great effect. A fire ship set fire to one of the Turkish vessels (I); and as a violent wind rose at the same time, the whole Ottoman fleet got consumed, except for a couple of ships, which the Russians took hold of with their rowing boats and which they managed to preserve from the widespread fire.
>
> All the inhabitants of Scio witnessed this awful scene, and the light of the conflagration was such, that they could discern the least events from the depths of the port. All the vessels were on fire, and successively exploded, as the fire reached the stocks of gunpowder: the sea was covered with victims, who swam through the debris and the flames and tried to reach the shore: the artillery of the Turkish vessels, which was loaded, became a new way of destroying, and wrecked almost all of the city and the fort of Tchesmé. (92–95)

The text goes on for two more paragraphs to articulate the political implications of this action, but these were already widely known. The Ottoman defeat at Çeşme was not only a turning point in the war, but also an important sign of Ottoman vulnerability. What I'm more interested in is how the initial deployment of the map's detached precision seems to authorize the narrative distantiation of the above passage. Here image and text are working together to suppress any kind of affective response. Choiseul-Gouffier's key rhetorical move here is to talk more about the propagation of flames and fire, less about the sailors dying on board ship or drowning in the harbor. This has the disturbing effect of turning the battle into a spectacle of light, heat, and, of course, smoke.

This rendering of the battle as a spectacle of fire is modified further by Hilaire in the next plate (Figure 71). His *Vue du port et de la ville de Chesmé* (*View of the*

VUE DU PORT ET DE LA VILLE DE CHESMÉ.

A.·P.·D.·R.

Figure 71. *Vue du port et de la ville de Chesmé*, plate 51 in Choiseul-Gouffier, *Voyage pittoresque de la Grèce* (1782), engraving. Courtesy of the Getty Research Institute, Los Angeles.

Port and the Town of Chesmé) is curious because unlike Choiseul-Gouffier's representations of the battle it does not signal the date of the battle in the title. The generic title of the topographical view seems to imply that it is no different from any of the other views in the first section of *Voyage pittoresque*. But close examination of the engraving reveals that ships and galleys are still burning on the left.[31] The right side of the engraving is littered with hulks and sinking ships. In other words, the Battle of Çeşme appears to be still unfolding, or we have arrived on the scene sometime on the following day. Reminiscent of the first plate in the volume, this engraving hybridizes two or even three temporal moments. The left portion of the engraving seems to capture the immediate aftermath of the Battle of Çeşme on, say, 8 July 1770: ships are still burning near the shore. The right portion gives a sense of the harbor after the fires have stopped burning: the right portion of the image is literally a watery grave. But these two scenes frame a view of the town's minaret and its crenellated walls as they were observed by Hilaire and Choiseul-Gouffier in 1776. My sense is that this hybridization of historical moments gives the sense that the firestorm that destroyed the Ottoman fleet is figuratively still burning. With this engraving the *Voyage pittoresque* moves well beyond the empirical record of a specific journey of enlightenment. It has moved into the realm of wishful thinking, and here the desire for cultural appropriation takes a very specific form. Hilaire's engraving imagines a state of continual destruction for Ottoman culture and thus sketches in an opportunity for those, like Choiseul-Gouffier or Byron thirty years later, who would like to imagine a Greece free of Ottoman control. But more subtly, the desire for past moments to inhere in the present—like the smoke perpetually rising in the left of plate 51—applies as much to the destruction of the Ottomans as it does to the "continuation" of ancient Greek culture in the Enlightenment. It involves a complex collapse of temporal distinction and thus amounts to a historical sublation in which past, present, and future are suddenly disclosed in a fantasy of plenitudinous cultural identity. In the midst of all this smoke lies a well-polished mirror that Choiseul-Gouffier returns to again and again to shore up the all-too-obvious indications that time and the other are continually moving away from his grasp.

Lady Craven's Hellenic Diversions

"I Cannot Even Have a Little Finger or a Toe"

In a letter to his friend Horace Mann, dated 16 March 1786, the author and politician Horace Walpole, known now primarily for his gothic novel *The Castle of Otranto* (1764) and for his remarkable house at Strawberry Hill, notes that he has been following "the adventures of a certain Lady and her *cousin* Vernon . . . I comfort myself that I have never dealt with my heroine but in compliments or good advice—but this comes of corresponding with strolling Roxanas."[32] The "Roxana" in question here is the scandalous Lady Elizabeth Craven and the adventures referred to here would eventually be collected in her travel narrative *A Journey Through the Crimea to Constantinople*, which was first published in London in 1789 by G. G. J. and J. Robinson in a costly quarto edition with six engravings and a "map of the roads of Crimea." Walpole's remark offers a useful starting point for an introduction to Craven's text because of the double meaning of Walpole's preferred appellation. To call Lady Craven a "strolling Roxana" compares her not only to Roxolana, the famous wife of the sixteenth-century sultan Suleiman, and thus to a whole host of resilient fantasies regarding Eastern sexuality and Oriental despotism, but also to the eponymous heroine of Daniel Defoe's novel *Roxana* of 1724.[33] Defoe's novel is about the rise and demise of an English courtesan, who, in a famous scene, clinches an affair with the king by donning the costume of a "Turkish" woman. The masquerade is both heavily eroticized and thematically rich because Defoe deploys Turkish costume to figure Roxana's threat to the cultural and social order of early eighteenth-century Britain. As Laura Brown argues, Roxana is threatening because, like the supposed wife of the sultan, her erotic agency gives her access not only to the sinews of power, but also to a form of financial independence wildly at odds with normative British understandings of femininity and class identity.[34] As a "Fortunate Mistress"—Defoe's phrase—Roxana develops an entrepreneurial relation to her own virtue that simultaneously provides her with remarkable class mobility and denies her the safety net of reputable friends and relations.

But what are we to make of the fact that for Walpole, Craven was a "strolling Roxana"? At one level, the verb stroll carries the connotation of prostitution, but it also connotes travel. So the question can be refigured as, Does women's travel, particularly to the East, partake of the social opprobrium reserved for prostitution? This is a vital question because Craven's narrative is at pains to distance itself from the sexual scandals that precipitated her departure from England. We will return to these matters shortly, for there is another way of reading Walpole's remark that merits our attention. From as early as 1778, Lady Craven had been writing and translating plays, including Antoine de Ferriol, comte de Pont-de-Veyle's *La somnambule* (translated by Craven as *The Sleep-Walker*). Throughout the late 1770s and early 1780s, Lady Craven's plays were performed for the benefit of the local poor at Benham, near the Craven's seat at Newbury, and eventually farces such as *The Miniature Picture* and *The Silver Tankard; or, The Point at Portsmouth* were performed at Drury Lane and the Haymarket in 1781. By modifying the phrase "strolling player," Walpole is signaling Lady Craven's deep connection to both private theatricals and to the lower genres of theater, which would eventually undermine the legitimacy of the royal patent theaters. Throughout the eighteenth century, the patent theaters had exclusive rights to present comedy and tragedy in London, but a wide range of theatrical practices emerged that challenged this government-sponsored monopoly. Strolling players were the lowest members of the theatrical community, moving from town to town to organize shows outside the reach of the censor. As commercial entertainers, they shared a great deal with courtesans and prostitutes, who also threatened, through commercial means, the norms of legitimate sexual exchange that structured British society. Walpole is emphasizing something already nascent in the reference to Defoe's novel: namely, that Craven travels through the world behind a series of complex and potentially unsettling personae. Walpole's remark reminds us that the narrator of *A Journey* both is and isn't Lady Craven, and that much of the complexity of her book lies in the transit from historical personage to a self-styled theatrical citizen of the world.

It is at times difficult to imagine a more fascinating character. Elizabeth Berkeley was born on 17 December 1750, the youngest daughter of Augustus, 4th Earl of Berkeley. Seventeen years later she was married to William Craven, who would become Baron Craven in 1769. Monogamy was not their strong suit. They had six children and numerous affairs. What is interesting is that these infidelities were in no way discreet. In 1773, Lady Craven conducted a remarkably public affair with Adrien-Louis de Bonnières, duc de Guines. He was the French ambassador to London, and the affair was sensationalized in the *Town and Country Magazine*.[35] George Romney, competing with Sir Joshua Reynolds for the most fashionable sitters, was fully aware of Lady Craven's notoriety and her beauty when he painted her portrait in 1778. It was also during this period that she developed literary relationships with Horace Walpole, Samuel Johnson, and James Boswell. In 1783, Baron Craven formally separated from his wife by settling £1,500 per annum on her. She left England with her youngest son to reside near Versailles. Like Defoe's Roxana, her departure and her husband's subsequent actions against her meant that she was permanently alienated from her other children.

For his part, the baron faced no such scrutiny or disgrace. He had a public mistress, a Mrs. Byrne, who figures quite prominently in the *Journey*'s dedication: "Beside curiosity, my friends will in these Letters see at least for some time where the real Lady Craven has been, and where she is to be found—it having been the practice for some years past, for a Birmingham coin of myself to pass in most of the inns in France, Switzerland, and England, for the wife of my husband. My arms and coronet sometimes supporting, in some measure this insolent deception; by which, probably, I may have been seen to behave very improperly."[36] With this gesture, Lady Craven sets her text up as defense against what she calls "a treason to my birth and character" perpetrated by her husband and his mistress. Despite this retroactive gambit to restore her relative virtue, Lady Craven lived in France, like many other men and women of fashion, as a sexual expatriate. Forced to leave England because of sexual indiscretions, these aristocrats had the financial where-withal to circulate in European society without the social barriers imposed by strict codes of reputation and honor, but they were often permanently separated from their relations. Among these scandalous figures were important collectors of antiquities such as Sir Richard Worsley, who fled England in 1783 after it was re-vealed that he enabled the numerous adulterous affairs of his wife. A prominent antiquarian, he was traveling through Greece, Turkey, and the Crimea at the same time as Craven, and she arranged for part of his transit to the Crimea (214). Al-ready socially suspect, these men and women were heavily scrutinized in the Lon-don press for their cosmopolitan social ties. While living near Versailles, Craven became part of the social circles at court, wrote plays for the court theater, and appears to have captivated a number of men, including Henry Vernon, the rather unnotable fashionable lover who accompanied her on her travels to Russia and Con-stantinople, and Christian Frederick Charles Alexander, Margrave of Brandenburg-Ansbach-Bayreuth, to whom *A Journey* is dedicated and who would eventually become her husband.

The situation of these two men, both in Craven's life and in her travel narra-tive, is intriguing. The journey recorded by Craven's narrative is very much an erotic adventure: between 1783 and 1786, she traveled in Vernon's company, but his presence—and the sexual liaison it implies—is all but erased in the text. He is referred to near the end of the narrative, but reference was probably not that nec-essary when the book was published in 1789. As Katherine Turner argues, "By March 1786 Lady Craven's affair with Vernon had become public knowledge in London and Lord Craven had successfully discouraged her children from writing to her."[37] Furthermore, many readers in London would have known that by March 1787 Lady Craven, like Roxana in Defoe's novel, had moved up the social ladder and was openly living with the Margrave of Ansbach in spite of the fact that the invalid margravine was still alive. Shortly after the publication of *A Jour-ney* in 1789, the mainstream monthly *The Gentleman's Magazine*, with the benefit of hindsight drew attention to Craven's dedication to the margrave in order to in-sinuate that her "tender character of a *brother*" didn't quite capture the true nature of this relationship.[38] For readers aware of this sexual itinerary, *A Journey*'s very public dedication to the margrave and its suppression of Vernon reads as a pro-gress of vice in which every new relationship involves the reinvention of the cour-tesan. As in *Roxana*, that reinvention is interesting because it also reconfigures the social dynamics that surround her self-representation, and in this case that has significant political ramifications.

It is important to remember that Lady Craven went to France just as the Treaty of Paris and the Treaties of Versailles were bringing the American war to a close. From 1778 to 1783, France had been allied with the American colonists against Britain, and thus Lady Craven's history of affection for French officials and her life at court in Versailles immediately after the war meant that her patriotism was easily impugned. This period—which I have referred to elsewhere as post-American—was one of remarkable anxiety regarding Britain's national and imperial identity.[39] Because the American colonies used the language of political liberty to resist colonial oppression and because most Britons considered the American colonists as brethren, the rift in the Atlantic world deeply unsettled the very grounds on which fantasies of governmentality and citizenship were built. Across a wide range of media, Britons not only engaged in a thoroughgoing critique of martial masculinity but also began to reconfigure their relation to the cultural patrimony. Lady Craven's text is not immune from this scrutiny of gender and culture, and in quite conspicuous ways she interweaves emergent gender norms and patriotic exculpations with a focused claim on the cultural legacy of antiquity. The transit from 1784—the time of her journey—to 1789—the date of publication—follows a trajectory from social suspicion to increasingly normative class affiliation for Lady Craven. This is important because significant portions of *A Journey* are devoted to reconstituting Lady Craven's political affiliation with Britain. Her extended homage to George Eliott, the British governor of Gibraltar who heroically withstood a three-and-a-half-year siege by the French and Spanish forces during the American war, and her satire of French tactical errors in the final phases of that conflict are the most obvious examples of this strategy (60–72), but there are more subtle negotiations with the question of Anglo-French relations throughout the book. Lady Craven's access to foreign courts is generally managed through her French connections, and she directs a great deal of attention toward her various French hosts. This is especially acute during her stay in Constantinople, where she was the guest of none other than the newly appointed French ambassador, the Comte de Choiseul-Gouffier.

After taking up his post as ambassador to the Ottoman Porte in 1784, Choiseul-Gouffier established an academy of sorts in the Palais de France in Pera to prepare the second volume of *Voyage pittoresque*. In a letter dated 25 April 1786 from her *Journey Through the Crimea to Constantinople*, Lady Elizabeth Craven provides her reader with a preemptive explanation for her decision to snub the British ambassador to the Ottoman Porte to reside instead with the French ambassador:

> I have a double satisfaction of being *au Palais de France*; Mr. de Choiseul has been sick these six months and never been out, but his spirits are better, and upon my account he has opened his house, and goes out a little,

which cannot fail to do him good. He has some artists with him, whose pencils he has employed to collect all the finest drawings, coloured, of the finest ruins that exist either in Europe or Asia, where an artist could venture—Monsieur Casas, one of them, has been plundered by Arabs several times; but his beautiful and accurate drawings will gain him immortal honour. The Comte de Choiseul's collection is, perhaps, the only thing in the world of the kind, and he means, when he returns to Paris, to have all the ruins and temples executed in plaster of Paris, or some materials which will copy the marble in small models; to be placed in a gallery upon tables. (201)

According to Frédéric Barbier, Choiseul-Gouffier's embassy was accompanied by a host of scholars and artists. The most important figure in Choiseul-Gouffier's entourage was the painter Louis-François Cassas. Under Choiseul-Gouffier's supervision Cassas conducted a number of expeditions in the eastern Mediterranean, including an overland journey to Palmyra and Balbec, a trip to Egypt, and, in the company of the French archaeologist Jean-Baptiste Le Chevalier, an attempt to locate the ruins of ancient Troy. Cassas produced over two hundred views of the region many of which were collected into the second volume of *Voyage pittoresque*.[40]

But Craven's account of aesthetic sociability has another register as well.

At night when we have no visitors, and all the ambassador's business is done, he comes into my room, followed by Mr. Casas and a few more people, with large *portefeuilles* full of these most beautiful drawings, and we pass three or four hours looking over them, and conversing upon topics which are my favourites—It is a singular instance of good taste in a Frenchman, to have given himself up ten years ago to the finding and collecting all that is really best worthy of record, as to the ancient architecture—Mr. de Choiseul's *Voyage Pittoresque de la Grece*, and when he was but two-and-twenty, taking the most perilous journeys to find out new antiquities, if I may so call them, must endear him to all lovers of the fine arts. (202)

Lady Craven's celebration of the philhellenic activities of the French ambassador and of his immediate social circle in Constantinople is part of an important aestheticization of political relations that consistently misrecognizes the contemporary Mediterranean world in terms of the classical past. In spite of its ostensibly cosmopolitan environment, the social world of Pera was exceedingly aware of ethnicity, rank, and nationality, especially among Britons who had just lost an empire in the Atlantic and were dealing with the local aftereffects of the diminished global influence. As Lady Craven goes on to record, her place of residence caused no small

amount of concern: "I am told there is an English merchant here extremely of-
fended at my lodging *au Palais de France*, and says, if Sir R. Ainslie's house was
not good enough for me, he had a new house, which he would have emptied, and
let me have had it all to myself—It is an affront to the *nation*, he says—*A peeress of
England to lodge at the French Ambassador's!*—The English merchants are very good
to me; I believe they guess the respect and esteem I have for them" (214–15). As
we have seen, Lady Craven's French predilections are a matter of some consequence,
but here she contains the anxiety generated by her association with the French
ambassador by suggesting that any objection could only come from a merchant,
from one who did not share the aesthetic lingua franca that makes it so easy for
Lady Craven to socialize with her aristocratic French hosts. As Viccy Coltman has
argued, the very nature of aristocratic education, the cultural underpinnings of
the diplomatic class, was so permeated by a "classical mood" that one can posit a
shared repertoire of texts and artifacts that define a particular style of elite identity.[41] What the merchant in Craven's text doesn't realize is that she is choosing a
very specific deployment of the classical world that was contested by the less famous British ambassador.

It should now be clear that Lady Craven's residence at the Palais de France with
the Comte de Choiseul-Gouffier is apt. Like the *Voyage pittoresque*, her text is
explicitly racist in its estimation of the "Turks," and like her French host, she consistently represents Greece as an occupied land, crushed by Ottoman domination,
desiring to rediscover and reawaken its liberty. In his company, she travels to some
of the sites described and illustrated in Choiseul-Gouffier's book and eventually
ends up in Athens to contemplate the ruins of the Acropolis: "The Temple of
Minerva, in the citadel of Athens, was used by the Turks as a magazine for pow-
der, which blowing up has flung down such a quantity of beautiful sculpture that
I should be very happy to have permission to pick up the broken pieces on the
ground—but, alas, Sir, I cannot even have a little finger or a toe, for the Ambassador who had been a whole year negociating for permission to convey to Constantinople a fragment he had pitched upon, and thought himself sure of, will be
sadly disappointed" (256). What interests me here is how the question of war discloses itself in Craven's text. Her prose is such that an event that happened almost
one hundred years earlier—in 1687 the Venetians shelled the Ottoman fortifications on the Acropolis and a mortar blew up the Turkish magazine—appears to
be just unfolding, scattering valuable sculpture at her feet. In a sense, this temporal slippage is symptomatic; everything about Lady Craven and Choiseul-
Gouffier's relation to these fragments of the classical past is marked by an erasure
of the present moment. Craven's text is remarkably similar to Hilaire's engraving of
the Bay of Çeşme in *Voyage pittoresque* in which the Ottoman fleet continues to
burn years after the fleet's destruction. It is as though desire for the finger or the

toe—the smallest of fragments from the ancient Greek world—eclipses all other considerations. In fact, the possession of that finger or toe is part of a larger political desire not only to reclaim these "sacral spaces" from the Ottomans but also to refigure the world as a phantasmatic zone of ancient liberty.

The simultaneous enactment of political and antiquarian observation that marked his tour of the Greek islands and Asia Minor also characterized Choiseul-Gouffier's career at the Sublime Porte: his diplomatic objectives began to enact the desires to liberate Greece from Ottoman control that were encoded in the *Voyage pittoresque*. For a brief period, Choiseul-Gouffier's fantasy of extirpating Ottoman influence could be fulfilled by Russia's imperial designs. From 1781, Catherine the Great was in control of the trade passing through the Caspian Sea to Bukhara and on the way to India. By 1783, she had annexed the Crimea from the Ottomans and thus was on the verge of control of the Black Sea. The annexation was a source of persistent aggravation for the Ottoman Porte—the ulema opposed Russian control of the Crimea on religious grounds, and the increasing military presence in the Black Sea severely threatened the already diminished Ottoman military presence in the region.

British officials were extremely concerned by the opportunity that the Crimean annexation raised for both Russia and France. From the end of the American war in 1783 to the arrival of Lady Craven in Pera in the spring of 1786, Britain was in a condition of relative diplomatic isolation. With the loss of the American colonies, protecting Britain's holdings in India from incursions by the French and the Dutch became of paramount importance. As Jeremy Black observes, "At the same time as Britain was vying with the Franco-Dutch alliance for dominance over the maritime route to India, Russia and France, though from different directions and only episodically and very loosely in cooperation, were apparently becoming more influential over the overland route."[42] British officials were extremely concerned by the opportunity that this raised for both Russia and France. France had historically opposed Russian incursions on the Ottoman Empire, but in 1783, none other than Choiseul-Gouffier argued in a memorandum that France should "expand her influence in the Levant by increasing her trade there. He argued that it would be possible both to preserve the Turkish Empire and to develop trade with Russia via the Black Sea. In August 1784 Louis XVI wrote to the Sultan seeking admission to the Black Sea for ships flying the French flag; Choiseul-Gouffier had been given instructions to the same end on 2 June. The Turks refused, but Marseilles ships flying the flag of Russia were acceptable. In 1785 a French trading company was established at Kherson, at the mouth of the Dnieper."[43] This shift had significant repercussions: the Russians intensified their trading relation with France at the same time that they refused to renew Britain's access to Russian commerce. Since access to Russian resources was crucial to the health of the Royal Navy, this shift not only exacerbated Britain's diplomatic isolation in the period following the American war, but also palpably impaired Britain's capacity to restore its military and economic strength. For the entire period of Craven's journey, the diplomatic actions of her primary host in Constantinople were of grave concern to the ministry of William Pitt and to George III. For a nation still processing the effect of American decolonization these threats were profoundly unsettling.

A Journey does not discuss the diplomatic activities of Lady Craven's host, but they serve as an important backdrop to much of the text's subtle engagement with matters of foreign policy. When she discusses her audience with Catherine II at the Hermitage, or describes a visit to Potemkin's palace outside Kherson, it is important to recognize that she is conversing with political figures widely understood to pose a threat to British imperial interests. The political complexity of her text becomes extremely acute in passages such as the following:

> Cherson [Kherson] may in time become a very beautiful town, and furnish the borders of the Boristhenes with examples of commerce; that inestimable and only real source of greatness to an empire—I am not soldier enough to know what fault there was in the fortifications, so that they are intirely to be done anew—but by the active and studious spirit of Korsakof, I have no doubt that they will be executed in a masterly manner—
>
> I can conceive nothing so pleasant to a young soldier, as to be employed in places where his talents must create the defence and stability of newly acquired possessions. (158–59)

Is this an expression of envy? Or is it a warning about the substantial French and Russian gains in this strategically vital area? It is remarkable that Craven doesn't indicate that the commercial activity described here is that of a French trading company working in concert with the Russian military. When she explicitly registers her wish "to see a colony of honest English families here; establishing manufactures, . . . establishing a fair and free trade from hence, and teaching industry and honesty to the insidious but oppressed Greeks, . . . waking the indolent Turk from his gilded slumbers" (188–89), she emphasizes that she does not wish to see the expansion of British mercantile interests in the region to come at a cost to French policy and trade. Rather her economic commitment to free trade subsumes British mercantilism in a cosmopolitan fantasy that "considers all mankind as one family, and, looking upon them as such, wishes them to be united for the common good; excluding from nations all selfish and monopolizing views" (189).

Larry Wolff reminds us that for many of Lady Craven's readers her journey was a precursor of sorts to the widely reported journey of Catherine the Great from Petersburg to the Crimea in 1787.[44] Craven actually takes advantage of the preparations for Catherine's triumphal procession to the Crimea by staying in many of the accommodations being prepared for the empress. This raises an important parallel between the two women that needs to be explored. During this period, Catherine was exerting increasing amounts of pressure on the hinterlands of the Ottoman Empire. In the period following Russia's incursion into the Crimea in the 1770s, Catherine secretly negotiated with Austria an alliance with the aim of eliminating the Ottomans from Europe altogether. This vast plan neatly divided the Ottoman territories such that Russia would control Turkey, Thrace, Bulgaria, and northern Greece in what amounted to a renovated Byzantine empire. Austria for its part would lay claim to Serbia, Bosnia, Herzegovina, and Dalmatia. The plan also involved the active participation of Venice, which would control Crete and Cypress, and France, which would gain Syria and Egypt. The implications of the latter annexation would be catastrophic to British trading interests in the Levant. France's extraordinary potential gains were a direct result of a progressive abandonment of its traditional Ottoman allies in the region following Louis XVI's marriage to Marie Antoinette and its resulting intensification of the Franco-Austrian alliance. Hence the British government found itself in the unfamiliar role of protector of the Ottomans and was on the verge of declaring an ill-advised war against Russia all through the spring and summer of 1791.

Lady Craven's text was published prior to the Ochakov crisis of 1791, but it is interesting to consider how many of her desires mirror those of Catherine. Her journey through the Crimea is full of the language of colonization, only Craven's "possession" of these spaces is aesthetic. Similarly, Catherine's so-called "Greek Plan" has its counterpart in Craven's aesthetic desire to liberate the Hellenic world from Ottoman rule. What is remarkable is that Craven's aesthetic translation of Catherine's political actions and aspirations is brokered by an alliance with France that looks very much like the kind of commercial and diplomatic relation desired by British officials all through this period. This leads one to wonder whether the parallel is established either to demonstrate an opening for Britain in this region or to highlight the real benefits of a commercial/political alliance with Russia. In other words, Craven seems to be establishing a desire for substitution whereby Britain supplants France and joins Russia and Austria in the partitioning of the Ottoman Empire. This brings Craven's text in line with the generally Francophobic approach to foreign affairs, but intriguingly it does so by aspiring to the position and accomplishments of someone like the Comte de Choiseul-Gouffier.

"I Think and Dream of Nothing but the Statues"

French mediation between the Ottoman Empire and Russia was shattered by war between the two powers in 1787, a war that seriously challenged the balance of power both in the region and among the various allies in continental Europe. Thus readers picking up Craven's text in 1789 may well have expected an elucidation of this volatile historical and political moment. But, as many reviewers noted at the time, *A Journey* does not seem to offer much in the way of useful knowledge regarding the Crimea, Russia, or Constantinople.[45] The *Analytical Review*, Joseph Johnson's radical monthly, is particularly telling on this point:

> In the slight remarks she makes, we have not observed much discrimination, and reflections are *very* thinly scattered. It has been said by a periodical writer, "that people, in a certain rank, carry an atmosphere with them wherever they go." Vanity, and many other causes, produce also a thick mist, through which objects are seldom seen as they really are; all in the same light. At the different courts Lady Craven visits, she converses with polite princes; but the reader cannot gather any information with respect to their characters as men, or catch a glimpse of a prominent feature to know them again in another company.[46]

This notion of a traveling atmosphere or mist that distorts Lady Craven's view offers a useful way of theorizing her representation of foreign spaces and peoples. The reviewer here ties this distortion to Lady Craven's rank, thus implying that the very aristocratic qualities that grant her access to the cosmopolitan world prevent her from seeing it as anything other than a reflection of herself. Thus the narrative is limited both in its purview—it rarely goes beyond her subjective aesthetic responses to her surroundings—and in its relation to preexisting ways of seeing social relations. That she should be amenable to both Choiseul-Gouffier's erasure of present-day Greece and Asia Minor in favor of a warmed over fantasy of classical liberty and Catherine's desire to establish a second Byzantine empire is a sign of the importance of this aestheticization to the consolidation of rank. These aestheticizations of the East are deeply entwined with fantasies of aristocratic election that cross conventional boundaries of nationality. That Craven's narrative was published at the time of the French Revolution is extraordinarily important because these historical events bring her and the ambassador together on political as well as aesthetic grounds. They are both part of the ancien régime that would be celebrated by Edmund Burke in *Reflections on the Revolution in France* (1790). As Horace Walpole indicates in his private repudiation of *A Journey*, Lady Craven's reputation would never be fully repaired, but her affiliation with the ancien régime allowed for a somewhat counterintuitive refiguration from sexual expatriate to political refugee.[47] And the very signs that rendered her suspect in 1783—her vanity, her Francophilia, her commitment to fashion and the beau monde—became the marks of her aristocratic bearing in the early 1790s.

However, the radical reviewer for the *Analytical Review* subtly registers the obsolescence of this fantasy of superior rank by indicating that Craven fails to fully recognize the gravity of the scenes she encounters. Although it is unverifiable, the possibility that this review was written by Mary Wollstonecraft, who regularly contributed to Johnson's publication, is intriguing for it resonates with many of Wollstonecraft's critiques of aristocratic demeanor in both *A Vindication of the Rights of Men* (1790) and *A Vindication of the Rights of Woman* (1792). At play here is a long-standing critique of fashion and luxury that became highly acute in the 1780s. Britain's failure in the American war was frequently tied to charges of dissipation and gender insubordination in both its political and martial leaders. For someone like William Cowper, Britain's loss of the colonies was a providential retribution for moral decay at the heart of the nation itself.[48] For readers of Craven's *A Journey*, the importance of emergent gender norms to this critique has far-reaching implications. Her representation of Ottoman culture is very much a function of her class privilege, and although we can discern typical forms of ethnocentrism throughout the text, philhellenism provides an important key to her descriptions of Ottoman and Greek society.

Importantly, that philhellenic stance is established well before she arrives in Constantinople in the narration of her visit to the Tribuna in the Uffizi palace in Florence. This famous octagonal room contained the Venus de' Medici, widely considered to be one the finest antiquities on the grand tour, and Lady Craven provides two descriptions of her reaction to this work.[49] Her first remark isolates a set of general responses to the entire room:

> I hope you do not expect a very rational letter from me, as I have been three days successively to see the statues and pictures, and am so much delighted with them, that I am at a loss how to give an account of my feelings, otherwise than by telling you, that while I am in the Tribune, the vulgar idle tale of real life never once comes into my mind, and I feel quite happy—and if till now I have been sorry often, which I have felt conscious of having nice feelings, or what is commonly called taste, at this moment I am extremely glad of it—I think and dream of nothing but the statues, from the time I leave them till I see them again. (78)

This sense of the Tribuna as a site of temporal suspension where the subject blessed with taste withdraws into a more perfect realm is reinforced in the second passage: "in the humour I am in, I could almost be tempted to remain a prisoner for life, upon condition my *cachot* was the Tribune; and I would ask for no other company than the heavenly inanimate figures in it—their silence is so much more eloquent than language—their forms so harmonious.—I think you begin not to understand me, and as I am not at all certain, if your ear and your eye agree together, as mine do, I will not attempt to explain what may be felt, but not described" (81). Lady Craven's resistance to this temptation to retire to a harmonious realm beyond the reach of linguistic description comes from a memory of her children, set off by a resemblance of a nearby Apollo to her son William, from whom she was alienated by her marital separation. In other words, her encomium to the power of art is trumped by her profession of maternal feeling.[50] This is reinforced in a postscript to the letter that elevates the seventeen statues of the Niobe family in a nearby gallery over the Venus. With the conspicuous deployment of reproductive sexuality here we can see the text's subtle alignment with heteronormative fantasies of the family that can be traced back to Choiseul-Gouffier's *Voyage pittoresque*, but which would take on crucial significance in Britain's reimagination of empire in the post-American era.

One could argue that Lady Craven's reactions to the Venus de' Medici and the Sala della Niobe provide a useful heuristic device for unlocking much of this text. Eighteenth-century viewers of the Venus saw the sculpture's pose as simultaneously chaste and revealing, thus providing a crucial template for much female portraiture in the period. George Romney's famous portrait of Lady Craven from 1778 replicates the sideways glance of the Venus, and thus at least part of her pleasure in the room has to do with a dreamlike condensation of her own beauty with this iconic rendering of classical beauty that quite literally ruptures the temporal continuum. That rupture is repaired by an allegorical affiliation between her maternal alienation and Niobe's suffering for her dead children. In terms of Lady Craven's represented viewing experience, the intense concentric pull of the viewer closer and closer to the Venus in what amounts to a kind of narcissistic vortex is countered by the centrifugal force of the Niobe group.[51] Arranged around the perimeter of the room, each anguished figure in the Sala della Niobe pulls the reader away from Niobe, and the very distance between the sculptures activates the radial lines of empathy between the mother and each dying child. This complex itinerary of aesthetic rapture, erotic identification, and maternal suffering condenses the primary rhetorical strategies of the text into one symptomatic whole, and it is from here that we can understand her critique of Ottoman culture.

Readers of *A Journey* would have recognized its divergence from Lady Mary Wortley Montagu's celebrated *Turkish Embassy Letters*, which deployed Turkish society to generate a scathing critique of Augustan social and sexual ideology. Montagu's letters were based on her travels in Turkey in 1717, but it was not until 1763 that they were published as *Letters of the Right Honourable Lady M——y W——y M——e: Written, during her Travels in Europe, Asia and Africa*. Her text went through numerous editions and was widely discussed in the ensuing years. As

Katherine S. H. Turner argues, "both writers commend the respect and apparent liberty granted to Turkish women, but Montagu's account of their grace and beauty is vigorously contradicted by Craven."[52] As we will see, the question of female beauty is anything but a trivial matter in *A Journey*. In a provocative gesture, Craven both parodies and openly disparages Lady Mary's letters as fraudulent (105). This provocation prompted censure from all of the reviewers, but perhaps the most salient issue here is the degree to which all extent readings of Craven's text, and indeed its composition, are colored by prior knowledge of Montagu's letters. This is symptomatically disclosed in a letter sent from Walpole to Craven on 2 January 1787, when she was preparing *A Journey*:

> I am sorry to hear, Madam, that by your account Lady Mary Wortley was no so accurate and faithful as modern travelers. The invaluable art of inoculation, which she brought from Constantinople, so dear to all admirers of beauty, and to which we owe perhaps the preservation of yours, stamps her an universal benefactress; and as you rival her in poetic talents, I had rather you would employ them to celebrate her for her nostrum, than detect her for romancing. However, genuine accounts of the interior of seraglios would be precious; and I was in hopes would become the greater rarities, as I flattered myself that your friends the Empress of Russia and Emperor were determined to level Ottoman tyranny. His Imperial Majesty [Joseph II, the Holy Roman emperor], who has demolished the prison bars of so many nunneries, would perform a still more Christian act in setting free so many useless sultanas; and her Czarish Majesty, I trust, would be as great a benefactress to our sex, by abolishing the barbarous practice that reduces us to be of none. Your Ladyship's indefatigable peregrinations should have such great objects in view, when you have the ear of sovereigns.
>
> . . . Every fair Circassian would acknowledge that one English lady had repaid their country for the secret which another had given to Europe from their practice.[53]

The primary point of contention between Craven and Montagu pertains specifically to the beauty of Ottoman women. Beyond its labored jokes on the liberation of women from the sultan's harem, Walpole's response to Craven's harsh repudiation of Montagu's assessment of Turkish beauty amounts to an apology for Lady Mary on the grounds that her importation of the practice of inoculation from Constantinople preserved the beauty not only of the British fair but also of Craven herself from the scourge of smallpox. This apology opens onto a rather strange quid pro quo of feminine preservation where the debt incurred by Montagu for the

beauty-preserving practice of smallpox vaccination is repaid by Craven's incitement of Catherine and Joseph to "liberate" the harem. In what is admittedly a
joking letter, Walpole brings the question of female beauty into direct relation
to questions of state, and in this he is merely making explicit something that was
nascent in Montagu's letters and would figure quite prominently in Craven's text.

Like Lady Mary Wortley Montagu, Lady Craven is fascinated by the harem
and the hammam, but her account of Constantinople is fully framed by a detailed
vindication of the taste of Choiseul-Gouffier and the circle of artists living under
his roof.[54] The first thing she relates upon her arrival in Constantinople is the con-
vening of an impromptu academy in her room (201). The intimacy of this scene of
classical appreciation should give us pause, because it is a rehearsal of the erotic
economy that was introduced in the Tribuna passages. In this space, among these
men, Lady Craven asserts a very specific kind of aesthetic agency that animates
her attack on the Sublime Porte for its failure to recognize the value of the Greek
antiquities it owns. That attack is most explicitly articulated in letter 55 where
Craven describes the disappointment felt by her and her French companions when
their attempts to convey statuary from the Parthenon to the Comte de Choiseul-
Gouffier are foiled by an Ottoman official. As important as the explicit declaration
that the Ottomans "have really not the smallest idea of the value of the treasures
they possess, and destroy them wantonly on every occasion" is her scornful narration
of her interview with the governor's daughters and wife that follows (257–58). She
portrays the women as both superstitious and subject to bodily decay. The former
quality is a confirmation of her general belief in Turkish ignorance, but the latter
is part of a larger construct that ties back into the veneration of classical beauty—
and, by extension, her own.

Unlike Lady Mary, whose letters return again and again to the beauty of
the women she encounters in the bath and the harem, Lady Craven finds Turkish
women physically repulsive. Her visit to the Acropolis is immediately followed by
a visit to the local bath, and I think it is important to think of them in similar
terms. Just as her account of the decaying and destroyed statuary of the Acropolis
is framed by architectural prospects, so too is her description of the women in the
Bath framed by an architectural threshold:

> The Consul's wife, Madame Gaspari, and I went into a room which pre-
> cedes the Bath, which room is the place where the women dress, and un-
> dress, sitting like tailors upon boards—there were above fifty; some having
> their hair washed, other dyed, or plaited; some were at the last part of their
> toilet, putting with a fine gold pin the black dye into their eyelids; in short,
> I saw her Turkish and Greek nature, through every degree of concealment,

in her primitive state—for the women sitting in the inner room were absolutely so many Eves—and as they came out their flesh looked boiled— These Baths are the great amusement of the women, they stay generally five hours in them; that is in the water and at their toilet together—but I think I never saw so many fat women at once together, nor fat ones so fat as these. . . . We had very pressing solicitations to undress and bathe, but such a disgusting sight as this would have put me in an ill humour with my sex in a bath for ages—Few of these women had fair skins or fine forms—hardly any—and Madame Gaspari tells me, that the encomiums and flattery a fine woman would meet with in these baths, would be astonishing—I stood some time in the door-way between the dressing-room and the Bath, which last was circular, with niches in it for the bathers to sit in; it was a very fine room with a stone dome—and the light came through small windows at the top. (263–64)

In a passage specifically designed to counter Montagu's famous hammam letter, in which she too is pressed to liberate herself from her corset and regretfully states that she must join her husband "to see the ruins of Justinian's church, which did not afford me so agreeable a prospect as I had left, being little more than a heap of stones" (27.103; H 1:164), Lady Craven not only undermines the desirability of the women around her, but also keeps her readers' attention focused on the beauty of the Roman building that surrounds the scene. But this rhetorical maneuver is not without its ambivalence, for she lingers in the doorway between the present world of social and potentially erotic engagement and her fantasy of the classical past.

It is here that the specific terms of her derogation of the women are so crucial. The fatness of the women is overdetermined, and this passage, like an earlier one, links the women's ostensible corpulence to their posture. This posture is tellingly compared to that of a tailor laboring on the ground, and thus fatness and labor conjoin to form a kind of class-based revulsion. These women are decaying before Lady Craven's eyes, and the sign of their decay—fatness—is a function of their lassitude. In other words, these women have been destroyed by the cultural and social norms of the Ottomans. As she states, "till some one, more wise than the rest, finds out the premature decay of that invaluable gift, beauty, and sets an example to the rising generation of a different mode of life, they will always fade as the roses they are so justly fond of" (226). Judging Turkish society according to the norms of fashion, Lady Craven takes the signs of bodily comportment to be indicators of character. Importantly, she underlines that fatness is a way of being. Once that way of being is eradicated, a rather different care of the self can be inculcated to restore feminine beauty to its classical state.

This is why the account of the bath is preceded by a rather different description of a visit to two Greek brides shortly after Craven's arrival at Choiseul-Gouffier's household:

> Their custom is to receive every body who has any curiosity to see their wedding clothes. These were very magnificent, and the women pretty—and looked prettier from a singular contrast in the turn of their features—One had a true Greek face, her head small, her nose straight, large blue eyes, with dark or rather black eyelids and hair, and her eyebrows straight—her neck long and round, her person rather inclining to lean than fat—a soft and sad countenance—The other was fattish; had black lively eyes, with a cheerful laughing countenance, her blood seemed to ebb and flow with more vivacity than her sister's-in-law. Her mouth, rather large, shewed a fine set of teeth, while the one with a smaller mouth and prettier teeth, seemed as unwilling to shew them, or light up her fine features with smiles, as the black-eyed bride was ready to laugh upon every or no occasion—They had both very little red on, and the pallid skin of the delicate Greek was perfectly suited to the form of the one—the other blushed often—They might have served for good models for the Tragic and Comic Muse. I would Sir Joshua had been at my elbow, his compositions are fine enough to satisfy a youthful poet's imagination, but here his pencil might not have disdained to copy two such charming originals. (234–35)

Again this fawning invocation of Sir Joshua Reynolds, the premier portraitist of London's beau monde, is meant to counter Montagu's gently satirical incorporation of Charles Jervas, principal portrait painter to George I, into her earlier text (27.102; H 1:162). But the crucial thing here is that these women are understood to be the living embodiment of Melpomene and Thalia, the muses of tragedy and comedy. They are valuable as signs of the classical past and as indicators of the pernicious effects of Ottoman occupation. The story of women corrupted by Ottoman practices is an allegory for the destruction of a feminized Greek cultural heritage by hyperphallic Ottoman occupation. Craven emphasizes that the destruction of the Acropolis occurs because the Ottomans use the site as a military encampment and munitions dump. In other words, like much of the discourse on Eastern despotism, the corruption of gender and politics allegorize one another. In this light, philhellenism amounts not only to a desire to figure the classical past as a mirror for a rapidly receding fantasy of aristocratic nobility but also to a simultaneous desire to figure forth that fantasy in the aesthetic recuperation of ruins, whether those ruins are made of stone or flesh.

It is in this sense that we need to see Lady Craven's manipulation of her persona as a similar attempt to recuperate her ruined character. Like Choiseul-Gouffier and his associates' attempt to reconstitute the classical past through art, or Catherine's attempt to reinvent Byzantium through force and diplomacy, Lady Craven's narrative explicitly attempts to reconstitute her nobility. Within the terms set by the allegory, the despotism of the Ottoman Porte is comparable to the tyranny of her husband. But this allegorical connection is not based on comparable forms of power or governmentality, but rather on a shared inability to assess true value. The Ottomans fail to value the art of classical Greece, and Lord Craven fails to value his beautiful wife when he opts instead for a counterfeit "Birmingham coin." Bringing together the geopolitical and the domestic in this way under the strained notion of aesthetic taste renders Lady Craven's *Journey* a very unsettling self-justification. At one level, we could argue that through these means Craven is shoring up her own persona with fantasies of racial and class supremacy, but there is another more disturbing implication. What happens if we see the self-justification as something not solely confined to Craven herself, but rather extended to British national and imperial fantasy? In the period following the American war, many of the key components of British patriotic identity were themselves in ruins. Recent writings on aristocratic masculinity and on the representation of elite sociability in the postwar era have argued that the humiliation of the loss of the American colonies generated a host of compensatory fantasies of national election and a full-scale reevaluation of the aristocracy's role in both domestic and foreign policy.[55] In this light, could we argue that the "mist" that seems to surround Craven's account of her travels amounts to a symptomatic obfuscation that is part of a larger cultural project to put the American debacle in abeyance?

There are strong incentives to read the text in this way. First, it helps to establish a logic for linking such seemingly disparate historical circumstances as the siege of Gibraltar, the grand tour, the Russian occupation of the Crimea, the philhellenic activities of Craven's associates, the Ottoman colonization of Greece, and the everyday details of travel. Throughout the text, Craven brings the reader to the verge of serious political or social commentary, but then suspends the analysis either by following a digression or by simply allowing her letters to dissipate into line after line of ellipses. This tendency was marked in all of the reviews, but no-where more cogently than in the *Critical Review*:

> This journey, with all the advantages which female elegance and rank command, must have been the most delightful gratification to the philosopher, the antiquary, and the politician. Lady Craven amuses us by the ease of her narrative, and the minute circumstances, which would probably have

been overlooked by either of those characters. But we are amused only: she
travelled as lady Craven, and she saw objects in the true female view. The
observations are, in a few places, trifling, and the new facts are not always
considerable or important; while the language sinking into familiar ease,
is sometimes colloquial and inelegant.[56]

Here the reviewer is signaling that the trajectory of this journey could open onto
matters of great seriousness, but the reader only senses them on the periphery of
the text, because Lady Craven's attention is taken up with matters ostensibly only
of interest to women of fashion. But the fact that the reviewer can discern the
larger implications means that they are nonetheless present. So what we are faced
with is—to borrow a term from painting—a figure and ground problem. If we
ignore the central figure—that is, Lady Craven's immediate subjective responses—
and attend to the background figures—Henry Vernon, the Margrave of Ansbach,
M. de Choiseul-Gouffier—then there suddenly emerges an entire cadre of cosmopolitan men invested in styles of social and sexual exchange forged in the courts
of continental Europe in the period before the Seven Years' War. The styles of nobility were precisely those embraced by the officers and politicians who led Britain
to imperial splendor in 1759; who oversaw the disintegration of the Atlantic imperium in the 1770s and early 1780s; and who were now engaged in a complex
reconfiguration of empire in the Levant and in the Asian subcontinent.

As Horace Walpole's response to the publication of *A Journey* demonstrates all
too painfully, Lady Craven affiliates herself with these figures in more or less scandalous ways such that the entire assemblage of social relations and cultural affiliations returns to Britain in an unsettling form to quite literally encapsulate much
of what the middling orders, not to mention more radical constituencies, saw was
defective or obsolete in aristocratic subjectivity. Perhaps this is why Walpole is so
uncomfortable with the text, because it comes perilously close to anatomizing what
is wrong with the upper orders at a moment when the ministry, and most notably
Edmund Burke, were about to embark on a full scale encomium to the gentry of
a bygone era. As he states in a letter to Lady Ossory,

Lady Craven's *Travels* [sic] I received from Robson two hours ago. Dodsley
brought the MS to me before I came to town; but I positively refused to
open it, though he told me my name was mentioned in it several times—
but I was conscious how grievous it would be to her family and poor
daughters, and therefore persisted in having nothing to do with it. I own I
have impatiently cut the leaves in search of my own name, and am delighted
on finding it there but thrice, and only by the initial letter. When I have
the honour of seeing your Ladyship, I can tell you many collateral circum-

stances; but I will not put them on paper—I fear she may come to wish, or should, that *she* had not been born with a propensity to writing.[57]

Walpole's desire to distance himself from Craven, in spite of the fact that he encouraged the publication of *A Journey*, is a sign of how sensitive matters of aristocratic dissipation had become. In censoring his own letter, Walpole effectively screens himself from guilt by association, but in other letters written directly to Craven he encourages her to publish *A Journey*.[58] As Feliz Turhan has perceptively argued, Walpole's ambivalence can be directly related to his rank, but Walpole's discreet duplicity is not that distant from Charles Pigott's vociferous attack on Craven in *The Jockey Club* of 1792.[59] Pigott was an ardent radical and his text is a scurrilous attack on aristocratic luxury. Thus he quickly overlooks Craven's disparaging remarks on Ottoman culture and her explicitly nationalist praise of the British navy in order to attack her preference of the Duc de Guines over her "plain downright British husband" and her scandalous liason with Henry Vernon on her journey.[60] Pigott's critique, although coming from a different place than Burke's nostalgia and Walpole's ambivalence, is similarly committed to putting the dissipation and immorality of the upper orders in permanent abeyance. In Pigott, Lady Craven is used as one of many examples of what must be gotten rid of in order for Britain to reform its political and social institutions.

What is important to note here is that despite a heavy cultural investment in reactivating the nobility of the ancien régime as exemplars of moral and political stability on the one hand or shaming the cultural elites as the source of all that was wrong with British society, the management and resolution of the political problems facing Britain's eastern empire was very much in the hands of the middling orders. Craven herself recognizes this when she dreams of a colony of honest English merchants in the Crimea (188). Advent of war with France on the Continent resulted in two important developments in Egypt and India respectively that would render many of the geopolitical implications of Craven's text irrelevant. The first was Nelson's epochal victory over the French at Abu Qir and the successful repulsion of the French at Acre. And the second was the defeat of Tipu Sultan of Mysore in 1799. These two related events effectively ended the French threat to British imperial holdings in India and inaugurated a new set of diplomatic relations with the Ottoman Porte that would render Lady Craven's text somewhat obsolete.

That said, the dynamic relationship between gendered and racialized tropes in Craven's text is extraordinarily valuable, first, for pinpointing the sexual fantasies undergirding Choiseul-Gouffier's text and, second, for comprehending the importance of intercultural sociability and nonheteronomative forms of sexuality to those most invested in discrediting the French diplomat's aestheticization of politics. The linked deployment of reproductive sexuality as a figure for the potential to reinvigorate Greece and of the sodomitical Turk as a symptom of the barrenness of Ottoman culture in the *Voyage pittoresque* consolidated a preexisting set of tropes for political ends. Craven translated this binary opposition between reproduction and sodomy into an economy of female beauty with desirable Greek women at one extreme and repulsive Ottoman women at the other.[61] Choiseul-Gouffier's deployment of sexuality was thus differentially written onto the bodies of Greek and Ottoman women. In the remaining chapters of this book we will see how the very practices proscribed by Choiseul-Gouffier and Craven are activated to imagine not only radically different models of sociability but also modes of governance that substantively diverge from the forms of nationhood and empire that began to cohere in the wake of the French Revolution and the Napoleonic wars. As we look at the work of Mouradgea d'Ohsson, Robert Ainslie, Luigi Mayer, Antoine-Ignace Melling, and Lord Byron in the following two chapters, we will see how important intercultural collaboration and homophilic modes of sexuality are to their critique of emergent models of empire. As with this chapter, I will be interweaving French and British examples to emphasize how understandings of specifically Ottoman matters are intertwined with larger global problematics. Just as Choiseul-Gouffier's and Craven's texts are inextricably bound up with seemingly disconnected events in the Atlantic world, I will eventually argue that Byron's historical analysis of imperial politics in *The Giaour* tracks back to the very moment in the American war when it became clear that one mode of empire was receding and a new world order was in the offing. The ensuing transformation in global politics had devastating effects on the Ottoman Empire, but each of the remaining writers and artists I consider developed intricate modes of resistance whose formal and historical precision allow us to see beyond the foreclosures exemplified by Choiseul-Gouffier and Craven and thus imagined a vital future in the Ottoman dominions. As we will see, matters of gender and sexuality will provide crucial points of analytical leverage.

CHAPTER 7

Narrative Fragments and Object Choices

Antiquities, War, and the Vestiges of Love

Choiseul-Gouffier's *Voyage pittoresque de la Grèce* casts a very long shadow. Within the French bibliophilic tradition Mouradgea d'Ohsson's *Tableau général de l'Empire othoman* (1787–1820) and Antoine-Ignace Melling's *Voyage pittoresque de Constantinople et des rives du Bosphore* (1807–24) are closely modeled on Choiseul-Gouffier's text but both subtly diverge from his example at the level of form, content, and execution in ways that have quite profound ramifications for the overall rhetorical effect of the books. Elisabeth A. Fraser's *Mediterranean Encounters* argues that all of the engraved travel books published in France after Choiseul-Gouffier's *Voyage pittoresque* engage with its legacy. Her study is "a biography of Choiseul-Gouffier's book: an object's life story as it is appropriated, altered, and redefined by different users."[1] Both d'Ohsson and Melling remediate specific aspects of the *Voyage pittoresque* in order to stage complex representational and political interventions aimed at re-foregrounding Ottoman life. These elaborate publications demonstrate the degree to which Choiseul-Gouffier marginalized the social forms of the world he passed through. The French nobleman's ancient ruins are replaced with vibrant scenes of everyday Ottoman life, religious ritual, and state ceremony. His obsession with the peripheral zones of the Cyclades and the Dodecanese Islands are countered by a thorough reengagement with the urban and suburban spaces of Constantinople (Figure 72). In the process, Choiseul-Gouffier's project of reactivating classical models of architecture and liberty subtly morphs into a fascination with the hybrid possibilities of the modern world.

Elisabeth Fraser's groundbreaking account of the translational dynamics at the heart of d'Ohsson's *Tableau général* emphasizes the deep level of transculturation in this project. A full discussion of this massive text is beyond my purview here, but some brief observations provide a useful pivot toward this and the next chapter. D'Ohsson was an Armenian dragoman who worked for the Swedish embassy

Figure 72. Louis-Nicolas de Lespinasse, engraving, *View of Sa'dabad and the garden at Kagithane,* plate 84 in Mouradgea d'Ohsson, *Tableau général de l'Empire othoman,* vol. 3 (1820). Courtesy of the Library of Congress.

in Constantinople. His career took a remarkable turn shortly after the Treaty of Küçük Kaynarca, when he emigrated to Paris to oversee the publication of a multivolume illustrated account of Islam and of Ottoman governance. As Findley argues, the book was both conceived and received as a counter to anti-Ottoman sentiments widely disseminated by Baron de Tott's *Mémoires du Baron de Tott, sur les Turcs et les Tartares* (1784–85) and Constantin-François Volney's *Considérations sur la guerre actuelle des Turcs* (1788).[2] D'Ohsson himself no doubt recognized the continuity between de Tott's and Volney's anti-Ottoman positions and those of Choiseul-Gouffier.[3] D'Ohsson's intervention was explicit and direct. He modeled the *Tableau général* on *Voyage pittoresque de la Grèce,* and his subscribers would have encountered a rather remarkable repudiation of Choiseul-Gouffier on the title page itself (Figure 73). In the place of Choiseul-Gouffier's feminized figure of Greece lying supine on the ruins of antiquity (see Figure 58), d'Ohsson directed Moreau, the designer of the frontispiece to the *Voyage pittoresque,* to provide a bold, active rendering of Muhammad and the first four caliphs, or Rashidun, with the Ka'ba in the background, a Sunni image suitable to Ottoman religious tradition. The message is, I believe, blunt and clear: whereas Choiseul-Gouffier was invested in resurrecting a dead culture, d'Ohsson is depicting a vibrant, living religious society overseen by the current Ottoman sultan, long understood to be the supreme leader

Figure 73. Jean-Baptiste Simonet, engraving after Jean-Michel Moreau le jeune, title page, for Mouradgea d'Ohsson, *Tableau général de l'Empire othoman* (1787). Courtesy of the Thomas Fisher Rare Book Library, University of Toronto.

of Sunni Muslims. As a rejoinder to Choiseul-Gouffier's allegory of disjunction and alienation, d'Ohsson's assertion of ongoing cultural and social relations couldn't be more damning because it effectively counters an almost vampiric fascination with antiquity with a resolute investment in living continuity.[4]

This is important because the *Tableau général* is itself a performative repudiation of Choiseul-Gouffier's text. Employing many of the same designers and engravers who worked on *Voyage pittoresque*, d'Ohsson categorically avoided the representation of antiquities from the Ottoman periphery.[5] Instead he oversaw the remediation of Ottoman images, some collected from preexisting Ottoman miniatures and some solicited from contemporary artists working in Constantinople, into the most modern of printed media.[6] The large folio books being published in France at this time were the most advanced of their kind. D'Ohsson specifically went to Paris to partake in this media revolution. There is a specific drive toward the present and beyond, but significantly the *Tableau général* draws up that which came before in a very specific fashion. As an instance of media convergence it effectively acts as a historical sublation.[7]

ASSOMPTION DE MOHAMMED.

Figure 74. Jean-Baptiste Tilliard, engraving after anonymous sixteenth-century illumination, *Assumption of Muhammad*, plate 2 from Mouradgea d'Ohsson, *Tableau général de L'Empire othoman*, vol. 1 (1787). Courtesy of the Thomas Fisher Rare Book Library, University of Toronto.

Günsel Renda and Elisabeth Fraser have demonstrated the pervasive influence of Seyyid Lokman's *Zübdetü't-Tevârîh*, or *The Quintessence of Histories*, a late sixteenth-century illuminated manuscript, on both the illustration of religious narratives and some costume figures in the *Tableau général*.[8] D'Ohsson himself makes much of the sources for the illustrations, emphasizing repeatedly their provenance and the risk entailed in rendering some images. The degree to which d'Ohsson simultaneously marks the Muslim prohibition against image making and the manifest evidence of its contravention warrants our attention. The second plate in the book remediates an image from Lokman's illuminated manuscript showing the Miraj, Muhammad's night journey from Mecca (Figures 74 and 75). The engraving seems to be an exact replica of the Ottoman original, but sustained viewing reveals a hybridization of French and Ottoman visual paradigms. The overall spatial structure of the composition rehearses the multiple planes of the original, but the figures are modeled and thus have volume in an otherwise flat space. The angels seem to mesh

Figure 75. *Miraj, Muhammad's Night Journey,* from Seyyid Lokman's *Zübdetü't-Tevârîh* (Quintessence of Histories), illuminated manuscript (late sixteenth century), Chester Beatty Library, Dublin, T414, fol. 121. Trustees of the Chester Beatty Library, Dublin.

with Christian iconography, but Muhammad's face, in accordance with Islamic custom is not represented. Is this the description of an Ottoman artifact? At one level, yes, but at another level it diverges from a strict empirical rendering of the original. Fraser usefully goes to translation theory in order to argue for a certain "markedness" in illustrations like this. According to Madeleine Dobie, translation always leaves "marks" of the original and thus constitute a hybrid entity.[9]

But one could argue further that the movement from Ottoman illumination to preparatory French painting or drawing and finally to book engraving involves a remediation that has significant temporal implications. This is perhaps most evident in an example like this where the medial shift is so extreme, but we could contend that the act of remediation pulls all prior media into the present of the *Tableau général*. In other words, the very act of engraving this image pulls it into a different medial environment and the subtle changes—the addition of volume to Muhammad's horse, the new found depth in the galleries of the Ka'ba—begin to take on connotations of progressive reform. The Miraj illustration sublates the sixteenth-century illumination into the visual economy of late eighteenth-century engraving. As Fraser notes, d'Ohsson explicitly aligns the history of Ottoman printing to the present project; the transcultural relation is disjunctive, but for d'Ohsson it is part of an ongoing progression that enfolds the very book in the reader's hands.[10]

Returning then to the Miraj plate, we need once again to ask, what is this? It does refer to a historical Ottoman artifact, but it is not a description of it. It is both a continuation and a translation of some of that object's formal elements. But those forms seem to be in a state of productive, even progressive, transformation. The volumetric rendering of Muhammad's mount and the perspectival representation of the galleries heighten the flat planar rendering of the Ka'ba. The contrast amplifies Muhammad's exceptional status in the image. We could argue that media convergence has intensified the image for a specific kind of viewer, one who needs a fully rounded Muhammad—that is, a nonbeliever. This helps to explain why this plate can even be contained in the same book as the title-page illustration (see Figure 73). Everything in this book is driving toward the reader's perception of its present enactment and all but requires an endorsement of the collaboration that made it possible. Here collaboration is embedded in the colliding modes of production: Ottoman miniature painting is redrawn and engraved by French illustrators and engravers. Either through the foregrounding of actual artifacts or of native informants, d'Ohsson continually demonstrates the existence and virtue of transculturation.

Hybridity and intercultural collaboration, those aspects of Ottoman sociability that Choiseul-Gouffier sought to cancel, constitute d'Ohsson's weapon of choice. It is possible to detect at the level of form and composition a remarkable reorganization of Choiseul-Gouffier's project that turns its very rhetorical and narrative strengths against its narrow ethnocentrism. To the degree that d'Ohsson subverts Choiseul-Gouffier's text in the name of a specifically Ottoman life, then we also need to recognize that he does so by formally inverting a text committed not only to the extirpation of Ottoman rule but also to Ottoman forms of sociability. It is not an exaggeration to say that d'Ohsson was fighting for life as he would prefer to know it. From Choiseul-Gouffier's fitful imagination of death comes a different, yet cognate, affirmation of intercultural life.

Fraser, Renda, and others have opened the way for an extended analysis of d'Ohsson's intervention, but this chapter looks at almost contemporaneous repudiations of the *Voyage pittoresque*'s genocidal mandate that also foreground intercultural collaboration and formal transformation. They were staged or executed immediately prior to the Russo-Turkish War of 1787–92. However, in this case the engagement with Choiseul-Gouffier does not so much negate his obsession with Greek antiquity as push beyond its own self-inscribed limits. These repudiations of Choiseul-Gouffier were initiated and overseen by Sir Robert Ainslie and conducted by his artist friend Luigi Mayer. Ainslie was the British ambassador to the Sublime Porte during Choiseul-Gouffier's tenure in Pera. As we will see, *Voyage pittoresque* becomes a valuable artifact in Ainslie's resistance to French influence in the period immediately preceding the outbreak of the Russo-Turkish War of 1787–92, so in a sense this chapter contemplates the political efficacy of texts and images.

Ainslie and Mayer engage in levels of intercultural collaboration quite literally proscribed by Choiseul-Gouffier's and Lady Craven's anti-Ottoman dispositions. I will be arguing that these collaborations generate complex affective bonds that are intensified by the fact of war, both local and global. My consideration of Ainslie and Mayer throws us directly into the midst of the conflict between the Austrian, Russian, and Ottoman Empires in the late 1780s—a conflict that would go horribly wrong for the Ottoman military and permanently alter the political terrain of the Ottoman state. The analysis here will be targeted: I will not be attempting to discuss the entire period of warfare but will rather focus on one incredibly resonant object—a beautiful watercolor produced by Mayer in the summer of 1788. As we will see, the drawing in question, not unlike d'Ohsson's remediation of the Lokman illuminations, engages with both a historical artifact and its representation in a way that significantly alters the object for the present predicament. That the watercolor was itself prepared for later engraving only heightens its similarity to d'Ohsson's investment in the political possibilities of mechanical reproduction.[11] Deep reading allows us to recognize how specific objects and aesthetic strategies can constitute historical interventions. In other words, the style of analysis mobilized here is meant to stand as one strategy for thinking through this historical problematic.

In light of what we have seen thus far, Ainslie and Mayer's activities in the lead-up to and during the renewed war between the Ottomans and Russians are revealing. Ainslie's diplomatic engagements couldn't be more focused on the present crisis: he was an actant in this conflict. But Mayer's extraordinary watercolors perform readings of the past—both recent and ancient—that explicitly attempt to imagine the emergence of modernity in the interstices of multiple imperial formations. In the immediate vicinity, Ainslie and Mayer were witnesses to the struggles between the modernizing powers of Russia, Austria, and the Ottoman Empire; but they remain subjects and representatives of the preeminent imperial powers of modern Europe. When they intervene, they often do so as visitors from the future;[12] when they contemplate what is unfolding around them, they often do so as subjects mired in their own past formation. That said, what interests me here is how observers like Ainslie and Mayer, whose interests are ineluctably tied to those of imperial Britain, temporalize the conflicts between ostensibly less modernized imperial powers in the eastern Mediterranean and the Black Sea. Like many of their predecessors, they use the classical material at hand—or rather at their feet—to think through the violent transformations of modernity, but they do it otherwise.[13] Unlike Choiseul-Gouffier, they do not invest in fantasies of reconstitution but rather explore possibilities of hybrid sociability, of peace, and of same-sex desire explicitly foreclosed not only by *Voyage pittoresque de la Grèce* but also by the ultimate dissemination of their own work. As we will see, the transit from Mayer's topographical views to their subsequent engraving in the early nineteenth century will erase all traces of interculturalism. As we enter the new century, this chapter will be marked by the sadness that attends the momentary contemplation and ensuing foreclosure of an unrealized future. And that affective condition, that feeling, will provide a crucial launching point for considering the work of Antoine-Ignace Melling and Lord Byron at the end of the Napoleonic wars in this book's final chapter.

From Fantasy to Policy

For readers familiar with *Voyage pittoresque de la Grèce* it is perhaps surprising that I have paid so little attention to Choiseul-Gouffier's "Discours préliminaire." This short introductory text is a cornucopia of anti-Ottoman discourse, and in many ways it states explicitly many of the sentiments that are encoded in the book's engravings. I have forestalled consideration of this important text because it is the focal point of a complex representational intervention by the British ambassador to the Ottoman Porte, Sir Robert Ainslie. As Barbier argues, by the time Choiseul-Gouffier was writing the "Discours préliminaire" in 1782, the young aristocrat's interest in the region was no longer simply antiquarian.[14] Like other observers throughout Europe, Choiseul-Gouffier became more and more convinced not only that the Ottoman Empire was dissolving but also that the liberation of Greece was imminent. Throughout the "Discours préliminaire," that liberation is regarded as a world historical imperative rather than a particular political struggle for the amelioration of contemporary problems in the Aegean. For this reason, Choiseul-Gouffier's focus is on the reconstitution of ancient Greece: "I had read a hundred times the description of the appalling state to which Greece was reduced . . . : tales, accounts, history, everything suddenly got forgotten as if by magic; I felt the same way as if, after having witnessed its previous splendor, I suddenly came back to gaze upon its recent decline; I was crossing so many centuries interposed between what I was seeing and what I had read about its former prosperity, I could not get used to discovering the splendor of such renowned places on what was just debris" (iv–v). And it is for this reason that the language shifts so easily to that of enchantment and spectacle. For all the declarations of Greek servitude and slavery, Choiseul-Gouffier repeatedly reverts to theatrical metaphors for historical conditions: imperial succession becomes a "sudden enchantment" and thus politics becomes a spectacular clash of civilizations: "What a sight it was to see, between the civilized, yet enslaved, Asia, and the free, yet barbarous, Europe, a nation, weak in the first place, but soon powerful, emerging, arising, growing to combine the advantages of freedom and civilization, strip the latter of its savage rudeness, purge the former of the marks of servitude, raise to the highest levels the dignity of man" (iv). The dualistic rhetoric of civilization and barbarism is given urgency by Choiseul-Gouffier's repeated assertions that "le stupide Musselman" (v) is a particularly dangerous threat because he has no interest, no respect for the very generalizations so liberally deployed above: separated from the dignity of humanity, Ottoman "ignorance" is figured as a corrosive historical force.

But perhaps the most remarkable aspect of the "Discours préliminaire" is its explicit endorsement of Greek revolution. This endorsement is first broached historically: Choiseul-Gouffier praises in turn historical instances of Christian resistance to Ottoman control. But as Barbier argues, it gains specific traction when Choiseul-Gouffier calls for revolution and proposes the institution of the independent state of Péloponnèse in the Morea.[15] Choiseul-Gouffier's proposal comes with the explicit statement that this can be realized through Russian intervention:

> Perhaps this noble and grand plan has already been designed by Catherine II, by this Princess, for whom glory is the primary need, who raised Philosophy to the throne, and devoted it to man's happiness. Perhaps this august Princess, arranging the plan of this memorable revolution according to the wisdom she possesses, knowledgeable thanks to the experience of a twenty-year reign, and thanks even to the uselessness of her last attempt, better informed of the obstacles and means, better served by more faithful emissaries, perhaps she is about to seize again a glory which seems to be made for her, and of which she was only deprived due to foreign circumstances, whose influence will be destroyed, as soon as it will be planned. (xi)

Barbier glosses this passage as an instance of youthful enthusiasm, but this is more than the effusion of an antiquarian dreamer. To misrecognize Russian conquest as an act undertaken for the happiness of mankind thoroughly separates Catherine's motives from the realm of politics altogether. This would be an act of liberation whose fetishization of Liberty would have very little to do with the freedom of the residents of the Morea. In this regard the "Discours préliminaire" is very much of a piece with the rest of *Voyage pittoresque*; this is why it too—in its initial form— concludes with the phrase *exoriare aliquis*. What stands out here—in spite of its sanctioned ignorance about Russian imperial politics—is Choiseul-Gouffier's invocation of a specific scenario for the resolution of his frustrated desires. In a rather bizarre gesture, he elevates Catherine into an Enlightenment heroine capable of bringing all that "enchantment" has done to hollow out reason's legacy to an end. In this single act of appropriated realpolitik, past and present moments of enlightenment will be fused into one plenitudinous whole and the dialectic of enlightenment will be resolved.

This dangerous fantasy was applauded by many with minimal investment in Russian or Ottoman affairs,[16] but it met with almost immediate resistance from French and British officials charged with negotiating with both powers. The career diplomat Pierre Michel Hennin—also an enlightened man of taste—strongly advised Choiseul-Gouffier to tone down the anti-Ottoman rhetoric of "Discours préliminaire" to the *Voyage pittoresque* if he would hope to be appointed to the Ottoman Porte. As Barbier demonstrates, Choiseul-Gouffier attempted not only to recall as many copies of the "Discours préliminaire" as possible, but also to put into circulation two different revisions of the text.[17] These revisions eliminated references to revolution and to the Russians and fully suppressed the xenophobic representation of "the gross ignorance of the Turks." With each cut the "Discours" became progressively smaller and smaller, and presumably Choiseul-Gouffier became increasingly acceptable as a diplomatic envoy.[18]

However, these revisions did not matter where perhaps it mattered most. According to Abbé Guillaume Martin, Sir Robert Ainslie, the British ambassador to the Ottoman Porte when Choiseul-Gouffier was appointed, used the *Voyage pittoresque* to stage an unofficial diplomatic intervention:

> Before disembarking, several of our Frenchmen who came on our boat did not miss the occasion to say a few words about the way the ambassador of England had just behaved in order to make the French nation appear despicable to the [Sublime/Ottoman/High] Porte [. . .]. As M. Ainslie, ambassador of England, had learned that M. de Choiseul had been nominated to the embassy of Constantinople, he had got from Paris this *Voyage pittoresque de la Grèce* and, a little before our arrival, he showed a copy to the great vizier and another one to the réis-efendi, and recommended his dragoman to point out to them all the remarks made against the Ottoman government, in par-

ticular in the foreword; and to properly explain to them the engraving of the frontispiece that depicts Greece, and to tell them: Here is the man France is sending you. . . . Well! The evening of the day we entered the port, M. Ainslie presented himself at the Palais de France in order to visit M. de Choiseul whom he had just betrayed. He expressed to him his satisfaction about his happy arrival and treated him with gushing politeness and offered him many services. You can rely on diplomats, they said![19]

This was precisely the scenario that Choiseul-Gouffier's advisers in Paris feared before his appointment as ambassador. He had not suppressed all of the initial imprints, and the anti-Ottoman rhetoric of the text is hardly confined to the "Discours préliminaire."

Martin's anecdote portrays Ainslie as a cunning and duplicitous figure, and it wouldn't be the last time that he would be maligned by French observers during Choiseul-Gouffier's tenure at the Sublime Porte. Like Choiseul-Gouffier, Ainslie had extensive antiquarian interests, but unlike his largely inexperienced French counterpart, he was well versed in the nuances of Ottoman diplomacy.[20] It is not surprising to see Ainslie pushing his advantage to the utmost. But I am much more interested in the actual scene of reading here. With the grand vizier Hamil-Hamid poring over the frontispiece to the *Voyage pittoresque*, what precisely was the Venetian dragoman to say about the less than subtle indictment of Ottoman rule? Precisely how much close reading would be entertained in such a situation? The book was a valuable tool for Ainslie, and in this section of the chapter I am going to demonstrate how one visual element of Choiseul-Gouffier's text became the occasion for a highly revealing aesthetic intervention that is every bit as nuanced as Ainslie's political maneuvers.

The rivalry between Choiseul-Gouffier and Ainslie had immense geopolitical significance, and Ainslie's activities—both diplomatic and antiquarian—during the Russo-Turkish War of 1787–92 attempted to develop a counterdiscourse to Choiseul-Gouffier's bellicose advocacy of Greek liberation. As we will see, comprehending the artistic response of Ainslie and his painter colleague Luigi Mayer requires a subtle understanding not only of the visual strategies employed in the *Voyage pittoresque*, but also a specific reading of the "Discours préliminaire" and its seemingly innocuous headpiece illustration. However, before undertaking a genealogy of this counterdiscourse, we need to become more aware of the political struggles that pulled the Ottomans into yet another futile war with Russia and that colored every aspect of Ainslie's relation to his French counterpart.

In many ways Ainslie and Choiseul-Gouffier's "Eastern" careers were thoroughly intertwined. Ainslie was the British ambassador to the Sublime Porte of the Ottoman Empire from 1775 to 1793, and thus entered his post immediately following the humiliating defeat of the Ottomans in the Russo-Turkish War of 1768–74 and left shortly after the Russo-Turkish War of 1787–92. Even though Choiseul-Gouffier's appointment as ambassador came much later in 1784, his expedition to Ottoman-controlled Greece was almost precisely contemporary with Ainslie's first meeting with Grand Vizier Halil Hamid Pasha and Sultan Abdül-hamîd. As Ainslie accommodated himself to Turkish life and the business of the embassy, Choiseul-Gouffier amassed the research and the images for his *Voyage pittoresque*. In the process, he did not neglect to collect intelligence regarding Russian and Ottoman military capabilities in the region, thus betraying a close link between his aesthetic and political interests that would characterize his entire career. As we have already noted, Choiseul-Gouffier was, right up to his appointment as ambassador, an advocate for Russian-sponsored liberation of Greece.[21]

For his part Ainslie had explicit orders to avoid war. During the early part of his embassy, Ainslie was charged with furthering British trading interests and with keeping peace in the region. The sultan Abdülhamîd advocated closer political and commercial ties with Britain in order to offset Britain's long-established, if somewhat cold, relations with Russia. The sultan's openness to Ainslie's advances was heightened by Ainslie's own comfort with life in Pera. As the *St. James Chronicle* reported, "Being strongly attached to the manner of the people . . . in his house, his garden, and his table he assumed the style and fashion of a Musselman of rank; in fine, he lived *en Turk*, and pleased the natives so much by this seeming policy . . . that he became more popular than any of the Christian ministers."[22] Ainslie served during the reign of two very different sultans. Abdülhamîd was widely ridiculed by European diplomats as hopelessly ineffective, but Ainslie appears to have developed a close relationship with him. The friendship between Ainslie and Abdülhamîd is perhaps most forcefully registered in Ainslie's circular dispatch regarding his death and by the coolness of his representations of Abdül-hamîd's successor Selim III.[23] Selim III was young and vigorous and would eventually push the Ottoman state and its military on the road to modernization.

The question of modernity is central because the descent of the region into war can be understood as a conflict between empires in varying states of modernization. Virginia H. Aksan gives the most comprehensive account of the wars prosecuted among Austria, Russia, and the Ottoman Empire between 1768 and 1792. As she argues, all three powers came into this period marked by their relation to the global conflict of the Seven Years' War. "The period from 1740 to 1768 was one of the longest periods of peace for the Ottoman Empire in its entire history," Aksan notes, but this period of calm and prosperity came at an unforeseen cost.[24] By sitting out the Seven Years' War, the Ottomans were not party to the extraordinary technological and logistical advances pioneered in European and colonial campaigns in this period. The Ottoman sultan Mustafa III (1757–74) was well aware of the dangers this posed and for this reason imported French military men like Baron de Tott to help modernize Ottoman artillery and fortifications. However, this period also saw a shift in the Ottoman military itself from a professional fighting corps to a militia-based army. The latter was slow to mobilize and relied on local elites for supply. What remained of the janissaries was dispersed along the garrisons that made up the primary line of defense along the Danube River from Belgrade to the Black Sea.

As Aksan emphasizes, the Ottomans spent the entire period from 1768 to 1792 attempting to maintain this line against incursions from Russia and, to a lesser extent, Austria. Both powers came out of the Seven Years' War in full possession of the massed firepower and rapid field artillery developed in the 1750s. And Russia in particular had a cadre of talented officers and a highly trained standing army at its disposal. Austria became an increasingly militarized society in this period, but it pursued a less bellicose path in relation to the Ottomans—Aksan ventures that it was economically worn down by constant warfare in central Europe. However, Russia was in an expansionist mode. With the accession of Joseph II, Austria tended to get folded into the aggressive plans of its Russian allies. But contrary to the fantasy of enlightened conquest projected by Choiseul-Gouffier and other French observers, Russian incursions on the Danube often involved drawn-out sieges of Ottoman garrisons followed by horrific scenes of slaughter. The Russo-Turkish War of 1768–74 was a particularly brutal affair that permanently impaired the Ottoman military. Aksan argues that the epochal defeat of the Ottoman army at Kartal in 1770 and the incineration of the Ottoman fleet a few months later at Çeşme can be traced to an absolute collapse in Ottoman supply lines that was due to a relative lack of state modernization.[25] In this sense, Russian dominance in this period had as much to do with the inability of the Ottoman state to mobilize food, money, and arms as it did with any particular strategic superiority or tactical genius among the Russians.

Significantly, Russia's extraordinary gains in this period—the above-mentioned defeats, the annexation of the Crimea, and the ensuing victories at Ochakov and Ismail in the early 1790s—may well have impeded its own modernization. As Aksan argues, the annexation of the Crimea in 1783 proved to be both financially and politically costly. The annexation itself precipitated not only the Russo-Turkish War of 1787–92 but also ethnic resistance to Russian policies of colonization. What this meant is that these wars did not instantiate a flow of money into Russia from the Crimean principalities, and thus imperial expansion destabilized the economic underpinnings of metropolitan society.

Financing became an acute problem for the Romanovs in the 1780s, when the brilliant, and savage, conquests of Suvorov climaxed two decades of victories in the south for the Russians. . . . The Russo-Ottoman wars of 1768–74 and 1787–92 (the latter including a reluctant Austria from 1788–91), however, proved very destructive to Catherine's legislative and economic reforms, and generated opposition from noble and peasant alike. The 1773–74 Pugachev Rebellion in particular threatened to bring down the dynasty altogether. The Russian army, composed of mobilized and "freed" serfs, increased threefold in the decades under discussion, with a similar increase in expenditure.[26]

Aksan's narrative is salutary because it provides a more systemic and nuanced account of Russian gains and Ottoman losses than conventional celebrations of Catherine, Potemkin, Rumiantsev, and Suvorov. This not only suspends any easy slippage from hagiography to a misrecognition of war for enlightenment, but also emphasizes that the very notions of gain and loss are complex here. The Ottomans unquestionably lost territory, men, and strategic sites to the Russians in this period, but it was precisely these losses that enabled Selim III and his successor Mahmûd II to institute crucial reforms to the Ottoman military and to the Ottoman state. And the cost—both financial and political—of Russian victory in the region slowed the process of modernization and thus made Russia increasingly vulnerable in the nineteenth century.[27]

Ainslie saw Britain through much of this extremely precarious geopolitical conflict, and his place in the history of the Russo-Turkish War of 1787–92 is complex. Charged with the task of undermining Choiseul-Gouffier at the Porte without aggravating the Russians, Ainslie subtly persuaded key Ottoman officials that the trade agreement between France and Russia was actually a political alliance and that France could not be trusted to mediate between Russia and the Porte. This strategy, combined with the Ottoman's intense suspicion regarding Choiseul-Gouffier, drew Ainslie closer and closer to the Ottoman side of the conflict. Eventually, the French and the Russians complained that Ainslie was pushing the seraglio toward another war. According to his dispatches, Ainslie's advice to the seraglio was precisely the opposite,[28] but as the war party in the Ottoman cabinet began to gain ascendance, and as Abdülhamîd's influence waned, the sultan eventually found himself with few options. Ainslie had great trepidations about war between Russia and the Ottoman Empire. He was not convinced that the Ottomans were prepared for another major conflict with Russia, and the potential gains for France, should Catherine's Greek plan reach fruition, would permanently alter the balance of power in Europe, and perhaps around the globe. The best he could hope for was continued peace and the alienation of the French. The last thing Britain, or the Porte, wanted was a French mediation of the ongoing acrimony over the Crimea, because it would achieve by diplomatic means what Russia was prepared to do by force. With the departure of the antiwar minister Gazi Hassan to Egypt, Abdülhamîd found himself increasingly isolated. Faced with the choice of simply ceding territory In Europe or engaging in war, the sultan reluctantly entered the conflict, likely because he could not fend off the political power of the pro-war factions of the cabinet and the ulema.

When war was declared on 14 August 1787, almost all observers were surprised because very few believed that the Ottomans were in a viable position to once again engage the Russians. No one doubted that the Russians and the Ottomans were headed toward a conflict, but most saw the declaration as premature. As Ainslie wrote to the British ambassador to Russia William Keith, "The so much apprehended éclat between Russia and the Court has at last taken place, *most probably when least expected*."[29] Jeremy Black has argued that despite Ainslie's protestations that he did not encourage the Ottomans, a war that embroiled the Austrians in the Balkans could be seen to serve the interests of British foreign policy. At this moment, Britain was very much interested in countering French influence in the civil conflict in the United Provinces and entangling the Austrians in the east would go some way to complicate French intervention in Holland.[30] Taken from this global perspective, rumors circulated widely both in Europe and in Pera that Ainslie had a motive to privately push the Ottomans toward an ill-considered war. Ainslie and others refuted the charge, but the following example, from a dispatch from Ainslie to British foreign secretary, Lord Carmarthen, gives a sense of how slippery these denials can be: "I am supposed to have held a language tending to encourage the Turkes to think well of their own Force in comparison with that of Russia. It is true, my Lord, I ever thought it a duty incumbent on Foreign Ministers, to conduct themselves with discretion, and to avoid giving offence to the Courts where they reside. Consistently with this Rule, I have always spoken guardedly (particularly in publick) of the Ottoman Power, and of their Preparations carried on for upwards of fifteen months, both in Asia and Europe."[31] As Black notes with regard to this passage, the distinction between public and private destabilizes this denial just enough to render it cause for suspicion. But regardless Ainslie's private discourse would hardly be decisive. And there is no question that Ainslie, like everyone else involved, had no illusions about how this war would unfold. The Ottoman military was not well prepared, and the alliance between Austria and Russia meant that the Ottomans would have to fight on two fronts in the Balkans and in the Black Sea.

Narrative Fragments

Ainslie's dispatches, both prior to and during the war, capture much of this trepidation. After the obligatory winter holding pattern, he expresses his surprise at early

Figure 76. Luigi Mayer, *Veduta dell'Ok Meidan o sia Piazza de Freccie nel tempo che il sultano si diletta in quel esercizio* (1788), watercolor. Trustees of the British Museum.

Ottoman successes against Austria in the spring and summer of 1788. Significantly, we know from a different kind of source that Ainslie visited the grand vizier's military encampment in the spring of 1788. Ainslie's dispatches from this period are supplemented by a remarkable album of watercolors now held at the British Museum. The watercolors were produced by Luigi Mayer in 1788 for Ainslie shortly after the outbreak of war. Mayer was an Italian artist who trained with Piranesi in Rome and lived with Ainslie all through the 1780s in Pera. Mayer returned to England with Ainslie in 1794, and the two men collaborated on three major collections of views of the Ottoman dominions, Palestine, and Egypt.[32] The watercolors are unusually large. There are fifty-eight in all, numbered and titled in sequence. Ten are kept in a separate portfolio because they are too large to bind. The remaining forty-eight are bound in an extremely heavy leather-bound book. The series starts with views in and around Istanbul and then ventures farther afield.

The early watercolors in the series, for all their pastoralism, also show an empire preparing for war. The first topographical view shows the largely ceremonial encampment of the sultan on the outskirts of Istanbul (Figure 76). The watercolor is now substantially damaged, but in a sense the fragility of the watercolor resonates with the subject matter. The view is taken at a great distance, but one could argue that it baldly attests to the technological inferiority of the Ottoman military. This is a conglomeration of tents not a bank of field artillery. The tiny figures are dispersed across the field; there are no ranks or blocs of soldiers performing organized drill exercises. The title of the view identifies the troop movements as a form of exercise, but my sense is that the watercolor is doing everything possible to separate "exercise" from the all important massing of firepower associated with military prowess in the period. In a sense, the very dispersal of the composition performs this assessment of military weakness. I also think there is something at stake in the rendering of the encampment itself. The vast tents are a sign less of efficiency and order, than of obsolescence and excess. It is difficult not to look down from this height and see the rehearsal of an earlier era's military symbols and protocols.

This sense of obsolescence and excess is reinforced by two extraordinary watercolors of the grand vizier's military encampment, each of which is dated 19 March 1788 (Plates 23 and 24). These bright vibrant pictures record Ainslie's audience with the grand vizier Koca Yusuf Pasha, and in this sense they are highly ceremonial. There is a long tradition of audience pictures stretching back to Vanmour, but there are relatively few images of this kind. The first shows the sequence of tents leading to the grand vizier's divan, but it focuses the viewer's attention on the soldiers and cavalry flanking the approach to the first tent. Mayer is careful to catch the distinction between the types of soldiers, but one can't help but notice something awry in this ostensibly balanced composition. At one level the painting is divided neatly in half with a converging diagonal on each side. On the right side we have soldiers bearing pikes overseen by an older officer with a scimitar. On the left we have a row of janissaries, all holding muskets, overseen by an unarmed figure in the foreground. As the viewer's eye moves outward to each side, this distinction between ancient and modern modes of warfare is accentuated. In the right foreground, we have a disorganized—and in one section indolent—group of men armed with swords and the odd gun here and there. In the left foreground Mayer presents two pieces of rather forlorn field artillery; the weapons are being ignored by the horsemen immediately adjacent, who are watching a cavalry exercise/game in the background left. The cannons themselves do not look especially recent, and I would argue that the entire deployment of figures and armory in the picture captures the precarious state of affairs facing the Ottoman military at this moment. The fact that the grand vizier's tent, where the audience is being held, is aligned with the right side of the picture only confirms what is proposed in the left foreground—that is, that the Ottomans will be going into this war far too reliant on their ground forces, and these forces are not sufficiently armed or supported by artillery to meet the Russians in the field. From this perspective, the formality of Mayer's composition—those hard diagonals—and the exuberance of his palette emphasize that this military encampment is more visually than tactically impressive. The very luxuriance of the picture is a sign of bad things to come.[33]

A similar but related point informs the interior view of the grand vizier's tent, only now the appraisal moves from that of military prowess to political efficacy. At one level, this is a very clumsy picture—the roof of the tent is both visually decorative and architecturally confusing. It is obviously concerned with excessive ceremony, but I think the primary visual strategy here is about color. This is a study in red with each row of Ottoman officials accentuating the redness of the central group of Ottoman figures. In this context the multicolored coats of the European ambassadors marks their difference from their hosts. The exception, of course, is Ainslie himself and his retinue who are installed on the left in red. Ainslie's glance outward is a curious gesture—he is the only European figure not looking at the grand vizier. If his coat subtly aligns him with the Ottomans, does his glance away from what is transpiring in front of him mark his difference from the other European powers? It is perhaps going too far to make this a sign of exceptionalism or resignation, but it is interesting that other Ottoman figures in the picture also glance away from the central action—most notably the mufti on the right who looks straight out at the viewer. Is this perhaps a sign of dissent or of a lack of unanimity not only in the ulema but also in the diplomatic corps? If so, this has the curious effect of not only separating Ainslie from the other European diplomats, but also of aligning him with the antiwar party.

This is very slender evidence for declaring Ainslie's political affiliations, but, as we will see, one of the striking things about Mayer's pictures is the degree to which he aligns his party with their Ottoman guides and hosts, and in this case it means aligning oneself with impending failure. In other words, a kind of ambivalent affiliation is at work here. As the first image of the encampment indicates, Mayer does not see much of a future for the Ottoman military cause. But the second image of the encampment seems to tie Ainslie and his retinue to some of the Ottomans in spite of their ill-considered entry into the war. I would argue that the clear separation of Ainslie from the other Europeans, both by composition and by palette, also distances him from the bellicose grand vizier. But what are we to make of those sporadic glances—including Ainslie's—away from this central wartime ceremony?

This is a question without a definitive answer, but if we look further into the album of watercolors I think it is possible to reframe the question in a more compelling fashion. The watercolors in the sequence after the representations of the grand vizier's military encampment turn forcefully away from the present predicament of war to record Mayer's travels through a number of sites made famous by the activities of the Society of Dilettanti and by Choiseul-Gouffier in the *Voyage pittoresque de la Grèce*. Ainslie had extensive connections with the Society of Dilettanti and was a voracious collector of antiquities. He spent much of his embassy collecting ancient coins, and his letters to members of the Levant Company in Smyrna and Aleppo always contain a paragraph with directions for acquiring coins. The numismatic texts derived from the Ainslie collection are among the most important ever published.[34]

Aside from a group of paintings of volcanoes that take up the back third of the album, the bulk of the watercolors are of the Greek and Roman ruins at Ephesus and Samos.[35] At one level, it is not surprising that Ainslie and Mayer were drawn to these archaeological sites, but their engagement has specific objectives that can only be appreciated by considering the relation of the views collected in the album to prior representations of these spaces. With war already under way, Mayer made his way to a site of recurrent destruction on Ainslie's behalf.[36] The bulk of Mayer's archaeological views concern the ruins at Ephesus, a site that figures prominently in *Voyage pittoresque*. We will be considering Choiseul-Gouffier's engagement with the site shortly, but it is important to have a sense of the range of views taken by Mayer and of the kind of sociability inscribed in his work.

At one level, Mayer's watercolors of Greek and Roman ruins are highly conventional. In some cases, he replicates the very views taken by Pars, Hilaire, and other predecessors.[37] But as one works through the album of views, a crucial difference slowly becomes apparent. Mayer's work fully integrates the Ottoman guides into this project, not as impediments or counterexamples, but as collaborators. Unlike in Choiseul-Gouffier, where Europeans are consistently arranged with their backs to their Ottoman guides and where their enlightened activities of drawing and looking are contrasted with the indolent lassitude of the Ottomans (see Figure 62), Mayer's pictures frequently present European and Ottoman subjects working on drawings together (Figure 77). These scenes of artistic collaboration are extremely important not only because they imply a level of intercultural communication, but also because they strike out so boldly from the work of prior painters working in this manner. The most significant of these scenes of collaboration come in Ephesus (Plate 25). One of the earliest Ephesus pictures, *Veduta della gran tribuna del Tempio di Diana d'Efeso* (no. 25), subtly links an Ottoman guide and an European draughtsman to the immediately adjacent pair of Europeans exploring what was believed to be the Temple of Diana. I would argue that this image of European and Ottoman working together on the "enlightened" task of representing the ruin is the necessary precursor to a much more complex and powerful scene of collaboration. Eight images later in the album—in his last painting executed at Ephesus, entitled *Veduta di frammenti di scultura ed architettura, che si osservano nell'antica città di Efeso* (Plate 26)—Mayer forcefully recalls one of the most famous images from Choiseul-Gouffier's *Voyage pittoresque*.

Figure 77. Luigi Mayer, *Veduta dell'Anfiteatro o Stadio di Efeso . . .* (1788), watercolor. Trustees of the British Museum.

Figure 78. Headpiece to "Discours préliminaire," from Choiseul-Gouffier, *Voyage pittoresque de la Grèce* (1782). Courtesy of the Getty Research Institute, Los Angeles.

Choiseul-Gouffier only engages with one object from Ephesus in *Voyage pittoresque,* but it is deployed twice in the text. A piece of sculpture from Ephesus serves as the headpiece for Choiseul-Gouffier's "Discours préliminaire" (Figure 78). Engraved in this fashion, it would appear to be a bas-relief, and the caption sends us to a later plate that shows the sculpture in situ (Figure 79). It is the only antiquity presented twice in *Voyage pittoresque,* and it is worth pausing over this differential

Vue d'une Porte à Ephèse.

Figure 79. *Vue d'une Porte à Ephèse*, plate 121, in Choiseul-Gouffier, *Voyage pittoresque de la Grèce* (1782). Courtesy of the Getty Research Institute, Los Angeles.

doubling before turning to Mayer's radical re-presentation of the same artifact. The details of the sculpture are not the primary focal point in *Vue d'une Porte à Ephèse*. The array of sculpted figures are there atop the ruin, but what we really have here is a de facto triumphal arch in a state of temporal decay. Like so many of the plates in *Voyage pittoresque*, the adjacent Ottoman goatherds figure for the present displacement of the heroic past by a corrupt and less advanced society. This sense of loss is intensified for the reader who has already seen a detail of the sculpture as the headpiece to the "Discours préliminaire." In that opening text, Choiseul-Gouffier explicitly romanticizes Greece as the land of Homer and Herodotus, and the sculpture of course makes that argument manifest. The sculpture shows two of the most famous episodes from the *Iliad* roughly abutted against one another. On the left we have an image of Achilles with the dead body of Hector attached to the back of his chariot. Priam stands, almost doubled over, immediately next to Achilles who is shown bearing his shield. This is the dramatic moment in book 24 where Achilles relinquishes the body of Hector out of sympathy for his bereaved father. On the right we have Achilles, seated, holding his head in anguish. The body of Achilles's heroic companion Patroclus is not rendered in the sculpture, but is no doubt implied. Two sculptural fragments placed side by side that must also be understood as fragments of narrative are brought together for our consideration. And not just any narrative fragments, these two scenes from books 18 and 24 of the *Iliad* bear a causal relation to one another—Achilles kills Hector to avenge the death of his beloved friend—and play out a key repetition—Achilles's comprehension of Priam's plight is made possible by his own affective experience of grief for Patroclus.

But what are we to make of the fact that the headpiece image erases two other scenes from the version of the sculpture represented in the larger plate? Is there any reason to be concerned about what would appear to be a disjunction between a decorative motif in Choiseul-Gouffier's text and another decorative element from the building itself? Perhaps we can get some purchase on that question by looking at Mayer's view (Plate 26 and Figure 84). Mayer's striking composition is almost a deconstruction of Choiseul-Gouffier's image pairing: we have the gate (without the relief) in the background and a more detailed rendering of the sculpture in the foreground. Mayer's watercolor tells us something important about the history of this material object. The sculpture in question is a third-century Roman sarcophagus popularly known as the "Achilles sarcophagus" because of its subject. The sarcophagus had been dismantled in late antiquity, and its parts had been built into the Gate of Persecution at Ephesus, where they were drawn by many later travelers, including William Pars (Figure 80). All four sides of the sarcophagus were acquired by the sixth Duke of Bedford in 1824, and the object is now at

Figure 80. Tracing on oiled paper from a drawing by William Pars showing the Achilles sarcophagus at Ephesus, from an album of prints and drawings compiled by William Young Ottley (ca. 1791). (See Figure 37.) Trustees of the British Museum.

Figure 81. Fragment of the Achilles sarcophagus, Woburn Abbey. Courtesy of the Woburn Abbey Collection.

Woburn Abbey (Figures 81–83). Mayer's rendering of three sides of the sarcophagus demonstrates that Choiseul-Gouffier's engraving of the gate was a reconstruction, and it also clarifies how the headpiece image was so well observed. The components of the sarcophagus were on the ground and thus could be studied and drawn in great detail.

But there is more at stake than simply undercutting the truth claims of Choiseul-Gouffier's engraving. The picturesque flourishes of *Voyage pittoresque* had always already put any such claims in question. More significant, it allows for the pictorial articulation of a very different history. As opposed to an image of antiquity overgrown by trees and neglected by the Turkish goatherds, Mayer's image frames the sculpture with conspicuous signs of human destruction. In his *Travels in Asia Minor*, Richard Chandler remarked upon the violent history of Ephesus, and William Pars's images for *Ionian Antiquities* were notable for their unflinching

Figure 82. Fragment of the Achilles sarcophagus, Woburn Abbey. Courtesy of the Woburn Abbey Collection.

portrayal of destruction. Mayer followed suit, but, if anything, the argument was intensified. The rubble that dominates the upper right half of the picture plane testifies to the long history of strife in this region. The settlement at Ephesus was the site of recurrent conquest and decline. The sculpture itself is a sign of this because it is a fragment of the Roman city that was built over the destroyed Greek town. In this regard, the narrative elements of the sculpture form a link between two now-defunct imperial powers. Both the subject of the sculpture and the

Figure 83. Fragment of the Achilles sarcophagus, Woburn Abbey. Courtesy of the Woburn Abbey Collection.

multiple framing devices of Mayer's picture emphasize that the classical heritage is inextricably tied to the violent prosecution of war.

How war figures here is extremely complex. Mayer's paintings frequently place the artist in the pictorial plane. The artist and his Turkish interpreter play a crucial role in this picture because their attention is bifurcated (Figure 84 and Plate 26). The interpreter points to the arched gate and thus to the literal and representational history of the sculptural object: it used to be up there; it has been repeatedly drawn and painted as part of this archway. And his gaze addresses the viewer in a crucial moment of intercultural communication. But the artist is focused on what lies before him: on Priam, Achilles, and the dead body of Hector. He momentarily ignores the interpreter and his gaze directs the viewer's attention towards the narrative moment in which Achilles puts rage and cruelty behind him and accedes to a condition of heroic honor. In short, the two figures address the viewer in radically different but complementary ways. The interpreter's direct pictorial address calls on the viewer to reflect on the historical situation of this encounter with the artifact. The artist's absorptive gaze demands that the viewer look through his eyes at the narrative unfolding in the artifact. Staged as an in/out bifurcation the interpreter/artist pairing seem to enact a kind of dialectical engagement with these fragments from the ancient world.

It is important to recognize how different this is from the deployment of Turkish figures in Choiseul-Gouffier's *Voyage pittoresque* or in the *Ionian Antiquities*. In

Figure 84. Luigi Mayer, *Veduta di frammenti di scultura ed architettura, che si osservano nell'antica città di Efeso* (1788), watercolor. Trustees of the British Museum.

these precursor texts, ethnic others operate either as historical obstructions to the European desire to acquire antiquities and commune with the Greco-Roman past or as signs of the degradation of the present political dispensation. Either way the ethnographic subject is deployed as an alibi for European acquisition and control. In the Mayer album, ethnographic subjects facilitate access to the object and to the historical world. And perhaps, most important, Mayer's Turkish figures take an active role in the interpretation and analysis of the archaeological sites. Scenes of intercultural collaboration are not uncommon, but nowhere is the complexity of intercultural inquiry more powerfully registered than in Mayer's treatment of the theater at Ephesus. In contrast to the pictorial strategies of the *Ionian Antiquities*, Mayer does not give us an elevation of the theater or synoptic view of the site, but rather provides a series of views that hide the theater from the viewer in order to focus on the penetration of the space. A similar pair of engravings from *Voyage pittoresque* indicates the degree to which Mayer resists the by now familiar modes of pictorial appropriation practiced by Foucherot and Hilaire (Figures 85 and 86). Neither an abstract reconstruction nor occupation of the theater itself—in Hilaire's topographical view the observer is placed in the orchestra in front of the remaining fragments of the skene and thus is "on stage"—Mayer's pictures emphasize that these spaces and all that they represent are fundamentally beyond our reach. The careful manipulation of enigmatic codes is crucial to Mayer's art and in the boldest of his theater pictures, *Veduta dell'Ingresso principale die conduceira nel Theatre di Efeso* (no. 26) we are presented with the European traveler and the Turkish guides descending into the past together (Figure 87). The difficulty of accessing the theatrical space is an apt metaphor for the entire project of linking historical excavation to extant literary knowledge of these sites. In this case, the palpable destruction of the theater and the difficulty of accessing its space figure for the challenge of reconstituting the Greek and Roman theatrical corpus. And this is a challenge facing the Europeans as much as the Ottomans in these images.

With this in mind it is helpful to return to Mayer's rendering of the Achilles sarcophagus (see Figure 84 and Plate 26). The bifurcation of the interpreter's and the artist's gaze engages the viewer in a dialectical act of observation: one that attends equally to the narrative encoded into the sculpture and to the historical narrative marked out by the interpreter's gesture. In a sense, both men—and the viewer—are engaging with the vestiges of war and the passage of time. With this recognition comes another important disclosure. The homosocial engagement between interpreter and artist is replicated in the left-hand fragment and thus this entire section of the painting doubles back on itself. The homosocial relation between artist and interpreter mirrors that between Achilles and Priam. Both sets

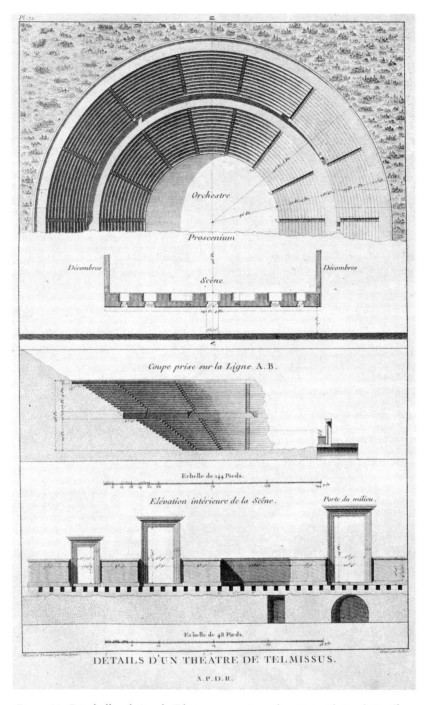

Figure 85. *Détails d'un théâtre de Telmissus*, engraving, plate 72 in Choiseul-Gouffier, *Voyage pittoresque de la Grèce* (1782). Courtesy of the Getty Research Institute, Los Angeles.

Figure 86. *Vue d'un théâtre de Telmissus*, engraving, plate 71 in Choiseul-Gouffier, *Voyage pittoresque de la Grèce* (1782). Courtesy of the Getty Research Institute, Los Angeles.

Figure 87. Luigi Mayer, *Veduta dell'Ingresso principale che conduccira nel Teatro di Efeso* (1788), watercolor. Trustees of the British Museum.

of men look in different directions and both sets of men are defined by their relation to the dead. In the scene of artistic production, the dead are figured by the fragments strewn about the painting—the very objects addressed by the artist's gaze and the interpreter's finger. In the narrative fragment, Achilles and Priam are triangulated by their relation to Hector's horizontal corpse. If one was to look only at this side of the picture, one would be tempted to argue that Mayer was simply celebrating Achilles—and by extension, the artist's—recuperation of martial honor from the horrible field of destruction and death.

But this intense engagement with the narrative fragment on the left side of the picture does not fully account for the image. The strong horizontal thrust of the sculpture itself generates another focal point for a different set of observers. Standing before the picture, the observers outside the frame (the viewing subjects) are afforded a different view centered on the remarkable pairing of Achilles and Andromache in the central and right fragments respectively. Drawn together by the repetition of their anguished gesture, these two figures call the viewer into a different pictorial hermeneutic. With no absorptive subject to mediate between the viewer and the object, we need to do some interpreting of our own. The right fragment shows Andromache mourning over the returned body of Hector—the great scene at the end of the *Iliad*'s book 24:

> First to the corse the weeping consort flew;
> Around his neck her milk-white arms she threw,
> And, Oh, my Hector! oh, my lord! she cries,
> Snatched in thy bloom from these desiring eyes!
> Thou to the dismal realms forever gone!
> And I abandon'd, desolate, alone!
> An only son, once comfort of our pains,
> Sad product now of hapless love remains!
> Never to manly age that son shall rise,
> Or with increasing graces glad my eyes;
> For Ilion now (her great defender slain)
> Shall sink a smoking ruin on the plain.
> Who now protects her wives with guardian care?
> Who saves her infants from the rage of war?[38]

The sheer lifelessness of his body is registered in the slackness of his limbs; her emotion is condensed into her gesture. But that gesture is repeated in the immediately adjacent Achilles, indicating that their grief is both causally linked and equal in significance. Put simply, the resonating gestures mark the extirpation of love, the horror of confronting the dead body of the beloved. And that sense of destruction and disarray is made manifest by the ruins in the background right. Which brings us to the most compelling element of Mayer's image.

Object Choices

The overall composition of the painting is dyadic. There is almost a vertical line separating the arched gate and the Hector/Priam fragment on the left from the pile of broken columns and the pair of fragments on the right. To put things reductively, the left side gives us heroic triumph (including artistic potency) and the right side gives us grief and destruction. But it is precisely this reductive formulation that allows us to see something about the narrative fragments. The central fragment, the scene of Achilles's grief is here presented as a metaleptic moment, an interruption in the narrative arc of book 24. The placement of the three blocks troubles the overall dyadic structure of the picture, and it does so by posing some intriguing questions about narrative time.

If we consider the adjacent fragments from left to right—and I think the rendering of the interpreter and the painter set this up—the story of Achilles returning Hector's body to Priam in the left fragment is interrupted by the scene of Achilles grieving for Patroclus in the central fragment. It is as though we have a sudden flashback that links two moments of affective response: Achilles's empathy for Priam's grief is linked to his own grief for Patroclus. An affective equation is built between the father's love for his son and the hero's love for his friend. The two adjacent fragments on the right side of the painting supplement this argument. Here Achilles's grief for Patroclus narratively prefigures Andromache's grief for Hector. An affective equation is built between the hero's love for his friend and the wife's love for her husband. In other words, the specific placement of the fragments attempts to conceptualize the precise nature of Achilles's affect: it is comparable both to the father's love for his son and to the wife's love for her husband. It quite literally lies somewhere between these two poles of attachment.

The relationship between Achilles and Patroclus is crucial to the *Iliad*: as Pope indicates in his commentary on book 18, Achilles has little interest in the prosecution of the war and thus the poem requires the horrible destruction of his closest companion to activate the hero. As Pope recognized, Achilles's love for Patroclus is—at the very least—a fundamental component of the plot. That said, it is in many ways the most enigmatic element of the poem. This enigma—in the Barthesian sense of a code that drives narrative desire—has generated myriad conflicting opinions. From the times of classical Greece through to the time of the Romans, the relationship was understood to be pederastic, although the ritual notion of *paiderasteia* was likely anachronistic for Homer's Ionian culture. Aeschylus and

Plato understood the relationship in these terms but disagreed on which figure was *erastes* and which was *eromenos*. Homer uses neither term, and it is clear that both characters have sexual relations with women slaves and captives. There is always the option of following Xenophon and seeing the friendship as one of devoted martial comrades. I believe that Mayer's painting does not follow any one of these readings but takes us into the heart of the affective enigma that may well constitute both the narrative and the ethical core of Homer's poem and of Ainslie and Mayer's historical predicament.

In this complex field of object choices, perhaps returning to the object—in a different sense—can help us make sense of why and how Mayer is engaging with the enigmatic relationship between Achilles and Patroclus. Mayer's rendering of the left and right fragments is remarkably close to the two long sides of the sarcophagus now in Woburn Abbey (Figures 88 and 89). Mayer's rendering of these blocks aspires to the condition of transparent facticity. However, close inspection of the central fragment reveals a startling deviation from the archaeological object (Figure 90).[39] What we have here is the key scene in the *Iliad* (18.275–82) where Patroclus's dead body is brought to Achilles. In terms of the overall composition of the sarcophagus, Patroclus's lifeless body on the top margin resonates with the recumbent corpse of Hector on the bottom margin. But Mayer's rendering eliminates the body of Patroclus and the nude figure carrying his corpse altogether only to replace them with a different pairing. The central soldier figure now carries a shield and the left part of the fragment features a standing nude facing right and a second partial nude figure facing left. These two new figures—one complete and one torn in two by what? shall we say time, or shall we say the war that everywhere surrounds the image?—hold hands. There is sadness, perhaps, in the posture of the nude man being led by the soldier, but certainly no confrontation with the dead body of the beloved. The two intermediate figures no longer recoil from the appearance of Patroclus's dead body, but rather seem to stare out at the viewer in a repetition of the interpreters' gaze. However, Achilles's gesture signals grief. What are we seeing here?

Significantly, Choiseul-Gouffier's detailed rendering of the sarcophagus also erases the body of Patroclus. It is unclear what the leftmost figure of the right fragment is doing. And with the erasure of the fragment devoted to the funeral of Hector and the expression of Andromache's grief, the right fragment in Choiseul-Gouffier's image is strangely unmoored from the narrative. Without Patroclus's body and without the implicit comparison between the gestures of Achilles and Andromache, Achilles's gesture becomes largely unreadable. His affective life is quite literally foreclosed and with it his motivation for entering the war. At this point it is difficult not to recall Choiseul-Gouffier's deployment of sexuality in *Voyage pittoresque*. As discussed in the previous chapter, Choiseul-Gouffier reads sodomitical

Fig. 41.   No. 146 III.

Figure 88. Comparison of left block from Luigi Mayer's *Veduta di frammenti di scultura ed architettura . . .* (1788) (*left*) to Arthur H. Smith's rendering in *A Catalogue of Sculpture at Woburn Abby: In the Collection of His Grace the Duke of Bedford* (1900) (*right*). Courtesy of the Thomas Fisher Rare Book Library, University of Toronto.

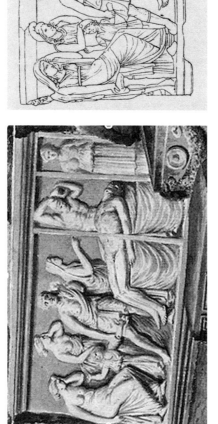

Fig. 43. No. 146 IV.

Figure 89. Comparison of right block from Luigi Mayer's *Veduta di frammenti di scultura ed architettura . . .* (1788) (*left*) to Arthur H. Smith's rendering in *A Catalogue of Sculpture at Woburn Abby: In the Collection of His Grace the Duke of Bedford* (1900) (*right*). Courtesy of the Thomas Fisher Rare Book Library, University of Toronto.

desire as a symptom of Eastern depravity, and thus it is a crucial component of his xenophobic attack on Ottoman governance. With so much of the sexual economy of Choiseul-Gouffier's liberationist rhetoric riding on this deployment of sexuality, Mayer's gesture here not only punctures the sexual fantasies that animate Choiseul-Gouffier's fetishization of the reproductive potential of Greek femininity but also undermines Choiseul-Gouffier's own claim to classical expertise. The strict partition of homoerotic desire from all things "Greek" renders Choiseul-Gouffier's veneration of Homer and Achilles incoherent.

In contrast, Mayer's addition of the rightmost fragment raises the question of Patroclus's death at the same time, or in spite of the fact, that his rendering of the central fragment refused to bring Patroclus's body into representation. It is a strange moment because it testifies to the ongoing existence of Achilles's love—in his object choice—in the face of that object's cancellation. It is as though Achilles looks across the face of that central fragment and sees a moment prior to Patroclus's death when the warriors stood hand in hand or a moment after his own death when he would join Patroclus in the underworld. Patroclus is ghosted by Mayer's painting, but he is recalled by the adjoining fragments: it is literally Priam's and Andromache's grief that makes Achilles's gesture legible and Patroclus's ghostly presence known. The distortion—or misrepresentation—at the very heart of Mayer's painting captures the fusion of memory and desire that characterizes a kind of love somewhere between that of a father for a son and husband for a wife. In other words, the fusion of memory and desire that defines the enigmatic love that inspires Achilles's most fearsome expressions of violence and his most tender moments of empathy. Regardless of what we can say about Mayer and Ainslie's own identities and their own attachment—and that is symptomatically vague—the treatment of the *Iliad* is deeply homophilic.[40]

In this context the incompleteness of the leftmost figure in the central fragment is extraordinarily resonant (Figure 90). Poised as it is on the central axis dividing the scene of heroic triumph on the left of the painting and the catalog of destruction on the right, this broken line, this figure severed almost perfectly in half, not only captures the hollowing out of the self caused by the death of the beloved, but also resonates with the embodied notion of divided love articulated in the *Symposium*. In a single moment of invention Mayer has made a crucial disclosure about the *Iliad,* about this archaeological site, and perhaps about his relation to Ainslie: in this poem, in this object, love as much as war will tear us apart. But what of the historical frame that relentlessly permeates this scene? It seems unlikely that this exploration of the desolation of war is meant to operate as an allegory for the surrounding geopolitical crisis in the region. Like the relationship between the sculptural object and the ground of the painting, it would appear that the viewer is being asked to work through the historical predicament in an adjacent

Fig. 39. No. 146 I.

Figure 90. Comparison of middle block from Luigi Mayer's *Veduta di frammenti di scultura ed architettura* . . . (1788) (*left*) to Arthur H. Smith's rendering in *A Catalogue of Sculpture at Woburn Abby: In the Collection of His Grace the Duke of Bedford* (1900) (*right*). Courtesy of the Thomas Fisher Rare Book Library, University of Toronto.

aesthetic zone. Hence my analysis shifts from calculations of interest, alliance, and force toward plangent questions of affective relations in the time of war. We are not being asked to look for hidden meaning beneath the image, but rather to recognize the meaning generated by adjacent fragments of narrative and by the close encounters between subjects and that which lies beside them. In this image, who and what lies next to whom makes all the difference in the world.

But this disclosure also hints at a very specific phantasmatic resolution of the larger conflict surrounding Ainslie, Mayer, and their Ottoman hosts. The torn figure at the center of the painting figures forth Achilles's own condition, because he is well on the way to death. When Achilles avenges the death of Patroclus by killing Hector, he seals his own fate as well as that of the Trojans. Hector, in his dying speech, predicts Achilles's death, but that death is not part of the narrative of the *Iliad*. He is killed by Paris's arrow, but in all of the versions of Achilles death, Paris's action is seen not as an act of valor but rather as an act of cowardice. Is it possible to see in the beleaguered state of the Achaeans throughout the first twenty-two books of the *Iliad,* in Achilles's initial reluctance to fight and his precipitous entry into battle following the death of Patroclus, an allegory for the perilous state of the Ottomans during Ainslie's embassy? It would certainly capture the weakness of the Ottoman position prior to the outbreak of war in 1787, Abdülhamîd's reluctance to go to war, the initial successes of the Turkish forces in 1788, and the disastrous loss at Ochakov later that year. And it would suggest that the decision to enter the war, like Achilles's decision to kill Hector, was linked to a sacrifice of

Figure 91. William Watts, mezzotint after Luigi Mayer drawing, *Fragments at Ephesus*, from *Views in the Ottoman Dominions... from the Original Drawings Taken for Sir Robert Ainslie, by Luigi Mayer* (1810). Courtesy of the New York Public Library.

the self to preserve the honor of the loved one. In this allegorical gambit, love for Patroclus translates into a complex affective attachment between the sultan, his allies, and his people that runs counter to traditional notions of Eastern despotism. Knowledge of the larger history of the fall of Troy would allow wishful observers to figure the Ottoman setbacks and the death of Abdülhamîd in 1789 as precursors to the ultimate destruction of the Franco-Russian threat. As strained as this allegory seems, it is perhaps the only phantasmatic response to the "Greek plan" that would suit British interests when Mayer's painting was composed. As with the aftermath of the Trojan War, what was needed was a dispersal of imperial competition, a clearing of the ground, prior to the phantasmatic invention of a new empire.

This, of course, did not come to pass; at least not in the ways figured forth by this image. But then this image itself was not allowed to rest. Ainslie and Mayer included an engraving based on this watercolor in the *Views in the Ottoman Dominions* of 1810 (Figure 91). The rendering of the sculpture is largely unchanged,

Figure 92. William Watts, mezzotint after Luigi Mayer drawing, *Part of the Grand Gallery of the Temple of Diana*, from *Views in the Ottoman Dominions . . . from the Original Drawings Taken for Sir Robert Ainslie, by Luigi Mayer* (1810). Courtesy of the New York Public Library.

but in the aftermath of Ottoman defeat in 1792 and the increasingly complicated place of the Ottomans in global affairs during the Napoleonic wars (the Ottomans were aligned with France in the Anglo-Turkish War of 1807–9), all sign of collaboration between European artist and Ottoman guide has been erased.[41] In fact, the Ottoman interlocutor has been replaced by another European and the clothing has been updated to dislocate this image from the immediate context of 1788. With this realization that the engraving is backing away from the drawing's more heterodox elements, we notice that the view of the sculpture has undergone a slight, yet decisive, change. The central half-figure who stands in for Patroclus now appears to have a female breast and with that alteration at least some of the drawing's homophilic qualities are put in abeyance. The other key scene of intercultural collaboration in the Ephesus sequence is subject to a similar revision (Figure 92). The Ottoman interlocutor is eliminated and the European observers are dressed with Regency flair. Whatever time these images are supposed to represent, one thing is certain: the time for open negotiation, collaboration, and affiliation in these spaces is under erasure. And that erasure is ineluctably tied to emergent sexual and racial orthodoxies at the heart of Britain's imperial project in the nineteenth century. As we will see, this remarkable revision of Mayer's watercolor, with all of its implied constraints on social and sexual relations, will provide a powerful heuristic for thinking about the practice of revision in two far more famous cultural artifacts: Antoine-Ignace Melling's *Voyage pittoresque de Constantinople et des rives du Bosphore* (1807–24) and Lord Byron's *The Giaour* (1813).

CHAPTER 8

Critical Disjunctions

The Intersection of Form, Affect, and Empire in Melling and Byron

> The work of Glory still went on
> In preparations for a cannonade
> As terrible as that of Ilion,
> If Homer had found mortars ready made;
> But now, instead of slaying Priam's son,
> We only can but talk of escalade,
> Bombs, drums, guns, bastions, batteries, bayonets, bullets,
> Hard words, which stick in the soft Muses' gullets.
> —*Byron,* Don Juan, *canto 7, stanza 78*

We could describe Ainslie and Mayer's repudiation of Choiseul-Gouffier's alignment of aesthetic fantasy and political policy as an act of geo-*poetic* resistance. Poetic in that they were engaged as much with the vexed historicity of epic form as they were with their more contemporary rival. As a reading of the *Iliad*, Mayer's watercolor depicting the Achilles sarcophagus at Ephesus recognizes the centrality of love to Homer's account of heroism and makes it speak to his own condition (see Figure 84 and Plate 27). If I am correct that the unabashed homophilia of Mayer's remediation of both the artifact itself and its representation in the *Voyage pittoresque de la Grèce*, then one can discern a palpable parallel with Montagu's letter book, itself a reading of the *Aeneid* that also comprehends the emotional dimensions of epic narrative. For both Mayer and Montagu, the demands of epic form come at a deep affective cost. Love and possibility are made visible through their cancellation. Montagu's text is as much a poetic rejoinder to her immediate precursors—Rycaut, Hill, Dryden, and Pope—as Mayer's watercolor offers a counter to Choiseul-Gouffier's phantasmatic investments in the liberation of Greece.

Both Mayer and Montagu are using the classical material at their fingertips to claim forms of artistic authority at variance with masculinist heteronormative notions of subjectivity and agency. And these norms are ineluctably tied to the shifting eighteenth-century sex/gender system. The preponderance of gendered and sexualized tropes in the archive of material we have been discussing is not incidental. In Vanmour we saw how marriage was deployed to allegorize the stability of the Ottoman state and how sexual license figured forth the disturbing potential of consumption in a changing world. In Montagu we saw how mobilizing the women peripheral to the epic tradition—the Trojan women, Dido, and Montagu's own authorial persona—allowed her to critically engage with the formal ordering of imperial violence. With the Dilettanti we saw the valorization of Montagu herself—a remarkable deployment of gendered authority in its own right at a moment when the propriety of female learning was under much scrutiny. In Choiseul-Gouffier the linked deployment of reproductive sexuality as a sign for the potential to reinvigorate Greece and of the sodomitical Turk as a sign of the barrenness of Ottoman culture couldn't have been more blatant. Craven translated this binary opposition between reproduction and sodomy into an economy of female beauty with desirable Greek women at one extreme and repulsive Ottoman women at the other.[1] Thus the deployment of sexuality in Choiseul-Gouffier was differentially written onto the bodies of women under Ottoman rule, "Greek" and "Turkish" alike. In this light, the emergence of nonnormative sexuality as the hinge around which Mayer's repudiation of Choiseul-Gouffier turns only gains further substance.

This chapter follows this deployment of sexualized and gendered figures into the early nineteenth century in order to bring us to the emergence of the kind of orientalist discourse first anatomized by Edward Said in *Orientalism* (1978). Building on the material discussed in previous chapters, I want to show how a sustained attention to form and history provides a way to think about two flawed masterworks of French and British Romanticism: Antoine-Ignace Melling's *Voyage pittoresque de Constantinople et des rives du Bosphore* (1807–24) and Lord Byron's *The Giaour* (1813). Unlike the other figures discussed in this book, Melling and Byron did not cross paths, although John Cam Hobhouse's account of his and Byron's tour of the Levant in 1809–10 indicates that they were well aware of Melling's architectural practice in Constantinople.[2] On the surface their works would seem to be radically dissimilar. Melling's vast elephant folio is in many ways the culmination of the French bibliophilic tradition and arose out of intense collaboration with the highest levels of the Ottoman court. Byron's "Fragment of a Turkish Tale" holds a privileged place in the criticism regarding not only the poetic fragment as a particularly Romantic form, but also the importance of sexual fantasy to Orientalist and Occidentalist discourse.[3] But at another level, this vast picture book and this fractured poem share many structural and formal similarities. One of my primary objectives in this chapter is to show how formal disjunction is crucial to both projects' attempt to deal with key historical problematics and that will require attending to the manifest difference between the illustrations and their explications in the case of Melling, and the poem and its notes in the case of *The Giaour*. In the former case, the explanatory texts that supplement Melling's marvelous views of Istanbul smudge their detailed celebration of quotidian Ottoman life into a dispiriting brand of Orientalism; in the latter, we find Byron curiously at odds with himself, trying to contain the implications of a poem whose volatility set the terms for much of his subsequent work. My readings of Melling and Byron show how a network of visual and verbal signs can simultaneously articulate the potential for transcultural hybridity and a regressive sense of imperial nostalgia. Ultimately this chapter hopes to show not only that studying nonliterary genres, visual media, and sociability can expand our understanding of canonical literature, but also that understanding European engagement with the Ottoman Empire is necessary for comprehending the global dynamics of French and British imperialism.

Melling's and Byron's books are very much conditioned by the weakened situation of the Ottoman Empire in this period but bear the imprint of Napoleon's military incursion into Europe and the Levant. That said, it will be impossible to disconnect this argument from Choiseul-Gouffier's gendering of the political, because both texts radically complicate our understanding of the sexual tropes that animate this archive. Melling directly engages with intercultural sexual desires to explore forms of imperial nostalgia; Byron queers the scene of desire not only to challenge Britain's emerging imperial practice, but also to wrestle with unresolved issues from its imperial past. Choiseul-Gouffier's *Voyage pittoresque* is regularly cited as an inspiration for Byron and Shelley's philhellenism, and David Roessel goes so far as to argue that the frontispiece sets the discursive parameters for the feminization of Greece right through the nineteenth century.[4] This discursive construct had tangible political effects during the Greek War of Independence in that European powers consistently figured their interventions as instances of white Christian men saving white women from their Muslim captors.[5] Nascent Islamophobia bolstered this historical fantasy, but my aim here is to show how these regressive tropes and discursive formations attempt—yet ultimately fail—to contain the emergence of nonnormative forms of sociability.

In both Melling and Byron, we can discern modes of intercultural sociability and sexuality that seek to cross or destabilize identity categories that were beginning to congeal into national and racial categories at precisely this time across western Europe. In these works intercultural sociability becomes aligned with queer sexuality because both become, in this moment, nonnormative, and as a result both are imagined, too, as reparative. What is so remarkable, I think, is that these affective bonds, much in evidence in the early eighteenth century—and in the early chapters of this book—are now under increasing surveillance.[6] Under the pressure of this emerging racial and sexual normativity, Melling and Byron devise formal methods for representing and enabling nonnormative social and sexual relations, but then allow these innovations to be overwritten and thus disciplined. Melling hands this task to his editor Lacretelle; Byron does it to himself with each successive version of *The Giaour*. But what this means is that important remnants of nonnormative relations can be excavated from their formal strategies, thus in a curious way their texts testify to the resilience of intercultural sociability beyond the strict enforcement of racial and sexual identity. In Melling, this will be most evident in the way that he renders space: it will be quite startling to see how the distortions that destabilized Vanmour's *View of Istanbul from the Dutch Embassy at Pera* become a conscious aesthetic decision in *Voyage pittoresque de Constantinople*. In Byron, we will find ourselves again contending with epic form, and with Montagu—whom he deeply admired—and Mayer will provide useful points of reference for our understanding of his poetic practice. Thus this chapter will not only bring our analysis of the deployment of sexuality throughout the book to a temporary conclusion, it will also bring many of our remarks on the politics of landscape, on the one hand, and the stakes of epic utterance, on the other, to a momentary close. I use the words "temporary" and "momentary" advisedly because the story I have been trying to tell does not rest. It is perhaps because foreclosure always implies the potential for openness that both Melling's book and Byron's poem have been amenable to contemporary readings aimed at building links between the past and otherwise forgotten futures.[7] But to comprehend this we need to return to 1788 and the immediate presence of war in the Ottoman Empire.

Melling's Volatile Hybrids

Despite victories against Russia's Austrian allies early in 1788, the Ottomans lost the key strategic position at Ochakov to Prince Potemkin and by the end of the year the tide had turned. Shortly thereafter Abdülhamîd died on 7 April 1789 and his bellicose young successor Selim III, in the words of Ainslie, "was to prosecute the warlike preparations by Sea and Land *with if possible additional zeal and vigour.*"[8] Selim III's war policy was a disaster for the Ottomans. A series of costly defeats ensued until the Turks surrendered to the Austrians in 1791 and the Russians in 1792. The ensuing Treaty of Jassy formally recognized Russian annexation of the Crimea. We know from various accounts of the later stages of the war that Ottoman resistance was fierce and that casualties were extensive. The storming of Ísmail, the most important Ottoman fortress on the Danube, in December 1790 gives some sense of how these battles proceeded. The fortress was defended by 35,000 men and 265 guns; the Russians attacked with 31,000 soldiers and 600 guns. The Russians very quickly overpowered the gates and walls, but then had to fight the Ottomans in fierce street-by-street battle. As Aksan states, "The *Serasker* and 4,000 men defended the last bastion but were slaughtered to a man. Turkish losses stood at 26,000 dead and 9,000 prisoners. Suvorov allowed his soldiers three days of looting, following one of the bloodiest confrontations in all Russian history."[9] It is perhaps not surprising that the Siege of Ísmail would become the subject of Byron's most strident antiwar statements in canto 7 of *Don Juan*.

Shortly after the composition of Mayer's watercolor, in the midst of all this bloodshed, another expatriate European artist living in Pera was asked to undertake an unusual intercultural collaboration. The Alsatian painter and architect Antoine-Ignace Melling was part of the original circle of artists and intellectuals who congregated around Choiseul-Gouffier after his appointment in 1784, but he eventually found regular work for the Russian ambassador Yakov Bulgakov[10] Bulgakov was one of Potemkin's protégés, and like the other enlightened ambassadors in Pera, he maintained a *dessinateur* as part of his company. Melling's work in Istanbul was remarkable by any measure. The body of drawings and paintings produced was extensive and boldly took as its object the city itself and the life of its inhabitants. He returned to France in 1803 with a vast archive of preparatory material that would form the basis for one of the greatest illustrated travel books ever produced, *Voyage pittoresque de Constantinople et des rives du Bosphore*.[11] Published in Paris between 1807 and 1819, no expense was spared in its production: a full set of thirteen *livraisons* and the text volume cost the subscriber 1,300 francs.[12] Melling's book is divided into two volumes. The second volume is composed of forty-eight plates of astonishing detail based on Melling's topographical and architectural drawings and a trio of maps, one of which scrupulously recorded from where each view was taken.[13] In its final binding the engravings were accompanied by a preliminary volume of textual commentary written by the historian Jean Charles Dominique de Lacretelle in consultation with Melling.[14] This latter point is significant because the text is replete with Islamophobic tirades on despotism and a highly predictable fascination with the harem that we can't necessarily impute solely to Lacretelle or Melling. In fact the commentary has a disturbingly supplemental relation to the images: composed years after the views themselves, the text buries the images in a layer of Orientalist dogma. So there is a struggle within the book itself between word and image that poses significant interpretive problems because there are cracks in Lacretelle's xenophobic representation of Ottoman culture that reveal an extraordinarily complex collaboration between

Melling and his Ottoman hosts. That his hosts happen to be Selim III and his sister Sultana Hatice (referred to as Hadidgé in *Voyage pittoresque de Constantinople*) makes this collaboration that much more compelling.

In spite of the fact of ongoing war between the Sublime Porte and Russia, it was through Bulgakow's connections that Melling found himself working for both Selim and Sultana Hatice. For Selim, Melling undertook a number of projects that integrated European ornament into the sultan's summer residence on the Bosphorus.[15] According to *Voyage pittoresque de Constantinople*, "The Great Lord . . . saw with great satisfaction the work of Mr. Melling, and he commissioned the artist to build for him, in Beschick-Tasch [Beşiktaş], a kiosk whose inside would have to be decorated in a European style" (1:98). *Voyage pittoresque de Constantinople* gives more detailed accounts of Melling's hybridization of European and Ottoman architecture, but Lacretelle's text frames the description of Melling's work at Selim's summer palace at Beşiktaş with opening remarks that transform hybridity into a hierarchy of design:

> The sight of an oriental palace deeply piques one's curiosity. An immutable despotism maintains such uniformity in the customs, the arts and the luxury of the Asian empires, that the abode of an Ottoman monarch can suggest to our imagination that of a Ninus or an Artaxerxes. In this way, the more modern building dons the imposing colors of the most remote Antiquity. . . . Finally, guided by the penchant that leads us toward all that is mysterious, we burn to enter the formidable enclosure where delight is *placée sous la garde de la terreur*. (1:98)

These opening remarks activate a whole set of fantasies regarding Eastern despotism that quite literally spirals out of control in the subsequent paragraphs. The longest paragraph in the commentary, under the pretext of describing one of the structural features of the palace, is devoted to the condition of the women "imprisoned" in the harem.

At turns leering and aghast, the text strangely expands upon what is not represented in the engraving (Figure 93). Melling's picture focuses our attention on the details of the palace as seen from the water; the plate commentary is dominated by an explication of what is behind its walls. But as the commentary unfolds it becomes clear that this rhetorical excess is staged in order to emphasize the difference of Melling's neoclassical restraint:

> One will undoubtedly feel deeply surprised when one sees this oriental palace beautified by a kiosk whose architecture cannot be found in the region where it used to shine in the old days. Maybe one day people will discourse

PALAIS DE BESCHIK-TASCH,
Séjour habituel du Grand – Seigneur pendant l'été.

Figure 93. Antoine-Ignace Melling, *Palais de Beschik-Tasch*, plate 28 in *Voyage pittoresque de Constantinople et des rives du Bosphore* (1819), engraving. Courtesy of the Getty Research Institute, Los Angeles.

on this part of Beschik-Tasch, and strangers will do it the honor to take it for a Greek monument. This kiosk and the gallery in the middle of which it is raised were built by Mr. Melling for Selim III. . . . The wooden-built kiosk, held by eight Ionic white marble columns, stretches along the entire length of the quay. The gallery is Corinthian. Selim III, who was rebuked for his fondness for European arts, applauded this kind of architecture, and awarded Mr. Melling a pelisse, which so far had been reserved for ambassadors or strangers in the service of His Highness. (1:99)

The less than subtle insinuation that Selim III prefers European to Ottoman culture comes with the suggestion that Melling is realizing Choiseul-Gouffier's dream not through revolution or regime change but through the inexorable force of modernization. It is a fantasy only marginally less xenophobic than that expounded in *Voyage pittoresque de la Grèce*. In the midst of the sultan's palace, this European architect is reconstituting the cultural authority of ancient Greece with the sultan's blessing. Again and again Lacretelle stages this as a heroic struggle: Melling and his patron have to struggle against "superstition" and against the narrow-mindedness of subaltern figures. The *kislar aga* looks on Melling's work with intense suspicion, and Lacretelle narrates how Melling was temporarily imprisoned before being liberated by Sultana Hatice herself.

What I want to stress here is the degree to which this discourse pushes well beyond Melling's illustrations. If we look at the engraving of the sultan's palace at Beşiktaş, the "Greek" or European elements of the building are barely discernible. In fact Lacretelle's attempt to specify the columns does not correspond to Melling's image. One is struck far more forcefully by the unity of form and function in Ottoman palace design. This disjunction between text and image is symptomatic of a larger problematic in *Voyage pittoresque de Constantinople* that becomes more apparent in the next engraving/commentary pairing in the book. I would contend that the engraving and the description of Selim III's palace sets the stage for the far more complex representation of Melling's work for Sultana Hatice. Lacretelle's description of how Melling entered Sultana Hatice's service shows the depth of intercultural sociability in and around Istanbul:

This princess, who was the sultan Selim III's sister, had always been the subject of her brother's most tender affection. It was her he entrusted with the wise plan that he had devised to gradually accustom the wild Muslims to European arts and civilization. She entered into all his tastes. She had been allowed to visit a charming house and some very nice gardens, that the Baron Hübsch, who was responsible for the King of Denmark's business, had had built in the village of Buyuk-Déré [Büyükdere]. Above all,

the gardens caught her attention: she felt the strongest desire to get similar ones; but where could one find in Constantinople an artist who could
fulfill the sultana's desire? The Baron Hübsch referred her to Mr. Melling,
who accepted the mission. (1.100)[16]

One could argue that this is simply yet another account of the sultan and his sister
looking to "Europeanize" themselves, but the implied relationships run counter
to the anti-Ottoman rhetoric deployed throughout much of *Voyage pittoresque de
Constantinople*. With little record left of his activities or of his final design, it is
worth contemplating the strange fact of Melling working away, living in his own
apartments adjacent to Hatice's residence, while the Ottoman military was being
systemically routed by the Russians.

Melling was installed in the quarters of Hatice's husband, whose post as the
governor of Erzuroum meant that he was frequently absent, but the sultan was a
frequent visitor:

> The Grand-Seigneur oftentimes visited his sister. . . . As the Sultana always
> looked for new ways to entertain her august brother, Mr. Melling offered
> to build a garden maze for her. The Sultana smiled at this idea, and showed
> great impatience as to see it carried out. The maze was planted with lilacs,
> roses, acacias, which rose very high in this region, and which may be
> trimmed into any shape. The curves were so thought through, that almost
> all paths led you back to the center and that the ways out were hard to
> find. The Sultan Selim, despite all his seriousness, enjoyed very much all
> the mistakes of this little labyrinth [*ce petit dédale*]. (1.101)[17]

It is fascinating that Hatice commissions a device for diverting her brother and
that Melling proposes a labyrinth. As the term *dédale* reminds us, labyrinths have
a classical pedigree stretching back to the Cretan labyrinth designed by Daedalus.
Unlike a branching maze, a labyrinth inexorably drives its user toward the center, but
the text emphasizes that Melling's proposed labyrinth is not easy to navigate.
Hatice's desire to entertain her brother is a subtle indication that the sultan was
desperately in need of uncomplicated pleasures. Selim III's eighteen-year reign
started in a state of war, but even after the Peace of Jassy in 1792 the Ottoman
Empire was in a continual state of unrest both from internal rebellions and from
the external vicissitudes of the Napoleonic wars. At the risk of comparing the great
and the trivial, I would contend that this garden is emblematic of much of Selim
III's predicament during this era. Despite the attempts of his predecessors—in particular, Mustafa III in the aftermath of the defeat at Çeşme—to modernize the
Ottoman military, the new sultan inherited logistical and technological short-

comings that rendered him unable to adequately meet his imperial rivals in the field. After the disastrous final years of the Russo-Turkish War, he had little choice but to embark on a complex and contentious program of reform. These postwar reforms extended well beyond the military into the very fabric of Ottoman society and culture, and they were marked by an explicit openness to European forms of modernization.

As Aksan emphasizes, the period after the Peace of Jassy was remarkable in that Selim III solicited suggestions for change from a broad range of voices.[18] Critique of the military and of the system of supply was scathing and the advisers most ascendant at court repeatedly argued that the Ottomans, as their Russian enemies had already demonstrated, could benefit from careful study of European models of organization in a range of fields. Selim III initiated a host of reforms, most important, to revenue collection, to the military, and to the system of grain supply. Aksan provides a clear outline of these specific reforms, but for our purposes Selim's actions can all be united under the rubric of centralization. The new order and the new army from which it took its name—*Nizâm-i Cedid*—was based on the imposition of laws designed to wrest power away from the provincial elites and from the janissaries whose corruption and dispersal had made the Ottomans weak in the face of Russian conquest. Instead of relying on a haphazard system of local supply to maintain troops, a central ministry was formed to oversee the transport and sale of grain. The structure of taxation was completely overhauled to ensure that the funds necessary for reform were readily available. And, most important, a new standing army under the direct control of the sultan, with recognizable regiments and protocols, was formed to operate as a counterexample of sorts to the corrupt system of janissaries and spahis. These military reforms were also highly technological and, as with his predecessors, Selim III brought in foreign expertise, largely French, to accelerate the Ottoman capacity to found cannon and train artillery soldiers. These centralizing and Francophilic reforms prompted significant resistance not only in the outer regions of the empire (most notably Egypt) but also in the inner circles of power. In the revolt of May 1807, the sultan and most of his inner circle were assassinated by the janissaries; on 3 June 1807 the *Nizâm-i Cedid* was eliminated by the new regime of Mustafa IV.

If we take Melling's cue and imagine for a moment the scenario of Selim III's diversion in Hatice's garden, the labyrinth, like the forces of modernization itself, keeps turning the sultan toward the center. With each turn it becomes increasingly difficult to find one's way back out to the surrounding Ottoman structure. The very hybridity of the project makes it a dangerous place for the sultan to play. As a metaphor, entering the labyrinth puts the sultan's status in question: the future of the empire turns on how he incorporates and navigates European organizational models; but his actions would be ultimately limited and proscribed by the prior governmental structures within which his motions were confined. With historical forces driving him toward centralization and thus separation from the past, Selim III would eventually have to face those forces who were not ready or whose interests were not served by modernization. In this context, the fact of the garden's disappearance both on the ground and in the archive is the objective correlative of Selim III's assassination and the elimination of *Nizâm-i Cedid*.

I'm using the labyrinth as a figure for Selim III's political predicament by focusing on the labyrinth's relation to the surrounding structure of the palace and showing a systemic breakdown that parallels the social challenges of implementing *Nizâm-i Cedid*. Lacretelle's commentary also opts for allegory but makes a symptomatic interpolation by inserting the most sensational sign of despotic corruption into the labyrinth itself. In his account, Lacretelle fills the labyrinth with harem women:

> The Sultan Selim, despite all his seriousness, enjoyed very much all the mistakes of this little labyrinth. The day the Sultan let the young ladies of his harem in the maze was a day of joy and folly. After playing for a little while, they started looking for exits in order to go back in the harem. As they were incessantly taken back to the same place, they thought that they were under the spell of an enchanter; but it seemed a pleasant prison to them, the garden resounded with their laughter, and their useless shouts to their companions. A few of them, who managed to find the only exit, cunningly enjoyed the confusion of the others. Finally, they successively recovered freedom; and, since that time, the greatest favor they could ask the Sultana was the permission to take a walk in the maze. (1:101)

In this sexualized fantasy of Ottoman usage, the labyrinth's centralizing power generates pleasure for Sultana Hatice's women by first trapping them in an "agreeable prison"—subtly distinguishing this entrapment from their regular condition—and then "liberating" them. This game of liberation works via the magic property of centralization and becomes the primary desire of the harem women. After they've experienced it once, they want more. In other words, this is a sexual fantasy of the potential of modernization to de-Ottomanize Ottoman society, and the emblematic technology comes from an architectural structure synonymous with ancient Greece. Lacretelle's argument reaches its logical conclusion when he suddenly invokes the countervailing presence of the *baş-ağa*: "The Basch-Aga, first Eunuch of the princess's harem, saw with great displeasure Mr. Melling's credit: he would lose his temper each time inventions would be proposed; and, to him, each embellishment that would be of European style seemed contrary to the Koran's laws" (1.101). In a different way, Lacretelle also captures Selim III's pre-

Figure 94. Antoine-Ignace Melling, *Portrait of Ottoman Woman*, ink drawing. Private collection. Bridgeman Art.

dicament: the labyrinth figures for the forces of European modernization and the *baş-ağa* stands in for those resisting Selim III's reforms. However, Lacretelle's highly sexualized and xenophobic presentation of the problematic leaves the garden well behind. In a sense, his sensational "socialization" of the labyrinth's use deflects attention away from Melling and Hatice's collaboration.

Hatice's garden was only the first commission Melling executed for the Ottoman princess. It would also appear that Sultana Hatice and Melling developed some kind of affective relation during this period, which came to an abrupt end with Napoleon's invasion of Egypt. The evidence of intercultural exchange is in many ways unprecedented because it takes the form of a correspondence between two figures normally proscribed from communicating with one another.[19] At some time during their association, Hatice and Melling exchanged notes written in an unusual form of Ottoman Turkish transliterated into Latin letters (with the exception of one letter in Italian). The letters are undated and their subject matter is highly quotidian. The everydayness of the letters has been a disappointment to those who would like firm evidence of an amatory relation between the sultana and Melling. The desire among historians and critics for such a relation is intensified by the existence of a drawing of an Ottoman woman on a divan covering her face with her sleeve (Figure 94). This is an unusual variant on the trope of the veiled woman because the "veiling" here amounts to a gesture quite separate from a specific article of clothing or a larger social convention. The fascinating element of this drawing is that the subject seems to be covering herself from the unwanted glance of the viewer, but the state of undress implies that she is comfortable with the gaze of the artist. In other words, the drawing seems to imply an intimacy between subject and artist in the moments before and after its rendering. And this implied intimacy has been temporarily interrupted by the preparation of the drawing itself for our consideration. The presumption that this is a portrait of Hatice is questionable, but its confirmation would fit into long-standing fantasies about European men in the harem. As we will see, this is not an incidental matter for Melling's *Voyage pittoresque de Constantinople*, but for the moment I want to forestall questions of sexual desire to consider the question of intimacy itself in this context. Without minimizing the importance of such an affective bond, it is worth considering the degree to which the correspondence and the drawing confirm the fact of intimate collaboration in the project of interculturalism itself. As we will see, Melling's work pursues the task of hybridization with great theoretical rigor and aesthetic flair. But to see this we need to look carefully at the structure that arose from and eventually surrounded this intercultural collaboration.

Throughout the 1790s Melling was involved in the renovation and design of Hatice's palace at Defterdar-Bournou on the Bosphorus. As Cornelis Boschma and Jacques Perot note, we can be much more precise about Melling's hybridization of Ottoman and European taste because we can refer to two architectural drawings and an engraving of the finished building. Melling's classicism is obvious from his frontal diagram for a section of the facade of the palace (Figure 95). As Boschma and Perot argue, the scales on the bottom left margins of the diagram indicate that Melling divided the structure into twenty-four sections according to precepts that can be traced back to Vignola's *Regola delli cinque ordini d'architettura*.[20] Vignola's treatise had an immense influence on French neoclassical architecture and its prescriptions for the various orders of architecture are evident throughout the design. The facade is divided into five vertical units each separated by pilasters. On the ground floor the pilasters are Doric; on the second story the pilasters, capitals, and the entablature are Ionic. The central three vertical units on the second floor extend outward and are supported by four Doric pillars, which are connected by a balustrade to form a pavilion. The decorative elements in the friezes of the entablature on both floors and along the roof are typical of any neoclassical building being built in France or England during this period. In short, one could easily glance at this drawing and mistake it for one of Nicholas Revett's or Robert Adams's designs, or the work of François-Joseph Bélanger or Claude-Nicolas Ledoux.[21]

But to do so would be to miss its most important feature. In keeping with the rules of the harem and with residential architecture in Istanbul, there are no windows on the ground floor. In the place of windows, Melling has designed niches

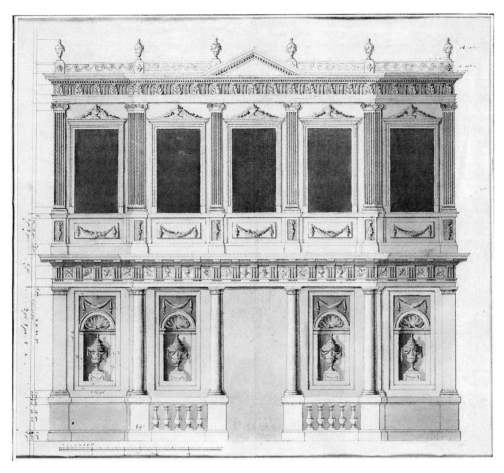

Figure 95. Antoine-Ignace Melling, design for facade of Sultana Hatice's palace on the Bosphorus. Private collection. Bridgeman Art.

for sculpted urns. The tops of these niches are decorated with inset stylized scallop shells and sculpted draperies. These niches simultaneously maintain the neoclassical proportions of the building and the sanctity of the harem. In this regard they are thoroughly hybridized features simultaneously figuring forth the idealized social order of two distinct cultures. The complexity of this hybridization is both aesthetic and historical. French neoclassical architecture returned to Greek models in order to emphasize planar qualities rather than sculptural volumes: planar proportion and the continual framing of devices enact the Enlightenment desire for clarity and organization. The irony of deploying sculptural insets, however classical in form, in the window spaces of the palace could not have been lost on Melling. The pilasters and tablets of this facade frame, even accentuate, a visual blockage; and in so doing, they accept this check on enlightened inquiry in the name of Ottoman social convention. It is a remarkable accommodation, necessitated no doubt

Figure 96. Antoine-Ignace Melling, design for Sultana Hatice's palace on the Bosphorus. Private collection. Bridgeman Art.

by his commission, but which for all of its classical trappings remains an image of a radical future.

The radicalism of the gesture becomes even more apparent when we consider Melling's other renderings of the palace facade, because we begin to see how the pavilion is integrated into the larger structure (Figure 96). Even in the partially colored forty-five-degree rendering of the building, where the details of the adjoining structures are barely sketched in, we sense the immediate contrast between the neoclassicism of Melling's facade and the typically Ottoman windows and rooflines. And the image also gives a sense of the differences in materials used in the construction of this hybrid entity. Both stories of the facade clearly have a marble facing; whereas the ground floors of the adjoining structures are brick and the second stories are of wood construction. The lustrous blue sky figures enlightened clarity of vision, but it also focuses our eye on the surfaces of the building, and thus the color of the structure itself emerges as a complex question. To encase the traditional wooden structures and decorations of Ottoman residential architecture with marble would be a material break with tradition. One is left with the sense that the problem of hybridization is resolved in the structural accommodations of the facade itself, but that Melling remains undecided about the final stylistic fusion.

His extremely detailed engraving of the palace in the second volume of the *Voyage pittoresque de Constantinople* would appear to demonstrate a resolution to the problem of hybridity (Figure 97). This engraving was executed at least a decade after the drawings; but Melling's facade appears almost unchanged, and the adjoining structures are now presented in the same level of detail. The high windows on the first stories and the protruding wooden second stories are typically Ottoman in character and design. The fact that this engraving immediately follows a similar engraving of Selim III's palace on the Bosphorus at Beşiktaş only makes this more apparent. Indeed, the order of the engravings is important here because the engraving of the sultan's palace establishes the precise terms on which Hatice's palace varies from the norm. Some level of integration between Ottoman and neoclassical decoration is afforded by the decorative elements on the long wall to the right of Melling's facade: each section in this wall replicates the vase and drapery elements of the sculptural niches in the facade in a larger set of arabesques. But above all it is the lack of color in the engraving that allows Melling to unify these elements. In other words, I would argue that the medium itself allows for a tenuous balancing act between neoclassical and Ottoman decoration across the length of the building so that we see the disjunctions but also imagine their structural and material coherence. Furthermore, the subtle movement from the sultan's to Hatice's palace that is enacted in the book's structure and in the movement of the boats in both images—the boats come toward the viewer from left to right in the former and move away from us from left to right in the latter—establishes a narrative of temporal progress and modernization. The fact that these images are retroactively constructed well after Melling left Constantinople only heightens the sense that what we are seeing here is a carefully constructed resolution to an ongoing problematic.

But there is more to be said about this engraving. In the foreground two groups of women depart by boat from Hatice's pavilion. There is a eunuch—the commentary identifies him as the *baş-ağa*—in the stern of the leftmost boat and a total of

PALAIS DE LA SULTANE HADIDGÉ
à Defterdar-Bournou.

Figure 97. Antoine–Ignace Melling, *Palais de la sultane Hadidgé*, plate 29 in *Voyage pittoresque de Constantinople et des rives du Bosphore* (1819), engraving. Courtesy of the Getty Research Institute, Los Angeles.

twelve veiled figures embarking for an unknown destination. The woman immediately adjacent to the *baş-ağa* is identified as Sultana Hatice. Aside from continuing
a sense of activity in the Bosphorus itself that is typical of the *Voyage pittoresque*,
this simple gesture also emphasizes that Melling's pavilion is a portal between the
inner and outer world of Hatice's residence. The door at water level becomes more
than simply the central organizing element of Melling's design, it now signifies a
point of entry, and in that sense becomes a central phantasmatic device for the
viewer's imagination of the harem. I would argue that the blackness of that harem
door in the engraving is the structural analogue to the veils of the women in the
boats. Melling is establishing a desire to see beyond these temporary blockages
that actually cancels the accommodation developed in his replacement of the
ground-floor windows with sculptural insets. What I want to suggest is that the
radical accommodation to Hatice's needs and desires implied by the initial design's
occlusion of the ground-floor windows has been superseded by an Orientalist desire to see and know what goes on behind them. No longer in Hatice's employ,
Melling's illustration of her palace starts to get reabsorbed into regressive fantasies
of harem life that preceded his collaboration with her.

As we have already seen, this sense of reabsorption into Orientalist fantasy is
accelerated by Lacretelle's commentary. Perhaps the most egregious example of
this accompanies the engraving of Sultana Hatice's palace, and, like many of
Lacretelle's additions, it turns on a narrative of sexual desire that allegorizes Selim III's Francophilia. Explaining that many foreign ministers wanted to see the
hybridization of neoclassical and Ottoman architecture in the palace, Lacretelle
narrates the visit of M. le comte de Ludolf, his daughter, and the aptly named
Mademoiselle Amoreux, the daughter of the French consul at Smyrna. There is no
interaction between the count and Sultana Hatice: she retires to private spaces while
he views the garden. In lieu of the father, his daughter and her friend accept Hatice's
hospitality and gifts are exchanged. But Lacretelle informs us that on the same day
Selim III was also visiting Hatice and that "the Sultan had a great desire to get an
idea of the skills that European ladies possess when it came to clothing. . . .
The Sultan, standing behind a grilled folding screen, saw these ladies without
being seen" (1:101). The sultan, "placed behind a grid screen," watches the two
young women entertain Hatice: Mademoiselle Amoreux plays on the harp and
both women dance. Significantly, both young women are associated with elegance,
decency, and dignity, but Mademoiselle Amoreux is presented as the spirited foil
to Mademoiselle Ludolf's calm disposition. In a sense they represent the alpha
and omega of European femininity. This scene of voyeurism is notable for two
reasons. First, it explicitly argues that Hatice and Melling contrive the scene for
Selim's pleasure. The text explains that Melling not only designed the parterre
so that the sultan could take up this position, but also that he was "instructed

to transmit to them testimonials of the Sultan's satisfaction" (1:101). And second, it implies that this voyeuristic moment exceeds all the pleasures at his ready disposal because these women represent more than sex. The entire scene is contrived to activate Selim III's Occidentalism and it does so via the most recognizable trope of Orientalism itself: scopophilia.

The reinvigoration of this scopophilia in the *Voyage pittoresque de Constantinople* is perhaps the most notable falling away from the visual restraint of the architectural drawings executed during Melling's tenure as Hatice's architect. Melling's cross-sectional illustration of Selim III's harem is the most obvious case in point (Figure 98). When the reader pores over this image and lands on the two women kissing on the right of the engraving and reads Lacretelle's lengthy discussion of the selection of the sultan's bed partner, one is basically placed in the same position as the sultan watching the two young French women above. In other words, the Orientalist scopophilia of this engraving sets the terms for Lacretelle's narration of the sultan's Occidentalist scopophilia in the textual explication. I would argue that what we see in the illustrations to *Voyage pittoresque* is a kind of overwriting of Melling's past collaboration with Hatice. But the fact that he presents his work on the Defterdar-Bournou Palace indicates that there is a complex attraction and resistance at play in the book. As we have seen that push and pull is manifest in the engravings themselves and in the textual explication of them.[22] However, the textual commentary often breaks beyond the representational paradigms of the illustrations by indulging in scopophilic narratives of erotic desire. But significantly these narratives of desire often mimic Orientalist tropes to underline the sultan's Occidentalism: his desire for modernization and his Francophilia. In this regard the harem and the sultan himself become nodes of rhetorical excess, and that excess has a very specific structuring effect on the overall composition of *Voyage pittoresque de Constantinople*.

My discussion of the engravings of the palaces at Beşiktaş and at Defterdar-Bournou has said little about their placement in the volume. They come midway through the second volume of *Voyage pittoresque de Constantinople*, and I would argue that the complex visual rendering of cultural hybridity in these two engravings and the cancellation of that hybridity in the textual commentary operates as a response to much of what comes before. The forty-eight engravings of the second volume can be divided into two sections: the first, comprising twenty engravings, focuses largely on the city of Istanbul itself; the remaining twenty-eight plates are devoted to views taken along the shores of the Bosphorus. As one moves from the maps that open the volume through to the end, the reader travels by water past the Isle of Tenedos through the Dardanelles to Istanbul where much of Melling's attention is on the seraglio. Then the reader travels from Tophane through the Bosphorus to the shores of the Black Sea. This water journey is only interrupted

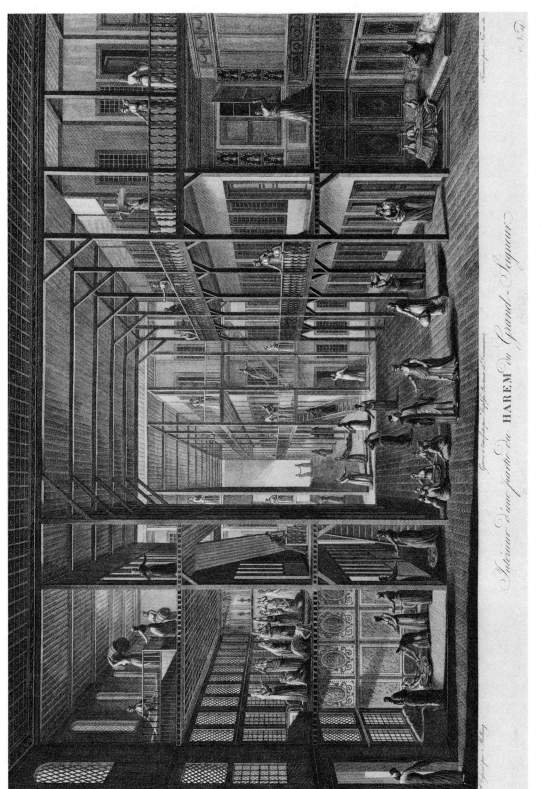

Figure 98. Antoine-Ignace Melling, *Intérieur d'une partie du harem du Grand-Seigneur*, plate 10 in *Voyage pittoresque de Constantinople et des rives du Bosphore* (1819), engraving. Courtesy of the Getty Research Institute, Los Angeles.

twice: once by a pair of architectural views at Tophane (plates 22 and 25) and finally by a group of waterworks, ancient and modern, that conclude the volume (plates 45 to 48). Put simply, the illustrations would appear to use the scopic tools of modernity—the elevated view, mapping, perspective, and the technology of engraving itself—to provide a controlled and highly detailed representation of the spaces and peoples of Istanbul and its environs.[23] Inge Boer's analysis of a typical topographical view is applicable to the project as a whole: "What strikes us in the landscape, however, is the apparent visibility of everything. The landscape is laid out before our eyes so that we can maintain the fantasy that nothing is hidden from our gaze. The effect is achieved by means of a bird's eye view of the scene, which results in longer perspectival lines. Unobstructed by elements in the landscape, it seems as though we can almost look beyond Constantinople." As she goes on to convincingly argue, this results in a visual distortion of the relationship between foreground and background, and a frequent erasure of the middle plane altogether: "The spectator is forced to move his/her eyes to contemplate the foreground. It is as if the foreground is produced through a wide-angle lens, so that an inconsistency within the overall visibility occurs. . . . In a sense, a bird's eye view and a wide-angle vision give us the best of both worlds, which is ultimate control."[24] Boer contends that as soon as one becomes aware of this conflation of viewing technologies one becomes aware of the constructedness of the image and this is undoubtedly true. But I would argue further, that the yoking together of these two visual modes is never fully achieved and they coexist in a constant state of disruption.

That disruption is complicated further by Elisabeth Fraser's argument regarding the convergence of Melling's views of the palaces on the Bosphorus and Ottoman wall paintings of the same subject. Fraser argues that the remarkable commitment to a wide-angle view amounts to a form of visual incorporation of a preexisting and prevalent Ottoman decorative art. It is from here that she contends that Melling is best approached as an Ottoman court artist.[25] The evidence she presents is evocative because there are clear parallels between these Ottoman paintings of palaces along the Bosphorus and Melling's engravings. My sense is that Melling has learned something about the disruptive potential inherent to the horizontality of these paintings, but he does not simply replicate their formal strategies. Instead their horizontality is strongly felt in the foreground of his engravings in a way that necessarily bends the middle ground and distorts the image. In other words, the engravings stage the differences between two representational paradigms and force the viewer to look in a way that shuttles between two specific modes of viewing. Melling's fusion of Ottoman visual style with conspicuously European landscape paradigms constitutes yet another volatile hybrid, and it testifies to the fact that there can only ever be a fantasy of control. Such a recognition goes some way to destabilizing the claims to Enlightenment clarity and visibility and subtly suggests the limitations of modernity itself.

Waterworlds

And yet in the midst of these visual disjunctions, one element of the book remains relatively constant: the ubiquity of water and the sense that Istanbul and the communities of the Bosphorus are linked by a complex aquatic sociability. Melling loves boats, and their presence is intimately linked to the book's most important political argument. Structuring the book as a waterway lends spatial coherence to the project, but Lacretelle's commentary indicates that there is much more at stake here than a geographical pilgrimage. The opening four plates—*Vue de l'isle de Ténédos, Vue des Dardanelles, Vue du château des Sept-Tours et de la ville de Constantinople*—are intricately tied to the history of the Anglo-Ottoman war of 1807. As Lacretelle is careful to narrate in the commentary to these images, a British naval squadron under the command of Vice Admiral John Thomas Duckworth entered the Dardanelles on 19 February 1807 in response to the Ottoman decision in the summer of 1806 to allow only French passage through the straits. Duckworth destroyed the Ottoman navy in the Sea of Marmora and anchored off of Istanbul, but the Ottomans responded by building powerful batteries with the help of Napoleon's ambassador General Sebastiani and French engineers working for Selim III. The artillery fire from the shore became so intense that the British fleet had to retreat on 3 March. Each of the sites in the first four plates played a conspicuous role in the aborted British invasion, so the book is reminding the readers of notable Franco-Ottoman successes. This is also why plate 7, *Vue de Constantinople, prise de la tour de Léandre* (Figure 99), has such conspicuous weaponry in the foreground (albeit presented in a celebratory capacity), and why plate 18, *Vue de l'arsenal de Constantinople* (Figure 100), essentially provides an anatomy of the restored Ottoman fleet. These are highly selective historical gestures because the Ottomans found themselves allied with both Britain and France at different stages of the Napoleonic wars. In a sense, attention is being drawn away from Napoleon's invasion of Egypt and the ensuing problems this generated for Selim III's rule. But I believe the gesture here is aimed less at offering a coherent vision of past conflict, than with figuring forth a future for Franco-Ottoman cooperation against rising British power in the post-Napoleonic world.

The key issue is less the particular victory over Duckworth than the fact that victory came through demonstrable collaboration between French engineers and Ottoman artillery crews. Under the rubric of modernization, this tactical victory finds itself aligned with Melling's own collaboration with Selim III and Sultana

VUE DE CONSTANTINOPLE,
Prise de la tour de Léandre.

Figure 99. Antoine-Ignace Melling, *Vue de Constantinople, prise de la tour de Léandre*, plate 7 in *Voyage pittoresque de Constantinople et des rives du Bosphore* (1819), engraving. Courtesy of the Getty Research Institute, Los Angeles.

VUE DE L'ARSENAL DE CONSTANTINOPLE.

Figure 100. Antoine-Ignace Melling, *Vue de l'arsenal de Constantinople*, plate 18 in *Voyage pittoresque de Constantinople et des rives du Bosphore* (1819), engraving. Courtesy of the Getty Research Institute, Los Angeles.

Figure 101. Antoine-Ignace Melling, *Selim III*, title page, *Voyage pittoresque de Constantinople et des rives du Bosphore* (1819), engraving. Courtesy of the Getty Research Institute, Los Angeles.

Hatice, and thus with the overall project of the *Voyage pittoresque de Constantinople*. The fact that these collaborations all precede the book's production is important because there is an unmistakable nostalgia for Selim III's Occidentalism that is announced on the title page of the first volume (Figure 101). With some sense of the ideological import of the frontispiece image to *Voyage pittoresque de la Grèce*, readers would have been struck by the difference announced by the portrait of Selim III, ensconced in the heavens, immediately preceding the formal title page and the gold-embossed Ottoman Arabic figure on the title page itself. As the "Préface des Éditeurs" states,

> We felt we had to put Selim III's portrait at the beginning of this publica-
> tion, because it is under his reign and thanks to his protection that
> Mr. Melling was able to do his great work: this prince was incidentally one
> of the most enlightened Turkish sovereigns and one of the dearest to Eu-
> ropean nations.
>
> The figure that one can notice under the title is Selim III's: it contains
> the words *Selim Khan ibn Moustafa mouzaffer daima*; in French: *Sélam, Khan,
> fils de Moustafa, toujours victorieux* [son of Mustafa, always victorious]. (1:2)

This opening gesture declares the book's primary divergence from Choiseul-Gouffier's *Voyage pittoresque de la Grèce*: the openness to Ottoman culture suits Melling's specific history as Selim III's architect and the larger historical separa-tion of France from Russia in the final stages of the Napoleonic wars. In the "Plan du *Voyage pittoresque*," Lacretelle argues that "in the *Voyage pittoresque* that we are announcing here, art and antiques will not be the primary topic" (1:2). Although the editors indicate elsewhere that the book was supported by Choiseul-Gouffier, it is clear that nostalgia for Selim III's project of modernization and hope for its continuation under Mahmud II has supplanted Choiseul-Gouffier's nostalgia for antiquity and his hope for the liberation of Greece. As we have already seen, the subsumption of Greek antiquity into French neoclassical design allows Lacretelle to bring many of Choiseul-Gouffier's aesthetic hierarchies in through the back door, but Melling's views of Istanbul seem to operate quite separate from this ear-lier anti-Ottoman position. Melling uses the generic parameters established by Choiseul-Gouffier to counter Choiseul-Gouffier's politics.

Indeed one could argue that Melling provides some of the most compelling images of the power of the sultanate at precisely the moment when its weakness necessitated a controversial openness to European models of modernization. The irony of this gesture should not go unnoticed because in many ways plates 7 through 10 and plate 12 are belated signs of the sultan's power. In fact these engravings are all images of Selim III. Plate 7 (Figure 99) shows the sultan's galley in ceremonial regalia touring the harbor. This image perhaps more than any other shows the com-plex problem of yoking together deep perspective with a wide-angle foreground. The bird's-eye overview allows Melling to provide a precise, detailed, and highly controlled image of Topkapi and the skyline of Istanbul. The horizontal expan-sion of the foreground allows Melling the room to handle Selim III's procession to the mosque in all its magnificence. One could argue that the former visual imperative is conditioned by the same Enlightenment desire to know that under-writes the map showing precisely where each view is taken from. But the latter visual strategy is aimed at capturing the effusive and elaborate sociability of the sultan. Linking the two generates a significant formal fracture (somewhere in the middle plane a massive spatial distortion occurs) that is addressed in the textual commentary. Rather than describing the image, Lacretelle's text becomes ob-sessed with fantasies of despotism.[26] What I would suggest is that the engraving presents two competing regimes of sight that instantiate a supplemental statement that attempts to contain the disruption by asserting a social and visual hierarchy. Lacretelle's supplement struggles to maintain the dominance of depth over hori-zontality, to legitimate the French Enlightenment desire to regulate this space by derogating the Ottoman sociability that seems to stretch the very image into its final shape. In short, the visual disjunctions and the text's sensational attempts to contain them are subtle evidence of the volatile hybridity of Melling's intercul-tural experiments. What started out as a melding of styles in his architectural commissions has transformed into a highly resonant deformation of the represen-tational presuppositions of topographical landscape itself.

The ensuing five plates are less unstable because they are less visually disjunc-tive: there is little foreground interference because we are staring directly—at times literally and at times metonymically—at the sultan. Plates 8 and 9 in *Voyage pit-toresque de Constantinople* are views of the seraglio from an elevated position (the latter plate shows an ambassadorial audience with the sultan; see Figure 102); plate 10 offers an unusual architectural cross-section of the harem (the text emphasizes that Melling had firsthand views of the space; see Figure 98) showing the typical activities of the women in different rooms. Finally, plate 12 shows Selim III in procession during the festival of Bayram (Figure 103). As we progress from plate to plate, we come closer and closer to the body of Selim III. With the exception of the harem cross-section—although his presence is both visually implied and textually asserted—the sultan is the ultimate object of representation, and thus everything is in some senses a function of his central power. But perhaps the strangest thing about this is that these remarkable "portraits" of the sultan's power only exist because of his weakness. Prior to the disastrous wars of 1768–74 and 1787–92 there isn't the same opening for this kind of artistic practice or for the kind of intercultural relationship implied by these illustrations. But I would argue that the traces of that interculturalism are felt throughout the bent space that seems to inflect every subsequent engraving in the book.

That said one could argue that the ultimate arrangement, execution, and pro-duction of *Voyage pittoresque de Constantinople* in Paris in the period between 1806 and 1819 owes as much to the resounding defeat of Napoleon at Waterloo and the ensuing transformation of European politics.[27] If the defeat of the Ottoman Empire

VUE DE LA SECONDE COUR INTÉRIEURE DU SÉRAIL.

Figure 102. Antoine-Ignace Melling, *Vue de la seconde cour intérieure du sérail*, plate 9 in *Voyage pittoresque de Constantinople et des rives du Bosphore* (1819), engraving. Courtesy of the Getty Research Institute, Los Angeles.

Marche Solemnelle du GRAND-SEIGNEUR, le jour du Baïram?.

Figure 103. Antoine-Ignace Melling, *Marche solennelle du Grand-Seigneur, le jour du Baïram*, plate 12 in *Voyage pittoresque de Constantinople et des rives du Bosphore* (1819), engraving. Courtesy of the Getty Research Institute, Los Angeles.

in the Russo-Turkish wars of the late eighteenth century set the stage for Selim III's Occidentalism and thus Melling's employment, then the fact of a weakened France and an ascendant British imperial power permeates the anti-British rhetoric of the textual commentary and the nostalgia of Melling's representation of the sultanate. Melling's nostalgia is as much for French imperial influence as it is for Ottoman modernization. Indeed the fact that he sees these two forces as coterminous unites the political and aesthetic objectives of the project into one phantasmatic whole. Perhaps this accounts for an unintended parallel between *Voyage pittoresque de Constantinople* and the sultan it patronizingly glorified. Just as Melling's elaborate engravings turned Istanbul itself into a figure for Selim III's failed attempt to modernize the Ottoman Empire, so too does the massive elephant folio stand as a vestige of failed French imperial ambition. A certain belatedness permeates both Selim III's and Melling's projects that necessitates the political excesses of Mahmud II's absolutism and the rhetorical excesses of Lacretelle's Orientalism.

Looked at this way, there is considerable incentive to extricate Melling's remarkable topographical views from their retroactive deployment in the *Voyage pittoresque de Constantinople*. Fraser does just this by reconstituting Melling's relation to Ottoman painting, his transculturalism, and ultimately his identity as a European painter for the Ottoman court. As with extant drawings for the facade of Sultana Hatice's palace at Defterdar-Bournou, we are fortunate in that many of Melling's drawings, gouaches, and watercolors, produced while in Hatice's employ, have survived; along with the record of their exhibition at the Salons of 1806, 1808, and 1810.[28] In other words, a parallel set of images was shown without Lacretelle's corrosive commentary. And, in some cases, Melling worked up fully realized paintings of select views. For example, the arsenal engraving in *Voyage pittoresque* was worked up in oils, and the diverse palette allows Melling many more options for capturing the hustle and bustle of the quay.[29] It is in these vibrant and colorful paintings that one can perhaps most powerfully feel the power that Orhan Pamuk has attributed to these images.[30] Freed from the ideological inheritance of Choiseul-Gouffier and of the social and political imperatives of post-Napoleonic French culture, these paintings and drawings attest to a level of visual engagement with Ottoman subject matter heretofore unrealized. Melling, like Vanmour many years earlier, is looking closely at the world around him, but his preference of landscape over genre painting allows for a requisite expansion in scale. In Vanmour, the tendency remains ethnographic, because the subject is society itself. In Melling, there is an attempt to capture the vast power, now receding, of the Ottoman Empire, and thus landscape aspires to the condition of history painting.

The most important of the paintings developed from Melling's drawings in Istanbul is *Vue de la pointe du Sérail et l'entrevue du général Sebastiani avec le Grand-Seigneur le 2 mars 1807*, and it demonstrates this complex aspiration (Plate 27).

The title is crucial. The painting transports the viewer to a moment on the eve of Vice Admiral Duckworth's retreat. The British fleet is anchored along the horizon on the left side of the painting; the right side of the picture offers a view of Topkapi Palace with Selim III and General Sebastiani meeting on the shore in the middle ground. The sultan is mounted on a white horse and Sebastiani and his fellow officers are dressed in full regalia. Melling has not represented the battery in action, but three of the Ottoman galleys in the foreground carry the mortars and cannons used to repel the British squadron. But more subtly, the picture's treatment of space and time is designed to capture a historical turning point: the orientation of the view (we are looking westward) and the pinkness of the sky indicate that the sun is setting on the British squadron's occupation of the harbor. By tomorrow the British ships will have weighed anchor and retreated to the Mediterranean. But it is important to recognize that the events represented took place four years after Melling's departure from Istanbul. In other words, its simulation of a key historical moment is retroactively composed to appeal to Parisian viewers cognizant of the British defeat.[31] The extraordinarily detailed rendering of Topkapi is no doubt based on drawings taken while Melling was in Istanbul, and there are numerous examples of Melling's drawings not only of galleys but also the sultan's procession. Bringing these elements together in this way is an act of historical invention aimed at celebrating the Franco-Ottoman alliance against the British.

But I would argue that this is more than the commemoration of a specific battle. This picture was likely executed sometime between 1808 and 1812 and thus coincides with a period when the Ottoman Empire seemed on the verge of chaos and when the French Empire was at the height of its power. Despite Selim III's success over the British, he could not contain unrest in the provinces. When the janissaries rose up against him shortly after the moment represented in this picture, Selim III was imprisoned and his cousin Mustafa IV became sultan. Within a year Selim III would be murdered and Mahmud II would take over the sultanate. When we broaden the historical frame, this picture is an elegy of sorts for Selim III, and it shows him on the verge of a rare moment of martial success. The intensity of Melling's pink sunset seems too effusive for a minor tactical victory over the British. But as a sign not only of the intimate association between artist and patron, but also of the cessation of Selim III's openness to modernization, then this glowing sky would seem to capture the afterglow of the Enlightenment itself. Within a short period of time that pink afterglow would fade to darkness as Napoleon invaded Russia in 1812 and get transformed into the virtuoso black-and-white engravings that make *Voyage pittoresque de Constantinople* one of the great artifacts of imperial nostalgia. And I would contend that its greatness, like the multivalence of the pink sunset in *Vue de la pointe du Sérail et l'entrevue du* général

Sebastiani avec le Grand-Seigneur le 2 mars 1807, lies in its capacity to capture the passing of two imperial encounters with modernity.

Byron's Obsolete Fragments

As one progresses through *Voyage pittoresque de Constantinople* it feels as though the historical events that determine the actual viewpoints in the first twenty engravings slip away like the water of the Bosphorus itself. The ensuing twenty-eight engravings seem to open onto a timeless realm beyond the geopolitical reverses that canceled Melling's affective relation to Selim III and Sultana Hatice. In this regard, the views of the Bosphorus exhibit the kind of historical evasion that we associate with nostalgia, and as I have suggested, I think it comes to allegorize a larger level of psychic avoidance; namely, the nostalgia for France's pre-Waterloo stature. With Melling we can see a reckoning with the vicissitudes of French imperial ideology from the losses in the Seven Years' War to France's global resurgence in the wake of the American war through to its rise and fall in the Napoleonic era. While Lacretelle's commentary devolves into the kind of Orientalist racism that would characterize much of nineteenth-century French writing, Melling's illustrations stand critically apart, exhibiting precisely the sense of collaboration and shared purpose that has been lost. It strikes me that this is a useful starting point for addressing the complex temporal and historical problematics articulated in Byron's *The Giaour*, for that poem too offers a puzzling mix of historical analysis and evasion. One of the strangest things about this manifestly strange poem is the tension between referentiality on the one hand and Orientalist fantasy on the other.

As numerous commentators have noted, Byron was committed to those aspects of *The Giaour* that had their roots in his own witnessing; he was intensely concerned that his descriptions be recognized for their descriptive and anthropological veracity.[32] The notes frequently refer to his tour of the Levant in 1809 and 1810 to claim firsthand experience with both the region and the poem's central events. And yet it is a poem whose narrative is riven by paradoxical contradictions and a palpable sense of unreliability. This contrast between the poem's claim to descriptive truth and its staging of narrative perspectivalism can be mapped onto the distinction between its apparatus—the advertisement and notes—and the verse. Like the disjunction between Lacretelle's explication of Melling's plates, Byron's paratextual remarks and the verse are often at cross-purposes, or more accurately, the relationship between the two is often slanted or skewed. The identity of the speaker in the paratext ranges from a seemingly objective commentator to Byron himself: nestled within the notes are autobiographical moments that almost overshadow that which is being ostensibly explicated. That said, we also see this tension within the poem proper; in other words, *The Giaour's* mediation of historical events and affective relations is doubly vexed. And that vexation is coterminous with the poem's critical relation not only to the extant representations of the Greek and Ottoman world but also to the normative models of sociability and sexuality in the Georgian period. As we will see, *The Giaour's* complex formal management of description and narration will allow us to think through the importance of these discursive modes throughout this book and thus offers an occasion to bring many of my previous arguments to a close.

My intention here is to focus on this particular poem in much the same way that I analyzed Mayer's watercolor of the Achilles sarcophagus. Rather than a broad-ranging discussion of Byron's Orientalism or of Romantic sexuality, I will be looking specifically at how Byron organizes the text to call into question virtually all of the cultural *doxa* that had by then accreted not only to notions of "Greece" and the "Turk" but also to norms of social and sexual relations in the Regency period. In other words, my interest has to do with how Byron the author finds a form and a genre to meet the crisis enveloping both Byron the subject and Europe more generally in the closing stages of the Napoleonic wars.[33] I am invoking the notion of crisis advisedly, because I believe *The Giaour* is a useful barometer for assessing how history, both global and personal, comes to be felt as a transitional state. To quote Lauren Berlant again, "Affect's saturation of form can communicate the conditions under which a historical moment appears as a visceral moment, assessing the way a thing that is happening finds its genre."[34] What is so striking for my purposes here is that Byron's historical critique extends back to the 1770s and exhibits a truly global reach; behind the veil of locality, Byron presents a coded analysis of British imperial culture from the moment of American decolonization forward. That may seem like a surprising claim for a poem so rooted in its time and place, but, as we will see, the poem not only targets specific chronological moments of global significance but also engages with prior discursive constructions to offer a genealogy of Britain's dispiriting imperial stance at the end of the Napoleonic wars. Thus Byron's poem, no less than Melling's illustrations, is marked by nostalgia, only it is for a moment prior to Britain's emergence as the dominant global power; and this can be seen in the poem's complex formal strategies. As we saw in our discussion of the aesthetics of ruination in the preceding three chapters, formal fragmentation has been repeatedly tied to crises in imperial history.[35] By reading form across visual and verbal media, my intention here is to show how the affective historicity of imperial nostalgia in the waning years of the Napoleonic wars inflects these works. Just as Melling's project is imbued by France's imperial rise and fall, so too is Byron engaged with unresolved matters in the history of British colonialism.

By highlighting the poem's form, I am merely rehearsing the reception of the poem from its earliest publication to the present day: the fragmentary presentation of the narrative has always been a crucial part of the reaction to *The Giaour*. Colin Jager's luminous reading of the poem in *Unquiet Things* makes one thing extraordinarily clear: paraphrasing *The Giaour* radically undermines its project, and yet virtually all criticism of the poem, from the earliest reviews onward, gives a summary of the plot.[36] This of course is an action authorized by Byron himself because he offers a summary in the "Advertisement":

> The tale which these disjointed fragments present, is founded upon circumstances now less common in the East than formerly; either because the ladies are more circumspect than in the "olden time"; or because the Christians have better fortune, or less enterprize. The story, when entire, contained the adventures of a female slave, who was thrown, in the Mussulman manner, into the sea for infidelity, and avenged by a young Venetian, her lover, at the time the Seven Islands were possessed by the Republic of Venice, and soon after the Arnauts were beaten back from the Morea, which they had ravaged for some time subsequent to the Russian invasion. The desertion of the Mainotes, on being refused the plunder of Misitra, led to the abandonment of that enterprize, and to the desolation of the Morea, during which the cruelty exercised on all sides was unparalleled even in the annals of the faithful.[37]

Byron expends thirty-one words on the poem's "story." Much of that story is not narrated in the poem: there is no corresponding narrative regarding the Giaour's violation of Leila. Her relationship to the Giaour is referred to but does not hold the status of an event. As Jerome Christensen states, "The purity of Leila is apodictic."[38] Leila's death, the first appearance of the Giaour, and his retreat to the Caloyer monastery are only obliquely rendered and significantly attributed to unnamed Muslim narrators. As numerous commentators have noted, the fragmentary narration of these events makes them the subject of readerly desire. Caroline Franklin argues with regard to the execution of Leila that the lack of narrative continuity only heightens the horror and the erotic effect of her death.[39] One could argue that there are only two fully narrated events, the killing of Hassan and the Giaour's account of the killing of Hassan six years later. This doubling of Hassan's death is, I believe, crucial because it opens up a gap within the story: what we have are two narratives of the same event, and they couldn't be more conflicted.

Within the "Advertisement" these narrative issues are fully subordinated to the much more elaborate historical placement of the story. Perhaps because the conflict over Leila is so cliché—both in its homosocial and Orientalist overtones—the "Advertisement" is far more fulsome about the precise historical moment of its occurrence. In fact, the preponderance of specific historical and geographical reference points in the "Advertisement" seems to set the stage for a historical poem, perhaps along the lines of *Childe Harold's Pilgrimage*. The "story" takes place shortly after 1779, and I think it is worth pausing over that specific chronological marker. The "Advertisement" places the story in a local spatiotemporal frame. The Treaty of Küçük Kaynarca of 1774 temporarily suspended hostilities between the Ottoman Empire and Russia. Venice, whose empire was all but extinct, still retained the Ionian Seven Islands, thus explaining the presence of the Giaour (an unnamed Venetian), but at the time of the poem the Russians still occupied the Morea (Peloponnesian peninsula). Their control over the region was far from clear: the rise of Muslim Albanian paramilitaries made this an interimperial zone of violent contestation.[40] It is hard to imagine a more unstable political time and place, thus the "Advertisement" emphasizes that the story is everywhere surrounded by violence and desolation of almost unrepresentable intensity.

But significantly it was only after 1794—that is, after the conclusion of the second Russo-Turkish War in 1792—that the Russians evacuated from the Morea, and the Albanians, or Arnauts, ravaged the peninsula. In other words, the "Advertisement" actually refers to two intensely violent periods of instability but blurs the boundary between them by using the phrase "for some time." This is significant for three reasons. First, by placing the murders of Leila and Hassan in the aftermath of the first Russo-Turkish War, Byron explicitly locates the story in a time of uneasy, nominal peace. The Treaty of Küçük Kaynarca was merely a hiatus that allowed the Russians to gear up for the much more decisive victory over the Ottomans in the second Russo-Turkish War. In this story, peace is a time of radical political uncertainty and death. Second, the Giaour tells his version of the killing of Hassan on the verge of the second Russo-Turkish War, thus any variation in its narration is imbued by the escalating animosity between the Ottomans and Russians in the mid-1780s. We have already seen in Chapter 7 that this was the period when Choiseul-Gouffier was attempting to realize his aesthetic fantasies by influencing Ottoman policy and when Ainslie was attempting to minimize the French ambassador's influence. The Giaour's confession and Mayer's watercolor are from roughly the same geopolitical moment.[41] This may seem like a tenuous connection, but, as we will see, many of Mayer's concerns are also Byron's, and in a sense, the poem's condemnation of the Giaour comes from an ethical space sketched out by Mayer's "reading" of the *Iliad*. In much the same way that Mayer's treatment of Patroclus's death invokes same-sex desire by veiling it and thus propels the viewer beyond the picture toward the affective relationship between Mayer and Ainslie, so too does Byron's activation of homoerotic desire behind the screen of homosocial rivalry propel the reader into the notes and toward Byron's non-normative sexual persona. Engaging with Mayer's drawing and Byron's poem requires that one move beyond the works into the world, both its intimate and global manifestations, that surrounds them. But fully comprehending this strange itinerary requires that we attend to the third historical resonance signaled in the "Advertisement" and then start asking some questions about what changes between the first narration of the killing of Hassan and the second.

If we look closely at the "Advertisement," we see that it is a circumlocution.[42] It uses spatial tags and event markers to say "shortly after 1779" without ever actually disclosing the date. The local coordinates are used as a way of invoking a moment whose global implications are important for understanding the poem's engagement with ancient Greece and the poem's fragmentary form. The entry of France and Spain into the American war in 1778 and 1779 respectively transformed that conflict into a global war. With decisive losses in India and the American colonies, and scandals at home that rocked British confidence in the war effort, 1779 was the beginning of the end of British imperial control of North America. We have already seen in Chapter 6 the impact of events in the Atlantic on Britain's global influence: this was a time of French resurgence in the Levant and their influence on Russia had palpable negative effects on the reconstruction of the British navy. Successful decolonization in the Atlantic had an extraordinary impact on the British economy, on imperial governmentality, and, perhaps most important, on British fantasies of governmental and martial efficacy.[43] Prior to the loss of the American colonies, British imperial fantasy mobilized a complex historical narrative regarding the migration of Liberty from ancient Greece to Venice to Great Britain to justify its colonial activities. This story of Liberty's movement was most vividly disseminated in James Thomson's poem of that name, but since American decolonization was grounded on the language of liberty, one of the possibilities facing a humiliated British polity in the wake of this civil war was that Liberty had migrated to more receptive shores.[44] Alone, bereft, Britain was beginning to look uncomfortably like Liberty's former domiciles.

The only traces of Liberty's grandeur left over from ancient Greece were the dismembered ruins that had so disturbed the Dilettanti: we could argue that Pars's entropic vision was being realized far too close to home. Byron's melancholic response to the ruins at Ephesus, Patras, and even Athens imbues his letters from his Levantine tour and was fully elaborated in the second book of *Childe Harold's Pilgrimage* and the opening two hundred lines of *The Giaour*.[45] Unlike his traveling companion Hobhouse, who was notoriously prolix in his account of the various ruined sites of Greece and Ionia, Byron only ever refers to Actium, Athens, Ephesus, or Alexandria Troas to emphasize the manifest sense of loss and desolation he associates with them.[46]

Likewise, the Venetian republic was a shadow of its former self: its power and its political significance were in an accelerated state of decay. It is no accident that the tormented figure of Byron's first Oriental tale is a troubled exile from the Serene Republic. The poem does not offer an explication of Venice's decline, but simply embodies it in the Giaour's morose alienation. I have argued elsewhere that there was considerable consternation among cultural practitioners in the final years of the American war and that in the 1780s Britain was in a similar state of retrogression.[47] The time of Byron's poem coincides precisely with this period of deep imperial anxiety in Britain, and it is telling that these moments of political and social insecurity are not explicitly addressed but rather textually repressed. This is not the place to rehearse the various symptoms of this post-American moment, but what is crucial for our purposes is the way that British imperial subjects reconfigured themselves and the way that British culture itself was reimagined to put this historical crisis in abeyance. In place of political arguments based on liberty and republican virtue, the emergent visions of empire became about territorial conquest and eventually religious salvation. Put simply, there was a shift from a Catonian understanding of Britain's republican prerogative to an alignment with Caesar's militarism. Marilyn Butler's cogent analysis of the poem's dialogue with events in India effectively argues that *The Giaour* is a revolt against the new rationale for and practice of empire based on a civilizing mission.[48] With India policy fully incorporating Charles Grant's dicta regarding the dissemination of Christianity and the suppression of Hinduism, imperial ideology had abandoned republican virtue in favor of Christian morality.[49] One of the key implications here is that heteronormative versions of the reproductive family would be effectively weaponized for emergent strategies of colonial control. Thus Byron's deployment of sexuality in *The Giaour* and elsewhere in the Oriental tales cannot be disconnected from his resistance to Christianizing models of empire. Caroline Franklin has exhaustively demonstrated how Byron's rupture with Georgian gender norms, especially in these poems, is both consistent and markedly visible.[50]

My addition to these arguments is to trace them back to the American crisis and the unresolved fate of Liberty's migration on the one hand, and to the historical/sexual fantasies we have excavated from the archive discussed in the preceding three chapters on the other. Byron's engagement with global politics, although veiled by his insistence on the local dimensions of the poem, goes back to the advent of decolonization itself and explores its psychic and political impact in this longer temporal arc. Just as most of the events in the poem are apodictic, its historical target, "1779," is not named but is everywhere a motivating factor. Like so many post-American engagements with decolonization in the Atlantic world, *The Giaour*'s exploration of gender instability and social insecurity mutually inform one another. Thus what we are looking at here is an extended critique of imperial policy and history, on the one hand, and a thorough analysis of how these geopolitical matters inflect affective dispositions and social actions.

If the poem's situation "shortly after 1779" signals a whole network of imperial anxieties, we also have to recognize that the poem was composed and modified at a historical moment, perhaps more than any other, that reactivated the unresolved emotional aftermath of American decolonization. I am referring to the War of 1812. As Troy Bickham states,

> the specter of the American Revolution haunted those who lived through the War of 1812. . . .
>
> From a global perspective, the War of 1812 was a continuation of the clash of American and British systems that became apparent during the Seven Years' War . . . and first erupted into armed conflict in the American War of Independence.[51]

Bickham's wide-ranging analysis demonstrates that the rematch between Britain and the United States attempted to settle unresolved issues: the Americans fought to reassert their postcolonial independence, whereas the British were attempted to erase earlier losses by curbing American ambition and rendering it a client state.[52] What is suggestive for the reading that follows is the degree to which competing rhetorics of liberty and vengeance permeated the popular representation of this conflict in Britain, for it is precisely the interplay between these concepts and feelings that Byron explores in *The Giaour*.

We would seem to be a long way from the poem, but I believe that Byron is engaged with these historical transformations not only at the level of allegory, but also quite literally in his deployment of the poem's eponymous hero. The poem is replete with representations of the disintegration of liberty and republican virtue.[53] This is most obviously the case in the poem's first 102 lines, most of which were added to the second edition of the poem, in which ancient Greek culture is placed irrevocably in the past.[54] As is well known, Byron constantly added more lines to *The Giaour* both in manuscript and in each successive printing, but its opening six lines were in place from the poem's inception:

> No breath of air to break the wave
> That rolls below the Athenian's grave,
> That tomb* which, gleaming o'er the cliff,
> First greets the homeward-veering skiff,
> High o'er the land that he saved in vain—
> When shall such hero live again?

(1–6)

Like the roundabout way the "Advertisement" locates the poem in space and time, these lines not only start the poem at a point spatially and temporally distant from its narrative events but also relegate the name of the entombed Athenian hero to the notes. The note is remarkably equivocal: "A tomb above the rocks on the promontory, by some supposed the sepulchre of Themistocles" (416). Everything that Byron would add in the second edition regarding the sepulchral quality of ancient Greek culture more generally is established here.[55] Themistocles, the great military strategist and leader of Athens, saved Athens and Greece from the Persians at the Battle of Salamis, but from the historical perspective of the poem's speaker his victory was in vain. Whether one reads this in terms of the Greek and Roman histories that Byron's readers would have been familiar with or in terms of eighteenth-century accounts of despotism, this is tantamount to saying that the victory that saved liberty and democracy from the threat of Eastern tyranny was only temporary.[56] But significantly, the notes signal something further: that Themistocles was banished from Athens as a traitor and thus was not allowed to be buried there. The identity of the bones in this tomb are the subject of doubt, and this doubt forces one to ask some questions about whether the Athenian's heroism even lasted as long as his lifetime.[57] There is a suggestion here that virtue will not return, and the notes insinuate that even ancient Athenians did not fully appreciate its value.[58]

With the "Advertisement" and the first seven lines, Byron has already declared Liberty's most sacrosanct homes to be little more than sepulchres. From this bleak starting point the poem quickly turns away from this historical dead end to a pastoral celebration of the landscape. The second fragment, which came into place in the second edition, opens with an apostrophe to Greece's "Fair clime!" (7), but it is not long before it is fully despoiled:

> Strange—that where Nature lov'd to trace,
> As if for Gods, a dwelling place,
> And every charm and grace hath mixed
> Within the paradise she fixed—
> There man, enamour'd of distress,
> Should mar it into wilderness
>
> (46–51)

This goes considerably further than Pars's entropic vision that we discussed in Chapter 5. In an extended metaphor, Byron compares the beauty of the ancient Greek ruins to the repose on the face of one who has just died:

> So fair—so calm—so softly seal'd
> The first—last look—by death reveal'd!

Such is the aspect of this shore—
'Tis Greece—but living Greece no more!
So coldly sweet, so deadly fair,
We start—for soul is wanting there.
Hers is the loveliness in death,
That parts not quite with parting breath;
But beauty with that fearful bloom,
That hue which haunts it to the tomb—
Expressions last receding ray,
A gilded halo hovering round decay,
The farewell beam of Feeling past away!
Spark of that flame—perchance of heavenly birth—
Which gleams—but warms no more its cherish'd earth!

(88–102)

Nigel Leask and Jerome Christensen make much of the "gilded" setting sun here: it runs through all of Byron's representations of Greece's fading presence, and it resonates provocatively with the fading sun in Melling's late paintings.[59] But the fact that Greece is feminized is no less important. On the one hand, the poem locates Greece's beauty in death; that in itself is a repudiation of Choiseul-Gouffier's gendering of Greek potentiality in terms of reproductive sexuality. But on the other, this passage, as Robert Gleckner and Jerome Christensen recognize, fully aligns Greece's ruination with Leila's nonliving state: this is why the description of the latter figures her in terms of marble (lines 495–503).[60]

These elements of the poem were all added at roughly the same time in the midst of the War of 1812;[61] they all operate outside the narrative of the poem; and they all firmly link ancient Greece with death. In all of these passages the chronotope of the poem—both its contemporary time and space—is fully alienated from the values and models of Greek antiquity, and that alienation is figured by the body of a dead woman whose beauty can be reconstituted by metaphorical description, but it is that aestheticization that activates the desires for exclusive possession that result in her murder. Byron's critique of the appropriative desires of antiquarianism couldn't be more blunt and can be applied equally well to Choiseul-Gouffier as to Lord Elgin.[62] But here the gendering is crucial because it so palpably engages with *Voyage pittoresque de la Grèce*, a text whose execution, publication, and message emphasize the ascendancy of French imperial desires in the wake of the American war. Choiseul-Gouffier's play for Liberty was linked to Britain's decline, and Byron responds by arguing that ancient liberty is no longer available to any suitor, except perhaps the Americans. It is a position that questions the very relation of ancient liberty to modern freedom and suggests that investment in the former is a historical misrecognition. In response to the post-American moment, Byron's critique imagines a new set of political and ethical possibilities that he aligns with George Washington and other revolutionary heroes prior to their corruption.[63]

This historical critique and its figural economy demand close scrutiny because they are linked to another cancellation of the Greek cultural patrimony, only its negation is less obvious and yet more formally significant. As part of the same set of additions that brought in lines 46–102, Byron also added lines 620–54. On the face of it these would seem to have little to do with the question of Greece and its revivification, or with questions of imperial governance; this verse paragraph comes immediately after Hassan recognizes the Giaour in his Albanian disguise bearing down upon him (595–619) and immediately before the poem jump-cuts to the Giaour killing Hassan (655–85). These inserted lines operate as a complex formal transit between the two doomed men: on the one side, we have Hassan and his recorded speech "'Tis he, well met in any hour, / Lost Leila's love—accursed Giaour" (618–19); on the other, the Giaour's first speech in the poem: "Yes, Leila sleeps beneath the wave, / But his shall be a redder grave" (675–76). In that transit from character to character, from recorded utterance to recorded utterance, something extraordinary happens. As violence erupts into the poem, and remember this is the chief narrative event of the story, Byron conspicuously mobilizes an epic simile, the very formal epitome of the poetic tradition from which he and the world around him are historically alienated. Unlike in *Childe Harold's Pilgrimage* where Homeric epithets are parodically mobilized or echoes of the *Odyssey* are bathetically engaged, this gesture moves past parody and bathos to discursive failure.

In a sense, it is here that we feel the cost of historical alienation, for the epic simile does not get incorporated into the narrative as a seamless enactment of the heroic, but rather instantiates a fracture in the narrative itself:

> As rolls the river into ocean,
> In sable torrent wildly streaming;
> As the sea-tide's opposing motion
> In azure column proudly gleaming,
> Beats back the current many a rood,
> In curling foam and mingling flood;
> While eddying whirl, and breaking wave,
> Roused by the blast of winter, rave;
> Through sparkling spray in thundering clash,
> The lightnings of the waters flash
> In awful whiteness o'er the shore,
> That shines and shakes beneath the roar;
> Thus—as the stream and ocean greet,

With waves that madden as they meet—
Thus join the bands whom mutual wrong,
And fate and fury drive along.

(620–35)

The failure of the epic simile is signaled by its disjunction from the space around
it. As the ensuing lines state:

The bickering sabres' shivering jar;
And pealing wide—or ringing near
Its echoes on the throbbing ear,
The deathshot hissing from afar—
The shock—the shout—the groan of war—
Reverberate along that vale,
More suited to the shepherd's tale:
Though few the numbers—theirs the strife,
That neither spares nor speaks for life!

(636–44)

The represented violence is not suited to the epic simile; it takes place in a pastoral world but, as the pun on "numbers" indicates, it is also alienated from a form
that "speaks for life." The poem is frantically looking for the classical form within
which to figure forth the battle between the Giaour and Hassan as either heroic
or somehow connected to life. The narrative is neither heroic in the classical sense,
nor can it open onto the redemptive possibilities of the pastoral.[64] This is why the
verse paragraph devolves into a Manichean conflict where love and death are mis-
recognized for another and the narrative fractures. What I would like to suggest
is that it is here that the alienation of Byron from Greek antiquity is felt most
acutely, because it is here that we see how the legacy of epic and pastoral is mobilized and found to be historically and affectively insufficient for the narrative. When
we recall the way that classical antiquity has been deployed either as a counterbal-
ance to Ottoman alterity or as a mediating discourse in which to assess cultural
difference, alienation from this cultural formation has seismic implications for how
alterity and identity will be negotiated. In terms of what we have seen elsewhere
in this book, the primary representational paradigms invoked by this space and by
this conflict prove to be inappropriate and thus fail. And that failure is more historically eloquent than any exposition of Byron's—and Europe's—alienation from
past models of republican virtue because it also has specific affective implications.

The fragment that ensues in which Hassan is butchered before the reader's eyes
has received elaborate treatment from Christensen and others that focuses on the

figural commutability between Hassan and the Giaour. What strikes me is that the killing of the Giaour is both narratively sensational and affectively unengaged. The obsolescence of the aesthetic and political models of Greek antiquity leaves the Giaour "alone," but significantly his solitude is not that of Achilles. The death of Patroclus activates Achilles's rage and the Giaour's killing of Hassan would seem to mimic Achilles's killing of Hector, but Byron does not allow the narrative to develop: there is no period of excessive defilement of the body of the enemy; there is no engagement with Priam; there is no affective outpouring from those close to Hassan because the social affiliations of the poem's primary Muslim character are so narrowly presented.[65] The poem merely shifts to the expression of the Giaour's isolation: "I am alone." In the face of his own lost political identity and in light of the loss of Leila and all that she connotes, the Giaour merely kills Hassan. I say "merely" because the act is an insufficient yet all-too-predictable response to the historical crisis enveloping both the Giaour and the narrative—and one could say the world within which this poem circulates. As Leask argues, "Byron's reduction of epic (or its vernacular form, ballad) to the fragmentary text of the Giaour's 'broken tale' is the formal equivalent of cultural degradation which is the poem's theme."[66] The poem has marked what epic was once able to do, what it once stood for, and then shown that all that remains in the contemporary moment is a cliché of xenophobic and homosocial aggression. Love and loss, both political and affective, are met with murder, and the resulting cultural vacuum is filled with homosocial rivalry— hatred now stands in for love. In other words, the poem enters an undead state, signaled by the famous invocation of vampirism in lines 747–88, but formally marked by a sudden shift in poetic procedure: fragmentation is replaced by repetition.

Interrupted Repetitions

The poem's nondevelopment, with all that it entails for the cancellation of heroism, is magnified by the poem's repetitive doubling back on the same narrative event. The first narration of the killing of Hassan fractures Greek poetic forms and emphasizes the Giaour's incommensurability with Hassan. It is here that the poem both theorizes and enacts a double alienation, first, of the contemporary world from the models of antiquity and, second, of the representative figures of Europe and the Ottoman world. After the fractured verse paragraphs that take the reader to the killing of Hassan, the poem settles into an extended soliloquy of sorts. The Giaour's confession, if that is what it is, constitutes almost half of the poem; its seamless utterance eventually recognizes a certain commutability between the Giaour and Hassan. In the process, the model of liberty that is mourned in the first half of the poem is replaced with a new kind of freedom based on Hassan's will to power, itself based on Byron's firsthand experience of Ali Pasha's capricious tyranny.[67] Despite the apparent coherence of the Giaour's utterance, his moral and political rationale for his behavior redefine liberty so that it is indistinguishable from tyranny. In this regard, the Giaour is more than simply brooding, he is a symptom of historical decline, perhaps even catastrophe.

This is nowhere more apparent than in the way that he retells the event of Hassan's murder. Careful comparison between the narration of Hassan's death in lines 655–88 and the Giaour's representation of the same event show a remarkable variation. As Jager summarizes, "this encounter demonstrates both an extraordinary intimacy between the two men and a careful delineation of difference. In the first instance, the difference was that Hassan killed Leila for tradition's sake, whereas the Giaour imagines killing her for love's sake. In this instance, as the two men stare into each other's eyes, the difference is that the Giaour's face hides behind a 'wounded mind,' while Hassan's face hides no such complicated interiority."[68] Jager is careful to emphasize that the former articulation of difference is imagined by the Giaour, but I would argue that the second is equally an effect of the Giaour's sub-jectivity. The distinction between these two accounts of difference is formally reg-istered: the first narration of the killing focuses on what the two men say; the latter telling is all about one man's gaze.

> He died too in the battle broil—
> A time that heeds nor pain nor toil—
> One cry to Mahomet for aid,
> One prayer to Alla—all he made:
> He knew and cross'd me in the fray—
> I gazed upon him where he lay,
> And watched his spirit ebb away:
> Though pierced like pard by hunters' steel,
> He felt not half that now I feel.
> I search'd, but vainly search'd to find,
> The workings of a wounded mind;
> Each feature of that sullen corse
> Betrayed his rage, but no remorse
>   (1080–92)

Hassan's represented speech is now summarized, and this shift in representation makes the evacuation of Hassan's subjectivity possible because no voice interrupts the Giaour's narration. But how do we read the one-sidedness of the gaze here? The Giaour "searches" Hassan's face to find a "wounded mind" that is a mirror of his own affective state. The Giaour desires "remorse" from Hassan, but can only find rage; but this doesn't square with the prior narration of the scene, where the Giaour is clearly aligned with rage and vengeance. In other words, the Giaour's remorse obfuscates his earlier motives and actions, and for this to be successful it is crucial that he project his rage onto Hassan. Jager sees this as reflexivity itself, but I think it is more like secondary revision—a process whereby the sudden recognition of the repressed similarity between the Giaour and Hassan is made temporarily manifest only to be renarrativized in a way that constitutes the Giaour's subjectivity. The misrecognition of Hassan thus becomes crucial to the Giaour's fantasy of subjective coherence and interiority. That this heavily racialized distinction is mapped onto tradition and modernity, fanaticism and secularism, is hardly surprising; nor is the fact that the Giaour cannot keep his character and disposition separate from Hassan for any extended period of time. He quickly becomes as fanatical as Hassan and states explicitly that he would have acted precisely as Hassan did with regard to Leila. Maintaining the separation between the Giaour and Hassan and all the dyadic relations they embody requires endless repetition, and thus the poem takes on the quality of a static loop. As Franklin argues, this is the crux of Byron's critique: "By this deeply ironic point-by-point comparison of the attitudes of Hassan and the Giaour towards Leila (and their joint guilt for her death), we see that the Venetian's romantic love retains many of the basic ideological assumptions of primitive patriarchy. The poem thus is paradoxically both a strong plea for female sexual autonomy, and an acknowledgment that as the fabric of society is built on the foundation of female chastity, woman will always be the chief victim of illegitimate love."[69] But Byron establishes a way out of this paradoxical repetition and reversion in the notes. As we will see, Byron's notes interrupt the poem's temporal continuum in highly productive ways and allow the reader to imagine other modes of operating in this space, both at the level of social practice and of representation, that may be more appropriate to this thoroughly modern world.

There are important implications here for the triangle of homosocial desire that links the Giaour to Hassan through Leila. As both men's object choice, she is the pivot around which each man's desire is directed and consolidated. But Byron's elimination of Leila from the narrative subtly unhinges the triangle.[70] Without Leila, the Giaour can only retroactively assert his possession of her by killing her killer. But that murder is itself not directly presented and is thus unreliable. Instead of Leila's murder, Byron chooses to represent—twice—the men's sublimated love for one another at the level of poetic form and affect and shows that this sublimation is a dead end. In other words, Byron's fragmentation of the tale casts doubt on all the motives for the murders while maintaining the inevitability of the poem's cascade of violence. This doubt is crystallized when the Giaour narrates the killing of Hassan because it is a failed anagnorisis—that is, a recognition that calls into question the very possibility of recognition as the way toward narrative resolution or catharsis.[71] We could say that the Giaour's dramatic monologue feints toward tragedy, but ultimately demonstrates tragedy's obsolescence in the modern world. When the Giaour looks at Hassan, he sees a fantasy of alterity that merely consolidates himself: recognition is suspended and turned around. The Giaour simply looks for himself in the other, thus occluding difference. What interests me about this is that its inherent narcissism is so similar to the antiquarian gaze. When Choiseul-Gouffier observes Greece or the Ottoman world, he looks with extraordinary intensity, but he sees either his own reflection in the ruins around him or an obstruction of sorts that we could simply call "Islam" or the "Ottoman Empire"—in quotation marks here because these are notions disconnected from either historical entity. This inability to see while looking as intently as possible is remarkably like that of the Giaour, and I would argue that it is categorically distinct from the kind of observations that Byron records in his letters and in his notes to the poem.

In the letters sent during the tour of the Levant, Byron consistently exhibits little or no interest in the classical ruins around him. As Roderick Beaton argues, he leaves it to Hobhouse to explore and record these sites of antiquarian knowledge, and when he does refer to them it is to emphasize their lack of interest, their unmistakable pastness.[72] In contrast, his remarks on Ali Pasha, on his immediate social interactions, on his sexual desires and escapades are detailed, motivated, and engaged. And this engagement also characterizes their mediation in Canto 2 of *Childe Harold's Pilgrimage*. To make a simple point, Byron was not only a detailed observer of Greek, Albanian, and Ottoman sociability and sexuality, but also an active participant in social and sexual actions that were only practicable in his present situation in Athens or Constantinople.[73] This, of course, includes his vividly recorded affairs with young men, especially Nicolo Giraud, during his residence in Athens. As Beaton states, "In Greece, where others did, Byron did too."[74] In other words, Byron is committed to the practice of everyday life in the spaces he visits, and he consistently contrasts living praxis to the vampiric conditions of those—like the Giaour and certain antiquarians—whose object choice is no longer living, but somehow not fully dead.[75]

This would be little more than a biographical observation except this same interest in present sociability progressively subsumes the notes to *The Giaour*. In the midst of the Giaour's account of the killing of Hassan, just prior to the actual narration of the killing, the reader is suddenly directed to the notes, where a lengthy discussion of the author's experience of "second sight" at Cape Colonna quite literally interrupts what is supposed to be the crucial anagnorisis. This note sends the reader off on a far more intriguing narrative whose implications are actually not that distant from the problem of intercultural relations that the Giaour is completely unable to engage or understand. The note to line 1077 is an interruption, but since the reader already knows the events being narrated in the verse, it almost comes as a relief; returning to the verse, the reader feels even more palpably the repetitive status of the Giaour's speech act. I would suggest that nothing undercuts or critiques the Giaour more forcefully and eloquently than this simple paratextual redirection, for it points to the ongoing life and future of the author function.[76] The Giaour's account of murder is simply not as compelling as Byron's somewhat flippant remarks. Thus the Giaour's soliloquy, although presented as a seamless utterance, is interrupted by an authorial/editorial voice that is clearly far more interested in matters of current social relations outside of the poem.

The emergence of this countervoice in the notes is significant because it counterbalances the loss of classical models, both discussed and enacted in the first half of the poem, with a kind of intercultural exchange firmly rooted in the present and formally articulated in Byron's paratextual strategy of interruption. This is why the poem itself ends with a note that in many ways subsumes the entire poem into the narrated experience of the editor/commentator. Emphasizing firsthand witnessing, the note to line 1334 takes us fully out of the poem and into the autobiographical narrative of the author. The characters in the poem have been replaced by a new kind of hero—the celebrity author—and thus Byron fully consigns the classical hero to oblivion because mobilizing these ancient figures and forms constitutes a dangerous historical obfuscation. Both of these major interruptions seem to erupt into the poem as from the future. No small portion of their power derives from the fact that they were added to the poem at a later stage and that they themselves explore the possibility of proleptically knowing what is going to happen. With history's repeated injunctions bearing down on the poem, it is significant that Byron so thoroughly thrusts the reader into a present moment that seems to have some purchase on the future. All of the poem's work on the "past," whether it be the narrator's description of the alienation from ancient Greece or the Giaour's attempt to give his account of the killing of Hassan, consistently subordinates history to what is about to unfold in the world outside and beyond the poem. The poem's temporal remove from the author/editor makes the poem itself an ancient fragmented ruin, the next Parthenon marbles, and thus posits or inaugurates a kind of futurity free of the poem's compulsive repetitions.[77] That fictional "beyond" includes future editions where new lines and new notes could seemingly be added at any time. In a sense, the regressive aspects of the Giaour's repetition are countered by the progressive possibilities inherent to mechanical reproduction and one of its chief effects—celebrity.[78]

In light of our earlier discussion of epic form, loss of epic representation's capacity to render this violent world in the first half of the poem constitutes a sign of modernity's inauguration in the second. Early in this monograph classical models offered a way of measuring alterity, of thinking through historical difference and change. Byron's demonstration that ancient models fail to have any traction here and now suggests that this strategy of using the past to either contrast with the Asiatic other or consolidate the European observer is no longer tenable. What remains is unrestrained will to power, or its reverse, nostalgic desire for that which is irrevocably gone. What I believe Byron recognized is that these responses are two sides of the same coin: the former is most vividly and palpably felt in Britain's emergent imperial stance in India, and the latter is everywhere in evidence in the aesthetic fetishization of antiquity.[79] We can imagine a coin with Wellington and Charles Grant on one side and Lord Elgin on the other. And Byron seems to have recognized the enduring value of such a practical and symbolic conjunction for British imperial self-fashioning. But he also understood that its endurance relied on a fundamental investment in martial efficacy and heteronormative sexuality—both of which have proven to be prone to dissolution and inversion. The instability of these strictly defined fantasies of gender and sexuality would have been historically evident to Byron because Britain had to work through a panoply of identity crises from "1779" onward and was in the midst of a particularly embarrassing period of overcompensation when he was working on this poem.

In the face of ongoing acts of imperial vengeance and increasingly strict monitoring of sexual, national, and racial identity, Byron offers something perversely different: a kind of celebrity authorial persona that endorses the need for and indeed the interest of continuing intercultural sociability and nonnormative models of sexuality. Everything in his career after *The Giaour* confirms this recognition: his critique of his own persona, his exilic example, his cosmopolitan stance, his vague yet vibrant sexuality, his revolutionary practice are all at odds with the forms of self-consolidation symptomatic of nineteenth-century imperial thought and policy. Although we cannot conclusively state that he saw the engraving of Mayer's Ephesus watercolor, Byron similarly subsumes a complex formal engagement with antiquity, a commitment to intercultural collaboration, an explicitly homophilic yet indeterminate approach to pederastic identity, and the same repudiation of imperial warfare that animated that earlier work into a new kind of countercultural gesture.[80] We could even go so far as to suggest that Mayer's self-representation in the foreground of that watercolor is a precursor to "Byron." Another way of saying this is to suggest that in the wake of the geopolitical transformations that essentially occluded liberty as a solely British provenance, Byron floats celebrity, here exemplified by his own authorial fame, as a surrogate for heroism. That Byron's surrogate celebrity keeps referring to a war-torn interimperial zone between the Christian West and the Islamic East is as productively vexing as his performance of masculinity, for it deploys this zone of uncertainty as a locus for the critique both of the specific historical situation in the Ottoman Empire and, in a more allegorical register, of British imperial policy in his present moment. This kind of floating persona carries with it an implicit critique of nostalgia and a demand that the reader remain fully engaged with relationality rather than fixed identity, for it is with the latter fixing that intersubjective and geopolitical violence unfolds both within the poem's narrative and within the poem's analysis of its world-historical moment.[81] We should not be surprised that both the poem and the poet were the subject not only of continuing co-optation and containment but also of enduring fascination and allegiance. He and his work point to a different world of difference to be either effaced or embraced.

Notes

Introduction

1. This is all the more striking when we recognize that there is already a long pictorial tradition of rendering this view. Similar views can be traced back to the earliest point of contact, and it featured prominently in Cornelis de Bruijn's widely circulated travel narrative. For an overview of the early modern visual record, see Amanda Wunder, "Western Travelers, Eastern Antiquities, and the Image of the Turk in Early Modern Europe," *Journal of Early Modern History* 7.1–2 (2003): 89–119. I use "Istanbul" and "Constantinople" somewhat interchangeably in this book according to how the city is named in the documents I am discussing.

2. My interest in the history of diplomacy, intercultural sociability, and the history of literary form has benefited immensely from Timothy Hampton's *Fictions of Embassy: Literature and Diplomacy in Early Modern Europe* (Ithaca, NY: Cornell University Press, 2012).

3. Rae Ann Meriwether, in "Transculturation and Politics in the Works of Lady Mary Wortley Montagu," *SEL Studies in English Literature, 1500–1900* 53.3 (Summer 2013): 623–41, makes a localized version of this argument, showing how the transculturation at the heart of Montagu's *Turkish Embassy Letters* impinges on her later political writing in the newspaper *Nonsense of Common-Sense*. Meriwether uses Montagu's analysis of veiling to understand her adoption of rhetorical anonymity.

4. There is, of course, extensive scholarship on these materials within the specialized disciplines of Ottoman studies.

5. Joseph Lew notes a similar distinction between early eighteenth-century representations of the Ottoman Empire and proto-Orientalist texts from later in the century in "Lady Mary's Portable Seraglio," *Eighteenth-Century Studies* 24.4 (1991): 432–50.

6. This title has been retroactively assigned and has become the conventional designation for Montagu's text, but as many commentators have indicated the title is a misnomer: over half of the text concerns observations of European and North African locales. For an extended discussion of the composition and publication of the Montagu's Letter-book, see *The Complete Letters of Lady Mary Wortley Montagu*, ed. Robert Halsband, 3 vols. (Oxford: Clarendon Press, 1967), 1:xvii–xx.

7. Lady Mary Wortley Montagu, *The Turkish Embassy Letters*, ed. Teresa Heffernan and Daniel O'Quinn (Peterborough, ON: Broadview Press, 2013), 100.

8. Denys Van Renen, "Montagu's Letters from the Levant: Contesting the Borders of European Selfhood," *Journal for Early Modern Cultural Studies* 11.2 (Fall 2011): 17.

9. The vast expansion in commercial relations in Central and South Asia gave Europeans some sense of the Mughal and Safavid empires and of the dynastic powers of China, but knowledge was a function of mercantile exchange. There were, of course, numerous empires and dynasties across the globe about which western Europeans had little knowledge and minimal interest.

10. For a thorough discussion of the way that the Habsburgs and the Ottomans operated outside Westphalian norms and precedents, see Mehmet Sinan Birdal, *The Holy Roman Empire and the Ottomans: From Global Imperial Power to Absolutist States* (New York: I. B. Tauris, 2011).

11. Palmira Brummett, *Mapping the Ottomans: Sovereignty, Territory, and Identity in the Early Modern Mediterranean* (New York: Cambridge University Press, 2015).

12. The work of Nahil Matar and Gerald Maclean has been crucial for reconstituting this history of exchange between early modern Europe and the Ottoman Empire. See Nahil Matar, *Turks, Moors and Englishmen in the Age of Discovery* (New York: Columbia University Press, 1999); and Gerald Maclean and Nahil Matar, *Britain and the Islamic World, 1558–1713* (Oxford: Oxford University Press, 2011).

13. Andrew Pettegree, *The Invention of the News: How the World Came to Know About Itself* (New Haven, CT: Yale University Press, 2014), 140–45.

14. Montagu's text references all of these precursor materials with great specificity.

15. This is not to suggest that epistolary form is not important to reading Montagu's text. That was established at an early point by Cynthia Lowenthal's seminal study *Lady Mary Wortley Montagu and the Eighteenth-Century Familiar Letter* (Athens: University of Georgia Press, 1994). The point here is that the letters' assumption of knowledge regarding the archive of books on the Ottoman Empire is one of the intimacy effects deployed throughout the Letter-book.

16. The term "Letter-book" refers to the leather-bound fair copy text that Montagu shared with her friends, which is now held at Sandon Hall. By using this term I want to emphasize its status as a manuscript book prepared for social exchange. For a discussion of this two-volume artifact, see the Introduction to the Broadview Edition.

17. It is only with the publication of Isobel Grundy's biography *Lady Mary Wortley Montagu: Comet of the Enlightenment* (New York: Oxford University Press, 1999), and, more recently, Denys Van Renen's "Montagu's Letters" that the full scope of her writing emerges. The new edition of the letters, produced by Teresa Heffernan and myself, was also aimed at prompting consideration of the text as a formal whole, thus drawing an equal measure of attention to its account of Habsburg Europe.

18. One way of stating this is to suggest that Said's *Orientalism* led us to project a more exoticized version of the "Orient" than really exists in Montagu's text. The Ottoman Empire is crucial to the way that Lady Mary understands Europe, but not because it stands for an absolute other, but rather because geopolitically it is actually involved in a war that is materially shaping the boundaries of Europe. In other words, Said's intervention, as crucial as it was, has caused us to focus so much on the discursive role of the Ottoman Empire in the making of Europe that we have ignored its material/geopolitical role in the making of Europe. And this is exactly the kind of robbing of agency from the East that critiques of *Orientalism* have focused on, albeit in a different discursive register.

19. Isobel Grundy's groundbreaking biography of Montagu forcefully made this point, but criticism rarely comments on the first twenty-five letters.

20. Berlant, *Cruel Optimism* (Chapel Hill, NC: Duke University Press, 2011), 10.

21. Berlant, *Cruel Optimism*, 16.

22. Caroline Levine, *Forms: Whole, Rhythm, Hierarchy, Network* (Princeton, NJ: Princeton University Press, 2015), 3.

23. See, for example, Ros Ballaster, *Fabulous Orients: Fictions of the East in England, 1662–1785* (Oxford: Oxford University Press, 2005); Srinivas Aravamudan, *Enlightenment Orientalism: Resisting the Rise of the Novel* (Chicago: University of Chicago Press, 2012); Robert Irwin, *The Arabian Nights: A Companion* (London: Tauris Parke, 2004); Marina Warner, *Stranger Magic: Charmed States and the Arabian Nights* (Cambridge, MA: Belknap Press of Harvard University Press, 2012); Saree Makdisi and Felicity Nussbaum, *The Arabian Nights in Historical Context:*

Between East and West (Oxford: Oxford University Press, 2008); Jennifer Schacker, *National Dreams: The Remaking of Fairy Tales in Nineteenth-Century England* (Philadelphia: University of Pennsylvania Press, 2003); Rebecca Carol Johnson, Richard Maxwell, and Katie Trumpener, "*The Arabian Nights,* Arab-European Literary Influence, and the Lineages of the Novel," *Modern Language Quarterly* 68.2 (2007): 243–79.

24. See Cynthia Wall, *The Prose of Things* (Chicago: University of Chicago Press, 2006); and Svetlana Alpers, *The Art of Describing: Dutch Art in the Seventeenth Century* (Chicago: University of Chicago Press, 1983).

25. See Benjamin Schmidt, *Inventing Exoticism: Geography, Globalism, and Europe's Early Modern World* (Philadelphia: University of Pennsylvania Press, 2015), 74–76.

26. Others, of course, have made many similar moves for later in the century. See, for example, Holger Hoock's discussion of empire, archaeology, and collecting in *Empires of the Imagination: Politics, War, and the Arts in the British World, 1750–1850* (London: Profile Books, 2010), 205–352.

27. For a cogent survey of the seventeenth- and eighteenth-century writings on the Ottoman Empire, see Teresa Heffernan, *Veiled Figures: Women, Modernity, and the Spectres of Orientalism* (Toronto: University of Toronto Press, 2016), 14–46.

28. This is actually the case from the earliest published accounts of Ottoman Empire. As Amanda Wunder demonstrates in "Western Travelers, Eastern Antiquities": "To the Renaissance European, a love of antiquity was a fundamental marker of civility, and it became one of the most important criteria by which Western Europeans judged the Turks" (91). Her readings of Augier Ghislain de Busbecq's *The Turkish Letters* (1581), Manuel Chrysoloras's *Comparison of the Old and New Rome* (1411), Pierre Gilles's *On the Topography and Antiquities of Constantinople* (1561), and other texts show that the European interest in the Ottoman dominions was always imbued with antiquarian desires. Gilles's text is particularly interesting in this regard, because, as Wunder notes, although the book attempts to "reveal only the classical layer of city's past," he nonetheless lists the significant Ottoman structures he is not describing, thus the ancient world is valorized but the present urban environment keeps asserting itself (102).

29. By using these terms, rather than present the past, I am adopting Walter Benjamin's skepticism regarding historicist narration. See Walter Benjamin, "Awakening," *The Arcades Project*, trans. Howard Eiland and Kevin McLaughlin (Cambridge, MA: Belknap Press of Harvard University Press, 1999), 462; N2a, 3; and Max Pensky, "Method and Time: Benjamin's Dialectical Images," in *The Cambridge Companion to Walter Benjamin*, ed. David S. Ferris (Cambridge: Cambridge University Press, 2004), 177–98.

30. New editions of Knolles's text came out in 1610, 1621 (with added material by Edward Grimestone), 1631 (with a continuation by Sir Thomas Roe), 1638, 1687, 1700 (with added material from Paul Rycaut). In other words, Knolles's *Generalle Historie* was constantly expanding. Jean Frederic Bernard, *Cérémonies et coutumes religieuses de tous les peuples du monde,* 7 vols. (Amsterdam: J. F. Bernard, 1723–37).

31. Johannes Fabian, *Time and the Other: How Anthropology Makes Its Object* (New York: Columbia University Press, 1983).

32. Aaron Hill, *A Full and Just Account of the Present State of the Ottoman Empire in All Its Branches: With the Government, and Policy, Religion, Customs, and Way of Living of the Turks, in General* (London: John Mayo, 1709), 29.

33. Benjamin Schmidt, *Inventing Exoticism: Geography, Globalism, and Europe's Early Modern World* (Philadelphia: University of Pennsylvania Press, 2015).

34. See entry for RIBA SD 155/4.

35. See Jason Kelly, *The Society of Dilettanti: Archaeology and Identity in the British Enlightenment* (New Haven: Yale University Press, 2009), 224–26.

36. See William St. Clair, *That Greece Might Still Be Free: The Philhellines in the War of Greek Independence* (London: Oxford University Press, 1972), 13–22.

37. Kishwar Rizvi, "Persian Pictures: Art, Documentation, and Self-Reflection in Jean Frederic Bernard and Bernard Picart's Representations of Islam," in *Bernard Picart and the First Global Vision of Religion*, ed. Lynn Hunt, Margaret Jacob, and Wijnand Mijnhardt (Los Angeles: Getty Research Institute, 2010), 174.

38. For an overview of the capitulation system, see Mehmet Bulut, "The Ottoman Approach to Western Europeans in the Levant During the Early Modern Period," *Middle Eastern Studies* 44.2 (March 2008): 259–74.

39. Michael Talbot has produced an extremely valuable synthesis of virtually all of the English and British ambassadors' accounts of these rituals in "British Diplomacy in the Ottoman Empire During the Long Eighteenth Century" (doctoral thesis, SOAS [School of Oriental and African Studies], University of London, 2013). See Sir George Larpent, *Turkey: Its History and Progress; From the Journals and Correspondence of Sir James Porter* (London: Hurst and Blackett, 1854), 284–95.

40. In the late seventeenth century, the Ottoman court had moved to Adrianople (Edirne). Mustafa II retained this practice, but shortly after the accession of Ahmed III the court returned to the capital and only used Adrianople as a summer retreat.

41. National Archives, State Papers (SP)/78, Letter 32. All subsequent references to this account of Sutton's public audience with the grand seignior on 10 March 1701 are to this manuscript.

42. For a detailed explication of the events depicted in this series of paintings, see Olga Nefedova, *A Journey into the World of the Ottomans: The Art of Jean-Baptiste Vanmour, 1671–1737* (Milan: Skira, 2009), 129–42.

43. The painting is also arguing for Damad İbrahim Pasha's precedence over Ahmed III.

44. Berlant, *Cruel Optimism*, 3.

45. Walter Benjamin, "The Task of the Translator," in *Selected Writings: Volume 1*, ed. Marcus Bullock and Michael W. Jennings (Cambridge, MA: Belknap Press of Harvard University Press, 1996), 253–63.

46. Mary Favret's *War at a Distance: Romanticism and the Making of Modern Wartime* offers the most sustained and suggestive account of the temporality of wartime.

47. See Virginia Aksan, "The Ottoman Absence from the Battlefields of the Seven Years' War," in *The Seven Years' War: Global Views*, ed. Mark H. Danley and Patrick J. Speelman (Leiden: Brill, 2012)

48. In this regard, my overall argument acts as a supplement to the recent attempts to analyze the Seven Years' War in light of globalization theory. The global implications of that conflict are not just a result of who participated and where battles were fought: they are also the result of who did not participate and where battles were not fought. Using a truly global frame of analysis means that there is not an outside to this war and that the truly global geopolitical sea change that accompanies the end of the war affects everyone, even nonparticipants.

49. The implication, of course, is that the openness of Ottoman society to male same-sex practices was a result of Ottoman women's lack of physical attractions.

50. Marilyn Butler, "Byron and the Empire in the East," in *Byron: Augustan and Romantic*, ed. Andrew Rutherford (New York: St. Martin's Press, 1990), 78–96.

51. One of the corollaries of my argument in Chapters 5 and 6 is that the debates about appropriation and intercultural sociability that animate the debate about the Elgin marbles actually precede their acquisition and that in its initial form the debate included the very figures erased from contemporary discussions, namely the Ottomans.

Chapter 1

1. Birdal, *The Holy Roman Empire and the Ottomans*, 135–36.

2. Despite a certain historiographical persistence, the "decline thesis" has been overwhelmingly disproved. See Douglas A. Howard, "Ottoman Historiography and the Literature of 'Decline' of the Sixteenth and Seventeenth Centuries," *Journal of Asian History* 22 (1988): 52–77; Douglas A. Howard, "With Gibbon in the Garden: Decline, Death and the Sick Man of Europe," *Fides et Historia* 26 (1994): 22–34; Cemal Kafadar, "The Question of Ottoman Decline," *Harvard Middle Eastern and Islamic Review* 4 (1997–98): 30–75; Ali U. Peker, "A Retreating Power: The Ottoman Approach to the West in the 18th Century," in *Power and Culture: Hegemony, Interaction, and Dissent*, ed. Ausma Cimdiņa and Jonathan Osmond (Pisa: Edizioni Plus Pisa University Press, 2006), 69–86; Jane Hathaway, "Rewriting Eighteenth-Century Ottoman History," *Mediterranean Historical Review* 19.1 (2004): 29–53; and Dana Sajdi, "Decline, Its Discontents and Ottoman Cultural History: By Way of Introduction," in *Ottoman Tulips, Ottoman Coffee: Leisure and Lifestyle in the Eighteenth Century* (London: I. B. Tauris, 2014), 1–40.

3. For a fascinating account of diplomatic engagement between the Ottoman Empire and Europe prior to this moment, see Daniel Goffman, "Negotiating with the Renaissance State: The Ottoman Empire and the New Diplomacy," in *The Early Modern Ottomans: Remapping the Empire*, ed. Daniel Goffman and Virginia Aksan (Cambridge: Cambridge University Press, 2007), 61–75.

4. For a thorough discussion of the transition in Ottoman diplomacy, see Rifa'at Ali Abou-El-Haj, "Ottoman Attitudes Toward Peace Making: The Karlowitz Case," *Der Islam* 51 (1974): 131–37.

5. E. Natalie Rothman's groundbreaking work in "Interpreting Dragomans: Boundaries and Crossings in the Early Modern Mediterranean," *Comparative Studies in Society and History* 51.4 (2009): 771–800, has focused historical attention on "how dragomans positioned themselves as mediators adept at crossing political and ethno-linguistic boundaries" (773). See also her *Brokering Empire: Trans-Imperial Subjects Between Venice and Istanbul* (Ithaca, NY: Cornell University Press, 2011).

6. See Virginia Aksan, *Ottoman Wars, 1700–1870: An Empire Besieged* (Harlow, UK: Pearson, 2007), 25–28, for a brief discussion of the transformational character of the Karlowitz negotiations; and Virginia Aksan, *An Ottoman Statesman in War and Peace: Ahmed Resmi Efendi, 1700–1783* (Leiden: E. J. Brill, 1995), for a more extended discussion of Ottoman diplomacy.

7. In "Ottoman Concepts of Empire," *Contributions to the History of Concepts* 8.1 (Summer 2013): 44–66, Einar Wigen argues that "empire" is a foreign concept to Ottoman politics and shows how Ottoman rulers laid "claim to three titles that may be called *imperial*: *halife*, *hakan*, and *kayser*. Each of these pertains to differents *translations imperii*, or claims of descent from different empires: the Caliphate, the steppe empires of the Huns, Turks, and Mongols, and the Roman Empire" (44).

8. Birdal, *The Holy Roman Empire and the Ottomans*, 6–7.

9. As Suraiya Faroqhi summarizes in *The Ottoman Empire and the World Around It* (London: I. B. Tauris, 2010), 2: "In Islamic religious law (*şeriat*) and also in Ottoman official writing, it was customary to describe the world as being made up of the Darülislam ('the house of Islam') and the Darülharb ('the house of war'). Into the first category belonged not only the domains of the Ottoman sultans themselves, but also those of other Sunni Muslims such as the Usbek khans or the Mughals of India." Faroqhi argues that in spite of this convention, in the absence of actual war, the borders between these two worlds were remarkably porous for largely pragmatic reasons having to do with the complex integration, if not incorporation, of the Ottoman economy into the emergent European world economy.

10. See Rifa'at Ali Abou-El-Haj, "Ottoman Diplomacy at Karlowitz," *Journal of the American Oriental Society* 87.4 (1967) 498–512; and Abou-El-Haj, "Ottoman Attitudes Toward Peace Making," 134.

11. See Jean-François Lyotard, *The Differend: Phrases in Dispute* (Minneapolis: University of Minnesota Press, 1989). Lyotard defines "differend" as "a case of conflict, between (at least) two parties, that cannot be equitably resolved for lack of a rule of judgment applicable to both arguments. One side's legitimacy does not imply the other's lack of legitimacy" (11). For an extremely evocative analysis of the application of the differend to intercultural politics, see Mohammed Ramdani's introduction to Jean-François Lyotard, *La guerre des Algériens: Ecrits, 1956–1963* (Paris: Galilée, 1989); and James Williams's discussion of Ramdani's argument in *Lyotard and the Political* (New York: Routledge, 2002), 9–13. See also Bart Vanenabeele, "Lyotard, Intercultural Communication and the Quest for 'Real People,'" *Language and Intercultural Communication* 3.1 (2003): 20–35.

12. *Post Man and the Historical Account* (London), 27 September 1697.

13. See Jean Nouzille, "La champagne decisive du prince Eugène de Savoie en Hongrie en 1697," in *La paix de Karlowitz, 26 janvier 1699: Les relations entre l'Europe centrale et l'Empire Ottoman*, ed. Jean Bérenger (Paris: Honoré Champion, 2010), 157–78, esp. 169–70.

14. *Post Man and the Historical Account*, 2–5 October 1697.

15. *Post Man and the Historical Account*, 2–5 October 1697.

16. *Post Man and the Historical Account*, 16–18 December 1697

17. *Post Man and the Historical Account*, 16–18 December 1697.

18. *Post Boy* (London), 6–8 September 1698.

19. See Birdal, *The Holy Roman Empire and the Ottomans*, 135. According to Bas de Boer, *Jacob Colyer: Mediating Between the European and the Ottoman Worlds* (Belgrade: Embassy of the Kingdom of Netherlands, 2015), 12: "The Ottoman Empire would only accept these conditions [*uti possidetis*] when they felt that no possible way to benefit from this war would exist. As Colyer states in a letter to his friend Gisbert Cuper (1644–1716): 'This nation cannot be dealt with until it goes down in a devastating defeat' [Jacob Colyer to Gisbertus Cuper, Constantinople, 1 January 1697, in National Archives, The Hague, Collectie Cupers, entrance 1.10.24. inventory 12]."

20. The best comprehensive account of what the treaty meant for the Ottoman Empire is Abou-El-Haj, "Ottoman Diplomacy at Karlowitz" (1967).

21. Modern discussions of the treaty usually refer to the present Serbian town of Sremski Karlovici by its German name "Karlowitz," but most of the eighteenth-century sources use the alternate German spelling of "Carlowitz."

22. *Post Boy*, 1–3 December 1699.

23. John-Paul Ghobrial, *The Whispers of Cities: Information Flows in Istanbul, London, and Paris in the Age of William Trumbull* (London: Oxford, 2014). Ghobrial's book focuses specifically on the movement of news within the Ottoman Empire and the flow of news from Istanbul to London and Paris. For an extremely valuable history of the news in this period, see Pettegree, *The Invention of the News*. Pettegree singles out the Battle of Lepanto as one of a few events that instantiated the desire for news across all of Europe (140ff.).

24. It is important to remember that manuscript newsletters remained in circulation well into the eighteenth century, and there is even evidence of hybrid newsletters that fuse print and manuscript intelligence. As Rachael Scarborough King has demonstrated in "The Manuscript Newsletter and the Rise of the Newspaper, 1665–1715," *Huntington Library Quarterly* 79.3 (Autumn 2016): 411–37, the *Post Boy* and the *Post Man* incorporated extra blank sheets for manuscript addenda. See Gary Schneider, *The Culture of Epistolarity: Vernacular Letters and Letter Writing in Early Modern England, 1500–1700* (Newark: University of Delaware Press, 2005).

25. See Kenneth Meyer Setton, *Venice, Austria, and the Turks in the Seventeenth Century* (Philadelphia: American Philosophical Society, 1991), 405, for a discussion of both the official

reports of Carlo Ruzzini, the chief Venetian negotiator, and the related collection of documents and letters (both originals and copies) now available in a large vellum-bound volume in the Marciana, MS It. VII, 399 (8625), *Congresso di Carlowitz (1699) e Carte parente di una missione di Carlo Ruzzini nella raccolta Marciana.*

26. In the map that accompanies the *relazione*, he is identified as Ionnes Baptista Nicolosi—Giovanni Nicolosi.

27. Setton, *Venice, Austria, and the Turks*, 405.

28. Lord Paget to Right Honourable to James Vernon, dated from Carlowitz, 16/26 January 1699, National Archives, Kew, State Papers, SP 97/21, Letter 37. Paget's letters give both Julian and Gregorian dates.

29. Ghobrial, *Whispers of Cities*, 57.

30. Paul Rycaut, *The History of Turks: Beginning with the Year 1679; Being a full Relation of the Last Troubles in Hungary, with the Sieges of Vienna, and Buda, and all the several Battles both by Sea and Land, between the Christians, and the Turks, until the End of the Year 1698, and 1699; In which the Peace between the Turks, and the Confederate Christian Princes and States, was happily Concluded at Carlowitz in Hungary, by the mediation of His Majesty of Great Britain, and the States General of the United Provinces* (London: Printed for Robert Clavell and Abel Roper, 1700). The publication of this text was advertised as early as November 1699. See *Post Boy*, 9–11 November 1699. Subsequent references are to this edition unless otherwise noted.

31. Rycaut's *Present State of the Ottoman Empire* (1665) was frequently reprinted, sometimes with the addition of new material.

32. *Gründ- und Umständlicher Bericht Von Denen Römisch-Kayserlichen Wie auch Ottomannischen Gross-Bothschafften, Wodurch Der Friede oder Stillstand Zwischen Dem Roemischen Kayser Leopoldo Primo und Dem Sultan Mustafahan III Den 26. Januarii, 1699; Zu Carlowiz in Sirmien auf 25. Jahr geschlossen Und darauff auch an denen respectivè Höffen Zu Wienn und Constantinopel bestaetiget worden* (Vienna: Schönwetter, 1702). Hereafter this text will be referred to as *Bericht*. I am indebted to Ashley Singer for the translations of the cited passages from this text.

33. *Theatre de la paix entre les Chrestiens et les Turcs: Generale afbeeldingh der Handelplaats alwaar de Vreede tusschen de Christenen ende de Turcken is gestooten den 26. Jan. 1699* (The Hague: Anna Beek Exc.). Beeck was working between 1702 and 1709. This map is also part of an atlas by Anna Beeck and Gaspar de Baillieu entitled *A Collection of Plans of Fortifications and Battles* (1709).

34. The only exception is the engraving of Count Ottingen in the *Bericht*.

35. Paget to [?], 14/24 October 1698, SOAS, University of London [School of Oriental and African Studies] Paget Papers, PP MS 4, Box 3, bundle 18 [X/461]. The addressee is unspecified.

36. Paget to [?], 14/24 October 1698.

37. See also MS It. VII, 399 (8625), *Congresso di Carlowitz (1699) e Carte parente di una missione di Carlo Ruzzini nella raccolta Marciana*, "Extrait de la lettre de S. Exc My Lord Paget. d'allee de Belgrad du 4 Septbre 1698," 152.

38. Rifa'at Ali Abou-El-Haj, "The Reisülküttab and Ottoman Diplomacy at Karlowitz" (Ph.D. diss., Princeton University, 1963), 65.

39. Rycaut, *History of the Turks, Beginning in the Year 1679*, 562.

40. Rycaut, *History of the Turks, Beginning in the Year 1679*, 563. Intriguingly, these passages on the "void" are replicated in subsequent histories of the treaty, while much else of Rycaut's account is adumbrated. See, for example, David Jones, *The Life of Leopold, Late Emperor of Germany* (London: Printed for T. Newborough, J. Knapton, and R. Burrough, 1706), 278 and 280. Jones transcribes the date inaccurately, but the passages he cites are verbatim from Rycaut.

41. See Victor Turner, *From Ritual to Theatre: The Human Seriousness of Play* (Cambridge, MA: MIT Press, 1982); J. Huizinga, *Homo Ludens: A Study of the Play Element in Culture* (Boston: Beacon Press, 1955); Mihai I. Spariosu, "Exile and Utopia as Liminal Play: A

Cultural-Theoretical Approach," in *Philosophical Perspectives on Play*, ed. Malcolm MacLean, Wendy Russell, and Emily Ryall (New York: Routledge, 2015), 13–26.

42. For the specific language used to establish this neutral zone, see *Bericht*, 2. I wish to thank Ashley Singer for providing a translation of this passage.

43. It is interesting to consider this scenario as a paradoxical enactment of Giorgio Agamben's "state of exception." Both the Habsburgs and the Ottomans legitimated rule through a posture of perpetual war against their religious others. As Suraiya Faroqhi argues, "both early modern European states and the Ottoman Empire were organized for war as their *raison d'être*," thus the suspension of this norm to enact peace is the state of exception for these increasingly obsolete imperial forms (*Ottoman Empire*, 8).

44. See Abou-El-Haj, "Reisülküttab and Ottoman Diplomacy," 60–70, for a discussion of the preliminaries. The first six pages of the *Bericht* are devoted to the various machinations employed by the Austrian delegation to resolve conflicting claims to rank and privilege between the Poles and the Russians.

45. Abou-El-Haj, "Reisülküttab and Ottoman Diplomacy," 67.

46. Working as interim ambassador for the English Crown while Paget was in transit to Istanbul, the Dutch envoy Heemskerk presented peace proposals at an inopportune moment, and they were publicly mocked at one of Paget's earliest audiences with the grand vizier on 14 March 1693. See Abou-el-Haj, "Reisülküttab and Ottoman Diplomacy," 4–8, for a discussion of this bungled maneuver. Despite this inauspicious start, the public repudiation of *uti possidetis* in 1693 set the stage for the Ottomans' return to the issue in 1698. Reporting on a meeting with Mavrocordato, Paget states, "in the visit he [the Ottoman chief dragoman] told me, the vesier asked whether I was the person that had favourably brought some overtures for peace between the two empires. . . . He then told me (but as from himself) that it might not be improper to (if in my audience from the vesier I had a convenient opportunity for it) to take notice of what had passed (i.e., the unheeded proposals of 1693)." London, Public Record Office (PRO), SP 97/21, 4, quoted in Abou-El-Haj, "Reisülküttab and Ottoman Diplomacy," 9.

47. By cross-referencing we could argue that this image depicts the morning of 3/14 November—that is, the first day of negotiation—except that that meeting took place in a tent.

48. *Bericht*, 7 (trans. Ashley Singer).

49. Rycaut, *History of the Turks, Beginning in the Year 1679*, 563 (emphasis mine). The same passage appears in Jones, *Life of Leopold*, 280.

50. The complexity of Austria's situation is well captured by Charles Ingrao and Yasir Yilmaz, "Ottoman v. Habsburg: Motives and Priorities," in *Empires and Peninsulas: Southeastern Europe Between Karlowitz and the Peace of Adrianople, 1699–1829*, ed. Plamen Mitev et al. (New Brunswick, NJ: Transaction/Lit Verlag, 2010), 5–18. As the authors state, the Habsburgs were continually dealing with conflict on all four points of the compass, but at the time of Karlowitz the onset of war with the French in the War of Spanish Succession was a pressing concern. Ingrao and Yilmaz helpfully point out that Habsburg imperial control relied on support from an array of allies. This was in direct contrast to the Ottomans, who, for better or worse, were isolated—this meant that they could not turn to anyone for assistance, but it also meant that they could prosecute war or peace with little concern for other interests.

51. Abou-El-Haj, "Reisülküttab and Ottoman Diplomacy," 69.

52. Faroqhi, *Ottoman Empire*, 28.

53. William Paget, undated correspondence, PP MS 4, Box 4, bundle 23 [VII/132], 3. From the context, this letter had to have preceded the negotiations: it is commentary on the preliminary position of each of the parties.

54. For the culturally specific approaches to rendering space in the era leading up to the negotiations, see Palmira Brummeett, "Imagining the early modern Ottoman space, from world

history to Piri Reis," in Daniel Goffman and Virginia Aksan, *The Early Modern Ottomans: Re-mapping the Empire* (Cambridge: Cambridge University Press, 2007), 15–58.

55. Faroqhi, *Ottoman Empire*, 21.

56. After the Treaty of Karlowitz (1699) and the Treaty of Istanbul (1700), joint border commissions attempted to demarcate the territorial limits between the Ottoman Empire and the powers of the Holy Roman League. See Rifa'at A. Abou-El-Haj, "The Formal Closure of the Ottoman Frontier in Europe: 1699–1703," *American Oriental Society* 89.3 (1969): 467–75, for a discussion of this process and the ensuing resistance to the closure of the frontier. Abou-El-Haj's argument concurs with Faroqhi's understanding of the porous borders at this time.

57. Abou-El-Haj, "Ottoman Diplomacy at Karlowitz" (1967).

58. For the canonical account of the importance of mapping and textual information for the visual economy of seventeenth-century Dutch art, see Alpers, *The Art of Describing*, 119–221.

59. In an era when the sultan so forcefully appropriated floral signs, one could argue that these tulip-like finials subtly signal the provenance of the tent.

60. If we believe the geography of the Venetian map, then we would be looking from the north and thus would be looking at Paget's doorway.

61. Rycaut, *History of the Turks, Beginning in the Year 1679,* 562.

62. There is also a way in which the engraving uses the conventions of the wonder cabinet to organize bits of information. I am indebted to Sophie Gee for this observation.

63. See Rycaut, *History of the Turks, Beginning in the Year 1679,* 561–62.

64. Paget to Lord Jersey, 10 January 1700, PP MS 4, Box 3, bundle 20 [XIV/48].

65. Paget to Mr. Yard, 15 August 1700, PP MS 4, Box 3, bundle 20 [XII/103].

66. Birdal, *The Holy Roman Empire and the Ottomans*, 138–48.

67. These processions were famously recorded by Evilya Celebi and figure prominently in Vanmour's and Melling's works. I will be drawing attention to seventeenth-century practices here because they are contemporaneous with the Karlowitz treaty, but procession as performance of Ottoman state power both predates and post-dates the era under discussion here. For some sense of the continuity of practices, see Aksan, *An Ottoman Statesman*.

68. Nurhan Atasoy, "Processions and Protocol in Ottoman Istanbul," in *The Sultan's Procession: The Swedish Embassy to Sultan Mehmed IV in 1657–1658 and the Rålamb Paintings*, ed. Karin Ådahl (Istanbul: Swedish Research Institute, 2006), 169.

69. Antoine Galland, *Voyage à Constantinople (1672–1673)* (Paris: Maisonneuve et Larose, 2000), 122. I am indebted to Julie Alusse for her assistance with the translation of this text.

70. *Post Man and the Historical Account*, 2–5 October 1697.

71. There is lengthy bill in Paget's papers outlining the extraordinary expenses entailed in maintaining a retinue for his progress to the conference site. See PP MS 4, Box 3, bundle 18 [XI/380].

72. *Post Man and the Historical Account*, 24–27 September 1698.

73. Rycaut, *History of the Turks, Beginning in the Year 1679,* 561.

74. See Geoff R. Berridge, "Dragomans and Oriental Secretaries in the British Embassy in Istanbul," in *Ottoman Diplomacy: Conventional or Unconventional?*, ed. A. Nuri Yurdusev (Houndmills: Palgrave Macmillan, 2004), 151–66, for a history of these functionaries.

75. Paget had brought this possibility to his first audience with the grand vizier in 1693. The grand vizier for his part ridiculed Paget's proposals by referring the ulema to an earlier set of proposals clumsily brought on behalf of the English by the Dutch ambassador Coenraad van Heemskerck.

76. Abou-El-Haj, "Reisülküttab and Ottoman Diplomacy," 67. Abou-El-Haj states that Mehmed Efendi's account of the proceedings gives detailed lists of these processions.

77. Rycaut, *History of the Turks, Beginning in the Year 1679,* 562.

78. Rycaut, *History of the Turks, Beginning in the Year 1679,* 563.

79. Rycaut, *History of the Turks, Beginning in the Year 1679,* 563. Rycaut's account incorporates some newspaper reporting almost verbatim. See *Post Boy,* 1–3 December 1698.

80. Rycaut, *History of the Turks, Beginning in the Year 1679,* 563.

81. See *Post Boy,* 1–3 December 1698.

82. As Roland Barthes argues, all narratives are instantiated by an enigmatic code. See Barthes, *S/Z: An Essay,* trans. Richard Miller (New York: Hill and Wang, 1974).

83. See *Post Boy,* 1–3 December 1698

84. *Bericht,* 7 (trans. Ashley Singer).

85. Paul Cernovodeanu, "Le journal des travaux du Congrès de Karlowitz (1698–1699)," *Revue des Études Sud-Est Européennes* 19.2 (1981): 325–54.

86. These dates are confusing. Rycaut states that the Poles did not enter into negotiations with the Ottomans until 23 November/3 December.

87. For a discussion of this part of the negotiation, derived from Rami Mehmed Efendi, Karlofça mukalemesi, Istanbul, Istanbul Úniversititesi Kütüphanesi, Türk Yazmalari, 3514 18a, see Abou-El-Haj, "Ottoman Diplomacy at Karlowitz" (1967), 505.

88. Tisa or Tisza (river). Also spelled "Tysa" in this text.

89. Titel is located fifty kilometers east of Petrovaradin.

90. English: Slavonia.

91. Osijek.

92. Petrovaradin.

93. Drava (river).

94. Sava (river).

95. Bosut (river).

96. The river Timiş (in Romanian), or Tamiš (in Serbian).

97. Bega (river).

98. PP MS 4, Box 16, bundle 72 [I/15]. As with the material published by Cernovodeanu, the document is originally in French although dates are given in Latin. Paget is referred to as "Milord." I am indebted to Julie Alusse for her assistance with the translation of this text.

99. As Cernovodeanu ("Journal des travaux") also notes, the secretary is likely British because he is using the Julian calendar.

100. As Lyotard states, "narrative is perhaps the genre of discourse within which the heterogeneity of phrase regimens, and even the heterogeneity of genres of discourse, have the easiest time passing unnoticed" (*The Differend,* 151). See Daniel Punday's remarks on narrative's relation to the "differend" in *Narrative After Deconstruction* (Albany: SUNY Press, 2012), 6–10.

101. As late as 1703 Paget is sending letters indicating his concern that border issues are still not resolved and that lack of attention to these matters will destroy the peace.

102. Cernovodeanu, "Journal des travaux," 354.

103. Paget dispatch, 16/26 January 1699, National Archives, Kew, State Papers 97/21, Letter 14.

104. Lord Paget to Robert Sutton, 21/31 January 1698/99, PP MS 4, Box 3, bundle 19 [XI/196], 23.

105. Rycaut, *History of the Turks, Beginning in the Year 1679,* 566.

106. Lord Paget to Robert Sutton, 21/31 January 1698/99.

107. Lord Paget to Robert Sutton, 21/31 January 1698/99.

108. See Rycaut, *History of the Turks, Beginning in the Year 1679,* 566, for a similar account of visitation and leave-taking.

109. The Kapela Mira (Peace Chapel) was built on the site of the conference and ostensibly replicates some of the architectural features of the negotiation tent: the building is circular, has four entrances, and the windows are purportedly patterned on the Union Jack flag to recognize Paget's mediation.

110. See Talbot's discussion of the importance of gift giving to diplomatic relations with the Ottoman Empire in "British Diplomacy in the Ottoman Empire," 181–215.

111. Rycaut, *History of the Turks, Beginning in the Year 1679,* 603.

112. Talbot, "British Diplomacy in the Ottoman Empire," 248–49.

113. Rycaut, *History of the Turks, Beginning in the Year 1679,* 604.

114. See SP/78 Letter 32, the relation of Sutton's public audience on 10 March 1701 with the grand signor, and the discussion of this account in the "Introduction."

115. The same is also true of the *Bericht.* The catalog of presents is exhaustive.

116. Rycaut, *History of the Turks,* 604.

117. Rycaut, *History of the Turks,* 605.

118. Talbot, "British Diplomacy in the Ottoman Empire," 201.

119. Talbot, "British Diplomacy in the Ottoman Empire," 202.

Chapter 2

1. Hill, *A Full and Just Account of the Present State of the Ottoman Empire,* 28–29.

2. See Chapter 1, note 2.

3. Alain Grosrichard, *The Sultan's Court: European Fantasies of the East,* trans. Liz Heron (London: Verso Books, 1998).

4. Aksan, *Ottoman Wars,* 26–27.

5. For much of the late seventeenth century, Mehmed IV and his immediate successors conducted the business of the court in Adrianople (Edirne). The court still regularly retired to Adrianople for the summer months during Ahmed III's sultanate. See Shirine Hamadeh, *The City's Pleasures: Istanbul in the Eighteenth Century* (Seattle: University of Washington Press, 2008), 3–27.

6. Ariel Salzmann, "The Age of Tulips: Confluence and Conflict in Early Modern Consumer Culture (1550–1730)," in *Consumption Studies and the History of the Ottoman Empire, 1550–1922: An Introduction,* ed. Donald Quataert (Albany: State University of New York Press, 2000), 91. Bruce McGowan, in "The Age of the *Ayans,* 1699–1812," part 3 of *An Economic and Social History of the Ottoman Empire,* ed. Halil Inalcik with Donald Quataert (Cambridge: Cambridge University Press, 1994), takes a slightly different view, emphasizing that domestic trade within the empire overshadowed foreign trade. McGowan's brief summary of the state of the empire is helpful, for he shows that the Ottoman enterprise was reasonably successful right up until the eve of war with Russia in 1768. Thus dividing the century not only dispels much of the European myths about decline in the early part of the century but also demonstrates why reform was so necessary in the wake of the Treaty of Küçük Kaynarca (639–45).

7. For the publication history of the various editions, see Lady Mary Wortley Montagu, *The Complete Letters of Lady Mary Wortley Montagu,* ed. Robert Halsband, 3 vols. (Clarendon: Oxford University Press, 1967), 1:xvii–xx.

8. See Alpers, *The Art of Describing.*

9. In "Turquerie: Culture in Motion, 1650–1750," *Past and Present* 221 (November 2013): 79–85, Alexander Bevilacqua and Helen Pfeifer show the strong links between the Ottoman miniatures painted by Musavvir Hüseyin and the costume images in Rycaut's *The Present State of the Ottoman Empire* and in Vanmour's *Recueil Ferriol.*

10. See Eveline Sint Nicolaas, "The Turkish Paintings of Ambassador Cornelius Calkoen (1696–1764)," in *Sultans, Merchants, Painters: The Early Years of Turkish-Dutch Relations* (Istanbul: Pera Museum, 2012), 47–75; as Sint Nicolaas states, the historical record of Vanmour's life in this period is scant, but "Vanmour's youth was probably not unlike the formative years of his contemporary Jean-Antoine Watteau (1684–1721), who was also from Valenciennes. As a

struggling, yet-to-be-discovered artist, Watteau spent several years working at a factory studio in Paris, where young artists produced prodigious amounts of art for a wholesale art dealer" (53).

11. The best accounts of Vanmour's career are Duncan Bull's essay on the artist in *The Ambassador, the Sultan and the Artist: An Audience in Istanbul*, Rijksmuseum Dossiers (Amsterdam: Rijksmuseum, 2003), 18–31; and Nefedova, *Journey into the World of the Ottomans*, 83–142.

12. Sint Nicolaas, "The Turkish Paintings," 51–52.

13. Sint Nicolaas, "The Turkish Paintings," 52.

14. See David Brafman, "Picart, Bernard, Hermes, and Muhammad (Not Necessarily in That Order)," in *Bernard Picart and the First Global Vision of Religion*, ed. Lynn Hunt, Margaret Jacob, and Wijnand Mijnhardt (Los Angeles: Getty Research Institute, 2010), 142–46. Out of a total of fifty-one engravings, Bernard and Picart used twenty-six of Vanmour's images, including all three of the large foldout engravings, *Mariage Turc, Enterrement Turc*, and *Les derviches dans leur Temple de Pera, achevant de tourner.* Because they are all reversed it is clear that Picart's team of engravers simply traced Vanmour's engravings.

15. Brummett, *Mapping the Ottomans.* The text was frequently pirated with nonauthorized editions simply making engravings from the printed text, thus many readers were first exposed to the images in reverse orientation.

16. See Thomas Jefferys, *A Collection of the Dresses of Different Nations, Antient and Modern*, 4 vols. (London: Thomas Jefferys, 1757–72).

17. For a discussion of the impact of *Recueil Ferriol* on later cultural materials and practices, see Jeff Moronvalle, "Le *Recueil Ferriol* (1714) et la mode des turqueries," *Dix-Huitième Siècle* 44.1 (2012): 425–46, http://www.cairn.info /revue-dix-huitieme-siecle-2012-1-page-425.htm.

18. Sint Nicolaas, "The Turkish Paintings," 55. A similar selection of costume paintings by or after Vanmour can be found in the National Trust Collection at Sissinghurst Castle in Kent, England. As the National Trust catalog states, "There are fourteen framed sets remaining, each with five vividly painted copper plates. The Sissinghurst set were owned by Marie-Gabriel-Florent-Auguste Choiseul-Gouffier (1751–1817)." http://www.nationaltrustcollections .org.uk/object/803040.10.3.

19. There are portraits of Ahmed III, Damad İbrahim Pasha, and the qadi in the Calkoen collection, and the audience paintings all contain portraits of the ambassadors who made the commission. See Eveline Sint Nicolaas, "From Sultan to Swindler: Seven Portraits from Cornelis Calkoen's Series of 'Turkish Paintings,'" *Rijksmuseum Bulletin* 59.1 (2011): 34–57, for a discussion of Vanmour's portrait practice.

20. See Wunder, "Western Travelers, Eastern Antiquities," for a useful discussion of the early visual record of contact with the Ottoman world.

21. There is a long history dating back to the sixteenth-century of albums showing views of cities with representative costumes in the foreground. See, for instance, George Braun and Franz Hogenberg, *Civitates urbis terrarium* (Cologne, 1575–1618). For an extensive discussion of early costume albums, see Bronwen Wilson, *The World in Venice: Print, the City, and Early Modern Identity* (Toronto: University of Toronto Press, 2005), 70–132.

22. See Corneille le Bruyn [Cornelis de Bruijn], *A Voyage to the Levant; or, Travels in the Principal Parts of Asia Minor, the Islands of Scio, Rhodes, Cyprus, &c . . .* (London: Printed for Jacob Tonson and Thomas Bennet, 1702), plates 34–39.

23. Wilson's remarks on classification explicitly link costume albums and botanical illustrations (*The World in Venice*, 92–100).

24. Wilson explicitly compares early costume albums to atlases (*The World in Venice*, 85).

25. Brummett, *Mapping the Ottomans*, 49–50, 63.

26. Charles de Ferriol, Jacques Le Hay, and Jean-Baptiste Vanmour, *Recueil de cent estampes représentant differentes nations du Levant: Gravées sur les tableaux peints d'après nature en 1707 et 1708 par les ordres de M. de Ferriol, ambassadeur du roi à porte; et mis au jour en 1712 et 1713*

(Paris: Le Hay, 1714), 12. All subsequent references to this text will be either to plate or page number and will be given in the text. For ease of reference I use the short title *Recueil Ferriol* throughout this chapter and the next. I am grateful to Julie Alusse for her assistance with the translation of this text.

27. Wilson, *The World in Venice*, 100.

28. The numbering of letters poses a problem because Halsband deletes the letter numbers and inserts real correspondence into the Letter-book. In all cases, I will be referring to letters as they are numbered in the Letter-book and presented in Lady Mary Wortley Montagu, *The Turkish Embassy Letters*, ed. Teresa Heffernan and Daniel O'Quinn (Peterborough: Broadview Press, 2013). When citing from the letters, I will present the letter number followed by the Broadview page numbers and then Halsband's (H) volume and page numbers in parentheses in the body of the text.

29. Madeleine-Françoise de Gontaut-Biron (1692–1739) married Jean-Louis d'Usson, Marquis de Bonnac (1672–1738), in 1715. He had arrived in Istanbul as the French ambassador in 1713 and wrote a memoir about his time there: *Mémoire historique sur l'Ambassade de France à Constantinople*. France, unlike England, was interested in ensuring that the Ottoman Empire remained a threat to the Habsburgs. The young bride gave birth to a boy in December 1716. Despite the tension between their husbands, Lady Mary and Madeleine-Françoise spent a good deal of time together.

30. See Atasoy, "Processions and Protocol in Ottoman Istanbul," 168–95.

31. As Zeynep Yelçe indicates, foreign ambassadors often viewed processions and ceremonies from separate private residences to avoid conflicts over precedence. See Yelçe, "Evaluating Three Imperial Festivals: 1524, 1530 and 1539," in *Celebration, Entertainment and Theatre in the Ottoman World*, ed. Suraiya Faroqhi and Arzu Öztürkmen (London: Seagull Books, 2014), 71–109.

32. Nefedova, *Journey into the World of the Ottomans*, 134–37, figs. 135–39.

33. These sights are described in virtually all prior and contemporary accounts of Constantinople. See for example de Bruijn, *A Voyage to the Levant*, 28–34; Hill, *Full and Just Account*, 137–39; Montagu, *Turkish Embassy Letters* (42.164–70; H 1:396–403).

34. Yelçe, "Evaluating Three Imperial Festivals," 88.

35. For some sense of the complex allegories and the sheer expense of court masque and pageantry during the reign of Queen Anne, see James Anderson Winn, *Queen Anne: Patroness of the Arts* (New York: Oxford University Press, 2014). See also David Bevington and Peter Holbrook, *The Politics of Stuart Court Masque* (Cambridge: Cambridge University Press, 1998); Martin Butler, "Politics and the Masque: *The Triumph of Peace*," *Seventeenth Century* 2 (1987): 117–41. Lisa Freeman provides a succinct introduction to the politics of public procession in England in the seventeenth century in *Antitheatricality and the Body Public* (Philadelphia: University of Pennsylvania Press, 2017), 11–32.

36. Yelçe, "Evaluating Three Imperial Festivals," 88.

37. For a description of this practice, see Hill, *Full and Just Account*, 108.

38. See Grosrichard, *The Sultan's Court*, esp. 55–84 for a discussion of the trope of the sultan's gaze in Orientalist texts of the eighteenth century.

39. Images from this section of the *Recueil Ferriol* feature prominently in the selections made for commercial clients such as the grouping displayed at the Amsterdam town hall and the grouping acquired by Choiseul-Gouffier. As we will see in Chapter 6, Choiseul-Gouffier's interest in the subject peoples of the Ottoman Empire is key to his philhellenism.

40. Ian Coller, "East of Enlightenment: Regulating Cosmopolitanism Between Istanbul and Paris in the Eighteenth Century," *Journal of World History* 21.3 (September 2010): 451–52, recognizes the importance of Franks to Vanmour's set of engravings but also offers valuable evidence regarding the divergence between representations of Franks in the Ottoman Empire and the practice of living in Istanbul as a French subject.

41. Isobel Grundy emphasizes that a shared sense of rank was crucial to Lady Mary's sociability; this is especially the case in her discussion of Montagu's visit to Fatima, the *keth-üdâ's* lady (*Lady Mary Wortley Montagu*, 148–49). Montagu refers to her as the "Kayha's Lady"; Fatima is the wife of the *sadaret kethüdasi*, the deputy of the grand vizier (34.132–33; H 1:349–50)

42. For discussions that link shopping, sexuality, and the public at a later point in the century, see Deidre Shauna Lynch, "Counter Publics: Shopping and Women's Sociability," in *Romantic Sociability: Social Networks and Literary Culture in Britain, 1770–1840*, ed. Gillian Russell and Clara Tuite (Cambridge: Cambridge University Press, 2002), 211–35; Conrad Brunström, "Sex and Shopping with Frances Burney," in *Queer People: Negotiations and Ex-pressions of Homosexuality, 1700–1800*, ed. Chris Mounsey and Caroline Gonda (Lewisburg, PA: Bucknell University Press, 2007), 86–98.

43. This same self-inclusion emerges when she discusses Jewish commerce later in the text:

I observed most of the rich tradesmen were Jews. That people are in incredible power in this country. They have many privileges above the natural Turks them-selves, and have formed a very considerable commonwealth here, being judged by their own laws, and have drawn the whole trade of the Empire into their hands, partly by the firm union amongst themselves, and prevailing on the idle temper and want of industry of the Turks. Every bassa has his Jew, who is his *"homme d'affaires."* He is let into all his secrets, and does all his business. No bargain is made, no bribe received, no merchandise disposed of but what passes through their hands. They are the physicians, the stewards, and the interpreters of all the great men. You may judge how advantageous this is to a people who never fail to make use of the smallest advantages. They have found the secret of making themselves so necessary, they are certain of the protection of the court whatever ministry is in power. Even the English, French, and Italian merchants, who are sensible of their artifices, are however forced to trust their affairs to their negotiation, nothing of trade being managed without them, and the meanest amongst them is too important to be disobliged since the whole body take care of his interests with as much vigour as they would those of the most considerable of their members. They are many of them vastly rich, but take care to make little public show of it, though they live in their houses in the utmost luxury and magnificence. (35.136–37; H 1:354–55)

The penultimate sentence indicates that the Frankish residents of Pera are as much a part of this economy as the Ottoman figures in the opening sentences.

44. In the painting executed for her sister, she is alone, and in the other she is with her son.

45. For further discussion of Lady Mary's adoption of Turkish dress, see Susanne Scholz, "English Women in Oriental Dress: Playing the Turk in Lady Mary Wortley Montagu's *Turk-ish Embassy Letters* and Daniel Defoe's *Roxana*," in *Early Modern Encounters with the Islamic East: Performing Cultures*, ed. Sabine Schülting, Sabine Lucia Müller, and Ralf Hertel (Burl-ington, VT: Ashgate, 2012), 71–80. On the issue of cross-cultural dressing more generally, see Onur Inal, "Women's Fashions in Transition: Ottoman Borderlands and the Anglo-Ottoman Exchange of Costumes," *Journal of World History* 22.2 (2011): 243–72.

46. For a powerful discussion of the theoretical implications of this aspect of costume il-lustration, see Wilson, *The World in Venice*, 127–32. As she states, "Costume illustrations in-vested moral values, ideality and social roles in the clothing that surrounded the body. But on the body costume is more than a frame; instead, clothing is the mediating surface through which the bodily and fragmented ego is integrated with the representations that sustain it" (130).

47. See Ballaster, *Fabulous Orients*, 65–68.

48. Mary Jo Kietzman, "Montagu's *Turkish Embassy Letters* and Cultural Dislocation," *Studies in English Literature, 1500–1900* 38.3 (1998): 537–51. Kader Konuk handles the hammam scene in terms of ethnomasquerade in "Ethnomasquerade in Ottoman-European Encounters: Reenacting Lady Mary Wortley Montagu," *Criticism* 46.3 (Summer 2004): 393–414, but because the focus is on imitators of Lady Mary much of the subtlety of the hammam letter is overlooked.

49. Elizabeth A. Bohls, "Aesthetics and Orientalism in Lady Mary Wortley Montagu's Letters," *Studies in Eighteenth-Century Culture* 23 (1994): 179–205.

50. Bohls is especially cogent on the significance of these comparisons; see "Aesthetics and Orientalism," 187–90.

51. Bohls argues that Lady Mary's decision to remain clothed maintains not only her feminine reputation but also her Occidental privilege and thus is another form of social avoidance ("Aesthetics and Orientalism," 194–95).

52. Vanmour painted Lady Mary twice. There is a smaller full-length portrait of her without her son and attendants that was either a study for the larger picture or was derived from it. The picture is in a private collection, but is reproduced in Nefedova, *Journey into the World of the Ottomans*, 125.

53. For an excellent discussion of these paintings, see Eveline Sint Nicolaas, "The Ambassador and the Sultan," in *The Ambassador, the Sultan and the Artist: An Audience in Istanbul* (Amsterdam: Rijksmuseum, 2003), 3–16.

54. See letters 38 and 39 (38–39.148–53; H 1:367–73).

55. See letter 32 (32.124–26; H 1:337–40).

56. See Diana Barnes, "The Public Life of a Woman of Wit and Quality: Lady Mary Wortley Montagu and the Vogue for Smallpox Inoculation," *Feminist Studies* 38.2 (Summer 2012): 330–62; Elizabeth Wanning Harries, "'An Experiment Practiced Only by a Few Ignorant Women': Lady Mary Wortley Montagu, the Smallpox Inoculation, and the Concept of Enlightenment," *Scriblerian and the Kit-Cats* 37.2/38.1 (2005): 40–41; A. F. M. Stone and W. D. Stone, "Lady Mary Wortley Montagu: Medical and Religious Controversy Following Her Introduction of Smallpox Inoculation," *Journal of Medical Biography* 10.4 (2002): 232–36; Isobel Grundy, "Medical Advance and Female Fame: Inoculation and Its After-Effects," *Lumen* 13 (1994): 13–42; Robert Halsband, "New Light on Lady Mary Wortley Montagu's Contribution to Inoculation," *Journal of the History of Medicine* 8.4 (October 1953): 390–405.

Chapter 3

1. Charles Perry, *A View of the Levant* (London: T. Woodward, 1743), 24.

2. Perry, *A View of the Levant*, 24–25.

3. For an excellent survey of the contemporary discourse on Sa'dabad, see Hamadeh, *The City's Pleasures*, 226–33. Hamadeh's monograph also contains superb eighteenth-century illustrations of the pleasure gardens.

4. Faroqhi, *Ottoman Empire*, 58–60.

5. One of the most important antigovernment activists in the ulema was Zulali Hasan Efendi, one of the chief *kâdîs* (or qadis) of Istanbul. Robert W. Olson, *The Siege of Mosul and Ottoman-Persian Relations, 1718–1743* (Bloomington: Indiana University Press, 1975), 74, summarizes his rift with Damad İbrahim Pasha as follows:

> Subsequent historians, most notably Mustafa Nuri Pasa, attributed Zulali's dismissal
> to the personal animosity between the *kadi* and the Grand Vezir. The conflict
> allegedly emerged during one of the festivities which Ibrahim staged frequently at
> Kagithane. At these gatherings one of Ibrahim's favorite pastimes was to toss gold

coins down the *yasmaks* (dresses) of the attending women—a skill at which the Grand Vezir was adept. One of the beautiful women whom Ibrahim "craftily deceived" (*hiyel-i-musamna*) and molested (*taarruz*) was the wife of Zulali Hasan Efendi. Mustafa Nuri states that this was the fuse which ignited the rebellion.

Mustafa Nuri's account is no doubt colored by his negative view of Damad İbrahim Pasha, but it is worth noting how similar the described acts of molestation are to accounts of libertine practices in England.

6. Sa'dabad was restored ten years later by Mahmûd I and used for another seventy years only to be destroyed in the early nineteenth century. The fact that the buildings are no longer extant is one of the reasons that there remains confusion about its architectural style. See Hamadeh, *The City's Pleasures*, 28; and Hakki Eldem, *Sa'dabad* (Istanbul: Kültür Bakanliği, Devlet Kitaplari Müdürlüğü, 1977).

7. See Salzmann, "The Age of Tulips," 83–106.

8. See Can Erimtan, *Ottomans Looking West? The Origins of the Tulip Age and Its Development in Modern Turkey* (London: I. B. Tauris, 2008).

9. As we have already seen in the previous chapter, this burgeoning world of luxury goods is copiously documented in Lady Mary's Letter-book.

10. Sa'dabad's importance as a political sign extends far beyond its brief existence. The historiography of the twelve-year grand vizierate of Damad İbrahim Pasha is in many ways dependent on the interpretation of this polarizing figure and his violent end. In one of the foundational texts of Ottoman history, *Netayic ul-Vukuat*, Mansurizade Mustafa Nuri Pasha presented a fierce critique of the grand vizier that is not that distant from that of the rebels. As Can Erimtan summarizes in *Ottomans Looking West*, Mustafa Nuri "is highly critical of Damad İbrahim Paşha, accusing him of lack of military zeal, mismanagement, avarice, nepotism and an unhealthy appetite for pursuing hedonistic pastimes—pastimes which involved tulips" (12). These "tulip entertainments," like Sa'dabad itself, were for Mustafa Nuri and his predecessor the historian Ahmed Cevdet metonyms for the dissipation that ostensibly weakened the empire during this period. In contrast, presentist narratives indebted to the nationalist rhetoric of Ahmed Refik, whose book *Lale Devri* coined the phrase "Tulip Period" to describe this era, construct İbrahim Pasha as a modernizing force whose openness to European culture and technology signaled a brief period of enlightened cosmopolitanism in the Ottoman Empire. Thus in this view, the elimination of İbrahim Pasha amounts to a rejection of modernity, to a return to religious rule. This has been an extraordinarily influential reading of these events in part because it so easily turns the "Tulip Period" into a brief period of progress, precocious or otherwise, in what is otherwise seen as a long historical decline. Refik and scholars following in his footsteps such as Fatma Müge Göçek suggest that Sa'dabad's architecture is modeled on that of Versailles and thus explicitly argue that the Patrona Halil rebellion was directed against Damad İbrahim Pasha's openness to European and, specifically, French influence. See Fatma Müge Göçek, *East Encounters West: France and the Ottoman Empire in the Eighteenth Century* (New York: Oxford University Press, 1987). As Dana Sajdi argues in "Decline, Its Discontents and Ottoman Cultural History: By Way of Introduction," in *Ottoman Tulips, Ottoman Coffee: Leisure and Lifestyle in the Eighteenth Century*, ed. Dana Sajdi (London: I. B. Tauris, 2014), 1–40, Refik's celebration of the cultural achievements attained under İbrahim Pasha's patronage are part of a post-Ataturk nationalist argument and thus need to be carefully scrutinized. And Can Erimtan has not only discredited the argument that Sa'dabad was based on Versailles, but also presented a compelling argument that sees the structure in terms of similar structures in Isfahan and places the palace's construction in the context of Ottoman/Safavid rivalry. Can Erimtan, "The Perception of Saadabad: The 'Tulip Age' and Ottoman-Safavid Rivalry," in Sajdi, *Ottoman Tulips, Ottoman Coffee*, 41–62. See also Hamadeh, *The City's Pleasures*, 229–35.

11. See "An Account of the Rebellion and Revolution which happened at Constantinople the 28th of September 1730," in Perry, *A View of the Levant*, 64–115. Perry's account is largely based on the English translation of a French account published at The Hague. *A Particular Account of the Two Rebellions Which Happen'd at Constantinople in the Years MDCCXXX, and MDCCXXXI* . . . (London: Printed for G. Smith, 1737), like its French source, is remarkably similar in perspective to Ottoman accounts. For a discussion of these similarities and of the overall anti-insurgent politics of the contemporary historiography, see Felix Konrad, "Coping with 'the Riff-Raff and Mob': Representations of Order and Disorder in the Patrona Halil Rebellion (1730)," *Die Welt des Islams* 54.3–4 (2014): 363–98.

12. Perry, *A View of the Levant*, 26.

13. The word "merely" signals a slight equivocation in Perry's text, and an implicit subtext links the two structures. Because Mehmed IV assumed the sultanate at age six, the executive power over the empire was conferred onto the grand vizier. Like Ahmed III, he was deposed by an uprising and the later sultan explicitly referred back to the earlier deposition as an example of the dangers of investing too much power in the grand vizier. By placing these two structures side by side in his text, Perry seems on the verge of invoking this history of excessive consumption and instability, but like his hesitations over what to call these structures his text exhibits a certain level of diffidence. See Suraiya Faroqhi's comments on these rebellions in "Crisis and Change, 1590–1699," part 2 of *An Economic and Social History of the Ottoman Empire*, ed. Halil Inalcik with Donald Quataert (Cambridge: Cambridge University Press, 1994), 618.

14. Olga Nefedova, in *A Journey into the World of the Ottomans*, makes a similar argument about the source of Vanmour's knowledge (105). See also Duncan Bull's essay on the artist in *The Ambassador, the Sultan and the Artist*, 18–31.

15. See Babak Rahimi, "*Nahils*, Circumcision and the Theatre State," in Sajdi, *Ottoman Tulips, Ottoman Coffee*, 90–116. For further discussion of circumcision and marriage ceremonies, see Yelçe "Evaluating Three Imperial Festivals," and Efdal Sevinçli, "Festivals and Their Documentation: *Surnames* Covering the Festivities of 1675 and 1724," in *Celebration, Entertainment and Theatre in the Ottoman World*, ed. Suraiya Faroqhi and Arzu Öztürkmen (London: Seagull Books, 2014), 71–109 and 186–207 respectively. As Sevinçli argues, "*surnames*, or books recounting wedding and circumcision festivities organized in the names of Ottoman sultans, have attracted the attention of scholars," but considerably more research needs to be done with these sources (186).

16. See Hanneke Grootenboer, *The Rhetoric of Perspective: Realism and Illusionism in Seventeenth-Century Dutch Still-Life Painting* (Chicago: University of Chicago Press, 2005), 136–40.

17. That this mirrors the distinction between Foucault's two regimes of sexuality should not go unnoticed. See Michel Foucault, *The History of Sexuality*, vol. 1, *An Introduction*, trans. Robert Hurley (New York: Vintage Books, 1980), 106–7 and 115–31.

18. See Hill, *Full and Just Account*, 124–28; de Bruijn, *Voyage to the Levant*, 89–90; Montagu, 36.143; H 1:362.

19. Rahmi, "*Nahils*, Circumcision and the Theatre State," 93–94.

20. As I have already discussed in the Introduction, this resistance can be traced in the audience paintings as well.

21. For a cogent discussion of the question of veiling in Montagu, see Teresa Heffernan, "Feminism Against the East/West Divide," *Eighteenth-Century Studies* 33.2 (2000): 201–15.

22. Fifty years later Luigi Mayer would treat the same subject with similar verve.

23. This is markedly different from the audience paintings where the sultan and the grand vizier are visually separated from the other figures. Each inhabits a carefully delineated space.

24. In this regard it is an extension of the related painting *Banquet of Distinguished Turkish Women* (Rijksmuseum), which populates a similar space with similar groupings of elite women and their slaves. In both pictures the movement of figures closely matches the movement of things.

25. She quickly unwinds this erotic fantasy by turning to a brutal description of "the bleeding body of a young woman, naked, only wrapped in a coarse sheet, with two wounds with a knife, one in her side, and another in her breast" (43.173; H 1:407).

26. Bull is more optimistic about this possibility than I am. The possibility that Vanmour saw engravings of Watteau's work remains a tantalizing possibility and has inflected the titling of some of the paintings. The titles for Vanmour's genre paintings have been imposed by later collectors and curators.

27. Again the title is something of a misnomer.

28. See Max Horkheimer and Theodor Adorno, *The Dialectic of Enlightenment* (Stanford, CA: Stanford University Press, 2007), 1–65.

29. We could think of these two pictures as akin to Montagu's ridicule of Pope's desire for a Circassian slave.

30. For a day-by-day account of the rebellion, see Olson, *Siege of Mosul*, 65–88.

31. Olson, *Siege of Mosul*, 75.

32. Olson, *Siege of Mosul*, 69.

33. See the discussion of the conflict between Zulali Hasan Efendi and Damad İbrahim Pasha in note 5 above.

34. See the report of the British ambassador George Hay, 8th Earl of Kinnoull, "A Short Account of what passed during the first ten Days of the Rebellion which begun [*sic*] at Constantinople on Thursday September 17 O.S. 1730," in State Papers 97/26.154; and State Papers 97/26.197, National Archives, Kew, for his account of Patrona Halil's assassination.

35. There is a third painting of the Patrona Halil rebellion that depicts the moment when women of the harem come to collect the bodies of the slain vizier and his aides from the rebels. See Nefedova, *Journey into the World of the Ottomans*,140.

36. Ghobrial, *Whispers of Cities*, 122–58.

37. See Ghobrial, *Whispers of Cities*, 153–55.

38. Kinnoull to His Grace the Duke of Newcastle, 27 September 1730, State Papers 97/26.147.

39. Cornelis Calkoen to the States-General, 13 November 1730 (Arch. S. G. Barbarijen, 6942), quoted in G. R. Bosscha Erdbrink, *At the Threshold of Felicity: Ottoman-Dutch Relations During the Embassy of Cornelis Calkoen at the Sublime Porte, 1726–1744* (Ankara: Türk Tarih Kurumu Basimevi, 1975), 95.

40. Kinnoull to Newcastle, 27 September 1730.

41. Quoted in Bosscha Erdbrink, *At the Threshold*, 93.

42. Kinnoull to Newcastle, 27 September 1730.

43. Kinnoull to Newcastle, 27 September 1730.

44. Kinnoull to Newcastle, 27 September 1730.

45. Sandys to Charles Delafage, Esq., 30 September 1730, State Papers 97/26.158.

46. See Günsel Renda's remarks on these portraits in "The Court and the Empire Observed," in *The Ambassador, the Sultan and the Artist: An Audience in Istanbul* (Amsterdam: Rijksmuseum, 2003), 34.

47. See Sint Nicolaas, "From Sultan to Swindler."

48. Kinnoull to Newcastle, 1 January 1731, SP 97/26.197.

Chapter 4

1. Grootenboer, *Rhetoric of Perspective*, 141.

2. Grootenboer, *Rhetoric of Perspective*, 136.

3. Wortley's successor Abraham Stanyan was also involved in the mediation, but as Bas de Boer argues in *Jacob Colyer: Mediating Between the European and the Ottoman World*, 18–22, Colyer was the Ottomans' preferred mediator in 1718 because of their experience with him in 1699.

4. Pope frequently attacked Montagu in verse as "Sappho." For a discussion of Walpole's scorn, see Jill Campbell, "Lady Mary Wortley Montagu and the 'Glass Revers'd' of Female Old Age," in *"Defects": Engendering the Modern Body*, ed. Helen Deutsch and Felicity Nussbaum (Ann Arbor: University of Michigan Press, 2000), 213–51.

5. Margaret J. M. Ezell, *Social Authorship and the Advent of Print* (Baltimore: Johns Hopkins University Press, 1999), 12.

6. See Ezell, *Social Authorship*, 61–83.

7. See Robert Halsband and Isobel Grundy, eds., *Lady Mary Wortley Montagu: Essays and Poems and "Simplicity," a Comedy* (Oxford: Clarendon Press, 1993) for Lady Mary's nonepistolary writings.

8. As noted above, I will be referring to letters as they are numbered in the Letter-book and presented in Montagu, *The Turkish Embassy Letters*, ed. Heffernan and O'Quinn (Peterborough: Broadview Press, 2013). When citing from the letters, I will present the letter number followed by the Broadview page numbers and then Halsband's volume page numbers in parentheses in the body of the text.

9. See Lowenthal, *Lady Mary Wortley Montagu and the Eighteenth-Century Familiar Letter*, on Lady Mary and the female epistolary tradition. See also Robert Halsband, "Lady Mary Wortley Montagu as Letter Writer," *PMLA: Publications of the Modern Language Association of America* 80.3 (1965): 155–63.

10. One could also claim, as Ezell does in relation to Motteux's *Gentleman's Journal*, that the epistolary form of the text is itself a trace of social authorship because so much scribal exchange was framed by letters. See Margaret J. M. Ezell, "The *Gentleman's Journal* and the Commercialization of Restoration Coterie Literary Practices," *Modern Philology* 89 (1992): 323–40.

11. For the publication history of various editions, see Halsband's edition of *The Complete Letters of Lady Mary Wortley Montagu*, 1:xvii–xx.

12. It does not appear in Halsband's presentation of the letters; neither do the letter numbers at the head of each letter.

13. See Srinivas Aravamudan, "Lady Mary Wortley Montagu in the Hammam: Masquerade, Womanliness, and Levantinization," *ELH* 62.1 (1995): 69–104; and Ballaster, *Fabulous Orients*, 65–90.

14. This is from Astell's inscribed remarks at the end of the letter book. They were printed in the 1763 edition as part of "Preface, by a Lady."

15. The exception is Elizabeth Kelley Bowman's essay "The Poet as Translator: Mary Wortley Montagu Approaches the Turkish Lyric," *Comparative Literature Studies* 50.2 (2013): 244–61. Significantly, Bowman emphasizes the importance of Virgil to Montagu's sense of lyric and of translation.

16. Alexander Pope, *The Correspondence of Alexander Pope*, ed. George Sherburn (Oxford: Clarendon Press, 1956), 1:407.

17. See Fabian, *Time and the Other*, 25–36.

18. Considering the state of women's education, "limitation" seems hardly the right word. According to Isobel Grundy, Montagu learned Latin at a very early age. See Grundy, *Lady Mary Wortley Montagu* (London: Oxford University Press, 1999), 15.

19. Helen Deutsch, "Lady Mary Wortley Montagu's Ecstatic Poetics," *Eighteenth Century: Theory and Interpretation* 53.3 (Fall 2012): 333.

20. Pope himself claimed something similar in his preface.

21. Jean Dumont, *A New Voyage to the Levant: Containing an Account of the Most Remarkable Curiosities in Germany, France, Italy . . . and Turkey . . .* (London, 1696), 268.

22. See Halsband's edition of *The Complete Letters of Lady Mary Wortley Montagu*, 1:389 n. 1.

23. See Kietzman, "Montagu's *Turkish Embassy Letters* and Cultural Dislocation."

24. This is also visible in letter 34.

25. Brummett, *Mapping the Ottomans*.

26. See Julia Kristeva, *Strangers to Ourselves* (New York: Columbia University Press, 1991), 1: "the foreigner lives within us: he is the hidden face of our identity, the space that wrecks our abode, the time in which understanding and affinity founder. . . . The foreigner comes in when the consciousness of my difference arises, and he disappears when we all acknowledge ourselves as foreigners, unamenable to bonds and communities."

27. But that value is mediated through Empress Amalia: the women perform for her, not for the emperor Charles VI, and she is in control of the prizes. In other words, the emperor is only ever in a voyeuristic relation to the games.

28. *Aeneid*, 5.485–544.

29. *Virgil's Aeneid*, trans. John Dryden (New York: P. F. Collier and Son, 1909), 199.

30. Lee Frantantuaono, *Madness Unchained: A Reading of Virgil's "Aeneid"* (Lanham, MD: Lexington Books, 2007), 145–46. For the most detailed account of the comet, see John T. Ramsey and A. Lewis Licht, *The Comet of 44 B.C. and Caesar's Funeral Games* (Oxford: Oxford University Press, 1997), 61ff.

31. David Ross, *Virgil's Aeneid: A Reader's Guide* (Oxford: Blackwell, 2007), 101. "This 'Julian star' (*sidus Iulium*) soon became a fixture on coins and seals. It was placed by Octavian over the statue of Caesar in the Forum and was represented on the pediment of the planned temple of the new god (not completed until 29 BC), which itself, with its altar in front, marked the spot where his body had been cremated. The comet became iconographically as important as the representation of *pietas* to be seen in Aeneas' flight from Troy" (Ross, *Virgil's Aeneid*, 101). Lady Mary emphasizes her expertise in Roman coins in numerous letters.

32. Ramsey and Licht, *Comet of 44 B.C.*, 52.

33. Richard Morton, "'Bringing *Virgil* over into *Britain*': John Dryden Refigures *Aeneid* 1–5," *Studies in Eighteenth-Century Culture* 27 (1998): 158.

34. *Virgil's Aeneid*, trans. Dryden, 199–200.

35. *Virgil's Aeneid*, trans. Dryden, 206. See Morton, "'Bringing *Virgil*,'" 158–60.

36. See Richard F. Thomas, *Virgil and the Augustan Reception* (Cambridge: Cambridge University Press, 2001); and Richard M. Morton, *John Dryden's Æneas: A Hero in Enlightenment Mode* (Victoria: University of Victoria Press, 2000).

37. Johnson's differentiation of Homer and Virgil is apposite here. See W. R. Johnson, *Darkness Visible: A Study of Vergil's "Aeneid"* (Berkeley: University of California Press, 1976), 47–48.

38. Like Johnson, one could speculate that Montagu would have comprehended the predicament of both Turnus and Aeneas and its difference from the closure of the *Iliad*. See Johnson, *Darkness Visible*, 114–34.

39. Charles VI is no Octavian.

40. Johnson, *Darkness Visible*, 154.

41. Johnson, *Darkness Visible*, 154.

42. Edward Wortley to Joseph Addison, Pera, 2 August 1717, *State Papers*, 97/59, National Archives, Kew. To avoid confusion I will refer to Edward Wortley Montagu as "Wortley" in the text and in subsequent notes.

43. Edward Wortley to Joseph Addison, Pera, 22 August 1717, *State Papers*, 97/59, National Archives, Kew.

44. Rae Ann Meriwether argues that these meditations on war continue well after Lady Mary's return to England and traces their vestigial presence in her periodical journalism. See Meriwether, "Transculturation and Politics," esp. 632–33.

45. Some Whigs advocated for a standing army, but the account of military corruption is not at all distant from classic Tory positions taken by Harley and Bolingbroke. Note how Montagu underlines that the failure of the sultan to regulate the law is due to distance. And how the sultan here, as the apogee of sovereign power, becomes in his very extremity the test case for sovereignty in Hobbes. Aaron Hill, in *A Full and Just Account of the Present State of the Ottoman Empire* (1709), had already described the Ottoman Empire as Leviathan: "when a Man who seriously reflects on what he sees, becomes a Witness of the numberless Attendants, Trains, and Carriages of the *Turkish* Armies, he cannot but with Wonder bless that God, who curbs in Mercy the Ambitious Arms of this prodigious Government, and has kindly plac'd a powerful Hook in the presumptuous Nostrils of their Great *Leviathan*" (28–29).

46. Here is Wortley's account of the situation:

> This Pasha's predecessor was stabb'd and cut into small Pieces by the Janissaries in the Market Place. Their chief reason was his not having agreed to their desire of plundering the German Country from whence at that time, and when I went by, they bought the greatest part of their Provisions. From his not complying with them, they argued that he was not enough enclined to carry on the War. They stab'd a Citizen in the streets while I was there for no reason but his being a Christian. Not one man was asked any question about either of these Facts, and the Pasha used no other method to hinder these disorders which differed little from a mutiny but giving them money in great quantity.

Edward Wortley to Joseph Addison, 10 April 1717, SP 97/59, National Archives, Kew. It should be noted that where Montagu diverges from her husband is in her account of the symbolic violence done to the kâdî and, by extension, to the state. As a representative of the state, Wortley remains silent on the precariousness of the law and chooses instead to focus attention on violence directed at what he perceives to be ethnic alterity. Montagu is far more interested in how the janissaries' violence undermines the state's claims to stability and order.

47. For a wide-ranging discussion of hospitality in the *Turkish Embassy Letters*, see Judith Still, "Hospitable Harems? A European Woman and Oriental Spaces in the Enlightenment," *Paragraph* 32.1 (2009): 87–104.

48. Grundy, *Lady Mary Wortley Montagu*.

49. George Sandys, *Sandys Travels, Containing an History of the Original and Present State of the Turkish Empire . . .* , 7th ed. (1615; London: Printed for John Williams Jr., 1773).

50. For Fabian's argument, see *Time and the Other*.

51. *The Twickenham Edition of the Poems of Alexander Pope*, ed. John Butt, 12 vols. (London: Methuen; New Haven, CT: Yale University Press, 1939–69), 7:14.

52. Aaron Santesso, "The Conscious Swain: Political Pastoral in Pope's Epic," *Eighteenth-Century Studies* 37.2 (2004): 264.

53. Montagu would eventually become one of Walpole's most loyal supporters, and her husband would become thoroughly anti-Walpolean. However, at the period immediately following Queen Anne's death it is difficult to place Montagu's politics.

54. Pope for his outspoken Toryism and Lady Mar for her affiliation with her Jacobite husband.

55. The most notable are his literal erasure from Achmet Beg's house in letter 25 and his conspicuous position of externality in letter 27. Montagu is quite literally removed from the

scene of hospitality and cosmopolitan exchange in the hammam by her husband's desire to see the relics of empire.

56. Santesso, "Conscious Swain," 264.

57. Not to be confused with Belgrade. Belgrade-Village was a resort outside Constantinople.

58. *Aeneid*, 6.444.

59. *The Works of Virgil: Translated into English Prose, as near the Original as the different Idioms of the Latin and English Languages will allow . . .* , vol. 2 (London: Joseph Davidson, 1754), 144.

60. For a discussion of the term *kadın*, see Leslie P. Peirce, *The Imperial Harem: Women and Sovereignty in the Ottoman Empire* (Oxford: Oxford University Press, 1993), 108.

61. *Iliad*, 24.896–980.

62. Carolyn D. Williams, *Pope, Homer, and Manliness: Some Aspects of Eighteenth-Century Classical Learning* (London: Routledge, 1993), 133–45.

63. One could argue that Pope's extensive notes constitute another site wherein he resists the text itself. By retaining a space for commentary, Pope in a sense guarantees a space of opposition to those elements of the Greek warriors' actions that he finds most disturbing.

64. By resisting an uncritical nostalgic alignment with the Greeks, Pope nevertheless activates nostalgia for a pastoral Tory idyll.

65. James Ellison, "Sandys, George (1578–1644)," in *Oxford Dictionary of National Biography* (Oxford: Oxford University Press, 2004).

66. George Sandys, *Travels*, 16.

67. Sandys, *Travels*, 17.

68. Sandys, *Travels*, 19.

69. The end of this passage exhibits an almost Wordsworthian reticence, but this is a recurrent rhetorical gesture in the Letter-book. As in her remarks on Hobbes's state of nature, Montagu does not explicitly conclude the thought, but rather forces the reader to fill in the gap in the text by attending to the subsequent example. This rhetoric of deflection and retroactive constitution parallels the way that the entire letter book deals with the trauma of the fall of Belgrade and the loss of Achmet Beg.

70. The Sigeion metope has a curious afterlife that quite literally connects the major figures in this book. Montagu was one of the first Europeans to write about it (she recorded the inscription as well); Edward Wortley Montagu removed a related object; William Pars drew the bas-relief; Richard Chandler schemed for the removal of both the stele and metope; Choiseul-Gouffier successfully negotiated with the local aga for a firman for their removal but was vigorously resisted by Sir Robert Ainslie and the local Greek population. Only when Lord Elgin backed up the firman giving him leave to take the artifacts with the threat of force was he able to quell local resistance to their removal. As Fredrik Thomasson concludes, "The Sigeion stele and the bas-relief of five female figures were the first pieces of what soon became Elgin's famous collection." Thomasson, "Justifying and Criticizing the Removals of Antiquities in Ottoman Lands: Tracking the Sigeion Inscription," *International Journal of Cultural Property* 17.3 (2010): 499.

71. Srinivas Aravamudan, in *Tropicopolitans: Colonialism and Agency, 1688–1804* (Durham, NC: Duke University Press, 1999), reads the passage as follows:

> Shocked by the fact that the classical monuments in Carthage are being used by the locals as granaries, Montagu suffers something of an ideological breakdown with respect to the women of the Maghreb. . . . In search for classical reassurance at the point she reaches Carthage, Montagu's reality cannot stand very much of humankind. In retrospect, it would be too easy to either accuse Montagu of an avoidance mechanism or overstate the case in favor of her radical brilliance by ignoring the racial ephemera. But from the vantage of her own historical moment, her travels

appear as a tentative ideological step that, for the most part, levies "positive" orientalist empiricism against the gothic extravagances more typical of eighteenth-century English orientalisms. (188)

72. The Treaty of Passarowitz of 1718 only temporarily abated war between the Ottomans and the Austrians. Future conflict would also draw in the Russians.

73. Johnson, *Darkness Visible*, 131–33.

74. For a crucial discussion of how the vulnerability that is constitutive of desire and sociability is exposed by death and translated into forms of aggression that must be resisted to prevent endless violence, see Judith Butler, *Precarious Life: The Powers of Mourning and Violence* (New York: Verso, 2004), 19–49.

Chapter 5

Note to epigraph: Richard Chandler, *Travels in Asia Minor; or, An Account of a Tour Made at the Expense of the Society of Dilettanti* (Oxford: Clarendon Press, 1775), 88. All subsequent references to this text will be presented in parentheses in the text.

1. See Aksan, *Ottoman Wars*, 88–89, 198–99.

2. Troy Bickham, *The Weight of Vengeance: The United States, the British Empire and the War of 1812* (New York: Oxford University Press, 2012), 17.

3. Douglas Fordham, *British Art and the Seven Years' War: Allegiance and Autonomy* (Philadelphia: University of Pennsylvania Press, 2010), 5. For a broad discussion of these historical and cultural developments, see also Frans De Bruyn and Shaun Regan, eds., *The Culture of the Seven Years' War: Empire, Identity, and the Arts in the Eighteenth-Century Atlantic World* (Toronto: University of Toronto Press, 2014).

4. Fordham, *British Art*, 5.

5. One could argue similarly that France's losses in the Seven Years' War had a significant impact on the events that led to its entry into the American war in 1778 and its imitation of the American Revolution in 1789. And it is against these earlier losses in America that one can comprehend the explicitly imperial aspirations that eventually overwhelmed France during the Napoleonic era.

6. Fordham, *British Art*, 5.

7. In this regard, many of my arguments in this chapter are consonant with Noah Heringman's work on "deep time" in the eighteenth century in *Sciences of Antiquity: Romantic Antiquarianism, Natural History, and Knowledge* (New York: Oxford University Press, 2013).

8. Richard Chandler, Nicholas Revett, and William Pars, *Ionian Antiquities, Published, with Permission of the Society of Dilettanti* (London: T. Spilsbury and W. Haskell, 1769), ii. All subsequent references to this publication will appear in parentheses in the text.

9. *The Antiquities of Athens* was the first major Dilettanti publication and had a profound impact on eighteenth-century theories of art and on archaeological inquiry more generally. Archaeologist and art historian Johann Joachim Winckelmann's work is heavily indebted to this publication, and it set many of the parameters for philhellenistic publications in Britain, France, and Germany.

10. Kelly, *The Society of Dilettanti*, 194. For an overview of the society's sociability and its activities, see Bruce Redford, *Dilettanti: The Antic and the Antique in Eighteenth-Century England* (Los Angeles: J. Paul Getty Museum, 2008).

11. Bruce Redford, "The Measure of Ruins: Dilettanti in the Levant, 1750–1770," *Harvard Library Bulletin* 13.1 (Summer 2002): 6. We will be looking at Choiseul-Gouffier's *Voyage pittoresque de la Gréce* and considering its relation to the Dilettanti publications in the next chapter.

12. See Kelly, *The Society of Dilettanti*, 192–205, for an account of the dissemination of information gathered on the Ionian expedition. Because Kelly offers such a thorough account of the architectural commissions arising from the expedition that aspect of Revett's work in particular will not figure prominently in this chapter.

13. See Zirwat Chowdhury, "'Imperceptible Transitions': The Anglo-Indianization of British Architecture, 1769–1822" (Ph.D. diss., Northwestern University, 2012). Chowdhury argues that the genre of topographical views of architecture was itself transformed just prior to the Ionian expedition by the work of Paul and Thomas Sandby. There was much debate as to the importance of landscape representation for establishing the aesthetic effect of architecture. Sandby was cognizant of the close proximity between this kind of landscape painting and ordnance survey. As Chowdhury states:

> After accompanying the Duke of Cumberland in his Scottish campaign from
> 1745–46, Sandby continued to work in the Duke's service thanks to his appointment
> as ranger of Windsor Great Park; he was finally appointed deputy ranger in 1764. In
> his first lecture on architecture, Sandby underscored the topographical salience of
> surveyorship, and distinguished it from architectural practice when he explained that
> surveyors made "elegant compositions [on land] for the landskip [*sic*] painter's
> imitation," whereas architects made "architectural ornaments" in the landscape. In
> both instances, he privileged the picturesque aesthetic informing the practices of
> surveying and architecture in order to suppress the military salience of both.
> Positioned at the intersections between the Board of Ordnance and the RA, Sandby
> knew all too well the military significance of designing topographically and architec-
> turally. (8)

14. The second installment was published as *Antiquities of Ionia, Published by the Society of Dilettanti, Part the Second* (London: W. Bulmer, 1797). It was broken into two volumes: the first volume rearranged the 1769 *Ionian Antiquities*, and the second added a significant amount of heretofore unseen material, including the Laodicea engraving.

15. The Paul Mellon Collection of British Art at Yale University has a number of Pars's brown-wash studies. In part because of the unreliability of measuring technology and in part because of an incipient tradition from Addison through Burke toward an aesthetics of sensation, these kinds of topographical landscapes were valorized over abstract elevations. Chowdhury, "'Imperceptible Transitions,'" states:

> Moving away from the traditional formula of plans, elevations and cross-sections,
> the RA soon began to promote the exhibition of architectural drawings in perspec-
> tive. As Sandby's own discussions of proportions and his surveying work in Scotland
> and Windsor had revealed, the perception of the dimensions of a building was
> greatly contingent on the viewing possibilities permitted by its surroundings. . . .
> Endorsing the topographical drawings that he and his brother had embraced in their
> practice, Thomas Sandby argued that perspective drawings did not merely heighten
> the visual effect of the building over a simple elevation, but could explain its
> proportions more clearly than the latter genre. Versed in the conjoined roles played
> by surveyors and architects, even though he himself spoke of their separation,
> Sandby advocated perspective drawings in an effort to bring the two practices into
> greater confluence. Furthermore, with an emphasis on spectators, rather than
> abstract geometric principles, Sandby was bringing architectural theory into an
> eighteenth-century British habitus. (14–15)

Because the composition of *Ionian Antiquities* would have predated Sandby's 1769 lectures at the Royal Academy, the topographical views and the elevations coexist in a productive dialectical relationship.

16. I am indebted to Zirwat Chowdhury for this suggestive observation.

17. In the second volume of *Antiquities of Ionia*, the site is described as follows: "In its present state it exhibits so confused a scene . . . that not a spot could be found where a view of it might be taken either satisfactory or picturesque" (32).

18. Pars may also be signaling the Ottomans' own self-understanding as the inheritors the Eastern Roman Empire—i.e., the Byzantine Empire, or Rûm. See Wigen, "Ottoman Concepts of Empire."

19. Frank Salmon, *Building on Ruins: The Rediscovery of Rome and English Architecture* (Aldershot: Ashgate, 2000), 41. See also Eileen Harris and Nicholas Savage, *British Architectural Books and Writers, 1556–1785* (Cambridge: Cambridge University Press, 1990), 49–55 and 491–95.

20. Andrew Wilton, "William Pars and His Work in Asia Minor," in Richard Chandler, *Travels in Asia Minor*, ed. Edith Clay (London: British Museum, 1971), xxiv.

21. See Frank Salmon, "Stuart as Antiquary and Archaeologist in Italy and Greece," in *James "Athenian" Stuart: The Rediscovery of Antiquity*, ed. Susan Weber Soros (New Haven, CT: Yale University Press, 2006), 102–45.

22. Kelly, *The Society of Dilettanti*, 225.

23. Kelly, *The Society of Dilettanti*, 227.

24. Kelly, *The Society of Dilettanti*, 230.

25. Quoted in Kelly, *The Society of Dilettanti*, 227.

26. Holger Hoock argues that the alignment of Britain with ancient Greece was a crucial part of British imperial fantasy in *Empires of the Imagination*, 205–71. He tracks this phenomenon in the archaeological endeavors of a slightly later period by looking specifically at the expeditions that supplied much of the British Museum's collection of antiquities.

27. The victory at Plassy in 1757 was arguably more significant in the *longue durée* of British imperial activity, but it did not have the same immediate impact on imperial ideology as Wolfe's victory at Quebec.

28. See Fordham, *British Art*, 165–72; and David Solkin, *Painting for Money: The Visual Arts and the Public Sphere in Eighteenth-Century England* (New Haven, CT: Yale University Press, 1993), 263–65.

29. See Virginia Aksan, "What Ever Happened to the Janissaries? Mobilization for the 1768–1774 Russo-Ottoman War," *War in History* 5.1 (1998): 23–36. The janissary corps was undermined by crises of payment and supply. Their supplementation by local forces known as *levend* also complicated matters of command.

30. See McGowan, "Age of the *Ayans*," 658–72, for his discussion of the escalation of violence and disorder in the provinces.

31. See Chandler, *Travels in Asia Minor*, 230 and 242–45. After first offering protection at a considerable price, the ağa at Hierapolis attempted to extort further money from the travelers. When the janissary escorting the expedition referred to the *firman* of the sultan, he was ignored and the threats escalated. The janissary "warmly urged the peril of our present situation" (243) and frantically moved them out of the region.

32. See Chowdhury, "'Imperceptible Transitions,'" for a discussion of this kind of historical erasure in the work of Paul and Thomas Sandby.

33. Like Mary Favret's plangent analysis of "wartime" in *War at a Distance: Romanticism and the Making of Modern Warfare* (Princeton, NJ: Princeton University Press, 2010), I am vitally interested in how the experience of peace's temporality is inseparable from its mediation.

34. Solkin, *Painting for Money*, 267.

35. *Lloyd's Evening Post, and British Chronicle*, 1–3 May 1769.

36. The catalog for 1769 Royal Academy exhibition lists the seven pictures by catalog number and title: no. 77, *An Arch at Mylassa, in Asia Minor*; no. 78, *A Ruin at Troas, Asia Minor*; no. 79, *The Propylia, or Entrance of the Acropolis at Athens*; no. 80, *The Castalian Spring at Delphi*; no. 81, *A Temple in the Island Aegina*; no. 82, *The Cave of Archidamus, near Athens*; no. 83, *Miletus, with the Ferry over the Meander* (10). In my ensuing discussion I refer to the titles used by the British Museum Prints and Drawings department, where Pars's paintings from the Ionian expedition are preserved.

37. Greg Smith, "Watercolourists and Watercolours at the Royal Academy, 1780–1836," in *Art on the Line: The Royal Academy Exhibitions at Somerset House, 1780–1836*, ed. David Solkin (New Haven, CT: Yale University Press, 2001), 194. The line, which came to dominate the curatorial logic of the Royal Academy shows at Somerset House, was also at play in the Pall Mall show. Pars's pictures would have been spatially marginalized by the larger works in oils. History painting and grand manner portraiture were the focal point of the exhibition. After 1780, when the Royal Academy moved to Somerset House, the exhibition space was divided into three: the Great Room and Anteroom upstairs and the Exhibition Room of Sculpture and Drawings on the ground floor. This was widely interpreted as a hierarchical division with drawing, architectural design, and sculpture literally subordinated to the paintings upstairs.

38. See Nicholas Savage, "Exhibiting Architecture: Strategies of Representation in English Architectural Exhibition Drawings, 1760–1836," in Solkin, *Art on the Line*, 201–16. As Savage states, there was much uncertainty about how best to present and exhibit architectural design.

39. This fluttering between Greece and Rome is reminiscent of Montagu's tendency to overlay the Homeric landscape of Asia Minor with allusions to Roman structures and literature that we discussed in Chapter 4. One could also read this overlay as participating in the ongoing debate regarding whether Greece or Rome was more aesthetically preeminent. As Kelly argues, this was a key backdrop to Stuart and Revett's argument for the importance of ancient Greek models in *The Antiquities of Athens*. See Kelly, *Society of Dilettanti*, 162–66.

40. According to the catalog for the Royal Collection, http://www.royalcollection.org.uk /collection/405416/the-departure-of-regulus:

> This is one of three pairs of neo-classical history paintings, painted between 1769 and 1773, commissioned by George III to hang in his "Warm Room" (a private sitting room) at Buckingham Palace (OM 1152-7, 405416-7, 405683-4 and 407524-5), along with one modern scene, the *Death of Wolfe* (OM 1167, 407297). This one pairs off with the *Oath of Hannibal* (OM 1153, 405417) of 1770. The first commission was placed in February 1768 when West showed the King his picture of Agrippina with the ashes of Germanicus which he had just completed for Robert Hay Drummond, Archbishop of York. The King commented upon the rarity of the subject and proposed "another noble Roman subject . . . I mean the final departure of Regulus from Rome"; he then commenced to read Livy's account of the story to the artist. Regulus, the Roman consul and general, was taken prisoner by the Carthaginians in 255 BC. He was sent back to Rome to discuss peace terms and an exchange of prisoners. However, Regulus distrusted the peace negotiations and insisted on returning to certain torture and death in Carthage. West's painting is set within a neo-classical composition that reflects—amongst other things—the Raphael Cartoons in the King's collection, which West greatly admired. From 1763 to 1787 the Cartoons hung in the Saloon at Buckingham House where West—and other artists—could have seen them.

After first defeating the Carthaginians both at sea and on land, Attilius Regulus was taken prisoner by Xanthippus, a Ladedaemonian general. According to Livy, "Regulus being sent by the Carthaginians to Rome to treat for peace, and an exchange of prisoners, binds himself by oath to return if these objects be not attained; dissuades the senate from agreeing to the propositions: and then, in observance of his oath, returning to Carthage, is put to death by torture." Book 18, in *The History of Rome: Books Nine to Twenty-Six, by Titus Livius*, trans. and notes by D. Spillan and Cyrus Edmonds (1849)

41. Solkin, *Painting for Money*, 268–69.

42. Wilkite activism argued for a broader franchise and for an increased role for the press in scrutinizing parliamentary affairs. For a useful summary of Wilkes's career, see John Sainsbury, *John Wilkes: The Lives of a Libertine* (New York: Routledge, 2006).

43. See John Barrell, *The Political Theory of Painting from Reynolds to Hazlitt* (London: Yale University Press, 1986), 69–162, for the canonical account of Reynolds's role in politicization of history painting and the Royal Academy's mission.

44. Solkin, *Painting for Money*, 273.

45. See Holger Hoock, *The King's Artists: The Royal Academy of Arts and the Politics of British Culture, 1760–1840* (Oxford: Oxford University Press, 2003), 150–64, and for extended discussion of the Royal Academy's place in the formation of British national fantasy and the politicization of art during the era leading up to and including the American War. See also Hoock, *Empires of the Imagination*, 39–82.

46. Empirical accuracy is not an immutable fact. As we will see in the next chapter, Choiseul-Gouffier's representation of the same artifact in plate 90 of the *Voyage pittoresque de la Grèce* looks nothing like Pars's version.

47. See Jules David Prown, "Benjamin West and the Use of Antiquity," *American Art* 10.2 (Summer 1996): 28–49; and Alexander Nemerov, "The Ashes of Germanicus and the Skin of Painting: Sublimation and Money in Benjamin West's *Agrippa*," *Yale Journal of Criticism* 11.1 (1998): 11–27.

48. Pars would hardly be alone here. Iain McDaniel's *Adam Ferguson in the Scottish Enlightenment* (Cambridge, MA: Harvard University Press, 2013) recognizes that Ferguson's analysis of the power struggle between civil and military authority in the *Essay on the History of Civil Society* of 1767 was staged with the Seven Years' War very much in mind, but he argues that Ferguson's historical analysis generated a deeply pessimistic view of the future of commercial society:

> Against Smith's positive vision of wealth's compatibility with liberty, or Robertson's picture of a balance of power among modern commercial monarchies, Ferguson outlined a nightmarish scenario in which Europe would come to be dominated by wealthy but despotically governed machine-states, whose future would resemble that of imperial Rome or, alternatively, China. . . . The result was a major rival to the more prominent histories of civilization usually associated with Hume, Robertson, or Smith, and a much-diminished confidence in the capacity of modern constitutional or civilized states to avoid the consequences of empire, revolution, and despotism that had destroyed the states of antiquity. (8)

For Ferguson the Roman example was crucial. McDaniel powerfully shows how Ferguson's readings of the transition from the republic to the principate undergird his critical understanding of the future of Britain's commercial empire and his sense that Britain would essentially rehearse the Roman descent into military rule and despotism.

49. Preface to *Ionian Antiquities*, ii.

50. This tension is mirrored by a public conflict between Sandby and Chambers at the Royal Academy regarding the representation of architecture.

51. Redford makes a similar point in "The Measure of Ruins" by referring to Lawrence Lipking's notion of "the ordering of the arts" (6).

52. Redford, "The Measure of Ruins," 6.

53. As Redford argues in "The Measure of Ruins," Revett, who oversaw the etching, engraving, and printing of Pars's watercolors for *Ionian Antiquities*, used every technique available to ensure that "the plate does justice to the precision of Pars's original—witness the etched passages that capture the effect of watercolor wash as a means of rendering the condition of stone" (30).

54. Significantly, these Turkish figures were removed, at great expense, when *Ionian Antiquities* was republished as the first volume of *The Antiquities of Ionia* in 1821. The Society of Dilettanti must have found the presence of the stonecutters disruptive enough to commission new engravings based on Pars's design.

55. This sense that the Ottomans were actively destroying antiquities can be traced all the way back to the earliest accounts of Constantinople. See Amanda Wunder, "Western Travellers, Eastern Antiquities, and the Image of the Turk in Early Modern Europe," *Journal of Early Modern History* 7.1–2 (2003): 89–119.

56. See Heringman, *Sciences of Antiquity*, 77–144.

57. Redford, "The Measure of Ruins," 30.

58. See Kelly's rather different analysis of this reconstruction in *The Society of Dilettanti*, 189–90.

59. Redford is right to stress the "culture of measurement" in Revett's plates to the antipicturesque strategy of the Society of Dilettanti folio. As he states, this fetishization of precision led Harris and Savage in *British Architectural Books and Writers* to conclude that the *Ionian Antiquities* was "not inspiring," and that is worth considering for reasons other than those stated by Redford in "The Measure of Ruins," 31. The assumption that these works should be inspiring is itself part of a larger ideological formation linking Britain to ancient Greece. What I am hoping to capture here is the moment where that linkage feels both forced and tenuous; and that requires looking beyond Revett's work to that of Pars.

60. See Salmon, *Building on Ruins*, 43–52, for a related discussion of the place of imagination in reconstituting the past.

61. See Redford, "The Measure of Ruins," 12–13, for a detailed discussion of the etching and engraving techniques characteristic of Dilettanti folio.

62. It is important to recognize that the Society of Dilettanti decided that the key response to this desire was to commission engravings for an explicitly reproducible medium.

63. See Fordham, *British Art*, 22.

64. For overviews of the cooperation between Britain and Russia in the Russo-Ottoman War of 1768–74, see M. S. Anderson's "Great Britain and the Russo-Turkish War of 1768–74," *English Historical Review* 69.270 (January 1954): 39–58; and his more specific discussion of naval affairs in "Great Britain and the Russian Fleet, 1769–1770," *Slavonic and East European Review* 31.76 (December 1952): 148–63.

65. *An Authentic Narrative of the Russian Expedition Against the Turks by Sea and Land . . . by an Officer on board the Russian Fleet* (London: S. Hooper, 1772), 8–9. All subsequent references to this text will be presented parenthetically in the text.

66. For a detailed discussion of the war, see Virginia Aksan, *Ottoman Wars*, 138–56; and Aksan, "The One-Eyed Fighting the Blind: Mobilization, Supply, and Command in the Russo-Turkish War of 1768–1774," *International History Review* 15.2 (May 1993): 221–38.

67. Jonathan Grant argues that "Russian victories over the Turks beginning the 1770s should be attributed less to Russian technological superiority than to tactical innovation, since the wonder weapon turned out to be the bayonet." See Grant, "Rethinking the Ottoman 'Decline': Military Technology Diffusion in the Ottoman Empire, Fifteenth to Eighteenth Centuries," *Journal of World History* 10.1 (Spring 1999): 199. For an even more pointed and specific critique of the decline thesis and the Russian wars, see Virginia Aksan, "Breaking the Spell of the Baron de Tott: Reframing the Question of Military Reform in the Ottoman Empire, 1760–1830," *International History Review* 24.2 (June 2002): 243–77.

68. Chios.

69. The narrator's rhetorical gestures here are comparable to West's representation of the mob in the *Departure of Regulus from Rome*.

70. Scipio's clemency is a chief example in Machiavelli's *The Prince*, chap. 17. As Redford argues, Wood's preface to *Ionian Antiquities* explicitly argues that the Society of Dilettanti promotes *virtù* ("The Measure of Ruins," 5). See J. G. A Pocock, *The Machiavellian Moment: Florentine Political Thought and the Atlantic Republican Tradition* (Princeton, NJ: Princeton University Press, 1975), 462–552; and J. G. A. Pocock, ed., with the assistance of Gordon J. Schochet and Lois G. Schwoerer, *The Varieties of British Political Thought, 1500–1800* (Cambridge: Cambridge University Press, 1993), 211–319, for the canonical discussion of the place of virtue in the British political tradition prior to and following the American war.

71. For thorough discussions of the differential outcomes of the Russo-Ottoman War of 1768–74, see Aksan, *An Ottoman Statesman*, 100–169.

72. See Faroqhi, *Ottoman Empire*, 31, regarding the "disastrous" peace Treaty of Küçük Kaynarca; and Aksan, *Ottoman Wars*, 155–60.

73. See Redford, "The Measure of Ruins," for the importance of lighting to the Dilettanti folio.

74. Some images were engraved in 1780.

75. Joan Coutu, *Then and Now: Collecting and Classicism in Eighteenth-Century England* (Montreal: McGill Queen's University Press, 2015), 216.

76. This engraving from *Ionian Antiquities*, with notes by Pars, is pasted into a bound drawing book owned by William Ottley and now preserved in the British Museum. On the same page are ink drawings by Pars of the Achilles sarcophagus. The same sarcophagus that fascinated Luigi Mayer twenty years later and about which I have a great deal to say in Chapter 7.

77. See Thomasson, "Justifying and Criticizing the Removals," 493–517. As he states, Pars produced a drawing of the metope in 1764, and Chandler was working on a strategy for the removal of the bas-relief and the famous Sigeion inscription that Lady Mary also discusses in the letter book (see *Travels*, 146–47). As noted in Chapter 4, n. 70, these two objects tie together almost every major figure in this book: Lady Mary wrote about them, Pars drew them, Chandler schemed for their removal, Choiseul-Gouffier successfully negotiated with the local ağa for a *firman* for their removal but was vigorously resisted by Sir Robert Ainslie and the local Greek population. Only when Lord Elgin backed up the *firman* giving him leave to take the artifacts with the threat of force was he able quell local resistance to their removal. As Thomasson concludes, "The Sigeion stele and the bas-relief of five female figures were the first pieces of what soon became Elgin's famous collection" (499).

Chapter 6

Note to epigraph: Lord Byron, *The Complete Poetical Works*, ed. Jerome J. McGann (Oxford: Clarendon, 1980–93), 2:202. Byron is echoing the "Discours préliminaire" from Choiseul-Gouffier's *Voyage pittoresque de la Grèce*.

1. I am invoking Frédéric Barbier's *La rêve grec de Monsieur de Choiseul: Les voyages d'un européen des Lumières* (Paris: Armand Colin, 2010) no less than Lady Craven's dreamy engagement with ancient Greek sculpture in the Uffizi in her *Journey Through the Crimea to Constantinople* (London: G. G. J. and J. Robinson, 1789).

2. J. S. Pritchard, "Chabert de Cogolin, Joseph-Bernard de, Marquis de Chabert," in *Dictionary of Canadian Biography*, vol. 5, *1801 to 1820* (Toronto: University of Toronto Press, 1983), 175–76.

3. See Barbier, *La rêve grec*, 57, for the orders. See also Léonce Pingaud, *Choiseul-Gouffier: La France en Orient sous Louis VI* (Paris: Alphonse Picard, 1887), for an early account of Choiseul-Gouffier's career.

4. See Barbier, *La rêve grec*, 35–60, for Choiseul-Gouffier's intellectual development and for an account of his commitment to enlightened sociability.

5. Quoted in Barbier, *La rêve grec*, 57.

6. Odile Cavalier's catalog to the Musée Calvet d'Avignon's exhibition *Le voyage en Grèce du comte de Choiseul-Gouffier* (Paris: Editions A. Barthélmy, 2007) provides separate essays on the contributions of each member of the expedition. Pierre Pinon's discussion of Foucherot's contributions is especially illuminating (41–45). The catalog also has useful summaries of the work of other figures in Choiseul-Gouffier's circle—notably Louis-François Cassas and Louis-François-Sebastien Fauvel. Jean-Baptiste Hilaire's name is frequently rendered as J. B. Hilair in the engravings.

7. See Barbier, *La rêve grec*, 119–40, for his excellent account of the book's compilation and production.

8. *Bibliothèque des sciences et des beaux-arts* 48.2 (1778): 491–92; quoted in Barbier, *La rêve grec*, 141. Thanks to Julie Alusse for her help with the translation here.

9. Elisabeth A. Fraser, in "Books, Prints, and Travel: Reading in the Gaps of the Orientalist Archive," *Art History* 31.3 (June 2008): 342–67, argues that despite the book's simulation of Choiseul-Gouffier's itinerary it is possible to resist the book's Orientalist imperative by attending to gaps in the text. In other words, the strong push to take the reader on a journey is interrupted by the book's conditions of production and its multiple discursive and visual modes.

10. See Palmira Brummett's discussion of Choiseul-Gouffier's maps in *Mapping the Ottomans*, 308 and 325–26.

11. See Sarga Moussa, "Le débat entre philhéllènes et mishéllènes chez les voyageurs français de la fin du XVIIIe siècle au début du XIXe siècle," in *Revue de Littérature Comparée* 68.4 (1994): 418.

12. This is especially notable when the *livraisons* are compiled into a whole text. As Barbier discusses in some detail, the *livraisons* were published separately and each *livraison* was reviewed separately. When the twelfth installment was published in 1783 subscribers would then be able to bind the entire collection into a whole. See Barbier, *La rêve grec*, 124–30 and 140–44.

13. Marie-Gabriel-Florent-Auguste de Choiseul-Gouffier, *Voyage pittoresque de la Grèce* (Paris: 1782), plates 47 and 48. All subsequent references to this book will be recorded in the body of the text; Choiseul-Gouffier's prose will be cited by page number and the plates will be given by number and title. I am endebted to Julie Alusse for her assistance with the translations of Choiseul-Gouffier's text.

14. Choiseul-Gouffier was the author of an important dissertation on Homer, so he is essentially credentializing himself here.

15. These are plates 3, 9, 12, 17, 24/25, 26/27, 34, 48, and 58.

16. Greek island now known as Ios.

17. The debts to Rousseau are manifest.

18. Sarga Moussa makes a similar argument regarding the deployment of reproductive sexuality in *Voyage pittoresque*. See 418–20.

19. David Roessel, *In Byron's Shadow: Modern Greece in the English and American Imagination* (Oxford: Oxford University Press, 2001), 59–68.

20. The "Explication" is on an unnumbered page immediately following the frontispiece illustration.

21. A military historian, Hanson is a Senior Fellow at the Hoover Institute and a strong advocate for the "war on terror." This passage is from his private papers, published online. See

Victor Davis Hanson, "History and the Movie '300,'" (2006), private papers, posted on carnageandculture.blogspot.com/2007/03/victor-davis-hanson-history-and-movie.html. For a lively denunciation of this reductive account of Greek history, see Thomas E. Jenkins, *Antiquity Now: The Classical World in the Contemporary American Imagination* (Cambridge: Cambridge University Press, 2015), 110–20.

22. There is much debate over the implications of this distinction. John Ruskin, for instance, argues that immovable laws are less germane that situational orders:

> Also obedience in its highest form is not obedience to a constant and compulsory law, but a persuaded or voluntary yielded obedience to an issued command. . . . His name who leads the armies of Heaven is "Faithful and true" . . . and all deeds which are done in alliance with these armies . . . are essentially deeds of faith, which therefore . . . is at once the source and the substance of all known deed, rightly so called.
>
> . . . As set forth in the last word of the noblest group of words ever, so far as I know, uttered by simple man concerning his practice, being the final testimony of the leaders of a great practical nation.

See *The Complete Works of John Ruskin*, vol. 24, *Modern Painters: Volume the Fifth* (New York: Bryan, Taylor, 1894), 211–12.

23. See Barbier, *La rêve grec*, 132, for a discussion of the importance of this phrase.

24. Plates 112 and 113.

25. Ovid, *Metamorphses*, 9.663–65:

> Sic lacrimis consumpta suis Phoebeia Byblis
> Vertitur in fontem, qui nunc quoque vallibus illis
> Nomen habet dominae, nigraque sub ilice manat.

26. The title "ağa" can apply to either a civil or military leader in the Ottoman Empire. Choiseul-Gouffier is referring to Hasan Çavuşoğlu.

27. Hasan.

28. See Marianne Hamiaux, "Les marbres de la collection Choiseul-Gouffier au musée du Louvre," in Cavalier, *Voyage en Grèce*, 95–107, for a discussion of Choiseul-Gouffier's appropriation of marble inscriptions, reliefs, and statuary. Many of these objects are now in the Louvre, including a separate cache of materials in the Petite Malmaison. See Christiane Pinatel, "Les plâtres de la collection Choiseul-Gouffier à la Malmaison," in Cavalier, *Voyage en Grèce*, 109–19.

29. Catherine the Great was sensitive to Choiseul-Gouffier's subtle critique of the Russians. See Barbier, *La rêve grec*, 153–67, for a careful assessment of the book's political impact.

30. Brummett, *Mapping the Ottomans*, 325–26.

31. Barbier, *La rêve grec*, 56, suggests that the warship in this section of the engraving is *L'Atalante*. It is difficult to decisively identify the ship's colors, but if this is the case then the temporal involutions of this engraving are that much more unusual. In the argument that ensues, I contend that this engraving constitutes a form of wishful thinking—i.e., that the destruction of the Ottoman fleet continues indefinitely. If this is a representation of Chabert's ship, then the image also constitutes a retroactive desire to be present at the Battle of Çeşme.

32. Horace Walpole, *The Yale Edition of Horace Walpole's Correspondence*, ed. W. S. Lewis, 48 vols. (New Haven, CT: Yale University Press, 1937–83), 25:632–33.

33. For a thorough discussion of the Roxolana narrative in Knolles, see Ballaster, *Fabulous Orients*, 59–70.

34. Laura Brown, *Ends of Empire: Women and Ideology in Early Eighteenth-Century English Literature* (Ithaca, NY: Cornell University Press, 1993), 146–57.

35. See *Town and Country Magazine* 5 (1773): 246.

36. Lady Elizabeth Craven, *A Journey Through the Crimea to Constantinople* (London: G. G. J. and J. Robinson, 1789), [iv–v]. All subsequent references to Craven's book will be given parenthetically in the text.

37. Katherine S. H. Turner, "Elizabeth [née Lady Elizabeth Berkeley], Margravine of Brandenburg-Ansbach-Bayreuth . . . ," in *Oxford Dictionary of National Biography*.

38. *Gentleman's Magazine*, March 1789, vol. 59, part 1, p. 237.

39. See Daniel O'Quinn, *Entertaining Crisis in the Atlantic Imperium, 1770–1790* (Baltimore: Johns Hopkins University Press, 2011).

40. For a thorough discussion of Cassas's bibliophile publications, see Elisabeth A. Fraser, *Mediterranean Encounters: Artists Between Europe and the Ottoman Empire, 1774–1839* (University Park: Pennsylvania State University Press, 2017), 47–94.

41. See Viccy Coltman, *Fabricating the Antique: Neoclassicism in Britain, 1760–1800* (Chicago: University of Chicago Press, 2006); see also Coutu, *Then and Now*. Another class dynamic is at play here as well. The British ambassador Robert Ainslie was from a merchant-class family, and thus Craven may well have been avoiding him on the grounds of rank. Ainslie's own classicism would have been perceived as aspirational.

42. Jeremy Black, *British Foreign Policy in an Age of Revolutions, 1783–1793* (Cambridge: Cambridge University Press, 1994), 49–50.

43. Black, *British Foreign Policy*, 51.

44. Larry Wolff, *Inventing Eastern Europe: The Map of Civilization on the Mind of the Enlightenment* (Stanford, CA: Stanford University Press, 1994), 123.

45. Readers interested in the politics of the region would have had to turn to Baron François de Tott's *Memoirs of Baron de Tott: Containing the state of the Turkish Empire and the Crimea, during the late war with Russia; With numerous anecdotes . . .* (London, 1785); or William Coxe's *Travels into Poland, Russia, Sweden, and Denmark: Interspersed with historical relations and political inquiries . . .* (London, 1790).

46. *Analytical Review* 3 (1789): 177–78.

47. Walpole, *Correspondence*, 34:36–37.

48. See William Cowper, *The Letters and Prose Writings of William Cowper*, ed. James King and Charles Ryskamp (Oxford: Clarendon, 1984), 1:555–56.

49. See J. R. Hale, "Art and Audience: The *Medici Venus* c. 1750–c. 1850," *Italian Studies* 31 (1976): 37–58, for related English responses to the Venus de' Medici.

50. Craven's subtle negotiation with the problem of virtue and pleasure resonates with John Barrell's analysis of how the Venus confounded notions of masculine public virtue in the period. See John Barrell, *The Birth of Pandora and the Division of Knowledge* (Philadelphia: University of Pennsylvania Press, 1992), 63–87.

51. There are numerous accounts of viewers holding and caressing the statue.

52. Katherine S. H. Turner, "From Classical to Imperial: Changing Visions of Turkey in the Eighteenth Century," in *Travel Writing and Empire: Postcolonial Theory in Transit*, ed. Steve Clark (London: Zed Books, 1999), 119.

53. Walpole, *Correspondence*, 42:183–84.

54. See Turner, "From Classical to Imperial," for a detailed reading of the relationship between Montagu's and Craven's texts.

55. See Robert Jones, *Literature, Gender and Politics in Britain During the War for America, 1770–1785* (Cambridge: Cambridge University Press, 2010); Hoock, *Empires of the Imagination*, 39–130; Martin Myrone, *Body Building: Reforming Masculinities in British Art, 1750–1810* (New Haven, CT: Yale University Press, 2005), 193–251; and O'Quinn, *Entertaining Crisis*.

56. *Critical Review* 67 (1789): 282.

57. Walpole, *Correspondence*, 34:36–37.

58. Walpole, *Correspondence*, 42:181–84.

59. See Feliz Turhan, *The Other Empire: British Romantic Writings About the Ottoman Empire* (New York: Routledge, 2003), 43.

60. Charles Pigott, *The Jockey Club; or, A Sketch of the Manners of the Age, Part the Third*, 2nd ed. (London, 1792), 159–60.

61. The implication, of course, is that the openness of Ottoman society to male same-sex practices was a result Ottoman women's lack of physical attractions.

Chapter 7

1. Fraser, *Mediterranean Encounters*, 5.

2. See Carter V. Findley, "Mouradgea d'Ohsson (1740–1807): Liminality and Cosmopolitanism in the Author of the *Tableau général de l'Empire othoman*," *Turkish Studies Association Bulletin* 22.1 (Spring 1998): 33–34, for a discussion of the political reception of Mouradgea d'Ohsson's text in France.

3. On the complex link between theories of despotism and French diplomatic policy, see Thomas Kaiser, "The Evil Empire? The Debate on Turkish Despotism in Eighteenth-Century French Political Culture," *Journal of Modern History* 72 (March 2000): 6–34.

4. Roderick Beaton, in *Byron's War: Romantic Rebellion, Greek Revolution* (Cambridge: Cambridge University Press, 2013), 34–37, cannily reads Byron's deployment of the vampire myth in *The Giaour* as an apt allegory for Byron's understanding of Greece's undead state in that poem. He doesn't make the connection to Choiseul-Gouffier, but I will be elaborating on this argument in the Chapter 8.

5. For detailed discussions of the composition of *Tableau général* and of d'Ohsson's career more generally, see Carter V. Findley, "Writer and Subject, Self and Other: Mouradgea D'Ohsson and His *Tableau général de L'empire Othoman*," in Sture Theolin et al., *The Torch of Empire: Ignatius Mouradgea d'Ohsson and the Tableau Général of the Ottoman Empire in the Eighteenth Century* (Istanbul: Yapi Kredi Yayinlari, 2002); and Findley, "Mouradgea D'Ohsson (1740–1807)," respectively.

6. For a discussion of d'Ohsson's contemporary sources in Constantinople, see Fraser, *Mediterranean Encounters*, 113–17; and Findley, "Writer and Subject." Günsel Renda has written extensively about d'Ohsson's principal source in the Ottoman court in "Illustrating the *Tableau général de l'Empire Othoman*," in Theolin et al., *Torch of Empire*; and in "Ressam Konstantin Kapidagli Hakkinda Yeni Görüsler," in *19. Yüzyıl İstanbul'unda Sanat Ortamı*, (Istanbul: Sanat Tarihi Dernegi, 1996), 139–62. Kapidagli was a painter in the court of Selim III, and he is almost certainly the source for d'Ohsson's double-sized plate of Mecca, although the French remediation of the Ottoman image produces an extraordinarily hybrid image. As Fraser notes, d'Ohsson also discusses these sources in the prospectus, in the "Preliminary Discourse," and in the course of the second volume.

7. I am diverging from Jay David Bolter and Richard Grusin's resistance to the linearity of Hegelian sublation in their discussion of media convergence in *Remediation: Understanding New Media* (Cambridge, MA: MIT Press, 1999), 55. My sense is that it is because the newer formation is still "in its becoming" that the remediation of the older Ottoman materials is so compelling.

8. Fraser, *Mediterranean Encounters*, 117–23.

9. Fraser, *Mediterranean Encounters*, 113. See Madeleine Dobie, "Translation in the Contact Zone: Antoine Galland's *Mille et une nuits: Contes arabes*," in *"The Arabian Nights" in Historical*

Context: Between East and West, ed. Saree Makdisi and Felicity Nussbaum (New York: Oxford University Press, 2008), 25–50.

10. Fraser, *Mediterranean Encounters*, 107–9.

11. See Walter Benjamin, "The Work of Art in the Age of Its Technological Reproducibility," in *The Work of Art in the Age of Its Technological Reproducibility and Other Writings on Media*, ed. Michael W. Jennings, Brigid Doherty, and Thomas Y. Levin (Cambridge, MA: Harvard University Press, 2008), 19–55. In both d'Ohsson's remediation of Ottoman painting and Ainslie and Mayer's remediation of Mayer's watercolors we are confronted with the uncertain politics of investing in auratic art at this moment. As we will see, in our reading of Mayer, engraving reveals both the political potential and the political constraints placed on the art object. I think a similar argument applies to d'Ohsson's remediations.

12. This is one way of thinking about the French dissemination of military technology in this period. De Tott and others come with technology and advice from afar and are frequently frustrated that the Ottomans are not yet ready to employ these innovations.

13. I am invoking Foucault's sense of comprehending Enlightenment to avoid its legacy that he articulates in "What Is Enlightenment?" in *The Foucault Reader*, ed. Paul Rabinow (New York: Pantheon, 1984), 32–50.

14. Barbier, *La rêve grec*, 159–61.

15. Barbier, *La rêve grec*, 157–58, provides a useful summary of Choiseul-Gouffier's redaction of Christian resistance to Ottoman rule and emphasizes the degree to which it conforms to the Enlightenment thought of philosophes like Talleyrand.

16. See Barbier, *La rêve grec*, for its reception among the philosophes.

17. See Barbier, *La rêve grec*, 162–67, for a discussion of the three versions.

18. For an introduction to Choiseul-Gouffier's diplomatic career, see Virginia Aksan, "Choiseul-Gouffier at the Porte, 1784–1792," *Studies in Ottoman Diplomatic History* 4 (1990): 17–34.

19. Abbé Guillaume Martin, *Voyage à Constantinople fait à l'occasion de L'ambassade de M. le cte de Choiseul-Gouffier à la Porte Ottoman, par un ancient aumônier de la marine royale . . . ,* (Paris: François et Louis Janet, 1819). Cited in Barbier, *La rêve grec*, 182.

20. There is some evidence that Ainslie also had espionage experience prior to his appointment to the Sublime Porte.

21. On this point, see Kaiser, "The Evil Empire," 25–29.

22. *St. James Chronicle* (London), 9 December 1790.

23. Ainslie sent a circular dispatch to all of the ambassadors in Pera on 8 April 1789 that opened as follows:

> I avail of the earliest opportunity to acquint you, tht on Monday 6th instant between nine and ten o'clock in the evening, Sultan Abdul Hamid was taken ill with an apoplectic stroke, which baffled every effort of physic and carried off that Monarch at half past six o'clock yesterday morning in the sixty-eighth year of his age and the sixteenth year of his Reign. The Grandees assembled for the occasion in the Serglio paid homage at eight o'clock to Sultan Selim the Third, heir to the throne, born in ? where accession was published in the Palace, and announced to the Public by the Cannon of the Seraglio. The remains of the deceased sovereign were interred at twelve the same morning. He left only four children, two princes and two Princesses, and I am told none of the Sultanas are pregnant. Sultan Selim is possessed of a manly person with a hale-robust-constitution. His genius is accounted superior to the common run, and the Publick and been long impressed with every favourable ideas of the qualifications and disposition of this Prince. It is impossible to say what effects this revolution may produce in the Polticks of the Porte, and in the situation

of its Ministers, but I am apt to think this change in the Ottoman Throne will influence in prosecuting the war with unusual vigour, *in order to try the fortune of the new Sovereign*, and in that case if he is well advised, he will be particularly cautious of making changes which might discourage his subjects and alarm the Friends of this Empire, who have contracted engagements with the present set of Ministers. Be that as it will the first order issued by the new Sultan was to prosecute the warlike preparations by Sea and Land *with if possible additional zeal and vigour*, and the Captain Pashaw has already received particular marks of his approbation.

National Archives (UK), Kew, FO 261/1, letter book, Sir Robert Ainslie to Secretary of State (FO 261/1.

24. See Aksan, *Ottoman Wars*, 129–79; quote at 130.

25. Aksan, *Ottoman Wars*, 147–54.

26. Aksan, *Ottoman Wars*, 136.

27. See Aksan, *Ottoman Wars*, 265–66.

28. Jeremy Black has taken up the issue of Ainslie's culpability in the progress of the Ottomans toward an ill-advised war in his essay "Sir Robert Ainslie: His Majesty's Agent-Provocateur? British Foreign Policy and the International Crisis of 1787," *European History Quarterly* 14.3 (1984): 253–83. He argues that Ainslie may have privately influenced the grand vizier, but there is nothing in the official record to suggest this.

29. Sir Robert Ainslie to Keith, 16 August 1787, BL Add 35539, emphasis Ainslie's; cited in Black, "Sir Robert Ainslie," 274.

30. See Black, "Sir Robert Ainslie," 258–64, for his discussion of the complex diplomatic strategy linking British resistance to French policy in the United Provinces to Austrian policy in the Balkans. Black makes a compelling argument that a war involving Austria on its eastern borders would serve British interests in Dutch civil war. However, such a unified global strategy seems to go against other assertions that Ainslie was relatively isolated from the British foreign secretary, the Marquis of Carmarthen (his ministerial overseer).

31. Ainslie to Carmarthen, 24 November 1787, PRO FO 78/8 f.251.

32. See *Views in Egypt, from the original drawings in possession of Sir Robert Ainslie, taken during his embassy to Constantinople by Luigi Mayer; Engraved by and under the direction of Thomas Milton; with historical observations and incidental illustrations of the manners and customs of the natives of that country*, elephant folio (London, 1801); *Views in the Ottoman Empire, chiefly in Caramania . . .* (London, 1803); and *Views in Palestine . . .* (London, 1803–4).

33. The left background shows a tourney of sorts—cavalry playing with the *djerit*—that would have been recognizable to readers of Choiseul-Gouffier. A full-size engraving based on a design by Hilaire, plate 76 in *Voyage pittoresque*, shows precisely this martial game.

34. See Domenico Sestini, *Lettere e dissertazioni numismatiche sopra alcune medaglie rare della Collezione Ainslieana*, 4 vols. (Leghorn: Masi, 1789–90). Sestini's studies of the Ainslie collection were supplemented by subsequent volumes and treatises.

35. The volcano pictures are clearly designed with a book project in mind. Three of the drawings made their way into *Views in the Ottoman Dominions, in Europe, in Asia, and Some of the Mediterranean Islands, from the Original Drawings Taken for Sir Robert Ainslie, by Luigi Mayer* (London: Printed by T. Bensley, for R. Bowyer, 1810). Aside from views of specific volcanic formations, Mayer also records "volcano culture" by showing how volcanic rock is incorporated into local architecture and how the largely Catholic population of the Greek and Italian Mediterranean address the eruptions in rituals.

36. We know that Ainslie did not accompany Mayer for the entire trip because there is a continuous correspondence between the embassy and London throughout the summer of 1788. See FO 7 8/9.

37. This is particularly true of the views of Samos.

38. Homer, *The Iliad*, trans. Alexander Pope, ed. Reuben A. Brower and W. H. Bond (New York: Macmillan, 1965), 24.906–19.

39. Mayer does not represent the fourth fragment of the sarcophagus.

40. See D. S. Neff,'s "Bitches, Mollies, and Tommies: Byron, Masculinity, and the History of Sexualities," *Journal of the History of Sexuality* 11.3 (July 2002): 395–438, for an invaluable overview of the sexual dispositions of the late eighteenth and early nineteenth century. Neff discusses the term "homophilic" in note 2, and, like him, I am employing it to maintain a distinction between historical practices and the advent of "homosexuality" as a category in the late nineteenth century. The key point here is that homophilic desire, as explored in Mayer's drawing, has a *heterodox* relation to normative gender and sexual codes in the period.

41. The erasure of the link between Ottoman and British viewer here has an interesting parallel to the "hidden" terms of the Treaty of the Dardanelles negotiated by Robert Adair in 1809. It contained "separate and secret articles" that dealt primarily with France and Russia. Britain pledged to support the Ottomans should France declare war on them, including sending a fleet to the Mediterranean for that purpose. Britain also agreed to provide military supplies if France threatened the Ottomans short of declaring war. Regarding Russia, Britain offered to help secure a peace with Russia should this be possible before the Ottomans were able to end their war.

Chapter 8

1. As noted earlier, the implication is that the openness of Ottoman society to male same-sex practices was a result of Ottoman women's lack of physical attractions.

2. See John Cam Hobhouse, *A Journey Through Albania, and Other Provinces of the Turkey in Europe and Asia, to Constantinople, During the Years 1809 and 1810* (London: J. Cawthorn, 1813), 2:863.

3. *The Giaour* is a crucial text for Saree Makdisi's recent theorization of Occidentalism in *Making England Western: Occidentalism, Race, and Imperial Culture* (Chicago: University of Chicago Press, 2015); and for the discussion of Orientalism in Nigel Leask, *English Romantic Writers and the East: Anxieties of Empire* (Cambridge: Cambridge University Press, 1992); and Peter Cochran, *Byron and Orientalism* (Newcastle: Cambridge Scholars Press, 2006). For discussions of the poem's fragmentary form, see David Seed, "'Disjointed Fragments': Concealment and Revelation in *The Giaour*," *Byron Journal* 18 (January 1990): 14–27; and Marjorie Levinson, *The Romantic Fragment Poem: A Critique of a Form* (Chapel Hill: University of North Carolina Press, 1986), 115–28.

4. David Roessel, *In Byron's Shadow: Modern Greece in the English and American Imagination* (New York: Oxford University Press, 2002), 59–68.

5. See Gayatri Chakravorty Spivak, *A Critique of Postcolonial Reason: Toward a History of the Vanishing Present* (Cambridge, MA: Harvard University Press, 1999), 287.

6. Perhaps the most vigorously documented instances of this kind of sexual surveillance pertain to colonial India.

7. See Orhan Pamuk's remarkable homage to Melling's engravings as signs of Istanbul's history. Elisabeth Fraser's interest in Melling is similarly redemptive. For readings of Byron that highlight the relationship between his sexuality and the poems, see Abigail Keenan, *Byron's Othered Self and Voice: Contextualizing the Homographic Signature* (New York: Peter Lang, 2003); and Louis Crompton, *Byron and Greek Love: Homophobia and 19th-Century England* (Berkeley: University of California Press, 1985). Jeffrey L. Schneider, in "Secret Sins of the Ori-

ent: Creating a (Homo)Textual Context for Reading Byron's *The Giaour*," *College English* 65.1 (September 2002): 81–95, uses the poem as a touchstone for queer strategies of reading.

8. See Ainslie's circular regarding the sultan's death in National Archives, Kew, Foreign Office 261/1 0003.

9. Aksan, *Ottoman Wars*, 167. Aksan quotes Austrian Field Marshal Laudon: "It is beyond all human powers of comprehension to grasp just how strongly these places [Ottoman defensive works] are built, and just how obstinately the Turks defend them. As soon as one fortification is demolished, they merely dig themselves another one. It is easier to deal with any conventional fortress and with any other army than with the Turks when they are defending a stronghold" (167).

10. Melling arrived in Constantinople in 1785.

11. Antoine-Ignace Melling, *Voyage pittoresque de Constantinople et des rives du Bosphore: D'après les dessins de M. Melling, architecte de l'empereur Sélim III, et dessinateur de la sultane Hadidgé sa soeur*, 2 vols. (Paris: Treuttel et Würtz, 1819). All references to Melling's text will be provided in the text by volume and page number. The volumes are not numbered so I have followed bibliographic convention and have designated the volume of textual commentary as volume 1 and the volume of engravings as volume 2. Likewise the commentary is not paginated; I have set the first page of the preface as page 1 and numbered continuously from that point. I am indebted to Julie Alusse for her translations of this text.

12. See Fraser, *Mediterranean Encounters*, 132–38, for a detailed discussion of the book's production. The multivolume *Description de l'Égypte*, produced over roughly the same time period as Melling's *Voyage pittoresque*, is the most obvious comparator. The preeminent project of its kind, the work was instigated by Jean-Antoine Chaptal, the French minister of the interior, in response to a decree by Napoleon following the invasion of Egypt and was produced by a team of roughly 160 scholars and scientists. The first edition took over twenty years to complete.

13. Melling's engravings and maps, freed from their xenophobic commentary, feature prominently in Shirine Hamadeh's *The City's Pleasures*, as illustrations of Istanbul's eighteenth-century urban and suburban architecture.

14. In *Antoine-Ignace Melling (1763–1831), artiste-voyageur* (Paris: Editions Paris-Musées, 1991), Cornelis Boschma and Jacques Perot state that the commentary was written by Pierre-Louis de Lacretelle, the elder bother of Jean Charles Dominique de Lacretelle, but the "Preface" indicates that it was M. Ch. Lacretelle. Fraser also notes that Melling's secretary Joseph-Antoine Cervini may also have been involved; see *Mediterranean Encounters*, 135.

15. A great deal has been written on the precise nature of Western influence on Ottoman architecture in the eighteenth century. As noted already in Chapter 3, there is an ongoing debate as to whether the palace at Sa'dabad mimics French or Persian palace design; the debate dates back to Ayda Arel, *Onsekizinci yüzyil Istanbul mimarisinde batililasma süreci* [Westernization process in eighteenth-century Istanbul architecture] (Istanbul: Istanbul Teknik Universitesi, 1975); and Fatma M. Göcek, *East Encounters West: France and the Ottoman Empire in the Eighteenth Century* (New York: Oxford University Press, 1987). Göcek's position is developed further in *Ottoman Westernization and Social Change* (New York: Oxford University Press, 1996), but her analysis of Sa'dabad has been persuasively countered by Erimtan in "The Perception of Saadabad"; and by Hamadeh, *The City's Pleasures*, 228–35. As Ali Uzay Peker notes, a similar debate inflects much of the writing on later eighteenth-century projects. See, for example, Ali Uzay Peker, "Western Influences on the Ottoman Empire and Occidentalism in the Architecture of Instanbul," *Eighteenth-Century Life* 26.3 (Fall 2002): 139–63; Yasin Çagatay Seçkin, "Gardens of the Nineteenth-Century Imperial Palaces in Istanbul," *Studies in the History of Gardens and Designed Landscapes: An International Quarterly* 23.1 (2003): 72–86; and, most important, Hamadeh, *The City's Pleasures*. Melling plays a vital evidentiary role in Hamadeh's text.

16. This passage is also cited in Boschma and Perot, *Antoine-Ignace Melling,* 18.

17. Boschma and Perot, *Antoine-Ignace Melling,* 20.

18. Aksan, *Ottoman Wars,* 134 and 181–207.

19. See Frédéric Hitzel, "Correspondence Between Antoine Ignace Melling (1763–1801) and Hatice Sultan," paper presented at the International Congress on Learning and Education in the Ottoman World, Istanbul, 12–15 April 1999.

20. Boschma and Perot, *Antoine-Ignace Melling,* 20.

21. See Kelly, *The Society of Dilettanti,* 194–205, for a specific discussion of how neoclassical projects in England utilized knowledge gained from the Ionian expeditions.

22. Inge Boer forcefully makes this point in her "Reading Melling's *Voyage pittoresque de Constantinople,*" *arcadia* 38.2 (2003): 288–91.

23. As Emel Ardaman argues in "Perspective and Istanbul, the Capital of the Ottoman Empire," *Journal of Design History* 20.2 (July 2007): 109–30, single-point perspective did not enter Ottoman visual culture until the nineteenth century (110).

24. Boer, "Reading Melling's *Voyage,*" 293.

25. Fraser, *Mediterranean Encounters,* 145–52.

26. Boer, "Reading Melling's *Voyage,*" 290, traces the complex movement of pronouns in this passage.

27. See Jacques Perot, "Du dessin à la gravure: Le voyage pittoresque de Constantinople et des rives du Bosphore," in Boschma and Perot, *Antoine-Ignace Melling,* 33–43, for a superb discussion of the production of the book.

28. See Boschma and Perot, *Antoine-Ignace Melling,* 42 nn. 9–12, for specific details regarding Melling's Salon exhibition.

29. Or, perhaps more accurately, both painting and engraving are based on the same drawing.

30. Orhan Pamuk, *Istanbul: Memories and the City,* trans. Maureen Freely (New York: Alfred A. Knopf, 2005), 62–75.

31. One can speculate that this is one of the unidentified pictures exhibited in the 1808 Salon because at that point British victory in the Anglo-Turkish War would not yet have happened.

32. On this point see, Philip W. Martin, "Heroism and History: *Childe Harold* I and II and the Tales," in *The Cambridge Companion to Byron,* ed. Drummond Bone (Cambridge: Cambridge University Press, 2004), 91–94: "Writing to the distinguished Eastern traveller, Professor E. D. Clarke, who had complimented him on his accuracy, he remarked: '. . . *you* are one of ye very few who can pronounce how far my *costume* (to use an affected but expressive word) is correct.—As to poesy—*that* is—as "Men Gods and Columns" please to decide upon it—but I am sure that I am anxious to have an observer's—particularly a *famous* observer's testimony on ye. fidelity of my *manners & dresses*'" (93). For the complete letter, see *Byron's Letters and Journals,* ed. Leslie A. Marchand, 12 vols. (London: John Murray, 1973–), 3:199. All subsequent references to the letters will by given by volume and page number in Marchand's edition.

33. That Byron's subjectivity was in crisis is vividly captured in Neff, "Bitches, Mollies, and Tommies"; and in Crompton, *Byron and Greek Love.* For a valuable overview of the relationship between sodomy and genius, see Andrew Elfenbein, *Romantic Genius: The Prehistory of a Homosexual Role* (New York: Columbia University Press, 1999), 17–38.

34. Berlant, *Cruel Optimism,* 16.

35. Levinson, *The Romantic Fragment Poem,* 115–28.

36. Colin Jager, *Unquiet Things: Secularism in the Romantic Age* (Philadelphia: University of Pennsylvania Press, 2014), 191–94.

37. Lord Byron, "Advertisement" to *The Giaour,* in *The Complete Poetical Works,* ed. Jerome McGann (Oxford: Clarendon Press, 1981), 3:39–41. All subsequent references to the poem will

be to this edition and will be given by line number in the text. References to the notes or McGann's apparatus will be cited by page number.

38. Jerome Christensen, *Lord Byron's Strength: Romantic Writing and Commercial Society* (Baltimore: Johns Hopkins University Press, 1993), 97.

39. Caroline Franklin, *Byron's Heroines* (Oxford: Clarendon Press, 1992), 40.

40. At a crucial point in the story Hassan mistakes the Giaour for an Albanian, thus this paramilitary history is signaled in the poem. Outside the poem Byron associated himself with this population in his famous portrait in Albanian attire.

41. Byron and Hobhouse were extraordinarily well versed in both the travel literature and the antiquarian publications pertaining to the Ottoman Empire. The Dilettanti publications would have been in their repertoire. Because Byron actually explored Ephesus, it is very likely Byron knew Mayer and Ainslie's *Views in the Ottoman Dominions* (1810), which has an engraving of the Achilles sarcophagus drawing.

42. In this regard it is much like the Giaour himself whose name is relentlessly repressed. As Makdisi states in *Making England Western* with regard to the Muslim fisherman's recognition of the Giaour, "To recognize the Giaour is to grapple with an absence rather than a presence—hence his 'name' which is not a name, an individual designation, but rather a derivation from three different languages intended precisely to deny the individuality of the other. The absence of marking turns out to be a mark; the lack of identity is what identity turns out to be" (162). To translate this into the problem of chronology, we could say that the absence of a chronological marker turns out to be a mark; the lack of a history (of decolonization) is what (imperial) history turns out to be.

43. See Robert Jones, *Literature, Gender and Politics*; Hoock, *Empires of the Imagination*, 39–130; Myrone, *Body Building*, 193–251; and O'Quinn, *Entertaining Crisis*.

44. For key discussions of the American war as a civil war, see Dror Wahrman, *The Making of the Modern Self: Identity and Culture in Eighteenth-Century England* (New Haven, CT: Yale University Press, 2004), 238–43; and Jay Fleigelman, *Prodigals and Pilgrims: The American Revolution Against Patriarchal Authority, 1750–1800* (Cambridge: Cambridge University Press, 1989).

45. Jerome McGann has famously argued that in *Childe Harold* Byron is "obsessed with the idea of the renewal of human culture in the west at a moment of its deepest darkness. This means for Byron . . . the renewal of Greece as an independent political entity becomes [his] objective correlative for this idea." See McGann, *The Beauty of Inflections: Literary Investigations in Historical Method and Theory* (Oxford: Clarendon Press, 1988), 260.

46. As a letter writer, Byron is far more interested in recounting the social exchanges he has with those people he meets on his tour. His lack of interest in antiquity is palpable and consistent. As he states, "my researches, such as they were, when in the East, were more directed to the language & inhabitants than to the Antiquities" (*Letters*, 1:134)

47. Richard Brinley Sheridan was the foremost theorist of this crisis during the years of the American war, and Byron was a deep admirer of Sheridan's political and cultural work. In the immediate postwar period, it is William Cowper and Charlotte Smith who reckon most directly with the post-American condition, and significantly the former confronts the issue by rethinking epic conventions, while the latter reimagines pastoral discourse in quite radical ways. As we will see in the argument that follows, Byron also focuses his most decisive formal interventions on these poetic modes. See O'Quinn, *Entertaining Crisis*.

48. Butler, "Byron and the Empire in the East." See also Caroline Franklin, "'Some Samples of the Finest Orientalism': Byronic Philhellenism and Proto-Zionism at the Time of the Congress of Vienna," in *Romanticism and Colonialism: Writing and Empire, 1780–1830*, ed. Tim Fulford and Peter J. Kitson (Cambridge: Cambridge University Press, 1998), 221–42.

49. See Charles Grant, *Observations on the State of Society Among the Asiatic Subjects of Great-Britain, Particularly with Respect to Morals; and on the Means of Improving It* (London, 1813). Grant's pamphlet had been circulated extensively and discussed in Parliament before its publication.

50. See Franklin, *Byron's Heroines*, 39–41.

51. Troy Bickham, *The Weight of Vengeance: The United States, the British Empire, and the War of 1812* (New York: Oxford University Press, 2012), 16–17.

52. Bickham, *Weight of Vengeance*, 19.

53. Nigel Leask, *English Romantic Writers*, 27, argues that "in Byron's case . . . [there isn't] any form of benign or 'normative' ideal of colonialism or imperialism, which is rather criticized *tout court* from the moral standpoint of aristocratic classical republicanism." Virtue, of course, is the cornerstone of classical republicanism. My sense is that Byron stages his critique from this position but is remarkably immune from nostalgia.

54. See William H. Marshall, "The Accretive Structure of Byron's *The Giaour*," *Modern Language Notes* 76.6 (June 1961): 502–9; and Michael G. Sundell, "The Development of *The Giaour*," *Studies in English Literature, 1500–1900* 9.4 (Fall 1969): 587–99.

55. For a cogent overview of the intersection of philhellenism, travel literature to the Ottoman Empire, and Byron's poetry from this period, see Nigel Leask, "Byron and the Eastern Mediterranean: *Childe Harold* II and the 'Polemic of Ottoman Greece,'" in Bone, *Cambridge Companion to Byron*, 99–118.

56. Levinson, *Romantic Fragment Poem*, 119–20, argues explicitly that the form of *The Giaour* is modeled on Herodotus's *History*.

57. Marjorie Levinson has argued persuasively for the connection between the Giaour and Themistocles, as invoked in the opening of the poem, and further that their ambivalent treatment in the poem is linked to Byron's equivocal position regarding Napoleon at the moment of the poem's composition; see Levinson, *Romantic Fragment Poem*, 125–26.

58. A similar skepticism inflects his account of the ostensible burial mounds of Homeric heroes at Alexandria Troas. In a letter to Henry Drury, 3 May 1810, Byron wrote:

> The Troad is a fine field for conjecture and Snipe-shooting, and a good sportsman and an ingenious scholar may exercise their feet and faculties to great advantage upon the spot, or if they prefer riding lose their way (as I did) in a cursed quagmire of the Scamander who wriggles about as if the Dardan virgins still offered their wonted tribute. The only vestige of Troy, or her destroyers, are the barrows supposed to contain the carcases of Achilles[,] Antilochus, Ajax &c but Mt. Ida is still in high feather, though the Shepherds are nowadays not much like Ganymede. (*Letters*, 1:238)

Byron's doubt is double-edged: who is to say that Achilles is buried here, and if so what difference does it make?

59. See Christensen, *Lord Byron's Strength*, 100–101; and Leask, "Byron and the Eastern Mediterranean," 109–10.

60. See Robert Gleckner, *Byron and the Ruins of Paradise* (Baltimore: Johns Hopkins University Press, 1967), 105; and Christensen, *Lord Byron's Strength*, 97–99.

61. The insertions came in early July 1813. See McGann's commentary in *Complete Poetical Works*, 3:413.

62. Byron's animosity toward Elgin and to the removal of the Parthenon marbles was and is well documented. It is encapsulated in his poem "The Curse of Minerva" and features prominently in *Childe Harold's Pilgrimage*, canto 2.11–15. See William St. Clair, *Elgin and the Marbles: The Controversial History of the Parthenon Sculptures*, 3rd rev. ed. (London: Oxford University Press, 1998), for a thorough overview; and Gillen D'Arcy Wood, *The Shock of the Real: Roman-*

ticism and Visual Culture, 1760–1860 (New York: Palgrave, 2001), 121–71, for a compelling discussion of the Parthenon marbles in Keats and Byron.

63. Byron's admiration for the American cause is well known; his encomium to Washington in "Ode to Napoleon Buonoparte" is perhaps the most famous expression of this. See Joseph Jay Jones, "Lord Byron on America," *Studies in English* 21 (July 1941), for an overview of his opinions; and Martin Kelsall, "Byron's Politics," in Bone, *Cambridge Companion to Byron*, 44–55, for how his thoughts on America fit into his political views.

64. In a sense this confirms the failures of the early part of the poem.

65. This was not the last time that Byron would explore war in Ottoman territory through an engagement with Homer. Canto 7 of *Don Juan* represents the horrific siege and slaughter at Ismail with which I started this chapter in order to stage a displaced critique of the bellicose policies of British governments in the wake of the Napoleonic wars. Near the end of the canto he invokes "Oh, thou eternal Homer!" and then contrasts Homer's poetry with modern warfare. Byron's strategy not only shows that classical heroism is no longer possible but also suggests that poetic technique has been superseded by military technology. It is also clear that Byron is using the Battle of Ismail to allegorize European conflict zones. For an extended discussion of Byron's treatment of the Siege of Ismail, see J. R. Watson, *Romanticism and War: A Study of British Romantic Period Writers and the Napoleonic Wars* (Houndmills: Palgrave Macmillan, 2003), 187–94.

66. Leask, *English Romantic Writers*, 30. He continues, "Heroic action, distinguished by love and martial glory in the epic tradition, becomes in the modern world a bloody and vengeful pattern of action and reaction which confounds hero and villain and results in the destruction of the two men's mutual love-object, Leila the Circassian slave. The world of *The Giaour* is a world suppressed under the (modern) sign of imperialism" (30). The clearest index of the poem's distance from Homeric epic is the distinction between the response of Hassan's mother to the death of her son and that of Hecuba.

67. For Byron's discussion of Ali Pasha in his letters, see *Letters*, 1:226–29. These reflections are famously linked to his representation of Ali in canto 2 of *Child Harold's Pilgrimage*.

68. Jager, *Unquiet Things*, 198–99.

69. Franklin, *Byron's Heroines*, 47.

70. See Eve Kosofsky Sedgwick's *Between Men: English Literature and Male Homosocial Desire* (New York: Columbia University Press, 1985) for the canonical discussion of the erotics of homosocial rivalry.

71. Significantly, the Muslim narrator—the fisherman—can never quite recognize the Giaour either. See Makdisi, *Making England Western*, 162.

72. Beaton, *Byron's War*, 10–19. See, for example, the contrast between Byron's letter to his mother of 12 November 1809 in which he describes Ali Pasha or his letter to Henry Drury of 3 May 1810 and his cursory account of Ephesus in the letter to his mother of 19 March 1810 (*Letters*, 1: 226–40).

73. This is famously captured in Byron's letter to Henry Drury of 3 May 1810: "I see not much difference between ourselves & the Turks, save that we have foreskins and they have none, that they have long dresses and we short, and that we talk much and they little.—In England the vices in fashion are whoring & drinking, in Turkey, Sodomy and smoking, we prefer a girl and a bottle, they a pipe and pathic" (*Letters*, 1:238). The easy slide from the signs of bodily and sartorial difference to practices and dispositions is one manifestation of Byron's queerness.

74. Beaton, *Byron's War*, 21.

75. See Beaton, *Byron's War*, 34–37.

76. See Michel Foucault, "What Is an Author?" in *Language, Counter-Memory, Practice: Selected Essays and Reviews*, ed. Donald F. Bouchard (Ithaca, NY: Cornell University Press, 1977), 113–38.

77. This does not imply that poem thus gains some kind of auratic or cultic status, because the poem is so palpably a mediated entity, a product of commercial print culture.

78. For recent analyses of Byron and celebrity, see Tom Mole, *Byron's Romantic Celebrity: Industrial Culture and the Hermeneutic of Intimacy* (New York: Palgrave Macmillan, 2007); and Clara Tuite, *Lord Byron and Scandalous Celebrity* (Cambridge: Cambridge University Press, 2015).

79. See Hoock, *Empires of the Imagination*.

80. The theatricality of this gesture is not incidental. As Andrew Elfenbein cogently argues in "Byron: Gender and Sexuality" in Bone, *Cambridge Companion to Byron*, 56–76, Byron's gender performance and his theatricalization of masculinity was itself disruptive. For a subtle handling of how readers projected or interpolated their desires into the scene of reading Byron's poetry, see Elfenbein's *Byron and the Victorians* (Cambridge: Cambridge University Press, 1996).

81. Byron's gesture has much in common with Nietzsche's adoption of critical history as a counter to monumental history on the one hand and antiquarian history on the other.

Index

Acknowledgments

More than any other project I have undertaken, this book required that I broaden both my critical skill set and my cultural repertoire. My debts to friends and colleagues are extensive because they provided both the social network and the intellectual sounding board necessary to bring the argument into shape.

The project developed out of my collaboration with Teresa Heffernan on a new edition of Lady Mary Wortley Montagu's Letter-book for Broadview Press. Working with her on the letters at Sandon Hall and in her apartment in Toronto was truly inspiring. Early on, my friends Marcie Frank at Concordia University and Leah Benedict, who was then a graduate student at SUNY Buffalo, invited me to present the earliest versions of Chapter 3 and Chapter 7, well before I thought I could yoke these materials into one project. Two extraordinary historians of the eighteenth century, Donna Andrew and Virginia Aksan, read the first draft in its entirety and offered incisive, productive criticism. That Donna came at the manuscript with an eye to its implications for British historiography and Virginia brought expertise on Ottoman military history to bear on my work meant that all of my ensuing labors were aimed at bringing these two very different areas of inquiry together. That bridging endeavor was staged in the realm of cultural history, and I was blessed by funding from a Social Sciences and Humanities Research Council Insight Grant to see and read virtually every image and document, whether it be in Amsterdam, Venice, London, or Staffordshire. Without the help of librarians and curators at the Rijksmuseum, the Marciana Library, the National Archives at Kew, the Royal Institute of British Architecture, the British Library, the Prints and Drawings division of the British Museum, the Fisher Rare Books Library at the University of Toronto, and SOAS at the University of London, this book simply couldn't have been written. Eveline Sint Nicolaas, the curator responsible for the Calkoen collection at the Rijksmuseum, and Michel Bosson, the archivist at Sandon Hall, were crucial to my research on Jean-Baptiste Vanmour and Lady Mary Wortley Montagu respectively. Both stood by and discussed the respective works when I was first examining them, and then promptly responded to follow-up inquiries. At Sandon Hall, the Dowager Countess of Harrowby kindly gave access to Lady Mary's library and the 8th Earl of Harrowby granted permission to use the archive. In the closing phases of the project Mai Pham at Bridgeman Art, Maria Zinser at Sotheby's, Christina Egli at the Napoleon Museum Thurgau, Victoria Poulton at Woburn Abbey, Baris Kibris at the Pera Museum, Molly Haigh and Amy Wong at the Charles E. Young Research Library at UCLA, Philip Roe at the Chester Beatty Library in Dublin, and my colleague Sandra Parmegianí assisted with image acquisition.

As I developed the chapters, various friends and colleagues weighed in with consistently challenging and useful commentary. Thora Brylowe, Nina Dubin, Sarah Cohen, and Humberto Garcia were especially important at this stage. At a later date Ashley Cohen read another full draft, and her enthusiasm and helpful commentary enabled me to reconceptualize the entire project. Her role in the genesis of the book was decisive because it confirmed my sense that scholars of eighteenth-century imperialism could be drawn into a fully interdisciplinary inquiry into matters somewhat tangential to conventional histories of British or French imperial practices. I cannot thank her enough, not only for her brilliant notes but also for her continuing dialogue about the project.

At this point I received thorough and detailed reports from my readers at the University of Pennsylvania Press. One of the readers was an Ottomanist, the other was a literature scholar who works on empire in the eighteenth century; both made detailed interventions and asked for further engagement with the scholarship in their respective fields. I hope that I have satisfied their requests. Their generosity and care with my manuscript was remarkable and for that I am grateful.

I received these reports while on a fellowship at New College, Oxford. Michael Burden kindly invited me for a three-month stay, and it had an inestimable impact on both me and this book. To Michael and my friends at New College (Andrew Counter, Andrew Meadows, Megan Campbell, Ryan Hanley, and Julia Buhrle), thanks for a wonderful term. While I was in Oxford, Ros Ballaster, Alexis Tadié and Luisa Calè were incredibly hospitable. They shared coffee and meals and organized workshops on large sections of the manuscript. After reading precirculated materials, John-Paul Ghobrial, Alexis Tadié, Rathika Muthukumaran, Ashley Cohen, and Luisa Calè spent the afternoon in Ros's beautiful office at Mansfield College, and I came away with a wealth of intelligent, pointed commentary on Chapters 2, 3, and 4. A second workshop, held at the British Museum but organized by Luisa Calè through Birkbeck College, was a rigorous engagement with Chapters 5 and 6. Kim Sloan, Ian Jenkins, Tita Chico, William St. Clair, and Luisa (again), and others rigorously critiqued my work and as a result these portions of the book are much improved. That discussion was especially memorable because the staff of the museum arranged for the actual drawings, books, and engravings under discussion to be in the room. At the end of the workshop Ian Jenkins pulled me aside and offered simple, kind words of encouragement that have remained with me through the process of revision. Chapter 6 and 7 received similar scrutiny at the 2016 Annual Conferences of the North American Society for the Study of Romanticism (NASSR) at the University of California, Berkeley. I'm grateful to Kevis Goodman, Celeste Langan, and Janet Sorensen for the opportunity to precirculate the chapters and to Thora Brylowe, Jeff Cox, Jill Heydt-Stevenson, Humberto Garcia, and the other workshop participants for their invaluable feedback. It was in this context that the suggestion to write on Byron came forward and for that I am grateful. Components of Chapter 5 were presented at the Johnson Society meeting in Montreal and at the 2015 NASSR Conference in Washington, D.C. After the latter event, Peter Manning, who has always been supportive of my work on this project, sent valuable words of encouragement, and until now I have been unable to thank him properly. Chapter 7 has been presented on numerous occasions—at the University of Pennsylvania, as a special plenary at the Canadian Society for Eighteenth Century Studies in Edmonton and at Balliol College. Thanks to Suvir Kaul, Michael Gamer, Katherine Binhammer, and Fiona Price for organizing these events. Sadly, this book's best audience will not get to read it. The project was conceived at roughly the same time that I got to know Srinivas Aravamudan, and he offered an incredibly rich response to the version of Chapter 7 that I presented in Edmonton. His passing was an immense loss to everyone working in eighteenth-century studies. His combination of critical acumen, good humor, and generosity was an inspiration to me and untold others in the field.

In the final phases of the book's revision, Helen Deutsch and Lisa Freeman both read the entire first part, "After Peace," on very quick turnaround. Their commentary, as one would expect from two such formidable minds, went to the core of the argument and clarified key issues. I hope that I have lived up to the implicit expectations of their remarks. Like their intelligence, their kindness and friendship know no bounds. Likewise, Ashley, Thora, Humberto, and Zirwat Chowdhury were called upon to look at some late additions; I owe all of them a great deal.

Of course, nothing would have happened without the vigorous support of Jerry Singerman, Hannah Blake, and Erica Ginsburg at the University of Pennsylvania Press. I came to them with a very specific view of what this book would look like, and they have done their utmost to realize my desires. This is a book with many moving parts, and I was blessed with a tremendous copy editor: Jennifer Shenk handled the manuscript with extraordinary care and rigor. Thanks also to Andrew Bailey and Don Bruce, the associate dean and dean of arts at Guelph, who consistently supported my research during this period. My extraordinary research assistant, Leslie Allin, was involved in this project from the outset. I owe her a world of thanks.

I have decided to stage these acknowledgments as a narrative of the book's production in order to highlight the deeply social quality of scholarly inquiry. Conferring with people about the project has been immensely fun. But as everyone knows, it isn't only those directly connected with a book's composition and production—either through critical commentary or more practical advice—who help bring a project to fruition. I have been blessed with a supportive community of friends, academic and otherwise. In addition to those already named, I hope the following list goes some way to register my thanks for their stimulating friendship: Laura Rosenthal, Misty Anderson, Kristina Straub, Laura Brown, Alexander Regier, Felicity Nussbaum, Sonia Hofkosh, Kevin Gilmartin, Julie Carlson, Joseph Roach, Deidre Lynch, Robert Jones, David Taylor, Tracy Davis, Kevis Goodman, Mark Canuel, Sarah Zimmerman, James Mulholland, Kathleen Wilson, Alex Dick, Betty Joseph, George Bouloukos, Ramesh Mallipeddi, Emily Anderson, Fiona Brideoake, Jon Mee, Gillian Russell, Jon Sachs, Catherine Bush, Jennifer Schacker, Gena Zurowski, Julie Murray, Lauren Gillingham, Sandra Rechico, and Monica Tap. Many a wonderful meal has been spent in their company. A special thanks goes out to Celia Moore and Jordan Cushing whose doors were always open when I was in London.

Finally, I want to thank my friends and family in Toronto. Jo was the still center in a rather stormy period and generously enabled my extended time away in Oxford in 2016. But, most important, she and Gabe and Eli continue to show me how to live happily every day with their love, their optimism, and their strength. This book is dedicated with love to Eli the amazing one.